# Religion and Society at the Dawn of Modern Europe

## Cultures of Early Modern Europe

**Series Editors:** Beat Kümin, Professor of Early Modern European History, University of Warwick, and Brian Cowan, Associate Professor and Canada Research Chair in Early Modern British History, McGill University

**Editorial Board:**

Adam Fox, University of Edinburgh, UK
Robert Frost, University of Aberdeen, UK
Molly Greene, University of Princeton, USA
Ben Schmidt, University of Washington, USA
Gerd Schwerhoff, University of Dresden, Germany
Francesca Trivellato, University of Yale, USA
Francisca Loetz, University of Zurich, Switzerland

The 'cultural turn' in the humanities has generated a wealth of new research topics and approaches. Focusing on the ways in which representations, perceptions and negotiations shaped people's lived experiences, the books in this series provide fascinating insights into the past. The series covers early modern culture in its broadest sense, inclusive of (but not restricted to) themes such as gender, identity, communities, mentalities, emotions, communication, ritual, space, food and drink, and material culture.

**Published:**
*Food and Identity in England, 1540–1640*, Paul S. Lloyd (2014)
*The Birth of the English Kitchen, 1600–1850*, Sara Pennell (2016)
*Vagrancy in English Culture and Society, 1650–1750*, David Hitchcock (2016)
*Angelica's Book and the World of Reading in Late Renaissance Italy*, Brendan Dooley (2016)
*Gender, Culture and Politics in England, 1560–1640*, Susan D. Amussen and David E. Underdown (2017)
*Food, Religion, and Communities in Early Modern Europe*, Christopher Kissane (2018)
*Religion and Society at the Dawn of Modern Europe*, Rudolf Schlögl (2020)

# Religion and Society at the Dawn of Modern Europe

*Christianity Transformed, 1750–1850*

Rudolf Schlögl

Translated by
Helen Imhoff

BLOOMSBURY ACADEMIC
LONDON • NEW YORK • OXFORD • NEW DELHI • SYDNEY

BLOOMSBURY ACADEMIC
Bloomsbury Publishing Plc
50 Bedford Square, London, WC1B 3DP, UK
1385 Broadway, New York, NY 10018, USA
29 Earlsfort Terrace, Dublin 2, Ireland

BLOOMSBURY, BLOOMSBURY ACADEMIC and the Diana logo
are trademarks of Bloomsbury Publishing Plc

First published in Great Britain 2020
Paperback edition published 2021

Copyright © Rudolf Schlögl, 2020

Rudolf Schlögl has asserted his right under the Copyright, Designs and
Patents Act, 1988, to be identified as Author of this work.

Cover design by Tjaša Krivec
Cover image: France, circa 1896: Monk by the Sea, 1808–10 (oil on canvas), Friedrich,
Caspar David (1774–1840)/Alte Nationalgalerie, Berlin, Germany/Bridgeman Images

All rights reserved. No part of this publication may be reproduced or transmitted
in any form or by any means, electronic or mechanical, including photocopying,
recording, or any information storage or retrieval system, without
prior permission in writing from the publishers.

Bloomsbury Publishing Plc does not have any control over, or responsibility for,
any third-party websites referred to or in this book. All internet addresses given
in this book were correct at the time of going to press. The author and publisher
regret any inconvenience caused if addresses have changed or sites have ceased
to exist, but can accept no responsibility for any such changes.

A catalogue record for this book is available from the British Library.

A catalog record for this book is available from the Library of Congress.

ISBN:   HB:    978-1-3500-9957-9
        PB:    978-1-3502-4677-5
        ePDF:  978-1-3500-9958-6
        eBook: 978-1-3500-9959-3

Series: Cultures of Early Modern Europe

Typeset by Integra Software Services Pvt. Ltd.

To find out more about our authors and books visit www.bloomsbury.com
and sign up for our newsletters.

# Contents

| | | |
|---|---|---|
| | Introduction: Religion as a System within Society | 1 |
| 1 | Christianity in the *ancien régime* | 11 |
| | Symbiotic competition: Pre-modern ecclesiastical and secular rule in Europe | 12 |
| | Christian churches in Europe: Organizational forms | 17 |
| | Hierarchy and elites | 32 |
| | Parish clergy | 37 |
| | Failing reforms | 45 |
| 2 | Christianity and civil society | 55 |
| | Religion during the Revolution | 57 |
| | The great secularizations | 67 |
| | From privileged corporate body to association | 75 |
| | The invention of political religion | 85 |
| | Diffusion and expropriation | 101 |
| 3 | Christianity in modern society | 129 |
| | Organization and its consequences | 131 |
| | Religion as a social movement | 142 |
| | Piety | 153 |
| | Women in a male religion | 174 |
| 4 | Religion as culture | 193 |
| | Ideas and structures | 193 |
| | The problem of deism | 196 |
| | Religions and religion in the history of humanity | 204 |
| | Religion and the foundations of culture | 224 |
| | The religion of philosophers and theologians | 230 |
| | Shifts | 245 |

| 5 | Secularization: A valid concept? | 249 |
|---|---|---|
|   | The process of secularization as a concept | 249 |
|   | Differentiation | 252 |
|   | Inclusion | 254 |
|   | Communication and the creation of meaning | 256 |
|   | Observing processes of secularization | 258 |

| Glossary | 260 |
|---|---|
| Notes | 270 |
| Bibliography | 309 |
| Index | 340 |

# Introduction: Religion as a System within Society

The period from 1750 to 1850 was marked by profound social changes in central and western Europe, affecting political institutions as well as the basic processes by which society was formed.[1] The emancipation of the British colonies in America and their new constitution served as a trigger for similar upheaval in Europe: the institutional structures of the *ancien régime* were swept away in a revolution and two decades of wars between different states, from which a new 'civil' society emerged, developing its own political and social institutions to replace the old feudal structures. There were two ways in which European Christendom was involved in this upheaval and the subsequent attempts to develop new forms of social and political organization: on the one hand, the changes in social structures and hierarchies had profound consequences for the social forms of Christianity; on the other hand, European Christianity, in turn, also played a large role in reshaping society and its institutions. It is this transformation of the social aspects of European Christianity that is the subject of this book.[2]

Thus I am not concerned with the history of the individual churches in Europe,[3] but with the history of Christianity as a system within European society at the beginning of the modern age. This approach has two implications: society must be understood as more than just a community structured as a state, and religion must be understood as a social phenomenon, which can only be adequately grasped within the context of social structures. Anyone researching this topic will find that there is a multitude of individual studies on the early churches and on the history of personal piety as well as much discussion on religion. This body of secondary literature, however, is of little assistance when considering the approach outlined above.[4]

The academic disciplines of secular and ecclesiastical history have each viewed the subject of religion from different perspectives. As a rule, church history focuses on questions of institutional and ecclesiastical organization, in most cases ignoring the history of individual piety. As a result, 'society' only makes an appearance in contexts where it functions as a counterpart to religion and is only relevant when ecclesiastical institutions address social problems or when secular politics deal with questions relating to religious life. In addition to this, church history tends to approach its subject matter from the point of view of one particular confessional church, either ignoring others or treating them in a generalized way as one group.[5] Conversely, secular history – especially social history – tends to consider religion in the context of 'cultural development', thus treating it as a separate area of social reality and marginalizing and isolating it.[6] Religious studies also proved far less helpful a subject area than I had hoped when it came to providing a methodological and conceptual framework for my project. Research in that particular field continues to be marked by a desire to identify religion as different from other social phenomena through comparative studies of its particular characteristics or 'dimensions'. To do so, religious studies has, since the beginnings of the subject under Max Müller and Edward B. Tylor, developed typologies of religions and religious phenomena. These are either taken out of their historical context and analysed with a view to establishing an inherent developmental logic or are accommodated within the larger outlines of the development of civilizations, thus assigning religion a particular place within a normative framework. This also divorces religion from its social and historical contexts instead of taking these contexts as the starting point for understanding religion. Correspondingly, those scholars of religion who do analyse individual religions within a concrete, historical context refrain from using a general concept of religion.[7]

For reasons that go beyond the scope of this introductory discussion, I decided to adopt the communications- and media-theoretical approaches that systems theory offers as a conceptual basis of my analysis. Systems theory seems to me to offer the clearest set of terms to address the following core questions relating to society: how does society succeed in organizing itself through different categories of meaning and how does society guarantee the stability of this order? Systems theory assumes that social phenomena continuously reproduce themselves, and it thus does away with the idea that the stability and reproduction of patterns of social order result from the motives and interests of individuals, an idea which, in any case, is implausible, as a brief consideration of one's own actions shows. Moreover, systems theory takes into account that the particular characteristics and actions of individuals, groups and institutions are determined by their relationship to other people, groups and institutions; none of these, therefore, occur in isolation from one another. These relationships follow certain delineable patterns in a given historical context. Consequently, there are convincing arguments that a solid theoretical basis is necessary in order to examine questions relating to society.

In addition to this, systems theory explicitly considers reality to be the result of observations. No one knows what the world is like beyond our own observations, a circumstance which also applies to academic examination of the world. When engaging in such academic observation, one must, therefore, take into account the fact that the subject of observation is not a pre-existing, given social world, but that social reality is created and structured by observations and communication*. This is the approach I will be taking in examining how Christianity emerges and is shaped as a system within society. This requires a set of terms that offer the distinctions necessary to describe the production of a meaningful, structured social reality; they include the following: meaning, communication, observation, media, system, environment, semantics, descriptions from within a given system (self-descriptions) and those that are undertaken from the outside (external descriptions), differentiation* and complexity. I will make use of these concepts without necessarily using these exact terms and without engaging in any in-depth discussion of them.[8] A glossary is provided at the end of this book for various terms, and the terms contained in it are indicated by an asterisk in the main text when they are first used.

Studying the make-up and history of social organization also requires terms that convey a sense of those aspects of society with which one is concerned. These do not have to be the same as the terms that the people who are being observed use to structure and order their social world – in fact, they cannot be identical, at least not for historical studies, because the world has changed and because first- and second-order observations have different aims. Individuals communicate with each other and observe their world in their given social configurations, and in doing so, they reproduce these configurations. Their aim is to engage in successful actions and communication; that is to say, their expectations must be reasonably likely to come true and an individual's surroundings are thus observed in a way that contributes to this. For example, an individual may posit a causal link between unconnected events and thus create 'actors', in Bruno Latour's sense of the word. A researcher, on the other hand, is interested in the way in which this process occurs. The aim is to identify both the semantic logic on which distinctions are based and the semiotic strategies involved in first-order observation.[9] For this reason, systems theory advocates applying a functional analysis to social constellations and phenomena. Contrary to what is often claimed, the point of this is not to tie social events to particular interests; instead, systems theory assumes that function cannot be explained by intentions and interests and in extreme cases may not be reflected in these. One reason why social configurations, from relationships between two people to entire societies, are stable is because as a whole, and certainly from the point of view of individual participants, they cannot achieve an understanding of themselves. It is for this reason that the overall structure of such an entity is stable: since the nineteenth century, social theories have used the term 'ideology' to describe this circumstance.

Focusing on the function of social events and configurations has a further advantage: it identifies social phenomena as a response and resolution to certain problems and thus it allows one to look for other possible and equivalent resolutions, in turn making it possible to compare the consequences of such possibilities. This sheds light on the variety of social phenomena and the different forms of developmental logic they often follow despite identical initial situations. Compared to the normative concept of 'ideology', an approach focused on an analysis of function has the advantage of doing away with any notion of teleology.

At first glance, religion is a phenomenon that relates to individuals, and Protestantism has been concerned with an individual's relationship to God ever since the Reformation. More generally, religion enables individuals to give mundane events meaning by placing them within the context of the infinite, as Schleiermacher argued. Deriving meaning from religion in this way thus leads to a particular kind of relationship between the individual and the world and to the individual viewing themselves in a particular way. Ethnological research suggests that, in the early phases of social development, religion had the function of giving meaning to the unfamiliar and unexpected, thus accommodating it within the familiar world. This illustrates the circular nature of the basis of social order: a phenomenon or an event can only be unexpected if there are also events that do fulfil certain expectations; *their* predictability, however, can only be understood if they are contrasted with unexpected events, which they therefore presuppose.[10] The roots of religion thus lie with the very beginnings of human associative relationships and the formation of society.

It is easy to imagine that this initial contradiction developed in different ways when different individuals or groups communicated. The personification of certain phenomena as spirits, demons and gods is an obvious natural development. However, these could still just be phenomena relating to an individual's consciousness, that is, they could still just represent individual religious experience. It is for this reason that Schleiermacher assumes that individuals have a desire to share their own experience of the eternal with others and to communicate with others about the presence of the divine; the aim is, according to Schleiermacher, to reassure oneself that others, too, have experienced the same thing and that it is not an illusion.[11] Religion becomes a social phenomenon as soon as it is used to make sense of the world, but by exchanging experiences regarding the divine, individuals turn religion into a particular form of communication, and, from that point onwards, it can begin to develop into an institution that is separate from its environment. It is important to note that, whatever the details of the social evolution of religion – religious virtuosos may have played a significant role in this process – differentiation, that is to say, the process of developing into something that is distinct from its social environment, can only begin once individuals start communicating about their own religious interpretation of the world. As the original problem is not limited to a particular space or time and as it is not uncommon, differentiation can continue without any restrictions and will stabilize once the opposing pair of immanence (that which is contained within the world) and transcendence (that which transcends the physical, material world) can be used to address social problems.

This scenario was presented by Émile Durkheim in his research on the religion of the indigenous peoples of America and Australia. According to Durkheim, the social function of religion was to organize individuals in particular kinship groups according to totems, with biological kinship only playing a limited role in this process.[12] The religion of these societies does not simply reflect patterns of social order but is involved in producing them. It contributes to a community developing into a society that is more complex than it would be without religion. This is quite far removed from individual religious experience and its functionality, but it presupposes this experience as well as shaping it. Structurally, the reproduction of society relies on autonomous processes of consciousness.

This explains why an individual may not feel the need to create meaning through religion but why the creation of meaning in the context of the distinction between transcendence and immanence seems vital to societies, as does the subsequent differentiation of patterns of actions and institutions in those periods that historians currently have knowledge about. This is because of the many ways in which religion, once institutionalized, is involved in society's self-reference, social order and the way in which this order is viewed by the society in question. As a permanent ability to exert physical force is involved in ensuring this social order, religion is also associated with rulership and power, and these elements often become indistinguishable. From the beginning, the language of power has been based on religion.[13] For this reason, the social form of religion can only be understood if the relevant social structures are analysed and the semantics of religion only make sense if we also consider the way in which society describes itself.

This establishment of a social function has significant consequences for religion, and these can still be felt in the nineteenth century. The distinction between religious and secular spheres of action was a continuing problem that, in the West, neither Augustine's distinction between *civitas dei* and *civitas terrena* nor Luther's two-kingdoms doctrine* was able to satisfactorily resolve. On the other hand, this lack of distinction meant that religion continued to be involved in the formation of different social groups and the formation of social and individual identity. Having taken on a social dimension and the functions that come with this, religion became an instrument of social inclusion and exclusion.

This may compensate for the third problem associated with the social differentiation of religion. While religious creation of meaning initially occurs through an individual's relationship with themselves and the world, it also already requires society. Meaning cannot be created without communication and thus a social community. In the same way, differentiation turns into a social phenomenon. As soon as the systemic differentiation of religion gives institutional form to a construction made up of actions, with its stability dependent on a devout audience regularly and frequently participating in religious acts, only limited reliance can be placed on an individual's spontaneous need to create meaning through religion. This is likely to already have applied to cults, as the importance of a god was linked to how popular a particular cult site or temple was,[14] and it is a point that becomes even more important once cults become religions and once churches come into being. The latter process shows very clearly the extent to which successful differentiation and the evolution of social institutions depend on whether they are able to reproduce actions or experiences that are relevant within a given system. Within Christianity, a number of such incentives that are based on the distinction between immanence and transcendence, and thus are genuinely religious in nature, developed through the idea of salvation being dependent on grace. Original sin, the devil, provenance and the uncertainty of whether one would gain salvation or not ensured that the means of receiving grace were of continuous importance; these ideas also gave meaning to people's experiences in relation to the fundamental distinction between immanence and transcendence. Nevertheless, from the emergence of churches in Late antiquity, Christianity engaged in various ways of continuously carrying out missionary work within the population, presenting the worship of God as a public affair, which could thus be regulated and prescribed. This suggests that the problem continued to be relevant. Unlike, for example, the economy, which is driven by the desire to satisfy existing needs in the face of limited resources, religion appears to lack a symbiotic mechanism that triggers the need to create meaning through religion. This is because there are always alternative ways of endowing things with religious meaning. In the European Middle Ages, these alternatives were labelled as folly in an attempt to neutralize them.[15]

When, in the eighteenth century, the idea of a responsible individual gained force, this had a significant impact, both theologically and in everyday life, on the acceptance of a number of the ideas that facilitated the formation of meaning through religion – original sin, predestination and a concern for the poor souls in purgatory. This obviously placed the Christian churches in Europe in a difficult position. At the same time, the violent process of secularization brought down the Church's buttresses within the economic and political reproduction of society that had enabled Christianity's institutional differentiation. The history of church institutions and religious life in the first half of the nineteenth century focuses on the way in which religious differentiation was able to continue in the context of new forms of social organization. For this to be possible, profound structural changes in the institution and in religious occasions were necessary in order for the production of meaning through religion to continue.

This new context was created by a society whose modern structures distinguished it from the *ancien régime* that had perished in the Revolution. It considered itself to be a civil society with a number of defining features: the equality of individuals before the law; the distribution of wealth by means of largely unchecked markets and a state guarantee of property, which mitigated the troubling consequences of an unregulated market; and a change in governance from sovereignty over subjects to a form of political power based on and controlled by participation. Ever since Max Weber characterized modernity as the coexistence of different ethical spheres with their own rationality, this type of society has been described as polycontextual, that is, a society without a clearly defined centre. Social structures are now based on function and not hierarchy.

In the *ancien régime*, the monarchy – an entity that was separate from society – ensured certain patterns of social order. In the new political structures of civil society, however, this had to be done by society itself, and this led to mass media playing an increasingly important role when it came to social integration and the reproduction of structural patterns. This new set-up was described as the separation of state and society because sovereignty, now a question of politics, was also faced with the problem of differentiation.[16] In political language and social theory, the 'nation' replaced the *societas civilis*, becoming a cipher for the unit formed by the two different entities of state and society. This semantic shift illustrated how upheavals in the way society was structured were accompanied by new self-descriptions of society that reflected the changes in the process of sociation. There is no need to refer to the currently emerging conservatism in order to see that societies and social systems* tend to lack an understanding of themselves during periods of rapid and significant change. This led to a tendency to view new developments in the context of what had been.[17] This was not only done for ideological reasons: despite the revolution, the changes that took place occurred while the engine of social reproduction, as it were, continued to run, and thus every innovation and change was determined by elements, and their configuration, that had until just before been in use and had had a particular function.

This transformation of European societies is not the focus of my investigation, but it is of interest in that it provides the context and preconditions for the transformation of religion as a system within society. This also assumes that we are not dealing with a one-sided deterministic relationship or one of cause and effect, but with a case of simultaneous evolution, involving reciprocal effects.

Writing a history of European Christianity that focuses on religion as a system within society means that I cannot claim to be writing a history of events that is in any way comprehensive. Instead, the topic highlights, and shows the interest of, particular events and constellations in which the social aspect of Christianity as a system within society becomes evident. Similar considerations apply to the differences between Christian churches. These differences and oppositions are not of interest for their own sake; instead, it is relevant to consider the contexts in which these differences are highlighted and what effects they have. I have made use of confessional differences in order to examine when a given change is the result of previous developments within a particular church and when it is not specific to a particular church but is the result of a problem or configuration that does not relate to this. As a result, developments and configurations that are not confessionally determined can be identified.

This approach made it clear, again and again, that a modern civil society can be thought of both as a single unified entity and as a multiplicity of entities, with both aspects representing social reality. It was a unified entity in that the destruction of the *ancien régime* meant that European societies, which were based on the same traditions, faced the same challenges everywhere when it came to restructuring themselves. The basic outlines of this project – the creation of a new order – were the same across Europe and there were no national differences. At the same time, the responses to the challenge were put into practice in different societies, separated according to state. Each of these had their own histories, resulting in different visions regarding their development. Here, too, I could not attempt to provide a comprehensive history of the different national varieties of Christianity; this would have by far exceeded the amount of ground I could cover on my own and would have failed as a comparative history due to the very different states of research on the different areas. For this reason, I have focused on central and western Europe. In the east and the north, its boundaries are formed by the limits of the German-speaking territories, and the Mediterranean and the Atlantic coasts serve as southern and western boundaries. However, as my aim is not to write a history of Christianity, but a history of the problems faced by religion, I have made certain selections within this core area too. I have only taken into account national histories of Christianity if this was necessary. Only by considering the multiple versions of civil society, as far as thematic focus and the state of scholarship allowed, could a sense of the overarching common features be obtained.

The beginning and end points of the periods under discussion – 1750 and 1850 – are not marked by particular events. Instead, they are intended as a rough delineation of the period. The second half of the eighteenth century was of interest because it offered a view both of the institutional state of Christianity at the end of the *ancien régime* as well as of the upheavals that were already visible on the horizon. The first half of the nineteenth century, on the other hand, allowed me to include as much of the new arrangements regarding the relationship between religion and society as was necessary in order to gain an impression of the trajectory that the transformation of the social forms of religion would take in modern western European society.

This book is divided into five chapters. The first chapter describes the close links between Christian churches and, on the one hand, state rule in a society based on hierarchy and, on the other, the reproduction of a society founded on privileges and aristocracy. Neither Protestantism nor Catholicism provided any clear distinctions between religious and secular social orders, and both orders supported each other in their reproductive mechanisms. This did not, however, result in these two spheres of society pursuing the same interests and sharing the same motivations. From the 1770s onwards, tensions appeared, and continuously increased, in the symbiotic competition between churches, which themselves exercised authority, and secular power. This was particularly the case in Catholic areas. These tensions resulted in attempts at reform, with secular rulers extending their influence far into the everyday life of the church and its structures, as well as into ideas on piety, but this did not lead to a long-term solution that could reconcile the different interests.

The second chapter is concerned with the ways in which the institutional forms of Christianity were incorporated into the legal structure of post-revolutionary civil society. The chapter begins with a section on the French Revolution and its difficult relationship with religion. The major instances of secularization, by which churches were deprived of all their rights to govern and lost most of their property, formed an important prerequisite for the different churches to be incorporated into a civil society built on participation and to make a plurality of confessions possible. The subsequent innovations in secular and ecclesiastical law meant that one's own adherence to a particular creed increasingly became a private matter. Religion could no longer function as a means of social inclusion. It is precisely for this reason that Christianity played an important role in the reorganized political space of nation-state societies. All social theories, regardless of political preference, considered religion to be a prerequisite for modern associative relationships. In a political context, Christianity gained importance as a source of symbols and rituals useful for providing constitutional monarchies with a modern guise and for shaping the nation as an entity based on shared experience.

The third chapter then turns to the changes in institutional structure and in piety that Christianity was subject to during these radical shifts. It became apparent that a very broad range and combination of organizations and social movements – from the centralized and hierarchical world church with its missionary orders to the Methodist free church* as well as networks of associations that were not tied to any particular region and brotherhoods with an array of different aims – provided an appropriate response to the social integration of civil society. By necessity, however, these organizations and movements also entailed a publicly visible dramatization of membership, and this also influenced different styles of piety. Here, if not before, it becomes clear that secularization is not the opposite of religion but a constitutive component of the history of religious forms in the modern period. Piety was in need of new occasions and points at which it could be connected to processes of social inclusion. Family and the construction of a type of individuality suited to modern society took on this function. Such new forms of piety shaped the means of communicating with transcendence in such a way that they could serve to reflect the social integration of society through media. The fact that European Christianity became more feminine was also a result of such shifts. This change developed through an explosive and jarring combination of, on the one hand, the new roles women found in the church and, on the other hand, an aggressive misogynistic discourse about the piety of women.

The fourth chapter deals with religion as culture, tracing the semantics of religion found in self-descriptions and external descriptions from the period between around 1720 and 1850. They show tectonic shifts in the concept of 'religion' as well as in speculations on the origins of religion, in descriptions of the possible and desirable forms of religion, and, finally, in what the function of religion was considered to be.

Moreover, European expansion meant that new knowledge was continuously accrued, and, within the semantic framework just mentioned, this new knowledge was combined with the self-image of a Christian Europe and its Christianity. At the beginning of the nineteenth century, this was then consolidated into an abstract concept of religion. Christianity became culture because, in the context of a universal history of humanity, it came to be viewed as one religion amongst many. In this process, a semantic concept of religion developed that had no need of revelation and that released religion from its previous task of maintaining social order. Instead, religion was increasingly described as a prerequisite for and result of an individual's relationship with the world and with him or herself, a relationship which derived from the capacity of humans, as cultural creatures, to symbolize and create meaning. In God, the human spirit viewed itself. Feuerbach then posed the question concerning the pathology of self-images, which were placed within the context of religious meaning. After Schleiermacher's time, theological thought as a whole deviated very little from these concepts. To assume that God existed as a prerequisite for the world, as Schelling laid out once more in his philosophy of revelation, became an undertaking without any systemic resonance because it deprived individuals of their freedom. In all these areas, and as early as the eighteenth century, religion and Christianity became important points of reflection and media of self-description, through which a society in the process of modernization considered the forms of and prerequisites for forming associative relationships.

The conclusions in the fifth chapter summarize the main results regarding the concept of secularization. The conclusion reached is that secularization exists.

# 1

# Christianity in the *ancien régime*

The church was an indispensible means of displaying and legitimizing royal power in eighteenth-century Europe. Empress Maria Theresa (1740–80), for example, placed particular emphasis on cultivating the concept of *pietas Austriaca*, the particular Catholic piety of the House of Habsburg, which had been developed by her predecessors since the seventeenth century. The Vienna court calendar shows that in 1738 alone she attended solemn mass in Vienna and the surrounding area fifty-eight times and was present at fifteen processions, turning them into state occasions. She made two pilgrimages*, arranged seven visits of the court to the Marian column and finally arranged two fraternity feasts and two other feasts for the ladies of the Order of the Star Cross. Her display of piety was matched by the French king, Louis XVI (1774–93), the 'Most Christian Majesty'. During his coronation on 11 June 1775 in the cathedral of Reims, he was anointed with oil from the Holy Ampoule, brought into the cathedral by the Abbot of Saint Rémy with a magnificent entourage. Before this, Louis had taken the coronation oath, swearing to protect the church, to safeguard its privileges and rights, and to persecute those it proclaimed as heretics. Together with the other bishops and archbishops of the Gallican Church, the Archbishop of Reims also presented him with the sword, part of the royal insignia. This was a sign of his secular power, identifying Louis as the source of the law in his kingdom. Right down to the smallest detail, the coronation ritual expressed the idea that royal rule was entirely divine in origin, thus tying the monarch closely to the church and its priests. Church and monarchy supported each other, and they were to remain bound to one another through the sanctified person of the king. During the solemn mass which followed the coronation, the king therefore received both wine and bread during Communion; that is to say, he received the sacrament in the same way as the clergy.[1]

Even Frederick II, who placed more importance on Enlightenment philosophy than on religious faith, insisted on his episcopal rank when dealing with his consistories* and occasionally even styled himself *vicarius Christi*. He made use of the idea that this gave him the power to bind and release in order to claim authority especially regarding marriage law. There was a strong degree of irony to this, which was based on the awareness that, with state rule now seeking to derive its legitimacy through natural law, the role which religion played in shaping society, along with religion's consequences for the social community, should also be determined by and judged on the basis of that same natural law, which automatically meant on the basis of the needs of the state as well.

In eighteenth-century France, lawyers were also busy dismantling the remnants of medieval social order. The *sacre* in Reims was declared to be nothing but an edifying spectacle for the people, which no longer reflected the real foundations of royal power. Writing about Louis XVI, the French chancellor d'Aguesseau claimed that the coronation ceremony merely served as a reminder that the king should act in accordance with the Ten Commandments when carrying out his duties as a ruler. Diderot's *Encyclopédie* stated that the king's claim to power derived solely from his descent, as specified in Salic law. Furthermore, the function of the impressive display at the king's coronation was to educate the people and sanctify the king as a person so no one might seek to kill him later. Such a rationalization of the king's sacral aura also influenced royal practice. Louis XV (1715–74) had already refrained from healing scrofula, and, according to the sources, Louis XVI made only one attempt to prove the magical and religious power of his sacral kingship in this way. Joseph II also reinterpreted his role as ruler: he considerably reduced the number of churches he visited and cut back his attendance at public church services by two-thirds.[2]

These developments were not simply related to the question of how secular power derived its legitimacy. Instead, they reflected the fact that in a pre-modern society, religion, which shared the same feudal structures as the secular world, was not only closely connected to secular state rule but also competed with it. By the second third of the eighteenth century, the religious sphere, ruled by the church, and the sphere of secular power had diverged significantly. As a result, state power, which was becoming increasingly consolidated, no longer hesitated to intervene in church affairs and, if necessary, to limit the church's influence. Conversely, religion needed to find a new place for itself within society. Increasingly, it came to be seen as a social space whose aims and inner logic were no longer accepted without question by the rest of society.

## Symbiotic competition: Pre-modern ecclesiastical and secular rule in Europe

Inevitably, this transformation was a complicated and contradictory process, which involved all levels of social reality, from direct interactions between individuals to questions concerning the organization of institutions. The institutional forms of religion had always clearly reflected the fact that it was part of a society that was organized hierarchically by estates and that was essentially agrarian but included growing enclaves of commercial production and trade. In this context, the only way in which power could be established on a permanent basis was by monopolizing land ownership, linking this ownership with direct authority over people. In this way, the society of pre-Revolutionary Europe had evolved from the early medieval period, developing into a society with an aristocratic hierarchy. From the beginning of the modern period onwards, structural patterns relating to function increasingly gained importance. As a result, by the last third of the eighteenth century, the abolition of noble privileges was overdue and only seemed to be a matter of time. This had a fundamental effect on aristocratic, land-owning churches.

Of course, the historical dynamics of the relationship between secular and religious worlds in the pre-modern period were determined both by the ways in which the two differed and stood in opposition to one another and by the aspects in which they were identical. Latin Christianity continued to be influenced by the Jewish and Early Christian idea of an entirely transcendent god who no longer inhabited the world he had created. Latin Christianity could therefore present itself as being the complete opposite of this life and this world's order, and it could thus also serve as a grounding for criticism of the world and those who ruled and shaped it. By distinguishing between a holy and a secular sphere, and by also making this distinction within the secular world, Christianity contributed to the 'disenchantment of the world'. Moreover, for the history of Europe (as for the development of Christianity itself) it was significant that the immortal soul of man became the point at which man was connected to this one God, who observed the world. Thus, through their souls, every single person was granted a share in and access to the divine. Mankind had access to transcendence, as symbolized by Jesus, who was both man and god. In a secular context, this idea manifested itself in European history as a process of individualization and formed the basis for the inalienable rights of man, whereas, from a religious point of view, the duality of God and the divine soul meant that man was responsible for his salvation. The presence of sin in the world raised the question of why God allowed evil to occur and how one could be sure about the salvation of one's soul, problems which have influenced the history of theology and piety in European Christianity right into modern times.

The Roman Empire shaped the non-spiritual aspects of Latin Christianity. The result was a legally based, hierarchical church, which spread throughout the entire Empire, and which, on the other hand, continued to practise its faith as a parish-based church just as it had in the early days of Christianity. Both these aspects connected the church to the social world: the hierarchy of bishops provided a link to the ruling classes and the parishes connected the church with the lives of those that were subject to those rulers.

The Roman church exercised its power to rule based on laws and on a hierarchical structure; moreover, it had access to writing, preserved and transmitted in the monasteries. This meant that, initially, its organizational power structures were clearly superior to the fragile kinship- and follower-based alliances of the Early Middle Ages, whose power was grounded in violence and force. In 1139, the Second Lateran Council drew a clear line between the church and early medieval kinship structures by introducing compulsory celibacy for major orders. The church had received considerable amounts of property through donations and this was to be prevented from circulating within kinship groups. The church's hierarchy resulted in a network of decision-making processes that spanned all of Europe, with decisions based on the Codex Juris Canonici, itself in turn based on Roman law. The church's emphasis on writing meant that it came to dominate society's knowledge and memory, that is to say, its time.[3]

The church's property fell into four main groups. There was monastic property, which provided the material foundation for the many monastic communities, and there were benefices*, which provided a living for ecclesiastical office holders from the curate to the bishops and popes. Furthermore, donations were made by lay people or by clerics themselves, which were used for a variety of purposes, depending on the wishes of the donor. The profits from a donation might go towards paying for benefices as well as making up regular alms donations or paying for masses for 'poor souls' in purgatory. Finally, the church had maintenance funds, which were usually administered by laymen and which mainly served to ensure the upkeep of the church's buildings within a parish.

This was the basis of temporal authority and estates on which the Roman church had constructed a pyramid-like clerical hierarchy; the members of this hierarchy carried out the religious rituals, administered the sacraments and preached the word of God, and thus they became the mediators between God and the laity. In this way, the clergy also ruled the laity spiritually, or at least claimed the right to do so. In practice, then, the clergy's mediating role manifested itself in a clerical hierarchy, the different levels of which worked together according to a set of laws. At its centre, the Pope as *vicarius Dei* held authority over all the clergy (*potestas jurisdictionis*), had the final say in administrative matters and claimed a comprehensive right to judge all spiritual and secular matters of the church (*plenitudo potestas*). The Pope's judiciary and administrative powers were undisputed, but the bishops held the same power to ordain and administered both the spiritual and temporal instruments of power in the ecclesiastical provinces, each made up of several bishoprics. The priests, who were responsible for pastoral work and the administration of the sacraments, answered to the bishop, as the Council of Trent (1545–63) had repeatedly stressed. The Pope and the bishop had several other office holders and authorities at their disposal in order to help them in the duties of their office – for the Roman Curia, there was an administrative body with fixed structures, which from an early date distinguished between chancery (*cancellaria apostolica*), financial authority (*camera apostolica*), and judicial and disciplinary authority. From the High Middle Ages onwards, the bishops answered to a cathedral chapter of canons who were holders of benefices; they claimed the right to elect bishops, whose electoral capitulations required them to pledge that they would represent their own and the church's interests. Archdeacons ensured that the parish clergy obeyed the bishops, they dispensed justice and carried out visitations. Bishops sought to transfer their judicial and disciplinary powers as well as other administrative tasks to a judicial vicar or vicar-general as early as the Late Middle Ages. Unlike the archdeacon, whose powers of office were linked to the benefices he received as a member of the cathedral chapter, judicial vicars and vicars-general acted as deputies of the bishop, and they could therefore be selected on the basis of ability and suitability and could also be removed from office. In order to form a closer link with the parish clergy, the dioceses were divided into deaneries. These were led by a dean who came from the parish clergy and who was responsible for supervising the clergy and reporting to the bishop. The various monastic orders did not fit into the episcopal hierarchy of supervision and administration. Monasteries and the convents of the mendicant orders were organized into provinces with superiors and, in this way, they were subject directly or indirectly to the Pope. For this reason, they gained wide-ranging or complete exemption from episcopal authority, as in the case of the mendicant and knightly orders. This led to serious problems with regard to pastoral care by bishops and its organization.[4]

This structure, which extended across all of Europe, was held together by the church-specific law code of the Codex Juris Canonici and by the fact that the clergy had managed to distinguish themselves as a separate group, which reserved the right to carry out ritual practices in the church and which represented the first estate in society, with a number of privileges and, in the ideal case, a distinct way of life. Tonsure, celibacy and ordination – with four minor and three major orders – ensured that this group was clearly marked off from the rest of society. Access to this group was remarkably open – only those who were illegitimate or who had serious physical disabilities were barred from admission. However, there were certain prerequisites: members had to enter of their own free will; they had to prove their resolve, through an oath and a solemn vow, to take their assigned place in the hierarchy and obey their superiors; and they had to be willing and able to acquire an education. The prerequisites for entering offices within the hierarchy were also determined by spiritual qualification (ordination) and suitability (education). Of course, life in general and the power relations of pre-Revolutionary European agrarian society placed significant limitations on a person's chances of joining the clergy in that these prerequisites presented an almost insurmountable obstacle to the rural lower classes, in particular, but not to the nobility, whose members sought to obtain the higher offices and benefices for themselves. The frequently stark discrepancy between a candidate's actual qualifications and what was, theoretically, required could be resolved by a dispensation from Rome. Fees were payable for such dispensations, and so it was mainly the nobility who could afford to obtain them. In many cases, however, even a dispensation was not enough to clear the way to higher ordination – the office of auxiliary bishop, which became more common from the Late Middle Ages onwards, is mainly a result of this circumstance. Nevertheless, through its admission principles, the church as an organization did open up career paths and thus became an important enabler of social mobility. The church's intention to differentiate itself from the social structures of society and designate its own social space is indicated by the rejection of nepotism and a strict prohibition on taking payment for dispensing services relating to its temporal or spiritual authority, known as simony. On the other hand, these prohibitions also indicate how difficult this was.[5]

For this reason, it was important, both for the clergy and the laity, that the church remained a clearly delimited legal sphere. Spiritual rule also manifested itself as the right to make judgements, including ones that affected secular matters, and this was put into practice through a judicial structure with multiple levels. With regard to the laity, the church claimed the right to adjudicate in matters of marriage law and areas of property law if the problem related to marriage, usury or benefices. All offences against the faith (heresy, apostasy) as well as perjury and offences against the order of the sexes (adultery, bigamy, rape) were, of course, brought before ecclesiastical courts. The clergy were subject to the church courts in all matters. Civil proceedings before ecclesiastical courts were always brought in writing. In criminal cases, a distinction was made between cases that required an accuser and cases of inquiry, which could be initiated by the church authorities *ex officio* if there was sufficient grounds for believing an offence had been committed. Written proceedings and the process of inquiry proved to be important and influential innovations in the history of European legal organization and the power structures. While the church did not hand out corporal or capital punishment and turned serious criminals over to the *brachium saeculare* – the secular arm – the ecclesiastical courts represented instruments of authority, which placed noticeable restrictions on secular rule.[6]

Spiritual and secular existed in a kind of symbiotic competition, which was manifested in the church's secular authority and which derived its dynamic from them. The distinction between spiritualities and temporalities on a material level and the distinction between clergy and laity on the level of personnel never constituted more than a superficial compromise that hid the contradiction underlying it but could not serve to resolve the tensions that existed in the relationship between the church and the secular world. Because the church held property, it wielded significant secular power in addition to its spiritual claims of sovereignty. In this way, the church became a competitor to the slowly emerging state of pre-modern Europe. Conversely, secular rule extended into the church's sphere through its secular estates.

The church's right to tithes, which it had held since the Middle Ages, meant that it had an almost universal right to tax the laity. Occasionally, there were also other forms of indirect taxation. The church not only benefited from the economic profits that its manorial rights provided, but it also, as a rule, exercised the associated judicial rights. However, because the church declared that it did not wield the secular sword, its property was often administered by a secular reeve. Bishops, monasteries and the holders of ecclesiastical benefices often also had these rights by way of purchase, donation and occasionally usurpation. If this property was manorial property, it was, then, no different from the property of the nobility. The special conditions regarding constitutional law in the feudally structured Holy Roman Empire even meant that church property, if it was a direct fief from the king, could serve as the basis for the authority of territorial princes. In these cases, a distinction was made between the direct ecclesiastical revenue granted to the church official in question (*mensa*) and the accompanying imperial fiefdoms. However, as bishops, abbots and prelates of the Imperial Church, these church officials with their territorial prince-bishoprics and imperial abbeys participated directly in the state-building process and in this regard were equal to the secular princes.[7]

Pope Gregory VII had sought to separate church property and ecclesiastical offices from the influence of secular rule in the Investiture Controversy, but this had failed. The church's worldly property and goods continued to mean that its organization could not be entirely autonomous because all ecclesiastical positions were dependent on benefices. Lay people and secular rulers could, therefore, exert significant influence on the church by allocating benefices. Consequently, both sides were willing to enter into disputes. As a result of the compromises that resolved the Investiture Controversy, cathedral chapters now elected the bishop, an office which was particularly significant from the point of view of the princes. The relevant archbishop and the Pope invested the newly elected bishop in his spiritual office, but the king provided him with the corresponding secular assets. The church generally reserved the right to make the final decision when it came to granting offices and benefices, but the laity could influence the process if they held the right of patronage* for a particular position. They suggested a candidate in a process known as presentation, and this candidate was usually confirmed by the collator of the post, usually the bishop. The bishop then also inducted the candidate into his new position (investiture). Lay patronage was important with regard to parish priests, in particular.[8]

The way in which the Investiture Controversy played out showed that secular rulership had not yet gained much organized structure but was determined to shape events. In the Late Middle Ages, however, the authority of princes slowly began to be consolidated into states, and these emerging patterns in spatial organization were no longer in line with the geographical structures and the social order which the church had established.

This was clearest in relation to bishoprics. For this reason, the idea of creating bishoprics for individual territories in order to adjust diocesan boundaries to the structures of secular rule remained on the political agenda until the end of the *ancien régime*. Secular rulers must have found it particularly difficult to accept that the Pope, as head of the church, could extend his influence into their territory through the episcopal hierarchy. From the fourteenth century onwards, princes generally asserted the right over bishops and the Pope to approve instructions by the church's hierarchy; these could only be issued and were only effective if the relevant secular ruler had explicitly approved them. The clergy and church property, on the other hand, pointed to the distinction between clergy and laity, and between temporal and spiritual authority, in order to claim exemption from princely authority and rapidly developing fiscal sovereignty. The *recursus ab abusu* introduced significant changes into the church's legal system by allowing the clergy to appeal to a secular court of law regarding decisions made by an ecclesiastical court. The taxation of the clergy and their associated income had also mostly been implemented through the participation of the ecclesiastical estate in the colleges of estates since the fifteenth century.[9]

## Christian churches in Europe: Organizational forms

It was not until the Reformation that new options for the institutional form of religion and spiritual rulership in pre-modern society arose. Two of the main pillars on which the church's organization rested were torn down. The idea of a universal priesthood meant that the clergy lost their special status as consecrated mediators between God and men – now, the clergy were thought of only as ordained ministers. The reforming authorities in towns and principalities confiscated or secularized all church property or, at the very least, placed it under secular authority, with the exception of church maintenance funds. In doing so, they hoped to eliminate both the material foundations of organized church structures as well as the basis for the symbiotic competition in which they had been engaged. Both processes – the new definition of ecclesiastical office and the secularization of church property – called the traditional episcopal hierarchy into question and reinstated the principle of the parish church. However, the church as an institution needed a hierarchy of qualified office holders in order to survive in the long term, and the question was now who could occupy these positions of power. As ruling princes were usually quick to stake their claims in this situation, they gained a decisive advantage through the Reformation, which, overall, caused a lasting shift in the competition between secular and ecclesiastical rule in favour of the secular side. The symbiosis now turned into one-sided dependent relationships, although this did not happen everywhere or in the same way in all places. A range of possibilities lay at the disposal of those engaged in reform.

Intellectual humanism discussed a neo-Platonic gnostic interpretation of Christianity, which involved the option of a non-church-based form of religion, but this idea quickly became marginalized and suspected of being heretical. Such perennialism* did not disappear entirely, but for the subsequent pre-modern centuries it was of interest only to small groups of intellectuals with very little potential for exerting any organizing influence. Nevertheless, it was of lasting importance for the theology and piety of Christian confessional groups and for the development of the modern culture of knowledge.[10]

The other extreme was found in the Catholic areas and states of Europe. In these areas, Roman Christianity was able to retain its property to a large extent and it was therefore not forced to change its basic social and institutional structures. It was not until the process of confessionalization that the Catholic Church had to adjust to the fact that there was now a plurality of confessions, both with regard to its form as an institution as well as its piety. The episcopal hierarchy remained unchanged, and so the symbiotic competition between ecclesiastical and secular rule continued here. However, as secular principalities now had a much more considerable weight than the church, they could shape Roman Christianity to a regional or national church, depending on their influence. The Gallican Church in France is an example of strong state influence, whereas the churches in Catholic states of the empire indicate a milder version. This social shaping of religion was not restricted to those parts of Europe which continued to follow the old faith. In the British Isles, it combined with Calvinist theology to form the Church of England. In all of these cases, religion had to accept significant losses with regard to its authority in the secular sphere. From the sixteenth to the eighteenth centuries, the only area outside the Papal States in which religion could claim to take on the characteristics of a state was within the structures of the Holy Roman Empire.[11]

The Anabaptists had developed a radical version of the parish church as a result of the Reformation. However, they were soon marginalized and declared heretical because the combination of the principle of the parish and spiritually guaranteed salvation had the potential to be an explosive social force, which posed a threat, in particular, for communal social relationships in towns and rural areas.[12]

In those cases in which Protestant Christianity had lost its worldly property to the secular principalities but continued to institutionalize religion as spiritual rulership, it almost went without saying that territorial statehood served as a model for the institutional structure of the church. Lutheran theologians, in particular, thus had problems in defining the relationship and the boundaries between church and state. Reformed regional churches (*Landeskirchen**) were based on a different, presbyterial idea, but otherwise they did not differ much from the Lutheran ones.

During the process of confessionalization, Calvinism, based on the idea of a self-governing parish church with presbyteries and regional associations, only emerged where the state could no longer serve as a subsidiary organizing principle for a church that could not derive its power structure from secular assets anymore. This was the case in France, which was ruled by a Catholic monarchy. The Edict of Nantes of 1598 granted protection to the Huguenots but beyond this there was no basis for any competition or symbiotic relationship between Calvinism and secular authority. In those areas in which, since the sixteenth century, states had emerged as a federation of estates with very little centralized power, the situation was similar although it was also characterized by the inclusion of multiple confessions. This was the case in the Dutch Republic and in the Swiss Confederacy. The Calvinist churches of these areas were based on the principle of the presbyterial parish church and thus emphasized the second institutional principle that Christianity offered.[13]

## Hierarchy and property

Those Christian churches in Europe which were organized according to an episcopal hierarchy owned considerable property, and thus secular authority, church wealth and episcopal administration coincided. The Catholic imperial territory of Bavaria represents an extreme example of this: at the end of the eighteenth century the church owned around 52 per cent of the land that could be used for agriculture – one-third of this was estimated to belong to monasteries alone. In other Catholic regions of western Europe, church property fluctuated between 10 per cent and about 35 per cent. In France the church owned about one-tenth of the arable land, but there was also strong regional variation. While this is a comparatively low figure, the Gallican Church's wealth was conspicuous enough for contemporaries to suspect that it controlled one-third of the kingdom. In actual fact, on the eve of the Revolution, the Gallican Church's income equalled the *taille*, the tax which yielded the greatest income in the country. The church had income from agricultural land, levies from land and judiciary rights, and income from tithes, which represented around one-third of a farmer's profits. In 1782 the Bishop of Quimper received about 4,000 livres from his estates, 1,000 livres from his manorial monopolies and 8,000 livres, i.e. more than both of the first two categories combined, from the tithes in his diocese. The church was also involved considerably in property transactions in towns as it had, in some cases quite considerable, claims to property transfer fees. The bishop of Paris owned 500 streets, which were the source of dues if property was sold or passed on through inheritance. These fees were around one-third of the bishop's total income. In the Iberian Peninsula, the share of the church's agricultural property was slightly higher than in France, but income from other rights was less significant. In Castile, the church owned around 15 per cent of the land although there was significant regional variation here, too. In Galicia, it only owned 5 per cent of the land, but, in the provinces of Seville and Toledo, the figure was 20 per cent. Church land was usually broken up into plots and leased out, and large ecclesiastical latifundia were rare. In addition to income from land, the church received considerable amounts from tithes and from church lending, with the church in Castile ultimately receiving considerably more than one-fifth and probably more than a quarter of all agricultural and commercial income. In Italy, the church held more wealth in the south than in the north, with land ownership varying between 10 and 25 per cent. Here, the church did not own much property in towns, but its most significant source of income was, as in other countries, tithes.

In these central and western European areas, around one-fifth of the land appears to have been held by the church and around a quarter of the income generated ended up in the coffers of the church as a result of the church's economic activities and through its rights to levies and fees and its privileges as a ruling authority. The Anglican Church looked poor by comparison. It retained its feudal property rights after the Glorious Revolution, but it had already lost around 40 per cent of its property in the course of the Reformation through the dissolution of the monasteries.

Two peculiarities characterized the church's distribution of wealth and thus also the internal structure of the churches: high and low clergy had an extremely unequal share in this ecclesiastical wealth, and there were significant differences even within these two groups. Canons in French aristocratic religious foundations had between 3,000 and 10,000 livres at their disposal and the 750 or so abbots of the monarchy received an average of about 10,000 livres. Episcopal sees had the largest amounts of revenue. At the top of the list were the dioceses of Cambrai and Paris with 200,000 livres, Rouen and Toulouse were estimated to receive about 90,000 to 100,000, and dioceses such as Besançon or Vienne had an income of about 35,000 livres. This money had to pay for the entire administration of a diocese, but the amounts involved showed that those who decided on the allocation of benefices could exert considerable power.[14]

The late medieval form of spiritual rule in the Imperial Church had merged with the form of stratified statehood that had developed in the Holy Roman Empire since the end of the fifteenth century. Despite all disputes surrounding ecclesiastical property, it was then left to slowly fossilize. The Catholic empire and the Catholic Church supported each other. This is why the church had a share in the imperial state's structure. Although the church's sovereignty was contained within the feudal system of the Holy Roman Empire, the archbishops, bishops, abbots and prelates, who were registered in the Imperial Register and had a seat and vote at the imperial diet (Reichstag\*), were granted territorial sovereignty, which, following the Peace of Westphalia\*, meant that they were even entitled to forge external alliances. The so-called ecclesiastical electoral states accounted for about 15 per cent of the area of the empire. In the middle of the eighteenth century, however, they were a very mixed group with regard to prestige and power. Since the Golden Bull (1356), three (Trier, Mainz and Cologne) of the five archdioceses on the princely bench of the empire had held the right to elect the king; the archbishops of Salzburg and Besançon each held the title of prince of the empire along with twenty other bishops. In addition to these, another twelve abbots, whose imperial fiefdoms had granted them privileges which allowed them to rise from the prelature, sat on the princely bench at the imperial diet alongside the heads of the major knightly orders. The abbots and provosts on the prelates' bench preceded the counts and lords in the hierarchy of the empire. The way in which these ecclesiastical princes were incorporated into the hierarchy of prestige and legal position roughly corresponded to the different levels of political importance of the territorial states they ruled.

These different positions in the hierarchy, however, which corresponded to those found amongst secular nobles, were less important than the fact that these ecclesiastical domains were also part of a second, ecclesiastical structure and legal framework. They were integrated into the hierarchy of the church and the great European orders, and this meant that they were quite different in character and distinct from secular statehood. Their ecclesiastical authority meant that they could not be fully integrated into the empire, but their secular aspects meant that they could not form a national church. Although the dioceses in the empire were grouped into nine ecclesiastical provinces, the Imperial Church (Reichskirche*) as such was not a tangible organizational entity. It existed through the political structures of the empire, which, by a degree of necessity, meant that bishops and archbishops had to act as secular rulers even with regard to questions concerning church matters. The failure of the Febronian reforms in the 1770s would show this very clearly. A synod of bishops or a national council could not emerge under these circumstances.

For the same reason, membership of the Imperial Church protected the bishops neither against the Curial absolutism of Rome nor against the aspirations of territorial rulers to create state churches. Rome had three nunciatures in the empire (Vienna, Cologne and Graz); the nuncio in Lucerne was responsible for the Swiss Confederacy and the nuncio in Brussels for the Netherlands. Since their establishment in the last third of the sixteenth century, these *missi cum potestate legati a latere* had not only acted as diplomatic representatives of the papacy but had also, over time, acquired considerable jurisdictional and spiritual authority and intervened in regular episcopal jurisdiction. Nuncios were therefore much more than mediators between the Pope and the bishops. In addition, as they supervised all exempted ecclesiastical institutions on behalf of the papacy, they also acted as efficient agencies of papal centralism. However, this did not change the fact that the state-like aspects of the Reichskirche conflicted with its organizational autonomy as a church.[15]

In France, the process of state formation centred on the monarchy had shaped the Catholic Church into an episcopal church largely independent of Rome and oriented towards the monarchical centre of secular rule. The Concordat of Bologna codified this regime in 1516, doing away with the canonical election of bishops and granting the Most Christian Majesty the right to appoint all bishops and the major abbots. The King proposed a candidate (*nominatio*) and the Pope appointed him (*institutio*), although the examination of the candidate's suitability for office meant that the Pope retained the right to veto a particular appointment (idoneity). The position of the bishops was also strengthened. For nine months of the year, they held the patronage of all the minor church offices in their dioceses. In return, Francis I (1515–47) had renounced provisions in the Pragmatic Sanction of Bourges, which had regulated relations between the king, the bishops and the Pope since 1437. It had been particularly important for Rome that the superiority and regular meeting of councils were no longer mentioned in 1516. However, the provision that papal bulls could only be published with royal approval was retained. This was the basis for the development of a Gallican Church in which the Pope's authority was at best indirect even in spiritual matters; conversely, the king's position within the church was strengthened in the long term as it gave him access to over 800 well-endowed benefices. The king made use of these to bind the nobility to the monarchy. The *feuille des benefices*, in which these ecclesiastical positions were listed, thus resembled a land register of the king's noble clients, and the church, as a church of the nobility, had secured its position as a national institution.[16]

Louis XIV (1643–1715) had sought to further improve his position towards the end of the seventeenth century by not only claiming the secular income during the vacancy of an episcopal see but also claiming the bishop's right of patronage. In the subsequent dispute with Innocent XI (1676–89), the king initiated a meeting of representatives of the high and low clergy, which in 1684 issued the Four Gallican Articles in the 'Declaration of the Clergy of France', edited by Cardinal Bossuet. It freed secular rule from ecclesiastical influence, but made the Pope's spiritual sovereignty entirely dependent on the agreement of church councils, on church law and on the customs and laws of France. The Four Gallican Articles did not last, and their retraction in 1693 was a first step on the way to the cooperation between Pope and King against the Jansenism of the French clergy, which the Pope condemned in the bull *Unigenitus* in 1713. However, the conflict had shown to what extent the interests of the Gallican hierarchy and monarchical power overlapped.

Nevertheless, this did not change the fact that the social position of the Gallican Church was coming under increasing pressure. The estate courts, the *parlements*, continued to adhere to the spirit of the Four Gallican Articles throughout the eighteenth century, jealously seeing to it that episcopal jurisdiction remained limited to spiritual matters. At the same time, they interfered in the church's judicial rights by supporting every cleric who sought an appeal against a bishop's court before a *parlement*. From the middle of the century onwards, those who refused to pay tithes could, in most cases, rely on the goodwill of the *parlements*.

For this reason alone, and more as a defensive reaction than anything else, the view that secular and ecclesiastical power each had their own sovereign sphere gained increasing traction among the clergy. This is how the assembly of the French clergy formulated it in 1765 to justify the bishops' complete freedom in ecclesiastical matters. On the intellectual stage, however, this battle was already lost: referring to the state's duty of care for its citizens, the lawyers of the Enlightenment argued against any legal claims and authority that the church had that affected the daily lives of citizens. Marriage was increasingly a point of contention for lawyers in France from the middle of the century onwards. Because it was considered sacred, judges in the *parlements* could not dissolve it, and this created an area of law which was dominated by the episcopal courts and which had great relevance for citizens' property rights. Thus, long before the Revolution in the writings of secular jurists, it was already claimed that marriage was essentially a (dissolvable) contract.[17]

In the Contract of Poissy (1561), the monarchy had succeeded in making church property subject to the state's fiscal system. As a result of the meeting at which the contract was agreed, the French church undertook to pay a tax on ecclesiastical property in order to pay off royal debts. This was referred to as a voluntary contribution (*don gratuit*) in order to emphasize that church property was fundamentally exempt from taxation, and the church insisted on retaining control over the assessment of the level of taxation, as well as overseeing its raising and spending. Under Louis XIV, these 'voluntary' tax contributions became more frequent, and in return the king allowed the clergy to hold regular meetings every ten years. Once this arrangement had developed into a permanent tax bureaucracy, the meeting of the clergy became the Assemblée du Clergé de France. The synodal make-up of the Gallican Church was, at its core, based on the organization of the estates.

This basis continued to determine the structure of assemblies of the French clergy in the eighteenth century. Each of the 130 dioceses of the monarchy had its own tax chamber (*chambre ecclesiastique*), in which, in theory, elected representatives of the diocesan clergy were to decide on the tax burden of the high and low clergy. In actual fact, those who made the decision were appointed or co-opted, so that normally the bishop, two members of the cathedral chapter, two more canons from the diocese and two other clerics carried out the tax assessment. There were no appeals before the *parlements* against the decisions of these tax chambers, so that the diocesan clergy was at the mercy of a small group with a vested interest that came from within its own ranks. From the 1760s onwards, resistance grew amongst them against this serious disadvantage, and in some dioceses synodal resolutions were passed which led to a democratization of the tax chambers. However, there was no significant reorganization until the Revolution.

The situation in the General Assembly was an even greater source of irritation for the lower clergy. Each of the twenty-eight archbishoprics of France was represented by two bishops and two ecclesiastical representatives from the second estate. All of these delegates were elected. However, the bishops were usually selected on a rotational basis according to who had held the office the longest, and those who were elected as representatives of the ecclesiastical province were usually members of the nobility and, more and more often, young vicars-general. The office of vicar-general had been created in the 1720s and had quickly developed into a position held by those whose ambition it was to later become bishops. As a result, from 1750 onwards, the Assemblée consisted of a homogenous assembly of current and future bishops who were selected from among the aristocracy and who shared a strong sense of class as well as a network of aristocratic family relations. The lower clergy was excluded; in the entire reign of Louis XV, only one parish priest was admitted to the Assemblée Générale.

Whenever this body, representing a truly aristocratic church, met once a decade in Paris, the assemblies lasted at least three months and there was a considerable amount of work to be done. As an assembly tasked with approving taxes, it was entitled to put together the catalogue of complaints from the Gallican Church which was passed on to the king. Increasingly, the focus of these complaints was the interference of *parlements* in the legal sphere of the church. In addition to this, however, questions concerning the organization of the church as well as the preaching of the gospel and pastoral care were addressed. In 1775, the causes of the decline of religion in France were discussed and it was decided to improve the education and training of the clergy. In all these matters, the General Assembly acted as if it were a synod of the bishops of the church of France – a gathering that the king consistently refused to convene. When decisions had to be taken concerning questions of dogma or the proclamation of the gospel, the bishops discussed the matter behind closed doors, and they voted not in order of the rank of their dioceses, but according to the length of time they had been in office. Their main task, however, continued to be decisions on royal tax demands and the corresponding assessment of the clergy, and the social make-up of the General Assembly was clearest in this context. The high clergy of the monarchy had no qualms about letting their significantly poorer brethren shoulder the majority of the financial burden. While parish priests who earned 300 livres often had to pay one-fifth to one-sixth of their income in taxes, bishops with an income of up to 30,000 livres frequently only had to pay 1,000 livres in tax. Canons of aristocratic religious foundations enjoyed similar preferential treatment. This situation had already caused outrage in the first third of the century, but it was not until 1751 that the Assemblée Générale decided on a system of progressive taxation, consisting of eight brackets. However, while this remedied the previously arbitrary nature of taxation, it did nothing to change the fundamentally unfair distribution of the financial burden that taxation presented.

The General Assembly of the Clergy of France meant that the Gallican Church as an institution had a concentrated structure and autonomy encompassing the entire country, which was unrivalled in all other regional churches of Europe. This also had its disadvantages, however, for in no other part of Europe was the social contrast between the aristocratic group of bishops and the parish clergy as obvious nor did the church allow itself to be so clearly identified as part of aristocratic society, which was, in turn, of course dependent on monarchical state structures. In the last third of the eighteenth century, this was reflected in an unexpected way: the clergy as a group disappeared entirely from the discourse on the order of estates. Even before Mirabeau equated the nation with the third estate, the genealogist Mangard had stated in 1787 that there were only two estates: the aristocracy and the commoners. According to Mangard, the aristocracy encompassed the clergy because both groups enjoyed the same privileges. Loménie de Brienne, Bishop of Toulouse and Bordeaux as well as minister of state under Louis XVI, similarly argued that the nation consisted of the aristocracy and of commoners. He argued that the clergy belonged to the aristocracy on account of their achievements and abilities and should thus also be entitled to a say in the governing of the nation. This argument was intended to defend the status of the bishops but it inevitably led to the church being pulled into the abyss along with the nobility when society finally cast aside the *ancien régime*'s order of privileges.[18]

A church that was based on landed property and the guaranteed privileges that came with estate-based authority would necessarily be structured in a particular way. Nevertheless, there was significant variation amongst the regional churches in eighteenth-century Europe. Much depended on the situation in which the relevant state found itself. In Spain, the reign of the Bourbon kings, who had been in power since Philip V (1700–46), strengthened the tendencies towards the development of a national church. There were fifty-two episcopal sees, which were organized into eight ecclesiastical provinces, and a concordat concluded in 1753 with Benedict XIV (1740–58) confirmed universal royal patronage rights for all of these sees and for the major abbots of the kingdom. This meant that the Pope was only able to appoint office holders to fifty-two benefices directly, in addition to retaining control of the nunciature in Madrid with its opportunities of influencing affairs. The Spanish monarchs used their influence to develop an episcopate that was loyal to the monarchy, but the bishoprics were not all given to members of the aristocracy. From the beginning of the eighteenth century onwards, an increasing number of bishops came from Spain's monastic communities. Unlike in France, the church in Spain had no estate-based assemblies, which was due to the way in which ecclesiastical property was taxed. The Spanish monarchy had been able to secure a fixed share of the church's income from tithes, and thus there was no reason to assign the episcopate a fixed place in the order of estates. Furthermore, episcopal power was controlled by cathedral chapters, which as a rule acted with a sense of self-confidence, and by the exemption of Spain's influential religious houses. This led to foreign envoys remarking on the fragmented nature of the Spanish church in the eighteenth century, which, they said, was ruled by bishops with very little apparent interest in wielding power. However, the Spanish Inquisition continued to have considerable power both in society and in the church. It had started as a means of converting the Jews and had developed into a wide-reaching apparatus of power that was controlled neither by the bishops nor by the king; the Inquisition ensured that any offence against social and religious norms could threaten an individual's social and physical existence. However, the number of accusations and convictions decreased in the course of the eighteenth century, and from the 1760s onwards the monarchy was more willing to curtail the autonomy of this instrument of power.[19]

In the church of Italy, the immediate presence of papal power together with the many small divisions of secular territories in many ways had stood in the way of a post-Tridentine expansion of episcopal power. State power apparently had not been able to function as a supporting structural counterpart for the ecclesiastical hierarchy; as a result, although the organization of religion was characterized by the same structural elements that have already been discussed, corporate elements within the Italian church and a very varied system of proprietary churches often limited the influence of the church hierarchy. The papacy had lost most of the patronage rights it had originally held for all episcopal sees in Italy and, outside the Papal States, the Pope only appointed the bishops of Venice and Lucca, although even in these cases he had to take the views of the local population into account. In all other Italian kingdoms, principalities and city states, secular rulers had secured the right of presentation for bishoprics. The dioceses of upper Italy, which had been created in the Late Middle Ages, were often directly controlled by individual noble families. The dioceses were generally small. In the kingdom of Naples alone, there were 131 at the end of the eighteenth century. In the small territory of the Papal States, there were sixty-five sees. In the eighteenth century, instead of developing towards a civil society, Italy experienced refeudalization, but nonetheless, the number of aristocratic bishops was comparatively low. About one-third of the bishops of the Kingdom of Naples came from noble families, and in the Papal States the number of nobles decreased to around the same level in the course of the century. As in Spain, many bishops came from monastic orders and, in the Papal States, the majority were recruited from the Curia: the dioceses were always part of the system of alimentation at the papal court. The other dioceses were part of this network in that they had to pay one-fifth to one-third of their fairly limited income to Rome via different legal titles. However, the Curia did not develop any centralizing institutional or political influence outside the Papal States, and so Italy's church continued to be organized polycentrically.[20]

The Ecclesia Anglicana had developed from the unusual combination of a feudally based national church and a Calvinist creed. The reformation policies of Henry VIII (1509-47), which were initially somewhat irresolute, had meant that the English church had lost its monastic properties, but the entire systems of benefices and the episcopal hierarchy had remained intact. Both were the focus of the revolution and Civil War in the seventeenth century and, in addition, the church had since become exposed to significant competition from the voluntary churches of the different Protestant denominations. The Anglican Church continued to exist after 1688 as a church organized according to an episcopal hierarchy that formed a counterpart to the monarchy. Since the reign of Henry VIII, however, monarchs had had the ability to make the jurisdictional appointment of bishops, but did not carry out spiritual ordination. The Church of England thus increasingly resembled a political institution of the monarchy, which took the shape of a large Protestant sect protected and supported by the monarchy and which, through lay patronage, could also be utilized by the gentry as a means of exercising social power. Preachers and the gentry usually cooperated very well in the control and moral education of the general population; the church's judicial powers, however, had been severely curtailed. The church had hardly any legal influence left in the secular sphere since marriage was no longer regarded as a sacrament but merely as a contract. Although the cathedral chapters retained the right to elect bishops, the monarch's suggestion of who to appoint as bishop, and in many cases as dean, was binding, which meant that, like in France, the monarchy had access to an impressive amount of power and maintenance titles through a total of more than 1,000 positions subject to patronage rights. In the eighteenth century, following the prorogation of the convocation in 1717, the Church of England no longer had any estate or synodical body of its own. It was, therefore, not able to carry out its own assessment of taxation levels, and the Archbishop of Canterbury had since undertaken the redistribution of taxes. Thus, taxation of ecclesiastical property was taken for granted and did not require negotiation. Nevertheless, the Anglican clergy participated in shaping and exercising political power in the House of Lords and Parliament. The twenty-six bishops of the Church of England, all loyal to the king, were amongst the 213 peers in the House of Lords, and the entire clergy was eligible to vote in elections for the House of Commons. Despite this strong political position, the Church of England's religious and social monopoly had been undermined with the appearance of Dissenters and their focus on individual conscience as a basis for institutionalized religion. It was, therefore, necessary to further strengthen the position of the Church of England. In 1661, the Corporation Act prevented Dissenters from forming their own corporations and, in 1673, the Test Act prevented Dissenters from taking public office. Thus, a person's public reputation and any active participation in civic life depended by law on participation in Anglican Communion. The Toleration Act of 1689 then codified the combination of religious tolerance and the social marginalization of Dissenters. This was a position Dissenters were only able to escape gradually over the course of the eighteenth century. From 1718 onwards, they could take up public office under certain circumstances, from 1727, Dissenters could serve in the House of Commons and, in 1745, the ban on marriages between Dissenters and Anglicans was lifted.

Catholics were excluded from this expansion of religious tolerance and continued to be treated as political and religious enemies of the common good.[21]

## Parish churches and the state

Nowhere else in Europe was the formation of a Protestant church based so directly on the old social and organizational structures as in England, nor would this have been possible. However, it was not just a question of theology that decided whether religion manifested itself socially as a territorial, bureaucratically structured, confessional monopoly that was closely tied up with the institutions of the secular state or whether it took the form of a presbyterial parish church with only the privileges of a corporation and a loose relationship to the state.

The presbyterial parish church had prevailed where secular rule had not followed the model of the centralized princely state but had, as in Switzerland and the Dutch Republic, developed as a federation of polycentric autonomous estates with little centralized power. Under these circumstances it was hardly possible to force the entire population to accept one single confession. The Catholic and Reformed cantons in the Swiss Confederacy had only achieved a parity between the confessions after fighting wars and, in the Netherlands, a multiplicity of confessions had become possible in the seventeenth century simply because of the need to create as comprehensive a coalition as possible to counter the Spanish enemy. In any case, any existing church property in Reformed churches had been entirely secularized and handed over to secular authorities. Reformed theology's focus on the community supported this but ultimately also relegated the religious parish to second place behind political municipalities or parishes.

In the Netherlands in the mid-1570s, the revolutionary uprising had led to the Reformed estates placing all church property under the municipal authorities. The church maintenance funds (fabrica ecclesiae*) and all other estates that had previously been used to provide an income to the clergy were now administered directly by the estate councils and the authorities of the towns. They thus took on the responsibility of supervising church buildings and providing for preachers. Not long after, this responsibility was extended to the care of the poor and those in need of support. Consequently, church masters (*Kirchenmeister*) and almoners, supervised by the municipal authorities, were appointed in all towns, villages and hamlets in order to ensure the church's property and endowments were managed appropriately.

At their first revolutionary assembly in Dort in 1572, the estates had spoken of freedom of religion applying equally to Reformed churches and the Catholic Church. This ideal did not, however, survive the pressures of the war against Spain. Only a few years later the Catholics were forced into the defensive. By the 1580s, all of the United Provinces had banned public Catholic ceremonies and had confiscated Catholic Church property. In 1576, the provincial estates had committed themselves to adopting the Calvinist faith in the long term and had elevated it to the status of a publieke kerk* (public church). A sustainable way had thus been found to allow the concept of the parish church, tolerance and Calvinist state religion to exist side by side, and this situation lasted until the Batavian Revolution at the end of the eighteenth century. This public church was supported by state-administered church property. In addition, the estates committed themselves to levying church taxes if necessary. Only Reformed practices and Calvinist teaching were permitted in social institutions, schools, universities, the army, the navy and even the overseas trading companies. From the 1620s onwards, all public office holders had to commit themselves to Calvinism, but it was not until the eighteenth century that regents were required to be members of the public church. This was already a reaction to the fact that the public church neither held a confessional monopoly nor represented true confessional parity. In most towns, Anabaptists and Lutherans had had the right to have their own church buildings since the seventeenth century, and these were known as 'hidden churches'. The internal dynamics of Calvinist theology forced the public church to adopt flexible policies. Where the Protestant principle of universal priesthood was understood to mean that correct teaching and true faith were determined by one's own understanding of the Gospel, which had to be justifiable to one's conscience, the proliferation of sects and different denominations could not be stopped by theological means. In 1619, the Synod of Dort* confirmed the doctrine of predestination, thus ruling against the Remonstrants' theology of an individual's role in their own salvation. Remonstrant preachers were expelled, with their brotherhoods and congregations developing outside the public church from that point onwards. The Nadere Reformatie* ('further Reformation'), with its idea of spiritual rebirth, gave the Remonstrant theology of grace a mystical-spiritualistic colouring, and their Pietist conventicles* in the eighteenth century were also not part of the public church. In addition to these developments, religious refugees fled to the Netherlands in the eighteenth century: Protestants from Salzburg, Mennonites from the Swiss Confederacy, Jews from eastern Europe and Huguenots from France. Most importantly, however, roughly one-third of the population of the Dutch Republic had always remained Catholic. In the south, the Catholic population maintained a clear majority, but even in the large cities of northern Holland about one-fifth of the inhabitants claimed to be Catholic in 1775, a number which even increased towards the end of the century.

The principle of the public church did not lead to parity, but it combined the religious and social tolerance of other confessional churches with the privileges due to corporations enjoyed by the Calvinist church. It meant that other confessions were denied public support, but the municipal authorities and regents refrained from intervening in their communities, unlike in the other principalities in Europe that had decided to tolerate multiple churches. In the Netherlands, church and state had already become separate at this point. The situation was more complex within the public church as a balance needed to be achieved between the church's autonomy and the authorities' influence. This was evident in larger towns in which there were several churches. Here, the political organization of the town overlay and dominated the religious parish's own organization. In the eighteenth century, there was only one presbytery in Groningen for all three Calvinist churches. It consisted of the preachers, the elders and the deacons. In other cities, the elders were appointed for a limited term; in Groningen, they were appointed for life. Like the deacons, they were chosen through co-optation. Since 1736, this internal vote had taken place in secret, and the parish community were not allowed to participate in any way and did not suggest candidates. Preachers were appointed by the presbytery, but the town councils then approved them, which was the cause of frequent disagreements in the eighteenth century. The preachers took an oath on the municipal authorities, and preachers, elders and deacons, who were really supposed to be responsible for the care of the poor and socially disadvantaged, worked together to ensure church discipline. Together, several towns or parishes formed 'classes', resulting in a supraregional church association. Practically the only way in which the classes were assembled was in the conventions of preachers, and they had authority over church-internal matters and religious affairs (jus in sacra*). Above them in the hierarchy were the provincial synods, for which each class elected two preachers and one elder.

It had been the declared aim of Reformed church formation not to have a common *senatus ecclesiasticus*, but to permanently separate spiritual and secular rule. Nevertheless, care was always taken to ensure that enough members of the town council were elected to the committee of church elders, for which purpose Groningen had even had a quota in place until the last third of the seventeenth century. The regents sent their *comissarissen politiek* (political representatives) to the provincial synods, where they were entitled to have a say on the matters discussed, in order to protect the interests of the secular authorities.

Following the resolutions of the Synod of Dort in 1619, to which the States General had agreed, these provincial synods did not come together as a national synod again. The regents wanted to avoid establishing any kind of ecclesiastical competition to the already only loosely structured confederation of the Netherlands. Church structure thus was not influenced in any serious way by state structures and was more similar to a corporation. Because of this, the public church came to resemble a private association early on. In the eighteenth century, the Calvinist public church hardly differed from other Protestant denominations in this regard. It was therefore natural that there was a desire to deprive the Calvinists of corporation privileges, and this had already been discussed in the last two decades of the century. It was finally implemented as a result of the Batavian Revolution in 1793.[22]

Protestant church formation developed differently where the Reformation had been turned into a state matter by autocratic princely rule. The church system developed almost inevitably as an appendage to state bureaucracy on the one hand and, at the parish level, as part of the rights of aristocratic patronage holders on the other hand. The 'General State Laws for the Prussian States' (Allgemeines Landrecht* *für die Preußischen Staaten*) of 1794 therefore did not refer to individual churches (*Kirchen*) at all but referred to 'the structure of the church' (*Kirchenwesen*) in the provinces. Since the Hohenzollern had converted to the Reformed church in 1614, rulers in Brandenburg-Prussia could only claim the title of summus episcopus* (highest bishop, the title given to the governor of the church) over their Lutheran subjects as an additional element of their territorial sovereignty but not as an integral part of it. On an institutional level, this had led to the establishment of a Church Council, which had all the powers of the former Upper Consistory except with regard to marriage. The Church Council was soon disbanded again, and its responsibilities were taken over by the Privy Council. This meant that leadership of the church became entirely incorporated into the state's bureaucracy, and thus was affected by the internal development of state authorities. At first, a department for spiritual matters was established in the Privy Council. Frederick II (1740–86), however, founded a separate Department for Spiritual Affairs, to which a Lutheran and a Reformed minister of state were appointed. They worked closely with the Justice Department. Because the regional consistories had turned out to be overburdened, from 1750 onwards, Frederick renewed his effort to expand the Berlin authority into a Lutheran Upper Consistory. However, this never achieved any true independence but was headed by whichever minister of state was in charge of the Department for Spiritual Affairs. His responsibilities were limited entirely to ensuring that preaching and teaching were standardized and to the examination of candidates for the offices of parish priest. In 1748, the secular courts had taken on the responsibility of ensuring discipline within the clergy, and the administration of church property was undertaken by the Department for Spiritual Affairs unless individual local parishes carried it out.

There was no question then of economic or judicial autonomy in church matters for Lutherans. In addition, the structures ensuring church discipline, the very essence of the Reformation church, had been weakened in several respects. When the clergy were removed from the jurisdiction of the consistories in 1748, the king's officials were also no longer subject to church discipline within their parishes. The superintendents* appointed by the king could only carry out their visitations in order to report to the authorities under which they were placed. They, as well as the Upper Consistory, were denied independent disciplinary measures. Entirely separate from these structures was a military church that had developed from the time of Frederick I (1688–1713) and which was strongly influenced by August Hermann Francke's Halle Pietism*. It was headed by a Military Consistory with a field provost (Feldprobst*), who examined the military chaplains, ordained them and instructed them in their duties. Serving as a military chaplain for five years established a claim to a position which was allocated through royal patronage, and many superintendents came from the ranks of the military clergy. For this reason, the field provost had considerable influence on who held higher offices in the church.

This nationalization of church leadership corresponded to the expansion of structures of authority at the base of the church. In those areas ruled by manorial lords, Junker* (landed gentry) exercised their patronage rights as part of their general sovereign rights. Under these circumstances, the church could not influence the development of life in the parishes, and the faithful saw the church simply as another aspect of the authority to which they were subject. The situation was similar for the pastoral clergy: the church only existed as part of the state's administrative structure. Under these circumstances, it was hardly possible for the church to develop an independent institutional shape.[23]

The Lutheran church was not tied as closely to state institutions and social rule everywhere else. However, theologians and Protestant lawyers always found it difficult to formulate a church concept which combined the spiritual idea of *ecclesia* and mundane reality. The Lutheran ideal of the parish had provided the possibility of measuring those in authority against the gospels, but this idea was also based more on the identical nature of the two spheres than on their differences. In 1783, Daniel Nettelbladt used three keywords to describe the development of state law regarding the church, and these continued to be relevant in self-descriptions of Protestant church communities and their relationship to state authorities well into the nineteenth century. Initially, episcopalism had transferred episcopal rights to secular rulers, who became the *summus episcopus*. This stage was followed by territorialism, in which the ruler had authority over all religious communities in his domain by virtue of his unrestricted territorial sovereignty. However, this was limited to external church life and could not influence an individual's decision of conscience. Thus, the ruler's choice of confession was no longer binding for his or her subjects, and several confessions could coexist in his territory. The prerequisite for this, however, was that these confessions developed very little independence as churches and that they did not engage in dogmatic dispute amongst themselves or within their own communities. This was the reason for a demand by Samuel Pufendorf that all churches should be dissolved because they were hierarchical institutions and abolishing them would facilitate the coexistence of different churches under one prince's rule. Nettelbladt identified collegialism as the third phase. His principal example of this was the Württemberg Chancellor Christoph Matthäus Pfaff, who, in 1719, was the first to define the church 'according to its original form' as a 'free society of those who join together in communal worship of God according to the teachings of Christ'.[24] As a community based on convictions, this church had transferred its jurisdiction in external ecclesiastical matters to the state because otherwise it would be impossible to live life according to the gospel, given the many corrupt members of society. Such a religious community would be able to deal with its own internal affairs just as other groups in the state did. Thus, the church as an institution was not yet understood as an association but was already considered a privileged corporation which recognized the rights concerning the external affairs of the church (jus circa sacra*) as having been merely transferred to the state.

In the context of the last third of the eighteenth century, Nettelbladt's ideas described an ideal situation rather than reality. In actual fact, in the territory of the empire, only some Reformed churches showed developments approaching these ideas. In most cases, control by the sovereign had led to the presbyterial and synodal aspects of churches being weakened or integrated into the state's supervision of churches.[25]

The institutionalization of religion was increasingly under pressure in the second half of the eighteenth century because all of its different variants seemed outdated. In those instances in which it was still capable of forming state-like structures itself, it only managed with great difficulty to withstand the pressure of the processes of state building that were occurring all around. Where, through its hierarchy and property, it remained intertwined with the rules and privileges of the *ancien régime*, it was affected by aristocratic society and rule themselves coming under criticism. Where religion became institutionalized as an appendage to state administration, its independence and identity were questionable; furthermore, the less autocratic rulers resorted to religion as a means of legitimizing their own position, the more of a problem religion's dependence on them became. Finally, in those cases in which a religious community was given the privileges associated with corporations, it became clear that this was not compatible with a true coexistence of multiple confessions. As structures changed, the social place of religion and its social form changed accordingly.

## Hierarchy and elites

The connection between power and property, characteristic of eighteenth-century churches that were part of aristocratic society, was reflected in the distinction between clergy in higher positions and those in lower-ranking positions as well as in the way in which the secular hierarchy of the estates was copied within the church. However, another way in which the connection manifested itself was the fact that all offices, from that of bishop to that of pastoral clergy, took the form of benefices.

Benefices provided both authority and material provisions to the office holder through different rights to govern and rights of disposition that were not related to the nature of the office. Formally, developed organization separates both aspects, and thus the responsibilities and ability of the official become more important than extraneous maintenance entitlements. In this way, formal organization gains significant independence from its social environment.[26] For this reason, benefices can certainly be used as an 'organizing' tool, but the institution that is created in this way is 'embedded' socially, and this connection is closer, the less the institution is involved in selecting office holders and the more the environment has control of this process. Almost all pre-modern European churches operated a patronage system that allowed lay people to influence the appointment to a particular living. This undermined the church's own organizational logic quite considerably. It represented a continuation of the idea of medieval proprietary churches (*Eigenkirchen*), and meant that the rules of the social world were applied to the ecclesiastical sphere and had considerable structuring influence.

With the exception of the offices of cardinal and pope, there was no office in the Roman hierarchy that could not be allocated through patronage. The system of patronage also survived in the Protestant churches. Through its property, the church became an institution that could provide for members of society, and it functioned as an instrument of social power and a space for the social reproduction of elites. This played out in a number of different ways across Europe, but there were certain recurring patterns.

In his prize-winning treatise on the 'Flaws in the governmental constitution of the ecclesiastical electoral states' (*Mängel in der Regierungsverfassung der geistlichen Wahlstaaten*) in 1787, Joseph Edler von Sartori, government councillor in Ellwangen, described the disadvantages that clerical feudalism presented for the Imperial Church and any improvement of its state-like structures because it increased the influence of the aristocracy.[27] The episcopal thrones in the empire were all firmly in the hands of the nobility and, since the seventeenth century, no one from the middle class had succeeded in ascending to this level in the ecclesiastical hierarchy. Nine out of ten benefices in the cathedral chapters were also held by nobles. Here, too, the strength of an ongoing refeudalization could be felt: in the seventeenth century, the wealthy middle classes had still been able to realistically aspire to the status of canon. Not all groups within the aristocracy aimed to obtain benefices in the Imperial Church to the same extent and not all were equally successful. There had been remarkable shifts in the course of the eighteenth century, with the Imperial Church increasingly serving as a place for the younger sons of those sections of the nobility that suffered most from the development of territorial states. The higher levels of the aristocracy, on the other hand, became less dependent on the church as a means of securing positions for family members. This was also reflected in the emperor's politics. Under Charles VII (1742–45) and Maria Theresa, the influence of the cathedral chapters on elections had still required considerable diplomatic and financial energy. Joseph II then made a point of eschewing this instrument of imperial aristocratic policy.

Such redistributions did not reduce competition for benefices very much. Naturally, some aristocratic families tried to achieve as much continuity as possible in certain bishoprics, but they succeeded less and less. The Wittelsbach family successfully continued the family tradition in Cologne and the other low German bishoprics, but this could only be done with some difficulty and only up until the second third of the eighteenth century. In 1761, Pope Clement XIII (1758–69) refused to approve the Wittelsbach cardinal Johann Theodor as archbishop of Cologne. Families that belonged to the lower nobility were less successful at bringing benefices under permanent dynastic control, and if they did act with the relevant skill, as did the Schönborns up until the beginning of the eighteenth century, they turned the rest of the aristocracy against them.

If a candidate for an ecclesiastical office was related to the predecessor, this increased the candidate's chances of success. However, in general, the impression is that, for the younger sons of the nobility, gaining high ecclesiastical benefices in the Imperial Church was difficult and involved many risks and unknowns. A defining characteristic of the Imperial Church was that benefices were awarded through a combination of election, co-optation and patronage; for this reason, they played a particular role in the social reproduction of aristocratic society. It meant that it was possible to influence the process of filling a post, but the results could not be predicted. Ultimately, these procedures remained opaque for all involved. Large family networks were put to use in the election of bishops, and there are surviving letters that document precisely which cathedral canon could be influenced through which relative. All attempts to put close relatives at an advantage through positions as coadjutor bishops* or resignations in their favour of cathedral canons ultimately proved to be insufficient. Canonries that were held by one family with direct patronage rights, such as the Galen family established in Münster, Osnabrück, Minden and Worms, were the exception.[28]

Even if some families, such as the Droste zu Senden in the north or the southern German counts of Königsegg, were more successful overall than many others in the competition for benefices, this system of institutionalized unpredictability ensured that a large number of noble families were occasionally able to place one of their sons in the Imperial Church's network of benefices. In this way, these benefices made it possible to balance the risks of biological reproduction and the limited resources available for the material needs of noble offspring. It is not certain to what extent kinship, friendship and patronage* contributed to the formation of elites or particular groups, but they contributed significantly to stabilizing the economically and genealogically precarious situation of aristocratic families, especially those of the lower nobility, by making the benefices of high ecclesiastical office available for this purpose.

Conversely, this also meant that no specifically ecclesiastical career path developed in the Imperial Church and that there was, therefore, no specific ecclesiastical elite.

It was not education and ability that determined who obtained an office; instead, the highest offices were often held by nobles who considered themselves to be primarily gentlemen and princes. Meanwhile, it had become rare for a bishop to be entirely without academic education: two-thirds of eighteenth-century prince-bishops had studied theology or law for a few semesters at least. However, only a minority had graduated with an academic degree, and their theological education does not appear to have led to a sense of group identity. This is probably to do with the fact that the places in which they had studied were far apart, and the Collegium Germanicum in Rome actually became less popular in the eighteenth century. The Imperial Church thus had neither a spiritual nor an intellectual centre that could have created a sense of identity among its higher-ranking officials.[29]

There were regions in which the recruitment to the hierarchy of the Catholic Church was even more closely linked to the interests of noble families. From the fifteenth century onwards, proprietary dioceses* had been created in Italy, especially in the northern principalities, and it had become usual for the ruler to hold the right of patronage. The appointment of these proprietary bishops could be influenced by noble families or groups by means of particular rights and claims. Thus, the Mirandola family had created a proprietary church in their territory and, in the sixteenth century, this had been turned into a bishopric. This type of patronage had a legal basis, but there were also informal but very stable proprietary bishoprics. The bishops in Naples, for example, came from the same two groups within the old nobility for almost 400 years from the fifteenth century onwards. Throughout the Early Modern period, Italian noble families invested large amounts of money to increase the glory of their family and consolidate their Christian commemoration in the public consciousness. To this end they secured canonries, chaplaincies, honorary rights to reside in a particular monastery, chapels in Rome and other visible signs of piety, just as long as they were associated with a living.[30] In the eighteenth century, interest in these efforts waned considerably. There were hardly any new endowments and those who held benefices developed a very secular relationship with their ecclesiastical positions. Overall, however, the cohesion of families and kin groups within the organization of the church was still much more evident than north of the Alps. Italian aristocratic society made use of the network of ecclesiastical benefices and the geographical distribution of holy places as a space that structured their group, developing it into a unified entity that transcended kin groups. It is difficult to judge the extent to which this also influenced integration within the church; it certainly did not make up for the lack of institutional centralization in the Italian church.

In France, high ecclesiastical benefices were allocated exclusively by the monarch, and thus the Gallican Church was accommodated within a recruitment system by which the monarchy had turned the entire nobility into an elite body of military and administrative officials who were closely connected to the state. Within this framework, a religious oligarchy based on function was able to develop amongst aristocratic bishops in a process of secondary professionalization.

In eighteenth-century France, middle-class individuals also rarely attained the position of bishop. Only 4 per cent of the bishops appointed since the beginning of the sixteenth century were definitely not members of the nobility. After 1700, the bishops' lists of the Gallican Church contain only one bishop who was of middle-class origin. In another aspect, too, the Gallican Church was reminiscent of that of the Holy Roman Empire: from the reign of Louis XIV onwards, the higher-ranking aristocracy and other noble families closely associated with the centre of power, as well as the entire nobility of the robe, were found less and less frequently in the ecclesiastical hierarchy. Most bishops of the eighteenth century came from the provinces, not from families of the impoverished lower nobility, but from houses with relatively large estates. Often these families had already made a name for themselves in the army because, for a younger son, a military career was the only alternative to advancement within the church. Family members who embarked on a career in the Gallican Church often did just as well financially as their brothers.

Family ties also promoted the chances of a church career in France. Overall, however, family ties were of secondary importance compared to the suitability of a candidate. The monarchy itself took measures to prevent the development of a 'family church'. Since the time of Louis XIV, bishops had, on principle, been appointed to dioceses far away from their ancestral homes, much to their chagrin. The main obstacle that prevented family interests from permeating the ecclesiastical space of the church, however, came from the criteria that qualified candidates for office: only bishops who had completed their academic studies were admitted. On the eve of the Revolution, all bishops had studied at one of France's great universities, had attained the degree of master and then studied philosophy for two years at a *collège*. This was followed by three years spent studying theology either at a *collège* or at one of the episcopal seminaries. At the end of this course of study, candidates obtained a baccalaureate in theology and, in 1789, almost one-fifth of the bishops even held a doctorate. While studying theology, candidates received all holy orders and thus were also ordained priests when they completed their studies. This mandatory combination of academic and spiritual preparation produced a clergy that was well suited to serve the needs of the church and contributed to the development of a sense of group identity amongst the bishops. Most of the bishops who later met at the General Assembly of the Clergy of France already knew each other from their time as students. In the second half of the eighteenth century, almost two-thirds of the bishops had spent at least three years at Saint-Sulpice and we know that all bishops appointed after 1780 had received their theological training in Paris.

From the beginning of the eighteenth century, the office of vicar-general developed into a further mechanism that separated the ecclesiastical career paths from the ambitions and social reproduction strategies of noble families and even the mechanics of monarchical rule. Vicars-general had been appointed with increasing frequency by bishops since the 1720s, and very soon there were several of these episcopal commissioners in each diocese. At the end of the *ancien régime* there were twelve vicars-general in the diocese of Bordeaux and nine in Rennes and in Lisieux. They were appointed by the bishop, took over important tasks in diocesan administration, did not receive benefices and thus were directly subject to the bishop's authority. However, the fact that, from the middle of the eighteenth century onwards, only those who had served as vicars-general were appointed as bishops became significant: in this way, bishops themselves determined who could become bishops in the future.[31]

Royal patronage in the Gallican Church led to something of a paradoxical result. The combination of aristocratic interests, compulsory academic and spiritual training, and the increasing influence of the high-ranking clergy on recruitment to their ranks led to the creation of a confident oligarchy based on education and achievement with a sense of group identity that was reinforced through general assemblies. This oligarchy was part of aristocratic French society, centred on the monarch, but it was also able to act independently to a much greater extent than any other church group in Europe. Ultimately this meant it was able to act against the interests of the king and the state.

The Protestant churches of Europe – with the exception of the Anglican Church – only offered limited scope for the aristocracy's social reproduction due to the fact that they had no episcopal hierarchy and that church property had been secularized. In the eighteenth century, there were a few remaining benefices in cathedral chapters in the former episcopal sees of Protestant territories, but these could not provide sufficient material resources to fulfil this purpose. However, close personal ties between the political elites and the church continued to exist, as was to be expected given the close association of church institutions to state bureaucracy. It was, thus, legal careers rather than ecclesiastical ones that developed in the consistories and the spiritual departments. In the Reformed churches, this institutional connection between ecclesiastical and secular power did not always exist, and thus, where it was lacking, overlap between the two spheres in terms of personnel had greater weight. The network of individuals that made up the town council and the presbytery in Groningen has been outlined for the period from the seventeenth century to the beginning of the nineteenth century. In the municipal authorities, a political elite – an oligarchy – developed. The permanent council consisted of a maximum of three dozen men from families who controlled the political developments in the town for the rest of their lives, with some short interruptions. The Sworn Council represented a slightly less closed circle, but here too, master craftsmen of the various guilds had been, in practice, excluded from the middle of the seventeenth century onwards. About one-third of Groningen's town councillors belonged to the presbytery either before or at the same time as serving on the council; new members of the presbytery were co-opted and the body showed an even closer connection between state and church in terms of personnel: around half of its members were drawn from the political elite of the town. However, there was a clear pattern that determined the roles individuals could play in the presbytery. The deacons responsible for the care of the poor came from the broader but politically almost inconsequential community of the Sworn Council; members of the town's councils entered the presbytery, which headed the church and was responsible for prosecuting religious and social transgressions. However, the reverse – a member of the church leadership gaining access to the city's ruling elite – was rare. Instead, in Groningen, the presbytery and the office of deacon formed a firm part of the typical stages in a political career, which was entirely consistent with the way in which a political oligarchy that assumed close connections between ecclesiastical and secular realms viewed itself. Nevertheless, it was clear that this connection was becoming increasingly fragile, with personal links becoming less frequent in both spheres in the course of the eighteenth century. The office of deacon suffered the greatest decline in appeal for Groningen's politically influential upper class and, in the early decades of the nineteenth century, the elites of the public church and the town administration finally became entirely separate.[32]

In the Protestant churches, celibacy was no longer mandatory for theologians and priests, and they became part of the educated middle classes. As a result, the ways in which Protestant church structures were incorporated into society and church functions were exercised were much less obvious and direct than in the case of the Catholic Church. However, it was always the case that, at least with regard to leading officials, candidates were not selected according to the logic of a religious institution but following the recruitment patterns of secular officials and the ruling elites. This placed noticeable constraints on the ability of religion to develop its own formal organizational structure. It was only in the Gallican Church that the episcopal hierarchy had managed to gain a significant degree of institutional independence in the course of the eighteenth century, despite the fact that it was entirely incorporated into aristocratic society. One of the reasons that this was possible was the decline in interest in church benefices and senior church offices on the part of the ruling elites, but this was also a European phenomenon, which affected all republics and aristocratic societies, regardless of any differences between them.

## Parish clergy

The living conditions of the parish priests of all confessions were a prime example of the survival of medieval structures in European Christianity as late as the eighteenth century. The clergy who preached the gospel and dispensed the sacraments, thus allowing the laity access to salvation, received their spiritual office from bishops or territorial church authorities, but the majority of them lived on parish benefices, the allocation of which was often decided by laymen or other church institutions who held the right of patronage. In most cases, the churches that emerged from the Reformation and the process of confessionalization had not made a clear break with these medieval structures, and the only changes that had resulted from the idea of universal priesthood were certain changes to the office itself. The social pull which the system of benefices exerted had been severely underestimated. Ultimately, the Protestant clergy – ordained to serve the church and no longer bound by celibacy – carried out their calling in conditions that hardly differed from those of Catholic, celibate priests, and it was unavoidable that these circumstances would affect the way in which the office was carried out.

A parish priest usually received income from three sources: he was entitled to the use of any dues and produce from land associated with the vicarage, he received tithes, and he was paid stole fees for carrying out certain sacramental rituals as well as mass stipends. In the course of the preceding centuries, feudal society, with its desire to always preserve the old in anything new, had created a whole range of varied rights, claims and exceptions, which was often too complex for even the priest to fully understand. However, these elements all had some basic features in common. The first was that the actual figure of the pastoral clergy's monetary income could only be increased with difficulty and so had lost considerable purchasing power by the end of the eighteenth century. However, because inflation was driven mainly by agricultural prices, the loss of value in monetary income was more than compensated for by the increased value of any agricultural produce the clergy were entitled to. Second, the driving force – that is to say, population increase – behind this increase in value is not reflected as clearly in our sources, but parish registers indicate that the clergy also profited from this: every additional marriage, every birth and every funeral meant that they were paid additional fees. The third common feature was that conditions varied greatly from parish to parish and so, in all of the Christian churches, there was a large gap between those who had been lucky enough to obtain a good living and those who received very little. Finally, the fourth feature was linked to the fact that the right to tithes had always attracted the attention of lords and merchants: tithes were considered a reliable security and a low-risk object of speculation and thus could serve as a means of exchange between the different cycles of power, money and agricultural produce. The right to receive tithes had therefore been pawned, sold or simply usurped for centuries. This had caused lasting confusion regarding questions of ownership. In many cases, therefore, it was not the parish priests who received the tithes but the bishops, monasteries and secular rulers or merchants. In theory, those who held the rights would provide compensation to the parish priest, either in terms of money or agricultural produce, but it was obvious that in these circumstances only small amounts actually reached the priests. If an even larger share or even all of the rights associated with a living were controlled by an ecclesiastical or secular ruler, this presented a serious threat to the care of souls in the parish because there was a risk of the parish priest being paid less than the benefices actually returned in terms of income. This, combined with patronage rights that were held by individuals outside the leadership of the church, weakened the office of the parish priest and then also affected religious life in the parishes.

It must be added to all this that, at least in the countryside, the parish clergy were part of the subsistence economy of the village due to their benefices being based on agricultural produce. In this way, they competed with their parishioners when it came to the hard work of producing everyday goods. With bishops and consistories increasingly pronouncing it unseemly for clergymen to be engaged in the work of farmers, the clergy of any of the churches were less inclined to lead a farming life, thus leasing out the property associated with their post and other plots of land, because it was incompatible with their image of themselves and their position. Despite this, however, tithes and other levies meant that the parish clergy were part of a cycle of production and social exchange, which encompassed both secular and ecclesiastical assets, and being in the midst of village life made it difficult to lead the life of a spiritual authority removed from earthly matters. In the best cases, this meant that priest and parishioners were bound together by a sense of mutual understanding, but the situation also meant that there was enough potential for mistrust, disagreements and violent outbursts of anti-clericalism, which negatively affected pastoral care in the parishes.[33]

## Income and background

One-third of French priests only received a certain share of the tithes, known as the *portion congrue*, granted to them by the tithe holder. Until 1768, this was 300 livres, and after difficult negotiations in the Assemblée nationale, it was raised to 500 livres; it was then increased by another 200 livres just before the Revolution. This was enough to survive but it did not enable the clergy to lead a life that was appropriate to their class. In 1773, a priest in the diocese of Bordeaux made a list of all the necessary expenses of a clerical household, which added up to around 1,340 livres. This amount included 600 livres for food and wine, 200 livres for candles and wood, and a small allowance of 60 livres for books. The remainder was required to care for a horse – so the priest could reach those members of his parish who lived further away – and to keep a domestic servant, who was in charge of the household. In addition to this, the expenses included 80 livres as alms for those in need. This list appears to have been quite accurate: in Nantes, a survey instigated by the bishop resulted in a very similar calculation, amounting to 1,800 livres. Most priests of the diocese, however, did not receive remunerations of more than 1,200 livres and the poorest had to survive on 700. Priests in towns were usually considerably better off than those in the country: in the large parishes of Paris, such as Saint-Gervais or Saint-Leu-Saint-Gilles, the stole fees alone amounted to several times these amounts.

On the whole, therefore, the priests of the Gallican Church were not poor. A village priest with an income of usually just over 1,000 livres was part of the small, comfortably-off middle class; if his income was larger, he even belonged to the farming aristocracy. The problem was the comparison with other groups in the church. Considering the life of the aristocratic clergy and the wealth of the monasteries, most contemporaries believed that the pastoral clergy were not receiving a fair share of the church's income as remuneration for their efforts. A pamphlet from 1786 calculated that the income from tithes of all the monasteries and canons of France was sufficient for every parish priest to receive a minimum income of 1,428 livres.[34]

The pastoral clergy in the Holy Roman Empire had to contend with similar conditions. Parish priests in 'Old Bavaria' (Altbayern*), which encompassed Upper and Lower Bavaria, occasionally managed property which could match a small aristocratic feudal estate, and most parish endowments had farms attached to them which were similar to those managed by the upper farming classes. Parish benefices were significantly more modest in Franconia and Swabia, but the diocese of Augsburg used the tithes, which it had been able to obtain over the centuries, to increase parish allowances. In the diocese of Münster, most parish benefices were such that, even without income from tithes, parish priests had the same standard of living as the upper class of farmers.[35]

The situation was not much different for parish priests and their families in Protestant parishes, although their income was ensured in a slightly different way on account of changes made to church property during the Reformation. In most cases, the medieval system of benefices and maintenance continued. This was the case in the Anglican Church as well as in most Protestant churches in the Holy Roman Empire and in the Reformed cantons of the Swiss Confederacy. In other areas, such as the landgraviate* of Hesse-Kassel, secularized church property had been brought together into a centralized fund that was used to provide a combination of income from parish property and additional allowances. In rare cases, all church property was centrally administered, and the income it generated – both in monetary terms and in terms of agricultural produce – was used by consistories or presbyteries to pay the salaries of parish priests. In the United Provinces, this kind of centralization was the result of the revolutionary situation in the territory, but in the Duchy of Württemberg, all parish and church property was also administered by the consistory. This did not necessarily mean that salaries were monetary; this was only the case in towns, if at all. The country clergy continued to receive only small parts of their remuneration as money; most of it took the form of allocations such as wood, grain, wine and other items of daily use.

These variations made little difference to the actual material position of the families of Protestant priests. In Brunswick-Wolfenbüttel the old benefices structure had been retained. Four out of five (80.7 per cent) of all parishes had an income of 200 to 500 guilders, according to a calculation of the consistory in 1765. Around one-sixth of parish priests received more than 500 guilders. The situation did not differ significantly in Hesse-Kassel, despite church property being administered differently. The lowest income was around 300 guilders in the last third of the eighteenth century, and high-income parishes received up to 1,000 guilders, with the average being around 500 guilders. These amounts appear to have been roughly the same in the majority of Protestant churches despite the differences in the way priests were paid. In 1794, the rural priests of the canton of Zurich received, on average, 550 guilders from their benefices. At the same time, there were areas in which priests were extremely poor.

Memoranda of the Berlin Consistory from the end of the eighteenth century refer to the difficult material situation of the preaching clergy in the state of Prussia, who were said to be worse off than many craftsmen. This was true, but, more importantly, the statement reflects the clergy's view on the way of life that was considered to be appropriate to their station. Given that the church had become incorporated into developments in secular administration, the preaching clergy now aspired to the same way of life as state officials. In Protestant territories, such as Hesse-Kassel and Brunswick-Wolfenbüttel, the income hierarchy of the Protestant clergy had mostly been adjusted to the allowances of secular officials by the end of the eighteenth century. A country clergyman received roughly the same as reeves, the heads of communities or municipalities, or town clerks. Parishes in larger towns provided the priest with an income that was equivalent to that of the mayor, and superintendents or superintendents-general received the same as privy councillors trained in the law. This reflected in material terms the view expressed by the Zurich priest Leonhard Brennwald in 1795: 'The priest is a member of the body politic'.[36]

As a result, the social reproduction of the Protestant clergy now occurred as part of the generational cycle of mainly educated members of the middle classes who were already associated with the state. Around a quarter of clerics in Württemberg in the eighteenth century came from the families of higher- and lower-ranking civil servants and from the mayoral families of the country towns. Just under one-sixth came from lower middle-class craftsmen's families and only 8 per cent came from liberal professions, including the merchants. In other territories of the Holy Roman

Empire, the situation was similar. Most frequently, however, clergymen were the sons of other clergymen. At least four out of ten clergymen, and often half of all Protestant priests in the Holy Roman Empire and the Swiss cantons, had grown up in vicarages. This high percentage, which continued to grow until the last third of the eighteenth century, indicates an increasing sense of self-awareness and group identity, which marked out the clergy, especially given their close connection with the educated class and civil servants. Clergymen's wives were also often the daughters of clergymen, and the vicarage's offspring had access to the entire world of the educated middle classes. Of the clergy's children, one- to two-fifths opted for a career in the church; the others entered the legal profession or followed a different course of study. It was not until the end of the century that social barriers began to become apparent, and a growing number of parish priests' sons became craftsmen.[37]

This situation forms a strange contrast with the image found in autobiographies and other documents produced by Protestant clergymen, which paint a picture of flourishing clerical dynasties whose continued existence was in no way threatened. This image emerges as early as the end of the eighteenth century. These descriptions employed the ideals of a class order that had not been stable for a long time and, in this way, they conjured up a particular sense of group identity. In reality, however, the only thing that bound this group together was a common career path in a social milieu in which an individual's trajectory was determined by ability and in which social position was based on individual achievement. Clearly, ordination alone was no longer enough to justify any special group status.[38]

Much less is known about Catholic priests because the seven Holy Orders which were conferred on them through ordination gradually separated a cleric from the secular world; as a result, the social origins of the person who ultimately entered the service of the church were of no significance in relation to his office as a priest. Throughout all of the eighteenth century, the recruitment of priests was significantly influenced by the fact that this office was only one of a large number of ecclesiastical benefices, and not all of these required the recipient to be ordained as a priest. Of the 140,500 members of the Gallican clergy, only 39,000 worked as parish priests in 1789. There were 20,500 curates, and more than half (57.5 per cent) of those in the church lived and worked in monasteries and convents. In Spain in 1797, there were 148,500 men and women who had entered the church, with just over half (52.2 per cent) of them living the monastic life. Of the 71,000 secular clergy, only 22,000 worked as parish priests; another 60,000 priests received other benefices and 10,000 had only taken minor orders. In some Italian towns only one in ten of the many clerics carried out pastoral care.

Amongst the general population, members of the different social classes had greatly varying levels of access to these resources. For the reasons outlined above, the numbers and different interests are often unclear, and it was not until the end of the century that church plans for reform and external intentions to carry out secularization led to increased interest in the social background of the lower-ranking Catholic clergy. Across Europe, two facts emerged. First, it became clear that towns and middle classes played an important role in the number of spiritual callings. Second, it was also evident that a fundamental shift was underway and that an increasing number of parish priests came from a farming background. In France, an initial overview of the situation was made possible by the Revolution. It showed that around 40 per cent of parish priests came from towns, despite significant regional differences. Around one-fifth came from families of the educated functional elites (as in the Protestant churches); parish priests from a lower middle-class trade background represented a minority of less than 10 per cent. At the same time, there were dioceses, such as Coutances, Vannes or Tréguir, in which more than half of the parish priests came from families of *laboureurs* – full-time farmers. However, both in the country and in the towns it was usually the children of the richest families in the parish who decided to pursue a church career. In Italy, the situation was different. Here, it was mainly the children of craftsmen who felt a calling to become priests; in the south, the majority of clerics had always come from the upper classes of the farming community. Overall, from the middle of the century onwards, the interest of the Italian middle classes in ecclesiastical benefices waned considerably, and so the percentage of priests who had a rural background increased. In the dioceses of the Holy Roman Empire, on the other hand, the recruitment patterns for the lower clergy were similar to those in the Gallican Church. As in France and Italy, Catholic parish priests increasingly tended not to have a middle-class background, but this change did not become particularly noticeable until the last two decades of the century.

Underlying this social change in pastoral care was a much more significant crisis in terms of spiritual calling. It is difficult to say to what extent reservations about benefices as a system of maintenance were mixed with an increasingly distant attitude to ecclesiastical office. From the point of view of an individual and his family, the spiritual advantages regarding salvation that came with being a member of the clergy probably could no longer make up for the disadvantages of that particular way of life. As a result, the willingness to invest in the system of benefices also declined. The titles of candidates for ordination had been decreasing since as early as the first third of the century, and endowments of all kinds became rarer. For this reason, the spiritual crisis ultimately manifested itself as a crisis in the system of benefices.

Spiritual callings had always taken different directions in town and country. Wealthy inhabitants of cities ensured that their sons who had embarked on a career in the church received well-endowed positions as canons in collegiate churches or a different benefice that did not require carrying out pastoral work. The sons of country craftsmen and farmers, on the other hand, either entered the monastery or worked as parish priests. Overall, at the end of the eighteenth century, the decline in numbers was greater in the monasteries and convents than amongst the secular clergy. Only in the Iberian Peninsula did the numbers wanting any kind of position in the lower clergy remain the same up until the end of the century. In France, Italy and most of the Holy Roman Empire, on the other hand, the size of monasteries and convents had been decreasing since the middle of the century. By the last third of the century at the latest, this development coincided with a long-term decline in the numbers being ordained as priests, and in the archdiocese of Cologne this decline continued right up into the 1830s. This reflected the growing distance in both the town and countryside from ecclesiastical office and coincided with a crisis in the church's benefices, which had been a concern for the vicars-general since the middle of the century.

Protestant churches were also clearly not safe from such strains on the system of benefices. In the canton of Zurich, from the 1760s onwards, this had led to a decline in the number of candidates wanting to become parish priests. The waiting time for a first benefice had increased and there was uncertainty for candidates as to whether they would ever obtain a sufficient living. In Württemberg the numbers wanting to be parish priests was controlled by decrees, the last of these in 1780, which barred the sons of craftsmen and farmers from studying theology and becoming members of the Tübinger Stift, a Protestant seminary. However, despite this measure, there continued to be more candidates for the office than there were positions.[39]

**Patronage as a form of dominion**

Benefices did more than provide an income: they also entailed authority, which, in turn, affected the church's ability to shape and fill ecclesiastical positions. A deciding factor here was the relationship between the patron's right of presentation and the qualifications demanded by the church and whether the patron attempted to influence the way in which the office holder conducted himself both privately and professionally. This was, of course, only an issue if the right of patronage was not held by a Catholic bishop or Protestant consistories or presbyteries, but, often enough, this was the case. In the Catholic Church, lay patronage had survived everywhere. In many dioceses of central and western Europe, the percentage of the parishes for which the bishop held the patronage rights was under 10 per cent. Relics of the system of proprietary churches, such as the *chiesa ricettizia**  in southern Italy, meant that a large section of the clergy was not subject to episcopal authority. This overtly combined clerical maintenance with the material strategies of reproduction in large rural family networks.[40]

In the Protestant churches, the Reformation principle of a parish electing its priest only survived to a very limited extent on account of organizational consolidation and increasing inclusion into state structures as well as the abolition of benefices and their subsequent administration by a church or state authority as part of the church's property more generally. The right to appoint a priest had moved from parishes to presbyteries or synods, which operated independently of the parish, or lay with the consistorial authorities or the ruler himself. This development occurred in many Reformed churches. The free individual right of patronage, on the other hand, had asserted itself wherever ruling authority continued to depend on compromise with the nobility. In these cases, patronage rights continued to have a firm place in the nobility's economic and non-economic power and rights, with Brandenburg-Prussia providing a paradigm for this. The Upper Consistory could only fill those positions which were subject to royal patronage. In all other cases, it was usually aristocratic patrons who appointed the priest, even, in many cases, in towns. In the Anglican Church, the restoration of the episcopal hierarchy after 1688 meant that, here too, the interests of the gentry decisively influenced the appointment of parish priests.

All this meant that religious considerations and church interests played a very minor role in the appointment of parish priests, and it enabled the laity to have a frequently entirely disproportionate influence on church matters. This applied both to those seeking to obtain a benefice as well as to those in the position to grant it.

Theological qualifications or a spiritual attitude were not the deciding factors in obtaining benefices or positions as parish priests. Instead, complex social strategies of protection and clientelism, involving the candidates, their families and entire family networks, aimed to out-run the competition. Influencing decisions in one's favour and being presented as a candidate for a well-endowed living required much persuasion and, more significantly, social power – in the sense of collecting old favours and promising future ones – and contemporaries considered this to be something of an art form. Success attracted further success, and the sons of politically influential families rose higher and more quickly than many of their competitors. A family network that included both relatives who were members of the church and those who were not was particularly useful to Protestant preachers. For Catholic priests, celibacy meant that there were fewer direct family members available, and illegitimate sons, who until the seventeenth century had often succeeded their fathers to a living, had disappeared from the picture since concubines had finally been banished and sexual abstinence had largely been enforced. In any case, they were irrelevant when it came to filling parish positions in the eighteenth century. However, uncles made sure to advance their nephews' interests and helped smooth their way through the complex process of benefice allocation. As with the benefices of the higher clergy, resigning a benefice in favour of someone else was a tried and tested way of ensuring family continuity in a particular office. If one had a close relative who was a parish priest, it was easier to obtain a benefice and, in many ways, one had much stronger chances when competing for a better position.

Family clientelism and patronage did not necessarily mean the candidate lacked the spiritual inclination necessary to fill the post in question. Much more serious damage resulted if a patron's decision to present a particular candidate was quite obviously guided by secular interests. In such cases, the church's authority to examine candidates and ordain them did not prevent the appointment of incompetent priests, who lacked any interest in their office. In his memoranda to the Department of Spiritual Affairs, the Berlin provost Johann Peter Süßmilch painted a very dark picture of the military's influence. The biggest problem, it seemed to Süßmilch, was the fact that the highest military clergyman, field provost Decker, allocated all more or less well-paid benefices in the kingdom to his military chaplains and thus indirectly also filled all offices of superintendent. Süßmilch resignedly referred to a *hierarchia deckeriana* and saw no hope in taking action against it.[41]

There were also hardly any obstacles to sovereigns making use of their right of patronage as a way of exercising their power. In the eighteenth century, openly selling benefices could no longer be justified in the Protestant churches of the Holy Roman Empire, but the practice did still occur. The aristocracy had the priests on their estates sign certificates of appointment, which represented a serious interference in the way in which they carried out their office. Major General Ludwig von Pfuel obliged the priest he had appointed in Jahnsfelde in the district of Lebus to proclaim the true teachings of Jesus of Nazareth because, according to him, the Formula of Concord* of 1577, setting out Lutheran beliefs, was harmful in Prussia and had been rejected as it directly contradicted 'the free spirit of Protestantism'.[42]

Where the church and its priests were so obviously regarded by those in authority as a component of their personal dominion over the farming population, it was logical that careful attention was also paid to cost. In Lusatia, parish priests were not allowed to mention publicly the reduction in their salary determined by their certificates of appointment. In some cases, the position of parish priest remained vacant because it was considered too expensive to fill. The gentry's control of pastoral care had led to many positions in Anglican parishes remaining vacant. Poorly endowed positions were not filled, or those who occupied them considered them to be nothing more than a source of income to be combined with other benefices, at best appointing a deputy who was paid even less. This was a well-known problem throughout the entire century. In 1812, an investigation concluded that there were 4,813 parish priests who did not live in their parish or carry out their duties there. Only 3,694 had a deputy, and so around 1,000 parish positions were entirely neglected. Under these circumstances, it was little wonder that the Methodists enjoyed great popularity.[43]

The post-Tridentine Catholic Church offered a little more protection to its parish clergy than the Protestant churches, which could often barely be separated from the state. However, this in no way meant that ecclesiastical and secular authorities always cooperated as equals or even worked together harmoniously. The Reformation had dispensed with the sacrality of ecclesiastical office and, for this reason, Protestant clerics viewed themselves and their office more in terms of ability and education and stressed their own middle-class social background. The Catholic clergy, on the other hand, continued to remain secure in their knowledge that their ordination had sanctified them. Despite this, the structural similarities in their ways of life and social position meant that many of the differences between Protestant and Catholic priests had been smoothed out. Although the middle-class background of one group had declined, while that connection had increased in the other in terms of material provision and family ties, this did not change the fact that, up until the end of the eighteenth century, the social circumstances in which both Catholic and Protestant parish priests preached the gospel and dispensed the sacraments ran counter to the spiritual understanding of their office. In the Catholic Church, the idea of a spiritual calling had not been formulated until the seventeenth century, and it had originally been considered the confessor's and the bishop's – that is to say, the hierarchy's – responsibility to determine an individual's calling. It was not until the second half of the eighteenth century that the focus was placed on following the voice of God, with the idea emerging that this was the only way in which a candidate could gain certainty on whether he was following the right path.[44] At the same time, the spiritual nature of the office could not emerge without professionalization. Seen from this perspective, the church's rules regarding training and qualification and the discipline to which the clergy were subject appear more as an attempt to integrate the clergy more strongly into the body of the church than social structures actually permitted.

## Failing reforms

The more state structures became institutionalized and the more monarchs freed themselves from feudal structures in the course of the eighteenth century, the more a church which was a significant part of this multi-level state structure was viewed as a problem. From the middle of the eighteenth century at the latest, this led to monarchs in all of Catholic Europe unceremoniously intervening in the church's right to organize itself. In Spain and Portugal, royal authority over the church was permanently strengthened and, in the territories ruled by the Austrian Habsburgs and other Catholic areas of the empire, the result was the establishment of regional churches. Maria Theresa, Joseph II and Leopold, Grand Duke of Tuscany and later Holy Roman Emperor (1790–92), could be certain of having the support of at least some of the bishops and archbishops because the centralized hierarchy of the Catholic Church presented numerous hurdles from their point of view, too, for carrying out their office in a way that was compatible with the Tridentine canons. The possibilities available to the Curia of extending its power into the individual bishoprics, that is to say, Rome's widely spread financial claims and the nunciatures, were not popular with the bishops, and the idea of abolishing or at least limiting these agencies with the help of secular authorities was appealing. However, if the power and continued institutional existence of the Catholic Church was directly tied to this multi-level state structure, as was the case in the Holy Roman Empire, such attempts at reform resulted in extremely complex situations, both for the ecclesiastical hierarchy and for secular rulers. In the end, many things were set in motion but little was achieved. Prime examples of this are the Febronian reform congresses of Koblenz (1769) and Ems (1786) and the establishment of another nunciature in Munich (1785). The bishops were also inclined to accept the offer of cooperation with secular rules because they hoped that it would provide an opportunity for them to gain access to the monastic sphere. Most monasteries and abbeys were largely outside the control of the bishop because they were part of the organizational and disciplinary hierarchy of their orders, which spanned all of Europe. Many of the heads of the orders were in Rome and subject directly to the Pope's influence; as a result, the activities of monks and nuns were associated with the power of the Roman Curia. The Jesuits had already suffered the consequences of this situation in the middle of the century. This, incidentally, shows that the reforms were also directed towards articles of faith and forms of worship in addition to the attempts to strengthen regional and national aspects of the church's organization. The Council of Trent focused on a form of internalized piety that centred on Christ and His act of grace and, for the most part, rejected the idea of a magical manipulation of the world. The indecisiveness with which its provisions had been implemented since the last third of the sixteenth century was, for the most part, due to the way in which the Jesuits went about their pastoral care. However, much of what was set in motion in the name of the Enlightenment and was directed at baroque forms of piety was also directed against the autonomy and the obstinacy of the faithful, who insisted that the religion which they lived out should remain intertwined with their daily lives.

**France**

As long as the great abbeys of France served as a means by which the king could equip his nobility, the Gallican Church had no need to fear any direct political pressure to secularize the property of religious orders. For the religious houses, adversity came from a different quarter. Members of monasteries could obtain a dispensation from

Rome to move to an order that had a less strict rule or to return to the laity (*translatio ad laxiorum*). The numbers of those taking advantage of this possibility were increasing, and the bishops – quite rightly – took this as an indication of the dismal state of monastic discipline as well as recognizing in it the continued ability of the Curia to intervene in the affairs of the French church. Moreover, in several cases, the *parlements* had signalled that they were willing to uphold the complaints of members of monasteries against their superiors. As the *parlements* had already demonstrated their willingness to take sides in the controversy surrounding Jansenism, it seemed a very real possibility that church autonomy would collapse. In 1765, the assembly of the Gallican clergy reacted to these developments. There was to be a commission on religious orders, for which Brienne initially sought papal legitimization. In the end, however, it was established by a royal law in July 1766 and took the form of a committee composed of bishops with a mind to reform, advocates of the most important noble families and theologians. The committee's members collaborated to discuss how religious orders might be reformed.[45]

There was agreement on the idea that religious houses in which the spiritual life had been irreparably damaged due to a lack of discipline or because there were no novices should be closed. The French bishops were aware of this when, a short time later, they were asked to report on the state of the monastic houses in their dioceses. Because of this, many refused to do so, but others took the opportunity to display their enlightened attitude towards monasticism without considering it necessary to conduct full inspections of the individual houses and abbeys. Overall, however, the reports which reached the commission showed a nuanced picture of the state of the different orders and their position in the life of the church. The regular clergy, monks and nuns who were active in parish pastoral care and popular missions or who cared for the sick received the support of the bishops. Monastic religious virtuosos engaged entirely in the contemplative life, however, met with little understanding from the bishops or an increasing portion of the population. The fact that the Jansenists' Augustinian economy of salvation had already severely undermined the trust in a treasury of grace*, accumulated through monastic prayer and administered by the church, probably also contributed to this situation. Thus, while the reports took into account the work the Carthusians carried out in caring for those of unsound mind, it could not be ignored that the debts of the entire order placed a huge amount of pressure on the individual houses and that there were no new members entering the order. Similar verdicts were reached regarding the different mendicant orders. Most had gained the respect of bishops and parish priests as well as the faithful for the pastoral work they carried out, but in these orders, too, the reports identified a corrupt leadership that had no interest in spiritual matters; this was particularly the case for the Capuchins and the Augustinians. The Dominicans were not popular amongst the bishops. The order was known for its emphasis on scholarship and, as a result, was regarded as a breeding ground for Jansenism, which was very critical of the church hierarchy. There was little understanding for the fact that the order's houses, which were usually referred to as houses of study, mostly did not obey the requirements of monastic discipline. The religious houses associated with Cluny and Citeaux, which followed the Benedictine Rule, were considered by the bishops to be particularly suspect because competition between the different branches of the order and their aristocratic leadership prevented any effective reform of discipline. As a result, their houses usually had very questionable reputations. The General Chapter of the Cistercians was not strong enough to establish a sense of cohesion between the different houses.

Despite the significant criticism that had been voiced, the commission had relatively little effect. The duc de Choiseul was dismissed in 1770, which led to the commission's work increasingly losing political support. The most effective measures turned out to be two royal decrees: the first, from 1768, raised the entrance age for monastic orders from 16 to 21 for men and to 18 for women; the second, in 1773, placed the individual houses much more firmly under the bishop's authority. The bishop's permission was now required for regular clergy to be ordained and to take confession and preach, and the bishop was also to monitor the acceptance of pious endowments. Once impending decisions regarding individual orders and houses became clear, the network of client relationships and influence began to show its effect. Moreover, it turned out that one could not hope for the cooperation of the heads of the orders in Rome. For this reason, most of the disciplinary and organizational reforms that had been demanded of the Capuchins, Dominicans and Augustinians were not implemented. It took years for decisions to close particular houses to be put into practice. Nevertheless, the Augustinians lost 51 of their 345 houses, the Capuchins gave up only 22 of their 451 convents, and the Benedictines were more significantly affected: in 1787, 44 Cluniac houses were closed, the old Benedictines lost 37 houses, and the Mauristes 21 out of 191 houses. The serious reservations held against the Dominicans had few consequences. Only 20 of their 179 houses were closed. The situation was critical for the Dominican houses in Paris in the Rue Saint-Jacques and the Rue Saint-Honoré. A few years later, due to a lack of funds, the convent in the Rue Saint-Honoré decided to rent out its refectory for gatherings of the Club Breton, thus giving the Jacobins their names.

### The Jesuits

The work of the Gallican commission on religious orders could be seen largely as a process within the church; the disputes regarding the Jesuits, however, brought the tensions between the Catholic dynasties of western Europe and the Roman Curia to the fore. Through their missionary activities, the members of the Societas Jesu had become the natural representatives of a papal world church, which ran counter to the regalism of the Catholic colonial powers. In addition to this, Catholic monarchs also sought to legitimize their power through natural law, and the influence of the Jesuits, which had long been valued, was now considered inconvenient and politically undesirable at the courts of Lisbon, Madrid and Versailles. Even the Jesuit idea of piety did not seem to fit into these enlightened times. As early as the end of the 1750s, this led to disagreements in Lisbon regarding the Jesuits' role in the South American Indian reductions*. This resulted in the *Militia Christi* having to leave the court. In 1759 they were expelled from Portugal entirely and the order's property was confiscated. In Spain and France the order's position also became increasingly difficult. In 1762 the *parlement* of Paris ordered the Jesuits to be expelled, an order which was confirmed by Louis XV in 1764. In 1767 the order was expelled from Spain without receiving the slightest support from the bishops. Despite carrying out her own church reforms, Maria Theresa had so far not acted against the Jesuits, but now she made it clear that she would no longer support them. In order to avoid relations with the Catholic monarchs becoming even worse, the Curia had little choice but to give way to the political pressure that was being exerted. In 1773 Clement XIV issued the *Breve Dominus ac redemtor noster*, in which he provided a long list of misconduct and negative developments in the order so as to justify closing it down. The various European rulers were charged with the responsibility of enacting and supervising the *Breve*. This created a chance of survival for the Jesuits as non-Catholic monarchs and princes saw no reason why they should have to do without the Jesuits at universities and in secondary education. Frederick II prohibited the proclamation of the *Breve*, and Catherine the Great also ensured that the structures of the Jesuit order remained largely intact in her empire because she intended it to become the backbone of a Catholic Church in Russia that was organized independently of Rome. However, in those areas of central and western Europe that were under Catholic rule, the Jesuits had no choice but to join other orders after 1773 or to become secular clergy.[46]

## Habsburg

Even the Russian support of the Jesuits showed clearly that Europe's rulers were interested in church and religion mainly from the point of view of stabilizing and consolidating monarchical power. The institutional organization of the church continued to hold appeal as a useful and necessary medium of the monarch's power. Within the varied domains of the Austrian Habsburgs, the main challenge with regard to the church was, therefore, the problem of how to standardize its organizational structures and how to adapt them to the increasing bureaucracy and plans for reform of an enlightened state. When Maria Theresa took the first steps in this regard, she may have still hoped to persuade the Curia of the benefits of making changes. Certainly as early as 1751, she had already stated in her *Political Testament* that a sovereign should also take an interest in church property and, in 1759, she introduced a special tax for the clergy in order to finance the war with Prussia. It was this open seizure of the church's wealth that caused serious problems regarding the implementation and acceptance of her reforms and, subsequently, those of Joseph II.[47]

The following decade's contribution to this question mainly consisted of complicated memoranda of the state chancellor Count Kaunitz-Rietberg, although the lack of other reactions is probably also due to the war with Prussia and the difficulties in dealing with the subsequent defeat. In 1770, an ordinance to standardize education within the orders was first issued and, in the same year, Maria Theresa ordered the minimum age for taking up a professorship to be raised to twenty-four. In the following year, the Queen of Hungary and Bohemia limited the number of feast days for the first time and, in 1772, the ability of the monasteries to engage in economic activities was restricted. This showed that religious houses were now generally regarded as economic 'black holes', using an inappropriately large amount of society's wealth for unproductive consumption or, in the worst case, as a way of keeping the population in a state of superstitious ignorance. In order to prevent the monarchy's subjects from spending too much time away from work, 'overnight' processions were now also prohibited.

Joseph II, who had been a member of the government as King of the Romans since 1764, had already stated in several memoranda that he believed the reform of the church and of religion ought to play a central role in any attempts to reform the state administration and social conditions. The epoch-making defeat of Catholic powers by the Protestants, sealed by the Treaty of Hubertusburg in 1763, had demonstrated the urgency of significant social reforms. This explains why Joseph II took such a radical approach to transforming state and society from 1780 onwards.

By 1783 the most important measures had been taken to create a new relationship between the Catholic Church and society in the Habsburgs' hereditary territories and to bring about changes in the Catholic Church that allowed it to be fitted into the overall structure of the reforms. Seen from this perspective, the series of imperial edicts and patents can be divided into three main areas of reform.

One of the first aims was to separate religion from processes of social integration, which it had hitherto structured and been closely associated with. In order to achieve this, Joseph II issued several patents of toleration in 1781, which freed banned or marginalized Protestant and eastern Christian groups from oppression and allowed them, and Jewish communities, to form independent religious communities with their own schools under state supervision. The only exception here was the Eastern Catholic Church. The Catholic faith retained the monopoly of public religious worship, but private worship was permitted for other religious communities, and they were allowed to build churches, albeit without steeples and with the entrance facing away from the street. Religion could thus no longer serve as a tool of social exclusion and was also no longer the only means of inclusion. This was particularly clear in the various Jewish patents. Joseph II strengthened the autonomy of Jewish communities and schools, removing the obligation for Jews to display stigmatizing signs on their clothing, and most of the restrictions that Jews had been subject to with regard to commercial activity were lifted. In 1783, a patent decreed that marriage was a civil contract, made in the presence of a priest but, nevertheless, mainly a secular affair. For that reason, given certain conditions, it could be terminated through divorce. This also affected the ability of religion to act as a means of social inclusion. All of these decrees presaged the end of the unconditionally Catholic nature of the state and of society; for religion, this meant that it would soon find itself within a legal system in which the conditions of existence would be largely the same for all confessions.

Second, the edicts of Joseph II addressed those aspects of the Catholic salvation economy that were considered by the reformers to have negative social effects. The ecclesiastically administered treasury of salvation and the principle of righteousness of works had, together, led to large amounts of goods and wealth – through endowments and donations – accumulating over the centuries in different sections of the church and the lives of the faithful. They were, in the broadest sense, intended to enable prayers for Christian souls and thus they did not form part of the productive economy, as defined by the physiocrats. Similarly, time spent in prayer was now considered by both the laity and religious virtuosos to be time that could have been spent working. The prohibition on pilgrimages lasting several days and criticism of the many Catholic feast days were logical developments resulting from this opposition between increasing one's earthly gain and managing one's spiritual salvation. It was also natural to take action against the orders if the monks and nuns did not engage in charitable work or educate the young and only focused on prayer. The brotherhoods and lay congregations, which combined the diverse needs of the faithful for help and solidarity with permanent mutual care through prayers, could not be judged any differently: here, too, wealth was hoarded for pious purposes and there were limitations on its availability for worldly purposes. In January 1782, Joseph II issued a decree for the dissolution of the monasteries, but this mainly affected mendicant orders and contemplative communities. In 1783 the Hofburg decreed that the brotherhoods should also be abolished and that their members, if they so wished, should be brought together in a 'single community of love'. It should be noted to their credit, however, that these radical interventions in the Catholic economy of prayer and provision, to which around 600 religious houses had fallen victim by 1787, were not a direct means of enriching the state treasury. The proceeds from the dissolution of the monasteries went into a religious fund, which was mainly intended to support the parish clergy and to regulate the parishes. In order to improve the pastoral care of the faithful, parishes were to have minimum sizes and, if necessary, new parishes were established. In the years that followed, around 400 parishes were created, many of them in the fast-growing towns of the Erblande*, the hereditary lands. The assets of the brotherhoods were used by the parishes for the care of the poor and to establish primary schools.

Third, the Josephine state intervened in the structure of the Roman church in those areas in which its hierarchy and the ecclesiastical–secular mixture of its sovereignty rights ran counter to the consolidation and autonomy of state structures. As early as 1781, Joseph II took the first steps to regulate the dioceses, with the aim of depriving all bishops outside Austria of their rights within the *Erblande*, with these then passing to Habsburg bishops. This was a difficult situation for Rome, and Joseph used the Italian territories of the Habsburgs as leverage, denying that the Pope had any right to give away benefices in Lombardy. After several years of negotiations, during which Pius VI (1775–99) travelled to Vienna and Joseph II to Rome, an 'amicable agreement' was reached in 1784. This granted the state the right to bestow benefices, but state-appointed bishops had to be confirmed by Rome. This provided the basis for establishing two new dioceses in Linz and St Pölten, thus removing the *Erblande* from the jurisdiction of the bishop of Passau and the archbishop of Salzburg, Colloredo. The property of the bishop of Passau in the *Erblande* was confiscated on this occasion but later returned. Nonetheless, the spiritual princes of the Holy Roman Empire rightly took this measure as a warning of what threats they might face in the future. In effect, the new bishops acted as officials of the country, and Joseph II wanted this also to be the case for the lower clergy in the parishes. In 1783, a general seminary was established as a way of reforming training for the priesthood, and this development was mainly influenced by the Braunau Benedictine abbot Stefan Franz Rautenstrauch. It also formed part of Joseph II's attempt to change church structures in a way that would allow them to function as a support for the state's interventions in society. Given the institutional weakness of state power, the state's church policies had to be aimed at turning the church into a tool for the state.

Of course, significant parts of the clergy had reservations regarding such interventions in the church. Maria Theresa and Joseph II nevertheless received considerable support from among the bishops and the parish clergy for their reforms, and this was a key factor in the changes being successfully implemented until the mid-1780s. Bishops, such as Karl Graf von Herberstein, Joseph Philip Graf Spaur and even, to some extent, the Archbishop of Vienna, Cardinal Christoph Anton Migazzi, supported Joseph II because they were in favour of episcopal authority being strengthened in relation to the Curia, the nunciatures and, above all, the religious orders. In a pastoral letter, Herberstein explained to the parish clergy in his diocese of Laibach that the secular princes had always had the right to supervise the external affairs of religion because these were closely connected to the political situation. For this reason, he claimed, both the patents of toleration and the dissolution of monasteries were justified. In any case, the monastic system was nothing more than a human invention and so the closure of individual religious houses was no great misfortune for religion, especially if it resulted in better training for the clergy.

The argument underlying such statements showed clearly that any willingness within the church to carry out reforms was based on Jansenist convictions, which were disseminated particularly by the Viennes cathedral canon, Johann Baptist de Terme, by Max Anton Wittola, who produced numerous publications and was an influential censor, and by the radical head of the Seminary of Vienna, Melchior Blarer.[48] The Austrian Jansenists were in favour of a strict approach to penance and Communion in pastoral care, and generally argued for the pastoral office to be given greater support in the face of competition from religious orders and different forms of autonomous lay piety, which highlighted the sensual aspects of religion and ensured access to the means of salvation through prayer and good works to secure the intercession of Mary and the saints. As a result, there were serious reservations concerning all forms of Baroque piety – ranging from mechanically saying the rosary to pilgrimages and passion plays. These reservations were connected to a desire for church reform influenced by Enlightenment ideas. Because the Jansenists were anti-Curial and episcopalist in outlook, they cooperated with the state with regard to the latter's reform policies. Nevertheless, it became increasingly apparent that there was a world of difference between the willingness within the church to carry out reforms – regardless of whether those involved were Jansenists or 'merely' enlightened – and the way in which the state implemented such reforms. The cameralist and physiocratic dogmatism of those in the Hofburg who were engaged in writing memoranda and carrying out reforms meant that changes to lay piety and public worship were considered explicitly from a financial point of view. There were demands to bury the dead in mass graves and in body bags rather than in coffins and there were regulations regarding the exact number of altar candles, lest they become too great an expense; it is small wonder that these measures were met with little understanding. The faithful were outraged because it ran counter to their ingrained willingness and desire to spend good money to pay for their salvation; the reformers within the church felt like they had been used because their opposition to Baroque piety was in no way identical with this frugal economizing. As a result, from the middle of the 1780s onwards, the support for Joseph II within the church melted away, with Archbishop Migazzi leading the open resistance of the church's hierarchy and clergy against the way in which they were being instrumentalized. As a result, the interventions that had occurred were largely reversed by Joseph II himself in 1780. However, the regulation and closure of monasteries was upheld.

Joseph's younger brother Leopold, Grand Duke of Tuscany, and his successor as emperor, pursued a policy of reform in northern Italy that, in some respects, was even more radical. Here, too, the state's policy regarding the church was part of a political programme of social transformation which was intended to replace feudal rule with a constitutional order together with a national assembly. Accordingly, the intention was to establish a national synod that was to represent the future Tuscan national church. Leopold was supported and advised by a small but journalistically very active Jansenist theological elite at the universities of Siena and Pisa and by an episcopate willing to carry out reforms. Amongst the bishops, however, there was a range of attitudes, with the views of the moderate Ludovico Antonio Muratori and the radical Scipione de Ricci differing greatly. Ricci was appointed bishop of Prato and Pistoia in 1789 and immediately began instituting reforms there, some of which anticipated the measures taken by Leopold.

Unlike Joseph, Leopold wanted public discussion to underpin his reforms. In 1784, the eighteen bishops of the Grand Duchy received a fifty-four-point plan for reform and, in 1786, a synod was convened in Pistoia as a way of rehearsing, as it were, the planned national synod. This national synod was to consist of different sessions led by the Jansenist moral theologian Pietro Tamburini from Pavia, in which a comprehensive dogmatic and ecclesiological programme of reform with overt reference to the Council of Trent was to be discussed. This assembly was referred to as a 'comedy council' by contemporaries because Ricci had required the lower clergy of his two dioceses to play those attending the council and, accordingly, all had to dress as prelates. In order to achieve the desired outcome, votes were signed and not anonymous.

Accordingly, the decisions, although unanimous, gave little indication of how the programme of reform was received. Ricci's and Leopold's proposals all failed to be approved by the assembly of bishops convened in the following year. However, the reforms also failed because the faithful openly opposed them in the last third of the 1780s. Ricci barely managed to escape with his life when word got out in 1787 that he intended to remove the Virgin's Girdle from the cathedral of Prato. Angry peasants stormed the bishop's palace, vandalized Ricci's coat of arms and burnt the Jansenist missals and breviaries which were stored there. In 1790, Ricci was violently expelled from his diocese because he no longer had Leopold's support at that time.[49]

A characteristic feature of church reforms in the Habsburg territories was that they had been conceived of and decreed as part of a fundamental reform of society, the object of which was to destroy the feudal foundations of political and social order. For this reason alone, they were unparalleled in the other Catholic territories of the empire. However, there were bishops who did seek, in the spirit of enlightened Jansenism, to make significant changes to religious life in their dioceses in order to standardize the training of the clergy and improve monastic discipline. However, the basis of the church's structures in the ownership of property remained unchanged, even in those areas in which the establishment of a regional church was openly pursued, as was the case in Bavaria. The Curia even supported this because it made it possible to establish another nunciature in Munich in 1785; this was to counteract attempts by the episcopate of the empire to create a national church. Using the pseudonym Febronius, Nikolaus von Hontheim had outlined in 1763 the idea that an anti-Curial programme could be combined with internal church reform, and this idea had been discussed at the reform congresses in Koblenz and Ems. However, it became evident in Bavaria, too, that this combination was not politically viable. Faced with the idea of a national church, the bishops predicted even greater pressure from the archbishops and the archbishops were concerned about the predictable opposition from the bishops. Together, both groups feared that secular rulers would attempt to appropriate church property because all of them knew that the church's unwieldy structure was most easily broken up by secularization, which would have deprived the Catholic Church of statehood.[50] The penultimate decade of the eighteenth century had shown that, throughout Europe, the church, as an institution of power, was considered to be a serious obstacle to the development of state structures. However, it could not be reformed in isolation; precisely because it was part of aristocratic society, the two could only be restructured together.

2

# Christianity and civil society

Even before the radical nature of the French Revolution had unfolded in its entirety, careful observers could tell that it would assign a new place to church and religion in the newly emerging society. In his polemic, Edmund Burke, a perceptive and eloquent critic of the Revolution, took this as his cue to reflect at greater length on the importance that Christianity might have for the political and social order when it was not only respected by the elites but also part of people's daily lives. Burke was thinking of a form of Christianity that was tied to the institution of the church and, for this reason, he emphatically stressed the necessity of protecting the well-founded property rights of the church. Burke considered it scandalous how recklessly the French National Assembly had sacrificed church property to the financial crisis of the state and had deprived the clergy of their rights. This dismaying precedent alone was reason enough, Burke concluded, for the United Kingdom to ensure all the more strictly for the future that the property rights of the Anglican Church should be respected. The clergy of the Church of England were not to fear that they might be dispossessed of their income from church property and be reduced to receiving their pay from the state.[1]

Burke was to be proven right in that the Church of England did not in fact face a comprehensive expropriation of its assets in the first half of the nineteenth century. However, the firm traditionalist Burke was wrong in that even his kingdom's parliamentary monarchy could not avoid the necessity of placing the relationship between state and church on a new footing by the middle of the nineteenth century and, as part of this process, Parliament saw the need to intervene quite extensively in Church property rights and the use to which they were put. In addition to this, in his polemic, Burke had been careful to avoid mentioning the fact that, in its *Declaration of the Rights of Man and of the Citizen*, and following heated debate, the National Assembly had decided that a person's religious convictions were free and subject only to that person's conscience (article 10) and that a citizen's rights were thus defined independently of the particular creed the citizen followed (article 6).[2]

This may not have been particularly remarkable from a British point of view: this was a nation that had already learnt to tolerate and accept Puritan Dissent and Methodists, not only within the Church but also on a political stage, and the social and political integration of Catholics was no longer a question relating to different creeds but one that was considered a problem of national unity. In the context of the situation on the continent, however, the history of the French Revolution with regard to religion showed that the institutional forms of Christianity needed adjustment to the requirements of a society of sovereign citizens who were equal before the law. The legally established hierarchy of privileges had undergone a long process of dissolution, a process which was validated by the Revolution. Following the American model, the *Declaration of the Rights of Man and of the Citizen* and the different constitutions of the Revolution accommodated the development of a society of free citizens, which was structured according to a division of labour. It thus placed its trust in the regulatory powers of the markets and any limits on access to the variety of social activities and positions other than talent and industriousness were inadmissible. The fundamental rights of the *Virginia Declaration of Rights* and the French Revolution represented the normative consequences of social analyses such as those carried out by the physiocrats and, after them, above all, Adam Smith. The Romantics later focused on the consequences of this social order in their laments on the fragmentation of life and the individualization of an organically structured society. While adherence to a particular creed functioning as a means of social inclusion was more or less compatible with the mechanical solidarity of hierarchical and corporately structured social orders, it was clear that it would present a major disruption to the organic solidarity of a liberal civil society, precisely because of the multitude of confessions in Christian Europe. For this reason, it was difficult to continue to interpret freedom of religion in the same way as in the seventeenth and eighteenth centuries, when the catchword 'toleration' had meant accepting the presence of other confessions, which were in principle disapproved of and which existed in their own individual, mutually inaccessible legal spheres.

Another new feature of this period was the separation between political and economic power, a consequence of the principle of the sovereignty of the people. The powers of governance and the monarchic sovereignty of the pre-Revolutionary European state began to diffuse through a space of political action that was defined by constitutions and characterized by a political public informed through media and by political parties, elections and a ruling structure defined by the separation of powers.[3] A purely parliamentary system continued to be the exception in Europe far into the nineteenth century, and most constitutions that were written later concentrated much of the state's power with the monarch and the monarch's prerogatives. However, churches, which could derive governing rights from their economic possessions, had become a foreign body in the political order of sovereign citizens. This applied especially to the Catholic Church and, in particular, to the church of the Holy Roman Empire. This was the church which had managed to retain the greatest degree of statehood for itself up to the collapse, whereas, in the Gallican Church and the Mediterranean world, concordats had ensured that the church's potential to rule based on property had been integrated into monarchically controlled aristocratic rule. For this reason, the secularization of governance for which the French Revolution provided a precedent was a concern everywhere in Catholic central and western Europe at the beginning of the nineteenth century. Napoleon himself did no more than speed up history in this regard. He ordered those developments in his states that would have taken place anyway in the long or short term. This applies to the secularization of governance, but it was even truer of the secularization of a monastery's or spiritual foundation's property, which was always carried out at the same time. The proceeds of this secularization of property sated the fiscal appetite of the state, but the broad support that these measures enjoyed everywhere was due to the general opinion that they disposed of a form of piety and a way of life that was removed from reality and had become obsolete long before.

From the last third of the eighteenth century, all European churches had to accept the fact that religion was being assigned a new place within the means of social integration, and European societies were in the process of redefining the relationships between religion and power. This called for, and made possible, the reorganization of piety and religious life. First, however, the church had to regain some stability without having recourse to the accustomed degree of secular power. It also presented a complicated challenge for the Protestant churches, which had developed in close proximity to the state. In this process, it was of limited help that social theorists of all political persuasions began to place religion at the centre of their social theories. The fact that state power fully intended to continue to take advantage of the aura of the sacred in the future did not make the task faced easier for any of the confessional churches. The change in nature of the political and the forms of public worship of God continued to be inseparably connected in this way.

## Religion during the Revolution

Whenever the epoch-making shift that the French Revolution represented was positioned historiographically, the relationship between religion and revolution played a central role from the beginning. The way in which the Revolution dealt with the Christian-Catholic heritage of the *ancien régime* was identified as one of the driving forces of the revolutionary dynamic as early as the nineteenth-century Restoration*. Jules Michelet wrote the following in his history of the French Revolution in 1846: 'The Revolution is the continuation of Christianity and conflicts with it. It is at the same time Christianity's heir and its opponent'.[4] Michelet's statement brought together two questions: whether the Revolution itself had a religious quality and whether it was itself religion. In this way, the interpretation of the Revolution was closely connected with the relevant contemporary political conflicts regarding the relationship of state and church and of society and Christianity. How much space could the political heritage of the Revolution grant Christianity in each of these cases? By emphasizing the autonomous religious character of the Revolution, Michelet opposed an interpretation of events which tried to claim the Revolution as an expression of a particular type of socialism based on Christianity. This idea, similar to those of Saint-Simon, did not find much acceptance, but the question of the religious quality of the Revolution continued to be central to the history of its interpretation. For Alexis de Tocqueville, who continued to maintain that the French Revolution was political in character, its historically epoch-making aspect was also that it developed 'like religious revolutions' despite, as he emphasized, not primarily dealing with Christianity as a 'doctrine' but as a 'political institution'.[5] The first two major university-based historiographers of the Revolution, Alphonse Aulard and Albert Mathiez – one a republican, the other a socialist – developed this hypothesis in two studies at the turn of the century, one on the origin of the revolutionary cult and the other on the Cult of the Supreme Being.[6] In this way, the problem of revolutionary religion became the subject of academic analysis and was placed within the context of comparative religious science, an area which was just emerging. In later research, this led, on the one hand, to interpretations of the Revolution from the point of view of religious sociology and, on the other hand, to minutely detailed examinations of the Revolution's context and of its interpretation. The original question also changed. It was extended to include the possible religious dimension of political order and political events in the modern era, that is, the nineteenth and twentieth centuries. It continues to be an open question as to what extent the French Revolution created the preconditions for such a transfer of the sacred into the political space, establishing a model for future developments. For this reason, the concept of 'secularization' forms part of the basic vocabulary of the political and social language of modernity, and it would be difficult to imagine research in the historical and social sciences without this topic.

## The *constitution civile*

It became clear as early as 1787 that the property of the Gallican Church would have to play an important role in restoring the state finances, when the Assembly of Notables tried to find a way out of the crisis of reform in which the monarchy found itself. The refusal of the two privileged estates to clear the monarchy's debts by contributing to a special levy led to the downfall of Calonne. The thankless task of trying to persuade the monarchy's high clergy to agree to a compromise after all was left to his successor, Bishop Loménie de Brienne. However, he too failed to convince the general assembly of the church arranged in 1788 to break the opposition of the clergy. It was to some extent understandable that the bishops and abbots of France refused to cooperate. For months, there had been public discussion about the necessity of selling church property in order to rebalance the state finances, which were in debt to the tune of 140 million livres. As a precautionary measure, the church had already carried out an inventory of all its property titles. The contribution that was expected was in fact quite limited. The church was asked to contribute 8 million livres, which did not even amount to 5 per cent of its annual income from tithes and landed property. Under these circumstances, the reaction of the bishops and abbots was petty, not to mention short-sighted. With the inevitable declaration of partial state bankruptcy in August 1788, the monarchy lost control of the political process, and Brienne initiated a public debate on how to organize the Estates-General, which had been convened immediately.

At this point, the high clergy of the Gallican Church must already have begun to realize that their decision had been wrong. The parish clergy, who were financially disadvantaged and had little say in the decision-making process of the church, launched a flood of leaflets and pamphlets in the run-up to the elections in order to make themselves heard and to draw attention to their situation. Because the pastoral clergy continued to be held in high regard by the population, this action resulted in 208 of the just under 300 seats of the Estates-General due to the clergy falling to parish clergy.

In the period that followed, this pastoral clergy also acted in a way that showed they were entirely conscious of their status. They did not by any means think of themselves as part of the Third Estate and were waiting for the opportunity to redistribute political influence within the Gallican Church. For this reason, only a small number of the clergy supported those with no privileges when the vote on whether to change the Estates-General to a National Assembly was taken in June.

The fears which had led the majority of the clergy to reject the proposal turned out to be well-founded. By deciding to dissolve itself, the Estates-General had once and for all removed the political protection that surrounded the hierarchy of privileges in the *ancien régime*. In the countryside, rumours of an imminent counterstrike of the privileged ruling classes led to the eruption of violence towards secular and ecclesiastical landlords. In order to avoid the worst in the face of the Grande Peur, and with the approval of the clergy, the National Assembly abolished the privileges of the nobility on the night of 4–5 August. Out of consideration for the nobility, the only rights for which they were not to receive compensation were the rights to tithes. The remaining feudal rights were declared to be property and had to be redeemed. In this way, the old governmental order was abolished, but the monarchy's financial crisis was by no means over. The National Assembly broke the stalemate on 2 November 1789, when it voted, with an overwhelming majority, to nationalize ecclesiastical property and to auction it off to benefit the treasury. This proposal had been put forward by Talleyrand, the Duke of Périgord and Bishop of Autun. On 13 February of the following year, the vows of those orders that were not involved in education or in the care of the sick were nullified and their monasteries were dissolved. This completed the National Assembly's reorganization of the church's property rights and their entitlement to govern. It was an easy step to take because the National Assembly had been following enlightened criticism of the clergy in religious orders and ultimately could claim to be seeing through attempts at reform from within the church that had so far not met with success.[7]

This claim, however, was deceptive. The revolutionary National Assembly no longer wished to reform the Gallican Church but it wanted to fundamentally reorganize it in order for it to fit into a constitutionally based state. When, in the context of the discussion regarding monasteries, the Carthusian Dom Gerle put forward a motion declaring Catholicism the national religion, it failed; this had to be seen as a very bad omen.

Immediately after the abolishment of feudal privileges, the National Assembly had instituted a committee for church matters in August 1789. Its task was to develop a concept for the reform of ecclesiastical institutions. The proposal made in spring 1790 did at least meet with the approval of the parish clergy because the allowance from the treasury intended for pastoral work meant an improvement in the financial situation for most of their number even if fees for administering the sacraments were to be abolished. The bishops could also hope to come away unscathed one more time as their relationship with those who wielded power was fairly good. However, the rules of power play had undergone a complete change as political business was no longer conducted between members of the same estate but by the elected members of a National Assembly. This was also reflected by the committee's other proposals. Secular electoral bodies were to choose bishops and clergymen in future, and a council of priests was assigned to the bishops that oversaw the way in which a bishop exercised his office in the diocese. The Revolution was clearly in favour of a pastoral church controlled by the state; the church's hierarchy was, at most, to have a coordinating function but was hardly able anymore to carry out the canonically prescribed tasks relating to leadership and church discipline in preaching and teaching.

The discussion of the proposals in the National Assembly continued for more than three months, but no changes were made to these specifications. On 12 June 1790, the *Constitution Civile du Clergé* became law. Four sections outlined a new Catholic Church which was integrated into the constitutionally based nation. Part I reorganized the diocesan and parish structure, reduced the number of bishoprics by just over one-third to eighty-three and abolished all rights of intervention by non-French church superiors, thus including the Roman head of the church. Part II decreed that, in future, clergymen and bishops were to be elected by local committees, whose members were to be appointed by the National Assembly, and were then to be installed by the relevant state authority. Cathedral chapters were abolished and the office of the bishop, as had been discussed, was tied to a council of priests. The spirit of this arrangement undoubtedly demanded that this clergy, whose legitimation derived solely from the state, should display their allegiance by means of an oath on the nation, the law and the king. Sections III and IV provided the regulations on the salary of bishops and clergymen and stipulated that office holders should reside in their dioceses and parishes.[8]

There were a number of quite different causes for the conflicts which were now gradually beginning to escalate, and they involved sections of society – a society stirred up by the Revolution – that were vastly different. Three aspects must be distinguished. First, within the church, the structure of the hierarchy was being questioned, both with regard to the relationship between ordinary clergymen and bishops as well as between bishops and the Pope. The bishops demanded approval from Rome for the civil constitution or at least approval by a national church council.

Second, this demand also reflected the fundamental break that a national church, which derived its legitimation through the legislative will of an elected constituent assembly, presented in relation to the traditional ecclesiology of the Roman Church. As an institution from pre-modern times, the Roman church was based not only on its institutions but, above all, on its spiritual legitimation derived through the unbroken chain of Roman bishops spanning the centuries since the death of Christ and their appointment of all fellow priests. Protestantism and its Reformation theology had developed the idea that knowledge of salvation could be communicated through different media, that is, through an individual's experience of faith and through texts. This was out of the question in the Catholic understanding of what church meant. Thus, the French bishops, who had always been happy in their Gallican enclave, now demanded the Pope's involvement or at least the approval of the new church model through the resolutions of a national episcopal assembly. If this did not happen, the church would become a mere appendage of state power that lacked all attributes of its divine appointment. This characterized a basic dilemma that none of the Catholic churches in any of the constitutionally based European civil societies of the nineteenth century was able to resolve and that, practically by necessity, resulted in the development of Ultramontanism* in the Catholic clergy.

The third point was that the decisions of the Constituent Assembly, which considered itself revolutionary, reflected an understanding of state and society that was sustained by a vision of a purely secular human order. The only role the church could play within this order was as an institution that had been assigned certain administrative and social functions; religion was treated as a form of morality both with regard to how it was preached and how it was incorporated into daily life. The society of the Revolution considered itself to be the entity responsible for formulating and fulfilling a secularized promise of redemption. Accordingly, society now began to look for a form of representation and symbolism which could endow the absolute nature of its claim with the aura of the sacred. The question was what shape the religion created by a revolutionary nation should take.

## De-Christianization

This constellation of factors provided further fuel for the revolutionary process, especially outside the National Assembly. In Paris, as well as in the towns and villages of the provinces, there was a clash between the pious expectation of the church-going population, the uncertainty of the parish clergy and the aggressive desire for change from the revolutionary protagonists, who acted as commissioners sent by the National Assembly and as units of the revolutionary National Guard and worked with the backing of the local revolutionary committees. The situation became worse as early as summer 1790, especially in those regions of France where Catholics were faced with a confident Protestant population or where they took umbrage at the fact that the National Assembly had issued an order in September decreeing that the Jewish population was to enjoy the same civil rights as non-Jews. For their part, local revolutionary committees were urging the immediate enforcement of the civil constitution. The Pope continued to maintain his silence although his position in the matter had long since been settled. In September 1790, the bishops of France issued a statement regarding the civil constitution that could only be understood as a rebuttal of the law. The legislature, which had convened in September, now had to react to this statement, and on 26 November, opposed by most of its ecclesiastical members, it issued a decree which gave the clergy two months to swear the oath demanded or else be removed from office.

An open confrontation could no longer be avoided. Roughly half of the French clergy refused to take the oath, in many cases resisting serious pressure from the populace. Events took a particularly violent turn in the urban centres of the revolutionary movement, such as Paris and Marseille, but many village parishes also demanded that the clergy submitted themselves to the new order. These events have been analysed in detail in the scholarship on the period, showing that the regional distribution of the clergy who refused to take the oath results in a map of France which reflects the distribution of Catholic and secular areas into the second third of the twentieth century. Particularly strong resistance to the civil constitution on the part of priests and curates was found in the west, for example, where the clergy traditionally had a strong position. The percentage of those refusing to take the oath was also high in many towns because clerics could escape personal pressure more easily there. In the south, too, refusals to take the oath were numerous; here, Catholics were faced with large Protestant groups in the population, leading to Catholicism becoming a matter of identity. Revolutionary France, on the other hand, covered the Paris Basin and the area north and south of it and then, from there, extended south-east in a band that reached as far as the Mediterranean. In the departments in the south-west, too, a high percentage of clerics took the oath on the constitution.[9]

In the meantime, the hesitant Pope Pius VI had brought himself to issue a statement in which, on 13 March 1791, he condemned the civil constitution. This resulted in 22,000 clerics retracting their oath and the situation becoming even more complicated and hopeless. In many cases, the priests who had left their office could not be replaced. Thus, in many cases, there was no one to administer the sacraments. In other parishes, avowed supporters of the Revolution seized the opportunity to establish themselves in office and to exercise the spiritual office in a way which they considered appropriate in the revolutionary context. Priests married with provocative solemnity and some became involved in the work of the local revolutionary committees. At the beginning of 1792, clerics were attacked in those areas in which they continued to refuse to take the oath. In May 1792, the National Assembly increased the pressure on those priests unwilling to take the oath by threatening them with imprisonment and deportation. This measure was not, however, put into action until August 1792 when the Convention, which had resulted from the constitutional impasse, carried out the threats. Thousands of clerics now fled France and about 2,000 were deported. In September 1792, secular authorities rather than clerics were put in charge of keeping the civil registry and marriage was declared to be a contract which could be dissolved and a divorce granted if this was the will of the couple in question. The clerics had again lost an important function in the organization of society.

The clergy had been seen as a cumbersome obstacle in the way of revolutionary reorganization, but they were now summarily suspected of operating a counter-revolution both from within France and from the places to which they had emigrated. Conversely, the Revolution, it was imputed, wanted to follow its supposed destruction of the church by wiping out Christianity. The signal for the so-called campaign of de-Christianization was given on the nineteenth Vendémiaire of Year II of the revolutionary age (10 October 1793), when the revolutionary commissioner in the western departments, Joseph Fouché, issued a decree that prohibited carrying out Christian practices in public. This campaign was not only aimed at institutional Christianity. It was designed to shatter the traditions of Christian *memoria*, which had, up until then, joined the living with the dead – the object was to create the space for a national memory. Starting in the heart of rural France, a wave of violence directed towards the clergy, the church and religious ritual took hold of the entire country within half a year. Churches were shut down or assigned a new, secular function, church equipment was turned over to the secular authorities, cemeteries were vandalized, and statues and images of saints were deliberately destroyed. In the south, in particular, there were carnivalesque judgements of heretics and other instances in which church rituals were mocked in a way that was obscene in the eyes of the faithful. The violence that took place was destructive, but it also signalled commitment to the Revolution. Temples of Reason were founded; the local revolutionary societies devised new festivals that involved a liturgy through which the ideas of a revolutionary civil society could be represented and celebrated. In order to demonstrate their loyalty to the Revolution, many parishes decided to rename themselves if the old name referenced a saint or had a Christian etymology of another kind. Again, the locations of revolutionary place names show significant overlap with those areas in which there were constitutional priests. This is one of the reasons why it is unlikely that these events were entirely spontaneous. We know that the commissioners sent by the Convention initiated such actions in many places. In other areas, the initiative lay with the revolutionary guards, and the spread of de-Christianization in waves reflects their movement through France. Nevertheless, the process of revolutionary de-Christianization was not something that had been set off by Paris. A process had begun in the eighteenth century through which Christianity gradually lost its function as the foundation of and guiding principle in an individual's life. Revolutionary de-Christianization was particularly strong in those areas in which this process was significantly advanced, and those regions in which institutional Christianity was still strongly rooted in the population offered the greatest resistance to de-Christianization. In almost all places, however, it was women who showed their disdain for the 'red' priests of the Revolution, and frequently they even stepped in resolutely when clerics and church property were attacked. This gendered difference in the degree of loyalty to the church was to become one of the defining characteristics of Catholic piety in the nineteenth century.[10]

## The Revolution's cult

The gradual process from estrangement to open hostility between the Revolution and the church also posed problems for the revolutionaries. The question of how to achieve the marginalization of an overly institutionalized form of Christianity became increasingly less important: the discourse of the Enlightenment had been prepared amongst the intellectuals and, as the oath demanded of the clergy and the campaigns of de-Christianization showed, the detachment from habitual forms of Catholic piety amongst the population had already progressed significantly since the eighteenth century in some regions and particularly among the professional bourgeoisie. In these areas, the Revolution was supported by long-term developments. However, when it came to making use of symbols and rituals derived from church practice to give shape to the political sphere, a degree of resourcefulness was called for, as the conflicts with the church and the disassociation with Christianity made this difficult.

In this context, the Revolution took its starting point deep in the *ancien régime*. It was customary throughout Europe to open an assembly of estates with a church service, and the work of the Estates-General in Versailles had opened with a procession of the delegates to the church of St Louis. The National Assembly, too, did not initially break with this tradition of giving the political decision-making process a religious frame. Sessions always ended with a solemn Te Deum, and this had also been the case on the night of 4 August 1789, when feudal dues and church tithes had been abolished. Indeed, the clergy were initially some of the most loyal adherents to the idea of reorganization. Members of religious orders blessed the French Tricolour; parish priests provided a religious setting for the ceremony when liberty trees were planted.

However, as early as 1790, it became clear that the Revolution, as a process which involved the masses, drew on traditional forms of ritual and communal relationships (Vergemeinschaftung*) through festivals for an essential part of its dynamic and also derived its social definition from these. A consistent aspect of urban festivals had always been that pre-modern political communities had to come together time and again to collectively eat and drink in order to continue to be a community.[11] At every parish fair a performative communality was realized for the members of the parish through commemoration. These elements shaped the culture of craftsmen and journeymen, and even the court staged festivals in order to strengthen its own sense of identity. Despite the fact that a growing proportion of communication was carried out via written and printed media, the aspects described fulfilled the conditions for integration in a society which still understood and experienced the concept of society as something tangible that was enacted amongst those present. All social theory of the Enlightenment – first and foremost Rousseau – held this view.

For this reason, the Revolution quickly found occasions during which it could show off and develop a sense of itself. This included celebrations during which liberty trees were planted, a practice which had occurred as early as 1789. On 14 July 1790, the National Guard in the province of Paris held a celebration of brotherhood in which the king and his family participated together with the deputies and officials of the National Assembly. It became a model for manifold Festivals of Federation in all parts of the country. The successful businessman Palloy had discovered his love for the Revolution during the storming of the Bastille and referred to himself as Palloy the Patriot from that point onwards. He erected a wooden dancing stage next to the ruins of the Bastille, which became the focal point of a three-day public festival to commemorate the defeat of tyranny. This bacchanalian exuberance characteristic of the revolutionary celebrations was compatible with church participation, but it was entirely able to develop its full effect without any exaltation of its status through religious ritual.[12]

A further strand of revolutionary ritual unfolded in spring 1791 when it was decided to convey the remains first of Mirabeau and shortly thereafter of Voltaire to the Panthéon as heroes of the nation. This meant that, rather than choosing Notre Dame as the location of commemoration, a secular temple of remembrance was established; this fact alone indicates the chasm which had opened up between the church and the nation in the meantime. The first person to be buried in the Panthéon was Mirabeau. His translation and interment were actually still very much in keeping with courtly obsequies, involving a funerary procession structured according to estate and a funerary mass arranged along the lines of a church service. In some parish churches in the town, masses were even read for him. His final translation to the Panthéon in December, however, was a very sober, secular ceremony. In the meantime, Voltaire had been received into the Panthéon and, in this way, the place for a secular saint's cult was established. The relics of the philosophical apostles of humanity, it was written, were to be gradually gathered together here. The transfer of Voltaire, as a representative of the Enlightenment, was carried out without any kind of church participation, and it deliberately avoided any reference to church symbols or rituals. In order to represent the fact that the Republic had overcome the *ancien régime*, the funerary procession was modelled on those of antiquity. The Revolution intended to construct its own identity around the historic break with the past which it represented. The translation turned into a celebration for the entire capital, which involved a large part of the population. Those who could not take part were able to read about this communal experience in journals. These journals reported that there had been cries to the effect that the population now had a fatherland; it was reported and asserted that this citizens' festival could compete with anything that the great peoples of antiquity had ever staged; and it was stated that it was the task of the press to report all of this to the entire French population and to make it come alive for them.[13]

The process of consciously turning away from a culture of festivals based on Christian tradition and a way of reckoning time that was rooted in the church reached its highpoint in the establishment of a new order of time. In late 1792 the Convention commissioned the citizen Guilbert Romme to create a revolutionary calendar, the Decadi. A little under a year later, Romme presented the Convention with a report in which he suggested introducing a calendar based on the decimal system. The year was supposed to start on 22 September, the autumnal equinox, in order to give fitting expression to the civic and political equality on which the Republic was based. The decimal division of time and names of the months based on the seasonal progression of the year combined two of the most important principles of the enlightened hierarchy of values. In this way, the calendar became a symbol of the innovative nature of the revolutionary order, of its rationality and of the idea that it was incontrovertible because it was based on human nature. The intention was to provide the political order with an explicitly non-Christian *fondament sacré*.

The Decadi had trouble gaining acceptance over Sunday, but we know today that people increasingly accepted the revolutionary calendar in the years 1793 and 1794 and that later greater areas of life were included than was long assumed. However, the idea that the new calendar would really have provided sacred foundations for the political order did not convince the revolutionaries either. The Revolution had established an independent discourse in political and social language and the republican defeat of the *ancien régime* provided the Revolution with a myth that could be developed in order to present its own history in a particular way, but the power of the revolutionaries lacked the aura of the sacred, which the monarchy still had, despite all justification of the king's power according to natural law.[14]

At the same time as Fouché's decree was issued, marking the beginning of the violent process of de-Christianization, an attempt was made to remedy this lack of the sacred by holding a Festival of Liberty and Reason in Paris. The meticulously detailed planning left nothing to chance. The nave of the cathedral was hung with cloth in order to cover Christian images and symbols. A holy mountain had been raised as an artificial mound in the centre, and on this a temple of philosophy surrounded by busts of the great representatives of the Enlightenment had been erected. The torch of reason burnt in front of it. Actresses from the opera were sent to participate in the ceremony by climbing the mountain of the temple in white gowns and paying reverence to the philosophers there. There were hymns to liberty and speeches. Subsequently, the festival's 'congregation' formed a procession to the Convention accompanied by a living goddess of reason; the Convention then made the official decision to consecrate the cathedral of Paris as a Temple of Reason.[15]

Although this performance was more of an operetta than a ritual – the participation of actresses alone ensured that this was the case – in the disruption created through the process of de-Christianization, the Cult of Reason also gained a degree of popularity in the provinces in the months that followed. However, this was not sufficient as a sacred foundation for the dictatorship of the Convention. The available semiotics of the sacred remained infused with Christianity, despite all de-Christianization. When Jean-Paul Marat was murdered in July 1793, his heart was removed and kept in a vessel made of agate in the Jacobin Club. This vessel supposedly came from the royal treasury. Such a use of Christian symbolism in a completely different context was helped by the national cult of martyrs in other ways, too, but it did not develop into a liturgy for the new order.

Robespierre made one last attempt to do this in May 1794. He considered the anti-Christian thrust of the Cult of Reason to be politically damaging and he generally doubted that a social order could be founded purely on rationality. He declared to the Convention in November 1793 that the Cult of Reason remained an aristocratic affair and that it surrendered the nation to atheism: 'If there was no God, he would have to be invented'.[16] In May 1794, Robespierre presented the Convention with the plan for a Cult of the Supreme Being. He justified this idea by again pointing to the dangers that an atheist society faced, and he implored the political actors to take on the task of creating an order that would not continue to corrupt people but would lead them permanently to a life of virtue. This was aimed at the *encyclopédistes*' 'sect', in the spirit of Rousseau, and also against Robespierre's own political opponents. The idea of a Supreme Being was, he said, a continuous appeal to the human sense of justice and the idea would thus strengthen a republican society. According to Robespierre, the Revolution needed a national cult that was to educate the public and offer festivals through which people could glorify the divine. The nation's future liturgy was outlined in fifteen articles. The Cult of the Supreme Being was to proscribe tyranny, threaten murderers with punishment, comfort the misfortunate and free the oppressed. New festivals were planned in order to achieve these goals, the plan for which was to be drawn up by the Committee of Public Instruction and was to contain mandatory festivals relating to the Revolution as well as a long list of festivals relating to different virtues and to the natural cycle of the year.

The painter Jacques-Louis David was commissioned with planning and organizing the first Festival of the Supreme Being on 8 June 1794. He created a public festival of the Revolution and nature that was designed to be instructional. It was a work of art and incorporated the Tuileries and the Champ de Mars in Paris. The most impressive and uplifting moment was when Robespierre himself set an oversized statue of atheism on fire with a torch, which burnt away to reveal a slightly scorched statue of wisdom. David's meticulously detailed arrangements aimed to create collective enthusiasm and elation, but the intention was obvious to all those participating and observing events. On the Champ de Mars there was dangerous unrest when someone called out that Robespierre wanted to turn himself into a god.[17]

The Cult of the Supreme Being was then disseminated throughout the entire country through the directives of the Committee of Public Instruction and through David's planning. The Cult had relinquished the theatrical aspect of the Cult of Reason and had been turned into a complex aesthetic ritual that not only educated its participants but also involved them in events and could offer them the elevating experience of a situation which was removed from everyday life. The mandated festivals of virtue and of nature created an entire web of revolutionary liturgy, which covered the everyday life of the bourgeoisie. It is doubtful whether this endowed the revolutionary order with a sacred aura. The Cult of the Supreme Being collapsed with the fall of Robespierre on 9 Thermidor II. The subsequent attempt of the Directory to install a form of theophilanthropy inspired by the Free Masons did not meet with success. In February 1795, the Convention decided to readopt freedom of religious practice, but the separation of church and state was to be retained in future.

The Revolution had failed in its enterprise to provide itself with a new sacrality that was not inspired by Christian ritual and which could serve as the nation's religion. The Cult of the Supreme Being lacked the absoluteness and the sacrifice to the Revolution that was offered publicly on the guillotine on a daily basis. Cult and the Terror referenced each other, and together they immersed the Revolution in the unconditional nature of holy things; this was something that artificial cults designed to meet certain aesthetic tastes did not have the power to evoke.

However, a pluralistic, bourgeois nation-state society such as the one emerging from the Revolution clearly had no use for this kind of murderous sacrality of a totalitarian order. It needed something the Revolution had also successfully created and had tested on several occasions: a language and a way of presenting and communicating social integration in a society that was no longer organized according to a particular hierarchy, but which was held together through different media of communication. The revolutionary festivals and the revolutionary cults represented a mixture of public festival, educational oratory, and the interpretation and reproduction of the event through different media, and this mixture succeeded in effectively supporting the 'nationalization of the masses' in the nineteenth century.[18] The Revolution had resulted in a public sphere that was communicated by different media and whose social power transcended all types of liturgy under the conditions of a civil society. It appeared to be so successful that the major confessions asked themselves, in turn, what they could learn from the Great Revolution when it came to the public worship of God. The problem, then, was not that the Revolution looted the Christian archives of symbolism, but that, in the course of the reorganization of the church's institutions, its own ritual practice also had to be adapted to social change. This was the real reason that the Revolution represented the writing on the wall for European Christianity.

## The great secularizations

As General Bonaparte carried the Revolution from one victory to the next in Europe and established sister republics and satellite states from the Mediterranean to the Atlantic, the export of the Revolution meant that the material basis of the Catholic church's authority came under comprehensive attack everywhere, a development that had been feared since the resolutions passed by the National Assembly. In the case of the Papal States and with the arrest of Pius VI in 1799, the vision of a national episcopal church without a hierarchical centre flashed up briefly. Like the Protestant churches, this would have had to find organizational stability in a close symbiosis with secular state power. As a result, the measures that were now taken in Catholic states were only superficially linked to the reforms of the eighteenth century. These had been initiated by enlightened rulers and bishops in order to strike at parts of the church's wealth that represented a particular kind of church organization and a piety which was not considered to be conducive to correctly understood Christianity or to an enlightened state. This interest in having an ally had been discarded early on by the modern state, which had come into its own during the Revolution. The focus was now on beating off a competitor, and the symbiotic competition of the pre-modern period was unilaterally declared a thing of the past. The secularization of church property, which took place up until the middle of the nineteenth century, was thus mostly an open nationalization, and making the property of monasteries, brotherhoods and other pious foundations available in order to improve pastoral care in the widest sense was only a secondary aim.

Nevertheless, there were different ideas concerning the aims of these encroachments on church property. The way in which the states of the European Restoration sought to legitimize political power, which became widespread in Europe following the collapse of Napoleon's power but had been foreshadowed by Napoleon and his imperial reign, represented an important break in this regard. Institutional Christianity, contained within the church, was rediscovered as a support for the throne and as a bulwark against the threats which constitutions and the principle of popular sovereignty represented to the monarchy. In the satellite states established after 1800, this led to the restitution, in some cases already under Napoleon, of property expropriated under protectorates or sovereign rights secularized in revolutionary republics between 1797 and 1799. This already indicated how closely the structure of the church's wealth would continue to be linked to debates concerning political constitution. The cycle of secularization of governance as an element of constitutional policy followed by restitution repeatedly occurred wherever the question of political constitution continued to be discussed regardless of whether this was because the shape of the nation state had not yet been determined, as in Italy, or because of a difficult balance between an absolutist Restoration monarchy and liberal parliamentarianism, as was the case in Spain. In the territory of the Holy Roman Empire, restitution largely did not occur in the wake of revolutionary secularization of governance; this was because such a move would have put the post-Napoleonic order of the states at risk, and there was no desire to return to the political order of the Holy Roman Empire.

Secularization, however, could also be justified on the basis of socio-political arguments, as neither the concept of mortmain and its associated feudal rights nor the entailed estates of the nobility and the feudal burdens on family farms fitted comfortably into a liberal society made up of property owners with free capital and property markets. Thus, the church's income from tithes could present a reason for the state to intervene in church property in Protestant states, too, as the Anglican Church was forced to realize in the 1830s.

Even after 1800, most measures taken towards secularization could still be justified by the Josephine argument that they were actually measures to reform the church. In Catholic states in particular, the secularization of monastic property after 1800 was often justified by referring to necessary improvements in pastoral care and the education of the population. The same arguments were cited in the Anglican Church, which began the nineteenth century as a structure dependent on property-based benefices.

## Italy and Spain

In Italy, after the secularizations through the Revolution and through Napoleon, the most important act of restitution was the re-establishment of the Papal States decided by the Congress of Vienna in 1815. The Papal States developed into a reactionary theocracy under Pope Gregory XVI (1831–46), having had more moderate beginnings under Pius VII (1800–23) and Leo XII (1823–29); the church's previous property and feudal rights, of course, were restored in this context. The rulers of the other seven principalities and kingdoms that existed in Italy following Napoleon's attempts to consolidate the multitude of political subdivisions understood the way in which religion could provide legitimation for their own political power, but a secular concept of statehood and Josephine traditions prevented these territories from reverting to pre-Revolutionary conditions. After 1815, most states gradually concluded concordats with the Curia, which usually involved recognizing the processes of secularization that had occurred in the preceding years as legitimate, including Napoleon's abolition of tithes. The north, under Habsburg influence, was no exception. Sometimes, as in the Grand Duchy of Tuscany, a form of compensation was agreed upon and no further laws against the acquisition of property through mortmain were passed, or church property, assuming it had not already been sold, was returned, as was the case in the Kingdom of Naples. However, all property retained by the church in this way was entirely subject to secular law. Restitution went furthest in Piedmont-Sardinia, where an agreement was reached in 1828 on the basis of the Napoleonic concordat to return church estates confiscated under French rule. Here, too, monasteries had to undergo rigorous visitations from 1825 onwards, but these were carried out by the Curia.[19]

In Spain, state encroachment on church property predated French rule. In 1798, significant amounts of church property were sold in order to provide funds for the depleted state budget, although the Crown pledged to compensate the church for the loss by paying back the property's monetary value at 3 per cent annually. This appropriation of church property was connected to monastic reforms. Visitations were undertaken in more than 2,000 houses of religious orders around the turn of the century. In 1803, the Spanish bishops submitted proposals to the Pope to bring the monastic orders more strongly under the disciplinary authority of the bishops. This resulted in the mendicant orders in effect no longer being controlled by their superior generals, who resided in Rome. These developments had already combined aspects of an episcopally oriented church reform aiming at the establishment of a national church with the state's willingness to secularize church property as a way of accessing funds to alleviate financial problems. Nevertheless, the resolutions passed under Napoleon's brother Joseph Bonaparte in 1809 represented a new level of secularization, determining as they did that the property of all brotherhoods should be expropriated and all religious orders in Spain should be dissolved. None of these resolutions were put into practice, and French occupation was ended through active support from the church. The monastic clergy, in particular, had been heavily involved in guerrilla warfare. Joseph Bonaparte's direct attack on the church, however, did have a negative consequence, in that it instantly ended all willingness within the church to carry out reforms. Thus, the bishops initially hoped that the Congress of Deputies of the Cortes would free the church from state domination while allowing it to retain its economic and social privileges without any change. When Ferdinand VII returned from exile in 1814, this illusion had already been dispelled. The Spanish nation was firmly Roman Catholic, but the Cortes had abolished the sovereign rights of the nobility and the church and had ordered the dissolution of contemplative religious houses. The church now placed its hope in the king that he might reinstate the old rights of the church and keep his promise that he was going to restore the entire pre-revolutionary order. Ferdinand VII met these expectations to the extent that he granted generous restitution of church property, allowed the Jesuits back into the country and reinstated the Inquisition as an instrument of political censorship and regulation. However, none of this constituted a liberation of the church. The king had no scruples in making use of his universal right of patronage in order to instate bishops that were loyal to him and he did everything in order to prevent closer ties between the Spanish church and Rome. These actions, along with his policy of restitution, meant that the question of the state's relationship to the church became central in all subsequent debates concerning Spain's political order. The succession of liberal parliamentary rule (1820–23), Ferdinand's royal autocracy (1823–33), the power vacuum of the dynastic crisis (1833–39), the military regime under a general (1839–43) and the moderate constitutional monarchy of Isabella II were characterized by the fact that, in times when the monarchy had lost power, encroachment on church property was greater, while the monarchs subsequently tried to contain the consequences of secularization. By the middle of the century, however, their energy in doing so had clearly diminished. Ferdinand had re-established the more than 800 monastic establishments which had been closed down between 1820 and 1822 without compensating their buyers. The decisive blows against the church as a landowner came in 1836 and 1837. In 1836, all monasteries and all male religious communities, with a few exceptions, were dissolved and their property put up for sale. In 1837 all remaining church property became part of the national assets and was thus not only subject to state supervision but actually nationalized, as became clear four years later when more than 10,000 properties that had originally belonged to the church found their way onto the market. It was not possible to reverse these acts of secularization without risking a collapse of the entire system, and Isabella II therefore confined herself to putting an end to the confiscation of church property. As a result, the concordat of 1851 created a state church that held a fraction of its former economic power.[20]

## The Imperial Church

The secularization of the Imperial Church by the provisions of the Imperial Recess (Reichsdeputationshauptschluss*) of 1803 was preceded by a history of events dating back to 1648. Part of this history was the refusal of Rome to recognize the religious agreement of the empire made in the Peace of Augsburg in 1555 while, in the second half of the eighteenth century, it also supported the idea of a territorial state church, in contrast with the episcopalism of the Imperial Church. On the other hand, the secular estates of the empire had already repeatedly detailed how easy it would be for them to resolve political and religious conflicts by accessing the wealth of the Imperial Church. Territories of prince-bishops (Hochstifte*), such as Magdeburg, had already become victims of the compromises struck as part of the Peace of Westphalia. In addition to this, the Catholic territories were increasingly less inclined to restrain their fiscal appetites for church property, in particular that of the religious orders. This was supported by enlightened publications that, for economic, social and religious reasons, denied monastic clergy and nunneries the right to exist. In the League of Princes (Fürstenbund*) of 1785 the interests of the imperial estates openly opposed those of the imperial state, and this sealed the fate of the Imperial Church. The ease with which the Habsburgs and Prussia agreed with France in the Treaty of Lunéville in 1801 to access the property of the Imperial Church, in order to compensate for the imperial territories west of the Rhine that were ceded to France during the Revolution, thus did not come as a surprise.

The dams had been breached. No one wanted to miss the opportunity to obtain a share of the wealth that would now be distributed. Even prince-bishops who were affected by this appropriation of church property demanded that other prince-bishoprics should be transferred to them, without taking into account spiritual considerations. The Knights of Malta were also keen to receive compensation from church property. The Josephine programme of reform, together with the secularization of governance of ecclesiastical imperial estates, in its fiscal form, now had become imperial law.[21]

The distribution of the spoils began before the imperial resolution (Reichsschluss*) had been formally agreed. There was no significant public opposition to this, not even amongst Catholics. Two ecclesiastical electoral principalities, one prince-archbishopric, nineteen prince-bishoprics and around forty imperial abbeys were secularized. Commissions were formed in the secular territories in order to record the property of the monasteries and abbeys and to determine how the estates, buildings, inventory, libraries, works of art and ecclesiastical equipment should be used. These measures led to considerable financial gain. For the Kingdom of Bavaria, it is estimated to have amounted to over 20 million guilders. The state forests alone gained an additional 97,000 hectares. However, these sums were offset by the allowance that had to be paid to the members of monastic communities, the funds allocated to cathedral chapters and for bishoprics, and the amounts payable to the institutions that had been dissolved. Ultimately, then, the net amount that the state obtained was considerably more modest. A final account for Bavaria from 1825 thus only amounts to 3.7 million guilders, and similar amounts can be calculated for other states. For the successor states of the empire, the real advantage lay in the secularization of governance, as the symbiotic competition regarding sovereignty between church and state had now finally come to an end and the Catholic Church had lost its rights of state sovereignty.[22]

## England

It had not come to this in the years since 1830 for the Church of England, but the extent to which it supported the consequences of industrialization being ignored politically meant that the political public also came to consider it part of the establishment and that it was vulnerable to attack. The bishops of the Church of England had had a significant part to play in the fact that it took until the third reading for a moderate reform of the electoral laws, which were to give the workers in the industrial centres better representation in Parliament, to be passed by the House of Commons and the Lords in 1831. This resulted in a flood of pamphlets directed against the political class and fiercely attacking the bishops and their church. Lists were published which denounced the enormous sums of money that the bishops had at their disposal from their benefices. Many of these figures were made up but this hardly mattered as the bishops' income merely symbolized the problems that related to the way in which resources were distributed within the Anglican Church and the negative consequences this had for the spiritual life.[23]

It was a complex problem. First, it concerned the land owned by the church and its role in the agrarian economy of Britain. Second, there were the negative consequences that the benefice structure had for the spiritual care given to the faithful. Finally, through the question of how the church was financed, the problem affected the relationship between the church and Dissenters.

With regard to the first point, the Anglican Church was suffering the consequences of a development that the churches on the continent would no longer have dared to dream of: since the middle of the eighteenth century, the amount of land owned by the church had increased substantially. The reason for this lay in the church's claim to tithes. These were considered by Parliament to be securitized property rights, and so most of the enclosure acts that Parliament passed involved an agreement on compensation for tithes. As a rule, the right to tithes was exchanged for land and so the amount of land held by those with benefices had more than doubled since the middle of the eighteenth century. At the same time, the faster the agrarian economy grew at the beginning of the nineteenth century, the more those involved in economic policy and daily politics considered tithes to be an irritating obstacle in the way of a further intensification of agriculture. Adam Smith had already commented on this and Arthur Young, the agrarian economist, had agreed with his criticism of tithes. The church's right to tithes reduced the capital gains that could be earned from agriculture. When the prices for agrarian produce collapsed after 1814, the argument was turned around. Agricultural labourers blamed the tithing system for low wages and unemployment in general. For this reason, from the 1820s onwards, this source of the church's income was considered an anachronism that was believed to hamper economic development and lead to social injustices.[24]

Within the church, wealth had turned out to be a curse rather than a blessing. The income of the English parish clergy had risen considerably since the eighteenth century; in general, it had doubled and, in some cases, it had risen fourfold. This allowed the parish clergy to lead the lives of gentlemen. They took part in politics, were welcome guests at sociable gatherings held by the gentry and had led a life that was leisurely enough to conduct extensive and successful enquiries into academic questions or engage in writing. Lawrence Sterne and Robert Malthus were famed for their literary and journalistic work and not for any dedication to pastoral work. An ecclesiastical career had therefore become a desirable aim in life for the middle classes. However, it was the system of benefices and not the rise in income due to a strong economy which formed the basis for this social rise of the clergy. Just under half of all patronage rights were held by laymen in the 1820s; together, the Crown and bishops had the right to choose around one-fifth of all parish priests, and the parish clergy themselves held patronage rights for a quarter of all parishes. Parish benefices came at a price, and so there was a market for them. However, this meant, of course, that holders of benefices were keen to increase their returns on such an investment, and so the possibility of accumulating multiple benefices was extensively taken advantage of. For this reason, the improved economic situation of the parish clergy had not altered the fact that there were not enough clergy in the parishes. For a long time, positions in the parishes had remained vacant because they were badly remunerated; now they remained vacant because members of the clergy were accumulating benefices in order to preserve a socially valued position with regard to income and status. Thus, the proportion of vacant rectorates, or those that were only filled by substitutes, had actually increased in the first decades of the nineteenth century. All members of Parliament and the House of Lords were aware of the catastrophic consequences this situation had for the degree to which the population identified with the Anglican Church. Furthermore, this monetized system of benefices prevented the efficient use of the church's wealth. It was impossible to establish new posts for parish priests in the increasingly industrialized regions with their fast-growing population. Thus, pastoral care in those areas suffered, and it was difficult to compete with Dissenters and Methodists.[25]

However, it was not just for this reason that Dissent put pressure on the state church. The second main source of income for the church comprised contributions by the parishes, the amount of which was determined annually within the parish, but increasing numbers of Dissenters had been refusing to give their consent to the church rate since the turn of the century or had found spectacular ways of refusing to pay it despite legal sanctions. Municipal government was made more democratic in 1835, and this meant that the influence of Dissenters increased considerably in some town councils. The conflict concerning church rates now looked to become a serious threat to the Anglican Church. It had already become abundantly clear how badly it affected the ability to maintain old churches in a good state of repair and build new ones.

All of these aspects came together at the beginning of the 1830s. Influenced by revolutionary upheaval on the Continent, the view that a stable state church was required as a reliable support for the political and social order gained strength. Pressure on the church to reform increased, and the government and Parliament initially suggested that the Anglican Church was capable of solving these problems itself. In 1832, Parliament established a commission made up entirely of members of the clergy to reform parts of the church. However, the commission's work led to no substantial result and only resulted in an even more acrimonious public discussion surrounding the separation of church and state, the detrimental consequences of the benefices system for the church and the wealth of cathedral churches. This problem brought down an entire government, and it contributed significantly to the early dissolution of Parliament in 1834. Between 1836 and 1840, Melbourne was the first prime minister to have any success when, supported by a new Church Commission, he had three fundamental laws on church reform passed by the House of Lords and the Commons. The Church Act of 1836 was aimed mainly at the bishops, their economic power and their remaining feudal rights. They were prohibited from holding any benefices in addition to their office. Furthermore, the income from their office was set at a minimum of £4,000, and this was combined with a moderate adjustment of this income in order to equalize it to some degree, as it had, until then, differed significantly in different dioceses. Two dioceses were dissolved and two new bishoprics – Ripon and Manchester – were created in the heartland of industrialization. The bishops of Durham, York and Ely lost their right to judge cases of secular law. Finally, the law determined that the Church Commission was to continue its work for the time being, thereby creating a new, independent body of the church leadership positioned between Parliament and the ecclesiastical hierarchy. The Church Act was supplemented by the Dean and Chapter Act of 1840, which abolished a large number of benefices that did not require residency, did away with a number of other sinecures, prohibited the accumulation of more than four canonries and limited the number of canons in any given cathedral to twenty-four. The Pluralities Act of 1836 had already reorganized the benefices system of the lower clergy. It determined that they could accumulate no more than two benefices and the income from them was limited to a maximum of £1,000. The maximum number of parishioners in two parishes held by one person was to be 3,000 in total. In addition to this, the bishop had to approve any individual wishing to hold multiple benefices and the law in general tightened the rules on residency; if necessary, bishops could demand that two services were held on a Sunday. The clergy were prohibited from trading in commercial goods in order to provide as little distraction from their pastoral duties as possible. The law was supported by the enforced sale of the patronage rights of civil parishes to the church, which had already been decided in 1835 in connection with the Municipal Reform Act. This provided some income, but it was also intended to lessen the influence of the Dissenters on the selection of parish clergy. The main point of disagreement with Dissent, namely the church rate, however, was not abolished until 1868. The measures outlined focused on the consequences for the church of the benefices system and the way in which the church's wealth was organized; the Tithe Act of 1836, on the other hand, did away with that aspect of the church's feudal rights that was economically the most harmful. The church tithes were commuted on the basis of market prices for natural produce and had to be paid off. Land that had been newly developed for agricultural use was not to be subject to tithes, and thus the question of how to finance the church no longer proved an obstacle for the modernization of agriculture.[26]

It took years for each of these laws to be implemented, which prevented the Church Commission from being dissolved. The slow pace at which its work progressed confirmed the belief of the kingdom's political elite that the ecclesiastical hierarchy was not capable of managing the church's finances and property in a spiritually and socially responsible way. In 1850, a commission for the administration of church property began its work. It was part of Parliament, and the bishops had very little influence over it. This did not mean that church property was nationalized – Burke would have seen his views confirmed in that regard – but it represented a form of state supervision. Combined with the laws passed between 1836 and 1840, this development was aimed at neutralizing the economic core of a spiritual institution and changing it in such a way that it no longer presented an obstacle to the church's adjustment to the fundamental economic and social structures of civil society.

## From privileged corporate body to association

### Toleration

The division of European Christianity through the Reformation and the developments of different confessions had made it necessary as early as the late sixteenth century to find political and legal ways of ensuring non-violent relationships between the different churches in the emerging states of Europe. The Peace of Augsburg had combined the *ius reformandi* with the *beneficium emigrandi*, meaning that it was only the rulers who enjoyed freedom of conscience. However, this solution had proved to have too high a cost: as a result, groups were driven out of their home territories; entire populations of subjects were repeatedly made to change the confession they followed, openly calling the principle into question; and finally, there were confessional wars between principalities and civil wars. In the course of the development of a doctrine of sovereignty in the seventeenth century, these problems were combined with references to natural law, resulting in religious practice being defined as a public matter, and thus one that could be ordered by the state; this state Leviathan, however, was obliged to recognize an individual's freedom of conscience as long as it was only expressed as private opinions and as long as adherence to a creed that diverged from the official one was only practised in the concealed services of private households. The religious and toleration edicts of the eighteenth century were still based on this idea. It even enabled a distinction between churches as privileged public corporate bodies, on the one hand, and religious communities, on the other hand, which were only considered to be private corporate bodies, provided freedom of conscience was allowed to be expressed not just in the home but also through semi-public parish life.[27] This was expressed legally through the toleration patents of the 1780s, for example, those in France (1787) and under the Habsburgs (1781) as well as the Woellner Edict. With his religious edict, Johann Christoph Woellner had demonstrated that the principle of toleration as a way of distinguishing between different levels of publicness in divine worship could also be used to mitigate the institutional consequence of theological controversies within Protestantism and could even be used to support Lutheran orthodox* theology and practice of piety against Enlightenment thinking and the relativism associated with it.

In the relationship between churches of different confessions, toleration had always meant that one church was given the status of state religion, while the others were not prohibited but their religious truth was rejected and they were legally and politically discriminated against. Thus, the *Allgemeine Landrecht* of 1794 made a distinction between state-approved 'church societies', which had the rights of privileged corporate bodies and whose clergy had a position equal to that of civil servants, and 'tolerated' church societies, which were classified as 'permitted private societies'. Another consequence was that a private sphere free of state intervention was now defined, which was initially a sphere in which a whole range of religious convictions could be practised.[28]

As early as the eighteenth century, this understanding of the concept of 'toleration' was met with serious scepticism by some, who argued that this superficial legal compromise could not prevent conflicts in the day-to-day coexistence of different confessions. On the contrary, violent encounters actually increased when Catholics were suddenly confronted with over-confident Protestants or Protestants felt driven into a corner by Catholics. This had been shown by unrest in those Swiss cantons in which adherents of different confessions lived and in Swiss subject territories (Gemeine Herrschaft*), as well as by the upheaval that occurred in Habsburg territories after 1781 in parishes in which a significant number of individuals suddenly openly proclaimed their adherence to Protestant doctrines.[29] Such conflicts, of course, always reflected social tensions, but a particular concept, shared by Judaism, Christianity and Islam, lay at the core of religious violence throughout the history of Christianity: all three religions carried out the 'Mosaic distinction', deriving their own sense of religious identity from judging the gods of the others.[30] By combining faith, scripture and grace, Protestantism had connected this distinction with an individual's implementation of revelation in their religious practice; in this way, the distinction was no longer an absolute, transcendental, external one. However, the necessity of maintaining public order, to which Protestants always referred as a means of distinguishing correct religious belief from false, presented enough of a constraint. Catholic theologians, on the other hand, continued to insist up until the end of the eighteenth century that religious intolerance should be based solely on theological arguments, as there was no salvation outside the church of Rome.[31]

The Enlightenment castigated both phenomena as a form of fanaticism that was inimical to the spread of reason and to social peace. In doing so, the Enlightenment cast general doubt on whether a religion that was tied to a particular church and based on the absolute nature of its revelation, rather than a private, deistic conviction, could have a place in society at all. Rousseau called Roman Catholicism a 'religion of priests' and concluded that anyone who dared 'to say "there is no salvation outside the Church"' would necessarily have to be banished from society 'as there could no longer be a state religion' in Rousseau's day. In this statement and in his *Letters Written from the Mountain*, concerned with the rule of the Geneva Consistory, Rousseau succinctly made the point that republics, in particular, could not survive individuals suffering curtailment of their civil rights as a result of adherence to a particular confession.[32]

In the context of the principle of popular sovereignty, a plurality of confessions, which had previously been a concern with regard to social peace, became a problem relating to the political order. Up until this point, monarchs had given their state and their subjects a sense of confessional identity, which did not necessarily have to be the same as that of the individual and which could, as outlined above, coexist with other confessions. If the people became the sovereign, this sovereign would be confessionally divided, and so the question was whether this was possible and what the nature of the relationship between the different confessions needed to be so as to avoid the potential for political conflict. The situation was complicated by the fact that, after 1800, in most cases, political orders had developed that were based on constitutions, regardless of whether these were agreed, decreed or based on tradition. They related to civil societies in which the mix of confessions had become increasingly complex and confusing in the first few decades of the nineteenth century, on the one hand, as a consequence of the Napoleonic reordering of states and, on the other hand, as a result of migration movements which resulted from the increase in trade and industrialism. Together, these factors meant that toleration as a means of distinction could not simply be dispensed with because the monarchical principle relied on legitimation through a preferred religion. At the same time, however, toleration created new social and political tensions in a confessionally diverse population. Until the middle of the nineteenth century, a number of very different solutions were found for this problem, but they converged in the fact that popular sovereignty and confessional plurality could only be combined if one dispensed with having a state religion and if all churches were treated as nothing more than citizens' associations.

## The difficult plurality of confessions

Napoleon was the first to try to resolve these contradictions in order to secure his autocratic military rule. The concordat agreed with the Curia in 1801 recognized the Catholic faith of the majority of the French population and of their first consuls and confirmed the freedom to publicly practise religion, provided this was done in adherence to the general laws. The reference to the majority of the population being Catholic already implied the details subsequently laid out in the Organic Articles* regarding the relationship between the different churches: the freedom to practise one's religion publicly applied to all three Christian churches with no distinction made between them regarding their relative status. This recognition by the state came at a significant cost. Anything that was relevant to the public practice of religion – from feast days to clerical vestments and the internal organization of the churches including Protestant confessional statements – was subject to state supervision and regulation. The concept of the pre-modern state church had acknowledged the independence of the churches but had always assumed close personal connections between the religious sphere and that of secular power. Now religion had become a social organization that was separate from the state; the different confessional churches as 'cults' were placed on the same level and had equal status before the law. The norms of this sphere were determined by the needs of civil society.

In this way, it had become possible to secularize the state while, at the same time, turning religion and the organization of the church into a tool that could be utilized both by society and by the state. Joseph Görres later wrote that 'the church was incorporated into the abstract state as a sub-category of this abstraction'.³³ For this reason, all the 'servants of the cult' also became employees of the secularized state. The constitution of 1814 reinstated Catholicism as the state religion because, as François-René de Chateaubriand commented, the idea of the throne of St Louis without the religion of St Louis was absurd; however, despite the Restoration of the monarchy, individuals remained free to choose which church they belonged to and this choice did not affect their rights as citizens. Even in the Catholic state, Christian religion was no longer allowed to influence an individual's access to offices and rights in society and politics. The July Monarchy* returned to Napoleon's secular system and Napoleon III also continued in this tradition in the Second French Empire, although this did not prevent him from appropriating Catholicism as a way of securing plebiscite majorities. The functionalization of religion proved to be capable of development in the field of political culture, too.³⁴

In Italy and Spain, developments were slower – partly because the Revolution had been perceived as a violent assault and as God's divine judgement, but also because, in the emerging political conditions, it seemed expedient to make the largely Catholic population subject to Catholic states so that the church could continue to support secular power. In Italy, all seven kingdoms and duchies, in addition to the Papal States, that emerged from the Napoleonic order established Catholicism as the state religion in the concordats concluded with the Curia since the 1820s. This included the states in the north, despite the Josephine tradition being particularly strong there. The Protestants in Piedmont-Sardinia were not granted legal and political equality until the upheaval of 1848 started the process of national unity. Catholicism continued to be the state religion in Spain under all Spanish monarchs up to and including Isabella II, but the liberal interim constitutions of the 1820s and 1830s separated state and church. However, the attempts in 1837 to make the clergy subject to a civil constitution failed even under liberal auspices.³⁵

In central and northern Europe, which had been affected by the Reformation and thus was faced with the question of how the different confessions could coexist, there was significantly greater pressure to ensure the legal and political homogeneity of the citizenry through parity of the various confessions. The solutions that were found depended on the support the concept of a state church enjoyed. Even in republican Switzerland, most cantons held onto the idea of a rigid state church, either Catholic or Protestant, while at the same time allowing freedom of conscience. The necessary parity that had to be achieved in the former Swiss subject territories was implemented by reflecting these divisions in the structure of state bodies. In Graubünden, two-thirds of administrative posts in the canton were reserved for members of the Reformed church and one-third was assigned to Catholics. Appenzell was divided into two regionally different parts and, until 1836, Reformed Protestants and Catholics formed two separate legislative assemblies (Landgemeinden*) in Glarus.³⁶

The greatest potential for conflict was found in the Netherlands, a monarchy since 1815. Here, the former Austrian Netherlands, which were Catholic and had a large population, had been incorporated into the former States General, which were Protestant. The prerequisites for organizing relations between the confessions by constitutional means were quite promising. In 1796, the Batavian Republic had granted Catholics equal rights, and the Dutch constitution of 1815 also granted freedom of religion and conscience, although it made this subject to the requirements of public order. These precedents were not strong enough to counteract the tradition of state church law, which William I (1815–40) had adopted as a policy, or the utopian idea of a state church held by the Belgian Catholics. William I claimed the right to intervene in the affairs of the Catholic Church, as well as in those of the Lutheran state church and the Mennonites and Remonstrants, which he had marginalized. The Catholic bishops for their part refused to recognize the Dutch Constitution as they believed it violated the canonical rights of the church. A concordat of 1827 was supposed to ameliorate the situation by placing the election of bishops back into the hands of the cathedral chapters, but, despite this, William I continued to try to influence the election of the Belgian bishops. The monarchy also continued to control the seminaries and episcopal colleges, and those training to enter the clergy had to attend the college of philosophy established by the state in Louvain. This strained situation between the confessions had the potential to turn into a political conflict because of a drive to limit the king's power in favour of the States General. This made it possible for the Catholics in the south and the liberals in the north to forge an alliance, which resulted in the creation of an independent Belgium after the July Revolution. Its constitution enshrined freedom of conscience in 1831, and this applied not only to Christians, but also to Jews and, from 1835 onwards, to members of the Anglican Church. The separation of state and church no longer involved one church being elevated above the others as a state church; instead, the different confessions were granted full institutional autonomy, including the right to freely shape relations within each of the churches. The clergy of these confessions were employed and paid by the state. The freedom of assembly initially benefited the Catholic religious orders the most, but it also made clear that the structure of the confessional landscape was to be based on freedom of conscience. The reactions to these developments showed how much of a challenge this separation of state and church – carried out by Catholics themselves – represented. Pope Gregory XVI only dropped his opposition once the Belgian episcopate had declared that, in practice, the Catholic Church would continue to have the status of a state church. In his 1837 tract on the struggles between state and church, Görres described the 'doctrine of the complete separation of church and state' as an 'utterly reprehensible false doctrine', which led state and church to ruin.[37]

Developments in the British Isles were less dramatic, despite the denominational and confessional situation being far more complex. Since 1689, the different denominations had enjoyed their freedom, which had considerably increased up to the middle of the eighteenth century through the gradual relaxation of the Test and Corporation Acts, and the Methodists could still be considered part of the Anglican Church. Thus, at the beginning of the nineteenth century, the problem of freedom of religion only seemed pertinent in relation to Catholics. Here, however, the connection between parliamentary sovereignty, the capitalist mobilization of society and the necessary equality of the confessions became particularly important. Through the Act of Union of 1801, Parliament in London assumed responsibility for Ireland, whereas, up until that point, Ireland had been treated like a Crown land. It soon became clear that it was impossible to integrate a part of the Commonwealth into the parliamentary system if its population was denied political rights due to their particular confession. The tensions that resulted from this could not be ignored once the migration of Catholic Irish to the main industrial centres in England brought the conflict closer to the centre of political life. In addition, the fear of revolution had led to the reinstitution of the Test and Toleration Act in 1789. This also limited the ways of dealing with Methodism, which was increasingly venturing out of the legally protected space of the Anglican Church and was holding its own services with Communion in its parish halls. Dissent and Methodism, which had been putting considerable pressure on Parliament and the Lords since the 1790s as part of a campaign to abolish slavery, exemplified the success of the evangelical movement and, in order to avoid political tensions, there was a gradual removal of the measures by which Dissenters, Methodists and Catholics had been discriminated against. The New Toleration Act of 1813 represented a first step in this direction. It lifted the ban on forming religious corporate bodies, a ban which had been in place since the seventeenth century. Unitarians, who were frequently encountered amongst the Dissenters, were no longer barred from passing their property on through inheritance, and this did away with a significant and extensive social disadvantage to which the Dissenters had been subject and which had affected members of the middle and upper classes in particular. The New Toleration Act granted Methodist preachers the same rights as the Anglican clergy, and the Test and Corporation Acts were finally repealed in 1828.

Only one year later came Catholic Emancipation. Catholics in Ireland, who represented the majority of the population, had continued to be legally and socially marginalized following the union with Britain. The small Catholic parishes that existed in England had developed under the protection of manors that had remained Catholic, but beyond this, there was hardly any institutional integration. In Ireland, on the other hand, a confident episcopal church had maintained its position despite English rule and had even prevented an initiative in 1813 aimed at an agreement between Pope Pius VII and the British government. The not unreasonable worry had been that the church in Ireland would be exposed simultaneously to interference from both London and Rome. Since the last third of the eighteenth century, some of the more significant social disadvantages that Catholics suffered had already been removed: from 1778 onwards, Catholics had been allowed to buy property; from 1783 onwards, they were allowed to hold public office in Ireland; and from 1817 onwards, they were able to become officers in the British Army. However, in the long term, this was not sufficient to prevent increasingly confident political demands regarding Irish interests and identity. The discrimination against members of particular churches was used as a means of political mobilization by charismatic leaders such as Daniel O'Connell. O'Connell turned the Catholic Association – up until that point an organization of the upper middle classes– into a political mass movement. After some of the bishops had expressed their sympathy for the movement, the pastoral clergy followed suit. Parish priests opened their churches for election rallies, and although, as a Catholic, O'Connell was not allowed to sit in the Westminster Parliament, he was elected to the House of Commons in 1828. The alliance between a political emancipation movement and the Catholic Church had resulted in a situation which, it was believed, could be defused by depriving adherence to a particular confession of its potential for political and social conflict, much like in the Netherlands a short time afterwards. The more perspicacious of the Tories successfully opposed the Crown and the Anglican bishops and, in 1829, severe restrictions were introduced regarding political activity in Ireland. At the same time, Catholics in the Commonwealth were granted social and political equality. They could now sit in Parliament if they took an oath not to use this position to harm Protestantism and to protect the king from conspiracies. Extremely harsh voting criteria, however, ensured that only very few Irish Catholics reached the House of Commons. Apart from the positions of Lord Chancellor and Lord Keeper, as well as leading positions in the British military in Ireland, they now had access to all state offices. Religious orders, including the Jesuits, were allowed to take up their prayers and missionary work, albeit closely supervised, and the British government relinquished any claim to veto a bishop's election, a right that had been proposed in 1813.

Although the Anglican Church remained a state church, there had been a gradual increase in the political and legal equality of the confessions – including the different denominations. Catholics were able to establish a church system that was mostly free of state interference and, in 1850, they appointed the first bishop for England. Dissenters and the Methodists established themselves as free churches after the middle of the century. In the long term, this loosening of the connection between adherence to a particular confession and political and legal rights undermined the privileged position of the state church. By 1840, the royal oath of office before Parliament had changed considerably. The obligation to unconditionally protect the Anglican Church had been qualified significantly, with the king merely undertaking to influence ministers not to decree anything that would hinder church officials in their work. The desire to separate religious matters from political issues and legal rights was also evident in Parliament. In the 1840s, liturgical reform was discussed within the church hierarchy but could not be settled because the hierarchy did not possess any decision-making procedures or authorized agencies. As a result, Parliament refused to engage in the discussion. On the other hand, members of Parliament missed no opportunity to diminish the Anglican Church's constitutional functions and thus to reduce it to the same level as the other churches. Through the Poor Law of 1834, civil registers, previously held by Anglican priests, were put into the hands of secular parish authorities, and, from 1836 onwards, Dissenters and Methodists could be legally married without an Anglican priest. This reduced the significance of confession on an individual level and, in the long run, generally put in doubt the legal competency of religious bodies regarding this cornerstone of social order.[38]

In the former Holy Roman Empire, Napoleonic legislation regarding state church law had been influential enough to lead to freedom of conscience being included in the German Federal Act (Bundesakte*) of 1815. In addition, the Federal Act stated that adherence to a particular confession should have no influence on one's political and civil rights. The discussions which preceded the Federal Act had been concerned with drawing a distinction between state-approved 'religious bodies' and 'private communities', similar to the *Allgemeine Landrecht*. This resulted in a threefold division of the law concerning the confessional landscape of the German Confederation

(Deutscher Bund*), which was an essential component of the state church law of its members until the middle of the century. A distinction was made between church societies recognized by the state, on the one hand, and confessions that were private, that is to say, only tolerated, on the other. The former had the right to practise their faith publicly and enjoyed equality in all legal matters and with regard to civil rights. The latter were required to practise their faith in private and were usually also subject to certain restrictions of their political or citizens' rights. Among the confessions recognized by the state, it was possible to effectively elevate one to the status of state church or to designate it as such by law, but this did not affect the rights of the other confessions.

The way in which this fairly homogenized area of law was put into practice differed significantly in the various federal states, depending on the confessional mix as well as the state's constitutional development. In Bavaria, the Napoleonic solution was adopted and a concordat was agreed in 1817 which preserved the canonical rights and privileges of the Catholic Church that it had traditionally held. A subsequent edict, however, took greater account of the Protestant parts of the new kingdom and referred to the three Christian confessions as public religious communities; these were contrasted with religious groups that were merely 'societies' according to civil law. This distinction provided two points of reference regarding policies on religion and the church and, in the late 1830s and the 1840s, this allowed Karl von Abel's Ministry of the Interior to pursue an open clericalization of political life. Its high point was a decree of 1839 which required Protestant members of the Royal Bavarian Army to attend Catholic services and genuflect before the tabernacle.[39]

Because it was traditionally Catholic and had Catholic kings, Bavaria, to a certain extent, was a special case within the German Confederation when it came to the question of a state church. In reality, however, the situation was not much different for territories with Protestant rulers. This was despite the fact that Protestant rulers could not conclude concordats, and the question of religion was regulated internally by laws or constitutions and externally by bulls of circumscription*, which were negotiated with the Curia but were unilaterally declared by the latter. In this way, agreements were reached without having to enter into a contract with the Curia. The states in which this applied were Württemberg and Baden in the south-west and Hesse and Saxony. Freedom of conscience was granted everywhere and the three Christian confessions were given the status of privileged corporate bodies, with their members enjoying the corresponding rights as citizens. Placing the three churches on an equal footing in this way made use of a principle that had already been employed by the Holy Roman Empire in an attempt to resolve the conflict between churches in the Peace of Westphalia. It assumed that the different territories in the empire determined a state church and thus also presupposed toleration as a means of distinction. This was in every way a pre-modern approach and the state church law of the federal states very quickly turned out to be unsuited to contain both the dynamics of this new confessional coexistence amongst the population and the strength of confessional church development.

This situation became particularly problematic in Prussia. As there was no constitution, the *Allgemeine Landrecht* continued to apply in religious matters after 1815. Constitutional promises had not been kept and the population thus had no parliamentary representation but was entirely subject to the king. It thus could be hoped that the provisions regarding the civil equality of adherents of the different confessions in the *Allgemeine Landrecht* would continue to be sufficient. According to these provisions, any disadvantage to citizens who were members of a particular church had to be based on the law. This invoked the order of privileges of an estates-based society; accordingly, it became increasingly problematic as civil equality before the law became more accepted through the move to modernize and mobilize Prussian society, which was driven by both the political and administrative leadership. This resulted in a political problem because the structures of the different churches had also changed in the upheaval in the years after 1800; because the church was subject to strict supervision by the part of the state, these changes in church structure also played a role on a political level. The secularized Catholic Church went from being a church based on an aristocratic hierarchy to an episcopal church, which then also developed an Ultramontane orientation towards Rome and wanted to see its new institutional form implemented as freedom from state supervision. Protestant churches were trying to find a constitutional model that could support Christianity without this framework being part of the state directly. These structural problems resulted in conflict between the Prussian state and both the Catholic Church and the Protestant churches. In the former case, these conflicts revolved around mixed marriages and the Cologne Troubles (Kölner Wirren*), and in the latter case around church union, the order of service and church constitution.

The problem of mixed marriages was only superficially due to the different concepts of what marriage was – on the one hand, a Catholic sacrament and, on the other, a contract confirmed by the church that followed the legal concepts of the Protestant state. Freedom of conscience now meant that the churches became organizations with a particular membership that was no longer determined by family tradition or the ruler's beliefs. Civil subjects now decided which confession they would adhere to, and the only way in which churches could influence individuals now lay in education. For this reason, the conflict regarding mixed marriages had great potential for mobilization in western parts of Prussia, and this turned the dispute into a conflict concerning the fundamentals of state–church relations. The result was ultimately that Rome and the bishops from the Rhineland refused to marry Catholic women if any prospective children were to be brought up according to the father's Protestant faith, as Prussia decreed from 1825 onwards. In 1841, an agreement was reached with Rome, which finally resolved the conflict following bitter disputes and the expulsion of Bishop Droste Vischering. The agreement stated that it was solely up to the bishops to decide whether Catholic priests could participate in mixed marriages, and this accelerated the introduction of civil marriages. In addition to this, the Catholic Church had gained an important freedom: communication with Rome was no longer supervised by the state, and the state also limited its say in the election of bishops.[40]

The relationship between Protestant Christians and the state became more complicated when Frederick William III (1797–1840) planned to create a dogmatic and ritual union (Union*) between Lutherans and Reformed Protestants by changing the liturgy (Agende*). When the liturgy that had been in place in Lutheran parishes was introduced to Reformed communities in 1829, questions were raised as to whether there should be candles and crucifixes on the altar or not, whether pastors should wear a cassock or only tailcoats, and whether those taking Communion should cross themselves and kneel. The issue became contentious when a cabinet order of 1834 declared the liturgy of 1822 to be binding for all Protestant parishes.

Frederick William III had pursued the Union and the question of a church constitution as a political project. The church was to provide Protestant Prussians with a subsidiary space for social integration as this continued to be denied to them politically. In 1847, after intensive consultations, Frederick William IV issued a religious patent which recognized all religious communities that 'agreed in all essentials' with the three major Christian confessions. They were given the same authority as the recognized churches to carry out marriages that were valid under civil law. This allowed Old Lutherans* to form their own church outside the Union. Other confessions continued to retain only the status of private associations, but the religious patent introduced civil marriage for them and all other dissidents. Thus, civil marriage ceremonies now existed in all of Prussia as an alternative to church marriages.[41]

Given the situation regarding different confessions in the states of the German Confederation, this development was irreversible. The Constitution* agreed by the Frankfurt Parliament* therefore contained statements on the relationship between state and church that went far beyond the individual right of freedom of confession enshrined in the German Federal Act. There were no longer any legal differences between religious communities or privileges of one group over the others. The constitution also stated that 'there is no state church'. As a result, religious communities could come into being without needing recognition by the state. The distinction between privileged corporate bodies and mere sects, which, up until then, had been the deciding factor in the legal relationship between religion and society, no longer existed. Toleration as a form of distinction thus ended because it no longer had a place in the political and social order of a civil society. This society needed religious pluralism, at least with regard to Christian confessions. Civil society had placed religion in a homogenized legal space in which all religious communities had the status of associations. Individual religious commitment was now no different to other motivations and interests, which also found expression in a whole variety of associations. For religious communities and churches, this meant that they lost significant powers of social inclusion. Only civil marriages had legal force, and church marriages had to be held after the civil ceremony.

The Constitution of the Frankfurt Parliament did not initially become a reality. In most states of the Confederation, those in power considered the constitution, in many aspects, to have gone beyond what was thought to be prudent. The imposed Prussian constitution of 1850 returned to the distinction between recognized religious communities and spiritual societies without corporate rights, but the state continued to withdraw from this legal field. State patronage was abolished and Catholics were granted free communications with Rome. In addition to the patent of 1847, the introduction of a civil marriage law was announced, but this was not introduced until the Kulturkampf*. Nevertheless, this constitution, together with the religious patent, largely neutralized the political and social consequences of confessional differences. Like other constitutions of the period, it stressed the fact that religion in a civil society could no longer take the form of a state church. Its model was a free church consisting of members who had exercised a free choice of conscience. This corresponded to the secularized state, which refrained from interfering in the matters of religious communities but also ensured that adherence to a particular confession did not lead to differences in political or social rights and that religion lost its ability to include or exclude individuals socially except within a religious context. In this way, the pre-modern relationship between society, religion and the state was, at least theoretically, abandoned. Even if this was not yet the case everywhere in the mid-nineteenth century, Europe's confessional diversity had proved to be a decisive driving force in enabling the free-church model of a modern, secularized, liberal civil society.

## The invention of political religion

In 1799, in his *Reden über die Religion*, Schleiermacher informed the educated despisers of religion that he was not worried about the future: no period, he claimed, had ever accepted religion better than the current one. Friedrich von Hardenberg (Novalis) took a similar view. In the same year, he submitted a text to the *Athenaeum* in which he prophesied the imminent 'resurrection' of a new form of Christianity which would help to create a new Europe after its fall into anarchy. Goethe refused to print these insights, and they were not introduced to the public until 1826 when religion had indeed once again become formative for social order: the political Restoration of the nineteenth century had remembered the significance of the church as a support for monarchic legitimacy, and the ability of religion to bring together as yet fragile nation-state societies was valued. At the end of the eighteenth century, however, such diagnoses were by no means a given. Chateaubriand stated as late as 1826 that the Revolution had destroyed the Christian memory of Europe.[42]

The developments that followed were Janus-faced. The political order of nineteenth-century Restoration looked to the future by adapting its political style to the demands of a liberal civil society. However, at the same time, it also continued to draw its legitimacy from a tradition that pretended the events of 1789 had never taken place: the 'monarchical principle' modelled itself on a bygone world without seriously wanting it back. This bygone world was to banish the greater evil of popular sovereignty, as Friedrich Julius Stahl told the readers of his treatise which gave this principle its name. Accordingly, the monarchs presented themselves as 'citizen kings*' who initially ruled as affable patriarchs and finally turned the traditional foundation of their legitimacy into mere props of a Caesar-like form of populism.[43]

Considering the historical developments of this period, the use of this lost world as a model cannot simply be attributed to a continuity in elites and interests, although such continuity undoubtedly existed. Juxtaposing aspects of different times as if they were contemporaneous with one another and combining radical social modernization with traditional social forms and argumentation were the defining features of a society in the process of transformation, which had yet to develop its own character and modernity. For the time being, this society presented itself as the mirror image of pre-modern times. While this image was not a distortion as such, it did perpetuate two temptations: the first was to use the pre-Revolutionary European patterns of social order as a standard against which to unfavourably compare a society that was pluralist, linked up, characterized by a division of labour and controlled by the markets; the second was to shape current political and social institutions in a way that was still strongly influenced by the aims and principles of the pre-Revolutionary European *societas civilis*.

The society of pre-Revolutionary Europe had not thought of itself as a structure created and communicated by different media. Instead it had viewed itself as a hierarchically organized set of communal relationships between individuals and groups, in which law and sovereignty were derived from a divinely created order of the world and were not at the disposal of mankind. The early modern state's claim to sovereignty had already placed a strain on this political civil society and had inspired a defensive, 'conservative' theory of the political. Other aspects also illustrated the consequences of describing an ever more complex society as the community of those present. One example is the increasing importance placed on values and convictions as the basis of social coexistence from the beginning of the eighteenth century onwards.[44]

The rupture represented by 1789 led to an escalation of these problems, and it was no longer possible to treat them simply as a question relating to social theory. The Revolution raised them up onto the stage of social politics. Nevertheless, associative relationships continued to be experienced and understood mainly as communal relationships and so the nation – which was the name now given to the society that formed the state – was also constructed as the fervent association of the members of society. Politics was dependent in an unprecedented way on the liturgy of choreographed mass events in order to shape a public in which, according to the understanding of the time, writing and printing served to establish the 'complete presence'[45] of its members despite temporal and spatial distance.

It soon became apparent that this constellation helped religion to gain a new significance. Anyone who intended to continue to view the *societas civilis* as a conservative, counterrevolutionary utopia could find the most important arguments for their purpose in Christian natural law. The Christian (religious) community seemed to be a useful model in general for countering and overcoming the disintegrating and alienating forces of modern sociation, which had been unceasingly lamented since the Romantic period. For the political regimes of nineteenth-century Restoration, the obvious conclusion was to use religion as a legitimating force and to draw on the different confessional churches as a means of disciplining subjects. A monarchy that was integrated into a constitutional system knew that it was safest in a 'Christian state'. In this way, nations were presented as holy communities, which required a political religion in order to survive in the face of a realm of needs. This development came at a price. Apart from the state churches, which continued to be oppressive, churches and theologians now had to deal with the fact that religion had become a political choice. Political views now influenced discussions about theology and the constitution of the church.

**Society and morality**

Liberalism, which was in the process of emerging, was only interested in religion when it came to warding off clerical influence.[46] As a constitutive element of human associative relationships, religion became the focus wherever social integration was not based on the formal principles of political participation and equality before the law and was, instead, primarily understood as a problem relating to social values. As the example of Thomas Hobbes shows, the pre-Revolutionary European ideas regarding social integration mostly considered it to be a function of state sovereignty and thus it had been described in the context of power relations. Accordingly, then, religion was seen in negative terms. It had a social function as a state cult, which protected the might of Leviathan by endowing it with a holy aura, but otherwise it remained a private conviction, which was only relevant to society to the extent that the belief in an afterlife and the fear of the Last Judgement helped to assert the norms and laws of the state.

The idea of popular sovereignty and the division of powers had cut off this strand of the political self-description of European societies. Anyone who, after 1789, reflected on the questions of how a society could come into being, what was required for a given social order to be stable, what factors could form the basis of political power and what the prerequisites were for national identity could turn to religion as a special type of morality which would ensure that social order and political rule could also be constructed on the basis of consent. The importance that was assigned to religion and morality with regard to constructing a society thus indicated to what extent power was legitimized from within society and dependent on the consent of a majority.[47] Conversely, anyone who persisted in believing that the prerequisite for maintaining order in the long term and securing state authority was to remove any doubts concerning their legitimacy by referring to the idea that both were divinely derived would obviously think of society, state and religion as one organic unit. Finally, while social solidarity was not yet considered a problem at the beginning of the nineteenth century, it became a pressing problem the more clearly industrial modernity reared its ugly head of pauperism* and division, especially as people's loss in social status had become a threat to political order.

These three areas were the focus of a European discourse that had developed since the end of the eighteenth century. They connected the Catholic conservatism of Joseph de Maistre, Louis de Bonald, Chateaubriand and Juan Donoso Cortés with the ideas of Karl Ludwig von Haller, they linked the English Tories from Burke to William Gladstone with the 'Christian socialism' of Lamennais and Saint-Simon, and they united the German Romantics Friedrich Schlegel, Novalis and Franz von Baader with the conservative politicians Joseph Görres, Friedrich Julius Stahl, Friedrich Gentz and Frederick William IV, whose respective confessions were fundamental to their politics. The underlying structures of their arguments were similar, despite the differences in confession leading to polemical disagreement and limits on the extent to which the different sides took in each other's views. There is much evidence to show the widespread reception of political confessional publications in the 1820s, and this fact alone meant that it was possible to make oneself familiar with the other side's arguments. Knowledge of these arguments contributed considerably to the development of an intellectual, politically active network in which religious and political possibilities intermingled to such an extent that disagreements between the confessions were often covered up. Karl Maria von Radowitz, who undoubtedly held Catholic beliefs, was both a very close and trusted advisor to Frederick William IV and a close political friend of the Gerlachs, who were Protestant.[48] Different political cultures and their stages of development appeared to be a more important factor in determining with whom one disagreed and whom one opposed. This became all the clearer the more specifically the issue under discussion dealt with religion and churches.

**Society and family**

In order to drive out the 'chimera' of an 'artificially bourgeois' society and to outline a stable theory of the 'naturally sociable condition', as Haller had already announced in the title of his *Restoration of Political Science*, it was necessary for the conservative critics of post-revolutionary conditions to think consistently of society, state and religion as an organic entity that had always existed and whose existence and interaction were not derived from human action but already had its starting point in God's divine order of creation. This was the only way to avoid the idea of a 'social contract', which divided people, their interests and the order of society in such a way that they could be played off against each other.

This requirement meant that the ideas of the likes of de Bonald, de Maistre, Adam Müller and Haller shared a common rhetoric which referred to an opaque beginning. According to this, a person did not enter society as an individual but as the member of a family. The *societas civilis* of nineteenth-century Restoration thought did not consist of individuals at all, but always of families. A person learnt to be a member of society within the family and through family alone because the family provided the 'natural' relationships of authority that existed between the generations and because it was the origin of (natural) religion, understood as knowledge of God's existence and as ritual practice. Chateaubriand identified the origin of all communal relationships in the cult of the dead. People were made people only through the knowledge of God that the family passed on to its members, as de Bonald stressed, and he added that all social order could be traced back to the maxim 'Honour thy father and thy mother!'. According to de Bonald, the natural authority of parents taught a person that it was proper to respect power. Power and religion emerged from the family. The social order that had become necessary through the family was based on the family: the family was both cause and organizing principle. The state was necessary because families could be at war with one another. A nation was formed by families that had a common ancestor, and they formed a state if they decided to submit to the same laws. Cortés's 'divine state' was also based on the natural authority of the father in this way and the associated families that developed from it. These were divided into kinship groups and into provinces. It was hardly possible to ignore the fact that society was organized according to a division of labour around the middle of the nineteenth century, and so Cortés supplemented the localized structuring principle with professional classes in which families with the same social tasks were grouped. All of these 'natural' groups then formed the 'Catholic' state in which the monarch's throne was the symbol of the state's unity and its hierarchical order.[49]

Gladstone also only knew two natural and universal types of human communal relationships, which at the same time formed a moral unit and thus had a religious quality: the family and the state. However, defining a person's associative relationships exclusively through their family was not something that was obvious to English conservatives due to the arrangement of the body politic in the commonwealth and, in particular, the extent to which the English social order had been influenced and shaped by market and economic relations. A commonwealth was not distinguished from a slave plantation by way of the foolish fiction of a social contract, Coleridge wrote in his 1825 treatise *On the Constitution of the Church and State*, but by the unconditional idea of personal integrity and an individual's free will. Highlighting individuality in this way, however, led seamlessly, in this case too, to the outline of a society made up of individuals with property, motivated by 'personal interests' and divided into three classes. One consisted of the 'landed interest' of the landowners, the second of the 'moneyed interest' of craftsmen and merchants. The third comprised theologians, the clergy and all academics of society in order to provide a cultural foundation and to elevate society by turning it into a morally integrated community.[50]

## Against atomization

The common denominator of all of these outlines of organic sociation originating in the family was the fact that they were aimed against the idea and reality of a society integrated by market forces and by means of political and administrative structures communicated through various media; the reason for this opposition was the belief that only direct relations between people could create and permanently maintain the unity in feeling and convictions that led to coherence. Burke referred to the revolutionary festivals as 'mere tricks' when considering the rationalistic fragmentation into electoral districts and departments which the Revolution had undertaken in France. One's 'public affections' should instead be developed within the family. True patriotism did not arise from belonging to 'the Checquer, No. 71, or to any other badge-ticket' but could only come about if it started in the family and then was transferred to the 'habitual provincial connections'. This was where the 'inns and resting places' were to be found. Burke dealt with the impermanent nature of the civic spirit by connecting it to a topology of travel, which can only be imagined as a series of direct encounters. It was the communication that direct encounters entailed that made this commonwealth real, and the only way that a common idea could conceivably hold it together permanently was if things stayed this way.[51]

This connection between interactive sociality and a type of associative relationship based on values was fundamental to the reconstruction of the *societas civilis*. It was important enough for Haller to make it the fundamental principle underlying all three forms of government between which he distinguished. It went without saying that it applied to a state ruled by a monarch and structured according to class. In a municipality too, political sociation took place through the continuously updated presence of the citizens. The 'religious community', finally, which, if it became independent, was also a state, was based on 'the relationship of a teacher or spiritual leader with his disciples or the faithful'. Haller was concerned here to emphasize that a spiritual leader's charismatic authority was also of divine origin. This leader's superiority was based on 'a higher form of wisdom', which had been granted 'directly' by God. The social form of the spiritual community, however, continued to be the relationship between a teacher and his disciples, which depended entirely on their physical presence. Cortés subsequently followed Haller exactly in his writings.[52] This rhetoric of attendance and presence necessarily led to the idea that at every level of social integration – from the family to the class-based state – it was always the 'entire' person who had to be present in his or her undivided existence.

Burke's detailed criticism of the electoral system instituted by the Revolution was very astute because this system did not accurately reflect the social circumstances of the electorate or of those elected: it moved them outside their natural structures and groups and thus both sides 'will be frequently without any civil habitudes or connections'. The elections in the English counties, on the other hand, guaranteed this direct connection between the electorate and those elected in the best way possible.[53] This argument was directed at the impositions that functional differentiation brought with it: governance turned into politics because social power was separated from political power, and this fact became apparent in the organic unit of the sociated person being fragmented into a disparate bundle of different roles. This destroyed not only the unity of a person but sociality in general. For this reason, Müller stressed that a class-based state should be created which was based on the 'living citizen' as that citizen emerged from the family. The concept of a state should be based 'on a complete view of the living person or the theory of family' as the state *was* 'the extended person'.[54]

Viewed against this idea, the present could only be criticized as being 'de-socialized'. Radowitz declared that the 'old order of society' had been dissolved and that society was thus exposed to the 'atomization' of mechanical centrifugal forces such that the 'innumerable small instances of individualization in which capital and labour formed a community filled with life' had disappeared. De Bonald incorporated this diagnosis into a theory of cultural decay reminiscent of Rousseau which – as Novalis had also done – located the utopia of a 'truly Christian society' back in time in an idealized medieval period. The big landowners had convened more and more frequently, villages had come into being and, finally, towns had developed, bringing with them all those things that resulted when a large number of people came together in a disorderly way: luxury and the frivolous arts, including, finally, philosophy. In this way, the agricultural nation of France had turned into a nation of urban citizens amongst whom the arts flourished, 'but family, the state, religion, society, all has been lost in it'. The modern national state thus could not really be considered a society anymore. Müller believed that the 'extended sanctuary of Christian religion', which he considered the state to have been in the Middle Ages, was decaying because nations had given in to the temptation of money and the philosophy of pagan antiquity: 'Therein lies the entire secret of the downfall of all private and political life and of the European federation of states'.[55]

This perceived and experienced unity regarding a religiously suffused sociability was incompatible with the idea of writing. Writing hampered direct contact between people and was of no use for ordering society. De Maistre laid out in great detail that any founder of a state who had presented himself as writing laws had failed. Moses was an exception to this because his tablets of law were of divine origin, and they thus overtly illustrated the general principle that every kind of order came from God. For this reason, nations could not be founded with pen and paper, but only through tradition and divinely inspired action. At most, one could write down a foundation myth, but the order to which a state adhered could not be put down in writing. Such arguments emphasized the absolute pre-eminence of tradition over anything that had been instituted by humans. However, they also indicated that the 'bodily currents' of a society based on presence *could not be controlled or replaced by a written programme. At best, writing was acceptable as a tool for preservation but not if its use went hand in hand with the social shaping of communication. In the 'truly Christian times' which Novalis imagined, 'childlike trust' tied humanity to the pronouncements of the powerful. Churches were 'mysterious' and were 'decorated with encouraging pictures, filled with sweet scents and enlivened by holy, uplifting music'. Venerating relics gave people 'peace for their soul and health for their body'. By using this phrase, Novalis interpreted sociation as a synaesthetic experience, which depended by necessity on the immediateness of sensory experience. For this reason, the Reformation's emphasis on the Bible as the cornerstone of faith represented a break with serious consequences: 'This choice was greatly detrimental to religious meaning as nothing destroys its ability to irritate as much as the letter does'.[56]

Novalis connected this diagnosis to the rest of his history of the decay of the European nations, which had created the current crisis. The answer to this crisis given by those commenting on contemporary developments was a form of religion which was based on evidence experienced through one's own senses and which could, therefore, be believed in again. Friedrich Gentz stated in 1819 that peace, satisfaction and general prosperity could be guaranteed 'only if there was a successful re-establishment of the moral, that is religious, basis of society' because all rules imposed by a government were in vain as long as the 'voluntary submission of the mind to a higher, inviolate law can be brought about'. The theorists had phrased this insight into the inner coherence of a segmented and hierarchical society based on presence more generally: 'Religion is the cause of all society because outside it no power and no duties can be justified. Religion is, therefore, the fundamental constitution of any social condition'. This did not describe a precondition as such, but it determined the precondition that made it possible to conceive of forms of associative relationships which were considered to be modern within the social ideas of pre-Revolutionary Europe. The fact that this led to religion becoming political lay in the nature of the matter.[57]

**Political religions**

There was little in these texts about religion that was descriptive. Confessional identities were outlined and political programmes and social utopia were laid out. It was only from this point of view that the descriptions of the state of religion and society made sense. The way in which religion was imagined therefore was shaped by the problems which one wanted it to solve within the envisaged *societas civilis* as well as by the significance which was attributed to religion as a basis for social coexistence and the endurance of social order. The more emphatically society was considered to be a divinely based *societas civilis*, the more elaborate the use of religion as an explanation and justification became, and thus the social remained a function of the religious. Conversely, in ideas of society as a secular entity, religion was considered to be a function of the social. Thus, the range of things that religion was supposed to be capable of included civilizing mankind and making social order possible, lending legitimacy to power and ensuring laws were obeyed in this life because they were based on transcendent justice, and creating solidarity amongst individuals who otherwise shared little due to their different tasks in the world of work.

De Bonald had stated that it was through religion that one became human if it allowed one to understand that one was God's creation. Within the concept of a civil society that had its basis in God, this key statement could be interpreted both from an anthropological point of view as well as through the history of philosophy. Cortés summarized Catholic anthropological arguments as follows in the mid-nineteenth century. Christianity produces man by ordering human abilities in a way that makes it possible for society to form. It makes the body subject to the will, which in turn is subject to the intellect, and this in turn to reason, and this to faith – all are finally subject to love. Against this background, Chateaubriand described a history of civilization in the West, in which Christianity – as a faith based on revelation, in the form of the Catholic Church, and as a system of knowledge – had released those forces that led mankind out of the barbarity of heathen antiquity and had made possible the subsequent achievements in the arts, sciences and social institutions An enormous amount of material was presented to the reader to illustrate the importance of Christianity for the development of literature, the arts and the sciences and to demonstrate the formative power which Christian ecclesiastical rites had. The political order of European societies was also considered to be a product of Christianity. The clergy served as energetic and circumspect moderators of political power and the states, and even the principle of representation found in constitutions was apparently modelled on religious orders. Chateaubriand's Christian teleological approach to history was directed against the Revolution, but it could also be used by liberals. For the Italian Antonio Rosmini, whose books were placed on the index by the Curia in 1849, Christianity's achievement was that it translated the equality of men before God into social practice and thus gave modern society the only legitimate – and solid – basis. Christian equality had ended slavery in antiquity, as Chateaubriand had also pointed out, and communities that extended beyond the family had only become possible through Christianity because individuals were taken out of this family unit and given the possibility of associating themselves with 'equals'. This was the basis for the 'sacrality' of modern society, too.[58]

Despite this fundamental sacrality, nineteenth-century society badly needed the ordering power of an actively engaged Christianity. According to Chateaubriand, concluding his historico-philosophical vision, one only needed to look to the great cities with their suburbs and one would see that order could not be maintained there without religion preaching duties and morals for all areas of life. If the veneration of the gospel were to be abandoned, prisons and executioners would rule the towns. With regard to state power, Haller recommended princes earn the unshakable trust of their subjects by displaying their own religious sentiments clearly and publicly. Because people believed in Christianity's power to tame, this would be considered more powerful in containing a prince's absolute power than any constitution would. Conversely, it would also ensure the population's obedience because it would make the divine origin of secular power clearly visible. 'It ensures loyalty even where it could not be forced' and it showed that power was a 'favour from heaven'. In this way, the population would voluntarily subject themselves to the authority of a prince. Chateaubriand had given a historical justification for the same arguments when he claimed that the barbarian statehood of the Romans had only been civilized by Christianity.[59]

Haller's arguments in his work on the Restoration quite naturally led to the idea that religion could be put to use in a calculated way, which was very much opposed by Ultramontane conservatism. Thus, Joseph Görres felt nothing but contempt for 'those political clerics who court state power'. This could do no more than touch the surface of a society that had been led into anomie by the boundless subjectivity of reason. For this reason, in Görres's view, the Restoration could only be a stopgap at best, which sought to find a reflex of former unity: 'In this situation, it is monarchy, with its good and bad sides, which, as the expression of a fragmented nationality, at least carries the appearance of unity'. According to Görres, the alternative was to look to the personality of the monarch, which 'might lead to equally as personal and emotional an attachment' in order to 'gain a firm ground amongst all the movement and swaying of principles'. The effect of Christianity according to this line of argument was not to ensure social discipline amongst the subjects; instead the true (Ultramontane) church was working on resurrecting the *societas civilis* that was based on religion and in which social discipline would resolve itself in a harmonic, organic social order. A similar argument had been made by Lamennais before he developed his liberal views.[60]

Christianity occupied a different place in these ideas regarding society if the latter was no longer thought of as deriving from religion, but religion was thought of as the result of society. Gladstone identified an individual's love of themselves as the core problem of sociation. The negative consequences of this were magnified in society. Moreover, the possibility of mutual control decreased in society, and the increasing complexity resulted in a tendency to deny responsibility for one's actions. These thoughts said much about the structural differentiation and differentiation through media in modern societies and their resulting complexity. Burke had argued that the freer and more democratic public order was, the more important religion became, the reason being that only religion could prevent the population from following its base instincts in political matters. However, it was precisely for this reason that Gladstone considered it necessary to refer to morality and religion: 'The remedy has been recognized by the common, the almost universal sense of mankind, as being found in collective religion'. As a result of this structural condition, society was nothing more than a moral structure, and society should combine the power of morality with the holy principle of religion, in the same way that an individual's morality was sanctified through individual piety. Gladstone's arguments were more restrained when they concerned a nation, that is, a society that had developed an awareness of itself; as a state, the nation had found the means to autonomously shape its politics. According to Gladstone, the state was not a source of morality, but, on the other hand, it was more than merely an economic alliance. If it was not to become an intolerable curse on the people, it required a moral foundation. Legislature needed an ethical basis, and statesmen would only act in the interests of the nation if they felt responsibility before God, and subjects could be ruled better if the consequences of offending were not just vicious punishments but eternal damnation. Gladstone thus concluded that, overall, religion was compatible with the rationality of the state and that religion's true place was in the sociality of a nation. Religion and the state belonged together because the state was responsible for enabling the social coexistence of its people. This sociality was a deeply moral structure in terms of its problems, aims and motives, but true morality could only be achieved if it turned to religion. For this reason, a nation could only really develop an awareness of itself if religion was practised publicly. Individual piety was not sufficient in this regard.[61]

Coleridge made it even clearer that the state's relationship with religion was purely functional and that religion's inherent role was to socially integrate the nation. Christianity had been right in ending the Israelite's priestly rule as law was not subject to religion. However, a national church, as the third estate, was responsible for ensuring that the nation had a permanent civilized basis. According to Coleridge, this basis consisted of the following elements: all knowledge, especially in the physical and 'moral science'; the memory of society in which the achievements of civilization were stored in order to connect the present with the past; and finally a form of public education that instructed everyone in their rights so that they might also understand their duties. This extensive task could not be accomplished by the clergy alone, and thus the national church that was outlined in this historico-cultural phantasmagoria also included all scholars, with theologians taking a leading role as theirs was the most comprehensive science. The science of the divine encompassed the study of foreign languages and was dedicated to the preservation and transmission of the past so that significant historical epochs and upheavals among nations and peoples might be transmitted and the history books continued. Its subject area included the ethical sciences and the application of ethics to the diverse social relationships amongst individuals. Finally, as a field concerned with ideas, theology provided the philosophical foundations of all other sciences. Ensuring the favour of supernatural powers and taking care of any matters concerning the hereafter was, however, the task of priests. The leading role of theologians and priests in the presentation and development of national civilization, thus, was not their holiness but theology's role as the source of all knowledge that civilized mankind. Thus, the closer Coleridge came to his own present, the less significant the clergy became. The clergy of the Anglican Church were tasked, on the one hand, with providing hope to the monarch's subjects that they would be able to improve their situation and that of their children. On the other hand, the clergy were responsible for teaching the entire population the knowledge and skills they needed in order to become members of a community and thus free subjects of a civilized kingdom.[62]

These reflections show the extent to which the clergy of the Anglican Church considered themselves to be part of an intellectual class responsible for the nation's collection of ideas and knowledge. Thus, religion continued to be part of a public sphere which determined the inner cohesion and identity of the nation. However, Coleridge pointed out that religion only contributed to this with regard to the production of knowledge which was not specifically religious and that religion was thus in competition with other sciences and intellectual discourse. The connection with transcendence, by contrast, had become a private matter and was no longer of interest in a public context. Gladstone did not take his arguments this far. He continued to maintain that there was a moral dimension to sociation and he called this religion because it seemed necessary to him that it should take the shape of a national church.[63] In both cases, however, it was clear that the integration of a national society largely occurred through the means of participation in and procedures of the political system and that values were secondary in this context. The role of religion was restricted to the idea of a constitutionally based national church, but it was no longer considered to be a medium of fervent national communitization.

In a Protestant context, this would not be the case for a long time afterwards due to the differing political conditions on the continent. Philosophy attempted to succeed religion, and Fichte explained in his *Addresses to the German Nation* that a well-organized state did not require public religion and that an individual's religion, in any case, was the consequence of and not the precondition for the general morality that had been brought about by public education. However, if a new age was to be established, this could not be accomplished without religion, although Fichte did not refer to Christianity in this context. Müller showed a similar reticence. His *Elements of Statecraft* described an entirely class-based order of life, and Christianity's main role was to reorganize the relationships between European states. In the 270th paragraph of his *Elements of the Philosophy of Right*, Hegel also referred to the assertion that religion was the basis of the state as 'confusing'. Nevertheless, as his argument continued, he identified a place at which religion and the state intersected. Because religion created a relationship between man and the absolute on the level of emotions and faith, it relativized the general laws of the state and led to 'the demolition of all ethical relations' through subjectivity or at least created a permanent, inner distancing of individuals from the law which made them capable of engaging in conflicts. Moving on from individual piety to institutionalized religion, Hegel argued that it interfered in the matters of the state whenever its teaching covered subjects relating to the 'ethical principles and the laws'. Restricting religion to spiritual matters and leaving all secular affairs to the state, whose function was 'answering simply to our needs', was not appropriate to the concept of the state, as this came into its own in the general morality. Thus, religion should take second place to the state in the areas in which the two overlapped. The state was 'that which knows', but religion could only offer subjectivity.[64]

Friedrich Julius Stahl would have followed Hegel in his fundamental separation of church and state but not with regard to the hierarchy stressed by Hegel. Stahl wanted a 'Christian state' because only a form of Christianity that was practised publicly could stabilize the 'monarchical principle' of the constitution in the long term and guarantee that the estates-based *societas civilis* was not damaged any further by revolutionary elements. Religion served as a form of protection against political and social change, and the national culture needed to stay Christian, as any change to this risked turning the constitutional state into a democratic one and because the state was always determined morally. In this context, Stahl referred to the willingness to sacrifice oneself for the fatherland – a willingness necessary in times of war – and to respect for the authorities.

'Protestantism as a political principle' provided the foundations of a 'Christian state'. For Stahl, one of the historical achievements of the Reformation was that it had separated secular sovereignty from its connection with ecclesiastical power and established an independent form of divinely derived legitimacy of secular princes. In this way, secular power was also directly derived from God but changed from something inherited to an office and public calling. The second achievement was that the idea of universal priesthood and freedom through the gospel corresponded to a 'general citizenship' and 'greater political freedom of peoples', which was in opposition to the freedom of unbelief and rationalism. In this context, Stahl disputed the Ultramontane interpretation of history, which identified the political freedom that the Reformation and Protestantism provided as revolutionary freedom. By contrast, Stahl argued that this freedom consisted of 'voluntary obedience of the people' to strong authorities because the people recognized that these authorities were instituted according to higher laws. For this reason, it was not possible to equate the idea of general citizenship with the revolutionary concept of *égalité*; instead, the reverse was true, in that general citizenship required the 'natural social differences' to be taken into account. The 'Revolution destroys all differences in societies and all ties and professional groups, resulting in a wild form of unstructured civil society', but Protestantism supported the class-based organization of society and, at the same time, founded that 'higher, spiritual community' which created an 'organic' relationship between king and nation. Stahl considered this idea to have been put into practice in the 'Prussian State', in which king and people were united in the 'reciprocal awareness … that they served a higher duty and calling together'.[65]

This perceived agreement between a monarch and the people was coded symbolically through the use of the term 'love'. This bound both sides together and thus changed a necessarily institutional and indirect relationship into a trusting, personal relationship based on personal presence. In public discourse and writings about monarchs, the idea of 'love' had become a commonplace since the end of the eighteenth century, and it was well known that it could be built on religion. 'Religion' and 'love' became complex codes and cyphers in political discourse when talking about the development of social and political relations. The blending of the two was incredibly productive in this period, and it played a major part in blurring the boundaries between socio-political dreams and poetic imagination. Novalis built his state on 'faith and love', and Baader was convinced that the French Revolution had actually made it necessary to bring about a closer connection between faith and love in politics. Because 'the tie of love or unity, which connects several minds as the members of one and the same community freely and from an inner desire' could only 'be understood as the effect of a single, truly higher and central being contained in all these minds', attempting to solve the 'problem of a civil society' without the 'spirit of religion' was consequently absurd. Love of God was the basic principle of 'a truly free common life', and 'true theocracy' was approached through this 'incorporation of sacred elements into the profane'. Elsewhere, Baader applied this to the political order. A 'positive organic bond and association' was necessary between king and people in order for them to serve each other with 'love and passion'. This could be achieved, according to Baader, if both sides were mindful of the fact that they exist only through the grace of God and 'in serving whom they find themselves joined together and constituted as a nation in voluntary dutiful service'.[66]

The dream of the 'sacred covenant' meant that political and confessional differences were irrelevant to the details of the argument. If social relationships were thought of as personal relationships, religion became of interest as the precondition for all forms of sociality. For this reason, this imaginative vision found its way into utopian socialism.

Although the latter considered society to be a structural entity, there was also significant support for viewing it as a set of associative relationships. This was evident in the utopian visions and in the experimental attempts to anticipate society as small groups of friends. Saint-Simon used 'religion' as a cypher to capture the ambivalence of the idea of the social. He argued for a new society made up of what was productive and useful. Its social and economic order would be based on science but would not dispense with morality as this regulated relations between the individual and society. All forms of organization and all institutions would thus be based on morality, which, however, could no longer be motivated by judgement in the hereafter, but which was based on interest. His *Nouveau Christanisme* (New Christianity) defined the contents of this morality. It was to be the successor of all present Christian churches and confessions, which no longer fitted the times. The central point of Saint-Simon's teaching was that everyone should treat each other like brothers and act accordingly. In the face of current social conditions this dogma must manifest itself as the single great goal 'to ameliorate in the quickest way possible the lot of the poorest class' (*de l'amélioration la plus rapide possible du sort de la classe la plus pauvre*). Saint-Simon was certain that such a renewed form of Christianity would end religious indifference and bring together the poor and the wealthy in a new society.[67]

## The church as a political form

The interest which religion and Christianity attracted in publications by necessity evoked mixed reactions in the churches of Europe, as those commenting on European Christianity and religion were not dogmatists or church historians but came almost exclusively from the world of literature, publishing, politics, constitutional law and philosophy. Whenever clergymen and theologians, such as Coleridge or Lamenais, voiced an opinion in the debate, they either thought of themselves more as intellectuals than as parish priests or were already developing a detached relationship with the church, which ultimately would lead to them giving up their priesthood. Thus, the debate did not reflect opinions within the church and instead was a discussion about the church. This led to religion and Christianity becoming the raw material for projections and visions that took only very limited account of the way in which religion saw itself. It also meant that the establishment of confessional boundaries that motivated some of these texts was mainly political, and religion became a tool with which political distinctions could be made. This development and the institutional concepts show the extent to which religion had become available to the discourses of self-observation since the end of the eighteenth century. Through this treatment, European Christianity became a cultural phenomenon and, like all cultural matters, could thus be relativized.

This situation materialized despite the debate also concerning the question of how church structures might be stabilized. The Savoyard nobleman de Maistre was the first to point out that, with the sovereign state having deprived the Catholic Church throughout Europe of its governing rights, the Catholic Church could only survive as an institution and as a political force if it reinvented itself and gave itself a purpose which, at least superficially, put it on an equal footing with post-revolutionary statehood. This was the only way in which the church could attain an indisputable and appropriate place in the order of legitimacy created by the Congress of Vienna. De Maistre's genius lay in dispensing with any attempt to base the church's legitimacy on political models, instead outlining the formal characteristics of sovereignty and transferring them from politics to religion. In this, he was also influenced by his deeply charismatic and pre-Revolutionary understanding of monarchic rule. In *Du Pape*, de Maistre concluded that there were no new theological arguments to be made with regard to the Pope's infallibility. The real function of this dogma was institutional as infallibility in spiritual matters and sovereignty in secular affairs 'are two entirely synonymous terms. Both express that higher power which governs all powers and from which all powers derive; which governs and is not governed, which judges and is not judged' (*sont deux mots parfaitement synonymes. L'un et l'autre expriment cette haute puissance qui les domine toutes, dont toutes les autres dérivent; qui gouverne et n'est pas gouvernée, qui juge et n'est pas jugée*). This, de Maistre argued, did not represent any special claim on behalf of the church; instead, the church merely shared all rules and rights that applied to sovereignty in general, as every government was absolute. The moment it was possible to resist a government because it was in error or had committed an injustice, it ceased to exist. All subsequent statements made by de Maistre followed from this: his rejection of a church based on councils, his criticism of the regulations in concordats regarding national churches, and his statement that secular sovereignty was not true sovereignty if it made itself dependent on the will of the people instead of deriving itself from the will of God.[68] Haller followed these arguments and Cortés also adopted them. This was the outline of how conservative Ultramontane thought viewed the church throughout the entire nineteenth century; for the Roman church it proved to be particularly useful because, externally, it provided arguments against constitutionally based national churches and, internally, it supported the change from an aristocratic church to a hierarchical church headed by the Pope. At the same time, the particular legal status of the Ultramontane church became a fundamental ecclesiological category, and this provided additional support to Catholicism at a time when faith and piety were undergoing profound changes. Long after Friedrich Julius Stahl developed such arguments for Protestantism, Carl Schmitt summarized the development as 'Catholicism as a political form'.[69]

In his writing and his political activities, Friedrich Julius Stahl, an adherent of the German spiritual awakening (Erweckungsbewegung) whom Frederick William IV had made professor of constitutional and canon law in Berlin in 1840, represented the connection between religion and politics that was common in Berlin in the first half of the century: Stahl was involved in founding the *Kreuzzeitung*, a publication that was the main means by which the Prussian Conservative Party made its opinions heard. After the revolution, as a member of the First Chamber of the Prussian Parliament, he argued for a revision of the constitution and, as a member of the Protestant Supreme Church Council (Oberkirchenrat\*), fought for the supremacy of Lutheran orthodoxy. In 1845 he published his 'constitutional treatise' on the 'monarchical principle', stating in it that the main task of the monarchical principle was to ward off the 'political system of the west' and especially the 'aggregation of classless, purely numerically based popular representation'. Writing on 'Protestantism as a political principle' in 1853, in

*Der Protestantismus als politisches Prinzip*, Stahl then outlined the religious dimension of this ultra-conservative position.[70]

One starting point was what he called God's *Einkindschaft*, that is to say, the state of all men being God's children. From this were derived the independent rights of princes and the 'higher political freedom' of the different peoples. Both aspects, Stahl claimed, had been worked out clearly in the Reformation. In the two-kingdoms doctrine, secular power had also been recognized as being directly derived from God and thus had become the equal of spiritual power. In stating that secular power was instituted by God, Stahl was attempting to resolve the paradox outlined above. In the same way, the Reformation had provided a new basis for the political freedom of nations – not as revolutionary freedom but as 'voluntary obedience' of a people to the ruling authorities, whose dominion they recognized as a higher law because it was based on tradition. The Protestant concept of universal priesthood thus resulted in a general citizenship, which, however, did not involve intermediary representation of the state's subjects. In this way, the Reformation had reshaped the organic ties of the preceding, patriarchal conditions into a higher, spiritual community. In a world in which the revolution had succeeded in destroying these achievements, it was Prussia's task to preserve them. The basis of the Prussian state was the 'reciprocal awareness' shared by king and people 'that they served a higher duty and calling together'. This was why Prussia needed to remain a 'Protestant state'.[71]

The text was retrospective in nature. The times had moved on with the revolution of 1848 and the creation of a constitution, even if the latter had been imposed from above. However, Stahl's text illustrated the extent to which problems regarding the structure and legitimacy of monarchy in a modern society could be resolved through recourse to the semantics of religion because all problems and tension regarding the nature of the political order – including the paradoxical basis of monarchic legitimacy, the lack of a vision and of representation of the nation, and the questions regarding the basis of social integration – could be glimpsed underneath the threadbare mantle of a negative political utopia.

Frederick William IV also commented on these matters in detail, pursuing the idea of a Christian, monarchical, estates-based state in which an episcopally organized parish church took on the task of social integration. The two essays of 1845 in which he outlined this model were wide-ranging, referring to the idea of apostolic succession and the organization of early Christian communities, and he went to some lengths to reconcile this with the idea that the bishop's authority would derive from the king. Frederick William IV envisioned a special ceremony for this conferral of episcopal authority on the church, and he also addressed the social order of parishes. He did not think of them as communities of baptized and confirmed believers but as a community of the heads of households, also writing that it was important to ensure that the rabble were excluded.

This unconventional plan of an estates-based hierarchical system showed that Frederick William IV could not imagine an independent and autonomous church. It could not be reconciled with his idea of political order, just as any estates-based constitutional order conflicted with his religious convictions. His constitutional policies involving the provincial estates, whose loyalty and love should not be hindered by a written constitution, were a reaction to his father's governmental absolutism and were based on the organological semantics of the Romantic movement. In the same way, he envisioned an Apostolic church divided into provinces with a general synod presided over by the king, the most important point being that this church represented the 'reawakened church of the Apostles' as 'a gift from God that could not be invented by man and for which man could never give enough thanks'. This *corpus mysticum* also formed an organic body, in which the bishop, deacon and the community composed of family leaders came together as independent actors and 'were noticeable only in their effect on the entire body'. Frederick William, therefore, compared these offices or activities 'with those of the heart – the activities of the church elders or officials instituted by the Lord with the activity of the veins, which allow life to flow into the heart from outside; the activity of the deacons is similar to the work of the heart in breaking down the blood; the activity of the parish, however, is comparable to that of the arteries through which life flows from the heart to the entire body'. In the original apostolic order, the interaction of these three orders provided 'life to the body of the church and is united through the divine life that flowed through it'. The king was sure that such a church would 'certainly have a beneficial effect on the state and the people'. Accordingly, at the beginning of the first essay he had already described as 'mob rule' the synodal constitution of the 'Presbyterials', which was based on elections, arguing that it aimed to stage 'the same performance in the church... as some wanted to see staged in the state'.[72]

English conservatism had a very similar concern and made similar arguments, albeit with a different result. Here, too, the issue was the political form of Christianity. Coleridge acknowledged that the 'Christian Church' was a visible, universal community of saints, but, at the same time, it also existed in every nation and kingdom as a special public community. This made it a 'real and ostensible power', and as such it was part of the constitutional order. Coleridge, therefore, also distinguished between religion, which included all supernatural cults and ceremonies, and a national church, which was made up of its assets and the clergy. While religion was subject to parliamentary decisions, the national church itself played a role in shaping the policies of the two houses of parliament and its property was protected by them. Conversely, this meant that religion could only fulfil its tasks of civilizing the nation as long as it was integrated into the estates-based order of the nation. Coleridge's description was based on criteria for exclusion. The clergy of the national church were not allowed to be subject to any foreign power, and they had to be able to marry in order to participate in the social life of the nation. Consequently, the emancipation of Catholics threatened the existence of the national church, not because of dogmatic differences, but because the legal and social form of the Catholic Church did not comply with the constitutional order.[73]

In Germany, the existence of Lutheran state churches had led to different problems and thus the approaches being discussed were also different. Because it had become apparent that the Lutheran churches, and thus also in part the united churches, had no structure independent of the state, the discussion regarding the organization of the church focused on how it could be separated from the state. This measure was considered necessary because Frederick William IV believed that only an organizationally autonomous church would be able to shape a Christian state.[74]

However, he was still speaking as the spiritual head of a united church. State and church were to be separated but not church and religion. In literary and political writings, including those by Schleiermacher, the concept of religion mostly already encompassed that of the church, and this was the prerequisite for including religion in social visions. None of the writers from Novalis to Saint-Simon was still of the opinion that the existing Christianities and churches were able to hold nations together. Novalis considered the Catholic Church dead and suggested that Protestantism should make way for a 'new, permanent Church'. Fichte warned that any future form of Christianity must be reconciled with ancient philosophy for it to be of any use in raising and educating a nation. Saint-Simon laid out in detail why the existing three main Christian churches were not capable of dealing with the challenges of the time. His idea of a new form of Christianity was to be influenced by the current state of science and be organized along the lines of academic learned societies.[75]

The European societies of the early nineteenth century had taken possession of religion and Christianity in order to reach an agreement on their social and political order. This development also occurred where the aim was to restore the old order. One consequence was that religion itself had to become political and had to accept and engage with new political forms; another consequence was that the churches' role barely exceeded that of a bystander and, with discursive patterns having been expropriated, the same procedures were now applied to ritual forms. Rousseau had predicted this in his outlines of a civil religion*. In his reflections on a Corsican constitution, he recommended that the people should be occupied with magnificent national festivals in order to wean them off superstition. The time given to church festivals should also be greatly reduced, and this could be done without angering the clergy if they were included in the national festivals. Care need only be taken that the clergy's role was such that 'attention does not adhere to it'. The staging of politics in the nineteenth century took a very similar form.[76]

## Diffusion and expropriation

### The political space of participation

The French Revolution had rewritten the political constitution of European societies, but this was only a starting point and required further elaboration. In the following years, therefore, this led not only to a reorganization of states but also to numerous attempts to give practical institutional form to the idea of a political power based on participation. The road to representative parliamentary democracy with universal suffrage was arduous because it ran contrary to the interests of the elites of the *ancien régime* and the new middle classes. It was also full of obstacles because the principle of popular sovereignty meant that politics could no longer be directed at classes and subjects but at entire peoples that had evolved into nations. As a result, the political space had to be redesigned. A monarchy such as that in the *ancien régime* could implement its sovereignty and control by communicating with an elite who were spatially and temporally restricted, but fuller political participation required a political space that encompassed the entire territory, without temporal or spatial discontinuities, and included all groups and individuals. From the end of the eighteenth century onwards, this led to a homogenization of political space in much the same way as the mathematization of the natural sciences had led to the development of a homogenous physical space instead of separate, discontinuous locations. This transformation has been described as the emergence of a reasoning, critical public through the mass dissemination of publications on contemporary events. Within this public space, parties formed, consolidating organically the choices available, both in terms of content and individuals, for shaping the political and social order. As a result, any government that emerged from elections was faced with an opposition alternative.[77]

But developments had not yet reached this stage. The highest degree of separation into political camps had been achieved in the London Parliament, where general male suffrage had been introduced in 1832. Over the course of the next decade, the monarch's government became dependent on approval by Parliament. The balance of power in this constitutional order had unmistakably shifted in favour of Parliament. Censorship of the press had already largely ended at the end of the eighteenth century and, instead, a form of private liability had been legally defined. Nonetheless, every government up until the middle of the century tried to control the press. Attempts were made to deprive newspapers of their financial independence and to manipulate the flow of political information. Governments did so, knowing that their battle had been lost a long time before because newspaper publishers and journalists were becoming immune to financial corruption as increasing circulation and advertising ensured growing revenues. The prospect of high fines thus also lost its threat.

The media were far less present and stable in continental political spheres, and the same applied to the organization of these spaces. In the French chambers of the first half of the century, regional loyalties dominated the decisions of the representatives and so, despite the formation of different camps, no political parties developed. Since Napoleon, the French press had been subject to unprecedentedly severe censorship, which was relaxed to an extent during the Restoration, but attempts continued to be made to control the journalistic public through pro-government newspapers such as *Mercure de France*. Censorship was not completely abandoned, and other means of controlling information were also employed. In the states that succeeded the Holy Roman Empire a rich body of journals and newspapers developed, but, excepting the years 1813 and 1814, there was strict censorship until 1848, especially after the Carlsbad Decrees\* of 1817. The chambers envisaged by the constitutions, whether agreed upon or decreed, continued to be influenced by different classes, and so they represented a society that was strongly divided along regional lines. In addition to this, census suffrage meant that there was a further division between a hierarchically structured middle class and a politically excluded subject population. The political elites of Prussia were not willing to allow even this socially and regionally fragmented form of representation and refused to implement a constitution.[78]

This level of detail is necessary when considering the ways in which the challenges of a participatory political order were dealt with in order to understand how religion became a central medium of political communication during this restructuring of political space in the first half of the nineteenth century, a development which led to the symbols and performative practices of religion being expropriated. In order to relieve the tensions of this transformation of political space, the consensus very quickly developed in Europe that the 'monarchical principle' could serve as a foundation for legitimate political power. The sovereignty of monarchs was no longer based only on dynastic and transcendent means of legitimation but was also subject to the law through constitutions, and so monarchy was to ensure continuity in the political order while at the same time allowing popular sovereignty, which enabled the development of nations. This did not make the task of governing any easier for monarchs in the first half of the nineteenth century. It required social dynamics to be shaped, but, more importantly, monarchs were forced to maintain that their rule had legitimacy, despite the military conflicts in Europe between 1790 and 1815 leaving this notion visibly damaged. While it had previously been impossible to imagine any alternatives to dynastic continuity, this had now changed. It presented a particular challenge for Louis XVIII of France (1814–24), who had to deal with the fact that he owed his rule to the military defeat of the nation and who was faced with considerable problems when deciding how to present his kingship. The reign of George III (1760–1820) of England was considerably enhanced by the victory at Waterloo, but he still had to deal with the fact that the House of Hanover had only ascended the English throne half a century previously. Similarly, in the successor states to the Holy Roman Empire, Napoleon's rule only contributed to stabilizing the monarchy in certain cases. Only Prussia's Frederick William III was able to reject a constitution, based on the successful opposition to Napoleon. As Friedrich von Hardenberg wrote in his Romantic imaginative conception of monarchy, Frederick William crowned himself. This title of von Hardenberg's work, *Faith and Love*, printed in 1798, already made use of a cipher from his repertoire of tropes and enigmatic language, and it implied that Frederick William's coronation of himself created its own, in no way less difficult, problems of legitimacy and political order for the monarchy. In other monarchies, for example, Bavaria or Wurttemberg, the stigma of military defeats that had been suffered as Napoleon's allies was amplified by the fact that, despite long-standing claims to the throne by members of the ruling houses, it was Napoleon who had actually made them kings. Thus, they also felt the after-effects of the Revolution.

The obvious way of alleviating these shortcomings was an alliance between the 'throne and altar', but this turned out to be contradictory and difficult to put into practice in the political sphere. Returning to a glorious sovereignty by divine right contradicted the constitutional framework in which it had to be realized as did the fact that monarchy was increasingly justified with recourse to the individual ruler's actual achievements in government. Nor did a state church offer an easy solution because, at its core, it presupposed a separation between state and church. Monarchical rule was thus sanctified in different ways, but, in all cases, it represented a balancing act between different symbolic worlds that were difficult to reconcile with each other.[79]

This situation did not make the performative and discursive symbols of the Christian churches any less attractive to the political world. They also became important to the political groups that had opposed the monarchy during the Revolution. The concepts of what a nation was had arisen in the pre-modern era from the attempt to mark out local and regional identities. As soon as the idea was transferred to the superregional area of rulership over an entire state in order to provide a social parallel to the political concept of popular sovereignty, the question arose as to how it could be presented. The only way in which it could be given a sense of social reality, and thus gain weight as a political institution with strong structures, was if it was implemented in a way that could be experienced by the senses and if it was imagined discursively. To enable the population – which was larger than any individual could experience and was in this sense transcendent – to conceive of itself as a unit capable of political action, tangible spaces of representation and experience had to be provided to the extent that early nineteenth-century conditions of the media and communication allowed. Chambers, parliaments or the monarch were not in a position to do this: in parliaments, census suffrage divided the nation into citizens and subjects and only allowed the smaller group to have a voice, whereas the monarchy no longer stood at the head of an estates-based hierarchy but, for reasons of continuity, was dependent on support by the nation itself.

The idea of a nation also encompassed a vision of a new form of social and political communal relationships. The 'civil society' of pre-Revolutionary Europe had been imagined as a social hierarchy in which political rule was concerned first and foremost with keeping the peace internally and externally, guaranteeing certain individual and group rights, and safeguarding property. This was the classic description in social theory of the seventeenth century. In the eighteenth century, the idea of the common good had been added, but the basic principle of the model had not changed. The concept of the nation had distanced itself from this principle through a revolution and referred to a politically constituted society made up of a community of shared attitudes and beliefs that was continually in need of re-creation and that determined the thematic substance of its own sovereignty and thus of its will to shape political developments. This went beyond the mere preservation of justice and property. The nation emerged from itself, and this was a performative phenomenon: 'liberty, equality, fraternity' as well as the *Declaration of the Rights of Man and of the Citizen* stood for a political programme of the nation's emergence and self-improvement. It meant that this nation – because it governed itself and was no longer subject to external rule – committed itself to a convergence of attitudes, to be ensured in extreme cases through programmes of education. Once politically constituted peoples appeared as nations, they embarked on a quest to find an identity for themselves that was determined by content and which marked it out as a community based on shared values and memories, the latter point lending the nation a dimension that the *societas civilis* had lacked entirely.[80]

Thus the *societas civilis* did not have much to offer by way of symbolism or vision that could have helped in the discursive and performative creation of the nation. Europe's body of local traditions, which Rousseau had identified and employed as a possible reservoir, underlined the fact that this was a community based on shared attitudes and beliefs because, in these traditions, associative relationships were not created through institutions or media but because the *contrat social* was envisioned as an explicitly articulated consensus amongst individuals who were present in person.

In each of these three problematic areas arising from the discursive and institutional transformation of the political order that had occurred in Europe since the end of the eighteenth century, instances could be found which suggested that traditional

Christian ideas might be used to shape the political sphere.[81] The pre-Revolutionary European concept of divine right presented itself as a means of legitimizing the monarchy. The creation of a homogenous political space in a performative sense could be modelled on the practice of Christian churches: a calendar of festivals could be used to create a spatially stable 'community of experience' that could be perceived both by the senses and intellectually. Christianity in its different institutional forms had always been a community based on a particular set of beliefs and convictions, and this served the vision of a nation well. In Christianity, social differences only existed with regard to the chances of salvation associated with certain positions, but the universal burden of original sin and the idea of brotherly love neutralized these differences. The literal recurrence of Christ's suffering and death during the Eucharist provided the tradition on which Catholicism as a community was based. Protestant churches and denominations also derived a sense of identity as a community based on shared memory from repeatedly returning to the Word and continuously addressing their past historiographically. Thus, nations did not emerge as a religious phenomenon with holy characteristics, but it can be observed that religious traditions were employed in order to provide a social and imagined reality for the nation.[82] From the beginning, however, there were other elements that competed with religion in this regard, namely monarchies and dynasties as well as militias and the military.

**Monarchy**

Wherever pure sovereign power stepped onto the stage, it had already dispensed with the trappings of divine service and Christian symbolism at the beginning of the nineteenth century. European rulers met according to sophisticated ceremonial rules. While care was taken to present the monarchs' sovereignty as equal, the Christian foundations of the sovereignty played no visible role. There were many reasons for this; amongst other things, it avoided the problem of confessional differences. The restraint in this regard was probably also a symptom of the dialectical tension that had arisen between the office of monarch and the Christian elements within its basis. The Revolution had represented a break in continuity and, because of this, European monarchs had to refer back to the divine right of their dynastic ancestors. However, they had to do this mindful of the fact that political constellations were now fundamentally different from those of the seventeenth and eighteenth centuries.

The most obvious situation in which this became apparent was the coronation. Napoleon had set the standard here. He had commented that the nation was a fluid cloud of dust particles that could only be stabilized by burying several blocks of granite in the earth. The Catholic Church in France was to be one of these blocks of granite, in addition to a strictly regulated centralized administration and the plebiscites. However, the French Concordat did not grant the return of national assets to the church and the church was made strictly subordinate to the state in the Organic Articles. The associated catechism, in which pastoral and public worship of God were obliged to adopt an enlightened form of rationalism, also prescribed that the faithful should be instructed that love, respect, obedience and loyalty to their Emperor Napoleon were among their duties as Christians. Napoleon had been instituted as a sovereign ruler by God because God had created the empires of this world according to His will at different times in history. For this reason, honouring and serving Napoleon was therefore also a way of honouring and serving God.[83]

The cynicism that the words of the catechism expressed also underlay the carefully planned coronation on 2 December 1804. The Pope had been lured to Paris with the vague prospect of renegotiating the Concordat and the Organic Articles. After the entry procession and his reception by the French episcopate, Pius VII was made to wait in the church for more than two hours in the cold because his throne had not been fitted with any heating. Only then did Napoleon, his wife Josephine and their family and entourage enter the church, only to dominate the space and the whole ceremony, turning the entire clergy including the Pope into props. The coronation was part of a service in which the clergy genuflected, crossed themselves and gave blessings when the emperor indicated they should do this; at the same time, Napoleon and Josephine were at pains to show that the mass was celebrated without their participation by refusing to take Communion. During the coronation itself, the Pope was made to consecrate the insignia, designed to allude to Charlemagne, and, in his role as God's representative on earth as his words declared, give them to the emperor. He anointed the emperor with the holy oil, asked for heavenly blessing for the imperial couple and intoned the Te Deum, which the Catholic Church had also used to provide divine legitimation to monarchs in the *ancien régime*. Napoleon placed the crown on his own head and also crowned his wife. After the mass and the coronation, the Pope withdrew to the sacristy to avoid the impertinence of having to assist during the ceremony of the civil oath, during which Napoleon placed his hand on the gospels and confirmed the Concordat, the freedom to practise one's religion and the inviolability of the national assets. It was no wonder that a disappointed de Maistre afterwards referred to the Pope in a fit of rage as an apostate fool and Chateaubriand charged him with having given his blessing to usurpation through this ceremony. The church's later symbolic revenge was comparatively mild: the ermine worn by Napoleon during the coronation was used for cushions for the seats of the canons of Notre Dame in 1815.[84]

No subsequent ruler in nineteenth-century Europe went further in plundering and reappropriating traditional church symbols than Napoleon Bonaparte. However, the question of how the sanctity of the monarch's office and the divine wish to transfer this sanctity to a particular person should be staged continued to be a problem during the European Restoration. Louis XVIII was in favour of an aggressive resacralization of the monarchy. The *Charte Constitutionelle* issued by him in 1814 referred to a king by God's grace. But he soon learnt that the nation had a revolutionary past which the monarchy could not simply abandon. The coronation ceremony, which had been repeatedly scheduled, did not take place due to a series of coincidences. First, Napoleon's return destroyed all plans for a ceremony; then, a renewed attempt at holding a ceremony in 1823 that had already been planned in detail was prevented by the assassination of the duc de Berry in 1820. Finally, the bad state of the king's health did not allow him to undergo the strenuous ceremony. These adverse circumstances nevertheless illustrated that, in a nation divided into those who supported the monarchy and those who adhered to the principle of the Revolution, the office of the monarch could be based on no more than a divine right enshrined in the constitution, but not on actual ritual sanctification of the office and the person. Louis XVIII demonstrated his sensitivities to these issues with his policy of *oubli*, forgetting and leaving the past behind, and he thus also perhaps spared himself and the church the task of staging a performative contradiction that would have arisen had he taken an oath on the constitution as prescribed in the *Charte*. To do so would have highlighted the fault lines of the political order.[85]

Charles X (1824–30) did not take any such consideration. Already during his first throne speech in 1824 he announced his intention to be crowned and anointed in Rheims, like all French kings since Clovis. His reign should be founded entirely on the traditions of the institutions. The coronation was to be a spectacle of religion and legitimacy in which the exaltation of the king's majesty was to be balanced by the solemnness of the liturgical rite. Nevertheless, contemporaries remarked that the antique-like elements in the iconography of the temporary constructions with which the cathedral had been furnished did not go well with the neo-gothic elements inside the building and obscured the grandeur and clarity of the gothic construction. This complaint was made by Victor Hugo, who at that time was still a supporter of the monarchy and observed the coronation ceremony; later, when his political convictions had changed, he wrote of the coronation as a theatrical performance that had been staged in a church against a cardboard set.[86]

In this case, the credibility and persuasiveness of these rituals were weakened because of the tension between the sacramental sanctification during the coronation ritual and the secular basis of the king's legitimacy with all the imperatives of post-revolutionary state church policy. In Protestantism, benedictions* were no longer understood as a means of sanctification and instead were taken as invocations of heaven, but the transformation of the church into an element of the state, with the monarch at its head, did not initially change after 1800, and this led to a complicated and paradoxical relationship between the secular and the ecclesiastical foundations of a monarch's rule. The symbols used resulted in a circular frame of reference: the legitimacy which the ecclesiastical institution required in order to bless the monarch and provide the ruler with a connection to transcendence had to be borrowed from secular authority, with the office of bishop held in personal union with that of the ruler. It is thus significant that this connection with transcendence was supposed to be created by the imaged episcopal succession because the clergy no longer had the power to bind and release. The two clergymen who were to anoint Frederick William I of Prussia (1730–40), one Lutheran and one Reformed, had been appointed as bishops by Frederick William himself. However, the king first placed the crown on his own head himself and then had the bishops anoint him. By reversing the order of these actions, the king underlined that the ecclesiastical action was less important; however, this only served to highlight the extent to which this relationship of justification between ecclesiastical and secular power lacked any firm foundations.[87]

The fact that Frederick William IV, who was very religious, tried to organize the Protestant church in Prussia as a church governed by bishops was certainly linked to this paradox inherent in Protestant views on how monarchical rule was to be legitimized. Moreover, a more obvious conclusion to draw from this paradox was that ecclesiastical coronation rituals should be avoided altogether, as had been the case in the English monarchy ever since the Glorious Revolution, despite a hierarchy existing in the Church of England. Kings no longer underwent a coronation ritual in Prussia either, and even the celebrations on the occasion of the coronation of 1701 were very modest. Frederick William IV replaced the coronation with an act of homage, which corresponded to the way in which the state was constituted in that this was the only way subjects in a monarchy without a parliament or constitution could enter into a 'relationship of loyalty' with the monarch.

In these problematic circumstances, 'jubilees' took the place instead of coronation ceremonies. In Bavaria, regality was based on two things: Napoleon's elevation of the territory to a kingdom and the constitution issued by the king himself in 1818. The monarch's position was thus legitimized in a comparatively circular manner, and Maximilian I Joseph held elaborate celebrations to mark his silver jubilee in 1824. Frederick William II celebrated in a similar way in 1822 and, during George III's reign in England, such jubilee celebrations took place in 1795 and 1825. On the continent, these celebrations were organized by the monarchs and their administration and were closely choreographed; in England and Wales they were the result of various different private initiatives in the towns and villages, resulting in a whole network of festivities marking the relevant date. Despite these differences, the similarities between these celebrations are stronger. Bells were rung and church services were held, in which the sermon focused on the monarch and prayers were offered for the monarch and their family. Following this, the festivities usually continued outside the church context with banquets, charity events, staged activities for the general good and public festivals. This shift from the performative acts of a coronation ceremony heavily influenced by Christianity and the church in its choreography and ritual to jubilee celebrations across the entire country indicates that it was becoming more important for monarchs of the nineteenth century to create a space in which their own presence was felt throughout the kingdom than it was to sanctify the institution and consecrate the person.[88]

Probably because the sanctity of the institution was becoming more fragile, monarchs were all the more obliged to display their Christian piety publicly. This was not always easy, partly because they were 'unmusical with regard to religion' (Max Weber) but partly also because their pious convictions resulted in a form of spirituality that was at odds with popular religious practices; after all, monarchs had to take into account that their kingdoms were usually home to several of the Christian confessions and denominations. For this reason, in the first half of the nineteenth century, the issue was not just to display the personal piety of European kings but to show the significance they assigned to religion and the church as the basis and reference point of their policies. A decisive factor in this context, once again, was the problem of how monarchs could legitimize their power.

In this regard, France had experienced an extremely sharp break between Napoleon and the two subsequent monarchs of the Restoration. Napoleon presented himself as a successful general and, during the 100 days of his return, as a charismatic conqueror of his own nation who had never forgotten his revolutionary origins. Accordingly, the reference to France's Catholicism could not be taken seriously, as during the coronation, or it was marginalized in day-to-day politics. Napoleon did at least consider it necessary to convert a bath that adjoined his rooms in the Tuileries into a chapel, in which he attended mass on Sundays. The Restoration of the two Bourbon kings who came after Napoleon made reference both to the monarchy as an institution and to the re-Christianization of the nation that had resulted from the Revolution and its break with Christianity. Accordingly, the monarch's pious bearing merged with social policies based on the Catholic Church and its clergy to form a unified picture. Louis XVIII was fairly restrained in this context. He relied on the Revolution eventually being forgotten and avoided direct references to Napoleon's symbolic and political legacy despite the essentials of its social policies having been taken over by the monarchy in the *Charte* of 1814. Louis made very hesitant and cautious political use of Catholicism and the church, as his unsuccessful coronation shows. Instead, he restricted himself to emphasizing his personal piety.

A significant portion – more than half in 1821 – of the approximately twenty royal celebrations in Paris each year were religious festivals and presented the king as a deeply religious Catholic. The requiem mass for family members who had passed away was a simple ceremony, which was celebrated in the Tuileries on 31 December. The annual Mass of the Holy Spirit, which opened Parliament, was celebrated with significantly more public extravagance. The king, his family and the most important officials of the state entered Notre Dame in procession in order to ask for the Holy Spirit's blessing. The annual procession in honour of the Virgin Mary was an important event at which the king displayed his claim to represent the nation as a community of the faithful. Its origins lay in a vow made by Louis XIII, who had placed the entire country under the protection of the Mother of God when his heir was born in 1638 and had ordered that the procession should take place annually in perpetuity. The procession started at Notre Dame, returning there to end with a Te Deum. Louis XVIII attended the Corpus Christi procession, which encompassed the whole town, at the royal parish church of Saint Germain d'Auxerrois.[89]

Charles X maintained these traditions and extended the programme of religious celebrations. It was under his rule that Catholicism and the Catholic Church found a definitive place in the social policies of the Restoration. It has been stated that he lived the life of a cleric and expected the same of his subjects. He also retrieved the Revolution from oblivion and turned it into the nation's collective Fall, redemption from which could only be attained by means of the rituals of penance instated by the clergy and their church. In 1824, Charles successfully established a ministry of ecclesiastical affairs and public education while his predecessor was still alive, although extremely weak from illness. This ministry was headed by a bishop, representing the first step towards giving the clergy control of the entire education system except for the universities. Contemporaries referred to the Parti Prêtre and the Chevaliers du Foi having seized power. The Parti Prêtre was a clerical brotherhood strongly influenced by the Jesuits. It had formed in larger towns after 1803 for the purpose of popular mission and now, under Charles X, pursued the aim of making the church a decisive force in politics, the economy and society. Its direct political influence, however, remained limited even under Charles X. Instead, he relied on an aristocratic secret society of pious Ultras. The Chevaliers du Foi had formed in 1810 and, following the model of the Freemasons, were organized as a 'religious, political and knightly order' (*ordre religieux, politique et chevaleresque*), seeing themselves as a 'secret, aristocratic and devout movement' (*mouvement clandestin, aristocratique et dévot*). The organization's initiation ritual, oath, code words, ritual prayers, absolute secrecy concerning membership and centralized organization made this order a powerful political force with members who were influential in politics and writing, such as La Rochefoucauld and Mathieu de Montmorency, who were both grand masters. It is uncertain whether Chateaubriand was a member. From as early as the late 1820s, the organization influenced the make-up of the king's council and, under Charles X, members themselves were appointed as ministers.[90]

This direct politicization of religious and ecclesiastical institutions was a phenomenon found in all churches of all confessions everywhere in Europe in the first half of the nineteenth century. It also occurred in Protestant monarchies, such as in Prussia under Frederick William III and his son William IV. Their strong personal piety was the reason for their anti-revolutionary political conservatism, while at the same time presenting a problem when it came to the social integration of the nation. Unlike in France, there was no revolutionary tradition that needed to be countered, but the monarchy in Prussia had successfully opposed a constitutional order, and so the nation entirely lacked institutional and political spaces of representation. The obvious substitute for this was the church.

Woellner was head of the Department for Spiritual Affairs and had created a religious edict as well as a system of censorship that required the entire clergy and all philosophers to adhere to Lutheran orthodoxy. Upon Frederick William III's accession in 1797, he was immediately dismissed, and this was probably because Woellner's aim was to combine this strengthened orthodoxy with toleration towards Catholics and Jews. Frederick William III did not for a moment give up the emphasis on orthodoxy and continued to require the clergy to adhere to it. In 1802, he issued a cabinet order which required all Christian children to be baptized and, in 1820, a 'general plan' was instituted which aimed to combat liberal tendencies in government offices, schools, universities and consistories and to cleanse them of all 'erroneous teachings and of those who seduced and had been seduced'. The king had been considering the idea of introducing a unified liturgy for the Reformed and Lutheran communities of his kingdom since 1798, and he was interested in introducing one that was more sensory as the human soul could only rise up to the 'transcendental ... by observing', as Rulemann Friedrich Eylert, court and garrison chaplain in Potsdam and the most important advisor to the king regarding the liturgy, wrote. Religion had to be 'turned into feeling' which combined both the light of the intellect and the warmth of the heart. Frederick William became deeply absorbed in these questions, studied the Bible and the Eucharistic controversy of the Reformation, wrote prayers and composed texts which prescribed in detail the design of altars and church interiors. The future liturgy of church services should be dominated less by the sermon and more by the communal singing of men. In his plans, the king wrote enthusiastically of four-part choirs with up to thirty members. The king also hoped that the *Agende* would solve one of the fundamental problems concerning the way in which the Prussian church was constituted. According to part 2, title 11, article 46 of the General State Laws, the church consisted of 'church societies', i.e. parishes which were autonomous regarding the liturgy and order of service. This meant that Prussia's Department for Spiritual

Affairs, its superintendents and consistories only constituted a church administration, but not an independent regional church. Frederick William regarded the fragmented nature of this church as a symptom of the 'wrongness of a time which looks for salvation in disorder and refuses to gain strength through unity'. The king had even created a special brochure on the *Agende*, published anonymously, but nevertheless, the new liturgy failed badly because it provoked opposition from Lutheran communities, especially in the Reformed western parts of Prussia. A pastor in the County of Mark wrote that it would all end with burnt offerings on altars being reintroduced.[91]

Frederick William IV was as conservative with regard to his understanding of monarchy as his father. His convictions were also rooted in his deep religiousness, which was influenced by Awakened and Moravian ideas through his closest trusted advisors, Leopold von Gerlach and the conservative Radowitz. This had led him to adopt a scrupulous, self-examining piety focused on penance even while he was crown prince. He drew life from prayer, as he himself stated, and wrote a number of theological reflections and treatises and greatly supported the building of churches, thus presenting himself as a Christian ruler. His appearance at the Dombaufest in Cologne in 1842, which marked the recommencing of work on the cathedral, was the most spectacular example of this activity.

A group of men who had known and influenced him since his youth inspired and supported Frederick William in his efforts to turn politics into a form of service to God. They had not formed an anti-Napoleonic secret society, but a relaxed and sociable German Christian Dining Club (Christlich-deutsche Tischgesellschaft). It had been founded in 1811 by Müller and Achim von Arnim and included Kleist, Fichte, Brentano and Clausewitz as well as Johann Albrecht Friedrich Eichhorn, who was Minister of Culture from 1840 to 1848 and thus dealt with the matter of church organization, and Karl Friedrich von Savigny, who was Minister of Justice for the Revision of the Law later on. Von Gerlach and Baron de la Motte Fouqué also attended the monthly meetings of the dining club, at which political, philosophical and literary topics were debated or poems and literature recited and read aloud. Fouqué's novels about a fantastical and romanticized world of medieval knighthood deeply impressed the king. Von Gerlach, Frederick William's closest advisor, also contributed to this religious infusion of the political space in an organizing capacity. After the revolution he became the head of the so-called camarilla, not a 'knightly order', but a small, powerful group, which he mentioned in correspondence with his brother as early as 1838 and which went on to exert a considerable influence on the policies of the court in Berlin. His brother, Ernst Ludwig von Gerlach, also a member of the dining club, supported the religious infusion of public space in other ways: in 1828, he and Wilhelm Hengstenberg founded the *Evangelische Kirchenzeitung* and initiated the formation of a conservative party during the revolution, along with its mouthpiece, the *Kreuzzeitung*.[92]

Charles X presented himself as a fervent, humble and atoning member of his church and Frederick William IV portrayed himself as an inspired theologian; they did this in order to lend weight to their politics and to base them in transcendence, taking on roles that were available in the ecclesiology of their respective faiths. This also applies to George III of England, although political tensions were not as evident and thus politics and religion were not connected in the same way. The third Hanoverian king in London was a staunch Anglican and took his office as head of his church and as Defender of the Faith extremely seriously. He had the royal chapels in Windsor restored and attended morning and evening prayer there every day. The king attended Sunday services at St James's, and the newspapers regularly reported on this event. He recommended that his sons should read the Bible twice a day for the purposes of edification and introspection. This all indicates a firm, resilient faith which was a fact of life taken for granted and which also influenced his church policies. When Bishop Watson published an *Apology for Christianity* in 1776, George remarked that he had not known that Christianity needed such a defence. He was, however, entirely prepared to protect the orthodoxy of the Church of England. He considered the doctrine of the Trinity and the Thirty-Nine Articles to be the unshakeable foundation of the Anglican Church and regarded Socinianism, which questioned the doctrine that sins would be punished, as a threat to social order. The way in which he administered his patronage rights in the parishes and filled bishop's chairs also served to strengthen orthodoxy. Here his piety became public and directly political, since such decisions also affected the make-up of the House of Lords. It was also clear publicly that the charitable acts expected of a king were interpreted in a particularly religious way by George III. He supported missionary and Bible societies and became involved in the building of churches when it became clear in the new century that the pastoral care for his subjects was inadequate. However, there was of course no saints' or feast-day calendar that would have regularly brought the whole country together in prayer for the king.

In George III's view, the church and ecclesiastical administration were quite naturally within his political remit, and he took their institutional significance seriously enough to oppose the abolition of the Test Act in 1790 and Catholic Emancipation after the union with Ireland in 1800 because he feared that this would endanger the constitutional order of the commonwealth. This, however, did not prevent him from showing toleration towards Catholics and Dissenters in other areas, for example, by appointing Quakers to offices. For George III, religion was part of politics, and he acted as a Christian monarch and staunch Anglican, but he contributed little to inventing a new religious world of symbols to encode power and did not turn politics into divine service.[93]

Politics and religion intersected in the office and person of European monarchs of the first half of the nineteenth century, with politics taking over certain religious forms and semantics in the operation of power. The third aspect of monarchy, the dynasty, became another such point of intersection because here, too, Christian traditions helped to turn an element that had become alien to post-revolutionary politics into something that could be used for politics and political discourse in national societies. The dynasty proved complicated to deal with for two reasons. Dynasties had been invented to combine access to power and its resources with the biological reproduction of aristocratic society in a clearly arranged manner; it allowed individual family groups to highlight their claims to power over those of other families. Once royal power was based on constitutions, the idea of a dynasty became problematic as it so obviously represented a clear claim to power that it implied the dynasty would also be entitled to rule without a constitution or chambers. The concept of dynasty was also difficult because it evoked a hierarchically structured aristocratic society at a time when the nobility was faced with mediatization and the rise of new elites based on achievement and when former privileges, in the best case, had been reduced to compensable property rights. Dynasties could find a place in these new societies of individuals with equal legal rights and elites based on achievement by focusing on the family. Thus, dynasties and their individual members presented themselves to the nation in a form of new, public privacy. This was the prerequisite for establishing a functional relationship with the nation: dynasties benefited the nation, sacrificed themselves and even became martyrs for it.

Christianity was originally a community religion and emphatically not a cult practised in family groups. At the same time, the sacraments, prayers and requests for intercession supported an individual throughout the different stages of life – childhood, marriage, parenthood and finally mourning by the family – that characterized that individual as a person whose soul was committed to the family for commemoration and care through prayers. The royal calendars of feasts of the first few decades of the nineteenth century indicate that not every stage was equally suited to allow the dynasty to present itself as a family. It was customary to accompany pregnancies of queens with public prayers for a safe delivery, but this was part of the dynastic context as it was the construction of dynasties that had highlighted the role of coincidence in biological reproduction in the first place. Weddings, whether those of the monarchs themselves or of potential successors to the throne, also continued to be lavish dynastic court celebrations. The wedding of the duc de Berry to Marie-Caroline of Sicily, which was celebrated in Paris for ten days in June 1816, was a celebration which was entirely focused on the relationship between monarchy and dynasty right down to the emblems on display.[94]

The situation was entirely different when, four years later on the evening of 13 February 1820, the duc de Berry was attacked by an ordinary worker in front of the Paris opera house and died of his stab wounds later in the night. Although the assassin Louvell admitted under interrogation that he had intended to wipe out the royal family, the public subsequently experienced not the drama of dynasty, but that of the grieving royal family, one of whose members had been violently snatched away and had thus become a sacrifice for the nation. Such more or less spectacular deaths were the main occasions at which the dynasty presented itself as a family and its members as sacrificial victims, who could be sanctified by the providential semantics of the respective confessions.[95]

The death of the English Princess Charlotte after childbirth in 1817, that is to say, the death of the only legitimate granddaughter of the ruling king, outlines this phenomenon clearly. The press made the event known throughout the country and, within just a few days, established an image of the nation as a community in mourning who, in their emotional turmoil, joined the deeply shocked and wounded royal family. Throughout the country and in churches of all confessions, memorial services were held, and even the Church of Scotland held prayers – the first time this had been done for such an occasion. In the articles, speeches and sermons, the dynastic question was always present, especially as George III had celebrated a jubilee in 1801 and because the centenary of Hanoverian rule had been marked in 1814. Essentially, however, the focus was on the family, and the fact that members of the English royal family had received private funerals, without any public display, for most of the eighteenth century helped to maintain this focus. In the case of Princess Charlotte, another aspect came into play. The clergy and others spoke of her death as punishment for the sins of the nation: Charlotte's death had been an act of Christian sacrifice.[96]

In the case of the fatally wounded duc de Berry, on whom the dynastic hopes of the Bourbons had rested to a much greater extent, the idea that he had died for the nation was much more obvious. The assassination had been politically motivated and had obviously been an attack on the Restoration order. The duc, however, died the death of a pious husband surrounded by his family and the senior officials of state and church. Before he was called to God, he received the sacrament of penance, forgave his murderer and said farewell to his dearly beloved wife, who, as he announced, was pregnant. At least, this was the way it was presented, in great detail, in official and semi-official reports of his death. Very soon, engravings of his death began to circulate in which the emotional drama of the family was shown and in which the death of the duc already represented his apotheosis. The desire to construct a particular narrative was clear in those representations and reports in which people appeared who had evidently not been present. Two further ideas were connected with these constructions of a Christian death. On the one hand, a Christian prince, who had dedicated his life to charity, distinguished himself by military bravery and a strong character, and had otherwise led the life of an exemplary husband, was brought to life for the public through the printing press. In actual fact, everyone knew that the truth was different. During his lifetime the duc had been considered a slightly vulgar character, who loved life and women. Chateaubriand, who intervened in this campaign of the press, could not ignore this contradiction and compared the duc's weakness for women with the great Henry IV in order to stress that it had not affected the depth of his religious faith. He had died as a martyr and as such had entered heaven directly.[97] The pastoral letters of the bishops, read out at the memorial services held throughout the kingdom, had set the tone, presenting the Bourbons as the martyr dynasty of France, of superhuman greatness, and the murder as divine punishment for the population's lack of piety. They identified revolutionary ideas and the spirit of the times as the deeper cause of the disaster. Anyone who held such ideas was complicit in the duc's death.

However, it was unmistakable that these two romanticizations of the duc – one presenting him as a religious member of a Christian family and the other as a martyr – conflicted with each other. As a father and family member, the duc became a screen for the projections of political commentators and writers, through which the entire nation could come together as a community in mourning and could experience these emotions for one another and the monarchy. A flood of reports, pamphlets, poems and songs brought these events alive in the nation's minds and, through the ceremonies that were held, probably also turned them into a tangible reality. However, as a martyr, the duc de Berry only appealed to monarchist parts of the nation, excluding liberals and republicans. This division deepened in the months that followed. When the duc's widow gave birth to a son, this embodied political and dynastic hopes. The child was considered a visible sign of divine providence willing to complete the miracle of the Restoration. The Bishop of Grenoble phrased it in this way in a pastoral letter and ordered the Te Deum to be sung in the diocese. A national holiday was set for 1 May and occasioned numerous spontaneous celebrations. However, only a short while later, the national holiday to mark the little duc's baptism failed to elicit any public enthusiasm.[98]

However, the first case of the death of a family member being glorified as that of a martyr for the fatherland occurred in Protestant Prussia. Immediately after her marriage to Frederick William III, Queen Louise had become the focal point of the needs of a young, Romantic generation of intellectuals trying to find a religious language to describe political matters and thus to create new ways of imagining social order. Novalis wrote *Faith and Love* in this context and had it printed in the *Preußische Jahrbücher* (Prussian Yearbooks) in 1798. Employing a language of semantic contrasts, the text idealized the king and queen, united in love, to develop an image of the ideal relationship between state and society. The family was conceived of as a nucleus and as a model order. Sociation was to adhere to the principle of love and not self-interest. The text imagined a queen whose image and exhortations were present in the minds of those attending any wedding in the country and considered that 'this continuous mixing of the divine world with real life' would lead to 'true religiousness' and 'true patriotism'.[99]

Frederick William initially did not know how to deal with such an abundance of visionary imagination; he had learned people analyse the text and censured it. However, the text strongly influenced the idea of a patriotic figure with which one could identify and which was convincing because of its middle-class virtues and not its courtly ones. Recourse could be taken to this figure during the tribulations of Napoleonic times. Initially, Louise's conversation with Napoleon in Tilsit in July 1807 attracted hardly any attention although it was later elevated to a heroic act of national salvation. At the time, only one newspaper report mentioned it. It was followed by the flight of the king and the court and their return in 1809. Only now did a circle of artists close to the court, who were to a large extent identical with the Christian dining club, turn the queen into an artistic cult figure. During a performance in the National Theatre after the return of the royal couple, the stage was decorated with two marble busts, which represented the king and queen together on an altar. In March 1810 Heinrich von Kleist wrote a poem on the occasion of the queen's birthday, in which Louise was already presented as the queen of the world crowned with gold. After her death in July 1810, an official depiction of the funeral and the 'poems and commemorative sermons held on this occasion' was printed and sold in the post offices of the kingdom. It presented Prussia as a community united in grief for the queen. A cantata performed shortly afterwards in the opera house involved the unveiling of a bust of the 'perfected' queen, who was represented as a saint or the queen of heaven with a crown of stars. Another performance presented her transfiguration and entry into heaven. In his cantata, Brentano also addressed her as the 'exalted woman' who had gone to God. These motifs were repeated and combined with each other in numerous ways: in poems, ceremonies, designs for tombs, statues, half-length portraits and medallions. Louise was turned into a source of light that had been received into heaven. In theory this should have been stretching the limits of Protestant good taste. In his cantata, Zacharias Werner called the queen 'Luisa' in order to create a clear assonance with 'Maria'. The poem by the German poet Theodor Körner that was recited at the unveiling of Rauch's bust of

Louise, however, showed that, when religion was used in a political context, it was not a confessional but a cultural phenomenon. Körner also identified a population made up of sinners and, according to him, Louise had made the sacrifice that was necessary for the fatherland. When trying to reconcile the idea of a royal dynasty with that of a nation, even Protestantism created saints, martyrs and queens of heaven.[100]

**The nation**

The nation as the other element in this field of reference was not by definition a religious phenomenon, even if arguments of this kind often have been put forward in the secondary literature. The French Revolution had thought of it as a sacred community and presented it in this way, but the nation had also developed both as a political entity that was created by its institutions, its constitutions and its political processes and as a defensive community, with its army and the *levée en masse*. The Revolution had made use of the republicanism of antiquity as a semantic store for its own vision of what was political and what was national. It is, therefore, not possible to generalize and refer to the transcendental qualities of a nation in order to identify the extent to which religion as a performative process and discursive structure had a part in creating it. Instead, it is best again to identify the points at which different elements intersected and to examine each of these to uncover whether cross-connections developed at these points and how they might be characterized.

Nations as politically constituted, modern societies became social reality in three ways. First, they emerged from their political institutions and the political communication carried out by these; second, they had to become a space in which external delimitation and internal moral unity could be experienced on a cognitive and sensory level; and third, like many other communities, they required a shared memory as it gave the nation an identity, allowing it to distinguish itself from other nations. Religion was largely structurally amorphous and not institutional in this context. The nation could make use of its performative rituals of consecration, benediction and forms of divine worship determined by the church, ranging from church services, sermons and prayers to processions and ultimately an entire semantic field of symbols and myths. It was hardly ever the church as an institution that was relevant here; instead, its pious practices served as a storehouse.

The performative creation of the nation was amongst the most impressive forms of communicative and ritual forms by which religion helped the nation to become a tangible presence, and the religious core of anything national has been identified repeatedly in this process. In 1790, an 'autel de la patrie' had been erected on the Champ de Mars in Paris in order to celebrate the anniversary of the storming of the Bastille and the creation of the constitutional order, and the king's presence was also intended. A huge amphitheatre for at least 400,000 people had been built, with a raised altar at its centre. The entire construction referred back to antiquity through the use of columns and other emblems, and the inscriptions referred to the political structure of the nation and its constitution. The altar itself displayed a cross, and so the Catholic and sacral nature of the planned ritual was clear. Talleyrand, the bishop of Autun, read the mass for this altar of the fatherland together with 200 priests. Following this, Lafayette read out the oath on the Bible to the federates, and it was repeated by several thousand voices. The king also took the oath. Collective communication and the oath taken together created a brotherhood, which was undeniably the image of the nation that this performance created. For this reason, it truly was, at that moment, a confessional community and 'church'.

This symbolic construct was soon destroyed not only because the Revolution distanced itself and separated from the church but also because this vision quickly became incompatible with subsequent political and social developments. In 1791 a gathering in front of the altar to gain support for a petition was violently dissolved with bloodshed. The brotherhood began to seek out and persecute the heretics, their internal enemies, and the semantics of the altar were reversed. It was de-Christianized and all elements referring to the church were removed. In 1792 the order was made for altars of the fatherland to be erected in all parishes and to be inscribed with the declaration of human rights and the statement that the citizen was born for the fatherland and lived and died for it. The nation had become an abstract idea that spoke to the citizens and demanded blood sacrifice.[101]

The altar of the fatherland proved to be a popular if bulky item for export in Europe. Prussia was very interested, in particular during Napoleonic times. In 1792, Schadow created a design for a monument for Frederick II, which combined an antique altar with a statue of the ruler. Schadow's altar for Louise, erected in the Tiergarten in Berlin in 1809, also followed antique models. In an act of symbolic resistance to Napoleonic occupation, a painting by Johannes Gottlieb Puhlmann in 1807 presented a Germanic altar of the fatherland and a Germanic ritual act. It was obviously possible to import the altar into the world of Protestant symbols, but it was necessary to fill it with new meaning through references to antiquity and Germanic mythology. A Württemberg medal marking the constitution of 1819 also showed an altar from antiquity, framed by fasciae, above which the king and representatives of the assembly of the estates were shaking hands in a way that was reminiscent of the ancient marriage vow. Even if theologians might have claimed otherwise, this showed that it was the chancel and not the altar that was the leading symbol in Protestantism. One year after the Battle of Leipzig, victory over Napoleon was celebrated in Berlin with an altar erected on the parade ground. It was a military 'service', with the military's own liturgy of marching, drills and canons. Mixed into it there was a Protestant service with a sermon: the consistorial councillor and field provost Offetsmeier addressed those present, who then knelt in prayer, with bare heads, before singing the hymn 'Herr Gott, Dich loben wir' accompanied by gun salutes. This ritual created a defensive nation in which religion – as indicated also by the medal from Württemberg – taught respect for God but, above all, loyalty to the monarch. The field provost had placed particular emphasis on this in his address.[102]

It was clear that, within a political context, religion could not expect its symbolism to carry weight in its original religious sense. It had to accept that these symbols would be re-coded, distorted and syncretized with others. In this way, the nineteenth century created new types of political festivals which referenced the liturgy of church services but filled it with other symbolic elements or which employed church services and church bells as only one of a number of elements, and by no means the most important one.

The Wartburg Festival in Eisenach had been organized by the student fraternities (*Burschenschaften**) of Jena as one of these Protestant services with a sermon for 17 October 1817 to mark the Reformation's 300-year anniversary. The following day, the day commemorating the Battle of Leipzig, the students went up to the Wartburg and held a service-like celebration. One of the students, who had fought against Napoleon and had received the Iron Cross for his bravery, gave a speech. In the afternoon, a normal church service was held together with the *Landsturm*, the military reserve, in which the Battle of Leipzig was commemorated. In the evening, there was a celebratory bonfire, in which mock books by 'un-German' authors were burnt, including those of August von Kotzebue, who was later murdered. The following day, the fraternities who were present, from all parts of Germany, joined to hold a church service with Communion to strengthen their alliance. Following the assassination of Kotzebue, this was what allowed the authorities to claim that there had been a secret society.[103]

There was, however, no question of a secret society, but the students had succeeded in blending political and religious symbols and connotations to such an extent that the Reformation appeared as a patriotic act, as it had been phrased in the speech at the Wartburg on 17 October. At the same time, they had presented their patriotism as a religious conviction through taking Communion as a way of sealing their brotherhood. This amalgamation of different forms and references did, of course, represent an exception amongst the German national festivals, which developed into events for middle-class dignitaries, as, for example the Hambach Festival of 1832. They began with church bells, and a church service formed part of the festival, but the entire performance of the event focused on banquets, processions, speeches and bonfires. The festivals of the monarchy hardly differed from this. In English towns and villages, the emphasis was on charitable acts, but otherwise the rulers' jubilees were celebrated in much the same way as the national festivals or the arranged festivities for the monarchs in the territories of the German Confederation or in Restoration France.[104]

However, the Catholic parts of Europe had the advantage of having the structure of the church year and the saints' feast days at their disposal. These could be used to establish a calendar of national festivals during which, several times a year, church services and processions could also be used as means of representation by the monarchs. Even Napoleon made use of them. Following his coronation as emperor in 1804, he had a St Napoleon created, whose birthday fell on the Feast of the Assumption (15 August) and had to be celebrated. However, when Napoleon travelled to Vienna incognito in 1809 in order to experience the people's enthusiasm for their emperor in the most Catholic of places, he discovered it was restricted to the officially mandated measures. The same applied later on with the celebrations during Louis XVIII's and Charles X's reigns.[105] Regardless of whether monarchs could still credibly claim to represent the nation, such officially arranged religious events created a spatial and temporal framework spanning the entire nation, in which the transcendence of this unit became something the participants could perceive intellectually and through their senses. From the point of view of the central offices of the monarchy, this may have been even more important for the officials of the state than for the population as a whole. For this reason, in Bavaria, officials were ordered to attend such services for the monarch in full dress uniform. In many cases, the practice of substituting an absent person by means of images, which had, in theory, been banished from Catholic devotion to the saints since the Council of Trent but, in practice, had never been entirely rooted out, took effect in this context. In Augsburg in 1824, a temple of honour was erected on the occasion of the jubilee. In it, there was a shrine containing a covered image of the monarch, before which 'sacrificial flames' had been set up. These were lit by the town's dignitaries during a torchlight procession. The place and the organization of the event were reminiscent of the celebration of St Afra, which had taken place in 1805. The transfer of aspects of the cult of relics and of icons to royalty was also possible in Protestant thought well into the nineteenth century, and it even gained significance under constitutional law. The mantles worn by the royalty at Frederick William II of Prussia's coronation were said to have healing powers when they were divided and distributed amongst the population of Königsberg (Kaliningrad). This could be brushed aside as a curiosity, but the Prussian monarchs right up to Frederick William IV allowed themselves to be represented by 'images' during celebrations in their honour. On one of these occasions in Magdeburg in 1815, the image of the monarch along with his coat of arms, crown, throne and canopy were unavailable, and the event was postponed until it had been possible to assemble the necessary ceremonial equipment in order to celebrate the liturgy of homage.[106]

The nations developing in Europe were communities based on common memories and as such they could build on the memorial practices of the church's commemoration of the dead. As long as monarchs represented their subject peoples and the office was present in their person or, more specifically, their body, the burial of a king followed the lines of a *translatio*. As an event with legal constitutional significance, it transmitted the power of office from the dead king, present in the form of an effigy, to the new monarch. In those places in which attempts were made to preserve the legitimacy of the monarchy independently of a constitution, a monarch's burial was still carried out in this way in the first half of the nineteenth century. However, contemporaries already considered the event to be an antiquated spectacle when Louis XVIII died: his body was laid out in the Tuileries for five days, then there was a splendid funeral procession to Saint-Denis, where he was laid out for a further month before he was buried, following which the highest office holders of the monarchy proclaimed: 'The king is dead, long live the king'.[107]

The nation no longer saw its identity in the burial of a monarch but in a state funeral. Here, too, the Christian burial rite played a role, but because nations had regarded themselves as communities of sacrifice and defence ever since the French Revolution, they now also made use of the Christian cult of martyrs.

The French Revolution had shown that this by no means necessarily resulted in a fundamental sacralization of the nation but that, quite to the contrary, it could lead to a complete estrangement from religious matters. In 1791, the church of Sainte-Geneviève had been secularized in order to turn it into a temple of national education. The first person considered worthy of receiving a place in this hall of fame was Mirabeau, a formative figure of the National Assembly in this first phase of the Revolution. It had been his wish to be buried according to the Catholic rite, and so he received an ecclesiastical burial in the Panthéon. Voltaire, who was to be transferred there a few months later when the Revolution's relationship with the church was already becoming more fragile, was buried in a neo-classical rite created by David, in which the clergy were not involved, despite the radical thinker having expressly stated that he wanted to be buried in consecrated earth. When Rousseau was transferred to the Panthéon in 1794, a church ritual was unthinkable.

The revolutionary nation no longer looked to glorious role models in order to form its identity. Instead, it had begun to think of itself as a community of sacrifice and celebrated its martyrs. Accordingly, the ways in which this was done changed. The bodies of Marat and Lepelletier were laid out naked: their wounds and the blood that had flowed were put on display, with the bodies crying out for revenge and threatening all those who dared leave the path of revolutionary virtue. Brissot wrote as early as 1791 that betrayal was a danger to the traitor, and the martyrs placed truth at the centre of national identity. Their form of integration was based on exclusion, and they demanded that all other members of society be prepared to make the same sacrifice in order to defend truth. Two soldiers who had fallen fighting the enemies of the Revolution – one in Marseille and the other in Vendée – were now also admitted to the Panthéon in a ceremony once again designed by David.[108]

The concept of the nation required secular forms of commemoration. The subsequent eventful history of the Panthéon illustrates the deep divides that continued to exist between the concept of a nation and Christian forms of burial and commemoration of the dead, despite the martyr cult of the Revolution. Napoleon turned the Panthéon back into a church in 1806 but ordered that the church of Sainte-Geneviève should continue to be used as a burial ground for important men of the nation. A decree of 1806 regulated the way in which state funerals should be held, that is to say, the role of the military and the clergy, the order in the procession and the civil marks of respect. This decree remained in force for the entire century and was used extensively by Napoleon. In the short period between 1806 and 1814, there were over forty state funerals. The Dôme des Invalides was to be used as a burial place for the worthy victims of his many campaigns. Louis XVIII then returned the Panthéon to the church and Saint-Denis became the burial place of kings once again. The duc de Berry and the prince de Condé, who, as the head of the royal Armée des Émigrés, was given a state funeral, were also buried here. Under Louis Philippe, Sainte-Geneviève was once again secularized and transformed into a temple of the great men of the nation. For the heroes and victims of the July Revolution, however, a separate monument was erected in the Place de la Bastille with a statue of liberty. It initially contained the mortal remains of 504 victims of the Revolution, but these were transferred from this unconsecrated ground to Saint Germain d'Auxerrois with a huge funeral procession in 1840.[109]

The national cult of the dead in France meant a marginalization of church burial rites and an expropriation of Christian forms. Developments in the United Kingdom took a different course. The British nation developed much less of a need for a national cult of the dead than the French, as the 'private funerals' of the kings indicates. These funerals continued to be private as late as the middle of the nineteenth century, even if the public interest in them was increasing and the number of memorial events in the country had risen with every funeral since the death of George III. Because the king was given authority by Parliament, a *translatio* of royal power was not part of this political set-up. When William IV died in 1837, the crown was sent without further ado to the new queen in Scotland. The British nation mourned a 'great death' only in exceptional cases, such as Lord Nelson, Pitt the Younger and, in 1827, the Duke of York, who had been a great supporter of the Crown in Parliament. All three received state funerals. A common feature of these public funerals was that the navy and the army dominated the laying out of the body, its removal and the other public marks of respect. The clergy carried out the funeral service and the rites and were responsible for the sermon, but their influence even on these church-related aspects of the funeral was very limited. If the person in question was royalty, the dean of the chapel of Windsor handed over his key to the court's master of the ceremonies; the only thing the dean was able to influence was the liturgy, which, however, was largely determined by the Book of Common Prayer. This did not change until the reign of Queen Victoria when the church began to take on an increasingly important role in public life. When Wellington was buried in St Paul's Cathedral in 1852, Dean Millman organized the entire ceremony independently and the bishop of London later stated how dignified it had been, with the procession of the clergy appearing particularly impressive.[110] However, this performance of the nation as a community based on shared memory was not, at its core, a religious event even in this case. The church and the clergy participated, but that was all.

In the first half of the nineteenth century, there was no longer a religious core to the British national political order and semantic identity. The only times theological arguments were still put forward in parliamentary debates was when questions of public order in the strict sense were at issue. In their sermons, the clergy were neutral towards the political constitution, declaring its concrete form to be the work of man so that, even when the clergy dealt with the question of monarchy or popular sovereignty, their arguments were political and no longer biblical. On occasion, other notes were sounded, but even then they were muted. After the successful defence against Napoleon, divine providence and the chosen people were obvious references to make, and George III may have been convinced they were true, but they did not subsequently determine the national discourse. The sermons delivered at the great public funerals emphasized that the nation was subject to divine providence and that the suddenness of death was one of the ways in which this could be experienced. Death, therefore, was not divine punishment but a warning to the living. This kind of argument laid the ground for doubts that God would punish the sins of a nation at all. This idea was not voiced until the end of the century, but, even before that, there was no convincing reason to think of the nation as a community of sacrifice or penance in a religious sense. Public funerals were instead important opportunities to emphasize the transmission of emotions and to think of the nation as a compassionate community.[111]

A much more powerful amalgam of religion and national identity was developed in two other places in Europe in the first half of the nineteenth century: Catholic France and Protestant Prussia. During the radical phase of the Revolution, the nation in France had become a community of sacrifice. The question of truth that was key to this identity had religious qualities. Every subsequent construction of the *grande nation* had to refer back to and address this idea. Napoleon had been able to avoid doing so because his expansionist empire gave the nation a military identity and assigned the Grande Armée a key role in its performative representation. Following the Restoration, however, the ghosts of the revolutionary past made a powerful return, although Louis XVIII tried to banish them with his policy of *oubli*. They were powerful because the Restoration monarchy was a continuation of the old dynasty and thus had to address the way in which the Revolution had dealt with its ancestors. Here too, Louis XVIII avoided directly commemorating the murder of the king, but requiem masses were arranged for Louis XVI and Marie Antoinette. The queen's remains were allegedly discovered in a mass grave in 1815 and were transferred to Saint-Denis as relics. A chapel at the cemetery of St Madeleine was planned for the executed royal couple, but it was not built until the reign of Charles X. In sermons dating to as early as between 1814 and 1816, the entire French people were blamed for this crime and the return of the king was described as a necessary way of atoning for the regicide.[112] This set the tone for the sermons of the popular mission throughout the country, which were not supported by the state but were tolerated by the king.

Since nations were formed as communities based on shared attitudes and beliefs, it was natural from the start to think of them as areas in which Christian missionary activity could be carried out. This development can be seen in England, where missionary societies developed from the eighteenth century onwards. These societies also became discussion forums, in which the political, legal and religious identity of the nation was frequently debated, for example, as in the dispute regarding the abolition of slavery.[113]

In the territory of the empire, the state church in the Catholic monarchies meant that missionary activity did not take place until after the middle of the century. Missionary work in France began much earlier, and it became part of an anti-revolutionary redefinition of the nation. The congregations founded under Napoleon's rule had already set themselves the goal of 're-Christianizing' France. In 1816, a missionary society was established with royal approval to train priests for popular missions. Until 1830 they carried out such missions in more than 1,000 parishes and locations.[114]

The bishops and the missionary clergy considered this work to consist primarily of catechetical events which aimed at re-Christianizing the population by means of stirring sermons, prayers, confession, penance and processions. For most missionaries, however, it was obvious that the Revolution and the ideas that carried it were responsible for the decline of religion. Some of these missionaries, furthermore, were convinced that it was necessary to bring down the new political order so as to ensure that Catholicism could once again become a publicly influential power. Many sermons thus condemned the murder of the king and any participation in the Revolution as abhorrent individual and collective sins, which should now be confessed and repented of without delay and for which penance must be done. In many places, those active in the Revolution were publicly stigmatized and sometimes practically forced to convert. The nation of sacrifices and martyrs, through these sermons, had become a nation of sinners called upon to atone for the sins that had been committed. Unlike Louis XVIII, Charles X publicly supported this radicalization of missionary work and its arguments. In 1826, on the occasion of the Holy Year, he participated in a public penance procession. The year 1826 thus represented a culmination in this development. From now on, local resistance against the missionaries and their activities rose significantly amongst the authorities and the population. Just as the nation of martyrs had its enemies, so the nation of sinners also had its divisions.[115]

There was no division of this magnitude in Protestant Prussia as there was no counterpart to Protestantism. Unlike in the southern German states, where religion had not been used to motivate resistance to Napoleon because it was considered dangerous and contrary to state church convictions, Prussia's defence against the superior enemy was presented as a religious undertaking from the very first. The religious beliefs of the monarch played a role in this, as did those of his ministers and Romantic protagonists who gathered around the king. It may also be the case that the memory of the Seven Years' War was important. Frederick II had spent much propagandist energy on attempting to portray this war as a religious war against Protestant Prussia in order to justify his own position.[116] His arguments, however, were to gain an entirely new quality subsequently. It was also important that the connection between Pietism and pastoral care in the military had been very close ever since the time of Frederick William I, the Soldier King. In 1809, Frederick William III had revived the monthly church parade for the regiments. The infantry marched in front of the churches, gathered together their rifles, attended a service and then took their rifles again for the officer to take the salute directly in front of the church. In 1811, new regulations were introduced for a military church, which laid the foundation for the significant role that military chaplains were to have in the mobilization of the army and the civilian population for combat from 1813 onwards. When war was declared, the department responsible for religion and education issued an appeal to the Protestant clergy of the country to contribute to the success of the great cause by conveying to the souls placed in their care that no sacrifice in this war was too great and that 'body, life, goods and chattels, son and brother' should be given unprompted in order for 'the higher cause to succeed'. If 'such a holy fire' burnt everywhere in the fatherland, God would certainly give His blessing.[117]

What followed was an unprecedented commitment on the part of the church and the clergy to support the enthusiasm for the war. Soldiers were given a blessing before they left their parishes to fight on the battlefield, celebratory services were held after victories, flags were consecrated and there was a never-ending number of sermons. As many of these sermons, later printed, show, their core statements merged seamlessly with the religiously infused agitation of Ernst Moritz Arndt, Perthes and Jahn. Arndt had created a catechism for soldiers in order to put into practice his conviction that every 'drive to the sublime' was necessarily religious in origin. The entire discourse created an image of the fatherland as a community of sacrifice and the people as a defensive family. The soldiers died a death of sacrifice and martyrdom and, for them, their path into battle was a wedding procession to the altar of the fatherland. They waged a justified, holy war against an unbelieving enemy, and their victories indicated with certainty that the people had passed the divine test and would be protected by Providence in their quest for freedom.[118] Protestantism had clearly not forgotten its apocalyptic origins.

There was also some objection to the way in which the Protestant church was being utilized, but in this text the Protestant clergy and young Berlin intellectuals created a vision of the nation as a chosen people. This was a passing phenomenon, but it was sufficient to suffuse Prussian identity with these religiously encoded imaginings for a long time to follow.

**Religion and politics**

Religion provided ways in which the political framework and semantics could be given performative shape by constructing the identities of different peoples as political units and communities based on shared memory. However, religion also played such a large role politically in European societies of the first half of the nineteenth century because it was a comprehensively discussed political topic. This began with the transformation of the Roman church from a ruling estate into an institution that fitted into a civil society. In the Protestant case, it continued with efforts to establish churches as independent institutions, connected with disputes regarding the way in which one church was given legal preference over others. This practice was no longer appropriate given the complexity of social order, so toleration and equality, which ultimately only meant that there were multiple state churches, had to be turned into legal and political plurality. These conflicts culminated in a number of different but obvious topics, which centred on the role of the church in the education system, and thus also touched on the question of the readmittance of religious orders; mixed marriages and their significance regarding membership of a particular church; and finally the relationship between the different churches in states in which the presence of multiple confessions was now the norm.[119] These subjects were very significant in political discussions in the first half of the nineteenth century and endowed political processes within society with a significance that could be connected to interests and commitment in a way that resulted in the policies of monarchs, chambers and the decrees of the relevant administrative authorities venturing further into society and having a greater mobilizing effect than otherwise probably would have been the case.

The overall development of the political order in the first half of the nineteenth century was significantly influenced by the fact that religion became a cipher for one of the different options for shaping the political system. In the United Kingdom, the formation of political camps in Parliament by this point had already reached a different stage, but on the Continent, anyone who decided, for whatever reasons, to strengthen the monarchy's constitutional position could claim that this was also the church's position in Restoration France as well as in Protestant Prussia. The church as an independent and genuinely political option with a programme that had the potential to be adopted by political parties only emerged once this was no longer the case, for example, when the French monarchy acted in concert with revolutionary elements and the middle classes after 1830. Now was the point at which Montalembert could write to the French Catholics, pointing out their power to influence the composition of the chamber by voting for those candidates that promised to support the Catholic cause. In Prussia it took longer – twenty years too long, as Ernst Ludwig von Gerlach remarked in retrospect – for those who thought of Protestantism as a 'political principle' to form a politically conservative party that was based on this principle.[120]

In this way religion contributed to the structure of political discourse and the decision-making space, and this proved to be an important prerequisite for the politics of a constitutional order based on participation to undergo internal institutional and organizational differentiation. Even before liberalism or the social interests of the working class could be consolidated in an organizational way, religious and confessional interests provided the discursive and performative nuclei around which parties could form.

One of the reasons for the enormous political reach and the force religion had in shaping politics related to the media employed. Most political events, which, in the broadest sense were presented as church services, were particularly suited to being multiplied and disseminated in different media. In this way, the events were turned from something that those involved experienced into an event that was a 'public' reality encompassing all of society. Unless celebrations were centrally planned, it was often the press that encouraged them to be held, and through its reporting it then ensured supraregional coordination of the event and the creation of a coherent 'reality'.[121] It had been known since the *ancien régime* how significant the dissemination of such examples of interaction through the media was. It was an important way of imparting and spreading knowledge about courtly celebrations, the arrival of rulers, coronations and other events in which power was on display. Even more significant was the fact that it allowed the order of ceremony and the intended meaning of events to be constructed. Reporting on an event resulted in a separate media reality which, unlike the actual performance, had a high degree of independence. The new politics that existed now also made use of this. The Revolution had had its David, who created an image of the it. Napoleon had an official description of his coronation written and ordered a painting to be created by David, both depicting certain points differently from how they had actually occurred.[122] The question here is not one of forgery but of the construction of a particular social reality through certain media by means of 'accounts' and 'reports'. Every coronation, every journey undertaken by a ruler, every jubilee, every act of homage was described in at least one official report, in addition to all the other reports in the published mass media. Events that could be experienced directly were turned into media events. In the United Kingdom, too, reports on such celebrations, which were not usually centrally prescribed but were the result of private initiatives multiplied through publications, were summarized in a way that allowed an event to have a clear outline and significance even for those who had not attended it.[123]

It is characteristic of these reports that they attached great importance to the moods and emotions of those involved. Sociation was described here as fervent, deeply felt communitization and multiplied in writings. Precisely because they were communities based on shared attitudes and beliefs, that is to say, nations, early nineteenth-century societies constituted and thought of themselves as emotional communities. As far as the relationship between monarchs and subjects, in particular, was concerned, religion played a role not only because it provided and shaped occasions but because it provided important elements in the semantics of this emotional configuration: the love with which the monarchs turned to their subjects and the love that was expressed in the enthusiasm, grief, compassion and sympathy of the people for the fate of the ruler and his family were represented by a sentimental image of the family, which had received its first patriarchal contours in catechisms and sermons.[124]

This semantic productivity was one of the decisive advantages religion still had over its fiercest competitor in the shaping through performance and media of a participatory political order. The *levée en masse* became the symbol of a nation that had to defend itself against the monarchs of Europe, but the idea of a community of sacrifice was conjured up by texts that argued on the basis of religious actions and communal relationships. At the end of the eighteenth and the beginning of the nineteenth centuries, European wars were fought by armies that drew their members from general compulsory military service. Whatever the details of the arrangements in question, this gave the male part of the population a way of experiencing a sense of national belonging and togetherness that was perhaps more intense than that which could be experienced through political and religious festivals. The military therefore became increasingly important in the staging of politics even if, as in the United Kingdom, armies were also seen, almost as late as the middle of the century, as instruments of repression which assembled the roughest elements of society. Lord Wellington was convinced that the only way to turn such people into decent, useful soldiers and reasonably tolerable members of society was iron discipline, not enlightening or religious education. This conviction had a significant influence on the 'inner leadership' of the British Army right into the 1840s, and it determined the public view of the army.[125]

There were thus two developments, which mixed to varying degrees. On the one hand, the military was present at events that were actually acts of divine worship and thus took place in the sphere of the church. On the other, the military was slowly displacing religion, but this was only possible once politics was able to create its own system of meaning. Armies and military parades were impressive and could recall communal relationships, but they did not have the necessary semantic store to really conceptualize sociation. This development ultimately raises the question of what the consequences of this political form of church services were for religion. Considered from the perspective of the development of systems, a distinction can be made between positive and negative impulses, without it being possible to generalize and offset them against each other.

The integration of religion into a functionally determined social system was certainly promoted by the strong performative and semantic presence of religion in the public sphere. Religion was a central theme, and power often presented itself in a religious way in public. It is easy to understand why Schleiermacher wrote at the turn of the century that he was not worried about the future of religion. The development meant that religion was closely associated with the structural process of differentiation, on the one hand, and differentiation through media, on the other, in western European societies. This meant that it was possible to think of religion not just as a hierarchical church or sect-like denomination focused on the idea of the parish, but also as a social movement.

All of this, however, also exposed religion to second-order observation, thus laying it open to the suspicion that it was not all it claimed to be and was instead deception and ideology. This diabolical observation, which was already connected to the experiences outside Europe, perhaps affected religion to a particularly strong degree because it had, up until then, seen the world from an absolute point of view. In any case, this turned the nineteenth century into the century in which religion was criticized. The close connection between religion and politics resulted in many aspects in a secondary process of confessionalization. This continued to assign religion a place in the political space and perhaps also had internal mobilizing effects, but, additionally, it created problems that consumed a great deal of energy. This secondary process of confessionalization can be understood here as a compensatory movement that was caused by a destabilization of religion through communication and media because the constellation described here promoted syncretism of religious forms, which led to the religious code of communication becoming confessionally blurred. This resulted in a loss of semantic, symbolic and performative autonomy compared to other social systems. It also meant that religion could now be created, and the Romantics were the first to realize the opportunities this offered. The stabilization of social systems, however, depends on their code not being copied arbitrarily – inflation is not only an economic problem.

3

# Christianity in modern society

By the nineteenth century, the areas in which sociation occurred had changed compared to during the *ancien régime*, as had the means and media by which these associative relationships were reproduced. This was illustrated by the way in which the terms 'nation' and 'society' were used interchangeably in nineteenth-century socio-theoretical discourse. Three somewhat generalizing aspects of this change can be observed. First, communication through mass media became increasingly important for the reproduction of society as compared to communication directly and in person. Second, social spaces were restructured because sociation increasingly took place above the local level and, in the context of politics and the economy, on a global level. Third, integration no longer took place in social units that were characterized by the influence of ruling authorities and corporately ordered, and instead moved to organizational units, membership of which was voluntary.

As will become apparent, this opened up numerous possibilities for shaping the different confessional forms of European Christianity socially. However, some overarching patterns can be identified. For example, because of the change in the way in which sociation occurred at a local level, parishes became a problem. Parishes formed the institutional core of European Christianity, which not only determined the level of institutionalization but also the form of public worship. It was also mainly in communication at the local level that an individual's religiosity intersected with other areas of their life, making up that person's social identity. This, then, was where religion found its natural setting and it was also here that it was connected to the basic processes of social inclusion, affecting every individual.[1] Several developments, however, meant that the church could no longer simply be a parish church with an official hierarchy superimposed on it, regardless of how this hierarchy derived its authority. These developments were the reproduction of sociation beyond the local level; industrialization and a rapid increase in the population, leading to migration and the growth of towns; and social inclusion based on equality and voluntary activity rather than birth and corporate duties. Religion adapted new forms of social integration, for example, societies, media-based personal networks, and social movements and organizations, in order to adjust its institutional form to the new processes of sociation. In the case of social movements,[2] European Methodism probably had a pioneering role in transforming the model of Dissent into a flexible form of social integration, which became a decisive factor in shaping nineteenth- and twentieth-century European societies. The combination of organization and social movement allowed European Christianity to evolve into a world religion, but such shifts also meant that traditional elements of religious life changed, especially with regard to their function in the institutional reproduction of religion. Processions and pilgrimages had once given shape to sacred space at the local level and in regional contexts, but now they became media events that had a wider social reach and relevance. For the Protestant confessions, the organization of the church above the parish level through consistories or synods gained much greater importance than it had had during the *ancien régime*.

These tectonic shifts also affected individuals because they changed the conditions and means of social inclusion and thus the ways in which an individual developed. The most important aspect was the fact that voluntary choice gained a new significance, expressed in the role membership took on as a form of social inclusion. Being born into a particular church had been the normal way of attaining inclusion in the institutional, church-based religion of the parish, and it had been much more important than the idea of conversion. This corresponded to the mentality and practice of an order in which birth determined one's class and position. In the second third of the eighteenth century, missionary activity at home and abroad became one of the main activities of Christian churches. Abroad, it was a reaction to globalization, whereas missions at home were the result of organizations, societies, social movements and personal networks observing inclusion as social involvement based on individual choice, as was appropriate in a polycentric society of equal citizens. This dramatization was also reflected in the relations between the Protestant churches and Dissenters, and it underlay the escalating conflicts over mixed marriage and fuelled the dispute regarding church influence, in particular in the context of the developing elementary school system.

Because of this, the relationship between individual social identity and religion changed. Piety and the participation in public worship as well as personal conversion, if it could be observed as a deliberate decision, became elements from which a modern individual identity was fashioned, characterized by general traits being copied and combined with specific individual characteristics.

The transformations and shifts outlined here will be examined in more detail with regard to four distinct areas. The first area to be considered is that of church formation and the significance of organization and professionalization in the first half of the nineteenth century. The second section will deal with the flexible nature of religious systems, ranging from personal networks to organizations and social movements. Third, piety will be discussed as a way of giving social shape to transcendence. The fourth section will address the topic of individualization from the point of view of women, consider the possibilities that were open to them in the changing world of male religion, and examine the way in which men reacted to this.

Here, as in the other sections, the observational focus is the restructuring of social patterns of creating order. This means that determining the extent and reach of a religious revival, of a so-called second confessionalization, or of a precise quantification of 'secularization' is irrelevant; instead, our perspective focuses on why and how the frequency of religious communication became central to the reproduction of religion as a social system.

## Organization and its consequences

There are two major aspects involved in social units becoming organized institutions. First, internal communication must take the form of decisions, and second, the 'scope' of a social activity and, above all, participation in its decisions must be based on formalized membership. Membership, too, is usually subject to a decision. Here, the first aspect is of interest: decisions are usually made on the basis of communication that takes place in accordance with certain regulated procedures, excepting decisionistic directives or consensus-building rituals akin to palavers. Within a formal organization, this requires that a bureaucratic administration with defined powers and responsibilities processes information. Functionally, organizations define their relationship to the environment as consisting of a particular purpose, and thus internal bureaucratization requires the different roles within the organization to become professionalized.[3]

### The institution of grace

The Catholic Church of Europe, with its centralized structure focused on the Curia, the national episcopal churches and the clergy, had developed into a highly effective organization by the time of the *ancien régime*, even compared to state structures. The church had tiered powers of decision making and regulated processes by which to make decisions, the hierarchy of offices structured communication, and important positions within that hierarchy were filled by means of elections. Of course, in many cases, criteria other than those of functional suitability determined the outcome of these elections, which was extremely damaging to organizational efficiency. In the case of the pastoral clergy, it was even the rule rather than the exception that secular rulers decided who would be given a particular post. In addition, the network formed by the hierarchy was closer in some parts of Europe than in others. The national churches of Spain and France, which were governed by synods, did not have a close connection to the Curia. Elsewhere in Europe, political circumstances, restrictions relating to the presence of state churches and the fact that the church itself acted as a ruler resulted in a network of dioceses structured by means of metropolitan sees. These were connected to the Curia through nunciatures. Apart from this, however, Rome's influence was restricted to the confirmation of bishops elected by canons, the appointment of canons in particular cases and dispensing means of grace for a fee. The Council of Trent's model of a church that had a hierarchy centred on the Curia and a professional clergy overseen by the bishops had only been realized to a very limited degree.[4]

Napoleon's defeat had changed the general conditions in significant ways. The concordant of 1801 had abolished the order of France's national church, and the Curia was now faced with a church in western Europe that was completely fragmented and made up of individual bishoprics. At the same time, the Papal States had been saved as early as 1798 and re-established in their entirety at the Congress of Vienna in 1814. Thus, the state-like aspects of the Catholic Church were now concentrated in Rome, as the church's other sovereign rights had been abolished in the various different instances of secularization. This meant that states had to negotiate with the Curia if they wanted to regularize their relationship with the Catholic Church. As a result, the papacy became more significant in the context of international law, which then also influenced the papacy's position within the church.

The three Popes – Pius VII, Leo XII and Pius VIII – who occupied the throne of Peter in the first two decades of the nineteenth century, made use of this situation to consolidate their state structures, in line with Restoration principles, and to strengthen the authority of the Curia over the worldwide episcopal church. The means at their disposal were limited but effective because the bishops had nothing with which to counter this process. The first step was the restructuring of Curial agencies, which, amongst other things, meant the total subordination of the worldwide missionary system to the Sacred Congregation for the Propagation of the Faith (Sacra Congregatio de Propaganda Fide). The religious orders and later the congregations, rather than the clergy, were the instruments with which the Catholic Church sought to make its influence in the world felt because these were already structured, hierarchical organizations and could thus be directed more effectively by the Holy See. The reinstitution of the Jesuits in 1814 was a model for this. The nunciatures were developed into a network that monitored and controlled developments through regular reports on the bishops. After 1830, Gregory XVI took the step of ordering individual bishops to make *ad limina* visits, which, according to reports, were at times quite hostile. The extent to which the Holy See was suspicious of episcopal independence became clear when vicars or apostolic prefects, directly subordinate to Rome, were appointed in missionary regions instead of bishops.[5]

The reason for this situation was an ecclesiology which was focused on the Holy See and which understood the church, with its structures and offices, to be a literally holy institution, with its foundation through Christ being personified in the Pope. As a result, Rome was considered to be the doctrinal centre and the main source of all means of grace. When Leo XII proclaimed 1825 as a Jubilee, the worldwide Catholic Church was swept up in a wave of intense worship, which was channelled into indulgences, absolutions and privileges for churches, altars and brotherhoods that were to serve the salvation of the faithful. This made it very clear that this stream of salvation originated in Rome. It was the spectacular beginning of a policy of privileges and means of grace which the Church used in order to make it clear that it alone was the mediator between sinful souls and God. Intercessors also gained new significance. There was an increase in canonizations, and the Papacy promoted the veneration of Mary, Mother of God, who was considered the most important intercessor for the troubled souls of the faithful as there was hardly anything her son, seated at the Father's side, would refuse her. Dogmatically, this understanding of the role of the church was initially reflected in an increasingly quick succession of papal briefs and encyclicals. These criticized the state of the world following the fall from grace represented by the Revolution, as in the encyclical *Ubi primum* of 1824, but also emphasized the Papacy's paramount teaching authority. Similar encyclicals followed. In 1834, Gregory XVI voiced his opposition to liberalism and freedom of conscience and of the press. In 1854, the Immaculate Conception was declared to be dogma, an act which combined the Papacy's claim to be the highest teaching authority with an ecclesiological view according to which Rome was the source of all means of salvation and with the expectation of unconditional belief in the authority of the holy institution personified by the Pope.[6]

This was a decisive step towards the proclamation of the dogma of papal infallibility in 1870. It had been given theological justification at the beginning of the century in the writings of Louis de Bonald and Joseph de Maistre as well as in those of the Curia's theologians, such as Mauro Capellari, who described the Pope as a monarch as early as 1799. The establishment of this idea as dogma was marked by debate between the Roman Congregation of the Index and theologians who, at Catholic faculties throughout Europe, refused to accept an Ultramontane ecclesiology.[7] This dispute between Papal teaching authority and university academics did not become particularly serious in Germany until after the middle of the century, but there was already a sense of it when the encyclical *Singulari nos* of 1834 condemned Lamennais's theology as having been infected by democratic and liberal ideas and when, a year later, the writings of Georg Hermes, professor of theology in Bonn, were condemned as false doctrine because of his rationalist approach. The theology of infallibility was an appropriate self-description for a spiritual institution that had become a worldwide, hierarchical organization, defining its institutional reproduction and its claim to autonomy in regulating its own affairs. Structurally, it was the functional equivalent to the old sovereign rights, which had previously provided institutional stability, and it thus completed the transformation of the church into a different form of institutional integration.

From Italy to Ireland, the Catholic Church was reconstructed as an institution in a series of concordats with European states that were mainly negotiated between 1801 and 1830. The only exceptions were the two former Habsburg states of Spain and the Austrian monarchy, where such treaties were not concluded until 1851 and 1855. Where negotiations failed, as in the Netherlands in 1840, or were not even begun, as in the British Isles, the Catholic hierarchy continued to be represented by apostolic vicars.[8] The very form of these concordats pointed to the constitutional dilemma resulting from the end of the church's sovereign powers. The agreements were published as church laws – bulls of circumscription – and were then brought into legal force by a state law. This safeguarded the state's claim to be the only authority to regulate political and constitutional matters in society whilst also giving the church space to exercise institutional autonomy. It was a superficial compromise and was often already beginning to come apart as the concordats were being agreed. The French Organic Articles of 1802 represented a decidedly state-church-biased interpretation of the concordat that had been agreed the year before, and a similar situation obtained with regard to the Bavarian concordat and the law of 1817 and 1818.

In the first instance, the aim of the concordats was to determine a diocesan structure with metropolitan centres as well as the endowment of bishoprics, cathedral chapters and parishes to compensate for the previous secularizations. In addition, regulations regarding the appointment of bishops and episcopal authority over the clergy were introduced; this always meant determining the powers of the bishops in relation to secular authorities. Thus, the question of religious education and the education system in general, the clergy's role in education, and mixed marriages were also usually covered by the agreements.

The result was not a homogenous episcopal church, because state church claims were implemented in different ways in the various agreements. Thus, in the Kingdom of

Naples and in France, the bishops were appointed by the monarch, but in the territory of the former Holy Roman Empire, this power was returned to the cathedral chapters, albeit contingent on different procedures for the provision of information, which ensured that secular authorities had a decisive say in the matter. Canonical investiture was always assigned to Rome, which was therefore also able to exercise a veto. The bishoprics were only connected to one another through archbishoprics, although the establishment of provincial and regional synods had been an important topic during the Frankfurt negotiations with the southwestern German states in 1817–18.[9] Neither the states nor the Curia showed any interest in a democratic synodal church and, consequently, in national churches. After the French concordat, the Curia had forced fifty constitutional bishops to resign and had replaced them with Ultramontane bishops in order to finally put an end to the Gallican virus. When the French bishops attempted to resist Roman centralism around the middle of the century, Rome's answer was the encyclical *Inter Multiplices*, which reprimanded them for their opposition. Belgium was the only place in which the bishops made use of the scope that the constitution of 1831 gave them, holding an annual provincial council headed by the archbishop of Mechelen.

Within this framework, spiritual and institutional governing powers developed for the bishops, which allowed them to bureaucratize administration and worship in their dioceses and to make professional and disciplined 'assistants' of the parish clergy, as had been one of the demands of the Council of Trent. In Germany, they could count on the support of the state's church authorities, as these were of the view that pastoral care and religious education protected public order and the monarchy's power from the threat of liberalism.

The office of bishop was not as effectively removed from the grasp of the aristocracy as the end of a church of the nobility would have warranted. Although the Prussian concordat of 1821 did not specify that bishops or cathedral canons had to be members of the nobility, these posts often continued to be held by aristocrats. In France, by 1830, ninety of the new bishops were members of the aristocracy. Old and new office holders made use of the leeway they had. In most cases, the diocesan authorities were not very large bodies and were usually comprised of a vicar-general and a diocesan court that dealt with questions concerning marriage; these posts could usually be filled without the secular authorities being directly involved. Operational routines were formalized, and the cathedral chapters were incorporated into the diocesan administrative structures headed by the bishop. They thus no longer represented a competing second power. The archdeaconries, which had also held autonomous governing and judicial powers in the *ancien régime*, were dissolved, and so the governance of the diocese of its clergy was centralized and headed by the bishop with his collegiate diocesan administration.[10]

In Germany, at least, the deaneries were entirely different to the archdeaconries they replaced. Deans were often appointed by bishops despite the pastoral clergy insisting that they should be elected by and from amongst their own number. In addition to visitations carried out by the bishop, the rural deans also visited parishes and organized deanery conferences. These had nothing to do with self-regulation but were intended to provide further pastoral and theological training for the pastoral clergy, who were set problems to which they had to prepare written responses.[11]

One issue addressed by the concordats had always been the establishment of seminaries, in which the graduates of Catholic faculties at universities received practical training for their pastoral duties and were prepared for a clerical way of life and appropriate behaviour. There had already been initiatives to establish seminaries in the eighteenth century, but it was not until the 1830s that we can assume that the entire pastoral clergy in an area covered by a concordat had received training at a seminary. Candidates who had not completed an examination, which usually also involved the secular church authority because of the clergy's role within the education system, could no longer receive benefices. In France, a pastoral examination did not become obligatory until the middle of the century.

Before 1850, there was no lack of candidates entering the priesthood and, from 1830 onwards, there were indications that too many were doing so in the states of the former Holy Roman Empire. In Italy, too, the priesthood and benefices continued to be an attractive option even if the bishops did note that this interest was not necessarily combined with a willingness to undertake pastoral care. Bit by bit, the social make-up of the Catholic clergy changed. Up until the 1830s, most members still came from the middle classes of medium-sized and larger towns, a consequence of the educational barriers that had to be crossed in order to study theology at university. From the Vormärz period ('pre-March' period, preceding 1848) onwards, the clergy were also recruited from smaller towns and rural areas. The boys' boarding schools that had been established in some dioceses contributed to this by creating more educational opportunities and also extending the time during which young people could be shaped by the church.

There were dioceses and regions in Catholic Europe in which the parish clergy offered continued resistance to the professionalization and the discipline imposed on their ranks. In the aftermath of the revolution, around the middle of the century, serious displeasure was expressed in France, which prompted the Pope to support the bishops through an encyclical. The clergy in Belgium adapted more easily to the direction and control by ordinaries and, in Germany too, the professionalization of clerical training, the bureaucratization of diocesan structures, and the intensification of oversight and direction provided the prerequisites for the pastoral clergy to accept the Roman model of a centralized institution of grace. This new emphasis on spiritual institutional grace also increased the clergy's standing in the parishes, and the administration of sacramentals and other means of grace became the basis of the parish clergy's identity, their social position and their power. This generation no longer saw episcopal discipline and orientation towards Rome as a contradiction but as part of an Ultramontane worldview and understanding of their own position.

**Protestant state churches**

European Protestantism entered the nineteenth century with a much less organized and hierarchical institutional structure. At the local level, its discursive and theological integration took place through preaching and hearing the Word; at a regional and supralocal level, it occurred through the circulation of handwritten and printed texts. Social integration took place in communities. Patronage rights and economics meant that the parish was closely connected to the economic reproduction of pre-modern society, while the rights of self-regulation meant that it was interwoven with the social order of its members. This focus on the community came to be of particular significance in the nineteenth century because supralocal institutional integration had developed in close connection with pre-modern state structures, instruments of power and bureaucratic administration. Autonomous synodal structures had only been successfully established in Reformed areas such as the Netherlands, Scotland and some German territories. The English episcopal church had not been meeting for synods since the seventeenth century, but instead formed part of the political order as the Lords Spiritual in the House of Lords. The question of the extent to which Protestantism was even capable of forming a church that represented an appropriate institutional implementation of religious autonomy was, thus, entirely justified.[12]

The state church of the first half of the nineteenth century meant that this question, at times, was obscured from the view of Protestant theology. However, if one agreed with Schleiermacher's view that the Prussian reforms freed society from the state, one would also, after the collapse of Prussia, surely want the state-dominated association of parishes, confirmed again by the General State Laws in 1794, to be replaced by an institution which allowed the parishes to adopt presbyterial self-regulation and aimed to establish a church that governed itself on the basis of synods representing the parishes and the clergy. Schleiermacher was realistic enough to combine his proposals with consistorial elements that would have ensured the continued influence of the state.

Like the promise of political representation, these proposals did not become reality. The church order of 1816 included state church authorities that were headed by a state bishop, now called a superintendent, and garnished them with presbyterial and synodal elements, although even these were given a hierarchical structure. Only the parish priests were to be assembled at the district synods, led by the superintendent, and parishioners would not be represented. The participants at provincial synods were selected by the superintendent. However, it proved impossible to implement even this concept following the reactionary turn in the states of the German Confederation, with the Carlsbad Decrees being issued the same year. The establishment of presbyteries was reversed and neither district nor provincial synods were convened; a general synod was now entirely out of the question. The concept of a state bishop was revived with full regalia when Frederick William III appointed superintendents-general in 1829, some of whom were actually bishops. In doing so, the monarch clearly presented himself as the supreme bishop. The Protestant Church remained an institution that had hardly any independent organizational competence and instead borrowed it from the state.

The division for spiritual affairs of the Ministry of Culture headed the church and appointed consistories, which were made up more of lawyers than of theologians. At the lowest level of the hierarchy, manorial lords had more of a say than the parish, due to the continued existence of patronage rights and the lack of decision-making powers in the parish. When Frederick William III and his successor pursued a church union in order to institute a common liturgy, it became clear that Prussian Protestantism was in the process of handing over its theological autonomy to the state. The Westphalian church order of 1815 was considered by many to be an alternative because it included both a hierarchy of state bodies and a hierarchy involving presbyteries and synodal decision-making committees and because the synods had the right to make laws on spiritual matters but the state bodies were no longer allowed to initiate legislation in these matters. However, any momentum these provisions might have developed did not spread to the rest of the Prussian state. The renewed attempts to end the state dominance of the church – in place since 1841, with the Minister of Culture, Eichhorn, and Frederick William IV convening district, provincial and a general synod – failed because the fears concerning a self-organizing society were too great amongst the elites.

The separation of church and state became constitutional law in 1850, but the royal governance of the church was retained, and the Minister of Culture continued to exercise state power over the regional church. When the relevant department in the Ministry of Culture was elevated to the status of Evangelical Supreme Church Council (*Oberkirchenrat*), this was little more than a cosmetic change. It continued to be under the direct authority of the king. Provincial synods were not able to convene until 1869.[13]

Given the Westphalian church order, the development in the entire Prussian state may be an exception. In the Grand Duchy of Baden, too, since the constitution of 1818, additional decision-making bodies had been designated that were juxtaposed with the state authorities, and parish priests were chosen by the parish. The church union – both on an administrative and a theological level – between the Reformed and Lutheran parishes in the grand duchy had been the result of synodal resolutions and not the consequence of a royal decree. The church orders of other German territories also allowed the Protestant churches a greater degree of organizational autonomy.[14] Overall, however, German Protestantism remained under the guardianship of the state, albeit with varying degrees of freedom.

The history of the national churches of Scotland and England in the first half of the nineteenth century shows that other factors could also stand in the way of an autonomous organization of the church. Both the Church of England and the Church of Scotland were organized as parish churches. The parishes held property rights and they had obligations to provide for the poor, which meant that they were connected to the political and social life of the counties and cities. As a result, the clergy not only had a prominent social position, but they also played an important role in the local municipal authorities. On this basis, a presbyterial and synodal church developed in Scotland, whereas an episcopal church developed in England. The latter was also focused on a metropolitan see but had no means of self-governance. The fact that both of these churches were centred on the parish meant that, in both cases, the question of institutional renewal was seen primarily as a question of how church property could be redistributed. In order to increase the value of poor parish benefices, it was necessary to build new churches and to establish new parishes in areas that were experiencing rapid population growth due to migration. The Church of England was not in a position to make these changes on its own and had to rely on a parliamentary commission that began its work in 1834 and proposed the relevant laws by 1840. The General Assembly of the Church of Scotland, on the other hand, had been able to pass resolutions independently to reorganize the parishes, redistribute property titles and establish a residency requirement for the clergy in 1834. However, the Church of Scotland lost this institutional autonomy and unity due to this very issue a few years later in 1843 when the General Assembly split into an established church and a free church regarding the problem of what should take precedence: the parish's right to elect ministers or patronage rights.[15]

The Protestant clergy on the continent and in the British Isles possessed a sense of self-confidence based on a number of factors: the quality of their academic training, an acceptable standard of living if one held multiple benefices and, up to the mid-1830s, a middle- or upper-class background, provided one did not already come from a clerical family anyway. Until the middle of the century, around one-third of parish priests in the German states were the sons of clergymen, a figure which was already lower than that in the eighteenth century. Nevertheless, becoming a parish clergyman continued to be a means of social advancement and one that was becoming increasingly important. The weak point in the professionalization of Protestant religious virtuosos was the fact that only those who passed an exam – a state exam in most cases – could obtain the relevant education. In smaller states, such as Württemberg, the combination of theological study houses and pastoral seminaries meant that it was possible to bind individuals to the church early on through long, habitual moulding. However, this was the exception. The first theological seminary in Prussia, which was in Wittenberg, was not established until 1850; any previous attempts to set up training vicariates failed due to a lack of funds. As a result, many pastors took up their first positions after years spent working outside the church and had not received any kind of practical preparation. In the Church of England, the efforts of bishops to set up seminaries did not intensify until the 1830s. These seminaries were to provide an academic education for those theological candidates who could not afford to go to Oxford or Cambridge. However, the biggest problem faced by the Church of England was the fact that, due to the possibility of accumulating multiple benefices, roughly half of the 11,000 parishes had no resident parish priest or had poorly paid and disinterested curates standing in for the priest. The bishops' duties of visitation, set down by parliament in 1820, did little to change this, partly because the ordinaries showed limited enthusiasm for carrying out this duty until the 1840s. With very few exceptions, the clergy of the Church of England did not fulfil their pastoral duties until, around the middle of the century, church reform resulted in benefices being reorganized, residency becoming a legal requirement and accumulating multiple benefices being prohibited. For the continent, information on such collapses in discipline is scarce; presumably state oversight largely prevented them from occurring. Consistories were involved in examining candidates and organized regular visitations together with the superintendent, and laws prescribed the dress and appropriate way of life of the clergy. Until 1850, parish clergy in Prussia had to swear an oath to the king and were legally considered to be civil servants. If a member of the clergy transgressed, he could not hope for leniency on the part of the church authorities because areas of special ecclesiastical jurisdiction and exemptions had been gradually abolished.[16]

**Autonomy and membership as a problem**

In both major confessions, the church developed its structures in the first half of the nineteenth century by strengthening its organizational elements, but there were obvious differences. The Catholic Church expanded its aristocratically based official hierarchy, with one centralized, worldwide authority at the highest level. Offices at the intermediate and highest levels were partly filled by elections and this promoted functionality and professionalization. However, ties with the electing members became increasingly less important, as was illustrated by the cathedral chapters. The power to make decisions in spiritual and secular administrative matters was based on divine foundation, which was expressed through apostolic succession and elections. Within this framework, there was no space for reaching decisions through deliberation, and this hampered the development of synodal structures in the first half of the century, resulting in a church of dioceses and bishops. At the same time, however, it intensified the development of bureaucratic aspects as well as the professionalization of pastoral care, as the parish priests went from being enlightened teachers of morals to ordained administrators of a treasury of grace of a sacred institution. Ultramontanism[17] simply represented a natural habitualization of these conditions. In this way it was possible to expand and consolidate the Catholic Church as a largely autonomous organization despite it being a state church.

With this constellation, Protestant church formation in the first half of the nineteenth century became simultaneously easier and more difficult. It was easier because the state church provided an autocratic but ultimately secular hierarchy of office, which was what made it possible to extend the primary integration of Protestant church life in the local community to a nationwide level. Because of the significance of the local level, elections had a fundamentally important and positive function, which, when they served to allocate official and decision-making powers, went beyond merely increasing professionalization within a functionally oriented structure. They also always involved assigning a mandate for a specific purpose and fixed period of time. The fact that, in Reformed Protestant groups, decisions reached through presbyterial and synodal elements of deliberation remained an important factor in spiritual and administrative matters, while other Protestant movements at least aimed to include them at a national level, contributed to this. This is why the High Church plans of the Oxford Movement[18] and the evangelical group around Frederick William IV had autocratic, reactionary traits. Hengstenberg commented on the church models discussed during the revolution of 1848 and, in some cases, implemented briefly, by saying that there was a desire to surrender the church to the rabble. Thus, in the first half of the nineteenth century, the church structures of western European Protestantism were characterized by the juxtaposition of centralized and decentralized features. This was comparable to the Catholic Church, but the levels at which this occurred were different. The parishes were local and decentralized, but they were brought together by centralized structures that were determined by the state, personified by the bishops and superintendents, and further strengthened by entirely state-based levels of authority in those countries that had a corresponding tradition of bureaucratic administration. In these circumstances, a centralized church could only develop in conjunction with the state. Transnational integration occurred in different ways, as we will see later. Neither the deliberative decision-making process nor the emphasis on a mandate through elections hampered the professionalization of pastoral and administrative organizational roles, but these elements of self-organization could not develop into independent church structures, other than in a few exceptional cases. The state was involved in the organization of the church, preventing its independence as best it could and making the development of a church an impossible task.

Autocratic institutions with sovereign rights depend on obedience or at least on a visible acceptance of a hierarchy of powers. Organizations that do not have any sovereign rights, on the other hand can, at best, issue instructions internally. Externally, they have to rely on accepting and carrying out an audience role. This audience then acts voluntarily and must be motivated by the functional relationship of an organization to its environment. In addition to internal and external processes of differentiation and changes in the patterns of differentiation, the consequences of which will be discussed in the next section, this was one of the most important reasons for the new significance of membership. This significance of membership had been an important aspect of Christianity from its very beginnings and was expressed in the sacrament of baptism. The Reformation had not attempted to change this but, by opposing adult baptism, had made it clear that, with regard to membership, it did not believe in conscious decisions but in being born into the community. This corresponded to a social hierarchy based on birth and was compatible with an institutionalized church characterized by the influence of the ruling authorities, as the repeated changes in confession of entire territories following rulers' orders showed, but could no longer be maintained in the nineteenth century. The religious system offered a choice of confessions, denominations and syncretisms, but, above all, it was now undeniable that a lack of religion no longer meant – and could not be allowed to mean – social exclusion. In these circumstances, the justification of membership by birth and child baptism appeared questionable, especially given that the organized churches viewed attendance at public worship as a decision, and so directing patterns of behaviour became increasingly important.

The dispute concerning marriage that was carried out between the church and the state, as well as between different confessions, and the question of education illustrated the power these tensions had held since the end of the eighteenth century. The spectre of civil marriage had loomed large in Europe ever since the French Revolution and had put the churches to fright because it threatened to diminish their influence on the confessional life of married couples and, thus, also on baptism and the Christian tradition in which the children were raised. The energy expended on combating this challenge shows how seriously it was taken. After the defeat of Napoleon, the threat of civil marriage decreased significantly, the church regained control of the celebration of marriage and frequently retained jurisdictional authority in the matter, and civil registers usually were once again kept by parish priests. This was the reason why, until around the middle of the nineteenth century, questions regarding marriage rarely led to conflict anymore. Nevertheless, there were some exceptions, which indicated why the matter was important. The mixed-marriage dispute in Prussia was sparked off because Catholic bishops in the Rhineland, since the 1830s, had been instructing their pastoral clergy to celebrate mixed marriages only if the non-Catholic party to the marriage agreed to any children being brought up as Catholics. This placed particular pressure on Catholic brides. The dispute escalated to the extent that the archbishop of Cologne was arrested in 1837 because it was a topic that was particularly well suited to clarifying the relationship between church and state. However, the conflict had been triggered because Catholic bishops had broken with the tradition of coexistence and cooperation that had been practised since early modern times in the confessionally mixed areas of the Rhineland.

The situation in England and Wales at the time is not entirely comparable. Here too, mixed marriages had become a perceptible problem due to immigration by Irish Catholics. However, this only reinforced the original conflict between the Church of England and Dissenters concerning marriages. Dissenters considered it to be a form of discrimination that, despite civil disadvantages having been abolished in 1828 and 1829, their marriages still had to be conducted by Anglican clergymen and recorded in their registers. In 1836, Parliament introduced municipal registers of births, marriages and deaths and passed the Marriage Act two years later, which relieved Dissenters from having to be married by Anglican clergymen. This simply represented yet another stage in the separation of state and church.[19]

Such decisions, however, only exacerbated the problem of membership, and they highlighted the problem of access to elementary education. In the United Kingdom of the Netherlands, the nationalization of school education and teacher training and the explicit commitment at the beginning of the century that elementary school education should be confessionally neutral meant that, in the southern, Catholic parts of the country, demands for faith schools became a strong driving force for the violent separation from the rest of the country in 1830. The nationalization of the school system in the United Kingdom of the Netherlands was largely unique in Europe. State involvement in primary school education had only just begun in the last third of the eighteenth century, when it was made compulsory, but local communities were largely responsible for establishing and funding schools and formal teacher training did not exist nor was it on the horizon. It was not until the beginning of the nineteenth century that the state saw the school system as a means of increasing its influence in society. Familiar and habitualized religion was considered to be a basic factor in sociation and political order, and so the state's professionalization of elementary education existed in parallel with the influence and activity of the different confessional churches. In France, this led to an elementary school system that was based almost entirely on teaching congregations, in which the teaching was done by 'sisters'. In the Italian states, elementary education also remained firmly in the hands of the old and new Catholic teaching orders and educational congregations, while the state was responsible for the supervision of schools. This meant that religious education was a significant part of schooling everywhere, and attending mass, confession and other acts of faith and piety were a firm part of daily school life. In a way, attending school was a form of serving God. The situation was different in England and Wales in that king and Parliament did not become involved in matters of elementary education before the early nineteenth century. In the middle and upper classes, children were taught by private tutors or attended boarding schools. Local parishes and their manorial lords were considered to be responsible for the education of the lower classes. As a consequence, competition between the Anglican state church and Dissenters had been a decisive factor in the development of the elementary school system since the end of the seventeenth century. The Society for the Propagation of Christian Knowledge, which had formed as an evangelical response to the success of Dissenters in the Civil War and the revolution of 1692, was committed from the very beginning to establishing elementary schools and raised private funds for this purpose. Dissenting communities naturally sought to establish their own schools. At the beginning of the nineteenth century, a committee of the Privy Council was entrusted with supervising the school system. It was also decreed that all parish schools had to undergo regular episcopal inspections, with continued state funding, a newly instituted feature, being contingent on the outcome of the inspection. The Dissenters' schools did not have access to state funding. In 1811, the Church of England reacted to the Methodist British and Foreign School Society by founding a National School Society. The Methodist Society was to further expand this social movement's extraordinary success in the elementary education system, threatening the predominance of Anglican elementary schools. It was thus important for the Anglican Church that it should be able to continue to secure the lion's share of parliamentary school funding through the National School Society. In 1847, the different denominations reacted to the way this disadvantaged them by holding a school conference at which they demanded to be treated with equality, but this met with little success. In 1863, Dissenters were again excluded from the support programme by Parliament.

The churches of Europe still profited from the fact that the elites viewed religiosity that was actively practised as part of the foundations of society and political order. The revolution of 1848 reinforced this view. Thus, the Stiehl regulations of 1854, which were intended to reorganize the elementary schools in Prussia, regarded teachers as servants of the state and the church. The liberal educator Diesterweg, however, had already formulated an alternative model: it was possible to do without religious education in elementary schools because religious truth could be taught in every subject. This suggestion would have allowed individual religious choice in primary education.[20]

## Religion as a social movement

In spite of state church privileges, Christian churches were no longer the only options when it came to religion in the nineteenth century. Those who wanted to express their piety and who sought a connection with transcendence or even mercy from their God already had a multitude of practices and institutions to choose from. Research on this topic has formulated different categories for this diversity of sects, societies, brotherhoods, orders, congregations and associations. A closer look shows that all of these terms are, so to speak, contaminated because all are distinctions made by contemporaries within the religious system. They seek, on the one hand, to delimit religion from the non-religious environment, while, on the other hand, drawing internal boundaries between churches, confessions and other phenomena. The difficulties inherent in this field are illustrated by the incredible contortions of confessional church historiography and its blind spots. In order to understand the situation and bearing in mind what has been said above about organization, membership and voluntary choices, it is advisable to base one's own observations on a distinction that is independent of contemporaneous self-descriptions, i.e. a distinction between organization and social movement.[21]

Organization enables stable social systems to develop and allows systems to resolve internal problems and react to the requirements of their environment. Social movements, on the other hand, function differently. They replicate boundaries between systems within the system, in this way creating a counterposition. Those who occupy it believe they know more than the system and that they are in the right. Such a movement is often confronted by the system as an organization, leading to the organization's defects becoming apparent. Because of this, social movements always have an ambivalent relationship to this social form. Usually they cannot do without the system and they use it as a stabilizing mechanism, but if they are absorbed by it, this leads to serious problems regarding their survival. This is not only because it becomes difficult to show how the movement differs from its organizational environment, but also because both social forms operate in different ways. Organizations conceptualize themselves as 'decision-making enterprises' for decisive individuals.[22] Social movements dramatize membership as commitment to a common goal and, accordingly, they depend on presenting motives in a particular way. Social movements are kept alive by demonstrative and accumulated commitment, and thus they dramatize not only membership but also voluntary choice. In turn, however, this means that social movements can be used by both groups and individuals in order to lend stability to the idea of individuality as a type of distinctiveness that always reflects general traits. Accordingly, social movements need mass events, but the idea of direct communication between those who are present is only instrumentalized; in actual fact, those who are present are of secondary importance, with every meeting pointing to something greater than itself and becoming a performative act. Whatever happens and is communicated amongst those who are present is turned into an ostentatious display of different motives and the willingness to defend them. This requires the existence of more complex media. Associative relationships amongst those present are no longer sufficient in this context, and the events that occur must be communicated by means of other media. Social movements that spread more widely than the local level are media phenomena.

The advanced level of institutional consolidation and differentiation that religion, in the form of the Catholic Church, had reached in pre-modern Europe is indicated by the fact that such a copying of the system within the system was not possible or even necessary anywhere else. Up until early modern times, it had been possible to label such 'movements' as heretical, thus excluding them, to deal with them by force or to absorb them into the church through reforms of the religious orders or the church. Martin Luther's concerns were the first that could no longer be neutralized in this way. An important reason for this was the way in which religion combined with writing and printing, media suited to delivering their messages across great distances. Contrary to the original intentions, Luther's attempted criticism resulted in the formation of additional churches, and so the internal differentiation of religion now resulted in even more points of departure for differentiation or opposition. The post-Tridentine Catholic Church had built some reasonably strong defences against this with its centralized teaching authority and its sovereign rights, and so this phenomenon was mainly visible in the Protestant churches and the continued interpretation of the Word of scripture. The Pietism of Johannes Arndt and Jakob Spener and the English Dissenters illustrate the early stages of this social form's logic. Those who were 'quiet in the land' desired an internalized form of piety which the orthodox clergy were not willing to provide. They thus grouped around individual clergymen, and their *ecclesiolae* remained with the Protestant churches and parishes. This situation was sustainable because things did not develop any further than these 'little churches within the church'. This was more difficult to do with regard to the English Dissenters. Puritans, Quakers and Baptists raised certain theological problems, such as the Trinity, but, in addition to this, they turned the salvation economy, church structure and the question of voluntary membership into controversies together with predestination, adult baptism and independent presbyterially organized parishes. This led to autonomous communities forming around charismatic clergymen with their own houses of prayer, but the clergymen were still ordained within the church and the sacraments were also, in part, still administered within that context. These communities attracted Christians from the middle and upper classes if their positions within the traditional social order were affected by unsettling change, for example, when craftsmen became factory workers or farmers became proto-industrial country craftsmen. A decisive factor stabilizing the Dissenting movement was the fact that Dissenters, by law, were excluded from and disadvantaged in public life. Otherwise, their communities were isolated and only poorly integrated beyond the local level. As a result, although there were roughly 250,000 Dissenters in the eighteenth century, no particular social or religious dynamism developed. The example of Count Zinzendorf's Moravians also shows that, for such experiments in fashioning an institution to develop a permanent footing, they required protected spaces.[23]

## Methodists and German Catholics

It was not until the first third of the eighteenth century that circumstances allowed for a new interpretation of this social form that was acceptable in religious circles and spread widely, and this development occurred in Great Britain and Ireland. The capitalization of the industrial economy in some areas and agricultural production in general had generated significant migration and changed traditional patterns of reproduction. Thus, in some places in central and eastern England, the numbers of souls to be cared for by the Anglican Church had increased considerably. Due to the rigidity of the parish structure and the frequent absence of clergy, however, the Church of England could not respond to this situation in an appropriate way. Many of the faithful in the proto-industrial and mining regions justly felt that their spiritual needs were being neglected. Moreover, they were literally locked out of the churches, which were too small and whose seats were reserved for the established 'good' society.

At this point, John Wesley entered the stage. Born in 1703, he came from a clerical Dissenter family and must, therefore, have been familiar with the social logic of how partially autonomous religious communities formed. He studied theology at Oxford and came into contact with the Moravians on a trip to America and during a stay in Herrnhut. Neither this nor his theological training were able to calm his soul, which was torn to pieces by scrupulous self-observation. Afflicted by serious doubts regarding his faith, he began to preach in 1738 as a way of strengthening it. In 1739, he preached in the open air for the first time and, after only a short while, this led to him experiencing a revelation. Wesley became a manic, charismatic preacher, capable of deeply moving and inspiring his audience, something he recorded repeatedly in his journal. It is estimated that he held around 40,000 sermons and, being itinerant like the missionaries of the Bohemian Brethren, travelled around 250,000 miles.[24]

Wesley did not represent or proclaim a sophisticated theological programme in opposition to the Book of Common Prayer or the Thirty-Nine Articles, as he had no intention of founding his own church but wanted to improve the existing institution. His aim was to rouse the faithful to work towards escaping 'the future wrath of God'. Following the example of the Moravians, he tried to form 'bands' wherever he preached to bring together those who were affected by his words and wanted to change their ways. Under the strict supervision of a leader, believers in a band joined together in prayer and song and supported each other in systematically sanctifying and ordering their daily lives. Meetings began with mutual confessions of temptations, doubts concerning faith, sins and other lesser transgressions against a life directed towards salvation. Methodism became a movement in which daily life was lived in a consciously religious way and as part of a group. The mass gatherings for itinerant preachers' sermons ensured that the movement remained public, and anyone who wanted to become a member of the group simply had to declare their honest desire and acquire a class ticket. This also made it possible to participate in the love feasts that were held four times a year and which cultivated an organized form of sociability that consciously sought to differentiate itself from the rough culture of parish fairs and other public festivals at which alcohol and violent exhibition fights often played a role. Wesley very soon also produced a dignified funeral rite for his circles. Methodism provided a unique combination of religious activity and sociability, and Wesley brought together pious and tormenting introspection with a religious life of public morality that was shaped by the community. Wesley's focus was on attracting a large number of believers rather than creating an exclusive group, and thus there were no great theological or social barriers. At the same time, membership was shaped in such a way that it could become the focal point of either personal individuality or an individuality based on the group.

Wesley had an extraordinary sense and talent for institutional organization. Bands were combined into classes, which in turn were part of supralocal circuits. Wesley quickly appointed other itinerant preachers, who were not necessarily ordained by the Anglican Church; the only necessary qualification was to possess the charisma of one who had been awakened. He also appointed stewards and trustees from amongst the faithful to deal with administrative and financial matters and ensured that the clergy, who were always travelling, had assistants so that they might direct those amongst the laity who held offices. From 1748 onwards, he called together all preachers for annual conferences at which theological and organizational questions were discussed and recorded. These conference records were then printed and made public.

In this way, Wesley's movement and that of his itinerant preachers had come close to becoming its own church as early as the second third of the eighteenth century, especially since dedicated houses of prayer soon needed to be built as meetings could no longer be held in whichever rooms were available, and Wesley issued regulations to ensure that these buildings had a uniform design. As he continued to refuse to ordain his own Methodist clergymen, the members of the Methodist circuits continued to be dependent on the Church of England for Communion, baptism and marriages; as a result, Methodism continued to be a religious movement and not a church up until the first decade of the nineteenth century. In its institutional form, however, it was much better attuned than the state church to the dynamics of an English society that was losing its traditions. It has been estimated that, at the turn of the century, at times more people attended Methodist houses of prayer than were active in Anglican parishes. In 1811, after a number of disputes, Methodists began to ordain their own clergy, thus marking the point at which Methodism became a church in its own right. This was a dangerous and precarious step for any movement. Previously, the Primitive Methodists had split from the movement in 1808 and returned to preaching in the open, finding their followers amongst workers and the rural lower classes; established Methodism, on the other hand, became popular amongst the urban middle classes. This schism and others that followed did nothing, however, to hamper the success of Methodism. At the turn of the century, there were around 90,000 Wesleyan communicants, and their number grew to half a million half a century later, representing two million members. By this time, 11,000 prayer houses had been built. The old Dissenters had been overtaken long since, although their number had also grown. In the census of 1851, there were only 366,000 Baptists in 2,200 congregations.[25]

Becoming a member of a Methodist community meant taking responsibility for oneself and one's way of life. Thus, in the first half of the nineteenth century, Methodist congregations became an important place for emerging workers to engage in 'self-improvement', and certain parts of the industrial regions of central England were firmly Methodist. Methodists supported each other in developing a way of life in which time was used wisely, punctuality was valued and wages were not spent on drink in pubs and at fairs, on wrestling or cock-fighting, on bets, or on prostitutes. The temperance and abstinence movement and Methodism were very closely linked. Renouncing alcohol and turning to tea, as well as the concern for organizing one's time sensibly, were closely connected with the disciplined conditions of a working life that increasingly involved machines. In Methodist communities, however, these external constraints were transformed into a form of self-discipline and thus also into both small or more significant victories over oneself and one's own bad habits. This allowed the members to feel self-respect and gave the groups confidence, and it allowed a working-class culture to take root, which consciously set itself apart, bit by bit, from a less civilized environment.[26]

Wesley had been able to build on his charisma and that of the other itinerant preachers to create a strongly hierarchical institution, which was successful even when it became a church and which was able to prevent its form as an organization from interfering with the ideas of voluntary choice and commitment. This was partly to do with the fact that the material foundations of this confessional community were not landed property or other property rights or privileges, but the income generated from class tickets and donations, which could be put to use in a flexible way. Another reason was the fact that, even once Methodists had started ordaining their own clergymen and residential clergy had been established in some circuits, the principle of the itinerant preacher, who moved from community to community, was still upheld. All this required a high degree of commitment on the part of the faithful, not just in a religious sense but also with regard to the institution. Nonetheless, this clearly did not create a sense of being dominated or restricted by a hierarchical organization; instead, it conveyed a sense of control over the institutional structures. The fact that this was perceived as a social movement served to distract from any sense of autocratic control for a long time. The more obvious the elements of an institutional church structure became, the more important the institutionally assured participation of the laity was. The ability and willingness to make decisions now became as important as involvement. When Wesley reorganized the preachers' conference to the Legal Hundred in 1784, he filled the positions with clergy that he had designated, and there were no plans to involve the laity in the organization of the church. However, the demand for participation was now made at all levels. In 1791, the conference agreed that the laity should be involved in the appointment of local office holders, in accepting new members and in matters of discipline, including the decision to expel members. However, the extent of lay participation remained a controversial question, with the conflicts surrounding it resulting in the exclusion of members and secessions.[27]

Methodism had successfully provided a new institutional and social form within Christianity. It could not do without organization, but it used organization in order to transform the decision to become a member into responsible commitment to oneself and the community. Methodism thus not only created a particular way of life but also the associated motives, which manifested themselves publicly because Methodist piety displayed them. The threat that this competition posed for institutionalized Christianity became clear when Parliament passed the New Toleration Act in 1811, making it easier for Methodist houses of prayer to be built and for the clergy to preach in Anglican parishes. The intention was to prevent the rifts with the established church growing even deeper, but it was already too late.

There are no comparable phenomena on the Continent either amongst Protestant groups or, of course, in the Catholic Church, with the exception of the German Catholics* and the Friends of the Light as well as the cluster of Awakened communities in those Protestant regions in Germany in which there was a concentration of commercial activity and which were slowly being industrialized. The reason for this absence is the lack of any protected space in which such a development could take place and which the Anglican Church had provided for Methodism. The Continental state churches were more effective at controlling and supervising developments than in Britain and Ireland, and social and economic developments took place more slowly, so the conditions were different from those in which Methodism had spread in British society in the eighteenth century.

It was not until the 1820s, when the capitalist industrial transformation began to intensify in areas of proto-industrial cottage industry, that Awakened Protestant clergy, inspired by Pietism and often supported by Moravian preachers, were able to bring together conventicles in German states too. Their members were joined together by the experience of rebirth and met for prayer, songs and sermons. In Eastern Westphalia, for example, the police and the church had been monitoring such meetings and circles since 1811. The state was concerned that these groups might become politically active, whereas the consistories and superintendents were worried these conventicles would lead to the parishes disintegrating because conventicle members often withdrew from the frequently very rationalist and matter-of-fact business of established parish religion. In the 1830s and 1840s, mass sermons and mission festivals were held, with the 'bacchanalian business of conversion',[28] as some reserved contemporaries termed them, thus also attracting public attention.

The Pietistic revival, however, did not enjoy anything like the success of the Methodist movement, despite both clearly combining a desire for religious experience with social communitization in a way that allowed people who occupied marginalized and insecure social positions to gain a sense of self-worth and identity both as individuals and as a group. The Pietistic communities were scattered, and there were hardly any formalized connections, neither at a regional nor a wider level – even after 1850, groups were organized only as local associations. In proletarianized industrial classes, the workers' movement and early socialism* now came into view as alternatives. These included religious elements in their argumentation and their forms of sociability but transformed deprivation into driving forces of social and political protest. Pietism also lacked charismatic prophets like John Wesley, who had turned an institutional vision into reality. Johannes Ronge, a Catholic priest from Saxony, had understood this and, following the exhibition of the Holy Robe in Trier and the associated pilgrimage in 1844, which had been staged as a major event by the church, he published a protest again this 'festival of idolatry', which was printed in large numbers. He then began to travel and to preach, creating a national religious community which separated from the Roman hierarchy and was known as Deutschkatholiken (German Catholics). Its aim was to implement a practical, social form of Christianity that was based on rationalist theological thinking. Ronge attracted large crowds and he was particularly successful in those towns and regions in which there was a mix of confessions. The communities were organized as associations, and included both Catholics and Protestants from the milieu of lower-middle-class craftsmen. The question of mixed marriages, which had not been resolved in a satisfactory way, was particularly important to German Catholics, as was the confessional diaspora, which the German Catholics tried to resolve in their new communities. By 1847, more than 200 German-Catholic communities had been established with about 70,000 members, most of them in Saxony and Silesia. However, the movement had already passed its zenith at this point, a fact not changed by the increasing proximity of the group to the Protestant Friends of the Light. These had been seeking, since 1845, to connect religious and middle-class life through rationalist theology. From 1850 onwards, the two groups together promoted a new form of popular religion in a jointly published magazine, which was to be quite explicitly based on the rationality of this world. In 1859, the two groups officially merged to become the Union of Free Religious Communities.[29]

**Missionary associations and Bible societies**

These forms of organized religious movement that extended beyond a local level represented attempts by all confessions and almost all classes to give Christianity new strength in a changing society so that religion, the creation of communities and modern individuality could once again be combined. Institutionalized Christianity thus found itself in a new world. Its protagonists were forced to recognize that religion found itself in the midst of a society that, in Europe, was in the process of becoming secularized and ready to accept non-religious rationalities and that, outside Europe, was dominated by other religions. Another realization was that institutional alternatives to church worship were developing within Christianity and that individuals no longer considered religiosity and piety to be determined by social context, but instead by particular motivations that were expressed as decisions and observed as such by society.

Missionary work was an important response to this situation. Internally, it was directed at the secularized world and other confessions and religious alternatives; externally, it was aimed at the conversion of heathens.[30] Missionary activity also became an area in which voluntary work by lay people, mostly guided by the clergy, was organized in groups and associations that were independent but associated with the church. This also applied in the Catholic sphere, although the religious orders of the Catholic Church, the congregations and the brotherhoods already represented institutions that undertook missionary work and could accommodate the pious commitment of Catholic Christians. In this whole area, religion took on a very undogmatic, non-cultic and very worldly form. By collecting or donating money, by selling bibles and booklets, or by looking after the finances of a missionary society, individuals could express their faith through means other than prayer and outside the confines of church services in a way that was convincing to themselves and to others.

In England, two such societies emerged at the beginning of the eighteenth century as a result of the success of the Dissenters combined with the institutional weakness of the Anglican Church in the American colonies. In 1701, the Society for the Propagation of the Gospel in the Foreign Parts of the World was founded, followed by the Scottish Society for the Propagation of Christian Knowledge in 1708. Initially, these initiatives were not emulated in Britain, Ireland or the Continent. It was not until 1780 that the Reformed priest Johannes Urlsperger, together with other Awakened Christians, founded the 'Society for Christianity' (Christentumsgesellschaft) in Basel as a bulwark against the rationalist destruction of the Protestant faith. In 1815, it became the Basel Evangelical Missionary Society, which also maintained a large number of branches and subsidiary societies in German states. Its foundation in 1780 indicated clearly that, in future, competition between denominations and confessions would become the main driving force behind the foundation of missionary associations and societies. The Baptist Missionary Society was founded in 1782 as Wesley was beginning to restrengthen Methodism's centralized organization and, in 1783, the Methodist Society for the Establishment of Missions amongst the Heathen followed. The Quakers ventured into controversial territory associated with colonial expansion with their Society for the Abolition of Slavery, founded in 1787. The Anglican hierarchy and its clergy were very late in reacting to these developments: the Christian Mission Society was founded in 1799 after Congregationalist Dissenters had already established the London Missionary Society in 1797.

States on the Continent had been less engaged in colonization since the Seven Years' War, Napoleon's defeat and the first wave of decolonization in America, and so it took longer for missionary societies to emerge here. In 1822, merchants from

Lyon founded the Œuvre de la Propagation du Foi and, in the same year, its Protestant counterpart, the Société des Mission, came into being in Paris. In Germany, the Berliner Missiongesellschaft (Berlin Missionary Association) began work in 1824 and, in 1828, the Rhenish Missionary Society with four subsidiaries was founded. The Catholic missionary orders and some of the congregations working for them also sought to raise funds as well as support through prayer for their activities. The missionary organizations they had founded since the beginning of the nineteenth century often took the form of brotherhoods. Later, the Lyon Œuvre was often adopted as a model, but there were also local initiatives of individual clergymen with particular goals, for example, constructing a chapel in a particular missionary area. In this way, almost 250 Catholic missionary associations had been formed since 1818, but this development did not become a widespread phenomenon until 1840.[31]

The missionary zeal in Europe was not directed inwards until the beginning of the nineteenth century. In 1803, the British and Foreign Bible Society (BFBS) met in London. It was active throughout the Continent and also supported Catholic initiatives such as that of the priest Leander van Eß in the printing and distribution of cheap bibles. The Preußische Hauptbibelgesellschaft (Prussian Main Bible Society), founded in 1840, also cooperated with the BFBS until the question of the Apocrypha in German printed bibles caused a rupture in the relationship in the 1820s, with all contact eventually being broken off.[32]

All these societies established wide networks of subsidiaries and local associations in parishes in order to collect donations for their main purpose: distributing bibles or sending missionaries into those regions of the world which it was felt needed to be civilized by Europeans. To do this, missionary societies adopted quite different organizational forms. The British and Foreign Bible Society in London followed the model of a free association, with a constitution and a managing board that was elected by representatives of the local branches and had to account for the way in which financial contributions were used. The Basel company was set up more like a commercial business and managed by a group of seven Basel businessmen with a managing director. New members of the leadership were co-opted. There were annual conferences to which representatives of the supporting societies were invited. In 1821, a constitution was created, but the members did not receive any say in the running of the company. The Rhenish Missionary Society had no members at all. It was an association of four societies, which sent representatives in order to carry out their business. The member societies were also organized in different ways. The branch in Elberfeld had decided to accept no more than twelve members, and the Catholic Œuvre de la Propagation made use of diocesan and parish structures. In France, a governing board, which was split between Paris and Lyon, was responsible for distributing the extensive funds that came in from European dioceses in response to applications from the missionary orders and their individual projects. In the dioceses, the bishops appointed their own governing board, which brought together the donations and contributions collected and sent them on to Paris. The boards in the deaneries were convened to meetings by the bishop once a year.

For the members of the missionary associations, the sometimes very hierarchical way in which the concept of a 'free association' was interpreted did not negatively affect the idea of an 'attested Christianity', as the Basel society was referred to.[33] Membership was categorized according to the size of the donations that were regularly given for missionary purposes. The network of Catholic missionary associations, directed from Lyon and Paris, had perfected this way of differentiating between members, thus creating clearly visible indications of how willing an individual was to make a sacrifice and, accordingly, showing the intensity of their faith. Ordinary members were those who regularly paid a fixed contribution, and they were distinguished from special and perpetual members, who donated larger amounts. The clergy formed a group of their own. Members were divided into groups of ten, led by a 'collector'. Ten such groups formed a hundred, led by a priest. At the level of the deanery, these were again organized into groups of ten, with the bishop appointing a designated priest or the dean of the district to lead them.

These initiatives and networks of voluntary Christian involvement, which went beyond the local level and often transcended national borders, were bound together by annals or other regular publications that not only documented their financial success and explained how the donations had been used but also contained reports from the different local and regional groups as well as the missionary areas. This conveyed a sense of being part of a divinely ordained *mission civilisatrice* to promote worldwide conversion to the supposedly superior religion of Christianity and thus gradually bring the colonies onto the same cultural level as Europe.[34] At the same time, it created a sense of being part of a community of European Christians driven by the same religious zeal.

While Protestants could understand this as a sign of their awakening and as the realization of their philanthropic convictions, the Catholic institution of grace had at its disposal an even more powerful media machinery, which connected the individual believers to the worldwide circulation of the means of grace through the missionary organizations and thus made the individual soul part of a wide, never-ending stream of salvation. All Catholic associations were endowed with various indulgences, which could be obtained through donations and prayers. In some cases, such privileges were granted to individual altars; priests could grant indulgences themselves or distribute consecrated devotional objects. Moreover, people also knew that they were receiving the prayers of those in far-off countries who had been converted to Christianity. More than 2,000 masses were read daily in the Franciscan Ingolstadt Mass Association around the middle of the nineteenth century. The flow of money thus resulted in a return flow of means of grace, founded on prayer, and kept it in motion; this made the individual believer part of a worldwide community of salvation, which included both the living and the dead.[35]

Since the eighteenth century, in the majority of cases and in all confessions, these networks and movements that publicly displayed their Christianity were initiated by clergymen. John Wesley is an example of this, as is the Bishop of Lyon and his Vicar-General, who took up an idea of Pauline Mari Jaricot to create the Œuvre de la Propagation. The clergymen also usually determined affairs in the local branches of Protestant missionary societies. It depended on them whether a community of donors developed in a parish. Nonetheless, in these 'organizations' and 'societies', lay people had many opportunities to put their organizational talents to the test and thus to mark a particular social position within their local context and to define an individual role for themselves.

## Fervent and inspired networks

This function of religion probably also supported the formation of personal networks in which, from the beginning of the nineteenth century onwards, clergymen, together with lay people from the educated upper class, committed themselves to the cause of the faith and to the role of the Christian church in state and society. This combined Christian commitment and political options in a very direct way. The Chevaliers du Foi, who had been engaged in implementing the Restoration in France politically, had chosen to be a secret society and order of knights. Mostly, however, these personal networks were much more informal and acted less conspiratorially. People met regularly, exchanged ideas and trusted each other because they had known each other since they were students and because they had common goals and interests. In London, the so-called Clapham Sect had emerged from the 1790s onwards and was made up of 'converted' men and women of London's upper class. It had formed on the initiative of the banker Henry Thornton, who had been awakened and converted through the Methodist sermons of John Wilberforce. Thornton gathered about twenty men around him, some of whom had direct political influence as members of Parliament, and then effectively lobbied for the abolition of slavery under Pitt, the prime minister. The Oxford Movement, a network of church reformers that had developed since the 1830s, was also based on a small community of Oxford professors of theology and their students. The influence of these networks aroused suspicion, even if they did not act as secret societies. The Clapham Sect was accused of conspiracy, as was the group of staunchly religious men – with the brothers Gerlach and Friedrich Julius Stahl at their centre – who had gathered around Friedrich Wilhelm IV and his father. They were known as the camarilla*, reflecting their ability to exert direct and thus uncontrolled influence on the monarch. Similarly, in the Rhineland, a circle of Ultramontane converts, clergymen and writers, such as Clemens Brentano, had formed since the late 1820s, which ultimately sought to influence the election of the Bishop of Trier. In Munich, a group of professors, mainly of philosophy and (Catholic) theology, formed in order to oppose liberalism and rationalist theology by means of the journal *Eos*, founded at an earlier date by Franz von Baader. The journal *Der Katholik* was supported by a similar personal network around Josef von Görres, and comparable groupings can be observed in the Italy of the 1840s. Despite the influence of such groups, which at times was considerable, these networks in which the politicization of religion was pursued were a phenomenon typical of their time. They disappeared after 1850, when the social movement became institutionalized within the political system. Parties formed that were able to mobilize people with their combination of religion and politics.[36]

The institutional consolidation of forms of Christianity outside the established churches through organizational and charismatic integration changed European Christianity profoundly from the last third of the eighteenth century onwards. The connections between social movements, associations, societies, congregations, orders and brotherhoods, which operated across national and confessional boundaries, created a European Christendom that, despite its fragmented nature, could be perceived as a single unit through its organizational forms and the way in which it was communicated in printed media. Particularly in the context of missionary work, this was linked to a global claim and global actions, and so this Christendom became a world religion that competed with other world religions on the global stage.

Furthermore, these new social forms also opened up new possibilities for a religious and pious way of life outside the liturgical piety of the established church. Pious actions were compartmentalized, which meant that daily, secular life could be resacralized or at least come to be an expression of pious convictions or awakening and conversion.[37] All these activities, from joining a society and taking on offices within it to attending awakening sermons, were voluntary and thus perceived as decisions. This was a prerequisite not only for religion to organize itself, but also for religion and social *persona* to be combined in a new way. Religious confession could thus function as a marker of individuality and could define one's role. Religious experiences such as individual awakening or emotional communal experiences were not primarily means of internal differentiation within the religious system but of marking individuality. The result was a form of Christianity that was characterized by performative religious experiences and events communicated through different media.

## Piety

To humans in society, religion represents a sphere with its own laws and rationality. Its primary function is to shape the relationship between the world that can be perceived and that which lies beyond human sensory experience and secure knowledge. This transcendence consisted of two structuring elements in Christianity: 'God' refers to the areas that lie beyond the social and natural world, whereas the 'soul' refers to that part within humans that is only accessible to a very limited degree. Piety relates these two unreachable or transcendent entities to each other in such a way that, on the one hand, the relationship between this world and that beyond becomes something that can be experienced by human sense. At the same time, piety reproduces religion in its social form, but religion is more than piety. It extends beyond it to include dogma, the priesthood and organization. Piety, however, provides the link to the life and daily activities of those who adhere to the religion in question and is the point at which the development of the system overlaps with the reproduction of non-religious actions and meanings. Piety is a zone in which social forces are transformed and communicated.[38] Its social form is thus determined by three aspects: piety is associated with the reproduction of social order and the formation of social structures; it participates in the formation of social identity and inclusion; and it provides a social and discursive space in which the relationship between internal and external processes, that is to say, between the soul/psyche and the social world, can be debated.

This chapter outlines the history of piety in the first half of the nineteenth century with these three aspects in mind. In this way, it becomes clear that de-Christianization and so-called religious revival are components of the same process; that is to say, they are part of the transformation of piety and the public worship of God that aimed to adapt them to the associative relationships of modernity and to its discourses.[39]

A key term in shaping the relationship of piety to the human self-image was faith. From the Late Middle Ages to the Early Modern period, the concept had changed from merely being a relationship of loyalty to becoming an act made possible through grace. It was an inner, private process but was also linked to trust in a higher power and human cognitive abilities. This transformation of the concept was an important prerequisite for piety taking on a new form in the course of the Early Modern period. By dramatizing internal experience, it became one of the most important ways in which modern individuality was configured, an individuality that was pursued in Pietistic introspection, experiences of awakening and other written, autobiographical self-observations. From the seventeenth century onwards, the concept of the soul, which would then become the modern psyche, developed outside the religious sphere. In the eighteenth century, an important change was made to empirical psychology in that it aimed to differentiate between the observation of inner and outer experiences, from which individuality derived, on the one hand, and the contemplation of the divine, on the other. Introspection could only allow individuals to find themselves if they did not regard their life as leading to God but to themselves. Self-observation, biographical consistency and authenticity thus became a syndrome of the construction of individuality, which was still present in the nineteenth century and continued to have a connection with the religious sphere despite the discursive and institutional 'secularizations' that had occurred.[40]

This became important in the nineteenth century, because the new, functionally determined institutionalization of religion demanded decisions and motives that could be constructed in a socially attributable way. Conversely, modern individuality found this constellation to be more suitable than almost any other for combining the general and the specific in the process of copying and selecting. Religion, therefore, continued to be a social field in which the psyche remained directly involved in the formation and reproduction of patterns of social order and which, in turn, offered good opportunities for the psyche to construct itself as an individual and a social *persona* and present itself as authentic. An actively pious life could illustrate who a person was or wanted to be.[41]

This was one side of the dynamic that determined the history of piety in the nineteenth century. The other resulted from changes in relation to media.[42] It has already been shown how this affected the social reality of religion. The observations and experiences associated with it fundamentally altered the way in which the world was perceived and thus also affected the discourse on the relationship between the perceptible world and transcendence. It became conceivable that the human soul would embark on a journey after the body's death and move to a different planet in the universe without breaking off the connection to this world entirely. Piety and public worship of God developed in a communicative space in which the social conditions of transmission and communication were the subject of intensive reflection. These conditions, in turn, were reflected in social forms of piety and public worship, and practical piety was directly connected to the discourse on the role that different media played in sociation.

## The decline in the influence of the institutional church

The nineteenth century became a period in which religion moved outside the confines of the church. The church regarded participation in certain events as indispensable expressions of piety, for example, attendance at Sunday services, Communion in general, and Communion and confession at Easter, but fewer people were attending these events. The pace of this development in different regions varied significantly, and there were areas in Europe where only one-third of adults fulfilled the minimum requirements when it came to participation in services and Communion as early as the first half of the nineteenth century. In other regions, at least 90 per cent of the faithful still considered these things to be a natural part of their lives. Considerable data have become available on this in recent years,[43] and some general developments and trends can be discerned.

The move away from churches was a process that affected Protestants and Catholics alike to much the same degree. Only 40 per cent of adults in the Church of England and all other denominations attended Sunday services according to the census of 1851, a number that was actually quite high in the context of the nineteenth century. Until the 1840s, information here and there suggests lower levels of attendance, and from the 1860s onwards another one-fifth to one-third of the churchgoers registered in 1851 stopped attending services. This was despite the construction of churches and intensive pastoral care in Victorian England having considerably improved conditions compared to the first third of the century. In certain parts of France, 90 per cent of the faithful aged thirteen and above had attended confession and Communion at Easter at the beginning of the century, but the numbers had dropped considerably by the middle of the century and were usually two-thirds or less by around 1900. In those areas in which the quota in the first half of the century was already as low as 10–20 per cent, the decline was slower and, in some cases, numbers went up again. The German Protestant *Landeskirchen* compiled such figures for the first time in 1862, with significant regional differences. In Hesse-Nassau, attendance at Communion was around 83 per cent, but in Berlin it was down to only one-sixth. A large number of *Landeskirchen* occupied the middle ground, with around two-thirds or at least 40 per cent of the faithful attending Communion. Very soon after 1900, these numbers fell to around a third to a half and, in Berlin, they dropped even further, reaching 14 per cent in 1913.

These data are all the more important because institutionalized Christianity in both major confessions closely watched their membership, which was indicated by minimum attendance at public rites. Several countermeasures were taken. Thus, the structural framework for pastoral care was improved through the construction of new churches, the appointment of additional and better trained clergy, and a reorganization of the parish system. These measures were taken from the second third of the century onwards. From the middle of the century, pastoral care was also changed to reflect new challenges. The French bishops gave up their rigoristic position and began to recommend more frequent and regular attendance at Communion. This position was shared by the religious orders engaged in popular missions in German parishes since the 1840s. In the Church of England, the evangelical clergy, representing around one-third of the pastoral clergy at the middle of the century, encouraged the faithful to take

Communion significantly more than the three times per year that had been prescribed by the Book of Common Prayer for centuries.

From Vienna to Paris, Glasgow and Edinburgh, there was no difference between the confessions regarding the social characteristics of this move away from the church. The development was driven by the urbanization of nineteenth-century European society, and it occurred faster and was more sustained in towns than in rural areas. Industrialization was the second important driving force. In England in particular, this had already been abundantly evident in the first half of the century. At most, 2–10 per cent of Christians in the early industrial area around Coventry still attended Sunday services in the 1830s and 1840s. The census of 1851 showed clearly that it was the lower classes and the workers who had turned their backs on the church as a whole, even if some had joined the Methodists and other Dissenters. Third, religiosity and piety were important aspects of male and female roles, and so the move away from churches was symptomatic of a redefinition of the relationship between the sexes that had been in progress since the eighteenth century. Already in the last third of the eighteenth century, there had been a rapid decline in men in Catholic France and Germany leaving money for requiem masses or using religious wording in their wills, while women continued to hold on to these customs and forms. Religion and religious institutions proceeded to become more feminine in the nineteenth century, as a result of men abandoning the traditional forms of the institutionalized church and public worship more quickly and lastingly than women. The latter, on the other hand, not only held onto these elements but also tried out new approaches.

All this was observed. At the turn of the nineteenth century, Thomas Coke, an Anglican clergyman, wrote to the Bishop of London that a significant portion of society had developed a deep aversion to receiving Communion from the hands of an immoral clergyman. Coke had turned to Methodism and had carried out missionary work in America and on the Indian subcontinent. His verdict therefore was directed against the established church. Those who no longer attended Communion understood the word 'immorality' in a very broad sense 'as including all those who frequent cardtables, balls, horse-racing, theatres and other places of fashionable amusement'. He himself had experienced that it was futile to explain that the strength of an ordination did not depend on piety or even on the morality of a clergyman as these arguments were no longer persuasive.[44] Since the 1780s, statements such as Coke's together had developed into a discourse encompassing all Christian churches on the decline in public worship, the question of why religion was in such a bad state at all, and how it might be possible to reawaken the religious sense and piety of the people. Those who participated in this discourse by publishing their insights in treatises and journals were all clergymen and representatives of the church hierarchy.[45] There are a number of different emphases in these texts, depending on church politics, confession and denomination. In France, the Revolution was equated with the Fall of Man; in England, the growing distance between state and church was lamented; and, in Germany, Protestant arguments focused on the Woellner Edict and Catholic ones on the catastrophe represented by secularization. However, they all observed that religion and religious institutions found themselves in a world that had grown distant from and was hostile to them, and it was concluded that the new conditions would inevitably lead to a change in institutionalized religion and piety.

From the point of view of religion, this discourse summarized the fact that the world's relationship to religion was obviously changing. Internal views of religion developed that had the appearance of external assessments. This was done either from the point of view of a particular denomination, as in the case of Thomas Coke, or a connection was established between religion and its polar opposite. Friedrich Schleiermacher's phrase 'Speeches about religion to its cultured despisers'[46] was an example of this essentially diabolical observation mode. The change in perspective associated with the hypothesis of secularization was already evident in the language of many of these texts. One could only talk about religion from an observational point of view if one put aside religion's linguistic code and construction of identity. For this reason, texts no longer referred to churches and a decline in attendance, but discussed the importance of 'cult' and the 'temple' for religion. In all texts, Christianity, both in its pre-Reformation form and its modern manifestation, was placed within the context of the general history of religious institutions and religions against the background of a universal history of civilization.

Thus, to think of this process of de-Christianization and a decline in church attendance as a form of secularization was the result of an order of observation that became possible once religion and other social structures had become sufficiently differentiated from each other. The functional imperatives which both sides used to mark and stabilize this differentiation could then be perceived as different and incompatible. In his *Athanasius* of 1837, Görres warned that the Rhinelanders, who were otherwise such devout, church-going people, might forget 'the higher power as a result of industrial and political activity'. It seemed to him 'as if those external and generally highly respectable forces and aspirations threatened with overly great momentum to overgrow the internal and even more respectable ones entirely'.[47] Systemically and institutionally differentiated religion could also become a specific, separate area of an individual's life.

From the beginning, this discourse on the decline in engagement with the church was of interest from the point of view of statistics and social science. Even those who claimed that religiosity was an internal trait were also certain that it was reflected in an individual's external actions. Thus, if participation 'in religious acts noticeably decreases' in a population, this meant that religiosity in general was decreasing.[48] If the church was described as a 'church society', as was common not just in Protestantism, the number of members who actually actively participated became an indicator of that society's vitality and strength. For this reason, records began to be kept of the number of those attending Communion and services. By the middle of the century, statistical self-observation had become an established practice in German Protestant *Landeskirchen* and in the Anglican Church. In the United Kingdom, this resulted in the census of 1851, and in the German *Landeskirchen* it led to the surveys on public worship which were carried out at regular intervals from 1851 onwards.[49]

Similar developments in order to monitor membership did not take place in the Catholic Church, probably because of a different ecclesiology, which trusted in the sanctity of the institution, derived from its foundation. Here, the emphasis was on the ability to evoke religious enthusiasm and to mobilize the faithful on special occasions. Pilgrimages like the one to the Holy Robe in Trier or the Aachen pilgrimage from Cologne, as well as popular missions, were occasions on which the participants were counted or at least estimated, and the number of confessions heard, hosts administered or indulgences sold were proudly presented to the public.[50] Statistics concerning daily religious life, however, did not begin to be recorded until the end of the century.

The self-observation of religion gained a socio-scientific dimension in the discourse regarding the decline in church attendance because it began to make use of the concept of social classes. Nineteenth-century European societies resorted to this model when thinking about their own social order, translating the traditional concept of hierarchies into one of moral, political and economic differences, which made it possible to continue to describe modern society as a set of communal, interpersonal relationships. In the discourse on the decline in commitment to the church, this was reflected in the conviction that the lower classes in general, and the working class in particular, lacked any religious spirit and that nineteenth-century towns had become devoid of faith. The town was represented as the Whore of Babylon where, as in London, Paris or Berlin, there was a complete absence of God and a continuing disregard for His will.[51]

The clergy of all confessions commented on the process of urbanization and industrialization by means of these kinds of verbose, fantastical visions, which were an expression of the fact that the established church and divine worship had become separated from the reproduction of patterns of social order. The decline in commitment to the church was obviously the result of a structural dissociation, which had led to church attendance and church-based piety in many cases no longer being a useful way of reproducing individual roles, positions of status or entire ways of life. They had lost their social substance. The first signs of this had already been visible in the eighteenth century. Protestant church discipline declined because the social order of the villages was no longer reflected by the order in the parish, and the decline was fastest in those places that underwent the most profound changes, as has been shown for different places in Switzerland.[52] In the towns and rural areas that were being industrialized, new classes emerged, which were not included in the Christian idea of estates and had not been able to find an appropriate place within the daily life of piety in the parishes. Instead, they were attracted to Methodism and Dissent. Similar developments occurred in Catholic towns and villages. The educated wealthy middle classes were the first to distance themselves from traditional forms of providing for the life beyond, whereas the aristocracy adhered to old forms right up into the nineteenth century.[53] In the parish, a basic organizing principle in church structures was the combination of hierarchical social order and pious practice. This was reflected in patronage rights, in parish councils and presbyteries, in brotherhoods, orders of processions, funerary orders and in the allocation of pews. The changes in social order and in the formation of social groups that had been occurring since the eighteenth century meant that this combination had become an impediment to Protestant and Catholic church structures. The growth of parishes resulting from the increase in population and migration, especially in early nineteenth-century towns, played an important role in this development. But clear-sighted contemporaries felt that this was only a superficial symptom and that the real problem was the social configuration of the basic institution of the church. John Masen Neale, an Anglican clergyman close to the Oxford Movement, became infamous for storming those churches in which he worked after 1841 with an axe when he took office and smashing the locked pews in the presence of their owners in order to make space for the less wealthy members of his parish.[54]

**Piety in the context of the family**

In the nineteenth century, the nation had become a cipher for the fact that social order no longer occurred at the local level and, accordingly, the inclusion of individuals no longer took place in local communities or local groups. The fundamentals of the map of society were redrawn, and the entire body of socio-scientific and political terminology to which European societies of the nineteenth century resorted when describing and arranging themselves adjusted to the fact that social structures were now formed at a different level. References to a 'class society' thus were not just a memory of the estates-based order but reflected the fact that the formation of groups at a national and, later in the century, at an international level was the new process by which individuals were included in society. Religion and piety illustrate some of the consequences of this change. Piety and public worship remained or became an attractive means of inclusion if they highlighted membership of a group that went beyond the local level. There were two fixed reference points: one was the nation itself,[55] and the other was the authenticity of ways of life that involved a form of individuality that was the most important prerequisite of social inclusion into the range of different ways of developing functional orders. However, configurations which were related functionally to the structural and social relations of all of society were at least equally as important. This was often associated with the formation of systems, as in the case of the working class or the education system. It was unclear in the case of the family, which had become stylized as the core of sociation since the beginning of the century for a number of reasons: the family formed a point at which nature and sociation intersected; the family was regarded as an indispensable element of socialization; and it was considered to be the space in which emotionally based social relationships between authentic individuals developed, which were believed to be the basis of society as a whole. Family was the structural as well as the imaginary space in which individualization and sociation met.[56] Wherever religion and piety could be combined with the social and imaginary shaping of individuality, the attraction of religion in modern, nineteenth-century society increased.

For this reason, the family became one of the most important spaces in the nineteenth century where changes in religious practice and the reorganization of religion occurred. In the *ancien régime*, too, it had been regarded as a social space in which the father of the family ensured that his wife, children and servants fulfilled their religious duties. Now the rites of baptism, confirmation, marriage and burial that gave structure to a person's life increasingly became family occasions; in times of increasing social mobility, this helped to shape personal identity through commemoration and the ritual of a family celebration. 'Domestic days of commemoration' of successful family celebrations provided families with a history, in which family members could mark particular points and which also served to anchor their own biography. Thenceforth, these church occasions marking rites of passage gained unprecedented popularity.[57]

This is clearest in the case of funerals. In Protestant German parishes, the proportion of church funerals was below 40 per cent in 1862 and is likely to have been considerably lower at the beginning of the century as ecclesiastical and secular authorities had been standardizing this rite of passage since the 1830s. The churches developed new funeral liturgies which were aimed at making it a more solemn occasion. This was thus also an attempt to combat the traditional practice of giving the last benediction at home and following this by a funeral procession. It coincided with the authorities increasingly regulating the burial system and moving it under municipal control, as illustrated by burial grounds being moved away from churches to the edge of settlements and towns: instead of churchyards, there were cemeteries. At the same time, a middle-class burial culture and sentimental aesthetics concerning the grave developed, making the cemetery a place associated with family commemoration and giving an individual's life meaning. It also became a place in which the social position and biography of the deceased were increasingly important factors in the design of the grave and the inscription. At the end of the century, at most, one in ten burials in the Protestant regions of Germany took place outside a church context; however, this was not due to official intervention but to the way in which that particular rite of passage had become part of family and middle-class life, with the particular form that was adopted being that of the institutionalized church. However, the cremation of Freethinkers, which had become more popular since the 1880s, showed that a radical alternative to the general custom could also serve as a marker of individuality.[58] The need for the individualization of baptism and marriage was apparently less pronounced, with church rituals being the norm at the beginning of the century. This continued to be the case in nine times out of ten, despite the option of a civil marriage ceremony.

The firm hold of the church over these defining rituals of an individual's life could also carry risks, as Protestants realized in relation to confirmation. In the German *Landeskirchen*, confirmation only gradually became common practice from the 1830s onwards, and this affirmation of the baptismal covenant at the threshold to adulthood continued to be accepted even after the middle of the century. It is questionable to what extent it was actually regarded as a religious practice. We know from those who attended confirmation classes that these were often the point at which religious doubt arose for the first time because the young people attending the classes found it difficult to reconcile reason and intellect with what was being taught regarding religious beliefs. In the Anglican Church, the general practice of confirmation was uncontroversial, but the church ceremony merely provided an occasion for young people of both sexes subsequently to visit pubs and inns and behave like an 'unchristian and barbaric brood', as indignant clerics put it. By the middle of the century, this situation had improved, but it was clear that young people did not primarily consider the ritual to be a spiritual occasion and instead thought of it as a celebration and an opportunity to come into contact with the opposite sex. In addition, confirmation usually did not represent entry into church life. Especially in the lower classes, individuals often did not attend services or take Communion for years after this event marking the beginning of adulthood.[59]

In France, the Revolution had secularized these rituals so that, in 1834, around one in twenty married couples in the diocese of Versailles had not been married in the church. A campaign against this state of affairs was initially successful; moreover, while there had been a number of unbaptized children at the beginning of the century, this gradually changed until it was no longer the case. By around 1850, baptism, marriage and funerals were once again entirely in the hands of the church. The funeral ritual was subject to the same influences from the authorities as in Germany, and it was also turned into a family affair with its aesthetics determined by that context. In France, this was supported by a strong degree of commercialization, which detached the burial rite from the wider parish and turned it into an individualized family matter.[60] In the Third Republic, this individualization once again was understood as a conscious move away from the church. In Paris in the 1870s, one-fifth of the population was buried without church ritual, at times more than 10 per cent of marriages took place outside the church and only nine out of ten newborns were baptized.

The individualization of rites of passage thus was no longer necessarily expressed in Christian rituals nor did the increased significance of the family with regard to the sacraments and the special church occasions that structured a life, such as baptism, confirmation, weddings or funerals, result in more people returning to the church. This was because the social framework of the family had become more important than the religious community. In Anglican parishes, this led to some conflict. Up until the last third of the century, baptism and marriage were securely dominated by the church even if bishops complained that baptism had degenerated into a ceremony with superstitious features to a greater degree than any other church ritual. However, the faithful of the middle and upper classes persisted in conducting these rituals in a family setting separated from the congregation and their services even after the clergy attempted to change this practice from the 1830s onwards. Gradually, the clergy were successful in doing so and baptisms were carried out in the context of a service after the middle of the century, but it was still often only family members who attended.[61]

## Media and piety

In the course of the nineteenth century, new forms of worship and piety developed, slowly at first and then increasingly swiftly from the beginning of the 1830s. There were two reasons for this: first, the way in which the institutional forms of organization and social movement combined and, second, the use of the industrial printing press. From the 1830s onwards, religion quickly became a mass phenomenon. It was not just that mass media published texts on religion, but the institutions themselves and piety – as a particular way of participating in these institutions – developed their own kind of media reality. The institutional form and the way in which the media constructed this reality acted to stabilize and strengthen each other. The social reality of religion was increasingly also a reality of mass media.

The *Katholische Kirchenzeitung* (Catholic Church Newspaper) founded by Johann Baptist von Pfeilschifter in Aschaffenburg in 1829 aimed to create a space for Catholics from all over Germany to communicate, thus becoming a 'nation of brothers in the church ... that transcends political division and disunity'. The *Mainzer Katholik* (Mainz Catholic), the journal of Ultramontane Catholics, considered itself to be acting on a 'public battlefield' and, in 1843, published a review of the twenty or so years of the journal's publication and the good development of the Catholic press, in particular, since the Cologne Troubles. On the basis of this review, the author argued that 'Catholic journalism' was increasingly demanding.[62] In actual fact the history of the Catholic press had been very dynamic. Up until 1825, the theological journals that were published focused strongly on pastoral care and were aimed at the clergy and distributed only regionally in individual dioceses. In the first half of the third decade, however, eighteen new journals appeared and, in the second half, there were another nineteen, although many did not survive for very long. Of the ninety-two journals founded between 1815 and 1847, only about half still existed around the middle of the century. These journals mostly regarded themselves as voices of church politics; they were rarely liberal and instead confessionally based, they were directed at the clergy and the laity, and their aim was to appeal to the entire Catholic reading public. Many of these publications were organized by small groups and networks, such as the Mainzer Kreis (Mainz Circle), a group formed around Reis, Näff and Görres, who published *Der Katholik* (The Catholic), or the EOS circle in Munich, which produced the *Historisch-politischen Blätter* (Historical and Political Notes). Most of the articles in these magazines were written by clergymen, but one in five were already written by laymen. By the mid-1830s, the average print run was 1,460 copies, so that the twenty-two magazines published at that time already reached at least 200,000 readers.[63]

In German Protestantism, hardly any church-political journals emerged in the first half of the century. This may have been due to two factors: first, the Protestant church was divided both organizationally, through the *Landeskirchen*, and theologically; second, it was closely associated with the state. Even the Protestant church newspaper *Evangelische Kirchenzeitung*, founded by Ernst Ludwig Hengstenberg in 1827, was characterized by its semi-official closeness to the state and its defence of orthodoxy through a decidedly partisan theology. Such struggles for direction determined the landscape of Protestant theological journals long after the middle of the century. Ernst Wichern, who, since 1844, had been publishing the *Fliegende Blätter* (Flying Pages) as a newsletter of the Rauhes Haus* – a children's shelter that was associated with the 'Home Mission' – understood journalism as a platform for Protestant unity, an idea to which he aspired.[64]

The Protestant world was well aware that the printing press was an essential element in its form of faith and piety, and significant efforts were put into celebrating the Gutenberg anniversary in 1840. In keeping with this connection, apart from theological journals, European Protestantism mainly produced a large number of devotional books and treatises, which were then distributed amongst the faithful by the Awakened missionary, Bible and tract societies. These voluntary organizations highlighted the connection between journalism and an institution that operated above the local level. All of these associations required a newsletter or other forms of printed correspondence. When the Friends of the Light and the German Catholics joined forces in 1850, they also began a newsletter. Even the Methodists, who with their parish houses, festivals and sermons in the open field placed their emphasis on a form of piety that drew on the communication of individuals who were present in the same place, creating a supralocal level through its itinerant teachers, established their own printing empire, which produced and circulated the texts of sermons and songs as well as edifying literature.[65]

All this led to a noticeable increase in the production and circulation of printed pious texts since the end of the eighteenth century, and there was no significant difference in this regard between Protestant and Catholic regions, as a comparison between Catholic France, confessionally mixed Germany and the Anglican Church suggests. In the years after 1815, French publishing houses contributed between 300 and 400 religious titles to the books offered for sale by booksellers or colporteurs. During the Restoration and at the time of the duc de Berry's spectacular murder, this number temporarily rose to 1,000–1,200, but by the middle of the century it had gone down again to 600–800. It was not until the 1860s that the figures increased significantly once more. Thus, between 1815 and 1848, the proportion of religious titles in the total production of French publishing houses ranged between 8 and 14 per cent. It cannot be said, therefore, that religious books were disproportionately popular. The same is true of the situation in Germany. Around 1800, roughly 250 religious titles were on offer at the two book fairs in Frankfurt and Leipzig; in about 1830, the number was around 1,200, and this trend continued until 1850, after which the increase in numbers was very slight. As a result, here, too, in the first half of the century, only about every tenth book was religious. The proportion of literary fiction was three times as high. British book production shows the same pattern. From the first third of the century, it was driven by increasing literacy amongst the population, a decreasing cost of publication and expanding markets in the colonies. Between 1840 and 1900, the number of books printed annually increased by a factor of 2.5 from around 8.7 million to around 19.8 million. In the tradition of moral weekly journals, there was a significant number of books on how to conduct oneself, and Bible societies strongly promoted the dissemination of religious works. Nevertheless, in general, the proportion of religious books was actually slightly smaller than that on the Continent: between 1836 and 1896 it never exceeded 10 per cent and, in most years, it was 3–5 per cent. Even the above-average print run of religious titles did not increase the total share of religious texts in the available reading material by more than 10 per cent. Literary texts, on the other hand, made up 30–50 per cent of annual production in terms of the number of titles and their print run.[66]

The tastes of readers were reflected in the book lists of colporteurs and reports from lending libraries. The chivalric novel was significantly more popular than an edifying book or treatise. The clergy knew this, probably because many of them, including Catholics, also published works of edification or entertainment. On the other hand, considerable institutional zeal was shown in promoting the dissemination of religious reading materials. The tract and missionary societies have been mentioned already, but parish libraries were also established and confessional publishing houses were founded that published their own series of affordable devotional literature. This was a battle to defend readers against the detrimental effects of fiction and trivial texts by establishing a protected island of religious reading materials. Bishops and Catholic as well as Protestant priests never tired of condemning the immorality of novels and pointing out that the narrative suspense of a saint's life was entirely on par with that of a chivalric novel. These efforts were, however, in vain. The interests of the increasing numbers of readers moved the market for printed materials in a different direction. Religion had finally become a separate sphere of life in this area, too, once Protestant tract societies started producing non-religious titles in larger numbers.[67]

This should not lead us to underestimate the importance of tracts, journals or books of prayer and edification for the institutional form of religion in the nineteenth century and their influence in shaping and developing piety. The so-called religious renewal from the 1830s onwards was an organizational phenomenon, but with regard to its extent and form it was primarily a media phenomenon. The relevance of different media should be clear by now with regard to religious voluntary organizations that operated above the local and regional level. Sodalities and brotherhoods, which, until the 1830s, had a purely local focus and were only incorporated into wider structures through the institutional network of the order in question, were connected by regularly published journals the more Rome and the bishops sought to standardize, control and direct the focus of piety towards particular aspects, for example, devotion to the Virgin Mary or the Sacred Heart.[68]

Journals, newspapers and other printed works provided a fertile ground for the growth of a form of piety that was emotionally charged, expressive and often set in motion by charismatic leaders and which, since the 1820s, combined social spontaneity, religious fervour and institutional commitment in all Christian churches and denominations. The significant numbers who were attracted to miracle healers, such as the shepherd Heinrich Mohr, who worked in the West Prussian provinces, caused the authorities alarm and left them at a loss as to how to respond, but the popularity of such figures was only initially carried by local rumours. The rush of followers, which lasted for months, began when the first healings were reported in the newspaper. The spectacular pilgrimage to the Holy Robe in Trier in 1844 and the Aachen Pilgrimage, which also attracted large numbers of pilgrims, were more than well-organized mass events with a well-thought-out religious and logistical choreography: even for the pilgrims who were present, the events only became tangible as religious events because the healings were reported in newspapers and special publications authorized by the Church, which often summarized what the newspapers had written. These reports and representations not only described the events that had occurred but also painted a detailed picture of the experiences and feelings of the participants, including their motivation in participating, so that, from the 1830s onwards, a large number of models had become available that provided guidance on the conduct and inner experience of religious mass events.[69] The Methodists' events were disseminated through print media and are likely to have provided an example not just for European Pietists and revivalists. In the Catholic Church, for instance, these models of religious experience, developed and disseminated through different media, were probably an important prerequisite for the fact that, with the help of the state, processions and pilgrimages in France and Germany, which had previously been locally and regionally oriented, were successfully concentrated on large places such as Aachen, Trier and, from 1840, Lourdes. In Mediterranean Catholicism, religious life was fragmented locally to a much greater extent right into the twentieth century, due to less state influence in society and rates of literacy increasing at a slower pace.[70]

Texts and their mass reception were also able to lend a religious dimension to events that would otherwise not have been regarded in that way. The assassination of the duc de Berry and his subsequent representation as a martyr and pious spouse were such media events, and even the first nationalization of Protestantism in the Wars of Liberation cannot be imagined without printed sermons and the texts published by intellectuals.[71]

Printed materials provided models of a Christian way of life which members of brotherhoods and congregations could follow. Above all, however, they conveyed new styles of piety and various models of individual pious experience including the ecstatic piety of female visionaries and charismatic prophets. There were clairvoyants and prophets in France and England who hardly made any public appearances and attracted followers through print publications and correspondence.[72] The successes of the cult of the Virgin Mary from the 1830s onwards and the devotion to the Sacred Heart from the middle of the century brought together specific types of piety with explicit and detailed social role models and would have been unthinkable in the media conditions of the eighteenth century. The growing stream of printed images of religious events, which, since the eighteenth century, had been available to those of the faithful who could not read, ensured that the Queen of Heaven seen by the shepherd children in La Salette had the appearance one might have expected.[73] The wave of visionaries receiving stigmata was triggered by Clemens Brentano's 1831 report on Anna Katharina Emmerich, which described her visions and stigmata in detail. Görres deliberately ensured that a mystical and ecstatic model of piety became popular with the publication of his *Christliche Mystik*, the first volume of which appeared in 1836. Shortly afterwards, in 1839, the report on the suffering and visions of Maria von Mörl, from South Tyrol, was published. Görres had also taken significant interest in her. It is clear that Maria von Mörl became a role model for those women in the Bavarian *Oberland* and in Westphalia who experienced visions and stigmata in the 1840s.[74]

## Communicating with transcendence

The change in media in the nineteenth century, which influenced the social form of piety and divine worship as described above, placed particular demands on the way religion was practised and required this practice to reflect and elaborate on religion. In dealing with the transcendent, the question of perception, was, in any case, particularly important. The Lutheran concept of *sola fide* and Catholic penance also meant that the question of authenticity and the motivation underlying a person's devotion to God were core issues in communication with transcendence. There were a number of media-theoretical questions the answers to which would influence different concepts of prayer as well as ideas concerning the correct way of carrying out divine service and how visions, apparitions and stigmata should be viewed. Such questions included the following: how was a pious disposition expressed, how could it be awakened if necessary, what role did formalized and ritualized divine worship play in this, how did God and His saints communicate with humans, who else 'inhabited' the next world and was it possible to communicate with that world? The Christian religion in Europe clearly did not represent a self-contained sphere, either institutionally or discursively, and it was part of a larger context involving a spectrum which consisted of a magical and clearly only partially Christianized popular religiosity at one end and a scientific approach to faith expressed in mesmerism at the other. There were three areas in which different forms of religious communication through various media were tested: prayer, church service and the direct exchange between this world and the next.

There were differences between the confessions regarding the discourse about prayer.[75] In both cases, prayer and devotional books were important, but on the Protestant side writings on the possibilities of improving church services also played a role. However, a comparison of such writings from the second half of the eighteenth and first half of the nineteenth centuries does not suggest fundamental differences between the confessions. By the eighteenth century, 'magical' prayer was already a thing of the past, and it was not believed that the transcendent deity could be forced into submission through prayer, unlike during an earlier period – in the seventeenth century, Abraham a Santa Clara had still referred to prayer as fetters with which to tie the avenging hands of God. Deprived of this important aid, the faithful now had to meet the contingencies of life with a double strategy. First, prayer books provided a verbose discourse of theodicy, urging the faithful to regard strokes of fate and unforeseeable events as help and signs on one's individual route towards salvation, and to assign religious meaning to them by constructing causalities. The second point is that this involved placing a childlike trust in God the Father. This image of a trust-based father–child relationship continued to dominate the prayer and devotional books of the nineteenth century and, along with the theodicy discourse, it became a cipher for the idea that the faithful were responsible for successful communication and for establishing and stabilizing the religious meaning of their own lives.

However, the problems associated with sanctifying one's own life through continuous interpretation and permanent devotion to God were already being identified at the beginning of the nineteenth century. The argument was put forward that human attention was limited, and the many tasks demanded by a Christian life prevented an individual from devoting their life to God entirely. However, not even Pietistic or evangelical circles put forward the fundamentalist view that everyday life should be carried out according to religious imperatives. In the Methodist 'salvation industry', too, the individual rationality of different actions was recognized and efforts were restricted to executing them with an attitude agreeable to God.[76] Instead of transforming the world, the aim was to perfect oneself and to develop a particular attitude towards the world.

In this way, the prerequisites for prayer and piety were discussed, leading to self-referential elements entering prayer books at the beginning of the nineteenth century. It was argued that one even needed to pray for successful prayer, and prayer was increasingly no longer perceived as a request; instead, the faithful conversed with God in order to know themselves. Devotion to God and the banishment of forbidden desires from the heart continued to be unattainable for humans. Here, the reflective formation of modern individual identity, the social consequences of functional differentiation and the basic problem of all believers who turned to God converged. It was only from this point onwards that the significance and use of prayer and devotional books became more important, albeit very quickly. It went without saying that prayer and devotional books provided the basis for an individual's relationship with God. They suggested texts and formulations and provided instruction on the correct way of devoting oneself to God and on how to observe oneself. However, it was stressed increasingly often that prayer and reading were not the same thing. Reading printed texts aloud could not lead to correct prayer as a conscious and authentic address to God. Using a prayer book thus required a person to develop an understanding of the prayers and to then develop their own prayers on that basis. Pious reading was thus also subject to the 'loss of sensuousness' which characterized the reading of literary texts as this became increasingly more common. The advice was to acquire naturalness, much as the Romantic movement had suggested in a different context. One should learn sincere and fervent devotion to God in a methodical, considered way in order to achieve a pre-literate degree of naturalness which no longer showed any signs of being repetitive or mechanical.

In this way, prayer books acquired a paradoxical structure, which, however, turned out to be entirely suited to their function, given the changes in media. Prayer books were primarily performative texts because they produced what they contained. Reading the texts meant that what they described occurred. Increasingly, however, the texts also drew attention to their printed nature and to the fact that any authentic encounter with God or with oneself could not occur within the text or through reading, thus undermining the performative aspect of the prayer texts. In this way, prayer books took up the problem of certainty that was inherent in all communication with God by addressing the problem of how one might imagine an authentic relationship with God and directly experience Him at a time when religious meaning was available in mass-produced texts. By presenting themselves as texts within this context, prayer books prepared the practice of Christian religion for a world of mass publishing.

Church services were the second field in which the role of different media in religion was discussed. The starting point here was the problem of how to make membership visible, which had set the entire secularization discourse on self-observation in motion. It was argued that, while religion could not be reduced to the way in which public worship was carried out, it was nonetheless obvious that the declining numbers participating in it indicated a decline in religious sentiment. A large number of texts from the different confessions dating to the four decades after 1790 show that here, too, there were some predictable dogmatic differences but that the views of the clergy, who were usually the ones producing these texts, did not diverge greatly on the question of Christian piety.[77]

If the church was considered to be a (religious) society, then the primary purpose of church services was to make it a visible social reality. This logic could, however, also be used to argue that a church service should then also reflect the social order because the upper classes should serve as a model for the lower classes to follow. Teaching the basic tenets of the faith was regarded as the second important function of church services. The emphasis on this was considerably greater amongst Protestants, but Catholics also attached importance to making ceremonies and their relevance with regard to dogma and the salvation economy understandable. Thus, until the 1830s, there was lively debate concerning the use of the vernacular in church services. Protestants occasionally went even further: understanding edification as a general programme for education, they suggested that members of the congregation should read to each other from journals during church services. This reflected the continued influence of the Enlightenment, which had stressed the moral aspect of religion and had understood church services as a source of general and individual morality, with rituals being aids to developing it. Church services were generally regarded as something that preceded individual religiosity. The purpose of an appropriately arranged liturgy was to awaken religious feeling in the faithful. Occasionally, this conviction was associated with a social-anthropological view. The lower classes, in particular, required their senses to be stimulated because their limited intellectual capacity made it impossible for them to access religious truths through reason. In his autobiographical notes, the Archbishop of Trier, Hommer, addressed baroque forms of popular piety, in particular pilgrimages, and noted with some understanding that, because they worked so hard, the lower classes believed that only physically demanding activities were of any value. For this reason, they expressed their reverence for and devotion to God and the saints through activities that involved physical exertion.

The term 'popular piety' was the product of this ethnographic attitude and, as a rule, it did not involve the degree of sympathy that Hommer had shown. In the first half of the century, theologians and pastoral clergy who reflected on the form of church services emphasized the need for simplicity. Classicist beauty was a model to be aspired to, and all exaggeration and noise, including too great a degree of vividness, was to be avoided. Despite this, Protestant authors, in particular, did understand and stress the importance of sensory elements in the liturgy as a means of increasing the attractiveness of the service and its moral and formative effect. They argued for the use of bells and organs, recommended that greater importance should be given to hymns sung by the congregation, and occasionally advocated lending the Lutheran Words of Institution before Communion a new kind of mysticism through the use of incense. In order to strengthen the worship of God in everyday life again, a new sanctification of places and times was propagated. In the Catholic Church, this emphasis on the sensory aspects of the liturgy, which was based on the implicit contrast between intellectual activity and emotional states induced through sensory experience, meant that the calls for a vernacular liturgy became fewer. The argument was that, if Latin was not understood by those who attended, this gave a sense of mystery to the liturgy, the sacraments and the benediction, and this mysteriousness was the basis of believers' faith in the power of the strange words. An openly articulated desire to address psychological needs in church services underlay such arguments. It was argued that ceremonies and prayers should be arranged based on the feeling they evoked, and this contributed to an understanding of the service as a piece of theatre in which the faithful were the spectators.

Given the intensity with which these discussions were conducted in journals, tractates, extensive treatises and at meetings of the pastoral clergy, organized by bishops or consistories, the persistence of the traditional forms of the church service is remarkable. In the *Landeskirche* of Bavaria, there had been debate on how to achieve a 'refinement' of the service and lend it greater solemnity since the religious edict of 1821. In 1844, this led to a liturgy which contained very few changes compared to the one preceding it, despite a report of 1832 urgently recommending that the congregation should be involved more strongly in the service as it represented a 'reciprocal act'. The main consequences of these reforms were centrally standardized liturgies and prayers and, thus, local customs. As a result, there was an even greater sense that the liturgy and prayers represented an event directed by an ecclesiastical organization rather than one in which the believers who attended were involved.

In the Anglican Church, intentions to reform anything sensory and symbolic initially appeared to have greater success. The High Church Movement derived its arguments from the Tractarians and, in particular with regard to Catholic piety, was overwhelmed by 'a vision of Christianity as a ministry of symbols and its channels of grace' as well as by the unassailable foundation of the church's structure on historical fact and the latter's unbroken tradition, as Gladstone put it while in Naples in 1832. Historical research thus attempted to reactivate liturgical forms of early Christianity and the Middle Ages or the Eastern Church. Studying the history of the church and the liturgy became a theological act in itself. In around 1850, candlesticks and crucifixes reappeared on many altars. The clergy began celebrating mass in magnificent vestments again. However, here, too, historicization turned out to have its own dynamics, which were difficult to control. The tangible Christian traditions were by no means the only model when it came to the symbolism employed in the liturgy and the paraments; in addition, anything that could be learnt about pre-Christian Celtic traditions also often served as an inspiration. All of this ritualism was controversial and by no means influenced all public and organized Anglican piety. The opponents within the hierarchy and in politics were not only afraid of too great a proximity to Rome. Gladstone suspected that ritualism was a phenomenon of a general Victorian materialistic disposition: 'the preference of the rich for ornate churches and clergymen may represent not the spiritual growth but the materializing tendencies of the age'. Cultural criticism had become a double-edged sword. In 1872 the Privy Council banned a number of things from Anglican services: choir dress, the host, the mass celebrated facing the east and Communion under both kinds.[78]

This was a standardization of piety which was directed against the autonomy of local communities and in this respect differed little from what was happening in the Catholic Church. Changes in the church service occurred slowly, and none of the liturgical reforms of that century introduced a service that was one of the congregation. The discussion on how to improve public worship turned out to be a 'discourse on normalization' that continued to be part of the standardization of pious practices that was carried out by the official church beyond the local level. This particularly affected those forms of piety which had traditionally particularly involved the laity and local communities, as has been highlighted above for pilgrimages. At the beginning of the nineteenth century, dramatic presentations of salvation history in 'tableux vivants' and figures arranged to form particular scenes were still a characteristic of Corpus Christi processions, and these scenes were influenced by the conditions in the individual parishes. By the middle of the century, however, the procession had changed to one in which those in positions of social power presented themselves together with the Blessed Sacrament: the local elites, the military and then a populace that no longer participated in the procession as part of the religious *mise en scène*, but instead was ordered according to a bourgeois class system influenced by Christianity in which society was made up of men, women and specific age and professional groups. General and non-local aspects also prevailed over local elements in the brotherhoods and sodalities. Until the end of the eighteenth century, both had been establishments in which lay involvement had become institutionalized as the organization of special, pious practices, be they individual pilgrimages or the veneration of individual saints or the Sacred Heart. In this context, close local and regional networks of reciprocity had developed for the commemoration of the dead. In Germany's Catholic dioceses, the first half of the nineteenth century was characterized by attempts to create different unified brotherhoods, which no longer represented the local population but a 'general' form of social order: grammar schools, young, unmarried women, young men, married men, or those who were attracted by the global cult of the Virgin Mary or the devotion to the Sacred Heart. Piety thus became a collective concept, not just in an abstract sense but also in the way it was experienced socially.[79]

This collective aspect gradually gained a more defined content.[80] Religiosity was increasingly often referred to as a 'feeling' which, particularly among Protestants, only rarely related to a personal god but rather to the abstract notions of the infinite or the sublime. It could be observed in the beauty of nature and especially through an awareness of the infinity of the universe. Schleiermacher had described religion as a 'feeling and taste for the infinite' and thus had provided, very early on, a description of the kind of piety that allowed educated individuals to accommodate their religious sense within a world view that was increasingly influenced by scientific research.[81] There was only a small, hidden space left in this discourse for a god who worked miracles and intervened in this world through providence. This also became evident in the Catholic Church when church services were emphatically defended as 'adoration' of a personally present deity. Olympe Philipe Gerbert published a treatise in 1829 that laid out a patriarchal model, according to which the creature owes gratitude to its creator. He expressly opposed the idea of a mechanical universe, in which only an abstract divine force operated, because this took away the possibility of direct communication with an interlocutor who was actually present, through which mankind obtained salvation for their souls; the central event of a church service and the most important sacrament was, thus, the Eucharist.

This was a significant theological difference from the Protestant position, but it had no effect on the concept of piety. Enthusiasm is not the normal state of the human mind, John Henry Newman told F. W. Faber, the founder of the Catholic Brompton Oratory, who in an essay in 1854 called for more enthusiasm from the Catholics of England instead of the lukewarm kind of Christianity that hindered the 'progress of spiritual life'.[82] Newman's position was close to that of the Tractarians, who, despite their preference for symbols and rituals, emphasized 'soberness' as one of the essential characteristics of correctly worshipping God.[83] Underlying terms such as this was a debate about the relationship between the individual's experience of God and public, liturgic worship of God, which had been a feature of European Christianity in all its confessional varieties since Early Modern times and which gave careful consideration to the relationship between church services and religious feeling on another level. In the Anglican Church, those who believed that the function of church services was to channel the spontaneous inner feelings of the faithful and to control them had prevailed in the Book of Common Prayer of 1639. The individual soul was overwhelmed with the task of being good and pious, the defenders of the Book of Common Prayer wrote, which was why the book expressly banned individual prayer, allowing only prescribed and pre-formulated ones. The Puritans' rejection of this idea is well known, but only the success of Methodism built up enough pressure for the Anglican Church to give up insisting on the binding nature of the Book of Common Prayer in 1844 and to allow free prayer.[84]

**Perceiving the next world**

However, the fundamental position that religious excitement and rapture represented dangerous threats to the Christian faith and that religious feeling or an encounter with God should, at best, occur in the context of church ceremonies was not abandoned, because it was shared by all forms of institutional, church-based Christianity. In a Catholic context, this position had underlain the way in which Cardinal Bossuet had dealt with Quietism. Gerbert, who emphasized the personal presence of God in church services, also stressed that there was no individual inner union with God and that this was the purpose of Communion in a Catholic context. He was not alone in holding this view. Until well beyond the middle of the century, the discourse of French prayer books was dominated by anti-spiritualistic reflection on the correct form of piety. According to this discourse, piety should not lead individuals to neglect their professional duties. Protestant abhorrence of Pietistic rapture, trance-like experiences of religious awakening and free prayer was similar. In his *System of the Christian Certainty*, the Erlangen theologian H. R. von Frank tried to prove as late as 1884 that the mystical experience of awakening was not the result of an interaction with God, but rather represented an activation of what had previously been implanted in the believing individual through communal actions.[85]

According to this view, the process developed from the outside in. Christian souls who attempted to influence their emotional states themselves were regarded as a threat to church institutions. The social system insisted on only communicating with the psyche in a very specific way, influencing the psyche's state and experiences through particular rituals and texts. The institutions of European Christianity refused to see themselves as the result of individual mental experiences. It was important that the psyche should *not* become the dominant medium of the social form of religion. Accordingly, the relationship between the faithful and transcendence should be limited to 'adoration' or 'trembling' in the face of eternity, and it should be characterized more by observation than communication.

By erecting these barriers, Christian institutions created the need for a kind of religiosity in which religion, conversely, could be put to use as a medium of mental processes and in which direct contact with transcendence could be established. The framework for this was provided by a combination of only partly Christianized popular beliefs, developments in theological discourse and the scientific search for a connection between the senses and the soul, as exemplified by mesmerism and spiritualism. These elements overlapped, stabilizing and reinforcing each other.

In the first half of the nineteenth century, the clergy of all confessions and societies had to deal with the lively popular belief in ghosts and witches. Wise men with their special knowledge of medicine and healing as well as their ability to foresee the future were a problem for the local clergy, and church and state authorities had to face the appearance of prophets, who endowed their millenarian messages with charismatic credibility by claiming to receive them directly from the powers of the next world. Only a minority followed these charismatics, but the idea that unbaptized or unredeemed souls of the dead would appear as spirits in this world was a widely held belief of everyday Christianity up to the middle of the nineteenth century. Its way of coping with the human condition involved very tangible forms of religion, and thus transcendence made itself felt in this world in a varied range of ways. The only difference between Protestants and Catholics in this regard appeared to be that the former no longer believed in the power of the church's sacramentals, while Catholics continued to be convinced of the power of benedictions, exorcisms and prayers to ward off threats. Some hung up bulls' hearts in their fireplaces as protection against evil spirits entering, while others sought out the priest with requests to perform exorcisms to counter a persistent illness or to help establish contact with the spirits of the dead in order to find buried treasure.[86]

Theologically, things were more complicated. Even after the Bayerische Hexenkrieg (Bavarian Witch War) of the 1780s, the Catholic view was that a physical devil and his demons existed and were at work in the world and that poor souls who had not yet been definitely received into heaven or banished to hell went to purgatory, from where they were still able to access the world of the living. Since the Enlightenment, Protestant theologians had shown greater doubts as to the physical existence of the devil than regarding the personal nature of God, and they struggled to think of transcendence as having a particular topology. However, it was this point that appears to have made them susceptible to a neo-Platonic–gnostic discourse regarding the afterlife that had been made popular by Swedenborg since the middle of the century. One of this discourse's basic assumptions was that people in this world could experience the next world. These fantastical ideas received higher philosophical endorsement when Kant, in his *Dreams of a Spirit-Seer*, argued that there were different worlds that could be accessed through different modes of experience and perception. Thus, humans were part of an otherworldly spirit realm, even while they were still in this world. In his *Universal Natural History and Theory of the Heavens*, published in 1755, Kant wrote about the migration of the soul and took a scientific approach to the topography of the spirit world by suggesting that the planets might serve as resting places for souls on their journey. This created an image of the afterlife which could be used as a basis for further ideas. It attracted much scientific and theological imagination, and well-known Awakened Protestants such as Johan Caspar Lavater and Heinrich Jung-Stilling engaged with it extensively. In around 1800 it had been developed and popularized to such an extent that it could not only be found in treatises and cheaply available religious literature but had also made its way into Protestant collections of sermons.[87]

These shifts in theological imagination are linked to the beginnings of mesmerism because Mesmer developed his ideas and practice on account of the dispute with the exorcist Gassner, who attempted to drive the devil out literally by using the established methods of the Catholic Church. In 1784, the Puységur brothers discovered artificial somnambulism, thus providing a way of turning people who had enhanced cognitive abilities into mediums and, through them, of contacting the world which Kant had described in such memorable ways. In 1822, Dietrich Georg Kieser described the nerves as the basis of sensory perception and identified a ganglion that was responsible for the 'universal sense' and made somnambulant clairvoyance possible.

While doctors thus moved somnambulant clairvoyance out of a theological context, although also citing visions and apparitions as confirmation of their theories, theologians of all confessions made use of mesmerism as a scientific justification of miracles, private revelations and mystical experience of God. From 1854 onwards, Rome felt the need to draw a dividing line between itself and mesmerism in a number of documents. Mesmerist hypnosis was an admissible way of gaining scientific knowledge, but the subtle materiality of the spirits was rejected, and reservations were voiced about the 'technological' side of mesmerism because only God was considered capable of moving the spirits of the afterlife. Moral concerns were also raised about men inducing a state of unconsciousness and memory loss in women. We know that the clergy who acted as confessors and spiritual directors to the many female visionaries in the first half of the nineteenth century had fewer reservations. They were often very well acquainted with mesmerism and believed themselves capable of inducing visions in their charges at appointed times – in many cases, Friday was the preferred day of the week for this.[88] It was not only the practices that merged; there were also structural analogies in the framework of different media that organized the discourse and simultaneously framed and produced the phenomena. The many instances of stigmata that occurred from the 1830s onwards from Italy to France meant that the body became the primary guarantee that authentic contact with the afterlife had occurred, becoming more important in this function than as a medium of communication. The rigidity of the somnambulant medium's body in trance functioned in much the same way. Moreover, in both cases, contact with the afterlife became increasingly influenced by technology, due to these phenomena occurring at a time when the socially relevant media were changing at an increasingly fast pace. Whether it was exorcism, a pre-arranged vision, somnambulant hypnosis or spiritualist table-turning – which became a widespread practice in the middle classes across confessions after the middle of the century – all of these were processes in which the afterlife could be contacted in an active and selective way with the help of mediums. The transmission of this communication became technological. The psychograph was invented and recorded what somnambulant mediums perceived and learnt in the other world, and spiritualist table-turning involved a material aspect in that it made use of furniture in order to communicate with the spirit world. The 'higher guidance' to which the Upper Bavarian Redemptorists and other high-ranking men in the church supposedly submitted from 1848 onwards also communicated by means of a tangible, material medium. The seer Louise Beck had received stigmata in 1847 and had undergone several exorcisms before she became the most important medium of this male network. She wrote down the messages from the blessed spirit to whose leadership one had submitted and passed them on to her spiritual director. Those who desired guidance wrote to Beck, addressing their letters to the 'mother'. Beck produced the answers at night, writing while in an ecstatic state, without light, and following instructions from the Virgin Mary. The original request and the answer were sealed and returned to the sender.[89]

The degree to which the media framework of these spiritualist relationships with the afterlife was technological and functional was matched by the way in which the social context of these relationships was emotionally charged. It was determined by the relationship between genders, by family situations and by the dynamics of family relationships. Desire, emotions and interests often overlapped, potentially creating a psychologically dangerous mix. This applied both to the social biographies of the mediums as well as to the context in which their help was sought. Most Catholic seers – both those who experienced stigmata and those who did not, from Mörl in South Tyrol to Karoline Becker in Württemberg to Beck – have been shown to have had tense family relationships, a difficult marriage or a failed romantic relationship. The repeated appearance of the spirit of a dead priest in Krenzingen in the Black Forest was related to a complicated inheritance dispute in a particular village, in which the spirits involved themselves considerably. Mesmerism, on the other hand, was characterized by a desire to contact close relatives and deceased and beloved spouses. Christoph Martin Wieland reported how he experienced his wife's immediate presence for months after her death, with his rationalist refusal to believe in ghosts almost driving him mad. The reports from spiritualist meetings, which often brought together family members and relatives, also show that sexual taboos and emotional tensions were the implicit – or frequently articulated – topic of such family *séances*.

Piety is a sphere of meaning that has its own laws, but it requires media through which it can gain social form. For this reason, the relationship between internal and external processes during the states of ecstasy and trance that occurred during Methodist field preaching, in houses of prayer and during the penitentiary sermons of the Catholic clergy engaged in popular mission cannot be determined. However, with regard to visionary religion, the situation is clear. Here religion became a means of using the experience of communicating with the afterlife in order to develop the psyche within the emotional and social relations of civil society.

## Women in a male religion

Christianity was male. Its clergy and preachers, with rare exceptions in some denominations, were male, both in the Catholic and in the Protestant churches. Female spirituality was found in Pietistic prayer circles or was locked away behind the walls of nunneries. It was the father of the family who was responsible for ensuring that the church norms were implemented in society because he had the authority to rule over his wife, children and other members of the extended household, including servants (the 'whole house' or Ganzes Haus\*, as the concept has been termed by Otto Brunner). This was specified not just by church orders but also in secular police laws up until the end of the eighteenth century. The Pauline injunction that women should remain silent in the churches was taken seriously in all confessions and denominations, and it made little difference that Luther's outline of estates assigned women the roles of mother and educator – important with regard to a child's socialization, religious and otherwise – and that women were members of Pietistic prayer circles which allowed them to experience and communicate their spirituality. The processes of mobilization and differentiation associated with the capitalist and market-driven process of industrialization presented a challenge as they opened up new areas and possibilities of female social participation and, in almost all classes, multiplied the different possible ways of life. The role of women as well as the relationship between the sexes had to be renegotiated and redefined.

## The order of the sexes

This development concerned the basic configuration of social codes according to which the structures of European societies had reproduced themselves since the end of the eighteenth century. The family was considered to be the nucleus of social order because it was the only place in which legitimate relations between the sexes could occur. For this reason, even utopians like Charles Fourier took a reorganization of the relationship between the sexes as the starting point for their social models of the future. However, the family was also considered to be a model for political and social order in cases in which political power was autocratically based and supposed to act with patriarchal concern and where the idea of what was social consisted in emotional, hierarchically structured communal relationships. In the first half of the nineteenth century, there was often little difference in liberal or Catholic conservative terminology used to describe society. In his *Elements of the Philosophy of Right*, Hegel in 1820 described society, which was separate from the state, as a 'system of wants', and he wrote a section on the family because he considered it to be the basic form of social inclusion. In the family, Hegel wrote, the individual was not a person, but a member. Families appeared to be individual and particular elements when compared to society in general, which was a moral order in which an individual's freedoms were realized, but in actual fact, because morality as a bond first emerged in the family, membership of a family was no barrier to a person's entry into general civil society as a 'totality of needs and a mixture of necessity and caprice'. Instead it was its prerequisite.[90]

The dialectical loops show the tensions that had to be overcome at this point and the pressure civil society placed on the family as the primary level of sociation because it was required simultaneously to be the model for and counterpart of sociation. Men passed this pressure on to women, and religion was a decisive aspect of this. It played no role in Hegel's argument, because he only focused on it as a principle of 'subjective freedom', but this was different in political liberalism. Karl Theodor Wecker described the Christian family as a basic element of society and of a 'worthy state life'. A prerequisite for this was that women should be conscious of their particular religiousness because this secured their subordination as determined by God through natural differences. The Catholic view was even clearer: a Christian wife, and woman in general, was not inferior to the man in dignity, but was subordinate to him through the order of creation and the way in which nature had arranged the sexes. For this reason, Holy Scripture insisted in particular on the 'chastity, humility, modesty and piety of women'. From an ecclesiastical point of view, female piety was also of particular importance because it was a decisive prerequisite for the religious influence on children and their upbringing.[91]

Religiosity became the strongly dominant characteristic of a form of femininity which, since the 1780s, had been constructed in a wide range of discourses, encompassing medicine, social theory, literary texts, theology and practical religious texts. The observations of the clergy seemed to confirm this 'feminization of religion'. Woman had a heart that was receptive to all things sacred, a printed sermon of 1843 claimed. This was, it said, why women were the ones who listened most attentively to spiritual instruction, who attended confession the most frequently and 'entirely voluntarily', and who knelt before the altar the most devoutly.

If women had apparently found a new place in a male religion, the question arises as to where the institutional spaces in which this was possible occurred. The second point of interest is the discourse framing and shaping this change in the modes of inclusion for half the Christian population of Europe. Third, it should already be apparent that this had an effect on the social and Christian construction of femininity itself. We will be considering these changes from the point of view of religion.

**Charity, philanthropy and missionary work**

The entry for 'family' in the *Kirchenlexikon* edited by Heinrich J. Wetzer and Benedikt Welte stated in 1852 that the Catholic Church had prevented women from taking any ecclesiastical office and, in particular, from any kind of teaching authority, despite their special piety because this would not conform to their feminine nature.[92] The entry represented a Catholic point of view but the basic principle was shared by all European confessions and churches. For this reason, religion became more feminine in a very particular way which was not characterized as much by confessional or theological differences as it was by the dynamics of social processes of differentiation. This applied to the social field of religion itself, with new areas developing in which women could be active. However, it also applied to the social environment of religion, in which problems resulting from modernization processes appeared as functional fields of reference to which religion was a reaction. Commitment in such socially problematic fields could be interpreted as pleasing to God, while also clearly illustrating the social function of religion more generally. Capitalist industrialization and the associated migratory and liberating processes created urgent problems of inclusion that had not previously occurred in this particular and dramatic way. Where they had occurred, family and community structure had been sufficient to counter them and prevent them from becoming a more widespread mass phenomenon. Now, however, a new proletarianized unpropertied group with uncertain employment prospects had developed in the towns and the new industrial settlements, which in England at least were growing quickly. There was as yet no system of insurance that could help to lessen the risks that life posed to such groups, such as illness and the loss of income. In addition to this, craftsmen were also significantly affected by the economic changes, and the introduction of new technology such as mechanized looms presented a threat to those who worked in proto-industrial fields.[93] Religious charity and philanthropic efforts could now be directed at these groups, not only to support and help them, for example, in the case of illness, but also in order to 'educate' them and to teach them the skills, virtues and behaviour necessary for inclusion in a civil capitalist society. Mastering basic techniques such as reading, writing and arithmetic was increasingly becoming a minimum requirement for life in a society that reproduced itself through industry, urbanization and mass media. This meant that the political and social elites engaged in and encouraged the extension of elementary schooling, even if they were concerned about the socially destabilizing effects that educating the lower classes might have.[94]

It was well into the second half of the century before state authorities in Europe found themselves capable of shaping this structural and calamitous reorganization of

European societies at an institutional level in anything approaching an appropriate way. Before this, the social system was concerned with securing the dominion of those who owned property and it did not have sufficient resources to react to the structural reorganization in anything other than a defensive way, with liberalism and the *laissez faire* approach in political discourse doing no more than providing justification for an overly great structural strain on society. The focus on those with property is illustrated by protective tariffs and by the difficult debates on electoral and parliamentary reform in England that was to give greater consideration to the working classes. The problem of resources is highlighted by Guizot's law of 1832, which required all municipalities in France to set up primary schools and carry the cost of these.

Within religion as a social system, institutional dynamics were determined by other internal factors. Initially, these were the same in all confessions, as had become clear with the decline in ties to the official church. The fact alone that men of all classes increasingly stayed away from forms of worship and piety that took place within the church ensured that European Christianity became more feminine. The data available show that this applied both to Protestant and Catholic churches. It is evident everywhere that the ideas of sinfulness and dependence on grace that are central to the Christian economy of salvation were increasingly incompatible with male ideals of moral autonomy and personal responsibility.[95]

New places for women emerged where religious institutions reacted to changing patterns of differentiation and communication. They first developed where the social form of religion in a society of free and equal citizens emphasized organization and social movement, thus combining religious communication with ideas such as voluntariness and commitment as a way of recording membership. A second factor was the perception that religion now existed in a secular and largely atheized world, with catechesis and missionary work being the appropriate ways of approaching this world. Third, new opportunities emerged for women wherever pent-up religious energy was released through different media and communication, and somnambulist, spiritualist mediums and visionaries with stigmata appeared, who established contact with transcendence outside the institutional framework of the church.

The theological and symbolic traditions that helped to shape these possibilities differed to some extent amongst the confessions. Celibacy and works righteousness no longer held great importance in Protestantism, and so processes of feminization were usually driven by married women who were active in organizations such as charities, missionary societies and initiatives aimed at amelioration, and in Sunday-school teaching. The concept of 'philanthropy' that was strongly influenced by the traditions of the Enlightenment played a significant role in the way in which these women shaped religious life in British society outside the Anglican Church. Deaconesses who engaged in charity work and education only became more widespread in European Protestantism in the second half of the century. The spiritual equality and equal abilities of the sexes in Anabaptist traditions and Pietistic practices provided women in socially active Protestant movements with new possibilities of religious and organizational involvement. In a Catholic context, catechesis and missionary work had been carried out by religious orders until the end of the eighteenth century. Franciscan orders had been strongly involved in the care of the poor and the sick, whereas Jesuits and Dominicans had been active in missionary work and in the education of middle- and upper-class offspring. The education of upper-class girls had been in the hands of the congregations and third orders, such as the Congrégation de Notre Dame, the Congregation of Jesus (or English Ladies) and the Ursulines, since the seventeenth century. The male hierarchy of the church was not prepared to allow these women to take religious vows while living a life in the world, as the Jesuits had been permitted to do, and the Ursulines and the Congrégation de Notre Dame chose to become an organized order in the second half of the eighteenth century, while the Congregation of Jesus had been dissolved.[96]

The extent to which feminized religious spheres developed and the extent to which they were utilized clearly did not depend on confession but on the state and dynamics of social change. The degree to which society provided opportunities to act in a religious way and to shape one's life accordingly differed greatly. A comparison between France, England and Germany shows this very clearly.

In France, some seventy congregations for women were founded between 1800 and 1820, followed by sixty per decade up until 1870.[97] Men had comparatively little interest in this life determined and suffused by religion. Only seventy-four male congregations were founded by 1860. The communities were not usually very large but, because they increased significantly, there were more than 130,000 women living and working together in such groups by the end of the 1870s, while the number of men living a monastic life or a celibate life as part of a congregation was only around 30,000. Women not only joined congregations in large numbers, but they were also significantly involved in founding them. Roughly half of the congregations were founded on the initiative of women; a further 20 per cent were founded jointly by women and men, and only in 30 per cent of the cases were congregations founded by men alone. It was mainly middle-class women and the nobility who expressed their religious attitude and charity through such initiatives, although the nobility's interest diminished noticeably over the course of the century, while the commitment of economically active citizens increased. In every sixth case, individuals from a craftsmanship milieu were involved in starting a foundation. The church's role in proliferating congregations was minor compared to that of private individuals. One in five congregations was created by separating from another organization or by institutional branches being created. Founding a congregation always involved a considerable financial commitment that was seen as setting a good example for others. Work in charitable women's associations was supported by a steady stream of endowments and bequests, which continued to grow towards the middle of the century. By 1830, members of religious orders had received around 1.4 million francs and, in the first decade after 1850, 4.3 million francs were being donated annually. Around the middle of the century, the total wealth held by religious orders was equal to that of all the parish maintenance funds in the country. Most congregations were active in the towns and only one-third worked in smaller localities or in the countryside, but four out of ten worked in towns with over 5,000 inhabitants.

This was probably part of the reason why these communities were attractive to women who entered such a congregation and decided to take their vows after completing a novitiate. Only one-third of novices came from towns; the majority came from farms or were the daughters of craftsmen or small traders in rural France. Daughters of workers and day labourers were less inclined to choose this way of life, and it held no attraction at all for young women from aristocratic families, while for those from the rural middle and upper classes entering a congregation freed them from the requirement of leading a life that involved marriage and family and provided a way out of the context they had grown up in, permanently leaving behind their family environment. One of the rules of the congregations was that the sisters should never be assigned any work in the places from which they came.

Congregations allowed women to develop a working career. Only one in ten of the communities required its members to lead a contemplative life. In the other religious communities, women worked as nurses for the sick and elderly or, in the majority of cases, as teachers in municipal elementary schools. As a result, the French elementary education system was largely in the hands of the congregations right up to the time of the Third Republic. In 1850, they operated 10,000 schools, in which 680,000 children were taught the catechism and reading, writing and arithmetic. In the diocese of Lyon, two-thirds of all schoolchildren were taught by sisters from congregations. The congregations were particularly committed to teaching the catechism and to the literacy of girls. As early as 1850, the proportion of girls in their schools was around 45 per cent, and it increased even further in the following two decades. In the Loire department, nine out of ten girls who attended school were taught by teaching sisters. The Sisters of St Joseph resolved to educate 'strong Christian women' who were energetic, pious and ready to live an active Christian life. Lay people and male church officials thus regarded the congregations' sisters as carrying out missionary work because they were preparing women to participate, as wives and mothers, in the re-Christianization of the country, thrown into sin by the Revolution. In addition, their contribution to civilizing the proletarianized lower classes through their work in elementary schools was repeatedly acknowledged.

The women in the congregations thus had an important role in reorganizing and modernizing French society. This filled them with pride and self-confidence, which was deliberately encouraged by the training they received in their communities and which they passed on to others. When entering a community they had to commit themselves to unconditional obedience and submission to the hierarchy of a usually strictly managed, centralized organization, but as the sisters lived in small communities of up to ten women, their daily lives also allowed them a degree of freedom. It is difficult to judge how extensive this was, as the entire programme of training and the prescribed behaviour in the congregations was focused on internalizing discipline, duty and constantly fighting one's own internal 'damaging proclivities'. Therefore, professional activity during the day was framed by prayer, church services and exacting self-examination. The veneration of Mary played an important role in the congregations, in many cases already indicated by the congregation's name. While congregations did not allow women to live a free and independent life, they did enable them to find an independent place in the public sphere through their professional work. As late as 1870, a male member of the Old Catholic Church remarked on the motives of women founding and entering congregations, saying it showed a desire to attain blessedness not in the generally accepted way but by being different and having 'one's own dress, own rules, own occupation'. He thus suspected that, in addition to inclination and true vocation, individual motives included fashion and imitation, religious eccentricity and pride, and, generally, 'subjectivism'. Religion appears to have become an area in which individualization occurred and which allowed women to be included outside the context of marriage, the household and children. Most women did not consider the vows they took to be restrictive. Unlike in male communities, only one in five women left their community again, whereas in some male communities more than 50 per cent of members left, leading to the validity of entrance vows being limited to ten years in an attempt to halt this development.[98]

In public discourse, church authorities could claim that the numbers of women attracted by this combination of the active and the contemplative life indicated a revival of religion. In actual fact, however, this feminization of religion was a social phenomenon, as a look at other Catholic regions in Europe shows. The extent and strength of the congregations clearly depended on the degree of social change and not on how strongly Catholic a region was. Considering only the Marian congregations, 269 such associations were founded in France in the course of the nineteenth century, but in Italy, including the Habsburg territory, the number was fifty-eight and in Spain only forty-six. In Germany, twenty communities were founded. This picture does not change much, even if non-Marian congregations are taken into account. In Prussia, which included the Catholic Rhineland, twenty-three new congregations were founded between 1803 and the beginning of the German Empire. These had 281 houses, with around 2,500 sisters, resulting in a ratio in 1850 of just under five sisters per 1,000 inhabitants. In France, this had been reached in 1830 and, in 1861, the ratio was eleven sisters to every 1,000 inhabitants, the same as in Belgium. In Italy, on the other hand, there were only about four sisters for every 1,000 inhabitants as late as 1880. In Bavaria, around the middle of the century, such public activities of women still clashed with the traditional female role to such an extent that upper-class women in Munich asked their husbands for permission to engage in charitable work in public and preferred to carry it out away from the public eye rather than in the context of a society.[99]

In European Protestantism, the feminization of religion, supported by charitable, missionary and civilizing work, manifested itself differently. The Reformation had already done away with the idea that virginity had a particular value in salvational terms and had rejected monasticism. However, missionary, Bible, improvement and charitable associations provided a functional equivalent. They had developed in large numbers since the end of the eighteenth century, and became an area in which women could be active. As early as the first half of the century, 15–30 per cent of the membership of these societies was female and, after the middle of the century, this was often double that proportion. Societies and associations which specifically addressed women and their concerns, such as the Institution for the Employment of Needle Women, had an even higher proportion of female members. This was also the case, as a rule, in associations in which women were amongst the board members or which had been founded and were led by women. Up until the 1840s, there were only around two handfuls of societies of this kind and, like the Institution for Nursing Sisters founded in the 1840s, they focused on the particular situation of women. Women not only took on active roles in voluntary organizations, they also supported them financially through regular donations and endowments. The sums involved were usually a little smaller than those given by men, but the percentage of women amongst the donors roughly corresponded to their proportion of the membership overall.[100]

The English Woman's Journal noted in 1859 that charity was a field in which the 'unemployed energies of women' could be put to productive use,[101] and even the women actively involved, like Hannah More or Millicent Fawcett, were convinced that English society needed typical female characteristics such as morality, self-denial and compassion in order to recover. Women should remain women while engaging in these activities.

Nevertheless, the traditional role of women was also changing in this area through new occupations and tasks. Women proved themselves to be imaginative and skilled in charity events. They were appreciated for the care which they took as board members in managing the finances and, in many societies, women turned out to be particularly good at collecting donations and selling bibles and religious tracts. Women were particularly active and successful in visiting the homes of the poor. The Methodists had developed this combination of missionary work and interactive civilizing, and many charitable societies developed with the purpose not only of helping the poor and the sick through direct contact but also of teaching them how to lead a better life and enable them to help themselves. No effort was spared in this work. The London City Mission alone organized two million such visits in 1870 and had a budget of at least £20,000. In many societies, it became clear that women were more willing than men to take on the task of carrying out such home visits, and they did so with the intention of putting the households of the poor in order. From the middle of the century, the experiences gained through such home visits were collected in handbooks and manuals that were known as Ladies' Companions and which, from the point of view of liberal individualism, described a society deeply divided by class. Memoirs also show that women experienced the encounter with suffering and misery as a deeply religious experience. Mrs Gibson, a Methodist from Newcastle, wrote in 1837 that, for her, charity was a form of *imitatio Christi*, suffering with Christ, as He had suffered for mankind. Other women had awakened experiences on such occasions, which freed them from fears regarding religion and sin.[102]

It has been shown in the section on piety above that a system of societies with similar aims also developed in Protestant Germany, albeit slightly later and in a less intensive way. Women do not seem to have played a significant role in this. Initiatives such as the Frauen-Verein zum Wohle des Vaterlandes (Women's Society for the Good of the Fatherland), founded by Princess Marianne of Prussia in 1830 and aimed at alleviating the hardship caused by the wars against France, were the exception. Tentative attempts in the *Landeskirchen* to institutionalize the welfare work done by the church, with missionary and charitable duties, only emerged in the second half of the 1830s and were generally initiated by men.[103] Thus, Protestantism showed almost more clearly than Catholicism that the feminization of religion, which would allow religious motives to be combined with new professional roles and ways of life through missionary, charitable and civilizatory work, continued to be dependent on the dynamics of social modernization.

## Expropriated spirituality

It was for this reason that the traditions of spiritual equality and equal rights in the Protestant denominations and in Pietistic meetings could spread to new social spaces in England as early as the eighteenth century, with religion becoming a means of self-representation and public activity for women. The ecstatic piety of the Methodists clearly held particular attraction for women from the beginning, and Wesley ensured that this was taken into account in the services and in the organization of the circuits by delegating tasks. Wesley had circuits set up specifically for women. Overall, it is likely that more women than men gathered for prayers, sermons and spiritual exchange in the community halls. However, this changed at the beginning of the nineteenth century the more the Methodist movement began to turn into an organization. In 1802, the Methodists forbade preaching by women, and ordination was now entirely out of the question, a step only the Quakers had taken. Even in German Protestantism, the ordination of women was a strongly internalized taboo, and neither the Awakening movement nor the Friends of the Light or the German Catholics allowed women to become pastors, despite the dynamics of these reform movements having depended considerably on women from middle-class society. Women were allowed to preach in these communities, they spoke during 'free prayer' in the Awakened circles, and they convened meetings at which Pastor Ronge preached. Women could only take an active role where Protestantism took the form of voluntary organization or social movement. The activity of women in this context then could lead to new roles, in which piety could become a means of inclusion in entirely different social fields. The churches which enjoyed state approval offered hardly any such spaces, and women thus played no special role in theological reflections on worship and piety.[104] In all of Protestantism, the traditional role of women as wives dominated ideas concerning female involvement. This was because the decline in the salvational significance of virginity and the ideal of the pastor's wife who assisted and was subordinate to her husband were too strong.

Precisely because men in Christian Europe had doggedly held on to the right to shape communication with transcendence through the sacraments, they had to accept that there was a stream of mystical religiosity in which spontaneous and instant contact with higher powers was initiated predominantly by women and which had become a firm part of European culture. Even the misogynistic panic during the period of the witch hunts in Europe had done nothing to change this, and thus the magical practices of popular religiosity were still a female sphere. There seems to have been a desire to intensify this spirituality that was part of everyday life, a desire that was boosted by the political and social changes. The millenarian prophets in France and England and visions of the Sacred Heart, the Virgin Mary or other saints, which had increased since the beginning of the nineteenth century, mainly involved women. Where, at the margins, the religious sphere of communication overlapped with speculative science and medicine, women, too, were the ones who predominantly took on the role of the medium who established contact with the afterlife and its spirits. This was the situation in mesmerism, although the theorists of animal magnetism had not intended it to be this way in their writings. In spiritualism, too, it was mostly women who made contact with the otherworld during *séances*.[105]

Women who had holy visions and who received knowledge from the afterlife that went beyond what could be known in this world were given a voice they were usually denied, both by male religion as well as by the social order of nineteenth-century Europe in general. This voice could be used in a number of ways: to free oneself from marginalized social situations, to deal with family tensions or to defend oneself against an oppressive husband – all this could be combined with visions, with hypnotic and spiritualistic trance states, and above all with talking about them. The precarious social background of this extraordinary spiritual situation was matched by the precarious position of female spirituality itself. It remained a form of spirituality that was surrounded, controlled, criticized, suspected, manipulated and, where possible, institutionally fenced in by men. Women continued to depend on men who appropriated their speech. Stigmatized visionaries were looked after by father confessors as spiritual directors or by Romantic writers such as Clemens Brentano with his interest in Katharina Emerick. Somnambulant women surrendered themselves to magnetizers who practised hypnosis, and spiritualist mediums spoke at *séances* that were mostly attended by men. All variants of this spirituality were also faced with allegations of fraud: the authorities took measures against female healers and prophets; somnambulant women had to live with the suspicion that they were being manipulated by magnetizers and sexually abused while in a state of trance. Since the eighteenth century, the Catholic hierarchy had had a standardized procedure with which private revelations were tested for authenticity in order to avoid fraud or the work of the devil. Devotion to the Sacred Heart and Marian piety, both strongly and successfully promoted by the church hierarchy and Rome, went some way towards taming this special female spirituality by bringing it into the church and by making it part of everyday life.

## Phantasms of order and sin

The upstanding rationalist and former diocesan administrator of Constance, Wessenberg, had a treatise printed in 1835, in which he dealt with rapture as a general social and philosophical phenomenon. He generally believed its causes to lie in the idea that all material things were diabolical in nature and in the desire to make all commitment to an idea dependent on whether 'we derive pleasure from it'. He identified rapture as a widespread phenomenon of the time, found throughout society, in philosophy, politics and literature. Frequently, he argued, 'sexual urges' were at play without this being noticed. 'Women's mysticism', in particular, contained a 'secret capitulation between sensual and spiritual infatuation'. Women were 'even more easily inflamed by the fire of rapture' than men because of their liveliness and the fire of emotions. Men also could be cured more easily of rapture by the basic facts of science, an active life and experience.[106] In making these claims, Wessenberg was contributing to a discourse that took place as the traditional roles of men and women were changing and which identified these changes as a threat to the male position, which thus also threatened social stability. This encouraged the fraught imaginings which had framed the feminization of European Christianity since the beginning of the nineteenth century and which had produced it as a reservoir of codes and motives.

There was little difference in this regard between those who took a Catholic and pro-Restoration position and the evangelical clergy of the Church of England. One need only think of the writings of Frederick William IV and his conservative, Romantic advisers, which have already been discussed, in order to understand that this was a phenomenon in European discourse that tells us about the attempts to find a pre-social model of order with which one might respond to the political and social changes that were occurring. The family provided this model, with the pattern of authority displayed in the family reflecting a divinely willed order and, for this reason, the family was considered the point at which this social order reproduced itself and could be socialized. The ideas that were developed in this context were fundamentalist in nature because they made use of the Bible as a source of unassailable norms for social and political order. They were the result of a deep-seated fear that had taken hold of Europe's ecclesiastical and secular elites since the French Revolution.

The basic elements of this thinking had been prepared long before and only required reactivating in the nineteenth century. The natural state was not characterized by equality but by subordination, Robert Filmer noted in his arguments with John Locke, referring to the order of the sexes and declaring female succession to be a compromise which was necessary only in order to preserve society from disintegration and civil war. In his 1708 commentary on the catechism, the Archbishop of Canterbury, William Wake, took the Fifth Commandment as a basis for arguing that the family, ruled by the authority of the father, was the foundation of society, which also served as a model for a well-ordered state. The many tracts and sermons of the social and political theorists liked to refer to 1 Peter 2 and 3, which urged Christians to be subservient and obedient to the king and all other authorities, at the same time stating: 'Wives, in the same way submit yourselves to your own husbands so that, if any of them do not believe the word, they may be won over without words by the behaviour of their wives.' The issue at hand was not just the justification of monarchy but the basis of social and political power more generally. In his treatise on *The Complete Duty of Man* (1763), Reverend Henry Venn stated that a woman was required to submit to the will of her husband, regardless of whether she was more intelligent or more capable than him. The most she was permitted to do was to offer him advice. Otherwise, intellectual superiority would have to be considered the basis for authority, 'a notion big with confusion and ruin to society'. This construct was obviously not that simple for a theology strongly influenced by the idea of the natural state. In his *Principles of Moral and Political Philosophy*, William Paley, the archdeacon of Carlisle, wrote in 1799 that nature had made men and women largely equal according to their abilities and dispositions; they also had equal rights, but, nevertheless, the clear injunction of Scripture that women were to be subservient to men had to be followed. In the nineteenth century, such statements were supplemented by pointing out that this did not mean men were obliged to treat their wives as slaves.[107]

It was therefore an urgent and long overdue correction when Albrecht von Haller took the elements of this argument after the Revolution and reassembled them in another way, placing them on a different social foundation to the state of nature. He referred to God's act of creation and man's subsequent duty to obey God. Everything else derived from this: men's patriarchal authority over women and the entire household, the monarchical order of the state, and also the Pope's authority over his church, which was described as an analogy to the family by von Haller. The great thinkers of the Restoration, such as de Bonald, used this to outline the idea of a social order, including a political system, that was not only based on multiple patriarchal hierarchies but in which social and power relations could be understood as emotional relationships. The ruler's paternal love on one side corresponded to obedience, trust and childlike affection on the other. The idea of the family, therefore, did not lose its importance. Anglicans also considered it to be a sacred institution, with marriage at its heart, and, for this reason, marriage could not be considered a mere contract, which it would also be possible to terminate. The divorce law introduced by the Revolution thus became anathema to Restoration theology. De Bonald stated explicitly that the purpose of marriage was not to serve the lust of men and women but 'the production of children' (*la production des enfants*).[108]

Women as the wives who owed obedience to their husbands and as mothers of their children thus formed the central point of Catholic-conservative as well as Protestant-evangelical social theories. These could not, of course, overlook the fact that the world was changing, that liberal democracy was an alternative to monarchy, that society was no longer organized according to class, and that the family was no longer appropriate as the only driver of social reproduction, socialization and inclusion, because the elementary knowledge and skills had already been moved out of the family and into schools. At an individual level the consequences of this process of dissociation were described by the Romantics as a fragmentation of life into opposing spheres of rationality; this life could no longer achieve any unity and certainly could not be led as a 'Christian' life.

As a result of these discrepancies, political and social theology created a negative utopia in which the family, and in particular women, were expected to act as saviours from the supposedly calamitous consequences of the modern age. This applied to the relationship between the sexes as well as to society as a whole. The home and a faithful wife became a place of retreat, in which the man could take refuge from the storms of life and his professional duties. Here, in this paradise, one could preserve one's own identity. As William Wilberforce wrote to his wife at home during the parliamentary debates on slavery, 'it will be a comfort to me to know that you all who are, as it were, on the top of the mountain, withdrawn from and above the storm, are thus interceding for me who am scuffling in the vale below'. He had already laid out this theory of compensation in great detail in 1797 and had concluded that it was the warmth and affection of a woman that made it possible for a man who was dishevelled and harried by 'worldly airs' to allow religious sentiment and feelings to fill his mind. In the way that women served their husbands, they should also serve society as Christian mothers, who actively participated in missionary work, charity and elementary schooling. In France, the focus was on civilizing the working class and re-Christianizing a society in which the Revolution had encouraged the spread of atheism. Missionary sermons and Sophie Barat's initiative concerning devotion to the Sacred Heart addressed the latter point. The former was the subject of Catholic politics in the Restoration period. In 1846, de Bonald wrote to the parliament in Paris that the zeal of the members of congregations was needed because a moral *classe industrielle* was required, which was achieved by the instruction that young members of the working class received from those young women of faith. The same arguments were used by British Evangelicals. British society, shaken in its Christian foundations through industrialization, required a revival of Christian morals to prevent it from descending into anomie, and women were pivotal in this task. This idea was not unrealistic, given the degree to which women were active in congregations, Sunday schools, and charitable and missionary groups. The evangelical salvation industry was conscious of its success around the middle of the century. The Wesleyan Christian Miscellany declared in 1867 that drunkenness had been successfully combated, moderation and restraint were now the rule in all classes, there was less blasphemy and lack of faith, and true piety amongst both rich and poor had reached hitherto unknown levels.[109]

The consequences of assigning this fundamentalist Christianization of society to women also had to be taken into consideration. In 1844, the *Church Magazine* of the Baptist New Connection posed the question of how women could be most usefully employed within the church without contravening the apostolic injunction of 1 Tim. 2.12, which stated that women were not allowed to teach or have authority over men. The *Free Church Magazine* suggested that women, instead, could teach at Sunday school, visit the sick – although only in an emergency – and meet for prayer in order to open up their souls before God together. Care should be taken at these meetings, however, that women did not become too proud or self-confident, and, as always when women were given tasks outside the home, only those women should be chosen who would not engage in such activity for the sake of publicity or to promote themselves but who carried out such duties in obedience and service to God. Pandora's box had been opened and fear of what might emerge spread. In 1854, the socialist Michelet wrote a pamphlet directed against the influence of priests on women as it allowed the church to extend its influence into marriages. The text suspected priests and women equally of carnal desires and susceptibility to seduction, but it also gave structural reasons for this, amongst which it referred to the fact that women were tied to the home because of their role in raising the family but did not receive sufficient recognition for their work there. Christianity had placed the greatest importance on the family but had not raised mothers to the same level. It was up to the modern man, who was concerned for a better future, to do this in order to remove women from the grasp of the church.[110] Even for a socialist, the anxious concerns about the relationship between the sexes and the role of women were inseparably linked with the religiosity of women.

The visual arts realized this early on. Angels became female towards the end of the eighteenth century, and the messengers of God and protectors of mankind received female faces and the bodies of beautiful women. This was possible because religiosity had been discovered as the essence of womanhood and femininity. The temptress and the woman susceptible to sin and the devil apparently disappeared from the archive of discursive symbols.[111]

Things were not that simple, however. Two factors ensured that, despite the close connection between female identity and piety, women's religiosity continued to be viewed with suspicion and served as a surface onto which male fears and insinuations could be projected. On the one hand, medicine and psychology, both of which were becoming more professionalized, were advancing controversial constructions of femininity (as well as masculinity) as an essentially physiological reality.[112] This is of interest in the context of our discussion in that it also included female religiosity. On the other hand, and connected to the last point, there was a theologically based discourse concerning the connection between eroticism and piety, which reflected on the 'secret capitulation between sensual and spiritual infatuation', as Wessenberg had phrased it.[113]

Personal accounts and other sources from all confessions show that religious constructions of gender had moved from being the subject of discourse to influencing the deeper levels of identity construction. In England, religion played a secondary role in men's obituaries, coming after their profession and any offices the deceased had held. Experiences of conversion occurred late in life, usually not until the person was on their deathbed. By contrast, religion was a decisive element in the construction of social and personal identity in women's obituaries. The memorial cards from Catholic towns in the first third of the nineteenth century show the same pattern. The letters of men such as the Protestant Wilhelm von Kügelgen refer to the contradictions they experienced between reason and faith and to the impossibility of ignoring the objections of reason against the demands of faith. Women, on the other hand, wrote letters and diaries in which they expressed great contrition at being incapable of feeling true love for God and in which they despaired at the challenges to their faith. Men also generally did not engage in contrite and repentant self-accusations during confession. Instead, they openly admitted their transgressions, describing them as part of everyday life, while women's confessions were characterized by shame at their own sinfulness, which often actually prevented confession. According to the confession manuals of experienced confessors, women's confessions were short. The records of the Vienna asylum show that, in the first half of the nineteenth century, women felt the pressure of confession and religious despair more strongly than men. This led to women falling into depression more frequently, whereas men were more often diagnosed as suffering from manic states.[114]

Protestant and Catholic social theology had laid out in sufficient detail that women's sociation occurred through their role as housewives. Social inclusion for women took place through marriage. This was no great problem for Protestantism, where the pastor's wife could serve as a model. From the 1820s onwards, a large number of biographical and autobiographical works were, in fact, published that featured them as loving wives, committed Christians and mothers who brought up their children as church-going Christians. The entire spiritual press in England was permeated by the ideal of housewives who brought up children, and, from the 1830s onwards, this picture of women was painted in ever finer detail in 'improving magazines', which were printed in increasingly large numbers and were often aimed directly at women. This was also reflected in literature. Novels, which became popular among middle- and upper-class women, usually had a stereotypical plot in which young women faced numerous temptations, then had an experience of conversion and finally married, giving their children a Christian upbringing and carrying out the arduous task of civilizing and missionizing their husbands. This supported the theologians' arguments that women needed religion so that they could fulfil their duties as wives and mothers and, above all, be subservient to men, as stipulated by Scripture.[115]

It is striking that physicality and sexuality are mostly absent from the way in which the role of women was coded. These aspects had been moved out of the Anglican discourse, and prostitutes became the negative counterpart to wives. Their numbers had been growing significantly since the 1830s and, as early as the 1840s, they had increasingly become the object of evangelical civilizatory missions and voluntary religion. A significant section of the salvation industry concentrated on prostitutes, who were considered a warning sign of the modernity that also threatened Christian society in other ways. Prostitutes had no religion; their means of social inclusion were the monetized desires of men as well as their own bodies. Their profession exemplified an entirely market-driven relationship between the sexes and social conditions.[116] The phantasmic and hysterical discourse on the destruction of English society through prostitution provided a negative foil for the idea of a Christian housewife, absolving those who participated in the discourse of any necessity to address issues relating to her.

The situation was more complicated for Catholics. Celibacy and female chastity had encouraged the idea that the body was an impediment on an individual's route to salvation. This extended to ideas on morality in marriage, and Catholicism could not provide a positive model for the middle-class housewife. The more extreme aspects of a negative female anthropology, which also provided theological arguments for doubts that women were actually human, had largely disappeared by the eighteenth century, but prayer books from this period still show that hostility to the body, characteristic of Jansenist rigorism, had become embedded deeply enough in Catholic thought that even marriage fell under the suspicion of sinfulness. A monastic life was definitely preferable to marriage. Penitentials let women know very clearly that their 'sex... is particularly attacked by the soul's enemy from hell'. The 'infernal murderer of souls' was particularly intent on making women the 'female slaves' of his kingdom. In the nineteenth century, Catholic moral theologians interpreted this threat as referring to the physical body. A woman could never protect the dignity of her sex of her own accord, as its 'femininity itself will corrupt it'. Women therefore needed religion, as a prayer book from 1835 advised, and a woman remained sinful unless she turned away from the world entirely.[117]

The arduous development of a positive professional and class ethic was required in order for a positive role for women to evolve. This ethic allowed the professional life of Christian men also to become Christianized; the worldly, non-religious activities of men could thus be considered as contributing to the achievement of salvation as long as these activities were carried out in the correct spirit. In this way, the duties of women as subservient, self-sacrificing wives and Christian mothers could be interpreted as a form of inner-worldly asceticism. Prayer books and moral-theological treatises from the first half of the nineteenth century lay out these duties of women in great detail. The veneration of the Virgin Mary, directed by the church hierarchy, provided an important framework within which these elements could be assembled to create a positive and vivid role model. As early as the beginning of the nineteenth century, dedicated pastoral clergymen were pointing out that Marian feast days provided frequent and fitting opportunities to remind mothers of their responsibility for ensuring their children had a Christian upbringing. Mary, of course, was not primarily associated with motherhood at that point. In the devotional literature of the time, she is presented as a benevolent, powerful intercessor, as the Queen of Heaven and as Our Lady of Sorrows, in this way participating directly in the vicarious suffering of her son. Even though she was 'the Mother of God', the focus was not on her as a woman and certainly not as a housewife. The numerous legends associated with her primarily presented her as working miracles and did not depict her as part of any social reality. It was not until the 1820s that prayer books appeared in which Mary's humility, her love and her godliness were initially praised as 'ideals of true femininity' before all the gender-related stereotypes that had emerged were then recited. Mary was to help women in conforming to these norms, and women praying to Mary were now no longer unworldly saints but instead virtuous and chaste wives and housewives. This reassessment was underlined through Mariology, according to which Mary was claimed to be a 'second Eve', who had broken the chains of original sin and thus had removed the stain Eve had placed on women.[118] In this way, Marian piety became a social space that attracted women and provided them with an archive of possible identities and patterns of behaviour which could combine piety, individuality and social inclusion. It was precisely through this reference to original sin, however, that Marian piety also perpetuated the general suspicion with which women, because of their particular piety, were treated in the religion of men.

Attempts had already been made in the first half of the eighteenth century to standardize the process of canonization, which was relevant for developments in the nineteenth century. A central question was how to distinguish imaginary obsession from actual holy presence, especially in the case of women, who were apparently more likely to be subject to demonic influence. The main arguments in the eighteenth century were made by Eusebius Amort and Benedict XIV (1740–58), and, in the nineteenth century, these arguments were combined with a medical discourse that, on the one hand, was concerned with religious mania and, on the other hand, sought to find a scientific explanation for animal magnetism. In both cases, scientific interest did not initially focus on differences between the sexes, but the majority of individuals who underwent somnambulant hypnosis were women. Moreover, below the surface, there were connections between the theory of animal magnetism and possession by the devil and exorcism, as Mesmer had developed his theory in connection with the dispute over Gassner's methods (a Bavarian exorcist and witch hunter).[119] Wilhelm Ideler gave a provisional summary of religious mania as part of an empirical examination of case histories in 1847, closely connecting religious melancholy with a religious sense of sin and guilt. In their systematic examination of 'religious mania', doctors and psychologists also identified similarities between states of illness induced by a strong love of God and by obsessional earthly love. Thus, the psychological dimension of the erotic undertones of religious rapture and a mystical love of God were also highlighted here. This could affect both sexes, but Ideler's selection of cases made it clear that it was mainly the female psyche that was affected by melancholy and rapture.[120]

Moral theology and medical psychology were very close in this regard. Prayer books for women described scruples as the most harmful poison to female piety. Conversely, moral theologians made extensive use of the rapid growth in medical knowledge – on the one hand, to refine the casuistry regarding possible transgressions against God's laws and the natural order that were available to confessors in their handbooks and, on the other hand, to draw a finer distinction between those transgressions that were due to physical defects or reactions that could not be controlled and those that were ascribed to human will or transcendent forces, be they God, the saints, the spirits of the deceased or the devil himself. The Trappist monk and doctor, Pierre Debreyne, was particularly active in contributing to this field. He published a number of moral theological tracts, including a *Moechealogie* in 1846, which dealt with transgressions against the Sixth Commandment. In 1842, his *Essai sur la Theologie Morale* appeared, which was reprinted several times.[121] Debreyne was as familiar with the writings of the Church Fathers as he was with the works of contemporary psychologists and doctors. In his *Essai* he urged the clergy to devote their time to studying the latest scientific and, in particular, medical findings, and suggested that this should be facilitated by a special *societé*.

The *Essai* was intended for the pastoral clergy. The first part explained the theory of the temperaments to the reader in great detail, and a second section dealt with sexual transgressions. The third part focused on the moral theological dimensions of childbirth, and the fourth was concerned with all supernatural phenomena, from animal magnetism to hallucinations, and the different kinds of penance that could keep sinners from transgressing.

Debreyne's confessional doctrine reproduced all the elements of the physiological characteristics of gender, at the relevant points drawing connections to the sinfulness both of men and of women. The section on male masturbation was followed by a detailed one on clitoral, vaginal and uterine masturbation and finally also on conjugal masturbation, with the sinfulness of each being evaluated. Debreyne thought that women were nervous and easily aroused, which was why they could be led astray particularly easily by the wrong kind of education or through novels: shameless women, both young and old, were particularly susceptible to the devil's visitations as incubus or succubus. Debreyne also discussed stigmata on the basis of known and unknown cases as a specifically female problem, and followed this by strongly impressing on his readers that fraudulent mysticism was a particularly serious mortal sin. In his moral assessments of transgressions, Debreyne always took into account the latest medical findings: in the section on female masturbation he wrote a chapter on the pathological itching of the female pubic area; in another instance, he wrote that hallucinations could occur during pregnancy. Conversely, Debreyne knew that flagellation as a form of penance could have serious adverse health effects, with pain potentially being associated with illicit lust and floggings potentially serving to inflame the heat of the flesh in the first place.[122]

In this way, the casuistry of sin became a doctrine of the economy of hygiene and physical impulses that encompassed all parts of the body and the soul. Debreyne provided confessors with the knowledge and the instruments to research and map out this topography of desires and tendencies. In this way, the confession of sins changed into becoming an investigative act. General confession, which was being promoted more frequently, could thus serve to 'generate biographies', but it also had to be seen as an intrusion into the family, the imagined nucleus of civil sociation. This idea was also familiar to German liberals, and Michelet outlined it with a great deal of originality,[123] stating that the priest as a religious teacher and confessor represented a threat to family intimacy and thus to the position and authority of the head of the household, the husband. Furthermore, daughters as young as twelve had to entrust their deepest secrets to the priest, who, if he played it well, became the object of their first infatuation. In addition to this, the priest, bound to live a life of unnatural celibacy, had the ability to tie wives to himself by asking them, during confession, about details of their marriage that no woman could confess without being permanently filled with shame. This would then make them even more dependent on their confessor, thus creating a rift in the family which would destroy the fellowship of marriage.[124]

These ideas can be dismissed as an illusion, given what we know of confession from our sources: it was normally short and proceeded quickly through a confession manual. There are also indications that the growing distribution of these manuals and prayer books actually promoted a *culpabilization* of women in the first half of the nineteenth century, however, which could sometimes create a special tie between them and their confessors. Michelet's phantasm was fed by scandals, such as the case of Marie Zoe. In her general confession, which she made in writing to the famous priest of Ars in 1858, Zoe described how, having been raped twice, she had joined a congregation in her desperation and had begun a sexual relationship with her confessor there. Looking at herself and her life, she used the language of penitential and confessional manuals and regarded herself as the guilty party in all these sexual transgressions, including the violence she had experienced, because she had surrendered herself to the individual 'opportunities'. In this way, she stated, she had become a permanent, habitual sinner, and a sign of this was the fact that she had never made a complete confession but had always remained silent regarding her greatest transgressions, despite having to admit that it gave her pleasure talking about her evil deeds.[125] Any woman who took to heart what the prayer books and manuals of confession, written by men, told her had to see the devil and sin lying in wait at every corner: in daily physicality, in piety, in the contemplation of the divine and even in penance. Görres's *Christliche Mystik* of 1834 consisted of a multi-volume summary, consciously aimed at a non-specialist audience, of all things mystical and of current knowledge about access to the afterlife; its conclusion on the particular risks to women was succinct: 'Despite all moral freedom of the sexes, from which equal responsibility follows, nature is the deciding factor'.[126]

As for the Protestants, their moral theology was not free of such ideas either. In a German translation of Ludovico Muratori's treatise on imagination, which dealt with the troubled waters of mystical private revelation, the Protestant priest Georg Hermann Richartz had noted that women had a more vivid imagination than men. This was due to, on the one hand, their nerves being more easily excited, but it could also be related to an education that was less directed towards 'perfecting the intellect than increasing imagination' because the aim was to create pleasant and diverting companions for men. Women therefore had nothing with which to 'counter the excesses of imagination', and Richartz took as proof of this that women were extremely susceptible to religious enthusiasm but did not lead such movements because the female disposition was more inclined to 'suffer excitably than heal itself'.[127] Evangelical moralists also warned against the erotic implications of ecstatic piety in Methodism and different denominations, and their treatises discussed the particular stain on women through original sin. Special attention should be given to a Christian upbringing for girls in order to protect them from temptation and the devil. The Methodists combined their spiritual acknowledgement of women with a particularly rigid code of ethics and behaviour, which was largely concerned with premarital and extramarital sexuality. There was hardly any mention of the direct work of the devil here anymore, but instead there were references to tendencies and desires.[128] As a consequence of neology denying the devil any power other than perhaps causing natural disasters, Kant had located evil within humans themselves. Man was not evil because of tendencies or sensuality, but through free choice.[129]

Viewed from this perspective, the inescapable sinfulness of woman in Catholic imagination appears to have been the result of external observations by the devil and by men, and these could be addressed through the mechanics of penance. The Protestant construct was no less harmless because it focused on self-observation. According to letters written to Hahnemann, the founder of homeopathy, unmarried Protestants did not experience sexuality and married Protestants only in as far as procreation was concerned. These distorted views were also articulated in literature. The stories of middle-class marriages described wives whose desires and sexuality, in the best case, were an expression of their sacrifice to their husbands or, in worse cases, removed from view through unconsciousness. Wilhelm Traugott Krug provided an example of the first, Kleist's *Marquise von O*... a case of the second. There was no place for female desire outside marriage and certainly not within marriage. As a result, the Virgin Mary exercised a fascination even for Protestants. Women had to pay a high price for the use of religion as a means of emancipation.[130]

# 4

# Religion as culture

## Ideas and structures

Patterns of social order must ensure their own continued existence. In the continued reproduction of meaning, diverse human experience and actions must form different, distinct streams of communication. They must be identifiable as individual spheres that are internally coherent with regard to meaning and have their own rationality, and this identification must be clear both in terms of the practices within these spheres and to external observers. The same applies to religion. The prerequisite for its institutional development, that is to say, its differentiation from the environment, is that religious communication is distinct from other ways of acting and communicating and is recognized as such. This chapter will show that this problem is inherent to the object studied and is not one which historians have imported and applied to it from the outside.

The preceding chapters have dealt with the institutional transformation of religion in the context of fundamental social changes in Europe. In the course of these changes, major institutions were not simply reorganized or reinvented, but their very structures were transformed. Modern European society was organized according to functional imperatives which were incompatible with hierarchical organization. The destruction of this order affected not only the active reproduction of communication structures and institutions, but also their observation. This aspect will be the focus of this chapter, addressing the following questions. How is religion observed in this process of structural transformation? How do descriptions of religion change, and how do these descriptions relate to changes in the operative reproduction of religion?

The purpose is not to write a history of a particular term by examining its use in a series of different texts or perhaps genres, or to engage in an archaeology of discourse in order to reconstruct different knowledge systems and to find the unsaid in the said. Nor will this chapter address the core question of the history of (political) ideas: the 'reason' why 'ideas' are developed. This question results in concepts (terms) being associated with particular social and discursive situations and, thus, with particular interests; in extreme cases, they then can be identified as 'ideologies'. In the last section of this chapter, reference to the *German ideology* will show how this kind of observation of ideas developed from the observation of religion in an attempt to find a vantage point and distinctions that one was absolutely sure could not be identified with religion. Prior to Karl Mannheim's work, the sociology of knowledge adhered to this concept but then changed its focus from the origin of ideas to the question of their contribution to the construction, reproduction and transformation of social structures.[1]

This shift in the question is considered here from a particular perspective. The systemic description of communication and actions makes use of and is concerned with the idea of differentiation. Its aim is to investigate how, in particular social configurations, individuals create ways in which they differ from their environment and thus how they establish their identities. There are two underlying assumptions here. The first is that there is a difference between the operative reproduction of structure through communication and actions, on the one hand, and between the observation of such patterns of order on the other. This means that it becomes necessary to consider the 'reference point' of such observations. External observations view a structure from the outside and thus assign it to a world that has different structures, often in the context of 'society'. Self-observations, on the other hand, view particular orders from the inside and primarily relate to the operative reproduction within the structure itself.[2]

A system's observation of itself, therefore, is subject to the contradictory requirement of simultaneously being part of a communicative structure and differing from it. This involves the difference between communicative operation and observation as well as the question of the relationship between a system and its associated academic discipline, a question that is often difficult to answer even in modern functional systems. If one regards the rejection of theology as religious communication, and thus religion, at the very least, as an indication of system-internal differentiation, and one also understands the price that must be paid for theology becoming a discipline that is only able to engage in external observation, this is an analytical advantage. Distinguishing between different observational frames of reference thus allows us to formulate reasonable hypotheses regarding the functional relationship between operatively reproduced structures and observations and descriptions that are condensed into ideas or terminological concepts. Texts are then no longer examined simply with regard to their terminological strategy or ideas and one is no longer engaged in simply analysing discourse; instead, the aim is to understand the historical development of social configurations depending on the point of view of the observer. Niklas Luhmann highlighted this particular observation point by referring to 'semantics'.[3]

Self-descriptions can record all meaning and knowledge which is required for the operative reproduction of systems to function, both in relation to the identity of a system and its relationship to the world as well as in relation to how it changes and evolves. The identity of communicative constellations, which is stable over time and extend across different spaces, occurs according to a guiding distinction which determines the central meaning of a system. In this way, the conditions required for communication to continue are established and selected. Such constellations of meaning thus allow meaningful experience in relation to the system and, at the same time, structure expectations and the expectation of expectations. These guiding distinctions are rarely free of contradictions because of the emergence of systems, so the question also arises of whether the distinction between immanence and transcendence is an immanent one, which could mean one that is rational, or one that has a revelatory character. Below, a consideration of the writings of Hegel and Schelling will show that there is similar contradictory tension between God and the world. The guiding distinction must finally also be able to determine the boundary between a system and its environment both thematically and structurally. Thus, self-descriptions provide statements on the inner complexity and structure of a system, making it possible to view the world outside the system as different, while at the same time acknowledging that aspects of it may play a part within the system – in our case, as religion. This communication between a system and the world includes observations that have an external reference point – at least, this has been the case since system-internal, evaluative self-descriptions have been recorded and modified in printed form. Self-descriptions address external observations because they contain information on the world, even if this information is simply that the world sees the system differently to the way in which the system views itself. It is only under certain conditions of institutional differentiation and media situations that self- and external descriptions are found in separate texts and among different speakers; otherwise, they are frequently found together in the same texts.

Communication is subject to double contingency, and consciousness is part of the environment of social systems, meaning that it does not follow the system's imperatives of function and reproduction. As a result, in orders that are built on communication, choosing the most appropriate form of communication from amongst a range of options is a continuous and necessary process. The resulting slow or sometimes abrupt changes in structural patterns and complexity have to be tested for compatibility with the system's identity as soon as self-descriptions are available. These self-descriptions thus also by necessity are concerned with the ways in which systems can change and the limits on such change, negotiating the evolution of social configurations.

The present chapter analyses texts from the period between the first third of the eighteenth and the middle of the nineteenth century from this perspective, focusing on those that deal with religion as a social phenomenon. Given what has just been outlined, this examination will not limit itself to theological or philosophical, social-theoretical or 'historical' texts; instead, in keeping with the question regarding the position of the observer, it is concerned with analysing whether and how these different perspectives can be related to one another. The hypothesis is that both self- and external descriptions of 'religion' as a social communication structure reflect at least three fundamental shifts, which also required an adjustment of their semantics.

The first shift was the levelling of hierarchical patterns of social order and social order's functional reconfiguration, which resulted in a world of many perspectives, in which society as a whole only could be viewed from privileged viewpoints that involved the loss of information. Therefore, it is to be expected that the observation of observations plays a role in the relevant texts. This question is particularly apparent where reports and analytical description of the social phenomena of a world encompassing all of human history, explored comprehensively through colonial activity, confronted European self-awareness with an unimaginable multitude of alternatives and variants, which the self-perception of systems and societies had to take into account. This involved comparative ordering, which combined attempts to relativize phenomena and assign them places in a hierarchy, and this ordering was condensed into the ideas of culture and civilization that became central categories of social-theoretical thought in the first third of the eighteenth century. For this reason, this chapter will be concerned with religion as culture.

The growing importance of the concepts of organization and social movement were connected with this change and encompassed ways in which social configurations could be institutionalized. This probably led to a reassessment of the prerequisites necessary for stable social systems and to the perspective from which social patterns of order were described as shifting from stability to dynamism and change. Finally, it can be assumed that the growing importance of mass media for processes of social integration and inclusion led to changes in how society viewed the relationship between past, present and future. In this context, Reinhart Koselleck has spoken of the spaces of experience and expectation falling apart, but the way in which the past and the future were separated from the present, which is relevant for actions, only served to make these two time levels all the more conspicuous. Hegel took this into account in his concept of sublation (*Aufheben*).[4]

Self-descriptions are not commissioned unless social systems form as organizations in modern societies. Otherwise, they are just something that happens of its own accord, for example, in social theories, public polemics or theology. They are characterized by the perspective from which they describe the object in question. It is thus not possible to provide a hermeneutic and philological analysis of the entire semantic and argumentative structures of the texts that will be discussed in the following sections. Instead, the focus is on those that can be read as self- or external descriptions.

## The problem of deism

The biographies and political possibilities of those who, in the context of the discussion around natural religion in the United Kingdom, laid the foundations for a new concept of religion that was to be very influential in future descriptions of the phenomenon illustrated that Christianity, its churches and denominations were mainly viewed from the outside. These individuals included lawyers such as Matthew Tindal (1657–1733), internationally active military entrepreneurs like Herbert of Cherbury (1583–1648) and physicians such as John Locke (1632–1704). They knew from first-hand experience the law of power and the threatening dynamic that religious differences could have because they were from the upper class, like Charles Blount (1654-93), or were members of Parliament, like Cherbury. Conversion experiences seem to have played an important role. Tindal and John Toland (1670–1722) were both raised as Irish Catholics and then converted to Anglicanism.[5] Their writings on religion had in common a concern with finding a form for Christianity that would be compatible with a civil society capable of peaceful coexistence despite religious differences and that would be acceptable to individuals who relied on their senses to access the world and believed that empirical findings were a prerequisite for uncovering truth. Their writings thus were concerned with much more than just religious tolerance. Locke had demanded this tolerance in 1690, arguing that authorities in this world could only establish transcendental truth through violent conflict.[6] This was the justification for drawing a pragmatic dividing line between the social spheres of religion and politics, based on the experience of a bloody civil war which had suggested that state power would display its violent foundations as soon as it concerned itself with questions of transcendental truth. The internal differentiation of Christianity meant that religion had become an environment that could no longer be controlled by politics. Confessionally differentiated Christianity in its form as an institutional church had the potential to break up civil society, and this necessitated finding a new form of accommodating religion as a system within society.

## The religion of the *societas civilis*

Cherbury's *De Veritate*, printed in Paris in 1624, had already provided an important framework for this religion.[7] The possibility of acquiring religious knowledge through reason had been an integral part of Christian theology since Thomas Aquinas, and Cherbury shifted the question to take in not only knowledge based on reason but also sensory, empirical knowledge. According to Cherbury, recognizing things was a prerequisite for answering questions of truth, and recognition was based on the ability to distinguish between different things. In his argument, Cherbury referred to innate *abilities* of humans and not to innate ideas; thus, he concluded, things must generally match the ability to recognize them. Objects about which verifiable statements could be made thus were defined by having the right size, distinct characteristics, an appropriate position and a distance that was appropriate to the sense with which the object was perceived. The senses, for their part, should be impaired neither in their function nor their attention. Humans had four abilities that allowed them to process perceptions: natural instinct, internal and external imagination, and 'discursive thought', that is to say, the ability to deliberate. This, Cherbury believed, enabled humans also to test the truth of religious revelations. Reason should not be suspended in order to make space for faith. Without further arguments, Cherbury then laid out five points that he believed characterized true religion. First, it had to be monotheistic, positing one god as the highest being who had to be worshipped; religion had to be moral because, second, the combination of virtue and piety was the most important aspect of worshipping God and because, third, religion punished transgression through penance; fourth, religion had to include some form of justice after death that compensated for inequality in life; and, finally, as a fifth point, Cherbury rejected the truth claim of written revelation because it was impossible to know how accurately writers had examined the events that were reported. Claims could not be based purely on authority, but only on reason and experience. This rule applied also to faith, which should not be based only on the testimony of historians.[8]

Cherbury's treatise on the subject of truth had changed the fundamental concept of religion, shifting it in a number of ways, and these changes could be put to use wherever religion was observed in the context of society. In doing so, deists were looking for ways to explain radical structural and systemic changes that apparently could not be ignored, even when writing from an internal point of view and considering society in the context of religion, as was the case for William Warburton (1698–1779), an

Anglican clergyman and bishop of Gloucester. The conceptual shifts in question related, in the first place, to the subject of religion; second, to the way in which religious knowledge was gained; and third, to its social and institutional form and thus to the way in which it was practised. Cherbury had only considered the existing plurality of religions indirectly, and this later became a controversial topic, which contributed to the description of religion being historicized in a way that had not yet happened in Cherbury's writings.

Cherbury identified God, as the one Supreme Being, as the focus of religion. Thus, the semantic core of religion became a category of difference in that this one God required mankind as His creation to worship Him. The change was that this one God appeared to mankind only through His creation and that revelation through direct intervention in human affairs and the natural world was presented merely as a narrative the truth content of which had not been tested. This new generative elementary distinction, which was to serve as the basis for religion as a social phenomenon, also lastingly changed what was possible in this space of action and communication. The studies on nature carried out by physicotheologians* became theological, pious acts that were pleasing to God. In the first third of the eighteenth century, deists like Tindal referred to a 'natural religion' that human reason was able to derive through observing the nature of God and of itself as well as the relationship with God and among humans. They insisted that no revelation of any kind could add to the truths of natural religion, which was similar to the conclusion reached by Blount at the end of the seventeenth century. Blount had taken over his list of the features of true religion from Cherbury, making only minor alterations.[9] For Tindal, such statements meant that revelation was of secondary importance compared to natural religion because religion in general would be weakened if there were two sources from which human action could receive guidance.[10]

Redefining either the initial distinction or the focus of religion inevitably resulted in a different concept of what could guarantee certainty and thus establish truth. Acts of faith guided by the authority of Scripture or of an institution were replaced by empirical knowledge led by a form of reason that was no longer restricted by the Fall of Man in its reach and its ability to find its way. This moved religious experience and action into an entirely different context of meaning. At the same time, deists insisted that the relationship between observers within religion was important and that information should be derived from observing observers and not from the information these observers communicated. This was an obvious conclusion in a world in which the 'Gutenberg Galaxy' was constantly expanding.

The third shift related to the nature of religion in the social world of everyday life. In 'natural religion', piety no longer consisted of separate ritual acts that represented divine worship but, instead, it was the pursuit of 'human happiness', as Tindal wrote, which resulted from observing one's duties while taking into account human nature. In this context, Cherbury had referred to virtues and Blount used the term 'moral virtue'.[11] This represented a proposal for how religion could be given a new social form, thus adjusting the boundaries of this complex of actions and its internal structure to the changes that were on their way regarding patterns of social differentiation.

For this reason, reflecting on how religion could occur in society and society in religion could not be avoided, even if religion was chosen as a reference point, as in the case of William Warburton. In the dedication of his book on the *Divine Legation of Moses Demonstrated on the Principles of a Religious Deist*, Warburton delimited the boundary which separated the church from society.[12] He claimed to be writing against the author of the *Discourse of Free Thinking*, who, he stated, aimed to plunge the church into anarchy by telling the clergy that the same spirit of 'literary liberty' could rule in the church as in 'civil society', thus abusing the 'liberty of the press'. In the main, the treatise was concerned with offering proof that religion could only do away with a 'doctrine of a future state of rewards and punishments' if this was God's will. Warburton claimed to have chosen this topic as it offered the opportunity to directly demonstrate to the deists the necessity of divine intervention, and, in doing so, Warburton intended to prove that religion was 'absolutely necessary to Civil Government'.[13]

We will come back to this point but, for now, we must ask why Warburton thought it was necessary to provide these arguments at all. He quickly identified his main opponents: Pierre Bayle and Bernard Mandeville. Pierre Bayle, Warburton states, cited Pomponatus to argue that the doctrine of an immortal soul did not protect mankind from evil and Bayle even provided examples of people who openly denied that the soul was immortal and who, nevertheless, loved their neighbour. Bayle referred to Cardano to say that religion was an advantage to society, but by no means a necessity. Warburton then addressed Bayle's claim in detail that modern atheism was less damaging to society than religious superstition. Warburton's concern here was to show that man was not capable of virtue through self-love alone. Even if an atheist was capable of distinguishing good from evil, this did not mean that his or her motives in doing good were pure. Another important aspect for Warburton was the question of the order of the universe and society. Only an 'intelligent superior' could make actions moral through ensuring the necessary arrangement of things and events. Morality could not exist in a universe governed by chance, and Warburton transferred this idea to society. Even if one presumed an atheist's ability to recognize what was good, such people, driven by self-love, could not create social order. 'Self-interest' led to actions determined by fear and hope and thus 'caused all those disorders amongst men, which required the remedy of civil Society. And self-interest, again, operating by hopes and fears in Society, afforded means for the redress of those first disorders'. Warburton thus set up a contrast between, on the one hand, a community in which intrinsically virtuous people interacted with each other and, on the other, sociation among individuals guided by their own interests, with order and structure emerging from their interactions purely by chance – Adam Smith would refer to the 'invisible hand' only three decades later. Warburton thus viewed Mandeville's belief that it was entirely possible to demonstrate the 'public benefit' of 'private vices' as terrible iniquity and a diabolic wickedness as it would turn virtuous Christians into fools.[14]

Like the deists, Warburton was reacting to a social situation in which it was becoming increasingly clear that religion no longer played any role in shaping social order and that religious action did not serve to include or integrate individuals outside of a religious sphere. The deists thus proposed treating religion as if it were primarily concerned with morality and virtue, and Warburton, a man of the Church, followed this argument because, like the deists, he considered order to be the result of norms that placed restrictions on human action. Both sides thus deeply mistrusted the idea that interests, with their coincidental consequences, could fulfil the same role. Warburton's conclusion was to see religion as absolutely necessary for a politically ordered society, but, despite this, he did not oppose critics of Anglicanism, such as Lord Bolingbroke, who declared religion to be primarily of importance for political authority and advocated the introduction of a national religion that would overrule all other confessions.[15]

Warburton and the deists also agreed on another point: morality was based solely on man's free will, but this free will could only come about in a universe that was kept in motion by the will of God, while its events followed the laws of nature. Tindal had also stressed that God did not intervene in the course of events but allowed different occurrences to take place for the good of mankind so that humans might gain an understanding of their duties. The concept of humanity and of God that underlay these ideas was hardly compatible with the Reformation's doctrine of predestination,[16] and this was the point which represented the fourth important shift in deist discourse. Like the connection between religion and society through morality, it concerned the environment of religion, but, in this case, it focused on individuals. Natural religion did not assume that individuals were subject to decisions on salvation that had already been made. Instead, it considered Christians to be capable of distinguishing between good and evil and of exercising their free will to choose virtue on account of their belief in a future judgement after death. This was why Cherbury, Blount and Warburton continued to regard as essential the doctrine of the immortal soul and of a life after death, which could hold either reward or punishment for one's behaviour in this life. Warburton thus concluded that only a religion which involved these elements could ensure political peace in a civil society; however, it necessitated dispensing with the uncertainty of predestination and faith in salvation, instead trusting in individual freedom of choice. Furthermore, it envisioned individuals who were capable of acting virtuously on their own account, motivated by the prospect of judgement after death. A moral religion required both a society and an individual capable of morality. The fact that interests are also involved in moral decisions was not recognized.

**Theodicy**

This model had other advantages too. In 1748 the pastor Johann Joachim Spalding (1714–1804), himself the son of a parish clergyman, published a work on the destiny of man. He received much criticism for it, but judging by the number of editions that were published, it was one of the most influential Lutheran texts of the eighteenth century. One of his main opponents, Pastor Johann Melchior Goeze, declared Spalding to be a deist and accused him of ingratitude towards divine revelation because he had attempted to derive eschatological certainties through reason. Spalding had posed the question of 'Why do I exist and what should I reasonably be?' and had explored it in the form of a soliloquy. The different stages of this examination led him to distinguish between bodily and higher interests in the good, true and beautiful. Only if these interests were satisfied in the soul was 'a peace of mind and calmness brought about which is far above the attacks of external adversities'. Even this soul, at peace with itself, could not escape the condition of the world. Its peace was disturbed by ever-present misfortune and the indisputable injustices of the world. In this situation the soul was helped by being able to see the present life and eternity as parts of a larger whole, with injustices being addressed by a wise ruler of the worlds. The deist's idea of *justitia distributiva* in life after death appeared to be so plausible an answer to the problem of theodicy that it was also acceptable to Lutheran neology.[17]

A few years later, Samuel Reimarus (1694–1768) felt compelled to defend the 'noblest of truths' of the 'natural religion' against a multitude of works refuting it. Although he wanted to prove that Christianity included the truths of 'natural religion', enriching them with the secrets of Revelation, he argued that this revelatory form of Christianity was already dependent on 'natural religion', and he stressed that all the faithful were called to make use of reason. The element of a religion based on reason that he considered most important was the idea that God was present in His creation and that His providence shaped a universe that was otherwise not predetermined. Like Spalding, Reimarus considered the immortality of the soul to be more than a mere postulate; instead, it was a certainty which the soul could gain from self-reflection. Although he did not explicitly relate it to punishment or reward after death, Reimarus considered religion to be the basis of all moral behaviour and thus indispensable to sociation. Here, he also disagreed with Mandeville, replacing the 'invisible hand' with the Creator and His providence, which allowed negative things to happen without intervention. If vices sometimes brought advantages to human society, this did not come about 'because they are vices but through coincidence or rather through the providence of the creator, which is so strong that even those that strive to do damage to themselves and others must contribute to the general good without wanting it'.[18] Reimarus thus had gone beyond Spalding by providing an answer to the problem of theodicy that lay within this world. This was underlined by the additional information that an immoral individual always harmed himself and others more than he benefited them. In its self-observations, Protestant Christianity began to assume a society that was directed by proclivities and interests, and Protestantism thus described itself as a structure of meaning that was based on reason and provided the foundations for virtue in which transcendence was thus mainly reflected in inner-worldly aspects.

The deists' primary motivation in searching for a religion that could be accommodated within a civil society of virtuous citizens not yet guided by interests but by their free will lay in overcoming the problems that developed from the plurality of Christian churches, denominations and confessions. Cherbury and the other deists believed the solution lay in knowledge that was based on reason and could be universally exchanged, and they contrasted this with the idiosyncratic truth claims of revelations. Lord Bolingbroke had also called for the spheres of religion and politics to be separated by excluding from power, by law, those who based political decisions on their conscience.[19] As a politician, he was very aware of the fact that privileging reason above revelation and turning public worship into a morally neutral affair through a form of piety focused on virtue would not resolve the competition between confessions. Indeed, it actually would be viewed as a provocation by the existing confessions and denominations. For this reason, the entire debate about natural religion had a polemical aspect and led to implicit and explicit comparisons becoming an important methodological and rhetorical weapon in defining natural religion. From the start, this was associated with a historicization of religion. Cherbury had followed up his work on truth with an overview of all religions throughout history and in different parts of the world.[20] It was translated into English in 1705 and provided material for the debate that was already intense at this point.

Deists treated religion as a social phenomenon. In their search for the natural religion of the *societas civilis*, they were essentially writing as theologians, regardless of the frame of reference they chose for their observations. The machinery of their reasoning slowly ground to a halt in the mid-eighteenth century because it no longer distinguished between immanence and transcendence and, as a result, it became difficult to draw the boundary between itself and its social environment. This may be why Reimarus dealt with the human soul in more detail. He ascribed independent substance to the soul as well as the 'ability to recognize its different states'. In addition, it had an independent power of imagination, which allowed it to produce images of its own accord and not as a reaction of the senses to impressions or physical conditions. Reason, which processed information, was replaced by introspection as a way of achieving religious knowledge. Thus, transcendence appeared inside humans.[21]

**Religion as culture**

David Hume (1711–76) made no attempts to continue this construction of a rational and natural religion. Instead, his innovation was to examine religion within a different epistemological context, intended to highlight the weak foundations and illusionary nature of the old construction. In doing so, he essentially undertook the first external description of religion, as was clear from the introduction to his *Natural History of Religion*, in which he did not ask how religious truth could be recognized but why humans had religion in the first place. Accepting as a given that religion could derive from reason due to the multitude of evidence for an intelligent creator, Hume then focused on his actual undertaking. Given that religion was widely found among humans, but seeing as there were nations 'who entertained no sentiment of religion',[22] religion could not be regarded as a human instinct. The first religious principle, that is, reason as the source of religion, was thus actually a secondary principle.

The primary distinction Hume made in his observations was not between society and religion. Instead, Hume viewed man as a creatural being that had needs, urges and passions and was surrounded by a social environment; in order to achieve a state of reason, man had to undergo a civilizatory evolution that was not focused on a particular goal. Adam, Hume believed, had certainly recognized God in His greatness when he saw the universe, but subsequently man had gone through life as a barbaric, needy animal; that is to say, the state in which man appeared at the beginning of society, driven by so many needs and passions that there was not the leisure to admire the laws of nature or to pursue the question of what caused all those unaccustomed phenomena. This ignorant human being was frightened by anything that was new and by any form of change. Beginning to ponder the invisible forces that caused the vicissitudes of human life – from illness to the forces of nature – man developed the idea of spirits and forces in conflict with each other, which behaved in a very unpredictable and changing way towards humans. The first religious ideas therefore did not originate from a rational view of nature but from the insecurity of life and the hopes and fears that arose from them. The religion of human society was thus necessarily polytheistic. It was not based on a single founding revelation but was entirely the product of the human mind, which was ignorant and having to navigate an unpredictable natural and social environment with a body driven by urges and needs. The spirit world that humans created reduced this complexity to a manageable level. Subsequently, polytheistic ideas had not managed to proceed beyond this mode of observing the world. In Hume's opinion, the experiences and ignorance of an uneducated population had always prevented polytheism from developing into theism, which involved knowledge of a single creator and could always be developed on the basis of a rational observation of nature. It was reason and philosophy alone that allowed humans to do so, although success was wanting in some cases, according to Hume, as the plethora of Catholic saints illustrated. Hume took this as evidence that there had always been a consistent to and fro between theism and polytheism in human history.[23]

Religion was thus excluded from the history of civilizatory progress both of society and the human spirit. Society must take religion into account, and the human spirit strives to use philosophy in order to civilize religion; its success, however, is limited because philosophy cannot prevent humans turning to the gods, not with virtue and morality, as would be fitting for a perfect being, but instead seeking to win their favour 'by frivolous observances, by intemperate zeal, by rapturous ecstasies or by the belief of mysterious and absurd opinions', regardless of how subtly the gods are presented in the different religions.[24]

Against this background, Hume began to compare the consequences of polytheism and monotheism for society, always referring to monotheism as 'theism'. Hume considered the structural peculiarities and conditions of life to exist independently of religion and he thus regarded the historic back and forth between polytheism and monotheism as nothing more than an adaptation of thinking or of viewing the world; he thus, primarily, treated these two types of religion as different ways of interpreting the world. With regard to the truth claims made by religion, Hume believed that, when one polytheistic belief system encountered another, this tended to result in a division and hierarchy of responsibilities but hardly ever entailed open competition between cults. Theistic religion, on the other hand, tended towards intolerance and persecution of those who held different beliefs. Hume also believed that the lives people led under the two systems differed. An absolutely superior being made humans hesitant; a multitude of deities, on the other hand, provided support and encouraged humans in coping with their lives. Hume then dealt in detail with the ambivalent relationship between rational philosophy and religion. While polytheism produced only myths and narratives, the theological constructions of theisms were usually compatible enough with reason for there to be points at which they could connect to philosophy; however, this also held certain risks. Certainly, once theistic religions became religions of the book, philosophy risked becoming corrupted and a servant to superstition if it was too close to theology. Because theology had an inherent tendency towards disputes and controversies, philosophy would be confronted with the exclusion of heretical thought. Hume concluded that polytheistic religion was often easier for the intellect to understand, as it consisted 'only of a multitude of stories, which, however groundless, imply no express absurdity and demonstrative contradiction'. Precisely because such a religion was accessible to the common intellect, 'it happily makes no such deep impression on the affections and understanding'.[25]

By this point, at the latest, it was clear that Hume's ideas were only superficially similar to the epistemology of religion developed by the deists and their opponents. Hume's *Natural History* did not present religion as a predetermined component of a world which was still seen as created by God, which could be explored with reason and which could become part of human knowledge. According to Hume, religion was something that humans had brought forth themselves. He described it in the context of human nature, needs and intellectual capacity. The frame of reference of Hume's observations had shifted from a civil society that had been pacified to human perception of the world. Hume did refer to societal conflicts caused by theistic or polytheistic religions, but he no longer viewed them as the only aspects in need of debate when it came to the consequences of religion within social orders. Religion as a social phenomenon was now no longer based on knowledge gained through reason, but it had its foundation in human imagination. The assumption that divinity existed – whether as a single god or a polytheistic pantheon – was central to the creation of religious meaning, but it now also represented the difference between a correctly identified causality and one that had been misunderstood. In Hume's view, philosophy represented correctly identified causality as it was able to assess ideas of God according to this distinction. This showed deities to be the product of human imagination, elaborated as internally contradictory ideas in monotheistic religion or easily understood mythological narratives in polytheistic constructions. In the environment surrounding social order, religion did not primarily function as another ordering principle but as a means of interpretation, and this moved religion into the sphere of culture. It no longer supported the reproduction of social order through providing the motivation for virtuous behaviour but instead offered meaning, different world views and different attitudes.

Hume's conclusions were based on observations that had been rejected in deist discourse. Social order could develop without religion. Meaningful experience, purposeful actions and the coordination of expectations through communication all require a shared understanding of a world made up of natural and social coincidences. Hume also indicated the cost of including religion in such a social reality. It had to share its function of producing socially relevant meaning and reality with philosophy in the broadest sense. At the same time, this placed religion within the context of the historical development of the human mind. Unlike the deists' emphasis on knowledge through reason had implied, neither a single god nor multiple gods nor any knowledge of them were phenomena that transcended time. This deconstructive and relativizing approach to religion as a historical phenomenon linked Hume's *Natural History* to a multitude of texts on the history of civilization, the number of which had been continuously growing since the beginning of the eighteenth century.

## Religions and religion in the history of humanity

Deism had argued for natural or true religion as a rational abstraction of Christianity and repeatedly claimed that it was universal because the central elements of this 'natural religion' could be found in all known religions. Non-Christian religions thus were measured against a normative concept of Christianity. This perspective, which was entirely centred on Europe, continued to be central to the discussion of religion, but as Europeans appropriated other parts of the world – economically or by force – new knowledge made its way back to Europe and required new arguments in order to create a consistent picture of European identity in a world that was full of very different kinds of societies.[26]

The comparative history of civilization was important in terms of argumentation as it was able to highlight similarities and differences between various phenomena, allowing general conclusions. The resulting arrangements of similar and dissimilar phenomena were ordered on a timeline, as Buffon had done for plants and animals, and this resulted in the present becoming a world in which the non-simultaneous occurred simultaneously. This was linked to a desire to explain the 'family resemblance' of phenomena that the observer encountered in entirely different parts of the world at very different times and, conversely, to explain the variety encountered in one and the same place and at the same time.[27] In addition, it became impossible to write history as an account of progression towards salvation, as had last been done by Bossuet, if the multitude of non-Christian histories was to be included. Only if Christianity was replaced by mankind as a whole could these different histories be told as one meaningful story that related to an identifiable subject. The idea of providence was replaced with models of change involving causality, such as development or decline, which could also be supplemented by progress as a secular version of the earlier idea of perfection.[28] In order to combine this history with constructions of European identity in a way that assigned a historical place to Europeanness in the midst of all this diversity, it was an advantage if qualitative judgements could be passed on particular positions on a timeline, as this allowed the creation of hierarchies that could be viewed from different perspectives. This could be achieved through histories of civilization such as Giambattista Vico's (1668–1744) *New Science* of 1744 or Voltaire's (1694–1778) *Essai sur les Mœrs et l'Esprit des Nations* of 1756.[29] This combined a double approach to the different phenomena and events of human history by relating them to each other across space and historic time. Moreover, the historic time of coincidence was supplemented by a standardized time of necessity, thus providing a third approach to events and conditions. It was now possible for them to exist simultaneously in the present and in the past. This combination of three approaches solved two problems. An overview of the vast number of differences and similarities could now be gained because systematic orders with hierarchies arranged according to different perspectives could be combined. At the same time, the diverse knowledge being brought to Europe could be ordered in a way that prevented European identity from disintegrating in the face of the different relative perspectives.

## The early phase of historicization

In addition to the political and social state of societies, religion was a central focus in this context, and this inevitably changed ideas about it. The uniformity of this phenomenon could no longer be explained as an abstraction created by rational thought but had to be worked out comparatively – for Christianity too – through formal and functional similarities and genetically through shared developments. This changed the observational frame of reference of this phenomenon from civil society in Christian Europe to the entirety of humanity, made up of different civilizations. This meant that a natural connection between sociation and Christianity was no longer accepted without question and Christianity's place within human history had yet to be established. Moreover, as one religion among many, this comparison and its unpredictable results plunged Christianity, with its different institutional and theological forms, into the abyss that was the simultaneity of the non-simultaneous. It could not be predicted how Christianity as a religion with its own history could find a sustainable identity in that context.

Accordingly, the historicizing pluralization of the concept of religion was slow to develop. Cherbury's examination of truth in the mid-seventeenth century had been followed by his *De Religione Gentilium*, in which he laid out an overview of the different religions of the peoples, based on ancient sources and travel reports. It suggested that religion had originally been monotheist but had been corrupted by temptations and refashioned into heathen polytheistic religions of varying kinds; however, as a rule, its origins still could be discerned. This representation as yet had little historical depth because it was intended as a 'natural history of religion', illustrating Cherbury's ideas of 'natural religion'.[30] Two publications from the 1720s were also arranged as overviews: *Mœurs des Sauvages Amériquains Comparées aux Mœurs des Premiers Temps*, by the Jesuit Joseph-François Lafitau (1681–1746), printed in 1723, and *Ceremonies et Coutumes Religieuses de Tous les Peuples du Monde*, by the Huguenot engraver Bernard Picart (1673–1733), published in 1724 in Amsterdam. Picart's publisher believed readers would mainly be interested in the engraved illustrations and so this work represented a combination of things that were already known and in certain places relied on Lafitau.[31] Picart identified the worship of higher beings as the main feature shared by the many different religions, with an original religion based on reason having become obscured through a multitude of cults. As a Huguenot, he was interested in returning to the original purity of the concept of God, so that worship of God could also be brought back to its original simplicity. Lafitau's argument was more sophisticated. In his work, religion was only the focus of one section among others concerned with culture and the material culture of American 'savages', although it was by far the most extensive one. His starting point was the observation that there was no people, however barbaric, in all the known world and in all of history that did not have religion, despite the great diversity of customs and traditions. Whoever claimed otherwise was doing so in order to promote atheism or because they were ignorant of the ways in which other peoples lived; often those who described them had only had fleeting contact with them and did not know their language. Referring to Lactantius, Lafitau's conclusion was that the Creator – originator and focus of religion – had created religious inclination in the hearts of men. The First Parents had had a clear idea of their creator God up until the point at which they had sinned. Only then did the human mind darken to such an extent that abstract concepts had to be blended with sensory ideas, and thus the Supreme Being became a point on which man's instability and weakness could focus. This then led to the great diversity found in religion. It was important for Lafitau to point out that the essence had not been lost, that is, the knowledge of what religion was and the concept of a Supreme Being. On this basis, Lafitau laid out an overview of religious symbolizations, the types of worship associated with them, as well as the religious institutions, placing those from America next to those of antiquity and Old Testament Judaism. Lafitau emphasized the similarities between them, writing, for example, that the sun was a universal symbol of the deity and that the patriarchs of the Old Testament had also not yet imagined God as resembling humans but had turned monuments and places into symbols of Him.[32]

Lafitau's aim was not to construct a comparison that would result in a general concept of religion as he took such a concept for granted. By placing the religion of native Americans alongside that of the peoples of antiquity, he aimed to show that the former could be no more accused of religious barbarianism than the ancient Egyptians, Greeks and Romans. Similar forms of symbolization and divine worship were found everywhere as a result of the original true religion becoming corrupted. Thus, in the last paragraphs of the relevant chapter, Lafitau looked for evidence of Jewish and Christian practices in America and found circumcision, different kinds of baptism and even confession. He was particularly intrigued by a ceremony in Peru, which he believed also could be interpreted as the 'sacrament of the altar'. He also dedicated an entire paragraph to the worship of the cross among the ancient American peoples. He rejected the idea that the Apostle Thomas had preached in Brazil, Paraguay and Peru and also denied there was any proof that Portuguese ships with clergymen had landed there before the arrival of the Spanish. For Lafitau, these things showed that religion had a single origin, which also determined its form: religion was, according to its origin, pure and holy, its practice was strict, and it had been revealed for a particular purpose that 'assumed a being that was exalted above all else'. For Lafitau, the core of religion was a strict, ritualized cult of a personal god who 'cared' for his creation. To show this, Lafitau had created a colourful historical panel painting in which it was precisely the historical 'comparison' that prevented its subject from being historicized.[33]

One and a half decades later, the discussion about natural religion had created a situation in which it seemed necessary to historize the central ideas of Christianity in order to defend its peculiarity against all other religions and, above all, against philosophical neo-Platonic interpretations of the idea of God. William Warburton countered the Platonist Ralph Cudworth and his *True Intellectual System of the Universe*, in which a perennial philosophical concept of God was developed that was compatible with ancient atomism in an attempt to save it from accusations of atheism. Warburton wanted to show that philosophical constructions of God were misleading and, in doing so, he used the functionalist religious concept of the deists as a starting point. Almost the entire second volume of his *Divine Legation of Moses* was devoted to showing that only religions which included the idea of an immortal soul that was to experience judgement after death were suitable for a civil society. He examined everything ancient philosophers and legislators had said on the matter, although he explained he was aware that this might encourage the argument that religion had always been a 'creature of politics'. He even went so far as to show that, in the religions created by people out of fear, hatred and love after they had forgotten about the original revelation, the political order in which the religion in question existed – from the tribe to the political nation – was linked to the ways in which that religion imagined God, worshipped Him and functioned.[34]

Warburton considered this functional development to be connected to a process by which the idea of God became increasingly abstract, initially culminating in the Egyptian hieroglyphs. While previously objects and stars had been worshipped, the Egyptian hieroglyphs, which represented animals and other objects, were sacred characters, which were initially worshipped and thus treated like deities; as symbols, hieroglyphs were the focus of general idolatry. It was only in a second phase that these symbols became signs in which the signifier and the signified became separate entities, a development that arose because priests attempted to resolve the absurdity of worshipping heavenly bodies, animals and objects. In this way, this 'pagan church' created two groups of 'symbolizers'. One continued to engage in idolatry publicly (exoterically), whereas the other secretly (esoterically) developed the doctrine of an immortal soul and the abstract idea of a single god who emptied himself into the world, who could be found in all things and of whom the soul of man formed a part. This doctrine, Warburton stated, was summarized in the books attributed to Hermes Trismegistos but actually written by Egyptian priests.[35]

This doctrine risked resulting in Spinozism, and thus Warburton wanted to show that Moses as a lawmaker, with direct help from the revealed God, had made no reference to the immortality of the soul or judgement after death. In this way, Warburton intended to show that revelation was the second foundation of the Christian, abstract idea of God. Warburton also, quite incidentally, had denied that Judaism, which did not posit judgement after death, had the ability to create a civil society in 'normal circumstances', that is to say, without divine assistance.[36]

Warburton's complicated argument has frequently been misunderstood. In the present context, two aspects are of importance. Warburton realized that Christianity's truth by revelation could only endure if it was not subjected to historicization. Lafitau still had been able to take this for granted, but Warburton created a complicated and historically detailed argument because he could imagine how religious concepts developed once they were exposed to the abstracting efforts of the human mind and the laws governing the functionality by which social order developed. This process created a world of many religions, in which Christianity could only retain its special position if its competitors were viewed as having been poisoned by Egyptian pantheism.

**The long road to an abstract notion of religion**

Warburton's concerns were not unfounded. This became apparent once the first histories of humanity had been written as histories of civilization. Vico never used the term 'historical scholarship' in his text, but in various passages he made it clear that he was concerned with establishing the study of the common nature of peoples as a historical study. He understood history as a subject in its own right that required its own methodology, which differed from that of philology and philosophy. History could not be philology because a philologist's primary task did not consist in source criticism. It could not be philosophy, because philosophy was concerned with abstract, pre-existing concepts and not ideas that were derived from empirical study. Vico also referred to Bacon's *Cogitata et Visa*. For Vico, viewing the world of the different peoples 'as it is' meant observing that which was shared. This should make it possible to identify

God's providence in the world of human will, and so this new discipline could become 'a rational civil theology of divine providence'.³⁷

Vico's *Science* had the aim of providing a rational justification for divine providence, which was to give 'divine pleasure' to all who engaged in it. The key thing was the way in which divine providence was defined: it was not a manifestation of the primordial will of the Creator; instead, Vico identified it in the emergence of orders throughout history 'without human discernment or intent, and often against the designs of men'. A historical mind discovers these orders and their underlying causes through deduction and reflection and thus frees history from the grasp of Epicurean coincidence and from the chain of causality with which the Stoics had bound it to the 'will of the best and greatest God'.³⁸

Vico's historian derived divine pleasure from his work because he set himself up as an absolute observer who, by observing shared features, proved the necessity of events and thus provided an 'ideal eternal history'. According to Vico, the historian had a share in creating the 'common sense of the human race' if he could comprehend the man-made world with the greatest certainty. This discipline thus proceeded in the same way as geometry, 'which, while it constructs out of its elements or contemplates the world of quantity, itself creates it'. For Vico, however, human affairs were more real than 'points, lines, surfaces [or] figures'.³⁹

Vico's constructivist certainties were the result of his understanding of the subject, which matched his methodology. History was made by people with a free will, who, in an uncivilized state, were only capable of self-love, expressed primarily as uncontrolled violence at this stage of civilization. An individual's 'common sense' was based only on what was useful to them. This basic functional attitude then led to Vico's conclusion that similar ideas had arisen independently among different peoples. Natural law thus arose separately among the individual peoples, who were not aware of one another. Justice was not the invention of great lawmakers, but the result of the barbarian giants withdrawing to the forests in the post-diluvian period, founding families, engaging in violence and declaring their arbitrariness to be the law. For Vico, social order emerged from the process of sociation itself. All necessary things come into being through emergence alone, and this was why such processes reoccurred at different times and in different places.⁴⁰

These were the basic assumptions on which Vico constructed a social model involving three main elements: language, by which the human spirit emanated; the type of rule; and the legal system. In human history, each of these spheres in turn developed in three stages. The legal system, for example, developed from the mythological law of the gods, to the law of the heroes and finally to the law of natural equity in free republics. Individual states, constitutions or civilizations followed these cycles of development (which arose out of necessity), construction, prosperity and decay.⁴¹

Vico counted religion among the primary institutions that developed from the violence, fear and ignorance among giants' kinship groups in this post-diluvian world. The other primary institutions, according to Vico, were marriage, through which people make connections between each other, and funerals, through which the living create a connection with the dead by making them their ancestors. Religion was the foremost among these. It was not the result of revelation, but came into being through an emergent process driven by natural necessity, which came to be termed 'providence'. Religion was only connected to a creator god through a predisposition created in man, which compelled him to seek a higher being when he despaired of all help that nature offered. When this 'confused idea of divinity' was awakened in man, in his ignorance he ascribed it to beings 'to which it did not belong'. In this way and 'through the terror of this imagined divinity, they began to put themselves in some order'.[42] As a natural being, man entered the sphere of civilization through the bond, initially not understood, with something that was outside the natural world, creating a sphere of transcendence that was separate from nature and doing so out of despair at being at the mercy of nature and this life. Transcendence was created by man and had its roots in man's mental abilities. It appeared to him as a deity because man did not understand his own actions, which were based on fear and an excess of imagination.

After the Flood, religion then successfully tamed savage mankind. Vico applied a significant amount of imagination in detailing this point. For many centuries after the Flood, the soil was so damp that no 'matter capable of igniting' could develop in the air and thus there was no lightning. After a long period of dryness, the first flash of lightning came down above the wild giants, triggering a development in which the giants were tamed through the fear of the god they had themselves created and who gave them 'divine justice'. It was only now that there was a law that did not consist of violence.[43]

Religion then has two social forms: on the one hand, sacrifice, through the association with a deity, and, on the other hand, prophecy, in order to cope with the contingency of the unknown. In language, it is present in the form of myth. Theology begins as mythology and, according to Vico, can first be seen in Homer, whose *Iliad* refers to the period of the post-diluvian giants. Vico argued that the stories of the Old Testament Patriarchs also depicted the natural state of human history in their accounts of violence as a basis for order in family and tribal groups. This was not the only aspect in which Vico equated the Bible with the non-Christian myths of antiquity. He also explicitly denied that the biblical and ancient traditions, including ancient Egyptian ones, provided evidence of an 'ancient wisdom', *prisca sapientia*, that predated the Flood. Vico thus did away with any notion of a Judeo-Christian perennial philosophy that went back to before the Fall and that many of his contemporaries were intent on finding.[44]

The Hebrew religion developed from the prohibition of prophecy. Vico did not comment any further on this, but it marked Judaism out as special compared to other religions. Vico characterized Christianity as the 'revealed' religion but described its emergence and spread as a process characterized by violence, during which this religion had asserted itself in the face of Roman power through 'the virtue of the martyrs'. Subsequently, Christianity was instrumental in shaping a second barbaric age. Catholic kings created 'armed religions' everywhere in order to defend Christianity 'against the Arians ... and against the Saracens and numerous other infidels'. During the Crusades, this meant a return of the 'pious wars ... of the heroic peoples', and other phenomena of the heroic age of antiquity were reintroduced in a different form by Christianity: divine justice as canonical purgation and asylum in the form of ecclesiastical rule.[45]

Vico considered 'this world of peoples' to be characterized by monarchies, either 'barbarous' ones based on 'the vulgar wisdom of imaginative and cruel religions' or ones, as in Europe, which were based on Christianity and which were 'most humane in their customs'. However, this did not represent a final verdict on religion in the context of the history of civilization. In the last section of his *New Science*, Vico again stresses the significance of religion for the history of human sociation. It allowed the family structures of the heroic age to develop and supported aristocratic orders in communities. It provided a way of establishing popular governments and offered protection to princes in the monarchies that were established later. Thus, if the different peoples lose religion, 'they have nothing left to enable them to live in society'.[46]

This statement addressed the core problem of deism, but Vico's solution actually contradicted this statement. If one follows his outline, it becomes clear that religion only acted as a catalyst in the beginning during the taming of mankind through civilization. After this, humans tamed themselves through laws and political orders, and religion only served to support political power but lacked any direct civilizatory strength. Vico emphasized this when, with reference to Polybius, he discussed the question of whether philosophy could replace religion in the course of sociation. Only religion had the power to make people carry out good deeds out of physical urges. Philosophy, on the other hand, could do no more than simply encourage virtue. In the preceding section, Vico had again described the effect of providence, which ensured that humans, in following their urges, created order against their will. 'Men mean to gratify their bestial lust and abandon their offspring', but they actually succeed in bringing about the chastity of marriage, on which families are based. It is precisely this function that Vico also ascribed to religion, although he described an important limitation. False religions produced virtuous acts because the senses dominated the mind. In Christianity – the 'true' religion – the mind had to dominate the senses in order to achieve virtue; here 'divine grace causes virtuous action for the sake of an eternal and infinite good. This good cannot fall under the senses'.[47]

Unlike the deists, Vico had embraced Mandeville's view of the world. As a result, Christianity could not play a leading part in creating the order of the *societas civilis* because it assumed an idea of man that did not reflect reality, as Vico's entire *New Science* showed.

Vico had thus considered religion against the backdrop of the sensual nature of man and the necessity to civilize it, seeing this as a prerequisite for sociation. Voltaire on the other hand, writing just over a decade later, used reason to assess religion. His *Essai sur les Mœrs* was intended as more than a mere list of the deeds of rulers and events from human history; instead, only those examples should be recounted that had served to improve the history of humanity. Voltaire used 'civilization' as a criterion, allowing him to assign these events and cultural conditions in human history a relative place in the history of reason. History progressed as a continuous accumulation of knowledge through rational explanations of the world provided by arts and sciences and a simultaneous accumulation of human liberty. In this way, the simultaneity of a global present highlighted non-simultaneities in civilizations. This made it possible to identify a state of civilization amongst the 'savages' of America that mid-eighteenth-century European farmers had not yet attained.[48]

The focus of this history of civilization was mankind, which had retained the same instincts, self-love and basic striving for sociality throughout time, with Voltaire describing the last item as love for a female companion and for one's own children. Men had been given the gift of reason by God and were distinguished by the ability to learn because they were able to copy what they saw in the natural world. Language, developing from monosyllabic words and only gradually becoming polysyllabic as civilization progressed, was a prerequisite for the development of larger 'national' societies. Voltaire followed the prevalent theory that Chinese was the original language because it still consisted mostly of monosyllables. The history of civilization reached its first high point – and thus a place from which to increase its pace of progress – with Greek civilization. The Greeks invented the alphabet, allowing humanity to embark on collecting knowledge that consisted of the public use of reason and to pass it on over time and space. This was why the Greeks were the nation which used reason publicly, a practice that had been secret in other ancient populations. Despite growth in the arts and sciences now being possible, Voltaire claimed that European societies had not become entirely civilized even in his own day. Europe's presence was also characterized by the simultaneity of the non-simultaneous.[49] Reason would achieve a complete victory in the future that philosophers were working towards.

Writing about religion, Voltaire wrote that it was the third factor, in addition to climate and types of government, which influenced the mind of man and could thus explain the mysteries of the world. Before addressing the question of religion and its origins, Voltaire laid out the development that the concept of the human soul had undergone. He compared the original ideas concerning the soul with those still found among the peasant population: a more than confused, unsophisticated idea, but one that illustrated the way in which the nature of man, as it was before metaphysical reflection, transcended history. In the languages of ancient cultures such as the Syrians, the Chaldeans and the Greeks, the word for 'soul' always also meant 'life'. People were initially so occupied with their needs that they could not and did not need to contemplate an existence beyond the physical world. Dreams were the only means by which people saw beyond the world of life's everyday cares and concerns. Only once societies became more organized and a certain number of people gained the freedom to spend time thinking was it possible for dreams in which the dead appeared – whether father, mother or children – to result in an idea of the soul. The fleeting appearances of the dead were considered to be their souls because people were not yet capable of imagining beings that were entirely immaterial. Even for Homer, the soul was nothing more than an 'aerial image' of the body. The later Greeks then took over the concept of the underworld and of an apotheosis of the dead from Egypt, which led to the idea of another life beyond death developing, although this continued to be imagined not as a spiritual but as a physical form of existence. Plato was the first who had spoken of spiritual beings. Voltaire considered this to have been one of the biggest achievements of the human mind, although it would be challenged numerous times, and he stressed that even the Church Fathers continued to refer to a physical soul.[50]

Like Vico, who had presented the distinction between nature and a separate higher power as an achievement of the human spirit, Voltaire also connected the idea of the spiritual with the world in two ways. Its concept had not emerged through revelation but through philosophy, and it was based on a deception that created two realities and that had not been recognized as such. A person's ability to perceive with their senses and their imagination corresponded to the difference between reality and dreams. By imagining a soul, people created an immaterial image of themselves. This represented a secularization of religion with regard to its appearance and concept: religion reflected inner-worldly distinctions that had been created by the human mind in the face of a threatening natural world that was not understood. People developed ideas about hidden powers, attempting to gain their goodwill and creating the first cults for a multitude of deities and powers. Subsequent developments were closely linked to social order. More populous nations created deities for themselves that they recognized as 'lords': the Phoenicians had Adonai and the Syrians Baal. Although these protective deities were closely associated with individual states and although the different deities also fought each other if there were hostilities or war between the peoples, cultic polytheism did not lead to religious fanaticism. It was possible to appeal to the gods of the neighbouring people or even adopt them into one's own pantheon. The knowledge of a single god who created the world, on the other hand, is the result of 'cultivated reason' (*raison cultivée*). Like the idea of the soul and the spiritual doubling of the world, it is not produced by religion itself, and Cicero was the first to articulate it in antiquity. Theology developed as a way of answering the question of why there was evil in the world, and penitential rituals were created because humans were aware of their transgressions against social norms. Voltaire did not believe that the history of religious ideas and institutions could be explained by reason. It was not possible to find reason in 'folly' (*folie*).[51] The institutional components of religion in ancient cultures appeared to confirm this: idolatry as the worship of objects; prophecies and oracles; claims of miraculous occurrences; magic; human sacrifice, which Voltaire considered to have occurred amongst both the Jews and the Gauls; and finally mystery cults that reduced themselves to absurdity. In each of these cases, reason could apply its criticism. Miracles were inventions of misguided philosophers because they contradicted the mechanics of the universe, and magic, which was linked to astrology, could explain causalities, but culminated in witch hunts in Europe.[52]

With the increasing application of reason, no form of religion could continue to play an important role. War was far better at producing rational thought; at best, religion profited from the increased emphasis on reason. Thus, Voltaire considered monotheism and the rejection of theocratic forms of rule as an indication of the civilizatory state of a given culture, and these characteristics applied to Christianity as well as Islam and the Brahmin religions of India. As a rule, however, religion continued to be a hotbed of superstition that was reflected in human history by fanaticism, religious wars and the promotion of human servitude. European Christianity was no exception to this, having taken over too many aspects of Judaism: amongst other things, the idea of the devil and exorcisms. Voltaire repeatedly compared Christianity to the other great world religions. Although it was said of Asian religions that they represented a bizarre application of good doctrines, Christianity in Europe remained an obstacle to progress, barely matched by Islam in this regard. Voltaire stressed the 'genius' of the Arabs, whose conquests and expansions, led by Mohammed, certainly compared to those of the Romans. Voltaire regarded the Koran as a combination of religious dogma and laws which contained both sublime statements and many errors. The idea that Islam promoted human lust was nothing more than prejudice. The Old Testament King David had had relations with eighty women, whereas Mohammed had limited himself to four. All positive rules found in the Koran had models in antiquity: the prohibition of alcohol, the duty to give alms and the doctrine of God's absolute providence, which required a person to surrender entirely to God's will and which gave Islam a strong mobilizing power. However, Islam was not spared theological disagreements and schisms either.[53]

Much as in Vico's writings, the framework of civilization history within which Voltaire considered religion as a concept and a social phenomenon led him to doubt the positive contribution of religion, in general, and Christianity, in particular, to the sociation of humans. It made no difference in this regard that Voltaire assumed that man was capable of forming societies and considered that the development of structures required nothing more than an accumulation of knowledge, whereas, for Vico, the question of whether man was able to form a society in the first place lay at the heart of the matter. For this reason, Vico could claim that religion had a positive influence on this process, but only if it was focused on the sensuousness of humans and contributed actively to realizing 'providence'. In both Vico's and Voltaire's writings, religion was presented as a human product and a way of compensating for ignorance and a fear of contingency and threats. Externalizing the human spirit, which resulted in a whole world of secret powers, spirits and finally gods, did not simply serve to help humans, but also created an opposite force that exerted power over them. Both Vico and Voltaire referred to the diversity of the religious forms, which they had organized into groups on the basis of shared features, in order to demonstrate the universality of the nature of man, from which all these forms derived. Thus, the self-descriptions at this point already indicated the outline of a 'world system', which reflected the processes of colonial integration. This was a decisive point in the evolution of the way in which European societies thought about themselves, which could otherwise only be seen in relation to statehood or politics.[54] The comparative phenomenology of religions distilled a universal – and thus ahistorical – idea of man, which could serve as the subject of a history of civilization that examined the basis and mechanisms of sociation following functional imperatives. It became increasingly difficult to accommodate religion as a social system within this, and this phenomenology of religion indicated clearly how it could still relate to the world: as a monotheistic doctrine of virtue.

Lafitau, Vico and Voltaire had considered the historical development of human existence in three different but related contexts: the different forms of human sociation, the nature of man, and finally – given the diversity observed in both phenomena in the past and present – the question of whether there was unity in diversity. The peculiarity of the discourse on the history of civilization lay in framing this last question as a problem of the simultaneity of the non-simultaneous, on the one hand, and thus highlighting the nature of history as more than a sequence of unrelated events and conditions, while, on the other hand, admitting that the history of civilization had always recognized that not even a Eurocentric view could entirely eliminate the relativizing power of the comparison. These three different contexts were highlighted and related to one another in different ways by those authors who, since the mid-eighteenth century, had referred to the paradigm of the history of civilization, but they were never ignored. Religion always played a central role in these deliberations either as an important accepted fact of human sociation, as an element of what it meant to be human or in relation to its own historicity. This led to different views on the nature of religion and what it should be. The remainder of this chapter will highlight some of these developments up until the first decades of the nineteenth century.

Rousseau (1712–78) had a good sense of the degree to which contemporaneous European societies had differentiated. With this, he drew his well-known conclusions that were critical of civilization, but he also assessed the social phenomenon of religion from the perspective of different environments. Because this resulted in religion taking very different shapes and because it was difficult to reconcile these with one another, he divided his examination up into different texts.

In his *Contrat Social* (Social Contract), Rousseau set out to present a different solution from that of Thomas Hobbes for the problem at the heart of the *societas civilis*. Rousseau's basic assumption was also that humans essentially were not capable of forming and living in societies. For this reason, in his work the move from a state of nature to that of society disappeared between the end of one chapter and the beginning of the next, with Rousseau providing a cryptic statement at the beginning of the sixth chapter of the *Social Contract* that illustrated the contradictory nature of the process: 'I suppose men to have reached the point at which the obstacles in the way of their preservation in the state of nature show their power of resistance to be greater than the resources at the disposal of each individual for his maintenance in that state'. However, Rousseau did not conclude that a politically organized society was the solution to the problem, but rather that it served to unavoidably perpetuate it, forcing the individual into a situation in which freedom and individuality could only become a reality if political power, which according to Hobbes was external to the *societas civilis*, came from within society itself. The religion of this civil society should be a state religion because, as Rousseau stated with reference to Hobbes, there could not be two sovereigns – a secular and a religious one – in a civil society. Historically, any particular form of political state had therefore developed as a theocracy, in which it had not been possible to separate politics from religion. Rousseau's conclusion for his present day was to dissolve this theocracy while retaining the secular aspects and to suggest that the state should have a civil religion with state-defined dogmas. These should relate to the duties of the citizen, who would be encouraged to love these duties, and to civil morality. All of this would be recorded in an entirely civil creed. Anyone who did not 'publicly' believe in it would receive the death penalty. This civil religion had borrowed the implementation of norms and relentless persecution of heresy from sacral religion in order to stabilize state power and public order. It was, thus, a religion that was 'created' to serve the purposes of a civil society that ruled itself, and it had little or nothing in common with the existing, historical religion. In formulating these arguments, Rousseau had adapted the deist idea of a natural religion for the political sphere.[55]

Rousseau stated that a civil society could not be created with Christianity, because, while Christians considered each other to be brothers and children of one God, Christianity had no particular relation to the body politic. The Christian fatherland was not found in this world and so a union of true Christians could not result in a good and stable community. True Christians might make good slaves, but not good soldiers. At this point, the second function of a civil religion came into focus. It was a tie binding together the community and preventing sociated individuals from returning to the natural state. Priestly religions – Rousseau referred to Hinduism, Buddhism and Roman Christianity – on the other hand, only served to undo social unity. Even where they were national religions, they were deceptions.[56]

Rousseau referred to a third form of religion, the 'religion of man' or the Christianity 'of the Gospel', distinguishing it from priestly religion. The *Social Contract* only notes that it does not impede man's ability to live in society. However, Rousseau was convinced that – because a civil religion only viewed people as citizens – a religion of man was necessary. His idea of how this religion should look is illustrated in the 'Profession of Faith of a Savoyard Vicar' found in *Emile*. It opposed the materialist world view of Holbach and presented as a religious belief that moving matter required an intelligent force. Man could only develop a meaningful order, that is to say, one that could serve its purpose, if events in the world were not simply ascribed to coincidence but if there was a 'wise and powerful will' that ruled the world. Man, imagined as a sensualistic being, held this belief, based on knowledge gained through perceiving the world, because God could not be understood by human reason. Nevertheless, Rousseau considered it degrading to man to take revelation as a justification for religious certainty. Neither miracles, books nor the authority of a church could justify faith in a God who was separate from the world. This faith made it possible to worship a creator, and this worship filled the strength of the human soul with his divine being. This self-deification of humans through their faith in God was one of the reasons why it was possible for humans to realize their own nature in society and to recognize the true and the beautiful despite their passions, as man's chance of achieving moral behaviour lay in his freedom. The only thing that the 'religion of man' needed, besides reason, in order for man to realize his nature was a binding cult. However, this should not take the form of divine worship as God was not interested in this.[57] Thus, the 'religion of man' formed a counterpart to civil religion. The religion of the state was necessary in order to ensure normative stability in a society that ruled itself and in order to overcome man's opposition to sociation through a bond that held together the community. In the 'religion of man', the sociated individual recognized their own divine being through devotion to God. This allowed humans to fully realize their nature despite sociation.

The two religions that Rousseau had invented provided the solution to the divide between the nature of man and sociation, which was at the centre of Rousseau's social theory. In both cases, religion was viewed as a conscious human product in order to solve a clearly outlined problem. These two artificial religions had nothing to do with religions transmitted over time, and neither of the two had any need for transcendence in the usual sense of the word. In the case of the 'religion of man', it was only imagined to be real and could only be experienced through the divine subjectivity of man. Civil religion also made no reference to transcendence and, if it was to be found anywhere at all, it could only be equated with society. Rousseau's construction had put forward a basic question that would continue to occupy all social theories: if one assumed society was a community, how could one imagine the associative relationships of free idiosyncratic individuals? Conservative and socialist utopian ideas continued to rely on religion to achieve this purpose, as we have seen above (see Chapter 2, section entitled 'The invention of political religion').

In his treatise on the 'Origin and Foundation of Inequality', Rousseau had characterized the state of nature as a thought experiment that had to be carried out because one did not know the original state of man. Accordingly, he did not have much interest in the physiological history of human development or in a detailed history of civilization.[58] The same can be said of Johann Gottfried Herder's *Ideas for the Philosophy of the History of Humanity*, published between 1784 and 1791, although this considers much more historical material relating to civilizations on all continents than Rousseau's work does. Like Rousseau, Herder (1744–1803) connected the problem of man's sociation with his becoming human, referring to it as 'humanity', and took a historical approach to it. While Rousseau was interested in rediscovering mankind's disposition and purpose, Herder put forward a history of development in which the original dispositions of man were developed and perfected. The ideas on the history of humanity thus became a philosophy about man. In this way, the third approach to the phenomena of human sociation, the history of civilization, disappeared, and thus, in the third part of his work, Herder was able to create an extensive depiction of sociation processes, organized by continent.[59] The 'real' history of mankind consisted of the individual humanizing of man, which would not have been possible without religion. Thus, in addition to man's reason and his ability to learn – the refinement of his senses that allowed him to produce art and language – it was man's free will, his ability to reflect on things, and his attainment of humanity and religion that defined the way man is organized as a created being and thus the way man developed.[60] Herder used the term 'humanity' to refer to the purpose of man to realize his dispositions, to turn himself into a social being and to impose order on himself on the basis of this sociality.

Unlike Rousseau, Herder also addressed the question of how religion had developed. He considered it to be the highest form of humanity that man could attain, and he achieved it through the intellect seeking to understand cause and effect. Here Herder followed what had become generally accepted since Hume. It was mainly the threatening side of nature that was the focus here so that fear determined the invention of the gods. Because we do not truly know either ourselves or the world, all of this remains 'supposition and name', which turns into a true dream if cause and effect are repeated. Herder wanted to remove the derogatory connotations of the connection between religion and dreams, about which Voltaire had written, by presenting it not as an error but as a necessary consequence of man's limited perception and cognitive abilities.[61]

In searching for cause and effect, man finds the original cause but, because it lacks a defined shape, man cannot exert any power over it. As an intellectual activity, finding it is the highest form of humanity; a second step turns it into an exercise of the human heart if a person decides voluntarily to accept the law of God. In this second aspect, religion refines 'form and nature' when it is brought forth by humans. It allows humans to engage in sociation. Herder requires neither the original revelation nor Genesis, which he refers to as the 'oldest philosophy' of human history. Thus, religion is not invented, but it emerges at the very beginning of mankind's journey to itself, continuing in its essence to be tradition and not invention. Only priests can deceive and make up false secrets. In the same way that religion requires its own symbols in order to take on a social shape, it then also allows society to become visible and makes it coherent.[62]

Mankind's divine aspect is its ability to create symbols; this allows humans to combine language and reason in a way that creates thoughts, with language naming things and reason using them to calculate. However, human education and development does not primarily come about through new thoughts, but through 'imitation'. Science – and language itself – developed through imitation, and this is the prerequisite for there being a history of mankind as a whole and not just a history of one individual. Herder defined humanity not as a community based on common knowledge, as Voltaire had done, but as a community based on learning and education and consisting of chains of individuals. Only as part of this chain could man become man. In this context, education and learning are not simply a process of copying, but organic appropriation, so that culture and civilization are determined by differences and change.[63]

Just as Herder assigns man a place in history, he also assigns him a place in creation. Man is part of creation, not its crowning glory and not even its centre. He is only a 'middle creature' amongst the animals. By gaining dominance over them, man learnt most things from the animals. Comparative anatomy teaches us about similarities that make it possible to measure how close a particular genus is to humans. However, as 'the first of the creation left free', who, through his ability to walk upright and his freedom, was able to make himself the object of his actions and decisions, man shares features with God. In this regard, too, he is a middle creature: he is placed between the visible creation and that part of creation that goes beyond what can be perceived with the five senses.[64]

Herder insists that there must be a form of transcendence beyond this world that is the prerequisite for the existence of this world and for the nature of man. For this reason, religion, although produced by man, is not his invention or imagination but part of his disposition, and enacting it makes man able to live in society. This re-ontologization of a creator god, who was separate from the world but was accessible through reason, had no positive consequences for the assessment of Christianity. Herder described its development from Judaism and how it subsequently stabilized as a body of secret knowledge of a community held together by a common creed. Elsewhere Herder wrote of Scripture as an 'institution of God' because it helped to form traditions, but in Christianity Holy Scripture led to disputes and heresies as well as to priestly rule, which corrupted Christianity through the establishment of a cult.[65]

The environment in which Herder's religion found itself was that of the individual person and not society. His religion required no cult, and instead it realized itself in the relationship between each individual and their God, their world and themselves. This marked an important juncture in the discourse, more so than Rousseau's writing: if religion was no longer the central factor in man's sociation and in the creation and maintenance of patterns of social order, then, unless one considered it to be a mere error on the part of humans and human nature or the result of a continuing deception, religion could only be considered a socially relevant phenomenon if it and its origins could be connected to processes of individualization, which were now also becoming socially relevant. This appeared to be a viable model for the future, too, given the speed at which the changes relating to social differentiation liberated and presupposed the 'individual'. Schleiermacher was not the only one to develop his idea of religion from a feeling of utter dependency; mankind's innate *sentiment religieux* was also the starting point for Benjamin Constant's investigations in the history of religion.[66]

This shift, however, left a different problem unanswered: that of the plurality of the different forms in which religion had appeared in the past and present. Up until that point, the need for writing a world history of religion had been avoided by developing a history of monotheism, which eventually led to Christianity, and other religions had been considered only as polytheistic precursors if no creator god could be found in them. In view of the dynamic changes that had begun appearing in the relationship between religion and society since the 1780s, such arguments became increasingly less plausible and it was necessary to replace them with scenarios in which the plurality of religious options and the consequences for European Christianity could be considered.

The difficulties in accomplishing this change are illustrated by Johann Christoph Adelung's *Versuch einer Geschichte der Cultur des menschlichen Geschlechts* (An Attempted History of Human Culture) published in 1782,[67] two years before Herder's depiction of civilization history. At the time, Adelung (1732–1806) was a privy councillor in Saxe-Gotha. In his cultural history, he displayed the fruits of his theological studies and developed an image of the beginnings of mankind and the development of religion that tried to link the knowledge of the different stages of human culture, derived from the history of civilization, with Genesis and the other Old Testament books, although Adelung otherwise freed himself from the constraints of the biblical reckoning of time. He did not mention an original revelation or Adam's original knowledge, but he assumed that there had been an original monotheism that became more and more obscured as mankind progressed towards the Flood. Only one of Noah's sons had transmitted the knowledge of the one God, but amongst the tribes of the other sons, idolatry and polytheism became rife. Other stages that Adelung considered to be significant were Moses's cleansing of the concept of God as well as the subsequent moral improvement of religion through Greek philosophy, which had, finally, allowed the new Christian concept based on a theology of creation to emerge. Now, the world had a caring and loving god. Adelung then addressed the development of Islam, which he presented as deriving from Abrahamic religion, but he was mainly concerned to show that Christianity had been gradually distorted by priestly rule and a decline in morals. This situation had only been remedied by the 'activity of common sense' during the Reformation. Adelung's European history was designed as a history of Christianity, extended via the New Testament into the time preceding Christ.[68] Even though religion was viewed from a Eurocentric perspective, laying it out in this way meant that it was given a history which connected it with the stages and conditions of human culture. For this reason, Adelung was able to call for a historicization of Protestant theology at the end of his work, stating that it was necessary to consider whether that of the sixteenth century was still appropriate in the eighteenth century, given the significant difference between the two time periods.[69]

Philipp Christian Reinhard (1764–1812), who, after his time as a Jacobin, became a professor in Moscow, made the diversity of human religions the main subject of his 1794 study *Abriß einer Geschichte der Entstehung und Ausbildung der religiösen Ideen* (Outline of the History of the Origins and Development of Religious Ideas). In the preface, he stated that his primary aim was to establish why religion, which could be found everywhere in human history, could appear in such different forms. In the sixty-nine paragraphs of the book, he attempted to give an answer that derived all common elements in human history from the nature of man and attributed all differences to external circumstances. A shared feature amongst all people was the presence of religious ideas, and so these ideas must be based on human urges and the human soul. For this reason, religious ideas had developed from those dominated by the 'rough and sensual' urge into increasingly abstract concepts. Reinhard divided the developments up to the ancient Greek period into three phases: the first was an initial fetishism (rather than an original monotheistic religion) focusing on objects and stars; this was followed by a polytheistic pantheon inhabited by deified humans; the third phase involved worshipping the causes of striking natural phenomena. According to Reinhard, the development of religious ideas only followed an internal logic of religion to a limited extent. He referred to 'coincidence' and stressed the role of priests in the second phase and that of poets in the third phase. However, because he believed it could already be observed in Greek culture, he was certain that any anthropomorphic, personified idea of God disintegrated 'as soon as reason awakes'.[70]

Reinhard placed the history of religious ideas side by side with the development of man from a sensory to a rational being and, in this way, he presented religion as a secondary phenomenon in the development of human culture. This prevented him from being able to provide an answer to his original question.

It was not until Christoph Meiners (1747–1810), professor of philosophy in Göttingen, published his *Allgemeinen kritische Geschichte der Religionen* (General Critical History of Religion) in 1806 that the internal differentiation of religion was successfully used as a starting point both to define a concept of religion and to develop a history of the different forms of religion.[71] Like Reinhard, Meiners started out from the observation that there are many different religions but that they share a large number of similar features. He thus intended to break religions down into different elements and then to examine these individual elements in detail. He highlighted two main points: religious ideas – the 'act of recognizing higher beings' – and the 'services dedicated to them'. This led him to develop a general concept of religion which, he stated, should not be modelled on monotheism but had to be applicable both to religions with 'many gods' and 'one god'. In addition to the initial basic distinction, Meiners stated that assumptions must exist regarding the relationship between the higher beings and humans which explained how they were worshipped. This led to concepts such as orthodoxy and ideas concerning the level of piety required, but also unbelief as a way of doubting divine beings as well as superstition. By defining religion in this way, Meiners took into account the fact that religion both as a system of meaning and as a social institution could only achieve stability in its social environment if several of its borders were defined. His reference to unbelief, in particular, placed religion within a society that could also be secular. This was a religion observed both from the inside and from the outside. In this way, Meiners illustrated the definitional consequences of an abstract concept of religion.[72]

The details of Meiners's views on the development of how higher beings were imagined – beginning with polytheism and resulting in a true, Christian concept of a merciful God in another world – were not original nor was the fact that he described the history of Christian doctrine as a sequence of inconsistencies. However, in doing so, he developed a concept of the internal dynamics of the differentiation of religious ideas. He was undecided on whether religion had a single origin or whether it had multiple roots, but he was certain that, as with languages, it was possible to distinguish between original religions, religions derived from these original ideas and mixed religions. Climate, the quality of the soil and the genius of peoples effected changes in original religions, and thus similar conditions could result in similar religions, for example, those of the Egyptians and the Hindus. This differentiation of original religions produced mixed religions by means of missionary activity, migration and other forms of contact, an example being the religion of the Greeks. Meiners used this explanation to describe the consequence of the colonial spread of Christianity and Islam. He did not believe that it would not be possible for there to be a single religion amongst humans in the future because religions were 'subject to change' in those areas in which they spread, and this in turn led to mixing. In detailing these matters, Meiners created a developmental model of religion as a historical human phenomenon that treated its development as independent of the 'human mind' and its surrounding civilization, instead positing internal differentiation, independent creation of new elements by religion itself, and a rearranging and mixing of elements. This was a model borrowed from historical linguistics and it corresponded to the general assumptions regarding the evolution of social systems through functional social differentiation.[73]

Two decades later, Benjamin Constant (1767–1830) reformulated this idea from a different perspective. His view was that religion had emerged from the *sentiment religieux* and had become a positive, that is to say, institutionalized, religion because humans had felt the need to share with others their communication with higher powers. Its history depended on doubts and criticism of religion and above all, on the question of whether it had developed into a priestly religion or not. Constant believed the latter alternative to have become a reality as early as antiquity. Only the Greeks had managed to create a form of polytheism that was free and did not involve priestly rule and which allowed the *sentiment religieux* to develop freely. Constant considered the form of Christianity prevalent in his own present to be trapped between rational criticism of religion and priestly rule, but he believed that only a religion based on an individual *sentiment religieux* free of external constraints would be appropriate to the individuality of civil society, which was free and capable of development. Constant argued that religions led and administered by priests should be replaced by the social movements of sects; competition between these movements would allow the best form of religion to develop. This was a way of describing the evolution of an autonomous sphere of action, taking into account the requirements of individuality that sociation in the modern age posed.[74]

The history of civilization did not produce a truly consistent concept of religion, but it resulted in a number of shifts in the way in which religion was observed. All histories of civilization continued to assume that there was a creative god who could be recognized in nature. This normative monotheism is even found in Voltaire's writing, despite his view that religion and Christianity were an impediment in the history of civilization. In most cases, however, this monotheism was connected to the view that religion was one of the prerequisites for human sociation and could also contribute to civilizatory progress. Of course, in relation to the eighteenth century, this led to the demand that religion, as a doctrine of virtue and morality, should be given a form in which it was capable of fulfilling this function. It also meant that religion was given a place amongst other important institutions of civilization, such as law, state power or science, and that its 'functionality' was thus also assessed in the context of these spheres of rationality.[75]

Normative monotheism did not prevent transcendence from becoming an innerworldly affair at the beginning of the nineteenth century either, in that deities and transcendence itself were considered to be products of the human mind. Only Rousseau and Herder had continued to hold on to the idea of a personal god who existed outside or above the world, allowing human senses to experience creation. However, neither of them stated this directly, reflecting the idea in different ways: Rousseau by making this assumption a postulate of human self-consciousness and freedom, and Herder by leaving open the question of whether the God who existed was perhaps identical with the divine aspect of man after all. In this way, life after death became part of a cosmic continuum that also encompassed this world and was, at most, distinguished from it by the degree to which it was accessible to the human senses.[76] This also meant, of course, that this other world and the powers that inhabited it were judged by the rational criteria of this world. The majority of religious content and practices were thus accused of being ridiculous, absurd and irrational. Religion presented itself as a kind of knowledge of and rational insight into the nature of God which no longer really required any form of revelation. Anyone who continued to maintain that revelation reflected historical fact was either quick to state that religion could add nothing to the knowledge gained through reason or insisted that, conversely, reason was required for a correct understanding of knowledge gained through revelation.

If religion had become the result of a man-made distinction between this world and the next and if this distinction was not the result of reason but of man's ignorance and fear, then an original revelation and an original monotheistic religion, including a *philosophia perennis* based on Adam's original epiphany, seemed increasingly unlikely. By the beginning of the nineteenth century, they had disappeared almost entirely from outlines of the history of civilization. In this way, Genesis, as a prominent narrative background of man's origins, melted away into the mists of ignorance. The books of the Old Testament could now be placed alongside the myths of antiquity and historicized and examined in the same way.

Through the anthropological aspect of historiographic interest and through the shift of the transcendencies of this world, religion gained another dimension in addition to its function in the history of civilization. Increasingly, religion was understood as an individual relationship with God. Religiosity became an expression of modern idiosyncratic individuality that could be amplified to the extent that it was possible to refer to the divinity of man or at least to godlike nature.

This process of recoding had far-reaching consequences for the way in which Christianity was assessed. The violence that its exclusive monotheism exerted was stressed, the strangling of reason by priestly rule was considered, and its forms of worship were seen to display everything that could also be found in heathen and polytheistic religions. It was argued that Christianity in its traditional ecclesiastical forms was not appropriate for the modern world because it could no longer make any meaningful contribution to the formation of social order. It could no longer serve as a means of inclusion, and as a basis for a social *persona* appropriate to modern times, its contributions could only be disconcerting. For this reason, it was exposed to the competition of 'invented' religions, that is to say, civil religion and individual relationships with God.

Religion was only slowly influenced by a sense of historicity and thus changeability. When histories of civilization first began to be written, there was a strong inclination to de-historicize the phenomenon, with the result that, although the term 'religion' was used in the singular, the plurality of religion was always the focus. At the beginning of the nineteenth century, it became clear that the prerequisite for an abstract concept of religion was a combination of historicization and an understanding of the internal dynamics of differentiation that allowed the plurality of religion to become a single unit. Only then could the term 'religion' reflect the plurality and historicity of its different manifestations in a world that had become polycentric.

**Placeless Christianity**

From the point of view of European Christianity, this all appeared as destructive criticism of religion, which did not present any relationship between religion and the world that could be interpreted from a religious point of view. This was up to the theologians. Christianity's academic branch, however, was indecisive and evasive in its reaction. The idea of the devil was abolished and doubts were cast on original sin in order to make it possible to identify the faithful as morally responsible individuals.[77] The Catholic Enlightenment took action against any manner of worship that continued to focus on the financially driven circulation of means of grace instead of morality and introspection and that thus continued to feed suspicions of idolatry.[78] The moralization of religion can be seen as a response to the ways in which differentiation was reorganized, although it did not actually reflect eighteenth-century society but rather the model of integration and inclusion of the old European *societas civilis*. If it was referenced at all, the world of the present was only included as a distorted image. The libraries of Catholic priests allow us to gain a reliable impression of this.[79] Religion and church found themselves in a 'godless' world, and any attempts at re-spiritualizing it must have seemed hopeless to many. This resulted in a self-referential version of the discourse on secularization that the clergy of all confessions had engaged in since the 1780s.[80] It was difficult to make this version align with questions concerning the extent to which Christianity contained the world or concerning its functionality that had been posed by external observers.

Any theological contributions that addressed the arguments of civilization history directly were also defensive in character and did little to reposition Christianity in a world of multiple religions and a secular order, nor could they be read as proposals for a new form of Christianity that was suited to this situation. Charles Robert Gosselin published *L' Antiquité Dévoilée* (Antiquity Revealed) in an attempt to 'save' the Bible;

the second edition was published in 1808, with two further editions appearing before 1817.[81] He explicitly aimed to defend the Bible's chronology against Buffon and the geologists; above all, he rejected the idea that the account of the six days of creation in Genesis should be read as an allegory. Instead, he interpreted it as a space of time in which an almighty creator could accomplish the 'regeneration' of his creation. Thus, Greek mythology was no more than a personified history of Genesis. Gosselin's general conclusion was that human reason was incapable of finding out how the Earth had been created and thus it was necessary to trust Genesis on the matter.[82] A religion described in this way lost any sense of place and no longer played any role in the world as it was. At the same time as Gosselin, Reverend George Stanley Faber (1753–1854) attempted to rearrange the knowledge presented by civilization history in a similar way to Gosselin with the aim of retaining Christianity's elevated position as the only religion of revelation. To achieve this aim, Faber published a work on the origins of heathen idolatry in 1816, in which he presented a comprehensive comparative typology of the religious myths of all continents, essentially interpreting them as imaginings of family and gender relationships. The groups he developed served to prove that all of these religions had developed from one original, post-diluvian community which had dispersed across the globe on account of internal disputes and wars. Faber expended significant effort on aligning biblical chronology with secular history. This was particularly important to him because he wanted to present the religion of the Old Testament Patriarchs as the origins of Judaism, Christianity and heathen religion. He argued that it was only in Christianity that the idea of a Trinity had developed, and thus it was wrong to search for any ideas of the true God in heathen mythology.[83]

The self-descriptions of Christianity were more dynamic in relation to the worship of God, with this being reinterpreted in a number of ways. The idea of a punitive God whose predestination prevented some people from ever experiencing salvation was replaced by the image of a loving father whose children trusted and turned to Him. This was an affectionate and individual relationship which did not preclude performative ritual elements but was not based on them.[84] Instead, the emotions of the faithful were key and were gaining increasing significance as the third dimension of human consciousness alongside the intellect and reason. This was important in that it allowed religion to be associated with human characteristics other than reason and to become independent of ritual and correct practice. The question of content – of correct faith – was not addressed. This could have opened up another option that was generally ignored entirely when religion thought about itself. The possibilities presented by relating Christianity and the multitude of other religions in the world to one another were only used in a negative sense. From the point of view of European Christianity, with its confessions and denominations, these other religions continued to be error rather than religion.

## Religion and the foundations of culture

The history of civilization had mainly focused on the different phenomena associated with religion as well as its plurality and historical dynamics. There were, however, also texts that focused on other aspects. They presented the different forms of religion and its history as spheres that reflected on the origins of human culture in a form of sociality that was based on symbols and meaning. Three aspects were particularly prominent: the question of who practised religion, that of the foundations and forms of culture in human civilization, and that of the prerequisites in human nature that allowed culture to be produced.

**Self-revelation**

The notion of a *prisca sapientia* based on divine revelation, which was developed by the London Neoplatonists, was carried into the eighteenth century by John Hutchinson (1674–1737), amongst others.[85] In his 1730 book *Moses's Sine Principio*, he took as his starting point the question of why heathens knew more about some things than Christians if the latter had the truths of the Bible at their disposal. His answer was that heathens had a better understanding of how to 'read things' and thus how to use 'the light of the nature'. This idea allowed him to transfer the original revelation into the world by ascribing to Adam the ability to gain that knowledge of God through the observation of nature that the Bible later recorded as a direct revelation. As usual, this implied that, following Adam and Eve's expulsion from Eden, this knowledge had been lost by the time of Noah, resulting in a polytheistic age. In the context of our discussion, the way in which the mode of this original revelation was imagined is more important. The first human was not capable of receiving God's truths as a direct annunciation, and so God had to ensure that he acquired the ability to connect words and things. Thus, God gave man language and later writing. He helped Adam to relate sounds to actions and to the things that surrounded him. Gradually, Adam gained the ability to further divide the initial ideas and words and to create new combinations, leading to the creation of language. God then drew the attention of man to emblematic phenomena in nature, leading to an idea of the order and size of the world, and thus man was able to gain a sense of his distance from God. Hutchinson believed that techniques of memorization and the human ability to think in abstract terms were important prerequisites for this.[86] This was not a particularly complex theory of culture yet, but it did at least reflect on the arbitrariness of signs, the human ability to use language and the cultural significance of writing. Hutchinson became important for the eighteenth century because he supplied a version of the notion of an original revelation that was appropriate to his time and because he elaborated on the idea of the *prisca sapientia*.[87]

Meiners's treatise *Über die Mysterien der Alten* (On the Mysteries of the Ancients), published three and a half decades later, illustrated how these ideas could be related to cultural institutions.[88] He was not concerned with the *prisca sapientia*'s roots in an original revelation anymore but with the higher knowledge that had developed in ancient religions as soon as they were part of a more advanced civilization. Hunter-gatherer cultures only had fortune-tellers and magicians, but no priests. Because magic required knowledge that was difficult to acquire, a special caste was trained who were responsible for this aspect and, at the next stage of civilization, this caste produced the priests of temple-based religions as they appeared in Egypt and other cultures of the Near East. These priestly castes developed mystery cults in order to allow initiates to learn things that were not appropriate for the rabble, who continued to adhere to the public temple religion. These secrets involved three things: they related to the historical foundations of religion because they explained how heroes had become gods, they provided deeper insights into the nature of the world and the cosmos than the rabble were capable of understanding, and, finally, they formulated truths about the nature of God that contradicted the polytheistic temple religion.[89]

Meiners described the ancient mysteries as a body of knowledge about 'God and the world' that was the preserve of a small number of initiates; it consisted in carrying out rituals at night that 'de-deified' the gods in plays that deceived the senses and presented the stories of ancient heroes and their subsequent deification. In this way the gods who were worshipped in public could be overthrown and replaced by a philosophical concept of a single god. Meiners believed that this enlightened practice of deception by priests had been carried out not just in Egypt but also amongst the Phoenicians, the Chaldeans, the Brahmins in India and in the priestly religions of Japan and China.

Meiners's text became very important, especially in the Scottish Rite of freemasonry in the 1780s, illustrating that Meiners had created a semantic icon for the way in which enlightened thinkers saw themselves. Culture was produced by an elite and was only suitable for the common people to a limited degree if public order was to be maintained.[90] Secret societies such as the Strict Observance, the Rosicrucians and the Illuminati were the appropriate social expression for this aspect of the Enlightenment.[91] The quest everywhere was to find a form of religion that went beyond the usual Christian practice, and rituals which involved all the senses played as important a role as texts. The performativity of this form of commemorative theatre disenchanted the gods in order to replace them with a philosophical concept. The text contradicted itself and pointed to the future notion of idealism, namely that philosophy must become the religion of reason if it wanted to have any effect.

This was part of the 'pathogenesis' of the world of civil society, which was expressed here as general distrust of the written word.[92] It was the result of thinking of sociation as communication amongst those present, and it became a firm part of conservative social theory after the beginning of the nineteenth century (see Chapter 2, section entitled 'The invention of political religion'). On the other hand, the emergence of language and writing played a central role when it came to the cultural ability of humans and whether this was innate.

**Communication: God and language**

Hutchinson was not the last to insist on the media of both language and writing having been received directly from God. However, the Comte de Condillac's 1746 essay on the origins of human knowledge provided the discussion with a new basis.[93] Condillac (1715–80) first tried to combine the older notion of innate ideas with Locke's sensualism, referring to innate ideas that provided a foundation for the way in which humans related to the world; this allowed them to process other sensory impressions by reflecting on them and thus to produce new ideas. This *liaison des idées*, he argued, was what drove human development. Condillac attributed the development of language to the fact that man had been a social creature even before societies had formed. Adam and Eve had had the ability to communicate their concerns directly and without language, but post-diluvian man had to contend with the double contingency of consciousnesses that were no longer mutually accessible. The souls of humans, who were now exposed to the forces of nature, were only capable of perception and, because impressions gained in this way were combined with innate ideas, humans were able to gain knowledge that could be remembered. This assumed the ability to focus attention on different matters as well as the ability to image things. Communication came into being when members of the different sexes encountered each other and used shouts and gestures to express their feelings for one another. If these feelings were directed at the same object, it created a situation in which a sense of 'we' arose, and this allowed the shouts and gestures to become signs that could be repeated. Condillac stressed that this was not a deliberate invention, involving conscious action, but an emergent process in which signs became stable through such situations being repeated multiple times. In this way, the signs could be remembered and subsequently used with the intention of communicating.[94] Memory and the ability to identify things that were similar created a sense of expectation, and this led to sets of possibilities, which in turn gave meaning to specific events because they could also have turned out otherwise. However, at this stage, the process was still primarily based on human urges rather than the ability to reflect. For this reason, there was still a long way to go until the *parole* of arbitrary linguistic signs. Until that point was reached, humans expressed emotions through shouts and used bodily gestures to communicate with others on things concerning the world. The tools of language were gradually refined. The Greek epics presented a survival of this performative basis of human communication. It was not until much later that people sought to develop signs with which those who were not present could be reached. Hieroglyphs were a first such attempt. Condillac interpreted them as pictorial symbols which, through their use in religion, gained a second, secret layer of meaning. Outside a religious context, hieroglyphs had developed into letters through inattentive use.[95]

Just under a decade later, in his treaty on the origins of inequality, Rousseau rejected Condillac's history of how language had developed because he believed that a pre-social situation in which there was coincidental and fleeting contact between the sexes would not provide the stability required to create permanent linguistic signs. For it to develop, language thus required society. However, Rousseau did follow Condillac in thinking that the beginnings of communication through language lay in the human need to express emotions. Once sounds and gestures had reached the status of repeatable signs, general concepts shaped by the intellect could follow, enabling the subsequent development of abstract terms for genera and groups as well as the syntax of language. Rousseau then went on to refer to the 'almost demonstrable impossibility' that language was a human invention,[96] and later supporters of the idea that language was divine in origin, such as the parish priest Johan Peter Süßmilch, referred to Rousseau to defend their theory.[97] However, anyone who understood how Rousseau had tied language to society as the location of culture had to realize that what he had actually meant was that language was as unlikely as society itself.

Herder's arguments in his 1770 treatise on the origin of language were more direct.[98] They differed from Condillac's social model and Rousseau's idea of the externalization of human nature by linking the origins of language closely to Herder's positive anthropology. Herder described man's development from animal to human being as a continuum and a process during which humans' instincts and innate abilities lost their power and humans gained reason and the ability to live in freedom. Man's 'prudence' allowed him to develop language. Herder used this term to describe the relationship between humans and their senses. According to Herder, humans were able to focus their attention, select sensory impressions and observe themselves doing so. This control of their senses, combined with the human ability to reflect on things, allowed humans to give names to the different phenomena they observed. Man's ability to develop and use language as a way of naming things thus was based on an individual's reflective relationship with the world. Individual languages, on the other hand, were associated with groups. Man's ability to use language was social in that it was realized as a system of languages. Unlike Süßmilch and other authors who had participated in the call from the Royal Prussian Academy of Sciences for submissions on the origin of language, Herder argued that humans no longer needed language for God to teach them.[99] Language changed from being a means of establishing a relationship with God to one that determined the relationship between individual humans and with themselves, constructed by means of their intellect. In this way, culture became an expression of the human ability to engage in (non-religious) reflection, which humans used to find their place in a world that they had endowed with meaning.

Not long after Rousseau's treatise on the origins of inequality, the lawyer and parliamentary counsel Charles de Brosses (1790–77) described this situation even more clearly in his *On the Cult of Fetish Gods*.[100] In this examination of the religions of sub-Saharan Africa, which was translated into German in 1785 and coined the term 'fetishism' in religious studies, de Brosses followed Voltaire's civilization history by comparing contemporary phenomena in order to understand and thus disenchant the past. The Egyptian worship of objects and animals corresponded to the religious practices of African tribes that could be observed in the mid-eighteenth century and similarities existed in the religions of India or of the Celts. De Brosses was interested in them because they illustrated the general ways in which human thought processes developed at an uncivilized stage. De Brosses took it for granted that religion developed from fear and ignorance, and it was expressed in the worship of fetishes because man's relationship with the world was still dominated by imagination rather than the intellect. This power of imagination also led to dreams being considered reality. It created a world instead of understanding it, and it was what allowed humans to fall victim to deception by their senses in the first place. The 'imagined' meanings could only be separated from the relevant phenomena once the intellect determined man's view of reality and once reason could question the senses. Then meanings changed from being dreams to becoming a reality which humans could relate to using the signs they chose. Fetishes inevitably disappeared through this new relationship with the world and were replaced by deities that required symbolic representation because the human ability to think in abstract terms had increased. Rational ideas of God thus did not necessarily have to be derived from divine revelation. Monotheism within human history had many different origins, and divine revelation merely provided additional certainty.[101]

## Reflexivity: Symbols and myths

Religion had thus become part of the epistemic constellation that produced orders of knowledge characteristic of different civilizations. By the beginning of the nineteenth century, the conditions under which such questions could be discussed had undergone a number of fundamental changes. Until the 1780s, knowledge of non-Christian religions was based on imprecise travel reports, interested representations by missionaries and the information that ancient writers provided and which was repeatedly referred to. From a European point of view, there was little difference between Hinduism and Buddhism due to a lack of the relevant language skills to understand the texts and to translate and make them available to European intellectuals more generally.[102] In the 1780s and 1790s, this situation changed in relation to India, China and Japan as well as Egypt. The hieroglyphs had not been deciphered yet, but Napoleon's expedition had thrown fresh light on ancient Egyptian culture. The interest in non-European civilizations, especially those in Asia and the Indian subcontinent, increased noticeably once English trading colonialism changed to military and political colonialism. The languages of the world, their characteristics and relationships to one another thus became a source which could provide detailed information on the history of humanity and which could fill a number of gaps in the knowledge that had been available in Europe up to that point. Herder had not regarded language as an instrument of thought but as its determining factor. As long as religion was understood as one of the most decisive cultural products of humanity, religious texts could also be read in the hope of gaining information on the ways in which human culture had been produced as a creation of different ways of naming things, combining meanings and narration.

In 1812, the Heidelberg classical philologist Georg Friedrich Creuzer (1771–1858), who had also studied theology, published his *Symbolik und Mythologie der alten Völker, besonders der Griechen* (Symbolism and Mythology of the Ancient Peoples, Especially the Greeks).[103] His aim was to describe the 'physics', that is to say, the inner workings, of symbols and myths and, in order to do so, he made use of religion, especially of that of the ancient Greeks, in order to analyse the cultural 'ways of speaking' and their different peculiarities in the surviving texts. In this way, religion became the preferred social space for human symbolization. Creuzer distinguished between two fundamentally different epistemes. He identified Greek religion as symbolic and Egyptian religion as mythological, describing the former as an open and discursive practice of speaking and using signs that tended to approach things scientifically, whereas the latter was 'hidden speech', which derived from holistic, pictorial representations in which the complete picture was not presented simultaneously and not as a sequence. This contrasted with the Greek way of thinking, which was segmented, and thus made up of terms, and which was represented by the pile of pebbles symbolizing the god Hermes and by alphabetic writing. This distinction was the starting point, and Creuzer combined it, on the one hand, with a theory of the practical use of signs and semiosis and, on the other hand, a strictly ethnographic examination of religious myths and symbols, ranging from Egypt, Greece and India to Persia in the second edition of the work. Creuzer identified the idea of the 'mediator', which foreshadowed Christ, in the cult of Mithras. The physics of the symbol, on the other hand, contained a theory that treated writing in a pictorial way, with hieroglyphs depicting terms and letters depicting sounds, along with analyses of the semiosis in the allegories, metaphors and symbols that Creuzer found in the myths and religions he had examined.[104]

Creuzer described the process of imagination and symbolization by which people were able to talk about a reality that was not tangible, and he described how they used tangible reality in order to do so, creating narratives and symbols. Thus, the Christian idea of a sacrament was rooted in the Greek concept of a sign and in the practice of mysteries: it was not a holy process but a sign of understanding for those who believed in it and for initiates.[105]

In several places, Creuzer's work showed that his symbolism was also concerned with drawing the boundaries between disciplines. It was to provide a framework for philological examinations of religion, with which Creuzer wanted to distinguish the way in which philosophy had used ancient religion for its own ends since the Renaissance. This was in line with the general move towards differentiation in universities at the turn of the century. By thus outlining the social subject of a discipline dedicated to exploring the production of meaning, religion was placed within the context of culture as such. For Creuzer it was the main space in which human symbolization took place and it was thus the point at which the eighteenth-century discourse on the origin of religion and the social and cultural significance of language and writing intersected. Both were part of human nature; humans used their power of imagination and their reason in order to process reality, to recognize it and to endow it with meaning; they did this not just by representing reality through signs they had created but also by observing it as a carrier of meaning itself. This assumed a human and social ability to reflect on oneself and on human culture, an activity referred to as 'recollection' by Herder. Culture provided an internal environment for society, which replaced an absolute observer. In this process, religion had been reduced merely to a part of this space of reflectivity, but it was still of use to view this observation of observation. Even if transcendence had been created by humans, it retained its operative and semantic functionality. It allowed individuals and society to stand at some distance and view themselves from different perspectives.

## The religion of philosophers and theologians

Religion as a social phenomenon continued to be part of the way in which society reflected on itself when philosophers addressed the topic. For philosophers, too, religion offered a perspective from which society could observe itself as culture, that is to say, a historically and globally variable sequence and non-simultaneous juxtaposition of meaning and structures. The external views of religion that philosophers had expressed since the eighteenth century were different from previous external and self-descriptions, not just because they changed the phenomenon itself but also because, as philosophers, they took a fervent view of religion. The change in social patterns of differentiation meant that philosophy, which had encompassed any subject studied at the universities – from natural philosophy to metaphysics to theology and history – gradually separated into different disciplines, which now all claimed to be sciences. This required them to define separate fields of study and develop an appropriate methodology. The contribution of Kant (1724–1804) to this process was his *Conflict of the Faculties* of 1798, which indicated that philosophy acknowledged there were different spheres of rationality and areas of knowledge but was not yet prepared to abolish any hierarchy amongst them.[106] As the custodian of reason, and despite it being the lowest-ranking faculty, philosophy claimed a superior position in the disputes with those disciplines whose concern was merely to order society, such as medicine, law and theology; it thus reduced the other disciplines to fields in which the human mind was active in a purely mechanical way because these disciplines were based on the interpretation of texts the validity of which was based on authorization by a government. It was for this reason that theologians depended on philosophers to prove the necessity of God's existence. Even when it came to the question of the divine origins of revelation, theologians had to consult the historical division of the lowest faculty because it was a 'matter of history'.[107]

In his introduction to the second edition of his *Critique of Pure Reason* in 1787, Kant had prescribed a constructivist relationship with reality, based on the natural sciences, as a programme for metaphysics, and this presumably explained his optimistic view regarding philosophy's privileged position of observation.[108] Later philosophers found it more difficult because they focused on the self instead of reason. The *Älteste Systemprogramm des deutschen Idealismus* (Oldest Systematic Programme of German Idealism), attributed to Hegel (1770–1831), already gave a sense of where this would lead. The text states that philosophers required a sensuous religion, just as the 'great masses' did. A 'monotheism of reason' was necessary, and the philosopher should make his ideas 'aesthetic, that is to say mythological' in order for them to be of interest to the people. 'A higher spirit, sent by heaven, has to found this new religion among us; it will be humanity's last, greatest work'.[109] In order to maintain its position as the foremost intellectual discipline, philosophy, a rational mythology, had to become religion itself or at least concern itself with God.

## The absolutely free being

Religion was no longer criticized by philosophy; instead, theology's former servant incorporated it. This was made possible by determining the phenomenon in a new way and assigning it a different place in the social space. A Romantic statement claiming that religion was more than just morality and seeing it as only that would result in 'meagreness and drought':[110] this illustrated the fact that religion was no longer thought of as having a particular function in the process of sociation or as guaranteeing particular patterns of social order. The philosophy of German idealism and ideas that derived from it in the first half of the century observed religion as a phenomenon connected to the relationship of the human mind to itself and to the associated patterns of social individuation. It was a way of addressing structural changes that, as has been shown from different perspectives in other sections of this book, led to church-based Christianity now only providing partial social inclusion. However, this meant that religion was free to address a different problem posed by functional differentiation: how could a social *persona* capable of being included be formed into an 'absolutely free being'?

The 'Systematic Programme of German Idealism' had begun with the 'free, self-conscious entity' that allows the world to emerge from nothing, and it ended with a mythological philosophy as a religion.[111] In his preface to Hinrich's philosophy of religion of 1822, Hegel explicitly distanced himself from Kant and his philosophical approach to religion, but Kant's work had already changed the understanding of religion, making it possible for Schleiermacher and Hegel to develop their concepts in the first place. The basis for this was that Kant had examined religious experience and the question of God's existence as part of his programme of interpreting the world guided by the principles of natural science. As early as 1766, in his *Dreams of a Spirit-Seer*, Kant addressed the question of whether spirits existed and how humans could interact with them as a question of observing observation that was based on 'conceptions of experience' and that led to the conclusion that it was impossible to know anything about the spirit world because it was impossible as a human being to remember what one had felt and experienced as a spirit.[112]

Kant posed the question of God's existence in each of his three *Critiques* – the *Critique of Pure Reason*, the *Critique of Practical Reason* and the *Critique of the Power of Judgment* – providing comparable answers each time. With regard to the thing-in-itself, the greatest good and the highest nature and in relation to the laws of morality, rational thought declared the existence of God to be a reasonable and thus necessary assumption, which, however, did not *prove* God's existence. From the point of view of pure reason, the Supreme Being was nothing more than an 'ideal though a faultless one'. In terms of practical reason, a highest good was only conceivable if one posited a supreme nature that was capable of causing effects in a way that corresponded to the moral attitude of the individual. It was only the assumption that God existed which allowed humans to behave morally. Similarly, in the context of the power of judgement, a moral origin of the world was necessary for there to be laws of morality. Beyond this, however, there was no possibility of supporting humans in their 'belief' of God's existence.[113]

Thus the question of God had been reinterpreted as a question of how to apply theoretical thought. In the roof of his cathedral of reason with its nave and two aisles, Kant had decided to assign God a position in the eaves, and He did not appear anywhere else in the building. In 1793, Kant laid out the consequences of this technical theoretical distinction for a philosophical *Religion Within the Boundaries of Mere Reason*.[114] In the preface to the first edition of this book, he defined morality as being action that did not follow a particular aim. Its purpose is to have none. In order to unravel this paradox, seeing as will must always be directed towards a particular aim, the idea of a highest good is necessary 'to postulate a Supreme, Moral, Most Holy, and Allmighty Being'. In this way, it is possible to give our actions a purpose and thus to justify them to our reason.[115]

This represented a Copernican turn. It was no longer religion that formed the basis of morality but religion as a social fact was the result of the paradox inherent in morality. Philosophical religion, therefore, was no longer a matter only for philosophers but for the entire university. Its social form was the 'general church', in which those who took seriously their morality as a philosophical religion and lived according to its rules should come together as a family and as a 'voluntary community of the heart'. Because this 'community of the heart' did not need and also had to forego anything relating to church services, it would not have been a particularly visible community. Kant thought of church-based religion as a historical phenomenon, which in his time could only be justified if its aim was to establish religious faith more generally. For this reason, it was only church religion that had a universal history, but it was impossible to write a history of religion as morality that was implemented in everyday life as it was not a public condition and individuals could only become aware of it by practising it themselves. The philosophers' religion of morality had become a matter for the (free) individual who continuously reflected on the attitudes underlying his actions.[116]

## The spirit that observes itself

Hegel had largely followed Kant's concept of religion in his early writing, but in his *Phenomenology of Spirit* (1807) he made it clear that he no longer wanted to treat religion as the focus of a philosophy based on reason but that he identified religion as an area in which the spirit differed from self-consciousness. The concept of God was the result of the spirit engaging in reflection, allowing man's consciousness to view itself as if it were that of another entity; otherwise it would only be able to view itself as if it were something else.[117] This then led to the programme of religious philosophy which Hegel had been presenting in various lecture cycles since 1824.[118] In the preface to Hinrich's philosophy of religion, referred to above, Hegel had laid out in detail with reference to Kant's position why he was looking for a different approach to a philosophy of religion. 'Finite reason' could only be made to believe the stories that surrounded the 'eternal truth' if the matter itself, religion, was destroyed. But because the spirit continues to yearn for an undefined afterlife and because nothing could be got from 'a hollowed-out god', the only support offered to the spirit lies in the emotions: 'emotions are the only way left in which religion can exist'. This was directed against the theology of Schleiermacher, who had announced that he would be publishing a work on dogmatics, which Hegel perceived as competition. Accordingly, he sharply criticized the idea that 'emotion was the true and even only form' in which religiosity could still be authentic. Hegel disagreed with this because the essential purpose of the spirit was its freedom. A religion based on emotions, however, could only manifest itself as a 'feeling of dependence' so that a dog would have to be considered 'the best Christian' as dependency was his main state. Anyone who wanted to base religion on feelings would also have to allow 'the subject' to determine the content of these feelings. Religion could enter a person's heart as a feeling, but general ideas such as God, truth or freedom could not be based on the idiosyncratic subjectivity of an individual's emotions. For Hegel, religion could only be part of the world of the mind if the mind dictated is contents.[119] He thus accepted the subjective aspect which religion had gained as a feeling but he insisted that as a social phenomenon it was not just the sum of the emotions of different subjective consciousnesses; instead, it required the general nature of the mind in which historical and rational elements were brought together, preserved and elevated. Consciousness could only become aware of itself through its opposite, the mind, and vice versa.

In his *Phenomenology of Spirit*, Hegel had already presented his ideas on the matter. The preface stated that the word 'god' was in itself 'a meaningless sound, a mere name'. It could only gain meaning if it was not thought of as an existence or essence but as a 'something reflected into self, a subject'.[120] Since consciousness only knows the things it has experienced, it will only be able to access the mind (as well as itself) through experience. The mind thus has to become a different entity and become the object of itself. This conscious breaking up of immediacy, the estrangement from oneself and the return to oneself was the active movement that allowed consciousness to access the mind.

From this basic dialectical operation of distinguishing between another entity and oneself and the return of that which had been distinguished to that which was immediate, Hegel then constructed a philosophy of the mind in which the subject did not simply turn the world into its object; instead it only became the subject by observing the world from which it had separated, in the same way that the world only became reality and took on a particular shape by being observed. Hegel defined religion as the sphere in which the 'spirit knowing itself' appeared as its own 'pure self-consciousness'. However, this consciousness was not yet the same as the 'detached independent otherness', so existence and self-consciousness were initially not the same. Only once the spirit conscious of itself and the spirit of religion coincided was religion perfected. Then the spirit that was conscious of itself became a reality for itself and at the same time the object of consciousness, achieving its 'self-subsistence'. Accordingly, Hegel distinguished between three 'realizations': the concept of natural religion; 'religion in the form of art', in which all naturalness had been abolished; and a combination of the two, which he identified as 'revealed religion'. In the latter, the spirit that knew itself continued to be constrained.[121] Liberating it and enabling it to view itself on the basis of a 'detached independent otherness'[122] was clearly the task of a philosophy of religion that took the form of speculative theology, although, as philosophy, it had to insist that it was not religion.

Hegel's *Lectures on the Philosophy of Religion* were thus not concerned with the relationship between God and man but rather were intended to lay out what could be learnt about the mind if one started with the concept of God. Accordingly, in 1827, Hegel defined religion as the concept of God which was the absolute truth, 'the truth about all things'. As both God and the mind were an object of consciousness, they became each other's counterparts. Man's consciousness experienced God as one who revealed Himself and, for the subject, this experience manifested itself as a certainty based on faith and emotion with ideas and modes of thought that were determined by the objective form of religion. Hegel thought of the latter as a historical sequence of such relationships of the mind to itself, both on a subjective and on an objective level, and so he considered a perfected religion to be one in which consciousness experienced the unseparated-yet-separated relationship between man and God. Thus, Christianity represented the intended form of religion. To justify this, Hegel pointed to both the relationship between God and man and the Trinitarian concept of God, with which Christianity had realized the mind in its religious form. Here, the essence of the mind became its own object.[123]

These dialectical definitions did not result in Hegel creating a history of religion. His repeated treatment of 'specific' religions, which were supposed to give the 'coincidental', 'bizarre' and 'absurd' elements found in the different religions a sense of necessity, was a two-dimensional and predominantly geographical and typological overview of the knowledge that had been collected in Europe about Asian religions since the beginning of the nineteenth century.[124] Hegel's contribution to the external observation of religion was systematic. He attempted to save religion in its historical form from the criticism of reason by describing it as something in which the consciousness could see and experience itself as eternal spirit, thus allowing it to view itself as spirit. This movement occurred on the objective and thus social side as well as on the subjective and finite side. In religion, man's consciousness could experience itself as spirit; in philosophy it only observed itself. The understanding of social relations as emerging from distinctions which returned to themselves was preserved in Hegel's theory of God as a product of the consciousness and thus the definition of religion as a result of distinctions. Thus, the ontology of being dissolved into deliberate distinctions and relationships of observation.

## Potentia existendi

The challenge which lay in this for contemporaries became evident in Schelling's reaction. In his *Philosophy of Mythology* of 1828 and his *Philosophy of Revelation* of 1842 he argued that God develops independently of consciousness and that God is, therefore, not simply a being, but must have had an existence that preceded being and consciousness.[125] While Hegel – whose concept Schelling referred to as a 'negative philosophy' – argued that God resulted from consciousness separating from itself, Schelling sought to locate God in absolute transcendence once more by identifying Him with a *potentia existendi*.[126] God is God because there is nothing without Him; He alone is the power to exist. He is pure will, and as a force, He is able to create Himself as a being in the act of creation. Hence the world comes into being through God differentiating Himself from Himself. He is thus defined not as one but as 'several'. He is Himself both subject and object simultaneously, just as being is defined by this trinity: subject, object and the unity of this difference. Because God produces that which is different from Him – the world – consciousness is part of God in so far as it is a product of nature. For this reason, for Schelling the conceptions of God in European and Asian mythologies appeared as a 'pure inner figment of the imagination of human consciousness', but they are 'necessary conceptions' and not fantastical inventions. In the *Philosophy of Mythology*, he traces them from the original 'relative monotheism' to the polytheism of classical antiquity.[127] The philosophy of revelation, then, is devoted to proving that the original monotheistic idea of God was realized in Christianity.[128]

Schelling insisted that this process, which from a technical theoretical point of view was not fundamentally different from Hegel's, did not incorporate religion into academic reason, but instead that he had placed himself as a philosopher in a relationship to an existing god. He believed Hegel's 'negative philosophy' to be a thing of the past, whereas the future belonged to positive philosophy.[129] Things did not develop in this way, because positive philosophy rejected the scheme of subjectivization, first discernible in Kant's concept of religion and later expanded by Hegel, instead drawing the distinction elsewhere so that it became the counterpart of consciousness, which it turned into the object of the revelation in a 'non-divine' world. As Hegel had rightly seen, this deprived the spirit of its freedom. For this reason, mythology did not allow the self-observation of consciousness to evolve but instead gave space to the idea of God.[130] Schelling described the world, man and religion as a relationship of the divine to itself. The human process of sociation and the development of man's relationship with himself could make little use of this.

**Self-relationships**

Karl Rosenkranz (1805–79) wrote in 1831 that, in reading Schlegel, Schelling and Görres, he had never understood how contradiction had emerged in history. Only Hegel had allowed him to understand that consciousness was the object of development and that consciousness experienced itself in the development of recognition. The contradiction consisted in the development of consciousness and identity through an entity differentiating itself from itself. Rosenkranz then described the development of natural religion as the evolution of the original 'being outside oneself', which became possible for man by positing for himself a God from whom he could differentiate himself much like he could distinguish himself from nature. Self-relations became possible as a progressive separation from oneself. Man creates inner environments from which he can face himself; he needs only to have himself as the goal.[131]

A decade after Rosenkranz, Ludwig Feuerbach (1804–72) developed this programme for his investigation of the 'positive religion of revelation' with particular radicalism and clarity.[132] He wanted to present a 'critical philosophy' of Christianity, not a speculative philosophy of religion, nor a 'child-like mythology'. A prerequisite for this was to characterize philosophy's viewpoint as being different from that of religion. Religion and philosophy are the same thing in that they are 'ways of thinking'. However, philosophy thinks in concepts, whereas religion does so in pictures. It is 'dramatic' and, one can add, performative in its liturgical practice. It is not only the connection with the different mental faculties of the human mind – sensual imagination on the one hand and conceptual reasoning on the other – that allows philosophy to assert itself as a non-religion. Because the modern world has 'become master over' Christianity, transforming it from a figure of flesh and blood into a 'ghost', religion does not have to 'express', and this becomes the task of philosophy.[133]

This view expressed that secularization made religious philosophy possible and necessary. Because Feuerbach clearly located the two faculties of the human mind in the human 'psyche', he was able to distinguish his philosophy of religion from 'mythical pneumatology' or ontology. It became a 'pathology of the psyche' by examining the images of Christian symbols and thought with the methods of analytical chemistry. The meaning here is twofold: a pathologist exposes the internal 'organs' of the psyche and can thus also bring any disease to light, with this alone expected to have a therapeutic effect. Religion's beauty and usefulness cannot justify it being protected. One has to counter it with 'the water of reason'. It must then be added that, as a result, the theologian is left as a mere 'anthropologist', who considers religion's external features and thus cannot access the pathology or psychology of that which is being observed. The result is that the system remains opaque to itself in its academic enquiry and self-observation,[134] and it can only expect to gain any real information about itself from its environment and external descriptions.

The starting point then for defining religion is 'consciousness', which marks the difference between man and animal. This consciousness has a twofold aspect from the very beginning: it is the consciousness of man as a species and as an individual. As a result, humans have two lives: the internal life and the external life that relates to the species. Religion is part of the internal life; it is man's awareness of his infinite being as an infinite consciousness: 'You are God to the extent of your unrestricted self-awareness.' Every being has its god, 'its highest being in itself'. In as far as, and because, human consciousness develops a relationship with the mental aspect of a person's life, God exists.[135]

Religion is thus moved out of the social, species-related dimension of human life and into the psychological dimension. Man produces religion as the 'deification' of aspects of his being. These 'externalizations' become religion for him, and he becomes a religious man because he knows nothing about this. The *differentia specifica* of religion, therefore, is 'a lack': it is the misunderstood and unconscious self-knowledge of man. In it, man does not relate to himself but 'as to another being', and in this way religion's self-relation becomes self-alienation. The more divine a God becomes, the more negatively man views himself as man and the more he negates his own sensuality.[136]

This view includes a positive as well as a negative relationship of man to himself, which takes the shape of a relationship between God and man. In his first wide-ranging progress through Christian imagery, Feuerbach introduces those symbolizations which share features with the nature of man. These include the god who is concerned about the fate of men, who becomes man and suffers for humanity, as well as the Trinitarian God and the Mother of God – who represents the principle of love in the relationship between father and son. Pantheistic theology and mysticism also allow humans to develop a positive relationship with themselves. The former enables a relationship of humans with themselves as another entity; in the latter case, the relationship is with themselves as beings that are also physical. In this way, Feuerbach manages to identify humane elements in celibacy. The Christian who vows to remain celibate has no desire for sexual love because God serves as a replacement. In his subjectivity, that Christian sees himself as a perfect being who lacks nothing, not even the opposite sex.[137]

As Feuerbach then explains in a second part, religion conflicts with the nature of man whenever the relationship between God and man is mediated by a third party and man thus hands himself over as if he were another. This is the case with regard to the arbitrariness of the divine plan of salvation, and this is true also if God has created the world but it then follows the laws of nature. Religion is destroyed if mediating factors 'creep in': 'The machinist avoids direct contact with the deity'. Man also casts doubt on his own 'selfness' in proofs of God. Revelation is an insult to man because it turns the process of definition between man and God on its head and leads man to adopt a form of morality without a moral attitude. Hegel's speculative philosophy also contributes to the negative self-relationship of man. It turns man's consciousness of God into self-consciousness and thus returns God to man as his 'own nature': 'Thus it is acknowledged here what religion conceals and avoids through taking recourse to imagination, but it is done in such a way that this admission of speculation is still indirect, opaque and imperfect'. Speculative philosophy is still involved in religion – it is religion in the sense that it 'posits God as an objective being that is separate from us'. Hegel, Feuerbach argues, had found no way of expressing the identity of human nature with itself and thus he had retained notions of 'duplicity' and mysticism.[138]

This view is witness to a semantic and technical theoretical operation that involves a twofold paradox. Feuerbach claims that the identity of philosophy and the condition of the possibility of practising philosophy are an undisputable state of 'not being religion', but this only 'experiences' itself and knows about itself if it has religion as its object. However, by declaring religion also to be the poorly understood part of man's self-consciousness directed at itself, philosophy makes religion disappear. Philosophy thus lacks its object and the counterpart to its own identity. If philosophy wants to avoid becoming religion, this distinction must be established elsewhere. For this reason, following his criticism of Hegel's *Philosophy of Right*, which had already presented all the relevant arguments, Feuerbach also added a section describing the sacraments as an insult to man. The sacraments take man's ability to act and move it into nature through bread and wine; at the same time, they negate themselves because their effect cannot be experienced by the senses. Feuerbach wrote that, if the theological interpretation is removed from the performativity of these images, the daily acts of eating and drinking would allow an individual to experience himself in the unity of mind and nature. Eating and drinking 'are indeed in and of themselves religious acts'. Philosophy's new 'other' was now 'life': 'Thus, one need only interrupt the ordinary, common course of events in order to endow the common with uncommon significance and to give life as such religious meaning'.[139] Man had yet to make this sacred, but he no longer required religion to do this. From now on, psychology was responsible for man's internal, authentic self-relationships. Philosophy now had to reinvent itself as a philosophy of life. Religion had been 'released' from all social and psychological duties, having already lost its psychological function according to theory. However, even Nietzsche's *Ecce Homo* required it in order to give life and the body an aura of the absolute, with deities competing with each other: 'Dionysus versus Christ'.[140]

An alternative semantic set-up was developed by Karl Marx (1818–83) and Friedrich Engels (1820–95). Feuerbach's propositions already gave precedence to human practice over observation. *The German Ideology* then laid out that man did not initially encounter himself and nature in consciousness, but in the production of what was necessary for life. The social form of reproduction of life dictates the places from which the world can be observed as well as the distinctions that can be made. Like all other ways of describing the world, made possible through the division of labour, religion is thus tied to the conditions of material reproduction. One cannot, therefore, gain an independent position of observation through the contradiction that brings forth something through differentiation from itself. This contradiction must be replaced by the negation of the 'ruling' conditions. This, then, is neither philosophy nor religion but communism.[141]

In its examination of religion, philosophy highlighted the structural processes of differentiation that changed the function of religion because its relevance to the system shifted. Up until Feuerbach, it was associated with social inclusion through the internal life of a *persona* capable of inclusion and reflection. With Feuerbach's 'pathology' of religion, doubt was cast on this and responsibility for the point at which communication and consciousness intersected was given to a new discipline that focused on the psyche.

## Re-stating religion's foundations

The question that follows onto this inevitably focuses on theology. Since it also had to accept that these structural shifts had occurred, it accordingly had to process and work through the shape of religion. What else could be said of religion in an environment devoid of religion if the 'worldliness' of religion also continued to be taken for granted and considered necessary? The Catholic response was entirely performative.Even the texts that were written, such as *Athanasius* by Joseph Görres (1776–1848) or *Symbolik* (Symbolism) by Johann Adam Möhler (1796–1838), had a performative aspect. They did more than describe: they were intended to consciously produce and demonstrate.[142] Görres's text illustrated the independence of the ecclesiastical framework *vis-à-vis* state sovereignty and affirmed the universal claim of the Christian world order, to which the state was also subject. Religion appeared here as a fully hierarchical church surrounded by enemies. Möhler's contribution was to introduce distinctions according to confession. His *Symbolik* was dedicated to presenting the dogmatic differences in the confessional statements of Catholics and Protestants. Möhler regarded the Reformation as a necessary event in the history of Christianity because the truth only became visible in the dogmatic differences. It was not about finding a single truth, let alone a common one, but about showing and asserting it. This was a clear denial of an abstract, collective concept of religion that involved plurality.[143] This was matched by historico-philosophical outlines such as that of Friedrich Schlegel (1772–1829) in 1829, whose starting assumption returned to the idea that man was created in the image of God and who insisted on an original revelation and the divine origin of language as well as countering the progressive model of history with a cyclical concept concerned with return and restoration.[144]

The theology associated with this religion, which appeared as a church, now occasionally also referred to itself as 'religious studies' in its books. In terms of content, however, these books were neo-scholastic dogma and textbooks that provided the traditional recommendation that the inner life of man should be accessed through sensory impressions and exercises so that a religious attitude could develop there. This had been the pre-modern concept of the relationship between internal and external aspects of man.[145] Catholic transcendence continued to be beyond this world, but it made an appearance in the world through mediums. The interest in mesmerism and its media and the multitude of private revelations could make a particular kind of transcendence real and visible that could not be processed in its entirety by the self-referentiality of consciousness. All of this may be understood as a consistent refusal to reproduce the transformation of society in religion. However, it did enable a particular kind of criticism of the modern world. This then changed to produce an alternative world which thus became the performative negation of the actual world. This negation was also social practice.

Protestant theology saw itself as a science that did not want to break off the connection to other disciplines and thus took their criticism of religion seriously. This required accepting the way in which the different fields of knowledge had been divided, one advantage of which was the possibility to move controversial or aporetic issues to other disciplines. Schleiermacher (1768–1832) states in his *Glaubenslehre* in 1822 that theology and philosophy had parted ways. Ever since, the inquiry into creation has been assigned to philosophy and the 'higher natural sciences'. The idea of spiritual beings that could at least form an 'apparent body' and appear only temporarily in our world also 'does not involve any demonstrable impossibility'. Too little was known about other worlds and how they interacted.[146]

The consequences of such complacency, of course, comprised the necessity of determining one's own subject area and the position of theology within religion oneself. In his *Speeches*, Schleiermacher finally had rejected the 'enlightened' definition of religion as morality and had also distinguished it from metaphysics. Instead, religion needed to be defined precisely on the basis of being different from metaphysics and morality. Religion did not determine any obligations and it did not define any legal relationships either. Metaphysics defined the significance of infinity for man, and morality aimed to extend freedom into infinity. By contrast, the essence of religion was neither thought nor action, but intuition and feeling. Religion intended to observe the universe and to allow its influence to 'seize it and fill it in a state of childlike passivity'. Religion gave man a place in the universe, considered man to be the representation of that universe and saw the infinite in every individual thing. These ideas resulted in the notion that 'religion is the sense and the taste for the eternal', which allowed it to 'imagine all events in the world as the actions of one god'. Schleiermacher wanted to leave to metaphysics all speculation on the nature of this god prior to the world's existence, although his preface presented creation as an act of 'self-compulsion' of the deity that led to two conflicting forces operating in every existence.[147]

With his words, Schleiermacher went beyond the attempts to accommodate the concept of religion within the development of non-theological bodies of knowledge and argumentative rationalities by moving transcendence to a different position. Schleiermacher eliminated the concept of transcendence and replaced it with the question of how the world could be experienced in a religious sense, with religion being presented as a semiotic project for the individual. In this way, God became a 'generator of possibilities', allowing humans to engage in meaningful action and experience in an infinite world characterized by contingency, with this action and experience being designated as religion. Schleiermacher explicitly stated that religion was only 'one of the possible forms of intuition', drawing the obvious other consequence: such intuition depended on individual perspectives that were specific to that individual. In this way, miracles could be defined as events that were suited to being viewed mainly from a religious point of view. Thus, Schleiermacher had separated the concept of religion from orthodoxy, divine worship and immortality and had presented it as an observation of the world that related to God. This observation resulted in religiously disposed semiosis, which found its expression in religious moods. This necessarily implied the plurality of the subjective observation and experience of the world.[148]

These individual idiosyncratic religious feelings then came together because people felt the need to communicate with others about this experience, if only to reassure themselves that they had encountered 'nothing that was not human' and because the plurality and finite nature of one's own experience in the face of the infinite universe persuaded man also to experience it 'through an external medium'. In this way, religious feeling became a confession that did not occur through conversation in any arbitrary social setting but in special societies that were dedicated to this particular purpose. Here, the person moved by their experience stood up before the assembly to 'present their own intuition', acting as an object for the rest of those assembled but also taking them away with the person into their realm of religion. Religion was not something that could be taught; people could only be 'encouraged' to imitate others. In this way, man's innate predisposition to religion was set free again, having been hampered by the 'obsession with understanding'. Here Schleiermacher presented a Pietistically inspired church with the characteristics of a movement with members who were present as the true church of those who already had religion. However, the existing institution was needed for as long as there were people who were still looking for religion. Schleiermacher believed that these individualistic religions, which always related to others, would come together to form a community that would not have to be called a sect, because, to this community, 'the religious world was an inseparable whole'.[149] Schleiermacher's religion corresponded to the emerging abstract and collective concept of religion in the late eighteenth century and it ignored the fact that sociation no longer depended on communication between people who were present. Hegel identified this problem in Schleiermacher's concept very precisely.

At the same time, Schleiermacher adhered to the idea that Christianity was elevated above all other religions. However, he identified a kind of historicity and developmental dynamic in Christianity that was fed by a polemic force directed against itself and that possibly went beyond it. Individual elements of Protestant doctrine thus became mere 'possibilities of thought', whose persuasiveness could be put to the test.[150]

Schleiermacher had developed a concept of religion in which religious experience in a secular world was more than just a possibility; instead it always presupposed it as the counterpart to religion because it illustrated the 'lack and the purpose'. Schleiermacher did not mean a perception of the universe that was 'understood', but one that was felt and sensory and which could, if necessary, also exist without a 'deity'.[151] The particular challenge for later Protestant theologians was to relate this concept of religion to the philosophy of consciousness developed by Hegel and his followers.

In 1847, Ludwig Noack (1819-85) published his *Speculative Religionswissenschaft* (Speculative Religious Studies), writing that he did so to counter the view expressed in the *Deutsche Jahrbücher* that theology could be removed from the *Encyclopaedia of the Philosophical Sciences* and its subject matter, religion, be divided amongst philosophy and history.[152] With Hegel's arguments as a basis, Noack attempted to go beyond what Schleiermacher had argued, while also rejecting Hegel's impertinence of a philosophy of religion. He criticized the fact that Schleiermacher's definition of religion as an emotion did not become an 'objective position' of 'true thought', making a genetic definition of religion impossible. According to Noack, this problem was also found in Creuzer and Görres, and only Friedrich Christian Bauer had succeeded in examining the object of investigation thoroughly and conceptually as a historical phenomenon. Noack presented Hegel as the person who had completed what Schleiermacher had begun. By defining the absolute as the common focus of religion and philosophy, he had made it possible to write a 'genetic history of religion', which showed how the concept of religion manifested itself in external worship, making it possible to reproduce the development of man's religious consciousness. At the same time, however, Hegel had also destroyed religion because his philosophy of religion laid out how philosophy could take the place of religion. For Noack, this resulted in the necessity of a renaissance of religious studies, which he defined as the 'recognition through thought of the religious self in the thinking process of his self-realization'.[153]

This discipline of religious studies considered itself to be a religious act. It was not an 'external description' and was not intended to be a self-description in the strict sense; instead, it was a performative process that produced and observed at the same time.[154] Noack therefore defined religion in the context of a relationship between humans and God, arguing that it was religion that allowed humans to develop self-consciousness in the first place through a 'synthetic unity' with something 'that they were not'. Self-consciousness cannot guarantee this unity itself and is dependent on the absolute and its effect on the self-consciousness. Hegel had defined religion as a purely spiritual relationship between spirits, and Schleiermacher had considered emotion to be the foundation of self-consciousness and thus also of religion. Noack followed this, defining consciousness as an entity independent of the self, which humans experience as a 'life force' and as the 'revelation of God in the self'. Unlike with Hegel, religion is *not* one particular manifestation of the human spirit amongst other kinds of manifestation; instead it is found in a particular sphere of the mind.[155] Noack went on to develop this concept of religion in terms of a dialectical relationship between the self-consciousness and an external and assumed god, always rejecting Hegel's and Feuerbach's positions and referring to Schelling and Görres. Noack outlined the 'philosophical history of religion' that followed from this as an 'ethnography of the religious mind' and, now following Hegel again, as a 'history of the religious development of mankind' right up to the historical demise of the idea of religion in the world. Here, too, Hegel's idea of the history of religion being a directed process towards perfection was reversed and, thus, so to speak, 'de-secularized' or resacralized. The concept of religion was inherently truthful from the beginning, and history is the process by which all elements that are alien to this concept are removed from it. Noack refers to these stages of the revelation of truth, which he traces from fetishism to religions with a personal god (including Judaism), as 'direct', 'reflected' and 'free natural religion'. This process of purification, which gradually separated the divine from the finite, resulted in Christianity, the 'perfection of religion', which had been 'preformed' in the 'original germ of the religious mind'.[156]

In this way, religious phenomenology becomes a theory of signs like Auerbach's, which explains the ethnography of mythology as a 'continued prophecy of Christ'. As with Schlegel, who considered history to be structured according to cycles, in Noack's figurative concept, Christianity's elevated position is only compatible with a historicized understanding of religion if past, present and future are not completely separated from each other. In this regard, the terminology of the relevant semantics not only posed problems which affected all confessions to the same extent, but also provided solutions that were not specific to any confession. In order for Christianity's identity and superiority to be preserved despite the historical change in religions, it had to insist on an essential core that transcended history and which could only be posited and displayed.[157]

In 1824 and 1825, Eduard Zeller (1814–1908), a Tübingen theologian, presented the consequences of a historicist understanding of history for the identity of Christianity and for the significance of self-descriptions in this context of communication and observation in two treatises on the nature of religion and the perfectibility of Christianity.[158] Zeller initially presented his examination of the nature of religion as a conceptual history. It first focused on defining *theologia naturalis* from the Middle Ages onwards and then addressed Protestant theology, which, Zeller argued, had the task of highlighting religion as a *habitus practicus*, faith as trust (*fiducia*) and its basis as a God-given emotional disposition. Zeller took this as a starting point to distinguish faith from action and knowledge, stating that the devil was also capable of the latter; he then confirmed Schleiermacher, whom he believed to have found an appropriate way of doing this. The problem with Schleiermacher, however, according to Zeller, was that his solution resulted in the different faculties of human life becoming separated, and so Zeller moved on to Hegel, who, he explained, had defined religion as a particular type of thought and imagination. Zeller also criticized this definition because it ultimately presented religion as an imperfect type of insight. Having given a summary of Feuerbach's ideas, Zeller moved on to his own suggestion, which intended to avoid reducing religion to knowledge, action or emotion, instead presenting it as a form of the spiritual life that encompassed all its aspects, but the notion of which must take into account the subject's dependency on God. Through the subject's relationship with God, religion determines how the subject acts, feels and thinks. The objective form of religion – church and cult – is based on this subjective experience of the world.

If the objective form of religion was based on the relationship with God, which influenced all spheres of an individual's life, it had to be taken into account that it might change.[159] Zeller addressed this point in his second work on the 'Perfectibility of Christianity' (*Perfektabilität des Christentums*). He took as his starting point Protestant eschatology. When the 'birth of the new is approaching', the signs and portents of what is to be expected increase without there being a clear view of the future, making it impossible to tell whether it will continue the present or represent a break with it. Like other religions, Christianity was not yet perfect when it was founded, although the driving forces of change did not assume prophetic private revelations but a 'natural development of a principle of revelation inherent in humanity'. Medieval theology had expressed this trajectory towards completion as the idea of perfectibility, but the Reformation had shown that, as an idea of gradual revelation, it had become obsolete. However, the Reformation was also mistaken in thinking that it was restoring the 'original temple', and Protestant theology only came into its own once it became clear that it was not identical with the New Testament. Zeller demonstrated the different variants of this process of self-historicization by examining eighteenth-century theology and he concluded that all revelation is necessarily connected to the level of human knowledge. At no point, then, can dogmatics assume to know the 'perfected truth'. The consequences that were drawn from this differed, however. Schleiermacher thought it was possible to go beyond Christianity, while Schelling thought it was a necessary conclusion of transcendent idealism to abandon Christian doctrine. Feuerbach affirmed this because he considered Christianity to be a damaging religion. On the basis of this summary, Zeller drew the conclusion that Christianity's ability to evolve must in future not just be considered as a way of extending Christianity but also as a means of 'correction', both in relation to how it was taught as well as in relation to what was taught. In this way, it would become possible to think of perfectibility and revelation as the same thing. Arguing against the supernaturalists, he came to the conclusion that the perfectibility of Christianity should not be understood just as a perfection but as a 'real reorganization' and 'also in parts a reversal of what was taken for granted in the consciousness of its founders, not only in its form but also in content'.[160]

This was a decisive step in Zeller's description of Christianity as a historical phenomenon. He presented it as a social entity, and any changes in it should no longer be interpreted as the stepwise evolution of a 'being' that was already part of the plan in the original revelation but as an evolution subject to contingency and with its own dynamics. Its past could be described, but its future direction and results could not be predicted. This also meant that the question regarding the unity of this process could no longer be approached 'ontologically', and Zeller accordingly reformulated it as a question of the identity of a social phenomenon that was dependent on the viewpoints of different observers. If such a 'fluidity of religious consciousness' was assumed, the question arose as to how it had been possible for Christianity to 'remain itself in more than name for any length of time'. Thus, it had to be possible to recognize the 'identity of a principle' in the 'flow of phenomena', in the same way that a bodily organism renewed itself but could be 'recognized' as the same body. For this reason, it had to be possible for the religious life of a particular time period to be explained 'on the basis of the Christian principle', justifying the designation 'Christian'. Christianity's identity in its evolution as a religion now depended on the perspective from which it was observed. This forced the observer to accept that there would be a point in that future of infinitely progressing change at which 'humanity's thread to Christianity' would tear and its religious consciousness would adopt a new form. By contrast, the idea that the finite human history of religion consists in the Christian principle can then only be shown by the philosophy of religion and history.[161] This meant that Christianity required the secular thought process of philosophers in order to ensure its identity.

This statement revealed the internal contradiction of theology engaging in reflection and self-descriptions that were based on the system. In a world of many religions, Christianity could only maintain its special position in the history of mankind if it gave up the idea of infinity and thought of itself as finite. The text thus employed a performative contradiction. The open and undirected evolution of religion had to become teleological, but it did not appear that theology was capable of effecting this change. Philosophers of history and of religion are responsible for teleology and, thus, also for Christianity's unity and identity during the evolution of religious consciousness. Its identity can no longer be guaranteed by the individual self-descriptions of its theologians and requires teleological external descriptions of global, secularized society.

This destabilized the foundations of theology. In order for it to continue to be the science of religion it had to go beyond dogmatics and become the field of religious studies. In that way, it would be able, from within the system, to take an external view of Christianity in the context of religious plurality and non-religious elements. However, this presented theology with the contradiction inherent in self-descriptions: they are part of the system and its operative reproductions but must also attempt to separate themselves from them. For this reason, Zeller posed the question of how a 'philosopher' should behave if he was a 'servant of the church'. For the common people and more generally, religion was a 'matter of the heart' that was not compatible with the language of intellectual concepts. Because the people are aware of this difference, the theologian as a clergyman is always confronted with the 'accusation of hypocrisy'. This authenticity problem means that the words of the clergy are not understood in their 'direct and religious sense' but are taken dogmatically. Zeller suggested a solution to this, but it was somewhat contradictory: because science should be determined by truth rather than ideas drawing on sensory, everyday life, 'truth' needed to change. In order to convey that it was an 'idea' which benefited the clergyman in his personal life, it had to come before an educated person's rational judgement. If religion was defined as a matter of emotions, a theologian, who is beholden to truth, could only exercise his church office as an authentically held religious conviction if he presented religion as a conviction that does not require rational justification.[162] This 'acquired', deliberate naivety provided the same answer that could already be observed in Catholic approaches to re-stating Christianity's foundations. Saving Christianity in a modern world from conventionality derived from reflection and its 'arbitrariness' while also preserving the directness of emotions that had their origin in another entity presented two choices: either the act of believing (as an act) or the historicity of religion had to be made invisible. The safest thing was to do both, but it seems that Christianity was no longer in a position to do this on its own. It had become dependent on external observations by the secularized world.

These texts reflected the fact that the semantics Christianity employed when thinking about itself had arrived in a modern, polycentric society. It is remarkable how clearly religion addressed the general problem of how identity and change could be combined by social entities as they evolved in a functionally differentiated world. In doing so, religion had once again become a means by which society could reflect on its situation and, in this regard, it went further than contemporaneous philosophy and social theory because the problem of maintaining the system was more pertinent to it than other areas of society. The question was what form a religion could take if it was to consider itself Christian while also adapting to the idiosyncratic disposition of individuals and enabling them to understand experience and action in the (secularized) world as religious experience and action. Religion's particular challenge once again was to endow a considered identity with an authenticity and necessity that did not depend only on religion.

## Shifts

The semantics associated with religion between 1720 and 1850 document profound shifts in the way arguments were constructed in the symbolic and imaginary fields of self- and external descriptions of religion. The questions were, first, why religion was a phenomenon of human history; second, what its nature was; and third, what its function was. Before Hume, no one had expressed any doubt concerning the idea that religion was a constitutive and thus universal phenomenon of human sociation. This idea appeared to be confirmed by studying all historical sources and all peoples with whom European conquerors and colonizers had come into contact. It was an accepted idea that an original revelation underlay this universal phenomenon. This original revelation had given the first human couple and their descendants an original form of monotheism, which, however, had been forgotten after the Flood. Thus, once Noah's descendants settled in all parts of the earth, idolatry and polytheism developed and monotheism did not reappear until the Israelites experienced a new revelation. Hume's criticism of the reliability of travel reports threw doubt on the universality of religion in human societies and this became the starting point for his *Natural History of Religion*. In addition to this, Hume developed a more radical version of the deist alternative to an original revelation, described above, namely that humans had derived their idea of a creator god from observing nature. Hume turned this idea around, placing humans in the world as ignorant and helpless beings, rather than having people capable of recognizing the divine laws visible in nature. Man then externalized himself due to his ignorance and this resulted in religion. This idea that religion was a human projection and product with which humans projected their nature and their spirit into the world was decisive for the future semantics of religion and could be interpreted in different ways. Herder and Rousseau believed that it reflected man's ability to create symbols and connected it to the idea that religion brought forth man's own divinity. Hegel would not have disputed this, and believed religion and God to be the result of an externalization of oneself, that is to say, of the absolute spirit. Around the middle of the nineteenth century, the question was once again posed in a way that aligned with Hume's views: religion allowed man to produce a pathological image of himself and his divinity. To generalize, one could say that, at the beginning of the nineteenth century, humanity had religion because it had a god; in the middle of the nineteenth century, humanity had religion because (and in as far as) man considered himself to be a god.

The change in the concept of religion complemented this, occurring as a semiosis of meaningful configurations. In the beginning, it had been imagined as the result of processes of perception and reception, which encompassed recognition and the idea of an original revelation or the rational insight of natural religion as knowledge based on reason. According to Hume, the multitude of different forms of religion was the result and example of the human ability to develop symbols. In order to be the object of rational criticism, it could no longer be considered the result of rational insight. Starting with Hegel, religion came to be identified with a separate mode of thinking, which could be either sensory, and thus the opposite of reason, or performative, dramatic and pictorial, and thus different from abstract concepts. Religion could thus also become an emotion or could be considered an innate human *sentiment religieux*.

The question of individual salvation played a subordinate role in reflections on the function of religion as early as the eighteenth century. Deists considered it to be a necessary prerequisite for civil society. The belief in a life after death that would remedy the inequality and injustice of this life was to enable humans to live in an ordered society. Even Vico considered religion to be the first civilizing power that humans had produced themselves. Around the middle of the eighteenth century, the fact that a form of morality based on individual moral behaviour was considered to be important for social order already indicated that the *societas civilis* was moving towards civil society. Accordingly, Kant saw God as a guarantee enabling an individual's reason, morality and capacity for absolute judgement. The semiotic configuration of religion indicated a shift from recognition to the formation of meaning, and religion's function as a regulative idea combined this shift with the task of organizing a society that was increasingly viewed in terms of the ideas of Mandeville or Smith. Later, these two elements became separate entities again. The production of meaning through religion became a field for the mind to engage in reflection, according to Schleiermacher and Hegel, and this allowed the relationship of modern individuality with itself and with others to be articulated to the point of pathology. To this extent, religion was freed from the requirement of making modern sociation possible, and instead, it was now responsible for processing the consequences for an individual of this sociation. However, modern sociation also continued to be an enigma. The society of idiosyncratic individuals that was expected to order and shape itself required something to hold it together, a tie consisting not of fear of judgement after death or of morality but one made up of emotions. It also very clearly was no longer organized by authority, but by relationships involving transfer. For this reason, religion continued to be useful as a medium through which modern society could view itself and the ideas concerning its basis, and formative principles could be articulated and continuously updated. Finally, religion could also serve as the counterpart for other areas of cultural studies, allowing the latter to develop an identity whilst enabling religion to 'posit' Christianity.

5

# Secularization: A valid concept?

As much as there is agreement that the significant instances of secularization at the end of the eighteenth and the beginning of the nineteenth century represented a profound turning point in the history of European Christianity, views differ as to whether they were symptomatic of a long process of secularization in the course of which the importance of religion in society gradually decreased. The semantics of religion, which were traced in Chapter 4, indicate that the extent to which European societies were shaped by Christianity was a factor in the way they communicated with themselves regarding their own modernity. From the nineteenth century onwards, different concepts of secularization continued to provide an answer to this in one way or another. One could, like Karl Löwith, present the philosophy of history that was essential in the establishment of modernity as a secularized version of salvation history. Alternatively, like Hans Blumenberg, one could portray modernity as legitimate in its own right and not requiring religious explanations.[1] The course of these controversies cannot be traced in detail here, and this also applies to the attempts, in particular by historians, to resolve the aporias of the discussion by replacing secularization with de-Christianization in the hope of escaping teleology by focusing on developmental cycles.[2]

## The process of secularization as a concept

Instead, the various epistemologies of the term should be taken into account. There are three variants in the current discussion. It is understood (and criticized) as a normative concept, as a well-founded empirical one and, finally, as a constructivist observation. If the normative basis of the term is emphasized, the concept of secularization represents one of the great master narratives of modernity. Manuel Borutta has recently traced the emergence of the concept from the confrontation between European liberalism and Ultramontane Catholicism, revealing how it developed as the basis of an originally political programme that identified religion as a foreign body in a liberal state and its society. This political battle cry then migrated via religious studies into the emerging field of sociology and thus became a fundamental element in the sociological interpretation of modernity. Since then, social theory has contributed to this master narrative without reflecting on its polemical and political history. In keeping with this in a number of respects, Albrecht Koschorke analyses the concept of secularization as a hegemonic narrative, whose success and attractiveness consist above all in the fact that it does not define religion from within modern society, but rather relegates it to its edges or identifies it with an atavistic vestige of pre-modernity, which compensates for the distortions of modernity itself. In the present-day globalized age, secularization, as a teleological concept with a universal claim, provokes radical, fundamentalist counter-narratives, which serve to create an anti-Western identity in the societies of emerging nations, primarily in the Islamic world. Fundamentalism as well as the 'return of religions' thus appear as the consequences of a successful story of secularization, whereas the criticism and the growing doubts about it may be seen as resulting from and depicting Europe's loss of power and its increasing eccentricity in a polycentric world of 'multiple modernities' or even postmodernity.[3] These interpretations are plausible, but they do not address the question of whether the political genesis and function of a particular concept prevent it from being used academically or what alternatives there are to the idea of secularization. First of all, one would have to note that the normative, political associations of the term not only serve to make it immune to empirical findings, but actually attract this kind of contradictory information. On the one hand, present-day societies provide data on a dwindling interest in religion and a decline in religious practice, while, on the other hand, the idea of the return of religions in European societies and global configurations is frequently raised.[4]

For this reason, José Casanova and Talal Asad, while taking into account the normative implications of the concept, understand it as a primarily heuristic model, whose usability results from its suitability for classifying empirical findings and providing a context within which they can be defined. Casanova has concisely summarized the three elements of the term. First, the progressive differentiation of the spheres of life and values that characterize modern European societies leads to the exclusion of religion from most social institutions and areas of life. Second, this is connected with religion withdrawing from the public and political space of modern societies and becoming a private matter. Third, the road to modernity is marked by a fundamental disenchantment of the world, with the result that religious meanings are increasingly disappearing from social stocks of knowledge and interpretative contexts.[5] Max Weber emphasized that Christianity itself has vigorously promoted this disenchantment of the world since the Middle Ages.

The argument regarding differentiation is the least doubtful, although Asad emphasizes the public significance of religion in many modern societies as an argument against it. Casanova gives empiricism its due by decoupling the three elements of the concept from each other in order to take into account different, country-specific historical developments and configurations. This makes it possible to describe different variants and progressions that the process of secularization has taken in individual societies and their religions.

A concept of secularization elaborated in this way enables an empirically informed sociology of religion, but it is easy to overlook the fact that the concept of secularization already appears in it in two respects. Not only does scientific analysis presuppose it, but it is also already included in the empirical evidence (which the concept is intended to organize) because the facts which constitute this empirical evidence only become visible if a distinction is made between religion and non-religion. In this regard, one might refer to a liberal critic of Catholicism such as Johann Caspar Bluntschli, who analysed the relationship between state and church from a psychological perspective in 1844 and thus provided a phantasmatic orchestration of the Sonderbund War in Switzerland.[6] For Schleiermacher, too, the 'non-religious' was a necessary prerequisite in order to develop a sense and a taste for infinity; religion only became possible in the face of its absence and, conversely, the notion of 'absence' assumed that religion existed. Thus, addressing the question of religion as part of society outside the concept of a universal Christian world order and under the conditions of modern sociation – that is, according to Luther's reinterpretation of the Augustinian juxtaposition of *civitas dei* and *civitas terrena* as a distinction between spiritual and secular rule – always presupposed the distinction between religion and its secular counterpart, regardless of whether the question was treated in internal self-descriptions of religion or socio-theoretical external descriptions.

As a result of such theoretical arguments regarding difference, Niklas Luhmann's approach was to describe the academic and everyday condition of the world as the result of observations. Scientific concepts can then be regarded as distinctions employed in the observation of first-order observers, who produce a structured, meaningful social world in their communication and observations; in this world, religion exists side by side with, for example, the economy, and both are considered to be part of society.

In this way, secularization becomes a concept that indicates Christianity was already aware in the Early Modern period that it existed within a social environment organized according to other principles and producing meaning through a different kind of rationality to religion. This was a precondition for European Christianity to ultimately be able to semantically locate itself within an abstract concept of religion that was historically universal and morphologically plural. This cohesiveness manifested itself in the wave of religious self-descriptions that were published from the end of the eighteenth century onwards once this abstract concept was developed, and which lamented Christianity's position in the midst of a world of unbelief.[7] Moreover, a non-religious (philosophical, political and socio-theoretical) examination of religion had always required that its own position be distinct from religion, for which the semantics of religion provide ample evidence.

Secularization can thus be understood primarily as a category of observation rather than a teleological concept or normative stipulations, and it allows the social entity of religion to be regarded as distinct from others. As secularization does this in the context of society, it focuses on how this distinction is endowed with meaning, maintained and socially reproduced, that is to say, how religion gains social form. In the last third of the eighteenth century, Adam Smith separated the market economy from the state-controlled economy, introducing the term 'mercantilism'; as he demonstrated, this distinction was the precondition that allowed the economy to operate separately from politics, making it possible for an appropriate economic theory to be developed. Similarly, secularization can be seen as an effect resulting from a particular way of giving religion, as a category of meaning, a social form.

A scientific discipline that adopts the notion that secularization is an observational category focuses on a particular type of empiricism from the outset and does so from a particular perspective. The question that is pursued is how, under a particular set of historical circumstances, the difference between religion and other social spheres is produced operatively and how it is observed. This in no way implies teleological assumptions but, at most, represents the challenge to identify the conditions in a particular set of circumstances that may control the continuous selections which result in future conditions.

In relation to religion and society, this results in three areas in which theoretically relevant empirical data are collected. The most obvious area is the link between social differentiation and the institutional development and shape of religion. The second important area is represented by the nature and means of inclusion in religion, including the way in which social and psychological *personae* are formed; this is important because doubts regarding the universality of religion are more likely to occur on an individual than a social level, as the atheism discourse beginning in the Early Modern period illustrates. The third field is made up of the way in which external and self-descriptions present religion and religious elements as producing meaning because these descriptions not only outline how religious action could shape itself, but also, more importantly, how events could be experienced as religious events. In the following, the findings of the preceding chapters will be summarized briefly in relation to these three areas.

## Differentiation

Until the end of the nineteenth century the different social manifestations of European Christianity were closely connected to the reproduction of social and political order on many levels. Churches were organized as institutions of power or were closely coupled to Early Modern state structures of authority. Society's order of privileges, its power relations and the distribution of property were reproduced in clerical hierarchies and the system of benefices and patronage. After 1684, confessional territorial states attempted, often successfully, to enforce a particular confession in order to produce a homogenous population, and this was also an expression of the symbiotic competition between church and state. As the French Revolution erupted, the first breaks became visible. It foreshadowed the changes and shifts in the relationship between religion and society that were to occur by the middle of the nineteenth century in Western and central Europe*. Within a few years, French society was transformed from a collection of subjects dominated by a monarch into a fervent community that created its own political order. The nation became its potent cipher, violently driving church-based Christianity from the centre of society, excluding it from the most important aspects of the creation of political and social order, and seeking to destroy it as a means of social inclusion. At the same time, even the nation was convinced that stable associative relationships between patriots could not be achieved without religion and it thus invented the Cult of Reason and of the Supreme Being.

The great instances of secularization and the legal changes in the system of confessions and churches through concordats, the Organic Articles, constitutions or laws were the ways in which European states accommodated Christianity in a society of legally equal citizens and property owners by the middle of the nineteenth century, gradually turning churches and confessions from privileged corporations with sovereign rights into associations that brought together private interests. State and society were separate; the state had won its competition with the church, terminating the symbiotic relationship to its own advantage. Church structures could no longer act as ruling organizations, and this allowed new forms of institutionalized Christianity to evolve. In the Catholic Church, the end of the aristocratic church led to the professionalization of offices and allowed the purposeful expansion of pre-existing organizational elements. As a result, in a very short time, a world church developed, in which authority, the treasury of grace and dogmatic sovereignty were all centred in Rome. The Protestant church, which continued to be closely linked to the state, adjusted to a civil society and its processes of sociation through social movements, exemplified by free churches and a network of all kinds of societies. In both Catholicism and Protestantism, global confessions developed from participation in European imperialist missions to civilize other parts of the world. World religions did not develop during the Axial Age but in the course of nineteenth-century imperialist globalization.

Political and legal measures thus led to religion differentiating from other social fields; at the same time, individual confessions could continue to receive preferential and privileged treatment as state churches. Strong state control was also still possible, as was the use of religion for political means, as laid out in concordats and Organic Articles.

By the mid-nineteenth century, confessional state church law had led to religion increasingly becoming a private matter, but this differentiation did not mean that Christianity had disappeared from public and political spaces. The main reason for this was that the transformation of a society of subjects into a nation was not without its challenges, and this applied also to the adjustment of the old European autocratic monarchical governmental order to a participatory order without aristocratic rule. In both cases, areas emerged in which Christianity could act and participate in discourse, which ensured that it continued to play a role on the political stage although this did not mean that it had any significant political power. Christianity helped to present what had been the sacrality of the monarch as a form of personal piety. It was also used in order to encourage citizen subjects to love their citizen kings and to display this affection, and former dynasties made use of Christianity to present themselves to the political public as royal families. However, religion could no longer serve to legitimize a monarch's power, and thus jubilees and self-coronation gradually replaced sacral coronation rituals. Church-based Christianity also helped to create the homogenous sphere of action and experience that the new political order required, turning it into tangible experiences through festivals and church rituals. It provided symbols and rituals that allowed nations to worship at altars of the fatherland and provided their heroes and martyrs with state funerals, thus creating an image of the nation as a community of patriots related to each other through shared memory and a willingness to make sacrifices. However, with regard to the further increase in parliamentary democracy, it is perhaps even more significant that religion provided this public political sphere with a subject that provided structure but also provoked debate because the fundamentalist aspiration of shaping politics and the world exclusively on the basis of Christian norms – an aspiration expressed in all confessions and churches and not just in Ultramontanism – could be exploited as political options and alternatives with a significant mobilizing power.

Ideas on political and social theories dealt with these constellations in imaginative narratives and outlines. While these could be associated with particular political camps, the underlying basic topologies were very similar. They focused on a narrative of an ideal pre-Revolutionary European world in which Christianity was an integral ordering principle, doing so because this image could be used as a reference point for criticism of contemporary processes of differentiation and change. These ideas did not present social integration as a process facilitated by media and institutions, but as one that still depended on different types of sociation amongst individuals present in one place. Since Rousseau, there had been concerns that Dissent would allow individuals to refuse to participate in a society that produced and legitimized its own political order, in a sense resigning one's membership of society. For this reason, the nation was envisioned as a fervent community held together by emotional ties. Rousseau's civil religion could offer little redress here as it was still conceived of as an institution which would require people to obey laws and authorities, and it was thus still inspired by the *societas civilis* and deism. Conservatives and Romantic utopians devised new amalgams of Christianity and reason, which were to provide the basis for cohesion and solidarity between free individuals in the different nations. Thus, the new civil religions were not simply secularized derivatives of religion but inventions. At the same time, Zeller, a theologian from Tübingen, presented secularization as a historical and social process. He believed that Christianity's continued survival depended on how much longer it would be possible to experience and observe the world as shaped by Christianity.

In all of this, both the constitutional monarchy and the nation continued to be entirely secular concepts. Frederick William IV's religious failure was mainly political in his attempt to create a church union and introduce the *Agende* as a substitute for refusing to modernize Prussia politically. In these decades, there were indications in all western and central European countries that it would not be possible to use Christianity indefinitely as a source of symbolism for modernized processes of political integration. Competition came above all from universal conscription to the national armies. In future, it could offer the most important context of symbols and experiences for the nation of men. This was the background for the liberal theory of secularization to be formulated as a political programme. It was a reaction to the fact that, through the cataclysmic change from hierarchy to function as a means of creating social structures, problems and challenges arose which could no longer be solved within religion but which required religion as part of the solution. Liberalism aimed to put a stop to this.

# Inclusion

In all confessions, pre-modern piety had closely linked public worship with the reproduction of social order both at a local level and within the family. The mass and the Eucharist, church discipline, pew ownership, processions and brotherhoods represented this connection between social inclusion, social stratification and piety that was organized within the parish community. Once this connection was broken, the result was a decline in ties with the established churches on the part of the faithful, which, from the 1830s onwards, could no longer be ignored by the churches. The parish became a problem within the structure of the church because of urbanization and large-scale economic migration and because the processes by which social structures developed, thus making inclusion possible, moved from the local to the regional, trans-local and gradually also the global level.[8] Inevitably, this meant a change in the significance of piety and confessional adherence for social inclusion and exclusion. At the beginning of the nineteenth century, migration and the transformation in European power structures through war led to the emerging nations developing into multi-confessional societies. As a result, the combination of tolerance and spatial segregation that the confessional territorial states had used to regulate confessional mixing could no longer continue. In a nation that was intended as a participatory entity of individuals who had equal legal rights, confessional plurality required a plurality of confessions in the sense of negative equality. Membership of a particular confessional group should not be allowed to lead to advantages when it came to social inclusion, but it also had to be ensured that it did not lead to exclusion, especially in a political context. This principle had not been implemented entirely by the middle of the century, but Catholic Emancipation in the United Kingdom and the disputes regarding mixed marriage, civil marriage, a confessionally based education system and the legal status of one's confession as a private matter were stages in the process by which civil societies in Europe addressed the consequences of the division of Christianity into confessions that had competing, absolute truth claims. Confessions were expected to accept plurality, which meant that they lost their significance as a means of social inclusion.

The change in the social institutionalization of Christianity had similar consequences. Organizations and social movements no longer rely on membership by birth, which is sufficient for a corporation. Instead, membership had to be presented again and again as a decision and continued commitment of autonomous and responsible individuals. For this reason, the numbers participating in church activities and attending public worship and the frequency with which this was done were now monitored. Piety was produced as a mass event in Jubilee years, popular mission and spectacular supraregional pilgrimages, and the mass scale of these events was then reinforced and disseminated through media. A faithful individual who is a member of an organized faith community in a pluricentric society requires occasions for acts of faith and decisions. The papal briefs and encyclicals on the errors of the modern world provided these, as did the dogmas of the Immaculate Conception and papal infallibility. The dramatization of membership and commitment strongly encourages exaggeration and fundamentalist radicalism.

Just as adherence to a particular confession became a private matter, public and private divine worship also gained a new focus on the individual. Worship in churches could regain some of its attraction if it contributed to addressing the tensions and problems relating to the formation of individuality in the polycontextual order of a functionally differentiated society. Because the increased focus in religion on the family was initially intended to compensate for a lost sense of security, unity and orientation and was also implemented in this way in practice, it was expressed by a strengthening of the status of family, which Hegel described both as a model of society and its opposite. Piety now related to the family, as was illustrated by the increased significance of church occasions marking rites of passage and a new funerary culture. In the narrative of loss and deficiency, which modernity had created about itself since Rousseau and the Romantics, religion and family occupied complementary argumentative spaces. Both were institutions that had been inherited from an older, vanishing world and could thus be identified as areas that preserved an earlier order. They thus became places of refuge, with religion serving as such for the sensual female and the family fulfilling this function for the male active in public life. For men, their profession was the first means of social inclusion and the family thus became the counterpart to society. For women, who were responsible for turning this counter-space into that of a natural relationship that contrasted with society, religion was a means of sociation, although, at best, it allowed them to take on a marginal and lower-ranking position of dependence in the social order. In his *Psychologische Studien* (Psychological Studies), Johann Caspar Bluntschli, one of the first theorists of the liberal programme of secularization, represented the state as male and the church as female. This was an anxious reaction to the fact that the tectonic shifts in the structure of society caused by urbanization and early industrialization created problems that the liberal state and its society knew they could not solve. This task was left to Christian churches and groups, where it was assigned to women on account of a pre-Revolutionary understanding of gender roles. In this way, in all confessions, a new form of public piety developed in congregations and associations that were concerned with education, the care of the poor and missionary work. This opened up new ways of life beyond that of a caring wife or made new public spaces outside the home and family accessible. Social change had created a social situation for religion in which it contributed to the development of fissures in a patriarchal world. For this reason, the feminization of Christianity, which was primarily a feminization of piety and the different forms of piety and not one of church institutions, was accompanied by a misogynistic discourse that involved sexualized suspicion of female piety and a targeted *culpabilization* of the female conscience. Michelet's pamphlet on priests and women was the opposite counterpart to Bluntschli's psychology. Men of the church, such as Bishop Wessenberg, occupied the middle ground, denouncing female piety as rapture and secret infatuation. Christianity's contribution to formulating an idea of femininity – a male response to social change and to an anthropology that levelled out differences – was poisoned.

## Communication and the creation of meaning

In the course of the first half of the nineteenth century, Christianity became a phenomenon of mass media. Newspapers, magazines, the publications of associations, devotional books and prayer books allowed religious acts and experiences to be communicated through mass media. The media amplified religious events, shaped and popularized particular pious practices and emotions, and provided paradigms of religious experience, including visions and stigmata. This created a new sphere of public worship beyond church services, which developed as a social reality of religion supported by mass media. Socially, religion took place through media events. In this way, the degree to which every kind of divine worship could be perceived increased, and even the most private forms of communication with transcendence could still become communication in a social space. It was, therefore, not surprising that this private communication with transcendence became a discursive space of reflection and an archive of imaginative visions through which communication as a phenomenon of transmission could be contemplated more generally and experimented with. Animal magnetism assumed that there was another world that penetrated the body of this world with inscrutable fluidity, was present in this world and was accessible to the special senses of human mediums. From the first third of the nineteenth century onwards, religiousness was thus transformed into spirituality.[9] Doctors, surgeons, psychologists, philosophers and theologians engaged in the search for an organ within the body that was home to this sense for transcendence, but this quest must also be seen as reflecting the lack of any theory of sociation capable of explaining the communication of the social and its emerging structures through media rather than through communication between individuals present in the same place. The only thing that existed was a combination of the division of labour with the 'invisible hand' or a dialectic that dealt with the absolute spirit that permeated the world in an inscrutable way. Hegel was unable to explain how absolute poverty could spread while there was a state that guaranteed ownership rights and the rule of law, and this illustrated the powerlessness of such theoretical instruments in explaining a world that was shaped by successful mass media.[10] Karl Marx responded to Adam Smith by replacing the fluidity of the 'invisible hand' with the enigmatic concept of 'surplus value', but this did not lead to much theoretical headway being made. At the end of the century, Gabriel Tarde developed a theory of societies that produced their own social order, which was the first to take media into account, arguing that, at their core, the social and social structures developed from 'imitation'. It became apparent which theoretical direction Tarde was coming from when he characterized the way in which imitation worked as social somnambulism, referring to theories of hypnosis.[11]

However, this constellation did not just result in new combinations of religious action and experience to create meaning, such as communication with the world of the dead through mediums. It also changed the semantics of religion and the concept of transcendence. Hume and Kant caused the deist universe of ideas to implode, and this released religion from the function of ensuring social order and law-abiding behaviour by encouraging fear of judgement after death. In this way, the religion of the *societas civilis* had ended before the legal disbanding of the *societas civilis* itself. In external and self-descriptions, religions became establishments in which man, through his ability to symbolize, created himself and the world, thus allowing the spirit to develop relationships with itself and others. Hegel summarized this by saying that the reflexivity of the spirit occurred in a sensory way in religion, whereas the same process occurred through abstract concepts in philosophy. Schleiermacher, his opponent, accordingly suggested that emotions and not reason were the basis of religion. Later theologians realized that this would undermine the connection between the creation of religious meaning and other areas of life, and they thus argued that all human faculties were involved in the production of religion.

Philosophical and, in part, theological semantics conceptualized a form of religion in which man himself became God and God was a result of the spirit differentiating itself from itself. Religion's function was now to shape and stabilize the formation of individuality in a social and psychological *persona* suited for the polycontextual society of Vico, Mandeville or even Adam Smith.

Not only had transcendence been moved to within this world, it had found a place within man himself.[12] Religion could now be interpreted as individual creations of religious meaning, which then required communication in order, as Schleiermacher put it, for the individual to reassure themselves of what they had experienced. Schleiermacher referred to the sense and taste for the infinite, and this characterized the creation of religious meaning as a willingness and ability to observe events in the context of infinity and to endow them with meaning from that perspective, instead of ascribing them to mere chance or earthly causality. Feuerbach subsequently posed the obvious question that resulted from this, namely under what conditions this reflexivity could be carried out as religion, that is to say, the creation of religious meaning, and what configurations of religious symbols resulted in pathological images of the world and of oneself. His research into the archive of images and symbols of European Christianity led him to the conclusion that it was preferable to exchange the sense and taste for the infinite with a sense and taste for this life. This represented serious competition for transcendence, and so the difference between this world and another could now only be maintained rhetorically or brought about in other ways, for example, through a Dionysian state of intoxication.[13] This answer to the semantic secularization of religion was related to the Catholic response. The only way religion could now be produced was through performative acts which created a distinction from the continuous reproduction of the world as it was. Schelling suggested this in his philosophy of revelation as well as in his mythology, and the Protestant Noack also tried to present the science of religion – his term for theology – as a religious act once more, in which observation and operation coincide. He presented the historical phenomenology of religion as a type of theory of signs that was to provide certainty on the identity of Christianity at all points of its evolution. Religion could no longer assume transcendence. Instead, recreating it in a secular world became its main task.[14]

## Observing processes of secularization

A historical study that views religion as a particular way of producing meaning and as a particular form of communication, therefore, must take into account that the occasions and events for communication and the production of meaning in relation to a distinction that can be regarded as religion – preferably a distinction between immanence and transcendence – may also become rarer. Unlike, for example, the economy, politics or law, religion only has a limited ability to generate such events, which rigorously shape motivations and exclude alternative actions. At the beginning of the modern age, concepts that had long been successful became less plausible. Predestination and original sin conflicted with the imperatives of modern individuality because the latter's conception was geared towards identifying the uncertainties of life as economic, legal or social relationships. It thus subsumed all the contradictions of a modern life. However, the profound process of transformation also brought to light new problems, such as that of the relationship between men and women, social problems, the way in which the political sphere should be organized and the global diversity of religions – and also individuality. Distinguishing between immanence and transcendence could transform these problems into meaning, and they could then become the object of the kind of communication that was identified as religion. In relation to the evolution of the social form of Christianity, this was probably the most significant of the changes that have been observed. Secularization itself gained a new form because doubt was cast on the central distinction by which religious meaning was created, to such an extent that, by the middle of the nineteenth century, it was no longer clear how this distinction could be maintained. Moreover, Christianity now depended in a hitherto unprecedented way on the continued evolution of society (not of religion!) producing problems that could be addressed in a religious way. Despite successfully adapting to significant social change, Christianity as a system within society found itself in a new position. This led to structural conservatism and the attractiveness of fundamentalist options.

It was a contradictory situation. Religion was aware of the fact that its distance from the world had increased, as was observed externally too. This was one of the consequences of functional differentiation. At the same time, corresponding to the increasing polycentricity of society, the further development of religion became more and more dependent on the evolution of society as a whole. Identifying systemically integrated spheres of action requires, almost by necessity, a solid concept of society. Only if one disregards this, is it possible to overlook or ignore the fact that functional systems are specialized in producing solutions for problems that move any subsequent problems into other areas. The familiar public semantics regarding the environment represent this process. Functional differentiation simultaneously increases the integration of society (understood as an association of things that are different) and its complexity (as the selection of compatibility of the different elements).

It is not possible to make any definitive judgement on the consequences that this constellation had and continues to have for religion in a modern world. There are empirically valid indications that, for decades, there has been a continuous decline in religious practice and adherence to an associated system of values in all wealthy countries of this world that have social orders which afford their members security and the ability to plan their lives.[15] This would suggest that these societies provide increasingly fewer occasions for people to see compelling reasons to produce religious meaning in the traditional social forms. Historians will be unwilling to draw the obvious conclusion that religion may not be a universal phenomenon, but a historical one of human sociation. Historians cannot tell what individual or social problems will occasion the production of religious meaning in the future, nor can they predict the extent to which Christianity, for example, will be able to use this in order to develop its own system. They will also not want to speculate on what the results would be if Islam as a religion were to be examined by societies that are in the process of modernizing themselves. However, for now, historians can state that secularization and religion as a system within society exist: they can be observed.

# Glossary

| | |
|---|---|
| *Agende* (Prussia, 1821) | Unified regulations for the liturgy and church services in the Prussian States introduced by Frederick William III. The intention was to bring together Lutheran and Reformed parishes as a national church (Union). However, both sides offered significant resistance. |
| *Allgemeines Landrecht* | General state laws for the Prussian states. A law code for Prussia that had been created in a complicated process from the 1750s onwards and finally enacted in 1794. It codified the old estates-based society, but also had a number of traits that reflected a modern, civil legal and social order. |
| *Altbayern* | 'Old Bavaria'. The area encompassing the original parts of the Duchy of Bavaria: Lower and Upper Bavaria, as well as Bavarian Swabia. In 1648, the Upper Palatinate was added and then the Palatinate in 1779. |
| benediction | A 'blessing' in the Catholic Church that is (usually) given by a priest, who makes the sign of the cross, says prayers and sprinkles those present with holy water. The intention was to entrust certain people and things to the particular grace and care of God. This practice was not common in the Protestant churches and was regarded as superstition. |
| benefice | The land or other sources of income allocated to an official for personal use, usually in return for exercising his office. |
| bulls of circumscription | Papal decrees (bulls) in which the boundaries of dioceses were redefined. In the course of the concordat negotiations after 1803, several such bulls were issued to adapt diocesan boundaries to the new political boundaries. |
| **Bundesakte** | German Federal Act. The founding document of the German Confederation that was passed by the Congress of Vienna in 1815. It was the constitution of the German states that had been united as a confederation of states. In 1848, the Frankfurt Parliament created a constitution for the entire empire that overrode the Bundesakte. After the revolution had failed, it was reinstated in 1850. |
| *Burschenschaft* | Student association in university cities with particular rules governing the admission of members, their behaviour and the interaction with one another. |

## Glossary

| | |
|---|---|
| **camarilla** | The term means 'little chamber' and refers to an unauthorized and influential group of favourites surrounding a (monarchic) ruler. It was first used in the Spanish Restoration under King Ferdinand VII between 1814 and 1830. Later, the term was also used to refer to the circle of favourites and advisers to the Prussian king Frederick William IV. |
| **Carlsbad Decrees** | Measures to curb 'revolutionary activities' that were decided upon in Carlsbad during August 1819 by the states of the German Confederation. The catalyst was the murder of the Russian Consul General August von Kotzebue by the student Karl Ludwig Sand. Essentially, the measures included the monitoring of fraternities, surveillance of universities and their liberal professors, and surveillance and censorship of the press. |
| **central Europe** | A geographically undefined region between the European states in the west with access to the Atlantic and those states east of a line drawn from Poland to Hungary. |
| *Chiesa ricettizia* | A group made up of the clergy of a particular place who were supplied by a communal fund (*massa commune*). They usually lived with their own families. The *chiesa ricettizia* led to communal church structures that were largely outside the control of bishops and to the recruitment of clergy from families of the local parish. It occurred mainly in southern Italy (Basilicata) from the sixteenth century onwards. |
| **citizen king** | An interpretation of monarchy and kingship in the first half of the nineteenth century. In the aftermath of the French Revolution, monarchs no longer understood and presented themselves as the head of an estates-based society, but as representatives and caring 'fathers' of peoples and nations in a civil order. |
| **civil religion** | The term can be traced to Rousseau, who argued for the separation of religion and politics but was of the opinion that a political order would not be stable without elements of religious doctrine and public religious rituals. During the French Revolution, this view led to the Cult of the Supreme Being. From the perspective of religion, this concept could be perceived as a political instrumentalization of religion. |
| **coadjutor bishop** | A bishop of the Catholic Church who assists another bishop. Often, such a coadjutor has the right to succeed to the episcopal see. |
| **communication** | Communication does not mean the transmission of information and/or meaning between A and B. As used here, the term means that B initially identifies a message from A as such (B could also assume that it was not directed at them), accepts this message as information and then understands it. It is thus mostly impossible for A to predict how B will understand the message. This is dependent less on the message itself than on the particular circumstances that are currently relevant for B, that is to say, at |

what point in B's own history of progress it is received. All of this also applies to A from B's point of view. Communication consists in events, which pass as soon as they become socially relevant and which cannot be repeated. There is only new communication. If a person repeats something, they must also take into account that it may be perceived as a repetition and thus also be understood differently from the first instance. If one thinks of communication in this way as having inherent 'contingency' for all involved, the question of how social coordination is possible and how lasting social structure can develop requires a complex answer. This book observes religion with that in mind.

**consistory** — In the Catholic Church, the term refers to the General Assembly of Cardinals. In the Protestant (regional) churches it refers to a church court or authority.

**Constitution of the Frankfurt Parliament** — The constitution adopted by the Frankfurt Parliament in March 1849. It did not become law because of Prussia's resistance, amongst other things, but, nevertheless, served as a model for a liberal, democratic political order.

**conventicles** — Unofficial groups with heretical views and practices regarding religious faith. Since the Reformation, the term has been used in Protestant churches to refer to Pietistic gatherings for prayer and edification in private homes.

**Deutscher Bund** — See under Bundesakte.

**differentiation** — The establishment through communication of a difference that marks the boundary between a system and its environment. Systems always engage in differentiation from an environment, which also means that the environment is relative to the system. This environment, however, also can be a system. Religion is a large, functionally determined social system, much like the economy or the family. Organizations are another type of system, and interaction systems comprise a third kind that exists for as long as those involved are present (or react to each other as if they were present). Thus, organizations also always involve interaction systems. This poses a problem for the organization: it can either make use of this situation in order to progress or it can isolate itself from it. All social systems are engaged in differentiation within society, with the latter being defined as all communication that is mutually accessible. All social systems thus have other systems and society as a whole as their environment. Society's environment consists of the different systems and (as is only now being realized) nature. Social systems thus operate in a very complex environment even if it is only perceived selectively by the system itself. Differentiation, as the process by which the system and the environment are distinguished, replaces the distinction between the whole entity and its parts. The latter distinction does not, in fact, represent a difference but presumes identity and would thus be contradictory if viewed as a difference.

| | |
|---|---|
| **early socialism** | Also called utopian socialism. It includes outlines for a socialist social order from between the French Revolution and 1848, which developed models of an ideal state, a society of common property and advanced industrial production. Early socialists were termed as such by the later (Marxist) socialists, who saw themselves as 'scientific' socialists. |
| *Erblande* (**Habsburg**) | 'Hereditary lands'. Those parts of the Habsburg territory in which the dynasty reigned by hereditary right (core Alpine regions, Bohemia and Hungary). |
| *Fabrica ecclesiae* | Describes the church building itself as well as the assets intended for its maintenance. |
| *Feldprobst* | Field provost. Chief military chaplain in Prussia, who directed all pastoral care in the army. There was a Protestant and a Catholic field provost. |
| **Formula of Concord** | The settlement of theological disputes that arose after Luther's death, which was reached in 1577 after a lengthy preparatory period. It focuses on statements on free will and good works, but also on the person and nature of Christ. |
| **Frankfurt Parliament** | The elected parliament that met in St Paul's Church (*Paulskirche*) in Frankfurt for twelve months starting in May 1848 during the revolution of that year. It developed a constitution for a national German state and established a so-called provisional central government. |
| **free church** | A (Protestant) church that is not part of the church tolerated or privileged by the state. Membership is not usually by birth but by conscious choice. It is, therefore, also a voluntary church. |
| **Fürstenbund (1785)** | League of Princes. An alliance created on the initiative of Frederick II, initially involving Prussia, Hanover and Saxony. Soon after, fourteen other, mostly smaller territories of the Empire, joined the League. The goal of the alliance was the defence of the imperial constitution (against the Habsburgs) while also reforming it. |
| **Ganzes Haus** | 'The whole house'. A model of family-oriented life and economy developed by Otto Brunner and based on the economic literature of the seventeenth and eighteenth centuries. It was based on the idea of a mostly self-sufficient large-scale farm or country manor. The 'whole house' included a married couple, their children, elderly family members, servants and, in some cases, even relatives who lived and worked together under the authority of the *pater familias*. Demographic and economic historical research has shown that the 'whole house' did not reflect the social and economic reality of the middle and lower classes and only in certain exceptions reproduced that of the upper classes. It can therefore be understood as a Romantic idealization of the pre-modern, patriarchal family and as an (ideological) model of the self-description of pre-modern society. |

| | |
|---|---|
| *Gemeine Herrschaft* | 'Common dominion', Swiss subject territories. The territories jointly controlled and administered (as well as exploited) by the states (cantons) of the Swiss confederation. |
| German Catholicism | A religious and social movement in the states of the German Confederation starting in the 1840s. It focused on the parish and was similar to free churches; in this respect it was related to Methodism. |
| Halle Pietism | A focal point of Pietist movements in Protestant churches. Pietism in Halle was shaped by Philip Jacob Spener and, above all, his pupil August Herrmann Francke (1663–1727). Francke positioned himself against enlightened philosophy and theology and, amongst other things, founded an orphanage and the Francke Foundations to incorporate the message of the gospels in everyday Christian life. During the eighteenth and nineteenth centuries, the Francke Foundations became the centre of worldwide evangelical missionary activity. |
| *Hochstifte* | Spiritual territories in the Holy Roman Empire in which the bishop also exercised secular rule as a territorial prince. |
| Indian reductions | The consolidation of large parts of the indigenous population in stable settlements by the Jesuits in their mission areas in South America between 1609 and 1767. They are also referred to as Jesuit reductions. |
| July Monarchy | A term for the French monarchy beginning in 1830 after the July Revolution with the reign of King Louis Philippe I and ending with the founding of the Second Republic after the revolution of 1848. |
| *Junker* | A designation for landed gentry and manor owners in the Prussian areas east of the River Elbe. A political battle cry created by the liberals to describe their conservative and political opponents, who were viewed as reactionaries. |
| *jus in sacra/circa sacra* | Terms from German legal and church history. *Jus in sacra* designates the authority of a territorial ruler over the Protestant church in his territories. *Jus circa sacra* refers to the regulatory law governing all religious communities in the territory. |
| Kölner Wirren | 'Cologne Troubles'. The climax of the conflict between the Prussian state and the Catholic Church in the provinces on the Rhine. The focal point of the dispute was mixed marriage. Starting in 1830, the church refused to bless such marriages if a Catholic bride was not allowed to raise her children as Catholics. Archbishop Clemens August von Droste Vischering was arrested in 1837 because of this and only freed in 1839. Frederick William IV resolved the mixed-marriage dispute. |

## Glossary

**Kulturkampf**
'Culture struggle'. The political conflict in the German Empire between Bismarck and Catholics after 1878. This conflict between the secular state and the Ultramontane Restoration Catholic Church was, however, a European phenomenon and therefore also occurred in other states.

*Landeskirche*
A Protestant regional church organized and delimited in accordance with a particular territory, such as the various territories of the Holy Roman Empire. In England, a Protestant national church developed. The church in Spain and France is also referred to as a national church, but, in this context, it is important to note that Spanish and French bishops were also subject to the Pope as their spiritual head and thus did not follow the respective political authorities, at least when it came to spiritual matters (see also 'Ultramontanism').

*Landgemeinde*
Legislative cantonal assembly. The assembly of the (male) residents of a Swiss canton who were entitled to vote, held in the open air for political consultation and decision making.

**landgraviate**
Landgraves were princes and therefore took precedence over simple counts. As princes, they exercised sovereignty and territorial jurisdiction over their landgraviate.

**Lutheran orthodoxy**
The theological doctrinal system which was developed in the course of the consolidation of Lutheran state churches from about 1580. Numerous dogmas were issued and attempts were made to declare deviant teachings as heretical or, at the very least, to exclude them.

**Nadere Reformatie**
Dutch 'further Reformation'. A movement within the Dutch Reformed Church in the seventeenth and eighteenth centuries. It sought to model the daily and public life of Christians on the Bible and was related to English Puritanism and German Pietism.

*Oberkirchenrat*
The highest authority of a Protestant church (Supreme Church Council) and/or the person presiding over it.

**Old Lutherans**
Lutheran believers and congregations that refused to recognize the *Agende* and Union (see the relevant entries).

**Organic Articles**
The regulations issued by Napoleon in 1802 regarding the practice of religion in France. They complemented (and interpreted) the Concordat concluded with the Curia in 1801. After 1806, such supplementary provisions to concordats were also issued in other states.

**patronage**
Describes any kind of relationship of dependency between people in which a patron protects and promotes his client(s). The latter are obliged to offer the patron solidarity and support. In the Catholic Church, the saint to whom a church is dedicated at its consecration is the patron.

| | |
|---|---|
| **pauperism** | Term for the social and economic phenomena of mass poverty in the first half of the nineteenth century that were brought about in Europe by the transition from an agricultural to an industrial, capitalist market economy. |
| **Peace of Westphalia** | The peace treaty negotiated in Münster and Osnabrück over several years and signed in 1648, which settled the conflicts between the powers involved in the Thirty Years War. From the point of view of the history of religion, it is significant for recognizing the Reformed confession politically in the Holy Roman Empire. The imperial Edict of Restitution of 1629 was abolished, and Catholic and Protestant territorial properties were reorganized according to the situation of 1 January 1624 (with the exception of the *Erblande*). In confessionally mixed cities of the empire, government and administrative structures were introduced that took equal account of both confessions. |
| **perennialism** | An undefined term for the view that philosophical knowledge about the world is derived from an original set of statements that recur in changing forms. Often, the term specifically refers to esoteric knowledge or even knowledge available to Adam before the Fall that should be recovered in its perfection. |
| **physicotheology** | A rationalist form of theology and the doctrine of God originating at the end of the sixteenth century. It sought to demonstrate the existence and essence of God through the wonders of His creation. Physicotheologists therefore carried out detailed natural observation and research. The Anglican William Derham (1657–1735) was an important physicotheologian, who set standards for subsequent generations. |
| **pilgrimages (for example, to Aachen, Cologne and Trier)** | Journeys to these places and their important relics, such as the Holy Robe in Trier. Such journeys were increasingly organized as mass events by Rome from the 1820s, and they were associated with extensive opportunities to obtain indulgences. |
| **proprietary dioceses** | There were proprietary dioceses in the archdiocese of Salzburg. Their bishops were appointed, invested and enfeoffed by the archbishop of Salzburg. In this respect they were outside the ecclesiastical control of Rome. In Italy there were also bishops who were appointed by communities or noble estates. |
| *publieke kerk* | 'Public church'. The Calvinist Church of the Netherlands, which, unlike other Protestant churches, was not a state church. It is, therefore, also called a 'public church'. |

| | |
|---|---|
| **Rauhes Haus** | A social welfare foundation initiated in Hamburg in 1833 by Johann Heinrich Wichern (1808–81). It was originally an orphanage and was funded by wealthy Hamburg merchants and entrepreneurs. |
| **Reichsdeputationshauptschluss** | Imperial Recess. Resolution passed by the imperial estates and their deputies at the Old Town Hall in Regensburg on 25 February 1803, which determined that the secular imperial estates were to be compensated for territories ceded to France through the secularization of ecclesiastical and secular dominions. |
| **Reichskirche** | Imperial Church encompassing institutions and structures of the Catholic Church in the Holy Roman Empire. |
| **Reichsschluss** | Imperial resolution. Resolutions of the Reichstag (Imperial Diet) of the Holy Roman Empire. |
| **Reichstag** | Imperial Diet. A meeting of the estates or their deputies in the Holy Roman Empire that was initially convened intermittently and then made permanent from 1663 until 1806. This permanent Reichstag was located in Regensburg. |
| **Restoration** | After 1815, political efforts in all European states and a movement in political philosophy aimed at reversing the results of the French Revolution and Napoleon's reign. |
| **rights of patronage** | The rights and duties of a ruler or ruling authority with regard to a church. One of the duties, for example, was the upkeep of the church building. The rights may include the presentation of candidates for appointment to the parish. |
| **social systems** | Social systems are networks of communication that can be distinguished from an environment. Social systems are able to make this distinction themselves – it is not just apparent to an observer – and the distinction is reproduced in all communication relevant to the system. Social systems ignore communication that involves system-external distinctions. For example, since the Reformation, Protestants have no longer considered salvation as something that can be purchased. This distinction is realized in selection and restriction. Fewer things are possible in the system than in its environment. This also means that systems decide which information from the environment is relevant within the system. These restrictions can be realized in different ways: through speaker roles |

(for example, presence or membership), content (for example, particular topics and the way they are raised) or time (for example, the singularity or repeatability of connections). Social systems are made up of communication, and not people. People comprise a psychological and biological system and are thus part of the environment of social systems. Social systems must therefore deal with the internal dynamics of consciousness and its processes. Conversely, the same is true of consciousness: it must process the impositions of the social systems in which it is involved through communication. Social evolution thus accelerates (and can be tolerated by individuals in its social complexity) to the degree that social systems can be isolated from states of consciousness (motives, attitudes). In religion, this problem is illustrated in the debates concerning contrition (*contritio*/*atritio*) or a person's inner attitude during prayer. Social systems are not containers; instead, instances of communication can always be relevant in several social systems. This is one of the reasons why the relationship between religion and politics that is observed in this book becomes especially problematic.

**society based on presence/ associative relationships amongst those present**
Refers to historic societies that had social structures characterized by communication amongst individuals who were present. Writing was used in some fields, but it was not until the comprehensive use of printing that such societies were transformed, as could be observed in Europe from the beginning of the sixteenth century.

*summus episcopus*
The highest bishop of an episcopal Protestant regional church. The office was usually occupied by the ruler of the territory.

**superintendent**
Head of a Protestant church district of varying size and made up of several parishes.

**Synod of Dort (1619)**
A national assembly of the Dutch Reformed Church. Its main focus was the theology of Jacobus Arminius of Leiden. He denied absolute (and double) predestination and emphasized the participation of man in his salvation. His followers, who were called Arminians or Remonstrants, after their statement of faith, defended themselves unsuccessfully before the synod. After their refusal to submit to the synod, they were expelled from it and later excommunicated and removed from church offices.

| | |
|---|---|
| treasury of grace | All spiritual means (*spiritualia*) made available by the Catholic Church through the foundation of Jesus Christ by which the sinner can reduce the punishment for sins through contrition. The efficacy of *spiritualia* is grounded in the sacrificial death of Christ and in the prayers and works of the Blessed Virgin Mary and all the saints. This supply of good works and prayers circulates among all believers, who can themselves contribute to it through prayers and good works. Through this circulation, amongst other things, the church becomes a *corpus mysticum*. Indulgences and the sacrament of penance may also be used to mitigate punishment for sins. |
| two-kingdoms doctrine | A term coined in twentieth-century theology for Luther's claims about the relationship between God, the Church and secular rule. According to this doctrine, God's implementation of secular power creates as much order in the 'kingdom of Satan' as is necessary for Christian faith and devotion to God. This view was already controversial in the Reformation because, for Luther, it included the absolute obedience of the faithful to secular rulers in both secular and religious matters. According to Luther, there was no right to active resistance; at most, this was restricted to the 'inner' person, who had to obey God. |
| Ultramontanism | A position held by Catholics and Catholic officials who feel bound by the decisions of the Roman Curia ('beyond the mountains') rather than the political authorities of their own country with regard to religious and, in particular, political questions. This position was denounced by liberals. |
| Union | Church union. After 1815, Frederick William III aimed to unify the various Protestant churches in Prussia, which at that point had been considerably enlarged. The process began in 1817 with the call for the Reformed Church and Lutherans to celebrate the Eucharist together. The *Agende* (see relevant entry) issued by the king in 1822 triggered a bitter dispute, leading to the secession of the Old Lutherans. This was not settled until 1834, when the king declared that agreeing to the Union was not linked to approving the *Agende*. |
| *Vergemeinschaftung* | A social sciences term coined in the nineteenth century to describe forms of social ordering that were not determined by function. The term thus also tends to include pre-modern forms. |
| *Vergesellschaftung* | Sociation or associative relationships. Encompasses all forms of communication or the development of social structures. As used here, this term does not contrast with communitization but instead highlights that this is a continuous process which is realized through individual events (communication). |

# Notes

## Introduction

1.  Referred to here as 'sociation' or 'associative relationships' and translating the German term *Vergesellschaftung*\*.
2.  Where possible, quotations have been inserted from English editions and/or translations. The sources used are as follows: Edmund Burke, *Reflections on the Revolution in France*, ed. J. C. D. Clark (Stanford, CA: Stanford University Press, 2001), 257–272; Jean-Jacques Rousseau, *Social Contract* and *On the Inequality Among Men*, trans. G. D. H. Cole in *The Social Contract and Discourses* (London: Dent and New York: Dutton, 1913); Jean-Jacques Rousseau, *Émile*, trans. Barbara Foxley (London: Dent and New York: Dutton, 1911), rev. Grace Roosevelt and accessible via https://web.archive.org/web/20100622185927/http://www.ilt.columbia.edu/pedagogies/rouss eau/em_eng_bk4.html; Giambattista Vico, *The New Science of Giambattista Vico*, trans. from the 3rd edn (1744) by Thomas Goddard Bergin and Max Harold Fisch (Ithaca, NY: Cornell University Press, 1948); Johann Gottfried Herder, *Outlines of a Philosophy of the History of Man*, trans. T. Churchill (New York: Bergman Publishers, 1800); Immanuel Kant, *Conflict of the Faculties*, trans. Mary J. Gregor (New York: Abaris Books, 1979); *Oldest Systematic Programme of German Idealism*, trans. Karsten Harries in 'The Epochal Threshold and the Classical Ideal: Hölderlin contra Hegel', in *The Emergence of German Idealism*, ed. Michael Baur and Daniel O. Dahlstrom (Washington D.C.: Catholic University of America Press, 1999), 147–175; Immanuel Kant, *Dreams of a Spirit-Seer*, trans. Emanuel F. Goerwitz, ed. (with introduction and notes) Frank Sewall (London: Swan Sonnenschein & Co. and New York: MacMillan Co., 1900); Immanuel Kant, *Critique of Pure Reason*, trans. J. M. D. Meiklejohn, introduction A. D. Lindsay (London: Dent and New York: Dutton & Co., 1934); Immanuel Kant, *Critique of Judgement*, 2nd edn, trans. (with introduction and notes) J. H. Bernard (London: MacMillan and Co., 1914); Immanuel Kant, *Religion within the Boundary of Pure Reason*, trans. J. W. Semple (Edinburgh: Thomas Clark, 1838); Georg Wilhelm Friedrich Hegel, *Phenomenology*, trans. J. B. Baillie (New York: Harper & Row, 1967 [1910]); Friedrich Nietzsche, *Ecce Homo* (Portland, ME: Smith & Sale, 1911).
3.  See, for example, Kurt Dietrich Schmidt and Ernst Wolf (eds), *Die Kirche in ihrer Geschichte: Ein Handbuch*, vol. 1ff. (Göttingen: Vandenhoeck & Ruprecht, 1961ff.); Gerd Händler (ed.), *Kirchengeschichte in Einzeldarstellungen*, vols 3–4 (Berlin: Berliner Wissenschaftsverlag, 1990–2003); Hubert Jedin (ed.), *Handbuch der Kirchengeschichte*, 6 vols (Freiburg im Breisgau: Herder, 1962–79); Jean-Marie Mayeur, Luce Pietri, Charles Pietri, André Vauchez and Marc Venard (eds), *Die Geschichte des Christentums: Religion, Politik, Kultur* (Freiburg im Breisgau: Herder, 1991). In the following, I will occasionally use the plural form 'Christianities' because neither the terms church nor denomination can entirely capture the phenomena observed here.

4   There are exceptions, for example, Sheridan Gilley and Brian Stanley (eds), *The Cambridge History of Christianity*, vol. 8, *World Christianities, ca. 1815–1914* (Cambridge: Cambridge University Press, 2006).
5   For example, Kurt Nowak, *Geschichte des Christentums in Deutschland: Religion, Politik und Gesellschaft vom Ende der Aufklärung bis zur Mitte des 20. Jahrhunderts* (Munich: C. H. Beck, 1995).
6   Hans-Ulrich Wehler, *Deutsche Gesellschaftsgeschichte*, vol. 1, *Vom Feudalismus des Alten Reiches bis zur defensiven Modernisierung der Reformära 1700–1815* (Munich: Beck, 1987). The subsequent volumes do nothing to change this. A rather surprising misunderstanding is apparent, in that Max Weber's sociology, which does not use the concept of society, is used as a methodological paradigm for a history of society. See also Thomas Nipperdey, *Deutsche Geschichte 1815–1866* (Munich: C. H. Beck, 1983); René Rémond, *Religion und Gesellschaft in Europa: Von 1789 bis zur Gegenwart* (Munich: C. H. Beck, 2000) does not keep the promise its title makes: society is not discussed.
7   Max Müller, *Chips from a German Workshop*, vol. 1, *Essays on the Science of Religion (1867)* (New York: Charles Scribner, 1872); Edward Burnett Tylor, *Primitive Culture*, vol. 2, *Religion in Primitive Culture* (New York: Harper & Row, 1958 [1871]). More recent examples: Fritz Stolz, *Grundzüge der Religionswissenschaft* (Göttingen: Vandenhoeck & Ruprecht, 1985); Johann Figl (ed.), *Handbuch der Religionswissenschaft: Religionen und ihre zentralen Themen* (Innsbruck: Tyrolia, 2003). Historiographical adaptations are found in Peter Dinzelbacher (ed.), *Handbuch der Religionsgeschichte im deutschsprachigen Raum*, vol. 5, *1750–1900* (Paderborn: Ferdinand Schöningh, 2007); Burkhard Gladigow, *Religionswissenschaft als Kulturwissenschaft* (Stuttgart: Kohlhammer, 2005). On the history of comparative religious studies, see Eric J. Sharpe, *Comparative Religion: A History*, 2nd edn (Eastbourne: Open Court, 1986).
8   The following provide starting points for a large subject area: Niklas Luhmann, *Soziale Systeme: Grundriss einer allgemeinen Theorie* (Frankfurt am Main: Suhrkamp, 1984); Niklas Luhmann, *Die Gesellschaft der Gesellschaft*, 2 vols (Frankfurt am Main: Suhrkamp, 1998); Niklas Luhmann, *Einführung in die Systemtheorie* (Heidelberg: Carl-Auer-Systeme-Verlag, 2002).
9   Peter Fuchs, *Der Sinn der Beobachtung: Begriffliche Untersuchungen* (Göttingen: Velbrück, 2004); Bruno Latour, 'Gebt mir ein Laboratorium und ich werde die Welt aus den Angeln heben', in *ANThology: Ein einführendes Handbuch zur Akteur-Netzwerk-Theorie*, ed. Andréa Belliger and David J. Krieger (Bielefeld: Transcript, 2006), 103–134. Unfortunately, ANT does not theorize the concept of observation.
10  Niklas Luhmann, *Funktion der Religion* (Frankfurt am Main: Suhrkamp, 1977), 33–45; Niklas Luhmann, *Religion der Gesellschaft* (Frankfurt am Main: Suhrkamp, 2000), 7–52.
11  On Schleiermacher, see the references given in Chapter 4, notes 147–156. On the 'presence of God', see Walter Mostert, 'Glaube – der christliche Begriff für Religion', *Zeitschrift für Theologie und Kirche* 95 (1998): 217–231.
12  Émile Durkheim, *Die elementaren Formen des religiösen Lebens* (Frankfurt am Main: Suhrkamp, 1981). I diverge from Luhmann's suggestion at this point as Luhmann does not seem to me to make it clear enough that individual production of meaning has to be communicated. In my opinion, it is too weak to only refer to any production of meaning as always having been social. I am also not convinced

that religion's problem of contingency is in itself sufficient for the religious production of meaning to stabilize at a social level and for differentiation to begin. This is also the problem with the suggestion in Detlef Pollack, 'Was ist Religion? Probleme der Definition', *Zeitschrift für Religionswissenschaft* 3 (1995): 163–190, esp. 183–187. He is unable to explain why and how an individual problem should become a social one.

13   Luhmann ignores this aspect and only identifies the function of religion as providing solutions to understand the autopoiesis of meaning and structures. In my view that would not be sufficient for structural differentiation and would resign religion to the area of individual problems. Cf. Attila K. Molnár, 'The Construction of the Notion of Religion in Early Modern Europe', *Method and Theory in the Study of Religion* 14 (2000): 47–60; Jacques Derrida, 'Glaube und Wissen: Die beiden Quellen der "Religion" an den Grenzen der bloßen Vernunft', in *Die Religion*, ed. Jacques Derrida and Gianni Vattimo (Frankfurt am Main: Suhrkamp, 2001), 45–50. It is not possible to separate religion from politics. On this, see Giorgio Agamben, *Signatura rerum: Zur Methode*, trans. Anton Schütz (Frankfurt am Main: Suhrkamp, 2009), 94.

14   On the consequences of this observation for an ethnological concept of 'faith', see Thomas G. Kirsch, 'Restaging the Will to Believe: Religion, Pluralism, Anti-Syncretism and the Problem of Belief', *American Anthropologist* 106 (2004): 699–709.

15   Dorothea Weltecke, *'Der Narr spricht: Es ist kein Gott': Atheismus, Unglauben und Glaubenszweifel vom 12. Jahrhundert bis zur Neuzeit* (Frankfurt am Main: Campus-Verlag, 2010).

16   An example of this development is given in Reinhart Koselleck, *Preußen zwischen Reform und Revolution: Allgemeines Landrecht, Verwaltung und soziale Bewegung von 1791 bis 1848*, 2nd edn (Stuttgart: Deutscher Taschenbuchverlag, 1975); in this context, one might also refer to the second and third sections of the third part of Georg Wilhelm Friedrich Hegel's *Elements of the Philosophy of Right*.

17   For example, Alexis de Tocqueville, *Der alte Staat und die Revolution (1856)* (Munich: Deutscher Taschenbuch-Verlag, 1978), 14–17; and Benjamin Constant, *Werke in vier Bänden*, vol. 4, *Politische Schriften* (Berlin: Propyläen, 1972), 9–244 ('Principles of Politics Applicable to All Governments') – a text which gives a clear description of the social and political transformation, including its problems.

# Chapter 1

1   Jean Goy, *À Reims, Le Sacre des Rois de France* (Reims: Jean Goy, 1980), 95; Elisabeth Kovács, 'Kirchliches Zeremoniell am Wiener Hof des 18. Jahrhunderts im Wandel von Mentalität und Gesellschaft', *Mitteilungen des Österreichischen Staatsarchivs* 32 (1979): 126–134; John McManners, *Church and Society in Eighteenth Century France*, vol. 1, *The Clerical Establishment and Its Social Ramifications* (Oxford: Oxford University Press, 1998); Jeffrey W.Merrick, *The Desacralisation of the French Monarchy in the Eighteenth Century* (Baton Rouge, LA: Louisiana State University Press, 1990), 49–77.

2   Otto Hintze, 'Epochen des evangelischen Kirchenregiments in Preußen', in *Gesammelte Abhandlungen*, vol. 3, *Regierung und Verwaluntung: Gesammelte Aufsätze zur Staats-Rechts- und Sozialgeschichte Preußen*, ed.Gerhard Oestreich, 2nd edn (Göttingen: Vandenhoeck & Ruprecht, 1967), 74; Kovács, 'Kirchliches Zeremoniell'.

3   Hugo Rahner, *Kirche und Staat im frühen Christentum* (Munich: Kösel, 1961), esp. 205–280; Wolfgang Reinhard, 'Die lateinische Variante von Religion und ihre Bedeutung für die politische Kultur Europas: Ein Versuch in historischer Anthropologie', *Saeculum* 43 (1992): 232–240; Wolfgang Reinhard, *Geschichte der Staatsgewalt: Eine vergleichende Verfassungsgeschichte Europas von den Anfängen bis zur Gegenwart*, 2nd edn (Munich: C. H. Beck, 2000), 259–262.

4   Ludwig Buisson, *Potestas und Caritas: Die päpstliche Gewalt im Spätmittelalter* (Cologne/Vienna: Böhlau, 1958); Otto P. Clavadetscher, *Die geistlichen Richter des Bistums Chur* (Basel: Helbing & Lichtenhahn, 1964); Hans E. Feine, *Kirchliche Rechtsgeschichte*, vol. 1, *Die katholische Kirche*, 2nd edn (Cologne/Vienna: Böhlau, 1972), 201–205, 213–221, 299–354; Paul Hinschius, *System des katholischen Kirchenrechts mit besonderer Rücksicht auf Deutschland* (Berlin: I. Guttentag, 1869), vol. 1, 511–538, vol. 2, 38–49, 269–277, 285–291; Hubert Jedin (ed.), *Handbuch der Kirchengeschichte*, vol. 1, *Die katholische Kirche* (Freiburg im Breisgau: Herder, 1972); Gabriel Le Bras, *Institutions Ecclésiastiques de la Chrétienté Médiévale* (Paris: Bloud et Gay, 1964), 305–333, 365–376, 553–564; Wolfgang Reinhard, 'Die Verwaltung der Kirche', in *Deutsche Verwaltungsgeschichte*, vol. 1, *Vom Spätmittelalter bis zum Ende des Reiches*, ed. Kurt Jeserich, Han Pohl and Georg-Christoph von Unruh, 2nd edn (Stuttgart: Deutsche Verlags-Anstalt, 1983), 145–151, 153–157; Albert Werminghoff, *Verfassungsgeschichte der deutschen Kirche im Mittelalter*, 2nd edn (Leipzig: Teubner, 1913), 60–88; Alison Forrestal (ed.), *Politics and Religion in Early Bourbon France* (Basingstoke: Palgrave Macmillan, 2009).

5   Walter Croce, 'Die niederen Weihen und ihre hierarchische Wertung: Eine geschichtliche Studie', *Zeitschrift für katholische Theologie* 70 (1948): 257–314; Hinschius, *System*, vol. 1, 118–163; Albert Braun, *Der Klerus des Bistums Konstanz im Ausgang des Mittelalters* (Münster: De Gruyter, 1938); Feine, *Kirchliche Rechtsgeschichte*, 391–402; Wolfgang Reinhard, 'Die Kirche als Mobilitätskanal der frühneuzeitlichen Gesellschaft', in *Ständische Gesellschaft und soziale Mobilität*, ed. Winfried Schulze (Munich: Oldenbourg, 1988), 333–351; Aloys Schulte, *Der Adel und die deutsche Kirche im Mittelalter: Studien zur Sozial-, Rechts- und Kirchengeschichte*, 3rd edn (Darmstadt: Wissenschaftliche Buchgesellschaft, 1958 [1910]).

6   Hans-Jörg Budischin, *Der gelehrte Zivilprozeß in der Praxis geistlicher Gerichte des 13. und 14. Jahrhunderts im deutschen Raum* (Bonn: L. Röhrscheid, 1974); Helmut Coing (ed.), *Handbuch der Quellen und Literatur der neueren europäischen Privatrechtsgeschichte*, vol. 1 (Munich: C. H. Beck, 1973), 365–382, 835–848; Feine, *Kirchliche Rechtsgeschichte*, 271–294, 433–441; Paul Flade, *Das römische Inquisitionsverfahren in Deutschland bis zu den Hexenprozessen* (Aalen: Scientia Verlag, 1972); Gérard Fransen, 'Les Décrétales et les Collections de Décrétales', in *Typologie des Sources du Moyen Âge Occidental*, vol. 2, ed. Léopold Genicot (Turnhout: Brepols, 1972); Hinschius, *System*, vol. 4, 691–862; Reinhard, 'Verwaltung', 149–151; Achim Steins, 'Der ordentliche Zivilprozeß vor dem bischöflichen Offizial: Ein Beitrag zur Geschichte des gelehrten Prozesses in Deutschland im Spätmittelalter', *Zeitschrift für Rechtsgeschichte* 59 (1973): 191–262.

7   Albert Hauck, *Kirchengeschichte Deutschlands*, vol. 5.1 (Leipzig: J. C. Hinrichs'sche Buchhandlung, 1911), 132–142.

8   Wilhelm Kisky, *Die Domkapitel der geistlichen Kurfürsten in ihrer persönlichen Zusammensetzung im 14. und 15. Jahrhundert* (Cologne/Vienna:

Böhlau, 1906); Michael Kißener, *Ständemacht und Kirchenreform. Bischöfliche Wahlkapitulation im Nordwesten des Alten Reiches 1265–1803* (Munich: Ferdinand Schöningh, 1993), 17–144; Reinhard, 'Verwaltung', 165.

9 Daniel Dory and Raymond Verdier, *La Construction Religieuse du Territoire* (Paris: Éditions L'Harmattan, 1995); Reinhard, *Geschichte der Staatsgewalt*, 262–269.

10 Monika Neugebauer-Wölk, 'Esoterik in der Frühen Neuzeit: Zum Paradigma der Religionsgeschichte zwischen Mittelalter und Moderne', *Zeitschrift für historische Forschung* 27 (2000): 321–364; Wilhelm Schmidt-Biggemann, *Philosphia perennis: Historische Umrisse abendländischer Spiritualität in Antike, Mittelalter und Früher Neuzeit* (Frankfurt am Main: Suhrkamp, 1998); Rudolf Schlögl, 'Von der Weisheit zur Esoterik: Themen und Paradoxien im frühen Rosenkreuzerdiskurs', in *Aufklärung und Esoterik*, ed. Monika Neugebauer-Wölk (Hamburg: Meiner, 1999), 53–86.

11 Ronnie Po-chia Hsia, *Gegenreformation: Die Welt der katholischen Erneuerung 1540–1770* (Frankfurt am Main: Fischer Taschenbuch Verlag, 1998), 54–124; Kurt-Dietrich Schmidt, *Die katholische Reform und die Gegenreformation* (Göttingen: Vandenhoeck & Ruprecht, 1975); Hubert Jedin (ed.), *Handbuch der Kirchengeschichte*, vol. 4, *Reformation, Katholische Reform und Gegenreformation* (Freiburg im Breisgau: Herder, 1967).

12 Hans-Jürgen Goertz, *Die Täufer: Geschichte und Deutung* (Munich: C. H. Beck, 1980).

13 Marc Venard, *Das Zeitalter der Vernunft* (Freiburg im Breisgau: Herder, 1998).

14 Walter Brandmüller, *Handbuch der bayerischen Kirchengeschichte*, vol. 2, *Von der Glaubensspaltung bis zur Säkularisation* (St Ottilien: EOS Verlag, 1993); Wolfgang Mager, *Frankreich vom Ancien Régime zur Moderne. Wirtschafts-, Gesellschafts- und politische Institutionengeschichte 1630–1830* (Stuttgart: Kohlhammer, 1980), 89f.; Paul Gagnol, *La Dîme Ecclésiastique en France au XVIIIe Siècle* (Geneva: Slatkine, 1974), 134–155; McManners, *Church and Society*, vol. 1, 95–140; John McManners, *French Ecclesiastical Society under the Ancien Régime: A Study of Angers in the Eighteenth Century* (Manchester: Manchester University Press, 1960); Bernard Plongeron, *La Vie Quotidienne du Clergé Français au XVIIIe Siècle* (Paris: Hachette, 1974), 9; Armand Rébillon, 'La Situation Économique du Clergé à la Veille de la Révolution dans les Districts de Rennes, de Fougères et de Vitré', in *La Révolution Française*, ed. Georges Lefebvre (Paris: Alcan, 1930), 328–330; Michel Lagrée, *L'Histoire des Curés* (Paris: Fayard, 2005), 155–260; William Callahan, 'The Spanish Church', in *Church and Society in Catholic Europe of the Eighteenth Century*, ed. William Callahan and David Higgs (Cambridge: Cambridge University Press, 1979), 34–50; Juan Sàez Marin, *Datos Sobre la Iglesia Espanola Contemporànea 1768–1868* (Madrid: Editora Nacional, 1975); Peter Hersche, *Italien im Barockzeitalter 1600–1750: Eine Sozial- und Kulturgeschichte* (Cologne/Vienna: Böhlau, 1999), 121–123; Augusto Placanica, *Cassa Sacra e Beni della Chiesa Nella Calabria del Settecento* (Naples: Giuffré, 1970); Mario Rosa, 'The Italian Churches', in *Church and Society in Catholic Europe of the Eighteenth Century*, ed. William Callahan and David Higgs (Cambridge: Cambridge University Press, 1979), 70–72; Anthony Armstrong, *The Church of England: The Methodists and Society 1700–1850* (London: Rowman and Littlefield, 1973), 9–13; Alan D. Gilbert, *Religion and Society in Industrial England: Church, Chapel and Social Change 1740–1914* (London: Longman, 1976), 7f.; John H. Overton and Frederic Relton, *The English Church from the Accession of George I to the End of the Eighteenth Century 1714–1800* (New York: AMS Press, 1968 [1906]), 267–297; Norman Sykes, *Church and State in England in*

*the XVIIIth Century* (Hamden: Archon Books, 1962); Peter Virgin, *The Church in an Age of Negligence: Ecclesiastical Structure and Problems of Church Reform 1700-1840* (Cambridge: Clarke, 1989), 33-43.

15   Kurt Andermann, 'Geistliche Staaten am Ende des Alten Reiches', *Historische Zeitschrift* 271 (2000): 593-619; Günther Lottes, 'Die Geistlichen Staaten und die Herrschaftskonkurrenz im Reich', in *Individualisierung, Rationalisierung, Säkularisierung: Neue Wege der Religionsgeschichte*, ed. Michael Weinzierl (Vienna: Oldenbourg Wissenschaftsverlag, 1997), 96-111; Heinrich L. Raab, 'Wiederaufbau und Verfassung der Reichskirche', in *Handbuch der Kirchengeschichte*, vol. 5, *Die Kirche im Zeitalter des Absolutismus und der Aufklärung*, ed. Hubert Jedin (Freiburg im Breisgau: Herder, 1970); Karl Otmar v. Aretin, *Das Alte Reich 1648-1806*, vol. 3, *Das Reich und der österreichisch-preußische Dualismus 1745-1806* (Stuttgart: Klett-Cotta, 1997), 237-299, 516-522.

16   Pierre Goubert and Daniel Roche, *Les Français et l'Ancien Régime*, vol. 2 (Paris: Armand Colin, 1984), 23-31; Ilja Mieck, *Die Entstehung des modernen Frankreich 1450-1610: Strukturen, Institutionen, Entwicklungen* (Stuttgart/Berlin/Cologne/Mainz: Kohlhammer, 1982), 213-218.

17   McManners, *Church and Society*, vol. 1, 24; Dale van Kley, 'The Church, State, and the Ideological Origins of the French Revolution: The Debate over the General Assembly of the Gallican Clergy in 1765', *Journal of Modern History* 51 (1979): 629-666.

18   Pierre Blet, *Le Clergé de France et la Monarchie: Études sur les Assemblées Génerales du Clergé de 1615 à 1666*, vol. 2 (Rome: Gregorian University Press, 1959); McManners, *Church and Society*, vol. 1, 27f., 147-173; Gabriel Lepointe, *L'Organisation et la Politique Financières du Clergé de France sous le Règne de Louis XV* (Paris: Librairie de la Société du Recueil Sirey, 1923).

19   William Callahan, *Church, Politics, and Society in Spain, 1750-1874* (Cambridge, MA: Harvard University Press, 1984), 315; José A. Escudero, *Perfiles Juridicos de la Inquisicion Espanola* (Madrid: Universidad Complutense, 1992).

20   Rosa, 'Italian Churches', 67-76, 70-72; Christoph Weber, *Familienkanonikate und Patronatsbistümer: Ein Beitrag zur Geschichte von Adel und Klerus im neuzeitlichen Italien* (Berlin: Duncker & Humblot, 1988); Hersche, *Italien im Barockzeitalter*, 121-123; Placanica, *Cassa Sacra*, passim; Xenio Toscani, *Il Clero Lombardo dall'Ancien Regime alla Restaurazione* (Bologna: Il Mulino, 1979).

21   Armstrong, *Church of England*, 9-15; Gilbert, *Religion and Society*, 7f.; William Gibson, *Church, State, and Society 1760-1850* (Basingstoke: Macmillan, 1994); Gordon Rupp, *Religion in England, 1688-1791* (Oxford: Oxford University Press, 1986); Virgin, *Church in an Age of Negligence*, 109-191.

22   Ulrich Lampert, *Kirche und Staat in der Schweiz*, vol. 2 (Basel: Rütschi und Egloff Verlag, 1938), 6-96; Rudolf Pfister, *Kirchengeschichte der Schweiz*, vol. 2 (Zurich: Zwingli-Verlag, 1974), 638-647; Paul Wernle, *Der schweizerische Protestantismus im XVIII. Jahrhundert*, vol. 1 (Tübingen: Mohr, 1923), 1-90, vol. 2, 479-527; Jos Gabriels, 'Patrizier und Regenten: Städtische Eliten in den nördlichen Niederlanden', in *Bürgerliche Eliten in den Niederlanden und in Nordwestdeutschland*, ed. Heinz Schilling and Herman Diederiks (Cologne/Vienna: Böhlau, 1985), 37-64; Otto Jan de Jong, *Nederlandse Kerkgeschiedenis* (Nijkerk: Callenbach, 1972), 201-214, 246-319; Heinz Schilling, 'Das Calvinistische Presbyterium in der Stadt Groningen während der Frühen Neuzeit und im ersten Viertel des 19. Jahrhunderts: Verfassung und Sozialprofil', in *Bürgerliche Eliten in den Niederlanden und in Nordwestdeutschland*,

ed. Heinz Schilling and Herman Diedericks (Cologne/Vienna: Böhlau, 1985), 195–273; Heinz Schilling, 'Religion und Gesellschaft in der calvinistischen Republik der Vereinigten Niederlande – "Öffentlichkeitskirche" und Säkularisation: Ehe und Hebammenwesen; Presbyterien und politische Partizipation', in *Kirche und gesellschaftlicher Wandel in deutschen und niederländischen Städten der werdenden Neuzeit*, ed. Franz Petri (Cologne/Vienna: Böhlau, 1980), 195–250.

23 Erich Foerster, *Die Entstehung der Preußischen Landeskirche unter der Regierung König Friedrich Wilhelms III: Ein Beitrag zur Geschichte der Kirchenbildung im deutschen Protestantismus*, 2 vols (Tübingen: J. C. B. Mohr (Paul Siebeck), 1905–07), vol. 1, 44–82; Ludwig Ämilius Richter, *Geschichte der evangelischen Kirchenverfassung in Deutschland* (Amsterdam: Rodopi, 1970 [1851]), 230–247; Hintze, 'Epochen des evangelischen Kirchenregiments', 56–96.

24 Richter, *Geschichte der evangelischen Kirchenverfassung*, 208f.; Georg Ris, *Der 'kirchliche Konstitutionalismus': Hauptlinien der Verfassungsbildung in der evangelisch-lutherischen Kirche Deutschlands im 19. Jahrhundert* (Tübingen: Mohr, 1988), 6–8. On Nettelbladt and Pfaff, see Klaus Schlaich, *Kollegialtheorie: Kirche, Recht und Staat in der Aufklärung* (Munich: Claudius, 1969), 17–22, 65–132.

25 Foerster, *Entstehung der Preußischen Landeskirche*, vol. 1, 73f.; Frank Konersmann, *Kirchenregiment und Kirchenzucht im frühneuzeitlichen Kleinstaat: Studien zu den herrschaftlichen und gesellschaftlichen Grundlagen des Kirchenregiments der Herzöge von Pfalz-Zweibrücken 1410–1793* (Speyer: Mohr Siebeck, 1996), 620–652; Richter, *Geschichte der evangelischen Kirchenverfassung*, 219–225.

26 Niklas Luhmann, *Funktionen und Folgen formaler Organisation*, 3rd edn (Berlin: Duncker & Humblot, 1976), 23–54; Niklas Luhmann, *Organisation und Entscheidung* (Opladen: Westdeutscher Verlag, 2000), 23–54, 80–122, 279–302; Renate Mayntz, *Soziologie der Organisation* (Hamburg: Rowohlt Taschenbuch Verlag, 1967).

27 Joseph v. Sartori, *Statistische Abhandlung über die Mängel in der Regierungsverfassung der geistlichen Wahlstaaten und von den Mitteln solchen abzuhelfen* (Augsburg: Doll, 1787).

28 Peter Hersche, *Die Deutschen Domkapitel im 17. und 18. Jahrhundert*, vol. 2, *Vergleichende sozialgeschichtliche Untersuchungen* (Bern: Peter Hersche, 1984), 13–16, 89ff., 139ff.; Stephan Kremer, *Herkunft und Werdegang geistlicher Führungsschichten in den Reichsbistümern zwischen Westfälischem Frieden und Säkularisation: Fürstbischöfe, Weihbischöfe, Generalvikare* (Freiburg im Breisgau: Herder, 1992), 106–115, 392, 417; Rudolf Reinhard, 'Die hochadeligen Dynastien in der Reichskirche', *Römische Quartalsschrift* 83 (1988): 213–235.

29 Kremer, *Herkunft*, 139ff., 211ff.; Peter Schmidt, *Das Collegium Germanicum in Rom und die Germaniker: Zur Funktion eines römischen Ausländerseminars 1552–1914* (Tübingen: Niemeyer, 1984), 106–118, 162–170.

30 Weber, *Familienkanonikate*, 49–65, 117–147, 267–298.

31 McManners, *Church and Society*, vol. 1, 208–262; Norman Ravitch, *Sword and Mitre: Government and Episcopate in France and England in the Age of Aristocracy* (Den Haag: Mouton & Co., 1966); Michel C. Perronnet, *Les Evêques de l'Ancienne France*, vol. 2 (Lille: Éditions Garnier Frères, 1977); Augustin Sicard, *L'Ancien Clergé de France: Les Evêques avant la Révolution*, 5th edn (Paris: Gabalda, 1912 [c. 1893]).

32 Schilling, 'Das Calvinistische Presbyterium'.

33 Rainer Beck, 'Der Pfarrer und das Dorf', in *Armut, Liebe, Ehre*, ed. Richard v. Dülmen (Frankfurt am Main: Fischer, 1988), 107–143; Andreas Holzem, *Religion*

*und Lebensformen: Katholische Konfessionalisierung im Sendgericht des Fürstbistums Münster 1570–1800* (Paderborn: Schöningh, 2000), 198–203.

34   McManners, *Church and Society*, vol. 1, 321–346; Dominique Julia, 'Le Clergé Paroissial dans les Diocèse de Reims à la Fin du XVIIIe Siècle', *Revue d'Histoire Moderne et Contemporaire* 13 (1966): 195–216; Lagrée, *L'Histoire des Curés*, 252f.

35   Brandmüller, *Glaubensspaltung bis zur Säkularisation*, vol. 2; Werner Freitag, *Pfarrer, Kirche und ländliche Gemeinschaft: Das Dechanat Vechta 1400–1803* (Bielefeld: Verlag für Regionalgeschichte, 1998), 192–220; Holzem, *Religion*, 184–198.

36   Foerster, *Entstehung der Preußischen Landeskirche*, 75–78; Martin Hasselhorn, *Der altwürttembergische Pfarrstand im 18. Jahrhundert* (Stuttgart: Kohlhammer Verlag, 1958), 2–19; David Gugerli, *Zwischen Pfrund und Predigt: Die protestantische Pfarrfamilie auf der Zürcher Landschaft im ausgehenden 18. Jahrhundert* (Zürich: Chronos, 1988), 76f., 123–134; Luise Schorn-Schütte, *Evangelische Geistlichkeit in der Frühen Neuzeit: Deren Anteil an der Entfaltung frühmoderner Staatlichkeit und Gesellschaft; Dargestellt am Beispiel des Fürstentums Braunschweig-Wolfenbüttel, der Landgrafschaft Hessen-Kassel und der Stadt Braunschweig* (Gütersloh: Gütersloher Verlags-Haus, 1996), 227–287.

37   Gugerli, *Zwischen Pfrund und Predigt*, 141–206; Hasselhorn, *Der altwürttembergische Pfarrstand*, 24–35; Schorn-Schütte, *Evangelische Geistlichkeit*, 84–97; Luise Schorn-Schütte, 'Zwischen Amt und Beruf: Der Prediger als Wächter, "Seelenhirt" oder Volkslehrer; Evangelische Geistlichkeit im Alten Reich und in der Eidgenossenschaft im 18. Jahrhundert', in *Evangelische Pfarrer: Zur sozialen und politischen Rolle einer bürgerlichen Gruppe in der deutschen Gesellschaft des 18. bis 20. Jahrhunderts*, ed. Luise Schorn-Schütte and Robert v. Friedeburg (Stuttgart: Kohlhammer, 1997), 6–15; Malgorzata Grzywacz, *Familia Dei: Studien zum Erscheinungsbild der deutschen evangelischen Geistlichkeit in ihren Selbstzeugnissen und der Literatur von der Reformation bis zur Gegenwart* (Poznan: Naukowe UAM, 2002).

38   Gugerli, *Zwischen Pfrund und Predigt*, 44, 53, 185f.

39   Gilbert, *Religion and Society*, 7; McManners, *Church and Society*, vol. 1, 312–330; Hasselhorn, *Der altwürttembergische Pfarrstand*, 84f.; Hersche, *Italien im Barockzeitalter*, 116–121; Rosa, 'Italian Churches', 68f.; Rudolf Schlögl, *Glaube und Religion in der Säkularisierung: Die katholische Stadt – Köln, Aachen, Münster 1700–1840* (Munich: Oldenbourg, 1995), 155–168; Timothy Tackett, *Priest and Parish in Eighteenth-Century France: A Social and Political Study of the Curés in a Diocese of Dauphiné 1750–1791* (Princeton, NJ: Princeton University Press, 1977), 41–71.

40   Peter Hersche, '"Chiesa Ricettizia": Ein Modell kommunaler Organisation von Kirche in Unteritalien', in *Gemeinde, Reformation und Widerstand*, ed. Heinrich R. Schmidt, André Holenstein and Andreas Würgler (Tübingen: Bibliotheca academica, 1998), 293–308.

41   Freitag, *Dechanat Vechta*, 97f., 104–119, 193–201; Hintze, 'Epochen des evangelischen Kirchenregiments', 82f.; Holzem, *Religion*, 185f.; Konersmann, *Kirchenregiment und Kirchenzucht*.

42   Foerster, *Entstehung der Preußischen Landeskirche*, 50f.

43   Gilbert, *Religion and Society*, 94–97; Vivianne Barrie, 'Die Anglikanische Kirche', in *Die Geschichte des Christentums*, vol. 10, *Aufklärung, Revolution, Restauration (1750–1830)*, ed. Bernard Plongeron (Freiburg im Breisgau: Herder, 2000), 44–54.

44   McManners, *Church and Society*, vol. 1, 615f.

45   McManners, *Church and Society*, vol. 1, 571–614 provides further references to secondary literature on individual orders; Pierre Chevallier, *Loménie de Brienne et*

l'*Ordre Monastique 1760–1789* (Paris: Librairie Philosophique Vrin, 1959); Suzanne Lemaire, *La Comission des Réguliers* (Paris: Tenin, 1926).

46  Dale van Kley, *The Jansenists and the Expulsion of the Jesuits from France 1757–1765* (New Haven, CT: Yale University Press, 1975); Richard van Dülmen, 'Antijesuitismus und katholische Aufklärung in Deutschland', *Historisches Jahrbuch der Görres-Gesellschaft* 89 (1969): 52–80.

47  References to older and more recent secondary literature are found in Harm Klueting (ed.), *Der Josephinismus: Ausgewählte Quellen zur Geschichte der theresianisch-josephinischen Reformen* (Darmstadt: Wissenschaftliche Buchgesellschaft, 1995), XXIII–XLX; Bettina Braun (ed.), *Geistliche Fürsten und geistliche Staaten in der Spätphase des Alten Reiches* (Epfendorf: Bibliotheca academica, 2008).

48  Peter Hersche, *Der Spätjansenismus in Österreich* (Vienna: Verlag der österreichischen Akademie der Wissenschaften, 1977).

49  Adam Wandruszka, *Leopold II: Erzherzog von Österreich, Großherzog von Toskana, König von Ungarn und Böhmen, Römischer Kaiser*, vol. 1–2 (Munich: Herold, 1965), esp. vol. 2, 111–140; Charles A. Bolton, *Church Reform in 18th Century Italy: The Synod of Pistoia 1786* (Den Haag: Springer, 1969); Joachim Bahlcke, *Ungarischer Episkopat und österreichische Monarchie: Von einer Partnerschaft zur Konfrontation 1686–1790* (Stuttgart: Franz Steiner Verlag, 2005).

50  Aretin, *Alte Reich*, vol. 3, 237–297.

# Chapter 2

1  Edmund Burke, *Betrachtungen über die Französische Revolution* (Zurich: Manesse Verlag, 1986), 187–215.

2  For example, Walter Grab (ed.), *Die Französische Revolution. Eine Dokumentation* (Munich: Nymphenburger, 1973), 37–39.

3  Wolfgang Reinhard, *Geschichte der Staatsgewalt: Eine vergleichende Verfassungsgeschichte Europas von den Anfängen bis zur Gegenwart*, 2nd edn (Munich: C. H. Beck, 2000), 406–440.

4  Jules Michelet, *Geschichte der Französischen Revolution*, vol. 2 (Frankfurt am Main: Eichborn, 1988), 158f.; Wilhelm Alff, *Michelets Ideen* (Geneva: Droz, 1966).

5  Alexis de Tocqueville, *L'Ancien Régime et la Révolution* (Paris: Éditions Gallimard, 1967), 62–72; John Elster, *Alexis de Tocqueville: The First Social Scientist* (Cambridge: Cambridge University Press, 2009).

6  François-Alphonse Aulard, *Le Culte de la Raison et le Culte de l'Être Suprême 1793–1794: Essai Historique* (Boston, MA: Elibron Classics, 2003 [Paris: Felix Alcan Éditeur, 1892]); Albert Mathiez, *Les Origines des Cultes Révolutionnaires 1789–1792* (Paris: Société nouvelle de librairie et d'édition, 1904).

7  On these developments, see Nigel Aston, *Religion and Revolution in France 1780–1804* (Washington D.C.: Catholic University of America Press, 2000), 103–139; Jean Lefton, *La Crise Révolutionnaire 1789–1856* (Paris: Bloud et Gay, 1949), 37–56.

8  André Latreille, *L'Eglise Catholique et la Révolution Française*, 2 vols (Paris: Hachette, 1946–50), vol. 1, 87–104.

9   Timothy Tackett, *Religion, Revolution, and Regional Culture in Eighteenth-Century France: The Ecclesiastical Oath of 1791* (Princeton, NJ: Princeton University Press, 1986).
10  Michel Vovelle, *Religion et Révolution: La Déchristianisation de l'An II* (Paris: Hachette, 1976); Michel Vovelle, 'Die andere Entchristianisierung', in *Sozialgeschichte der Aufklärung*, part 2, ed. Hans Ulrich Gumbrecht, Rolf Reichardt and Thomas Schleich (Munich: Oldenbourg, 1981), 201–228; Horst Gebhard, *Liberté, Egalité, Brutalité: Gewaltgeschichte der Französischen Revolution* (Augsburg: Sankt Ulrich Verlag, 2011); Graeme Fife, *The Terror: The Shadow of the Guillotine; France 1792–1794* (New York: St Martin's Press, 2006).
11  François de Capitani, 'Schweizerische Stadtfeste als bürgerliche Selbstdarstellung', in *Stadt und Repräsentation*, ed. Bernhard Kirchgässner and Hans-Peter Becht (Sigmaringen: Thorbecke, 1995), 115–126.
12  Mona Ozouf, *La Fête Révolutionnaire 1789–1799* (Paris: Éditions Gallimard, 1976), 44–74.
13  Martin Papenheim, *Erinnerung und Unsterblichkeit: Semantische Studien zum Totenkult in Frankreich 1715–1794* (Stuttgart: Klett-Cotta, 1992), 213–238; quoted from Rolf Reichardt, *Das Blut der Freiheit: Französische Revolution und demokratische Kultur* (Frankfurt am Main: Fischer Taschenbuch-Verlag, 1998), 245f.
14  Michael Meinzer, *Der französische Revolutionskalender 1792–1805: Planung, Durchführung und Scheitern einer politischen Zeitrechnung* (Munich: Oldenbourg, 1992); Hans Maier, 'Über revolutionäre Feste und Zeitrechnungen', in *Wie eine Revolution entsteht: Die Französische Revolution als Kommunikationsereignis*, ed. Hans Maier and Eberhard Schmidt (Paderborn/Munich/Vienna/Zurich: Schöningh, 1988), 99–117.
15  Aulard, *Le Culte de la Raison*, 52–67.
16  Ibid., 215.
17  Ibid., 267–278, 307–322.
18  George C. Mosse, *Die Nationalisierung der Massen. Von den Befreiungskriegen bis zum Dritten Reich* (Frankfurt am Main: Ullstein, 1976).
19  Arturo C. Jemolo, *Chiesa e Stato in Italia dalla Unificazione a Giovanni XXIII* (Turin: Einaudi, 1965); Pietro Scoppola, *Chiesa e Stato Nella Storia d'Italia: Storia Documentaria dall'Unità alla Republica* (Bari: Laterza, 1967).
20  William Callahan, *Church, Politics, and Society in Spain 1750–1874* (Cambridge, MA: Harvard University Press, 1984), 73–209; on the early stages of the policies of secularization, see also Peer Schmidt, *Die Privatisierung des Besitzes der toten Hand in Spanien: Die Säkularisation unter König Karl IV in Andalusien 1798–1808* (Stuttgart: Steiner, 1990).
21  Karl Otmar von Aretin, *Das Alte Reich 1648–1806*, vol. 3, *Das Reich und der österreichisch-preußische Dualismus 1745–1806* (Stuttgart: Klett-Cotta, 1997); Heribert Raab, 'Der Untergang der Reichskirche in der großen Säkularisation', in *Handbuch der Kirchengeschichte*, vol. 5, *Die Kirche im Zeitalter des Absolutismus und der Aufklärung*, ed. Hubert Jedin (Freiburg im Breisgau: Herder, 1970), 533–554; the text is quoted from Ernst R. Huber and Wolfgang Huber (eds), *Staat und Kirche im 19. und 20. Jahrhundert*, vol. 1, *Staat und Kirche vom Ausgang des alten Reichs bis zum Vorabend der bürgerlichen Revolution* (Berlin: Wissenschaftliche Buchgesellschaft, 1973), 18.
22  Hans Müller, *Säkularisation und Öffentlichkeit am Beispiel Westfalen* (Münster: Mehren und Hobbeling, 1971); Andreas Holzem, 'Säkularisation in Oberschwaben:

Ein problemgeschichtlicher Aufriss', in *Die Säkularisation im Prozeß der Säkularisierung Europas*, ed. Peter Blickle and Rudolf Schlögl (Epfendorf: Bibliotheca academica, 2005), 261–299.
23  Owen Chadwick, *The Victorian Church*, vol. 1, *1829–1859* (London: Hymns Ancient & Modern Ltd, 1970), 24–33.
24  William R. Ward, 'The Tithe Question in England in the Early Nineteenth Century', *Journal of Ecclesiastical History* 16 (1965): 67–81.
25  William Ward, *Religion and Society in England 1790–1850* (London: Batsford, 1972), 8–15; Anthony Armstrong, *The Church of England: The Methodists and Society 1700–1850* (London: Rowman and Littlefield, 1973), 167–172; Peter Virgin, *The Church in an Age of Negligence: Ecclesiastical Structure and Problems of Church Reform 1700–1840* (Cambridge: Clarke, 1989), 160–180; Geoffrey F. Best, *Temporal Pillars: Queen Anne's Bounty, the Ecclesiastical Commissionars, and the Church of England* (Cambridge: Cambridge University Press, 1964), 239–345.
26  Chadwick, *Victorian Church*, vol. 1, 101–140.
27  René Pahut, 'Religionsfreiheit', *Theologische Realenzyklopädie* 28 (1967): 565–574; Étienne François, *Die unsichtbare Grenze: Protestanten und Katholiken in Augsburg 1648–1806*, trans. Angelika Steiner-Wendt (Sigmaringen: Wißner-Verlag, 1991), 190–244; Jan Hunter, *The Secularisation of the Confessional State: The Political Thought of Christian Thomasius* (Cambridge: Cambridge University Press, 2007).
28  Günther Birtsch, 'Religions- und Gewissensfreiheit in Preußen von 1780 bis 1817', *Zeitschrift für historische Forschung* 11 (1984): 177–204; Fritz Valjavec, 'Das Woellnersche Religionsedikt und seine geschichtliche Bedeutung', in *Fritz Valjavec: Ausgewählte Aufsätze*, ed. Karl A. Fischer and Mathias Bernath (Munich: Oldenbourg, 1963), 294–306; cf. in general Adolf Keller, *Church and State on the European Continent: The Social Service Lecture 1936* (London: Epworth Press, 1936), 151–268.
29  Oskar Sakrausky, 'Historische Beschreibung was sich anlässlich des Toleranzpatents in Arriach zugetragen hat', *Jahrbuch für die Geschichte des Protestantismus in Österreich* 102, no. 3 (1986/87): 3–91.
30  Jan Assmann, *Die Mosaische Unterscheidung oder der Preis des Monotheismus* (Munich: Carl Hanser Verlag, 2003), esp. 28–38.
31  Matthias J. Fritsch, *Religiöse Toleranz im Zeitalter der Aufklärung. Naturrechtliche Begründung – konfessionelle Differenzen* (Hamburg: Felix Meiner Verlag, 2004), 233–358.
32  Jean-Jacques Rousseau, 'Briefe vom Berge', in *Jean-Jacques Rousseau: Schriften in drei Bänden*, vol. 2, ed. Henning Ritter (Munich/Vienna: Hanser, 1978), 7–253, esp. 120ff.; Jean-Jacques Rousseau, *Gesellschaftsvertrag oder Grundsätze des Staatsrechts*, ed. Hans Brockard (Stuttgart: Reclam, 1979), 153 (IV, 8).
33  Joseph v. Görres, *Gesammelte Schriften*, vol. 18, *Athanasius*, ed. Wilhelm Schellenberg and Heribert Raab (Paderborn: Ferdinand Schöningh, 1998), 97.
34  The relevant sources are found in Ernst Walder, *Staat und Kirche in Frankreich*, vol. 2, *Vom Kultus der Vernunft zur napoleonischen Staatskirche* (Bern: Lang, 1953); Michael Erbe, *Vom Konsulat zum Empire Libéral: Ausgewählte Texte zur französischen Verfassungsgeschichte 1799–1870* (Darmstadt: Wissenschaftliche Buchgesellschaft, 1985).
35  Cf. notes 4 and 5 above.

36  Eduard His, *Geschichte des neueren schweizerischen Staatsrechts*, vol. 2, *Die Zeit der Restauration und der Regeneration 1814 bis 1848* (Basel: Helbing & Lichtenhahn, 1929), 590f.; Rudolf Pfister, *Kirchengeschichte der Schweiz*, vol. 3 (Zurich: Zwingli-Verlag, 1985), 251–260. Christina M. Schmid-Tschirren, *Von der Säkularisation zur Separation: Der Umgang des Staates mit den Kirchengütern in den evangelisch-reformierten und paritätischen Kantonen der Schweiz im 19. Jahrhundert* (Zurich/Basel/Geneva: Schulthess, 2011).

37  Görres, *Athanasius*, 21; Alois Simon, *Le Cardinal Sterckx et son Temps 1792–1867*, vols 1–2 (Wetteren: Éditions Scaldis, 1950); Willem F. Bakker, O. J. de Jong, W. Van't Spijker and L. J. Wolthuis, *De Afscheiding van 1834 en Haar Geschiedenis* (Kampen: VBK Media, 1984).

38  Cf. notes 8–11 above; on Catholic Emancipation, see Chadwick, *Victorian Church*, vol. 1, 7–24.

39  The sources are given in Ernst R. Huber (ed.), *Deutsche Verfassungsgeschichte seit 1789*, vol. 1, *Reform und Restauration 1789 bis 1830* (Stuttgart: W. Kohlhammer Verlag, 1957), 387–472; this work is also relevant to the points discussed in what follows. On Bavaria, see Heinz Gollwitzer, *Ludwig I: Königtum im Vormärz; Eine politische Biographie* (Munich: Süddeutscher Verlag, 1986), 513–537, 668–688.

40  Heinrich Schrörs, *Die Kölner Wirren 1837: Studien zu ihrer Geschichte* (Berlin: Dümmler, 1927); Rudolf Lill, *Die Beilegung der Kölner Wirren 1840–1842: Vorwiegend nach Akten des Vatikanischen Geheimarchivs* (Düsseldorf: L. Schwann, 1962).

41  Johann F. Goeters and Joachim Rogge (eds), *Die Geschichte der Evangelischen Kirche der Union*, vol. 1, *Die Anfänge der Union unter landesherrlichem Kirchenregiment 1817–1850* (Leipzig: Evangelische Verlagsanstalt, 1992), esp. 134–158, 220–256, 317–330; Erich Foerster, *Die Entstehung der Preußischen Landeskirche unter der Regierung König Friedrich Wilhelms III: Ein Beitrag zur Geschichte der Kirchenbildung im deutschen Protestantismus*, vol. 2 (Tübingen: J. C. B. Mohr (Paul Siebeck), 1905–07), 93–210.

42  Friedrich Schleiermacher, *Über die Religion: Reden an die Gebildeten unter ihren Verächtern (1799)* (Berlin/New York: De Gruyter, 1999), 58. Novalis (Friederich von Hardenberg), 'Die Christenheit oder Europa', in *Novalis: Werke, Tagebücher und Briefe Friedrich von Hardenbergs*, vol. 2, *Das philosophisch-theoretische Werk*, ed. Hans J. Mähl (Munich: Hanser, 1978), 732–750; François-René de Chateaubriand, *Essais sur les Révolutions: Génie du Christianisme* (Paris: Arvensa Editions, 1978), 459f.

43  Friedrich Julius Stahl, *Das monarchische Prinzip: Eine staatsrechtlich-politische Abhandlung* (Heidelberg: Mohr, 1845); Monika Wienfort, *Monarchie in der bürgerlichen Gesellschaft: Deutschland und England von 1640 bis 1848* (Göttingen: Vandenhoeck & Ruprecht, 1993), 194ff.

44  Rudolf Schlögl, 'Kommunikation und Vergesellschaftung unter Anwesenden: Formen des Sozialen und ihre Transformation in der Frühen Neuzeit', *Geschichte und Gesellschaft* 34 (2008): 155–224.

45  As described for esoteric groups and political associations by Ernst Mannheim, *Aufklärung und öffentliche Meinung: Studien zur Soziologie der Öffentlichkeit im 18. Jahrhundert* (Stuttgart: Frommann-Holzboog, 1979), 35–48, although he does not use the term 'complete presence'.

46  Jörn Leonhard, *Liberalismus: Zur historischen Semantik eines europäischen Deutungsmusters* (Munich: Oldenbourg, 2001).

47  William R. Gladstone, *The State in Its Relations with the Church*, vol. 1 (London: Gregg International Publishers, 1969), 93.
48  Joseph von Radowitz, *Ausgewählte politische Schriften*, vol. 1, ed. Wilhelm Corvinus (Regensburg: Habbel, no date); Friedrich J. Stahl, *Der christliche Staat und sein Verhältnis zu Deismus und Judentum: Eine durch die Verhandlungen des Vereinigten Landtags hervorgerufene Abhandlung* (Berlin: Oehmigke, 1858); Jakob von Gerlach (ed.), *Ernst Ludwig v. Gerlach: Aufzeichnungen aus seinem Leben und Wirken*, vol. 1, *1795–1848* (Schwerin: Fr. Bahn Verlag, 1903).
49  Carl L. v. Haller, *Restauration der Staatswissenschaft: oder Theorie des natürlich-geselligen Zustandes, der Chimäre des künstlich-bürgerlichen entgegengesetzt*, 6 vols (Aalen: Scientia-Verlag, 1964 [1820–34]), vol. 1, 90ff.; Louis de Bonald, *Législation Primitive Considerée par la Raison* (Paris: Librairie d'Adrien le Clere, 1847), 130, 160–165, 170–173; Juan D. Cortés, *Der Staat Gottes: Eine katholische Geschichtsphilosophie*, ed.Ludwig Fischer (Darmstadt: Wissenschaftliche Buchgesellschaft, 1966), 43.
50  Gladstone, *State*, vol. 1, 74; Samuel T. Coleridge, *The Collected Works of Samuel Taylor Coleridge*, vol. 10, *On the Constitution of the Church and State* (London: Princeton University Press, 1976), 18–28; cf. Panajotis Kondylis, *Konservativismus: Geschichtlicher Gehalt und Untergang* (Stuttgart: Klett-Cotta, 1986), 323–352; Ian Crowe, *Patriotism and Public Spirit: Edmund Burke and the Role of the Critic in Mid-Eighteenth-Century Britain* (Stanford, CA: Stanford University Press, 2012).
51  Burke, *Französische Revolution*, 345–347.
52  Haller, *Restauration*, vol. 3, 90ff., vol. 4, 3ff., vol. 6, vii–xiii; Cortés, *Staat Gottes*, 43–47.
53  Burke, *Französische Revolution*, 336–339.
54  Adam Müller, *Elemente der Staatskunst* (Berlin: Haug- und Spenersche Verlagsbuchhandlung, 1948), 398.
55  Ibid., 398–401; Bonald, *Législation Primitive*, 309; Radowitz, *Schriften*, 140; cf. Ethel Matala de Mazza, *Der verfasste Körper: Zum Projekt einer organischen Gemeinschaft in der politischen Romantik* (Freiburg im Breisgau: Rombach Verlag, 1999), 265–302.
56  Joseph de Maistre, *Considérations sur la France; Suivie de: Essai sur la Principe Générateur des Constitutions Politiques et des Autres Institutions Humaines* (Paris: La Société typographique, 1814), 211–240; Novalis, 'Christenheit', 732f.
57  Novalis, 'Christenheit', 732f., 737; Friedrich von Gentz, *Briefe und vertraute Blätter*, vol. 3, ed. Gustav Schlesier (Mannheim: Heinrich Hoff, 1838), 210; Bonald, *Législation Primitive*, 185; Albrecht Koschorke, *Körperströme und Schriftverkehr: Mediologie des 18. Jahrhunderts* (Munich: Fink, 1999).
58  Bonald, *Législation Primitive*, 130; Cortés, *Staat Gottes*, 50; Chateaubriand, *Génie*, 1077–1089; Christiane Liermann, *Rosminis politische Philosophie der zivilen Gesellschaft* (Paderborn: Ferdinand Schöningh, 2004), 398f.
59  Chateaubriand, *Génie*, 1089; Haller, *Restauration*, vol. 3, 77–99, vol. 4, 370f.
60  Görres, *Athanasius*, 72, 98.
61  Gladstone, *State*, 63, 89–105.
62  Coleridge, *Church and State*, 45–75.
63  Coleridge, *Church and State*, 44–46; Gladstone, *State*, 105.
64  Johann Gottfried Fichte, *Reden an die deutsche Nation*, ed.Reinhard Lanth (Hamburg: Meiner, 1978), 45f.; Georg Friedrich Wilhelm Hegel, *Hauptwerke in sechs Bänden*, vol. 5, *Grundlinien der Philosophie des Rechts* (Hamburg: Felix Meiner, 1999), 220–229.

65  Stahl, *Monarchisches Prinzip*; Stahl, *Christlicher Staat*, 12; Friedrich J. Stahl, *Der Protestantismus als politisches Prinzip* (Berlin: no publisher, 1853), 32–35.
66  Wienfort, *Monarchie*, 177; Franz von Baader, *Gesellschaftslehre*, ed. Hans Grassl (Munich: Kösel Verlag, 1957), 74–85, 139.
67  Claude-Henri de Saint-Simon, *Œvres Completes*, vol. 23, *Nouveau Christianisme: Dialogues entre un Conservateur et un Novateur* (Paris: Anthropos, 1966 [1825]), 117, 175.
68  Joseph de Maistre, *Du Pape*, ed. Jacques Lovie and Joannès Chetail (Geneva: Librairie Droz, 1966), 27–43, 129–137.
69  Carl Schmitt, *Römischer Katholizismus und politische Form* (Stuttgart: Klett-Cotta, 1984).
70  Cited in Gerlach, *Aufzeichnungen*, vol. 2.
71  Otto Dibelius, 'Friedrich Wilhelms IV und die Idee des christlichen Staates', *Die Furche* 22 (1936): 40–48; Gerlach, *Aufzeichnungen*, vol. 1; Stahl, *Monarchisches Prinzip*; Stahl, *Protestantismus*; Wilhelm Füßl, *Professor in der Politik: Friedrich Julius Stahl (1802–1861); Das Monarchische Prinzip und seine Umsetzung in die parlamentarische Praxis* (Göttingen: Vandenhoeck & Ruprecht, 1988), 31–50.
72  Ernst Ludwig von Gerlach, 'Friedrich Wilhelm IV: Zwei Aufsätze', in *Ernst Ludwig v. Gerlach: Aufzeichnungen aus seinem Leben und Wirken*, vol. 2, *1848–1877*, ed. Jakob von Gerlach (Schwerin: Fr. Bahn Verlag, 1903), 445–510; David E. Barclay, *Anarchie und guter Wille: Friedrich Wilhelm IV und die preußische Monarchie*, trans. Marion Müller (Berlin: Siedler Verlag, 1995), 50–60, 90–94, 128–136; Joachim Mehlhausen, 'Friedrich Wilhelm IV: Ein Laientheologe auf dem preußischen Königsthron', in *Vom Amt des Laien in Kirche und Theologie: Festschrift für Gerhard Krause zum 70. Geburtstag*, ed. Henning Schroer and Gerhard Müller (Berlin: De Gruyter, 1983), 185–213; Frank-Lothar Kroll, *Friedrich Wilhelm IV und das Staatsdenken der deutschen Romantik* (Berlin: Colloquium, 1990).
73  Coleridge, *Church and State*, 102–109, 138f.
74  See n. 72.
75  Novalis, 'Christenheit', 750; Fichte, *Reden*, 101ff., 177; Saint-Simon, *Nouveau Christianisme*, 182.
76  Jean-Jacques Rousseau, 'Gesellschaftsvertrag oder Grundsätze des Staatsrechts', in Jean-Jacques Rousseau, *Sozialphilosophische und politische Schriften* (Zurich: Buchclub Verlag, 1989), 380–391, 554–556 (draft constitution for Corsica).
77  On this topic and on the following two sections, see the overview of the history of institutions in Martin Kirsch, *Monarch und Parlament im 19. Jahrhundert: Der monarchische Konstitutionalismus als europäischer Verfassungstyp. Frankreich im Vergleich* (Göttingen: Vandenhoeck & Ruprecht, 1999).
78  On the press and censorship in the previous two sections, see Arthur Aspinall, *Politics and the Press, c. 1780–1850* (Brighton: Harvester Press, 1973), esp. 198–269 and 367–384; Hugh A. Collingham and Robert S. Alexander, *The July Monarchy: A Political History of France 1830–1844* (London: Addison-Wesley, 1988), 169–315; Hanley Wayne, *The Genesis of the Napoleonic Propaganda 1796–1799* (New York: Columbia University Press, 2005); Irene Collins, *The Government and the Newspaper in France 1814–1881* (Oxford: Oxford University Press, 1959), 4–65; a contemporaneous view is found in Henri Redhead Yorke, *Paris et la France sous le Consulat: Les Homes, les Institutions, les Mœurs*, trans. Guillaume Lerolle (Paris: Librairie académique Perrin & Co., 1921), 315–327.

79  On George III: Linda Colley, 'The Apotheosis of George III: Loyalty, Royalty and the British Nation 1760–1820', *Past and Present* 102 (1984): 94–129; Grayson M. Ditchfield, *George III: An Essay in Monarchy* (Basingstoke: Palgrave, 2002). On Ludwig XVIII: Sheryl Kroen, *Politics and Theatre: The Crises of Legitimacy in Restoration France, 1815–1830* (Berkeley: University of California Press, 2000), in particular 39–75; Natalie Scholz, *Die imaginierte Restauration: Repräsentationen der Monarchie im Frankreich Ludwigs XVIII* (Darmstadt: Wissenschaftliche Buchgesellschaft, 2006); Natalie Scholz and Christina Schröer (eds), *Représentation et Pouvoir: La Politique Symbolique en France 1789–1830* (Rennes: Presses universitaires de Rennes, 2007), in particular 159ff. (third part). On the successor states of the Empire in the German Confederation, see the overview in Hans-Ulrich Wehler, *Deutsche Gesellschaftsgeschichte*, vol. 2, *Von der Reformation bis zur industriellen und politischen 'Deutschen Doppelrevolution' 1815–1845/49*, 2nd edn (Munich: Beck, 1989), 297–322, and references therein.

80  On the semantics of the nation, see Reinhart Koselleck, Fritz Gschnitzer, Karl Ferdinand Werner and Bernd Schönemann, 'Volk, Nation, Nationalismus, Masse', in *Geschichtliche Grundbegriffe: Historisches Lexikon zur politisch-sozialen Sprache in Deutschland*. vol. 7, ed. Reinhart Kosellek, Werner Conze and Otto Brunner (Stuttgart: Klett-Cotta, 1992), 281–335. On the concept, see Niklas Luhmann, *Die Politik der Gesellschaft* (Frankfurt am Main: Suhrkamp, 2000), 210–222; Albrecht Koschorke, Thomas Frank, Ethel Matala de Mazza and Susanne Lüdemann, *Der fiktive Staat: Konstruktionen des politischen Körpers in der Geschichte Europas* (Frankfurt am Main: Fischer-Taschenbuch-Verlag, 2007), 258–267; Saskia Sassen, *Territory, Authority, Rights: From Medieval to Global Assemblages* (Princeton, NJ: Princeton University Press, 2006), 96–140.

81  Claude Lefort, *Fortdauer des Theologisch-Politischen* (Vienna: Passagen Verlag, 1999); Uwe Hebekus, Ethel Matala de Mazza and Albrecht Koschorke (eds), *Das Politische: Figurenlehre des sozialen Körpers nach der Romantik* (Munich: Fink, 2003).

82  To date, research on the matter offers little more than uncertain hypotheses. Cf. René Rémond, *Religion und Gesellschaft in Europa: Von 1789 bis zur Gegenwart* (Munich: C. H. Beck, 2000), 147–168; Jörg Echterkamp, '"Religiöses Nationalgefühl" oder "Frömmelei der Deutschtümler"? Religion, Nation und Politik im Frühnationalismus', in *Nation und Religion in der deutschen Geschichte*, ed. Heinz-Gerhard Haupt and Dieter Langewiesche (Frankfurt am Main: Campus Verlag, 2001), 142–169; Mosse, *Nationalisierung der Massen*, esp. 28f.

83  Johannes Willms, *Napoleon: Eine Biographie* (Munich: Beck, 2005), 319f.; *Catéchisme à l'Usage de Toutes les Églises de l'Empire Français* (Paris: Nyon & Nicolle, 1806), 58.

84  José Cabanis, *Le Sacre de Napoléon: 2 Décembre 1804* (Paris: Éditions Gallimard, 1970), 193–213; Willms, *Napoleon*, 383–398.

85  Scholz, *Imaginierte Restauration*, 58–71.

86  José Cabanis, *Charles X: Roi Ultra* (Paris: Éditions Gallimard, 1972); Françoise Waquet, *Les Fêtes Royals sous la Restauration ou l'Ancien Régime Retrouvé* (Geneva: Edité par Arts et Métiers Graphiques, 1981), 109–116.

87  Bernd Sösemann, 'Preußische Königsjubiläen als Ritual der Kommunikation: Dignitätspolitik in höfischer und öffentlicher Inszenierung von 1701 bis 1901', in *Preußische Stile: Ein Staat als Kunststück*, ed. Patrick Bahners and Gerd Roellecke (Stuttgart: Klett-Cotta, 2001), 114–124; Matthias Schwengelbeck, 'Monarchische

Herrschaftsrepräsentationen zwischen Konsens und Konflikt: Zum Wandel des Huldigungs- und Inthronisationszeremoniells im 19. Jahrhundert', in *Die Sinnlichkeit der Macht. Herrschaft und Repräsentation seit der Frühen Neuzeit*, ed. Jan Andres, Alexa Geisthövel and Matthias Schwengelbeck (Frankfurt am Main: Campus-Verlag, 2005), 123–162.

88  Werner K. Blessing, *Staat und Kirche in der Gesellschaft: Institutionelle Autorität und mentaler Wandel in Bayern während des 19. Jahrhunderts* (Göttingen: Vandenhoeck & Ruprecht, 1982), 70; Hubertus Büschel, *Untertanenliebe: Der Kult um deutsche Monarchen 1770–1830* (Göttingen: Vandenhoeck & Ruprecht, 2006), 50f., 241–292; Linda Colley, *Britons: Forging the Nation 1707– 1837* (New Haven, CT: Yale University Press, 1992), 217–232; Colley, 'George III'; David E. Barclay, 'Ritual, Ceremonial and the "Invention" of a Monarchical Tradition in Nineteenth-Century Prussia', in *European Monarchy: Its Evolution and Practice from Roman Antiquity to Modern Times*, ed. Heinz Duchhardt, Richard A. Jackson and David Sturdy (Stuttgart: Franz Steiner Verlag, 1992), 207–220.

89  Waquet, *Fêtes Royals*, 55–62; Scholz, *Imaginierte Restauration*, 39–58.

90  Cabanis, *Charles X*, 261–284, 317–328.

91  Thomas Stamm-Kuhlmann, *König in Preußens großer Zeit. Friedrich Wilhelm III: der Melancholiker auf dem Thron* (Berlin: Siedler, 1992), 356f., 478–486; Geheimes Staatsarchiv Preußischer Kulturbesitz Berlin, X Rep. 40-1497 and Evangelisches Zentralarchiv Berlin 7/2555.

92  Gerlach, *Aufzeichnungen*, vol. 1, 247; Arno Schmidt, *Fouqué und einige seiner Zeitgenossen* (Zurich: Haffmans, 1987), book 5, 303f., book 6, 421ff.; Kroll, *Friedrich Wilhelm IV*, 22–28.

93  Ditchfield, *George III*, 77–104; Clarissa Campell Orr, 'The Hanoverian Court and the Christian Enlightenment', in *Monarchy and Religion: The Transformation of Royal Culture in Eighteenth-Century Europe*, ed. Michael Schaich (Oxford: Oxford University Press, 2007), 317–342.

94  Waquet, *Fêtes Royals*, 68–70.

95  On this and the following sections, see Scholz, *Imaginierte Restauration*, 170–211; David Skuy, *Assassination, Politics and Miracles: France and the Royalist Reaction of 1820* (London: McGill-Queen's University Press, 2003), 144–172.

96  Michael Schaich, 'The Funerals of the British Monarchy', in *Monarchy and Religion*, ed. Michael Schaich, 421–450; John Wolffe, *Great Deaths: Grieving, Religion and Nationhood in Victorian and Edwardian Britain* (Oxford/New York: Oxford University Press, 2000), 15–22; Schaich, 'Funerals'.

97  Skuy, *Assassination*, 155.

98  Ibid., 230–232; Bettina Frederking, 'Auf der Suche nach dem "wahren" Frankreich: Das Attentat auf den Duc de Berry am 13 Februar 1820', in *Konstrukte nationaler Identität: Deutschland, Frankreich und Großbritannien (19. und 20. Jahrhundert)*, ed. Joseph Jurt, Daniel Mollenhauer, Michael Einfalt and Erich Pelzer (Würzburg: Ergon Verlag, 2002), 35–57.

99  Novalis, 'Christenheit', 287–304.

100  Clemens Brentano, *Werke*, vol. 1, ed. Wolfgang Frühwald, Bernhard Gajek and Friedhelm Kemp (Darmstadt: Carl Hanser, 1968), 204–217; Wulf Wülfing, 'Die heilige Luise von Preußen: Zur Mythisierung einer Figur der Geschichte in der deutschen Literatur des 19. Jahrhunderts', in *Bewegung und Stillstand in Metaphern und Mythen: Fallstudien zum Verhältnis von elementarem Wissen und*

*Literatur im 19. Jahrhundert*, ed. Jürgen Link and Wulf Wülfing (Stuttgart: Klett-Cotta, 1984), 233–258.

101   Kathrin Hoffmann-Curtius, 'Altäre des Vaterlandes: Kultstätten nationaler Gemeinschaft in Deutschland seit der Französischen Revolution', in *Anzeiger des Germanischen Nationalmuseums und Berichte aus dem Forschungsinstitut für Realienkunde* (Nürnberg: Das Nazionalmuseum, 1989), 286–289.

102   Hoffmann-Curtius, 'Altäre des Vaterlandes', 290–307; Hubertus Büschel, 'Vor dem Altar des Vaterlandes – Verfahren ritueller Sakralisierung von Monarch und Staat zu Beginn des 19. Jahrhunderts', in *Kultur, ein Netz von Bedeutungen: Analysen zur symbolischen Kulturanthropologie*, ed. Florian Steger (Würzburg: Königshausen & Neumann, 2002), 161–183.

103   Wichmann von Meding, 'Das Wartburgfest im Rahmen des Reformationsjubiläums 1817', *Zeitschrift für Kirchengeschichte* 97 (1987): 205–235.

104   Dieter Düding, 'Das deutsche Nationalfest von 1814: Matrix der deutschen Nationalfeste im 19. Jahrhundert', in *Öffentliche Festkultur: Politische Feste in Deutschland von der Aufklärung bis zum Ersten Weltkrieg*, ed. Dieter Düding, Peter Friedemann and Paul Münch (Reinbek: Rowohlt Taschenbuchverlag, 1988), 67–88; Cornelia Förster, 'Das Hambacher Fest 1832: Volksfest und Nationalfest einer oppositionellen Massenbewegung', in *Öffentliche Festkultur. Politische Feste in Deutschland von der Aufklärung bis zum Ersten Weltkrieg*, ed. Dieter Düding, Peter Friedemann and Paul Münch (Reinbek: Rowohlt Taschenbuchverlag, 1988), 113–131; Colley, *Britons*, 226ff.

105   Sudir Hazareesingh, *The Saint Napoleon: Celebrations of Sovereignty in Nineteenth-Century France* (Cambridge, MA: Harvard University Press, 2004), 3–12.

106   Blessing, *Staat und Kirche*, 78; Büschel, 'Altar', 173–175; Büschel, *Untertanenliebe*, 120.

107   Avner Ben-Amos, *Funerals, Politics and Memory in Modern France 1789-1996* (Oxford: Oxford University Press, 2000), 61f.; Laure Lévêque, *Penser la Nation: Mémoire et Imaginaire en Révolutions* (Paris: Éditions L'Harmattan, 2011).

108   Ben-Amos, *Funerals,* 32–45.

109   Ibid., 50–70.

110   Wolffe, *Great Deaths,* 15–75.

111   Robert Hole, *Pulpits, Politics and Public Order in England 1760-1832* (Cambridge: Cambridge University Press, 1989), 175–247.

112   Scholz, *Imaginierte Restauration*, 62–65.

113   Jürgen Osterhammel, *Sklaverei und die Zivilisation des Westens*, 2nd edn (Munich: Carl-Friedrich-von-Siemens-Stiftung, 2009 [2000]).

114   Ernest Sevrin, *Les Missions Religieuses en France sous la Restauration 1815–1830*, vol. 1 (Paris: Procure des Prétres de la Miséricorde, 1948), 114–125.

115   Kroen, *Politics and Theatre*, 76–108; Michael Phayer, 'Politics and Popular Religion: The Cult of the Cross in France 1815–1840', *Journal of Social History* 11 (1978): 346–365; Martyn Lyons, 'Fires of Expiation: Book-Burnings and Catholic Mission in Restauration France', *French History* 10 (1996): 240–264.

116   Hans M. Blitz, *Aus Liebe zum Vaterland: Die deutsche Nation im 18. Jahrhundert* (Hamburg: Hamburger Edition, 2000), 147–169.

117   Karin Hagemann, '*Männlicher Muth und Teutsche Ehre*': Nation, Militär und Geschlecht zur Zeit der antinapoleonischen Kriege Preußens* (Paderborn: Ferdinand Schöningh, 2002), 144.

118  On this more generally, see Peter Berghoff, *Der Tod des politischen Kollektivs: Politische Religion und das Sterben und Töten für Volk, Nation und Rasse* (Berlin: De Gruyter, 1997); Gerhard Graf, *Gottesbild und Politik: Eine Studie zur Frömmigkeit in Preußen während der Befreiungskriege 1813–1815* (Göttingen: Vandenhoeck & Ruprecht, 1993), 33–45; Hagemann, 'Männlicher Muth', esp. 272–296.

119  See, for example, the overviews given in Karl Egon Lönne, *Politischer Katholizismus im 19. und 20. Jahrhundert* (Frankfurt am Main: Suhrkamp, 1986), 51–84. Franz Schnabel, *Deutsche Geschichte im 19. Jahrhundert*, vol. 4, *Die religiösen Kräfte* (Freiburg: Herder, 1937), 97–202, is also still relevant.

120  Charles F. Comte de Montalembert, *De Devoirs des Catholiques dans la Question de la Liberté d'Enseignement* (Paris: L'Univers, 1843), esp. 66–77; Gerlach, *Aufzeichnungen*, vol. 1, 247; Collingham and Alexander, *July Monarchy*, 303–315; Edward Berenson, *Populist Religion and Left-Wing Politics in France 1830–1852* (Princeton, NJ: Princeton Legacy Library, 1984), 36–54.

121  Johann G. Wirth, *Das Nationalfest der Deutschen zu Hambach, unter Mitwirkung eines Redaktionsausschusses beschrieben*, 2 vols (Neustadt: Christmann, 1832), is an example.

122  Richard Schult, '"… das Schiff der Revolution in den von ihm bestimmten Hafen zu bringen": Jacques-Louis David und die Krönung Napoleons', *Geschichte in Wissenschaft und Unterricht* 12 (1992): 728–742.

123  Many examples are given in Büschel, *Untertanenliebe*; Colley, 'George III'.

124  Wienfort, *Monarchie*, esp. 186–203; Büschel, *Untertanenliebe*.

125  Kenneth E. Hendrickson III, *Making Saints: Religion and the Public Image of the British Army, 1809–1855* (Cranbury, NJ: Fairleigh Dickinson University Press, 1998), 25–56; Ute Frevert, *Die kasernierte Nation: Militärdienst und Zivilgesellschaft* (Munich: C. H. Beck, 2001), 27–49.

# Chapter 3

1  On inclusion and exclusion, see Niklas Luhmann, *Die Gesellschaft der Gesellschaft*, vol. 2 (Frankfurt am Main: Suhrkamp, 1997), 618–634.

2  Joachim Raschke, *Soziale Bewegungen: Ein historisch-systematischer Grundriß* (Frankfurt am Main: Campus-Verlag, 1995); Doug McAdam, John D. McCarthy and Mayer N. Zald (eds), *Comparative Perspectives on Social Movements: Political Opportunities, Mobilizing Structures and Cultural Framings* (Cambridge: Cambridge University Press, 1996); Niklas Luhmann, *Protest: Systemtheorie und soziale Bewegungen* (Frankfurt am Main: Suhrkamp, 1996).

3  Niklas Luhmann, *Organisation und Entscheidung* (Opladen: Westdeutscher Verlag, 2000); Dirk Baecker, *Studien zur nächsten Gesellschaft* (Frankfurt am Main: Suhrkamp 1997), 28–55; Niklas Luhmann, *Funktionen und Folgen formaler Organisation*, 3rd edn (Berlin: Duncker & Humblot, 1976).

4  Wolfgang Reinhard, 'Die Verwaltung der Kirche', in *Deutsche Verwaltungsgeschichte*, vol. 1, *Vom Spätmittelalter bis zum Ende des Reiches*, ed. Kurt Jeserich, Han Pohl and Georg-Christoph von Unruh, 2nd edn (Stuttgart: Deutsche Verlags-Anstalt, 1983), 143–176.

5   On this subject and in relation to the following section, see Hubert Jedin (ed.), *Handbuch der Kirchengeschichte*, vol. 6, *Die Kirche der Gegenwart* (Freiburg im Breisgau, 1978), 3–310; J. Derek Holmes, *The Triumph of the Holy See: A Short History of the Papacy in the Nineteenth Century* (London: Patmos Press, 1978), 15–160.

6   On this and on the following section, see August B. Hasler, *Pius IX (1846–1878). Päpstliche Unfehlbarkeit und 1. Vatikanisches Konzil: Dogmatisierung und Durchsetzung einer Ideologie*, 2 vols (Stuttgart: Hiersemann Verlag, 1977); Herrmann Joseph Pohlmeyer, *Unfehlbarkeit und Souveränität: Die päpstliche Unfehlbarkeit im System der ultramontanen Ekklesiologie des 19. Jahrhunderts* (Mainz: Grünwald, 1975); Otto Weiss, 'Der Ultramontanismus: Grundlagen – Vorgeschichte – Struktur', *Zeitschrift für bayerische Landesgeschichte* 41 (1978): 821–877.

7   Hubert Wolf, *Index. Der Vatikan und die verbotenen Bücher* (Munich: Beck, 2006), 84–201.

8   A. Hollerbach, 'Konkordat', in Adalbert Erler and Ekkehard Kaufmann (eds), *Handwörterbuch der Rechtsgeschichte*, vol. 2 (Berlin: Erich Schmidt Verlag, 1978), 1070–1074; Ernst R. Huber (ed.), *Deutsche Verfassungsgeschichte seit 1789*, vol. 1, *Reform und Restauration 1789 bis 1830* (Stuttgart: W. Kohlhammer, 1957), 417–450, which is also relevant for the following sections.

9   Dominik Burkhard, *Staatskirche, Papstkirche, Bischofskirche: Die 'Frankfurter Konferenzen' und die Neuordnung der Kirche in Deutschland nach der Säkularisation* (Rome/Freiburg im Breisgau: Herder, 2000), 439–470, 713–725; Karl Hausberger, *Reichskirche, Staatskirche, 'Papstkirche': Der Weg der deutschen Kirche im 19. Jahrhundert* (Regensburg: Pustet, 2008).

10  Joseph Müller, *Die bischöflichen Diözesanbehörden* (Stuttgart: Ferdinand Enke, 1905), 12–33, 113–126; Michael N. Ebertz, 'Die Bürokratisierung der katholischen "Priesterkirche"', in *Priesterkirche*, ed. Paul Hoffmann (Düsseldorf: Patmos, 1987), 132–163; Benjamin Ziehmann, 'Säkularisierung, Konfessionalisierung, Organisationsbildung: Dimensionen der Sozialgeschichte der Religion im langen 19. Jahrhundert', *Archiv für Sozialgeschichte* 47 (2007): 485–508; Joseph von Hommer, *1760–1836: Meditationes in vitam meam peractam. Eine Selbstbiographie*, ed. and trans. Alois Thomas (Mainz: Selbstverlag der Gesellschaft für mittelrheinische Kirchengeschichte, 1976), 275–299 and *passim*; Georg L. C. Kopp, *Die katholische Kirche im 19. Jahrhundert und die zeitgemäße Umgestaltung ihrer Verfassung mit besonderer Rücksicht auf die im ehemaligen Mainzer, später Regensburger Erzstifte hierzu getroffenen Anstalten und Anordnungen* (Mainz: Kupferberg, 1830).

11  Thomas Schulte-Umberg, 'Professionalisierung des katholischen Klerus: Forschungsstrategien und Perspektiven am Beispiel des Bistums Münster', in *Beruf und Religion im 19. und 20. Jahrhundert*, ed. Frank Michael Kuhlemann and Hans-Walter Schmuhl (Stuttgart: Kohlhammer, 2003), 28–50; Thomas Schulte-Umberg, *Profession und Charisma: Herkunft und Ausbildung des Klerus im Bistum Münster 1776–1940* (Paderborn/Munich/Vienna/Zurich: Ferdinand Schöningh, 1999), 132–225; Irmtraud Götz von Olenhusen, *Klerus und abweichendes Verhalten: Zur Sozialgeschichte katholischer Priester im 19. Jahrhundert. Die Erzdiözese Freiburg* (Göttingen: Vandenhoeck & Ruprecht, 1994), 64–71, 90f.; Ralph Gibson, *A Social History of French Catholicism 1789–1914* (London: Routledge, 1989), 56–92.

12  Alan D. Gilbert, *Religion and Society in Industrial England: Church, Chapel and Social Change 1740-1914* (London: Longman, 1976) and Stewart J. Brown, *The National Churches of England, Ireland and Scotland 1801-1846* (Oxford: Oxford University Press, 2001) provide overviews for Britain and Ireland.
13  The following are still insightful: Otto Hintze, 'Epochen des evangelischen Kirchenregiments in Preußen', in *Gesammelte Abhandlungen*, vol. 3, *Regierung und Verwaluntung: Gesammelte Aufsätze zur Staats-Rechts- und Sozialgeschichte Preußen*, ed. Gerhard Oestreich, 2nd edn (Göttingen: Vandenhoeck & Ruprecht, 1967), 57-96; Karl Kupisch, *Die deutschen Landeskirchen im 19. und 20. Jahrhundert: Die Kirche in ihrer Geschichte; Ein Handbuch*, vol. 4, 2nd edn (Göttingen: Vandenhoeck & Ruprecht, 1975), 51-61; Johann F. Goeters and Joachim Rogge (eds), *Die Geschichte der Evangelischen Kirche der Union*, vol. 1, *Die Anfänge der Union unter landesherrlichem Kirchenregiment 1817-1850* (Leipzig: Evangelische Verlagsanstalt, 1992), 55-62.
14  Frank Michael Kuhlemann, *Bürgerlichkeit und Religion: Zur Sozial- und Mentalitätsgeschichte der evangelischen Pfarrer in Baden 1860-1914* (Göttingen: Vandenhoeck & Ruprecht, 2002), 73-79.
15  Brown, *National Churches*, 190-246; Gilbert, *Religion and Society*; Anthony Armstrong, *The Church of England: The Methodists and Society 1700-1850* (London: Rowman and Littlefield, 1973), 164ff.; Peter Virgin, *The Church in an Age of Negligence: Ecclesiastical Structure and Problems of Church Reform 1700-1840* (Cambridge: Clarke, 1989); Robert D. Cornwall and James E. Bradley (eds), *Religion, Politics and Dissent, 1660-1832: Essays in Honour of James E. Bradley* (Farnham: Routledge, 2010); Kate Cooper (ed.), *Elite and Popular Religion* (Woodbridge: Ecclesiastical History Society, 2006).
16  Kuhlemann, *Bürgerlichkeit und Religion*, 62-72, 84-96; Oliver Janz, *Bürger besonderer Art. Evangelische Pfarrer in Preußen 1850-1915* (Berlin/New York: De Gruyter, 1994), 26-100.
17  Weiss, 'Ultramontanismus'; Karl Buchheim, *Ultramontanismus und Demokratie: Der Weg der deutschen Katholiken im 19. Jahrhundert* (Munich: Kösel, 1963), 36-82.
18  P. B. Nockles, *The Oxford Movement in Context: Anglican High Churchmanship 1760-1857* (Cambridge: Cambridge University Press, 1985), 146-170; S. A. Skinner, *Tractarians and the 'Condition of England': The Social and Political Thought of the Oxford Movement* (Oxford: Clarendon Press, 2004), 18-27.
19  Armstrong, *Church of England*, 37, 157-168.
20  An overview of the situation in Europe is found in the following works: Wolfgang Schmale and Nan L. Dodde (eds), *Revolution des Wissens? Europa und seine Schulen im Zeitalter der Aufklärung 1750-1825: Ein Handbuch zur europäischen Schulgeschichte* (Bochum: Winkler, 1991), 97-223, 513-579; Sarah A. Curtis, *Educating the Faithful: Religion, Schooling and Society in 19th Century France* (De Kalb, IL: Northern Illinois University Press, 2000); Horst F. Rupp, '"Jeder Lehrer – ein Religionslehrer": Über den Zusammenhang von Religion und Schule in Deutschland', in *Beruf und Religion im 19. und 20. Jahrhundert*, ed. Frank-Michael Kuhlemann and Hans-Walter Schmuhl (Stuttgart: Kohlhammer, 2003), 86-96.
21  On this, and in relation to the entire chapter, see Peter Beyer, *Religion in Globalized Society* (Arlington: Routledge, 2006), esp. 109-114.
22  This expression is borrowed from Hartmann Tyrell, 'Weltgesellschaft, Weltmission und religiöse Organisation – Einleitung', in *Weltmission und religiöse Organisationen. Protestantische Missionsgesellschaften im 19. und 20. Jahrhundert*, ed. Arthur Bogner,

Bernd Holtwick and Hartmann Tyrell (Würzburg: Ergon Verlag, 2004), 78; see also the references in note 2.

23 William Ward, *Religion and Society in England 1790–1850* (London: Batsford, 1972), 81–105; Martin Brecht, Klaus Deppermann, Ulrich Gäbler and Hartmut Lehmann (eds), *Geschichte des Pietismus*, vols 1–2 (Göttingen: Vandenhoeck & Ruprecht, 1993–95).

24 Armstrong, *Church of England*, 50–120; Reginald Ward, 'John Wesley', *Theologische Realenzyklopädie* 35 (2003): 657–662; David Hampton and Myrtle Hill, *The Evangelical Protestantism in Ulster Society 1740–1890* (London: Routledge, 1992), 8–16, 76–80; these references are also relevant for the following sections.

25 John Rule, 'Methodism, Popular Beliefs and Village Culture', in *Popular Culture and Custom in Nineteenth Century England*, ed. Robert D. Storch (London: Croom Helm, 1982), 48–70; Armstrong, *Church of England*, 171–175.

26 Rule, 'Methodism'.

27 Armstrong, *Church of England*, 167–172.

28 Josef Mooser, 'Konventikel, Unterschichten und Pastoren. Entstehung, Träger und Leistungen der Erweckungsbewegung in Minden-Ravensberg ca. 1820–1850', in *Frommes Volk und Patrioten: Erweckungsbewegung und soziale Frage im östlichen Westfalen 1800–1858*, ed. Josef Mooser (Bielefeld: Verlag für Regionalgeschichte, 1999), 27.

29 Andreas Holzem, *Konfession und Sektenbildung: Deutschkatholiken, Reformkatholiken und Ultramontane am Oberrhein 1844–1866* (Paderborn: Ferdinand Schöningh, 1994), 120–128; Friedrich Wilhelm Graf, *Die Politisierung des religiösen Bewusstseins: Die bürgerlichen Religionsparteien im deutschen Vormärz. Das Beispiel des Deutschkatholizismus* (Stuttgart: Frommann-Holzboog, 1978), 28–66; Sylvia Paletschek, *Frauen und Dissens: Frauen im Deutschkatholizismus und in den freien Gemeinden 1841–1852* (Göttingen: Vandenhoeck & Ruprecht, 1990), 30–46; Paul Ernst Lieberknecht, *Geschichte des Deutschkatholizismus in Kurhessen* (Marburg: N. G. Elwert, 1915), 5–81; Alexander Stollenwerk, *Der Deutschkatholizismus in den Preußischen Rheinlanden* (Mainz: Gesellschaft für Mittelrheinische Kirchengeschichte, 1971).

30 Stephen Neill, *Geschichte der christlichen Missionen*, 2nd edn (Erlangen: Verlag der Evangelischen Lutheranischen Mission, 1990), 165–213; Gerhard Rosenkranz, *Die christliche Mission: Geschichte und Theologie* (Munich: Kaiser, 1977), 193–237; Horst Gründer, *Welteroberung und Christentum: Ein Handbuch zur Geschichte der Neuzeit* (Gütersloh: Gütersloher Verlagshaus, 1992), part 2. Missionary activity as an aspect of the history of globalization in the nineteenth century is discussed in C. A. Bayly, *The Birth of the Modern World 1780–1914: Global Connections and Comparisons* (London: Wiley-Blackwell, 2004), 325–366; Jürgen Osterhammel, *Die Verwandlung der Welt: Eine Geschichte des 19. Jahrhunderts* (Munich: C. H. Beck, 2009), 1261–1266.

31 Jacques Gadille and Jean-Marie Mayeur (eds), *Liberalismus, Industrialisierung, Expansion Europas (1830–1914): Geschichte des Christentums, Religion, Politik, Kultur*, vol. 11 (Freiburg im Breisgau: Herder, 1997), 131–164; Peter Hinchliff, 'Voluntary Absolutism: British Missionary Societies in the 19th Century', in *Voluntary Religion*, ed. William J. Sheils and Diana Wood (London: Blackwell, 1986), 363–379; Brian Stanley, *The History of Baptist Missionary Societies 1792–1992* (Edinburgh: T&T Clark, 1992); John Roxborough, *Thomas Chalmers: Enthusiast for Mission. The Christian Good of Scotland and the Rise of*

*the Missionary Movement* (Edinburgh: Authentic Media, 1999); Sheridan Gilley and Brian Stanley (eds), *The Cambridge History of Christianity*, vol. 8, *World Christianities, ca. 1815–1914* (Cambridge: Cambridge University Press, 2006), 443–456; Wilhelm Schlatter, *Geschichte der Basler Mission 1815–1915*, vol. 1 (Basel: Verlag der Basler Missionsbuchhandlung, 1910), 193; Bernhard Arens, S.J., *Die katholischen Missionsvereine: Darstellung ihres Werdens und Wirkens, ihrer Satzungen und Vorrechte* (Freiburg im Breisgau: Herder, 1922); Robert Hoffmann, 'Die katholische Missionsbewegung in Deutschland vom Anfang des 19. Jahrhunderts bis zum Ende der Kolonialgeschichte', in *Imperialismus und Kolonialismus: Kaiserliches Deutschland und koloniales Imperium*, ed. Klaus Jürgen Baden (Wiesbaden: Steiner, 1982), 29–50; Eduard Kriele, *Geschichte der Rheinischen Mission*, vol. 1, *Die Rheinische Mission in ihrer Heimat* (Barmen: Missionshaus, 1928).

32 Wilhelm Gundert, *Geschichte der deutschen Bibelgesellschaften im 19. Jahrhundert* (Bielefeld: Chronos, 1987); Johannes Altenbernd, 'Bibelanstalt, Bibelbund oder Bibelgesellschaft? Bibelverbreitung und Vereinsgründung in der katholischen Kirche zwischen 1805–1830', in *Weltmission und religiöse Organisationen: Protestantische Missionsgesellschaften im 19. und 20. Jahrhundert*, ed. Arthur Bogner, Bernd Holtwick and Hartmann Tyrell (Würzburg: Egon-Verlag, 2004), 249–284.

33 Bernd Holtwick, 'Licht und Schatten: Begründungen und Zielsetzungen des protestantischen missionarischen Aufbruchs im frühen 19. Jahrhundert', in *Weltmission und religiöse Organisationen: Protestantische Missionsgesellschaften im 19. und 20. Jahrhundert*, ed. Arthur Bogner, Bernd Holtwick and Hartmann Tyrell (Würzburg: Egon-Verlag, 2004), 240.

34 Boris Barth and Jürgen Osterhammel (eds), *Zivilisierungsmissionen: Imperiale Weltverbesserung seit dem 18. Jahrhundert* (Konstanz: UVK, 2005), although the individual contributions in the volume do not lay any particular focus on missionary activity, which is discussed in more detail in Brian Stanley, 'Christian Missions, Antislavery and the Claims of Humanity 1813–1873', in *The Cambridge History of Christianity*, vol. 8, ed. Sheridan Gilley and Brian Stanley (Cambridge: Cambridge University Press, 2006), 443–458; Roxborough and Calmers, *Enthusiast for Mission*, 228–239; Heidemarie Winkel, 'Christliche Religion und ihre Sinnformen der Selbstbeschreibung: Mission und Ökumene als Grundpfeiler des Wandels religiöser Wissensformen', *Geschichte und Gesellschaft* 36, no. 2 (2010): 285–316.

35 Overviews are found in Urban Schwegler, 'Von Priestermission und Laienmitarbeit: Organisation und Bau katholischer Missionsgesellschaften auf dem Hintergrund der katholischen Weltmission. Am Beispiel der Missionsgesellschaft Bethlehem, Immensee (SMB)', in *Weltmission und religiöse Organisationen: Protestantische Missionsgesellschaften im 19. und 20. Jahrhundert*, ed. Arthur Bogner, Bernd Holtwick and Hartmann Tyrell (Wurzburg: Ergon Verlag, 2004), 397–423; Arens, *Katholischen Missionsvereine, passim*.

36 On the Chevaliers du Foi and the camarilla in Berlin, see notes 48 and 49 in Chapter 2; Nockles, *Oxford Movement*, 79–86; Armstrong, *Church of England*, 121ff., 130–145; Hans Kapfinger, *Der Eoskreis 1828 bis 1832: Ein Beitrag zur Vorgeschichte des politischen Katholizismus in Deutschland* (Munich: Pfeiffer, 1928); Christoph Weber, *Aufklärung und Orthodoxie am Mittelrhein 1820–1850* (Munich/Paderborn/Vienna: Ferdinand Schöningh, 1973), 26–54.

37 Both aspects are discussed in Beyer, *Religion in Globalized Society*, 29–61, 108–114.

38  There is currently no communication-theoretical model of piety. Maren Lehmann, *Inklusion: Beobachtungen einer sozialen Form am Beispiel von Religion und Kirche* (Berlin: Humanities Online, 2002).
39  Cf. the static treatment of these terms in Hartmut Lehmann (ed.), *Säkularisierung, Dechristianisierung, Rechristianisierung im neuzeitlichen Europa: Bilanz und Perspektiven der Forschung* (Göttingen: Vandenhoeck & Ruprecht, 1997).
40  Jean Wirth, 'La Naissance du Concept de Croyance (XIIe–XVIIIe Siècle)', *Bibliothèque d'Humanisme et Renaissance* 44 (1983): 7–58; Jens Ivo Engels and Hillard von Thiessen, 'Glauben: Begriffliche Annäherungen anhand von Beispielen aus der Frühen Neuzeit', *Zeitschrift für historische Forschung* 28 (2001): 333–357; Rudolf Schlögl, 'Öffentliche Gottesverehrung und privater Glaube in der Frühen Neuzeit. Beobachtungen zur Bedeutung von Kirchenzucht und Frömmigkeit für die Abgrenzung privater Sozialräume', in *Das Öffentliche und Private in der Vormoderne*, ed. Gerd Melville and Peter von Moos (Cologne/Vienna: Böhlau, 1998), 165–209, esp. 192–209; Rudolf Schlögl, 'Körper, Seele und Verstand: Medien der Subjektivierung in der Frühen Neuzeit', in *Der Mensch in Gesellschaft: Zur Vorgeschichte des modernen Subjekts in der Frühen Neuzeit*, ed. Michael Hohlstein, Rudolf Schlögl and Isabelle Schürch (Paderborn: Ferdinand Schöningh, 2019), 137–177.
41  Rudolf Schlögl, 'Rationalisierung als Entsinnlichung religiöser Praxis: Zur sozialen und medialen Form von Religion in der Neuzeit', in *Die Säkularisation im Prozess der Säkularisierung Europas*, ed. Peter Blickle and Rudolf Schlögl (Epfendorf: Bibliotheca-Academia-Verlag, 2005), 58ff.
42  Jochen Hörisch, *Der Sinn und die Sinne: Eine Geschichte der Medien* (Frankfurt am Main: Eichborn, 2001), 149ff., 180ff.
43  Hugh McLeod, *Secularisation in Western Europe 1848–1914* (New York: St Martin's, 2000); Olaf Blaschke, 'Abschied von der Säkularisierungslegende', *Zeitenblicke* 5 (2006): http://www.zeitenblicke.de/1/blaschke/index_htm (accessed 2 June 2006); Lucian Hölscher, *Geschichte der protestantischen Frömmigkeit in Deutschland* (Munich: C. H. Beck, 2005), 181–207; Rudolf Schlögl, *Glaube und Religion in der Säkularisierung: Die katholische Stadt; Köln, Aachen, Münster 1700–1840* (Munich: Oldenbourg, 1995), ch. III, 179ff.; Michael Pammer, *Glaubensabfall und wahre Andacht: Barockreligiosität, Reformkatholizismus und Laizismus in Oberösterreich 1700–1820* (Vienna: Verlag für Geschichte und Politik, 1994); Callum G. Brown, *The Death of Christian Britain: Understanding Secularisation 1800–2000*, 2nd edn (London: Routledge, 2008), 145–169; Owen Chadwick, *The Victorian Church*, vol. 1, *1829–1859* (London: Hymns Ancient & Modern Ltd, 1970), part I, 332f., 454–465, 514–519; Horton Davis, *Worship and Theology in England: From Watts and Wesley to Maurice, 1690–1850* (Princeton, NJ: Eerdmans, 1961); James Obelkevich, *Religion and Rural Society in South Lindsay 1825–1875* (Oxford: Clarendon Press, 1976); Gibson, *French Catholicism*, 158–192; Bernard Plongeron (ed.), *La Religion Populaire dans l'Occident Chrétien: Approches Historiques* (Paris: Edité par Paris, Beauchesne, 1976), 149–193; Jean Delumeau, *La Première Communion* (Paris: Desclée de Brouwer, 1987), 171–252; Jonathan C. D. Clark, *English Society, 1660–1832: Religion, Ideology and Politics During the Ancien Régime* (Cambridge: Cambridge University Press, 2000).
44  Ward, *Religion and Society*, 10f.
45  Friedrich Wilhelm Graf, '"Einfache Dechristianisierung": Zur Problemgeschichte eines kulturpolitischen Topos', in *Säkularisierung: Der europäische Sonderweg in*

*Sachen Religion*, ed. Hartmut Lehmann (Göttingen: Wallstein Verlag, 2004), 32–66; Sheryl Kroen, *Politics and Theatre: The Crises of Legitimacy in Restoration France, 1815–1830* (Berkeley, CA: University of California Press, 2000), 76–108.

46 Friedrich Schleiermacher, *Über die Religion: Reden an die Gebildeten unter ihren Verächtern (1799)* (Berlin/New York: De Gruyter, 1999); Rudolf Schlögl, 'Der Glaube Alteuropas und die moderne Welt: Zum Verhältnis von Säkularisation und Säkularisierung', in *Zerfall und Wiederbeginn: Vom Erzbistum zum Bistum Mainz (1792/97–1830). Ein Vergleich*, ed. Walter G. Rödel and Regina E. Schwertfeger (Würzburg: Echter, 2002), 69f.

47 Joseph von Görres, *Gesammelte Schriften*, vol. 18, *Athanasius*, ed. Wilhelm Schellenberg and Heribert Raab (Paderborn: Ferdinand Schöningh, 1998), 132.

48 Hölscher, *Protestantische Frömmigkeit*, 181f., 415, notes 2 and 8.

49 Hölscher, *Protestantische Frömmigkeit*, 182f.; Brown, *Death of Christian Britain*, 24ff.

50 Görres, *Athanasius*, 115–133.

51 Brown, *Death of Christian Britain*, 18–21.

52 Heinrich Richard Schmidt, '"Verfall der Religion": Epochenwende um 1700', in *Die Säkularisation im Prozess der Säkularisierung Europas*, ed. Peter Blickle and Rudolf Schlögl (Epfendorf: Bibliotheca-Academia-Verlag, 2005), 245–258.

53 Schlögl, *Glaube und Religion*, 252; Obelkevich, *South Lindsay*, 138f.

54 Chadwick, *Victorian Church*, 521.

55 Dieter Langewiesche, 'Nation und Religion', in *Europäische Religionsgeschichte: Ein mehrfacher Pluralismus*, vol. 2, ed. Hans G. Kippenberg, Jörg Rüpke and Kocku Stuckrad (Göttingen: Vandenhoeck & Ruprecht, 2009), 525–533.

56 Albrecht Koschorke, *Die Heilige Familie und ihre Folgen: Ein Versuch* (Frankfurt am Main: Fischer-Taschenbuch-Verlag, 2000), 187–215; Jacques Danzelot, *Die Ordnung der Familie* (Frankfurt am Main: Suhrkamp, 1980); Rebekka Habermas, *Frauen und Männer des Bürgertums* (Göttingen: Vandenhoeck & Ruprecht, 2000), 259–314.

57 Schlögl, 'Rationalisierung als Entsinnlichung', 62ff.; examples and further secondary references are found in Lucian Hölscher, 'Die Religion des Bürgers: Bürgerliche Frömmigkeit und protestantische Kirche im 19. Jahrhundert', *Historische Zeitschrift* 250 (1990): 595–630.

58 Hölscher, *Protestantische Frömmigkeit*, 202–207; Joachim Hoffmann, *Berlin-Friedrichsfelde: Ein deutscher Nationalfriedhof* (Berlin: Das Neue Berlin, 2001).

59 Hölscher, *Protestantische Frömmigkeit*, 201f; Obelkevich, *South Lindsay*, 131–135; Séan Ó Suilleabhain, *Irish Wake Amusements* (Dublin: Mercer Press, 1967), 19–23.

60 Gibson, *French Catholicism*, 164–167; Thomas A. Kselman, *Death and Afterlife in Modern France* (Princeton, NJ: Princeton University Press, 1993), 226–290.

61 Obelkevich, *South Lindsay*, 135–145.

62 Bernhard Schneider, *Katholiken auf die Barrikaden: Europäische Revolutionen und deutsche katholische Presse 1815–1848* (Paderborn/Munich/Vienna/Zurich: Ferdinand Schöningh, 1998), 66; Franz Dieringer, 'Die katholische Journalistik in Deutschland und ihre Aufgabe', *Der Katholik* 23 (1843): 1–17.

63 Schneider, *Katholiken*, 44–63.

64 Gottfried Mehnert, *Programme evangelischer Kirchenzeitungen im 19. Jahrhundert* (Witten: Luther Verlag, 1972), 11–25.

65 Davis, *Worship and Theology*, 144–182.

66 Blaschke, 'Abschied', paras 24–36; Claude Savart, *Les Catholiques en France au XIXe Siècle: Le Témoignage du Livre Religieux* (Paris: Beauchesne, 1985), 193–217; William St Claire, *The Reading Nation in the Romantic Period* (Cambridge:

Cambridge University Press, 2004), 551–569; Alexis Weedon, *Victorian Publishing: The Economics of Book Production for a Mass Market 1836-1916* (Aldershot: Routledge, 2003), 50–67, 91–95.

67 Hölscher, *Protestantische Frömmigkeit*, 270; Savart, *Catholiques*, 296–435; Martyn Lyons, 'Fires of Expiation: Book-Burnings and Catholic Mission in Restauration France', *French History* 10 (1996): 240–264; Rudolf Schenda, *Volk ohne Buch: Studien zur Sozialgeschichte der populären Lesestoffe 1770-1910*, 3rd edn (Frankfurt am Main: Vittorio Klostermann, 1988 [1977]), 143–147, 160–173, 186–226.

68 Norbert Busch, 'Die Feminisierung der ultramontanen Frömmigkeit', in *Wunderbare Erscheinungen: Frauen und katholische Frömmigkeit im 19. und 20. Jahrhundert*, ed. Irmtraud Götz von Olenhusen (Paderborn: Ferdinand Schöningh, 1995), 210f.

69 *Heiliger Rock Album: Eine Zusammenstellung der wichtigsten Aktenstücke, Briefe, Adressen, Berichte und Zeitungsartikel über die Ausstellung des Heiligen Rockes in Trier* (Leipzig: Mayer und Wigand, 1844); Wolfgang Schieder, 'Kirche und Revolution: Sozialgeschichtliche Aspekte der Trierer Wallfahrt von 1844', *Archiv für Sozialgeschichte* 14 (1974): 419–454; Nils Freytag, *Aberglauben im 19. Jahrhundert: Preußen und seine Rheinprovinz zwischen Tradition und Moderne (1815-1918)* (Berlin: Duncker & Humblot, 2003), 90–95, 142–180, 333–344.

70 Olivia Wiebel-Fanderl, *Die Wallfahrt Altötting: Kultformen und Wallfahrtsleben im 19. Jahrhundert* (Passau: Verein für Ostbairische Heimatforschung, 1982), 19–36; Barbara Stambolis, *Religiöse Festkultur: Tradition und Neuformierung katholischer Frömmigkeit im 19. und 20. Jahrhundert* (Paderborn/Munich/Vienna/Zurich: Ferdinand Schöningh, 2000), 9–41, 66–70; Walter Hartinger, *Religion und Brauch* (Darmstadt: Wissenschaftliche Buchgesellschaft, 1992), 105–121; Michael R. Marrus, 'Pilger auf dem Weg: Wallfahrten im Frankreich des 19. Jahrhunderts', *Geschichte und Gesellschaft* 3 (1977): 330–351; William A. Christian, Jr., *Person and God in a Spanish Valley* (Princeton, NJ: Princeton University Press, 1989).

71 On this subject, see the notes in the section entitled 'The invention of political religion' in Chapter 2.

72 John F. C. Harrison, *The Second Coming: Popular Millenarianism 1780-1850* (London: Routledge, 1979), 43–53, 57–63, 223; Judith Devlin, *The Superstitious Mind: French Peasants and the Supernatural in the Nineteenth Century* (New Haven, CT: Yale University Press, 1987); Thomas A. Kselman, *Miracles and Prophecies in Nineteenth-Century France* (New Brunswick, NJ: Rutgers University Press, 1983), 65–83.

73 Martin Scharfe, *Evangelische Andachtsbilder: Studien zur Intention und Funktion des Bildes in der Frömmigkeitsgeschichte vornehmlich des schwäbischen Raumes* (Stuttgart: Müller & Gräff, 1968); Adolf Spamer, *Das kleine Andachtsbild vom XVI bis zum XX Jahrhundert* (Munich: Bruckmann, 1930), 255–276; Ludwig Andreas Veit and Ludwig Lenhart, *Kirche und Volksfrömmigkeit im Zeitalter des Barock* (Freiburg: Herder, 1956), 59ff., 142f.

74 Clemens Brentano, *Sämtliche Werke und Briefe*, vol. 26, *Religiöse Werke (Part V): 1. Das bittere Leiden unseres Herrn Jesu Christ*, ed. Jürgen Behrens and Anne Bohnenkamp-Renke (Stuttgart: Kohlhammer, 1980); Joseph Görres, *Die christliche Mystik*, 5 vols, ed. Uta Ranke-Heinemann (Frankfurt am Main: Vito von Eichborn Verlag, 1989); Bernhard Gißibl, *Frömmigkeit, Hysterie und Schwärmerei: Wunderbare Erscheinungen im bayerischen Vormärz* (Frankfurt am Main: Peter Lang, 2004), 24–71, 155; Rudolf Muhs, 'Die Stigmata der Karoline Beller: Ein katholisches Frauenschicksal des Vormärz im Spannungsfeld von Volksreligiosität, Kirche, Staat und Medizin', in *Wunderbare Erscheinungen: Frauen und katholische Frömmigkeit*

*im 19. und 20. Jahrhundert*, ed. Irmtraud Götz von Olenhusen (Paderborn: Ferdinand Schöningh, 1995), 83–130, esp. 102f.

75  See Schlögl, 'Rationalisierung als Entsinnlichung', 56–60, on this section and for references to sources.

76  Schlögl, *Glaube und Religion*, 284–326; Brown, *Death of Christian Britain*, 39–57; Rule, 'Methodism', 48–70; Evan Cameron, *Enchanted Europe: Superstition, Reason, and Religion, 1250–1750* (Oxford: Oxford University Press, 2011).

77  Walter von Arx, 'Liturgische Reflexionen im Klerus anhand des Archivs für die Pastoralkonferenzen in den Landkapiteln des Bistums Konstanz', in *Liturgiewissenschaft: Studien zur Wissenschaftsgeschichte*, ed. Franz Kohlschein and Peter Wünsche (Paderborn: Aschendorff Verlag, 1996), 143–187; Hanns Kerner, *Die Reform des Gottesdienstes: Von der Neubildung der Gottesdienstordnung und der Agende in der evangelisch-lutheriscmhen Kirche in Bayern im 19. Jahrhundert bis zur erneuerten Agende* (Stuttgart: Calwer, 1994); Josef Hacker, *Die Messe in den deutschen Diözesan-Gesang- und Gebetbüchern von der Aufklärungszeit bis zur Gegenwart. Mit einem Überblick über die Geschichte dieser Bücher* (Munich: Karl Zink Verlag, 1950), 140f. Protestant sources: C. R. Ribbeck, *Ueber den Werth des öffentlichen Gottesdienstes und die demselben gebührende Achtung* (Magdeburg: Keil, 1800); Conrad Horst, *Mysteriosophie oder über die Veredelung des protestantischen Gottesdienstes …* (Frankfurt: Varentrapp, 1817); Georg Jakob Ludwig Reuß, *Neue evangelische Kirchenagende: Oder was zur gründlichen Untersuchung des protestantischen Cultus in der Kirche und für die Kirche billig zu dieser Zeit geschehen sollte* (Gotha: Beckersche Buchhandlung, 1821); Friedrich Ludwig Reinhold, *Ideen über das Äußere der evangelischen Gottesverehrung* (Neustrelitz: Ferdinand Albanus, 1805); Karl Gottlieb Brettschneider, *Clementine oder die Frommen und Altgläubigen unserer Tage* (Halle: Schwetschke, 1841); August Tholuck, *Die Lehre von der Sünde und vom Versöhner oder die wahre Weihe des Zweiflers* (Hamburg: Friedrich Perthes, 1823); Franz Christian Boll, *Von dem Verfalle und der Wiederherstellung der Religiosität mit besonderer Hinsicht auf das protestantische Deutschland*, 2 parts (Neustrelitz: Ferdinand Albanus, 1809); Friedrich Christian Thomasius, *Ueber Veredelung des christlichen Kultus durch Hilfe der Aesthetik: Mit Hinsicht auf die kirchliche Verfassung auf die preußischen Provinzen in Franken* (Nürnberg: no publisher, 1803); Josias Friedrich Christian Löffler, *Über den Wert und die Erhaltung des christlichen Gottesdienstes* (Jena: no publisher, 1811); C. D. W. Hoffmann, *Ein Wort über die herrschende Irreligiosität und einen zweckmäßigen Religionsunterricht als das wirksamste Mittel dagegen …* (Berlin: Frölich, 1804); *Die Lauheit des Zeitalters gegen Religion und Schrift …* (Leipzig: Bruder und Hoffmann, 1806); Wilhelm Traugott Krug, *Die Kirchenverbesserung und die Gefahren des Protestantismus …* (Leipzig: Baumgärtner, 1826); Franz Wilhelm Jung, *Beitrag zu Ideen über Kirche und Kirchengebäude* (Mainz: no publisher, 1814); Franz Hermann von Reinhold, *System der Christliche Gewissheit*, 2nd edn (Erlangen: A. Deichert, 1884 [1870–1873]). Catholic sources: Olympe Philipe Gerbert, *Considération sur le Dogme Générateur de la Piété Catholique* (Paris: Bureau du Mémorial catholique, 1829); Georg W. Friedrich Panzer, *Gesammelte Schriften einige Verbesserungen in der römisch-katholischen Kirche betreffend* (Frankfurt: Raspe, 1782); Josef Anton Weißenbach, *Von dem Mißbrauch beim Mariendienst und was da abzuschaffen, einzuschränken, beyzubehalten sey: Ein Hausbuch wider die Glaubensfeger* (no publisher, 1786); Ignaz Heinrich von Wessenberg, *Ueber Schwärmerei: Historisch-philosophische Betrachtungen mit Rücksicht auf die jetzige Zeit* (Heilbronn: Landherr, 1835); Joseph Geishüttner, *Versuch einer*

*wissenschaftlichen und populären Dogmatik* (Vienna: Doll, 1818); Wolfgang Menzel, *Christliche Symbolik*, 2 parts (Regensburg: G. Joseph Manz, 1854); Kopp, *Katholische Kirche*; Hommer, *Meditationes*, esp. 261f., 265ff.

78 Davis, *Worship and Theology*, 150–207, 215–284; James Bentley, *Ritualism and Politics in Victorian Britain: The Attempt to Legislate for Belief* (Oxford: Oxford University Press, 1978), 1–33.

79 Wiebel-Fanderl, *Wallfahrt Altötting*; Thomas Finkenstaedt and Helene Finkenstaedt, *Die Wieswallfahrt: Ursprung und Ausstrahlung der Wallfahrt zum Gegeißelten Heiland* (Regensburg: Pustet, 1981); Wolfgang Brückner, *Die Verehrung des Heiligen Blutes in Walldürn: Volkskundliche und soziologische Untersuchungen zum Strukturwandel barocken Wallfahrens* (Aschaffenburg: Geschichts- und Kunstverein Aschaffenburg, 1958), 125–180; Bernhard Schneider, 'Entwicklungstendenzen rheinischer Frömmigkeits- und Kirchengeschichte in der ersten Hälfte des 19. Jahrhunderts: Tradition und Modernisierung', *Archiv für rheinische Kirchengeschichte* 48 (1996): 57–195; Joachim Schmiedl, *Mariannische Religiosität in Aachen: Frömmigkeitsformen einer katholischen Industriestadt des 19. Jahrhunderts* (Altenberge: Oros-Verlag, 1994), 74–140; Alois Mitterwieser, *Geschichte der Fronleichnamsprozession in Bayern*, rev. Torsten Gebhard (Munich: Weinmayer, 1949), 94–135; Louis Châtellier, *L'Europe des Dévots* (Paris: Flammarion, 1987), 211–266.

80 See notes 76 and 77 for references relating to what follows here.

81 Schleiermacher, *Reden*, 80.

82 Mary Heimann, *Catholic Devotion in Victorian England* (Oxford: Oxford University Press, 1995), 26ff.

83 Ibid.

84 Ramie Targoff, *Common Prayer: The Language of Public Devotion in Early Modern England* (Chicago, IL: University of Chicago Press, 2001), 5–13, 118–130.

85 Heinrich Heppe, *Geschichte der quietistischen Mystik in der katholischen Kirche* (Berlin: Hertz, 1875), 331–377; Gerbert, *Considération*, 83–95, 193–233; Savart, *Catholiques*, 681–697; Reinhold, *Christliche Gewissheit*, vol. 2, 11–30.

86 Devlin, *Superstitious Mind*; Kselman, *Death and Afterlife*; Obelkevich, *South Lindsay*; Kselman, *Miracles*; Freytag, *Aberglauben*.

87 Diethart Sawicki, *Leben mit den Toten, Geisterglauben und die Entstehung des Spiritismus in Deutschland, 1770–1900* (Paderborn/Munich/Vienna/Zurich: Ferdinand Schöningh, 2002), 41–84; Ulrich Linse, *Geisterseher und Wunderwirker: Heilssuche im Industriezeitalter* (Frankfurt am Main: Fischer Taschenbuch Verlag, 1996), 27–54; Heinz-Dieter Kittsteiner, 'Die Abschaffung des Teufels im 18. Jahrhundert: Ein kulturhistorisches Ereignis und seine Folgen', in *Die andere Kraft. Zur Renaissance des Bösen*, ed. Alexander Schuller and Wolfert von Rahden (Berlin: De Gruyter Akademie Forschung, 1993), 55–92; Karl Aner, *Die Theologie der Lessingzeit* (Hildesheim: G. Olms, 1964 [1929]), 234–295; Helmut Zander, 'Höhere Erkenntnis: Die Erfindung des Fernrohrs und die Konstruktion der erweiterten Wahrnehmungsfähigkeit zwischen dem 17. und dem 20. Jahrhundert,' in *Trancemedien und Neue Medien um 1900: Ein anderer Blick auf die Moderne*, ed. Markus Hahn and Erhard Schüttpelz (Bielefeld: Transcript-Verlag, 2009), 17–56; Stefan Hoffmann, *Geschichte des Medienbegriffs* (Hamburg: Felix Meiner Verlag, 2002), 108–121 – also in relation to the following remarks.

88 Carl Joseph Hieronimus Windischmann, *Ueber Etwas, das der Heilkunst notthut: Ein Versuch der Vereinigung dieser Philosophie mit der christlichen Philosophie* (Leipzig: Cnobloch, 1824); Gißibl, *Frömmigkeit*, 53–56; Sawicki, *Leben mit den Toten*, 161f.;

Nicole Priesching, *Maria von Mörl (1812–1868): Leben und Bedeutung einer 'Stigmatisierten Jungfrau' aus Tirol im Kontext ultramontaner Frömmigkeit* (Brixen: Verlag A. Weger, 2004), 114–154.

89  Antoine Imbert-Gourbeyre, *La Stigmatisation* (Paris: Bouflet, 1984), 436ff.; Sawicki, *Leben mit den Toten*, 131–281; Otto Weiss, *Die Redemptoristen in Bayern (1790–1909): Ein Beitrag zur Geschichte des Ultramontanismus*, vol. 2 (Munich: EOS, 1977), 1009–1046; Priesching, *Maria von Mörl*, 102–114, 279–301 – also in relation to the following section.

90  Georg Wilhelm Friedrich Hegel, *Hauptwerke in sechs Bänden*, vol. 5, *Grundlinien der Philosophie des Rechts* (Hamburg: Felix Meiner Verlag, 1999).

91  References for the quotations are found in Rudolf Schlögl, 'Sünderin, Heilige oder Hausfrau? Katholische Kirche und weibliche Frömmigkeit um 1800', in *Wunderbare Erscheinungen: Frauen und katholische Frömmigkeit im 19. und 20. Jahrhundert*, ed. Irmtraud Götz von Olenhusen (Paderborn: Ferdinand Schöningh, 1995), 14f. – the article is also relevant in relation to the following section; Ruth Albrecht, Annette Bühler-Dietrich and Florentine Strzelczy (eds), *Glaube und Geschlecht: Fromme Frauen, spirituelle Erfahrungen, religiöse Traditionen* (Cologne: Böhlau, 2008).

92  Franz Laufkötter, 'Weib', in *Kirchen-Lexikon oder die Enzyklopädie der katholischen Theologie und ihrer Hilfswissenschaften*, vol. 11, ed. Heinrich J. Wetzer and Benedikt Welte (Freiburg im Breisgau: Herder, 1852), 820f.

93  David S. Landes, *The Unbound Prometheus: Technological Change in Industrial Development in Western Europe from 1750 to the Present* (Cambridge: Cambridge University Press, 1969); Heinz Gerhard Haupt (ed.), *Das Ende der Zünfte: Ein europäischer Vergleich* (Göttingen: Vandenhoeck & Ruprecht, 2002); Jürgen Kocka, *Arbeitsverhältnisse und Arbeiterexistenzen: Grundlagen der Klassenbildung im 19. Jahrhundert* (Berlin: Dietz, 1990); Klaus Jürgen Bade, *Europa in Bewegung: Migration vom späten 18. Jahrhundert bis zur Gegenwart* (Munich: C. H. Beck, 2002).

94  On the elementary school system, see the section entitled 'Organization and its consequences', note 20, and the section entitled 'Religion as a social movement', note 30.

95  References are found above in the section entitled 'Piety', notes 43–45; a summary is also found in Schlögl, 'Sünderin', 18–27; Hugh McLeod, 'Weibliche Frömmigkeit – männlicher Unglaube? Religion und Kirchen im bürgerlichen 19. Jahrhundert', in *Bürgerinnen und bürgerliche Geschlechterverhältnisse im 19. Jahrhundert*, ed. Ute Frevert (Göttingen: Wallstein, 1988), 134–156.

96  On the missionary movement, see the section above entitled 'Religion as a social movement'; on its significance for women, see Curtis, *Educating the Faithful*; Claude Langlois, *Le Catholicisme au Féminin: Les Congrégations Françaises à Supérieure Générale au XIXe Siècle* (Paris: Cerf-Histoire, 1984); Brigitte Basdevant-Gaudemet and Germain Sicard, *Les Communes Françaises: l'Enseignement et les Cultes de la Fin de l'Ancien Régime à nos Jours* (Paris: Honoré Champion Éditeur, 2005); Sean Gil, *Women in the Church of England: From the 18th Century to the Present* (London: SPCK, 1994); Frank K. Prochaska, *Women and Philanthropy in 19th Century England* (Oxford: Oxford University Press, 1990); Reilinde Meiwes, *'Arbeiterinnen des Herrn': Katholische Frauenkongregationen im 19. Jahrhundert* (Frankfurt am Main: Campus, 2000); Andreas Rutz, *Bildung, Konfession, Geschlecht: Religiöse Frauengemeinschaften und katholische Mädchenbildung im Rheinland (16.–18. Jahrhundert)* (Mainz: Von Zabern, 2006); Ute Gause, *Kirchengeschichte und Genderforschung: Eine*

*Einführung in protestantische Perspektive* (Tübingen: UTB, 2006), 163–200; Silke Köser, *'Denn eine Diakonisse darf kein Alltagsmensch sein': Kollektive Identitäten kaiserswerther Diakonissen 1836–1914* (Leipzig: Evangelische Verlagsanstalt, 2006).

97 On this and the following sections, see Langlois, *Catholicisme au Féminin*, passim, and Curtis, *Educating the Faithful*, as well as Geneviève Gadbois, '"Vous Êtes Presque la Seule Consolation de L'Eglise": La Foi de Femmes Face à la Déchristianisation de 1789-1890', in *La Religion de ma Mère: Le Rôle des Femmes dans la Transmission de la Foi*, ed. Jean Delumeau (Paris: Le Cerf, 1992), 301–325.

98 Curtis, *Educating the Faithful*, 65–80; Meiwes, *'Arbeiterinnen des Herrn'*, 234ff.

99 Hubert de Manios (ed.), *Maria: Études sur la Sainte Vierge*, 7 vols (Paris: Beauchesne, 1949), vol. 3, 474ff.; Meiwes, *'Arbeiterinnen des Herrn'*, 75–82, 260f.; Langlois, *Catholicisme au Féminin*, 310f.; Habermas, *Frauen und Männer*, 211–219.

100 Prochaska, *Women and Philanthropy*, appendix 231–251.

101 Ibid., 6.

102 Ibid., 6f., 22–45, 47–94, 118f.; Gil, *Women in the Church of England*, 77ff.; Tobias Brinkmann, 'Zivilgesellschaft transnational: Jüdische Hilfsorganisationen und jüdische Massenmigration aus Osteuropa in Deutschland, 1868–1914', in *Religion und Philanthropie in den europäischen Zivilgesellschaften: Entwicklungen im 19. und 20. Jahrhundert*, ed. Liedtke Rainer and Klaus Weber (Munich: Ferdinand Schöningh, 2009), 138–157.

103 Gause, *Kirchengeschichte und Genderforschung*, 163–179; Habermas, *Frauen und Männer*, 199–214.

104 Davis, *Worship and Theology*; Hampton and Hill, *Evangelical Protestantism*, 129–141; for references to secondary sources on German Catholics, Friends of the Light, and the Awakening movement, see above section entitled 'Religion as a social movement', notes 28 and 29.

105 In addition to the references given above in the section entitled 'Piety' in relation to popular religion, mesmerism and spiritualism, see David Blackbourn, *Marpingen: Apparitions of the Virgin Mary in Nineteenth-Century Germany* (New York: Knopf, 1994), 1–41; Walter Delius, *Geschichte der Marienverehrung* (Munich: Ernst Reinhardt, 1963); Robert Ernst, *Maria redet mit uns: Marienerscheinungen seit 1830* (Walhorn: Pfarramt Wallhorn, 1983); Raymond Jones, *France and the Cult of the Sacred Heart: An Epic Talk of Modern Times* (Berkeley, CA: University of California Press, 2000); Nicole Edelmann, *Voyantes, Guérisseuses et Visionnaires en France 1784–1914* (Paris: Albin Michel, 1995); Bettina Gruber, *Die Seherin von Prevorst: Romantischer Okkultismus als Religion, Wissenschaft und Literatur* (Paderborn: Ferdinand Schöningh, 2000); Antoine Imbert-Goubeyre, *Les Stigmatisées*, part 2 (Paris: Victor Palmé, 1873), 303ff. (lists those stigmatized) and passim – all of these references are also relevant for the following section.

106 Wessenberg, *Ueber Schwärmerei*, 78 and *passim*.

107 Gil, *Women in the Church of England*, 12–16; Schlögl, 'Sünderin', 33.

108 Raymond Deniel, *Une Image de la Famille et de la Société sous la Restauration (1815–1830): Etudes de la Presse Catholique* (Paris: Éditions ouvrières, 1965), 105–142; Gil, *Women in the Church of England*, 91–94.

109 Gil, *Women in the Church of England*, 29f.; Curtis, *Educating the Faithful*, 100; Jones, *Sacred Heart*, 131–135; Brown, *Death of Christian Britain*, 53f.

110 Brown, *Death of Christian Britain*, 67; Jules Michelet, *Le Prêtre, la Femme et la Famille*, 7th edn (Paris: Chamerot Libraire Editeur, 1861), 292–313.

111  Brown, *Death of Christian Britain*, 58; Gil, *Women in the Church of England*, 76f.
112  Karin Hausen, 'Die Polarisierung der "Geschlechtscharaktere" – Eine Spiegelung der Dissoziation von Erwerbs- und Familienleben', in *Sozialgeschichte der Familie in der Neuzeit Europas*, ed. Werner Conze (Stuttgart: Klett, 1976), 363–393; Claudia Honegger, *Die Ordnung der Geschlechter: Die Wissenschaft vom Menschen und das Weib 1750–1850* (Frankfurt am Main: Suhrkamp, 1991).
113  Wessenberg, *Ueber Schwärmerei*, 78.
114  Brown, *Death of Christian Britain*, 65, 91; Schlögl, *Glaube und Religion*, 296–326; Gause, *Kirchengeschichte und Genderforschung*, 167–177; Schlögl, 'Sünderin', 48; Edith Saurer, 'Frauen und Priester: Beichtgespräche im frühen 19. Jahrhundert', in *Arbeit, Frömmigkeit und Ereignisse: Studien zur historischen Kulturforschung*, ed. Richard von Dülmen (Frankfurt am Main: Fischer Tachenbuch-Verlag, 1990), 163–168; Edith Saurer, 'Religiöse Praxis und Sinnesverwirrung: Kommentare zur religiösen Melancholiediskussion', in *Dynamik der Tradition: Studien zur historischen Kulturforschung*, ed. Richard von Dülmen (Frankfurt am Main: Fischer Taschenbuch-Verlag, 1992), 228–234; Bettina Brockmeyer, *Selbstverständnisse: Dialoge über Körper und Gemüt im frühen 19. Jahrhundert* (Göttingen: Ferdinand Schöningh, 2009), 228–252.
115  Brown, *Death of Christian Britain*, 58–84; Margaret Beetham, *A Magazine of Her Own? Domesticity and Desire in the Women's Magazine 1800–1914* (London: Routledge, 1996), 45–89.
116  Prochaska, *Women and Philanthropy*, 184–220; Sue Morgan, *A Passion for Purity: Alice Hopkins and the Politics of Gender in the Late Victorian Church* (Bristol: University of Bristol, 1999), 92–98.
117  References are found in Schlögl, 'Sünderin', 27ff.
118  Schlögl, 'Sünderin', 31–40; Schmiedl, *Marianische Religiosität*, 17–26; Wolfgang Beinert and Heinrich Petri (eds), *Handbuch der Marienkunde* (Regensburg: Pustet, 1984), 823–842.
119  Ludwig A. Muratori, *Über die Einbildungskraft des Menschen: Mit vielen Zusätzen*, ed. Georg Herman Richartz, 2 parts (Leipzig: Weygand, 1785), 120–127.
120  Schlögl, 'Sünderin', 41f.; Anneliese Ego, *Animalischer Magnetismus oder Aufklärung: Eine mentalitätsgeschichtliche Studie zum Konflikt um ein Heilsprinzip in Frankreich* (Würzburg: Königshausen & Neumann, 1991), 1–33; Robert Darnton, *Der Mesmerismus und das Ende der Aufklärung in Frankreich* (Frankfurt am Main: Carl Hanser, 1968).
121  Wilhelm Ideler, *Der religiöse Wahnsinn, erläutert durch Krankengeschichten: Ein Beitrag zur Geschichte der religiösen Wirren der Gegenwart*, 2 parts (Halle: Schwetschke, 1847), part 2, 334f., 646f., 378f.; on the French discourse, see Frank P. Bowman, *French Romanticism: Intertextual and Interdisciplinary Readings* (Baltimore, MD: Johns Hopkins University Press, 1990), 106–121 ('From Historia to Hysteria').
122  Pierre Debreyne, *Essai sur la Théologie Morale Considerée dans ses Rapports avec la Physiologie et la Médicine* (Paris: Poussielgue-Rusand, 1844).
123  Ibid., 111–139, 141, 172f., 367, 379f.; for the traditional confessional manual to contrast with this see J.-B. Bouvier, *Dissertatio in sexo decalogi praeceptum et supplementum ad tractatum de Matrimonio*, 9th edn (Paris: Mequignon Juniorem, 1839), or J. Gaume, *Handbuch für Beichtväter*, 2nd edn (Aachen: Cremersche Buchhandlung, 1843).
124  Saurer, 'Frauen und Priester', 142 (on Rotteck and Welcker); Michelet, *Prêtre, passim*.

125  Michelet, *Prêtre*, x f., 210–217, 250–264, 277f.
126  Saurer, 'Frauen und Priester', 163–166; Groupe de la Boussièr, *Practique de la Confession. Des Pères du Désert à Vatican II: Quinze Études d'Histoire* (Paris: Cerf, 1983), 208–220, 229–238. Görres, *Christliche Mystik*, vol. 5, 87.
127  Görres, *Christliche Mystik*, vol. 1, 311–314, vol. 5, 81–87.
128  Gil, *Women in the Church of England*, 63f., 77–80; Nina Auerbach, *Women and the Demon: The Life of a Victorian Myth* (Cambridge, MA: Harvard University Press, 1982), 63f.; Brown, *Death of Christian Britain*, 61–67.
129  Kittsteiner, 'Abschaffung des Teufels', 79.
130  Koschorke, *Heilige Familie*, 187–203; Brockmeyer, *Selbstverständnisse*, 267–327; Theodor Mundt, *Madonna: Unterhaltungen mit einer Heiligen* (Frankfurt am Main: Athenäum, 1973 [1835]); Delius, *Marienverehrung*, 300ff.; Auerbach, *Women and the Demon*; Rita Morrien, *Sinn und Sinnlichkeit: Der weibliche Körper in der deutschen Literatur der Bürgerzeit* (Cologne: Böhlau, 2001), 226–287.

# Chapter 4

1  Reinhart Koselleck, 'Einleitung', in *Geschichtliche Grundbegriffe: Historisches Lexikon zur politisch-sozialen Sprache in Deutschland*, vol. 1, ed. Otto Brunner, Werner Conze and Reinhart Koselleck (Stuttgart: Klett-Cotta, 1972), xiii–xvii; Reinhart Koselleck, *Begriffsgeschichte, Studien zur Semantik und Pragmatik der politischen und sozialen Sprache* (Frankfurt am Main: Suhrkamp, 2006), 9–55; Achim Landwehr, *Geschichte des Sagbaren: Einführung in die Historische Diskursanalyse*, 2nd edn (Tübingen: Campus Verlag, 2004); Michel Foucault, *Archäologie des Wissens* (Frankfurt am Main: Suhrkamp, 1981); Lutz Raphael and Heinz Elmar Tenorth (eds), *Ideen als gesellschaftliche Gestaltungskraft im Europa der Neuzeit* (Munich: Oldenbourg, 2006); Martin Mulsow and Andreas Mahler (eds), *Die Cambridge School der politischen Ideengeschichte* (Berlin: Suhrkamp, 2010); Karl Mannheim, *Ideologie und Utopie*, 3nd edn (Frankfurt am Main: Schulte-Bulmke, 1952); Andreas Reckwitz, *Die Transformation der Kulturtheorien: Zur Entwicklung eines Theorieprogramms* (Weilerswist: Velbrück Wissenschaft, 2000), 147–169.
2  Niklas Luhmann, *Die Gesellschaft der Gesellschaft*, vol. 2 (Frankfurt am Main: Suhrkamp, 1997), 866–1149; Niklas Luhmann, *Ideenevolution: Beiträge zur Wissenssoziologie* (Frankfurt am Main: Suhrkamp, 2008), 234–252.
3  Niklas Luhmann, *Gesellschaftsstruktur und Semantik: Studien zur Wissenssoziologie der modernen Gesellschaft*, vol. 1 (Frankfurt am Main: Suhrkamp, 1980), 9–71, also on what follows.
4  Reinhart Koselleck, *Zeitschichten: Studien zur Historik* (Frankfurt am Main: Suhrkamp, 2000), 131–176; Georg Wilhelm Friedrich Hegel, *Hauptwerke in sechs Bänden*, vol. 3, *Wissenschaft der Logik* (Hamburg: Felix Meiner Verlag, 1999), 57ff.
5  Lalor Stephen, *Matthew Tindal: Freethinker; An Eighteenth-Century Assault on Religion* (London: A&C Black, 2006); R. D. Bedford, *The Defence of Truth: Herbert of Cherbury and the Seventeenth Century* (Manchester: Manchester University Press, 1979); John Dunn, *Locke: A Very Short Introduction* (Oxford: Oxford University Press, 1984); David Pfanner, 'Charles Blount', in *The Oxford Dictionary of National Biography*, vol. 6, ed. Matthew Harrison and Brian Harrison (Oxford: Oxford

University Press, 2004), 294f.; J. I. Israel, *Radical Enlightenment: Philosophy and the Making of Modernity 1650–1750* (Oxford: Oxford University Press, 2001); Wayne Hudson, *The English Deists: Studies in Early Enlightenment* (London: Pickering and Chatto, 2009); Jeffrey Wigelsworth, *Deism in Enlightenment England: Theology, Politics and Newtonian Public Science* (Manchester: Manchester University Press, 2009).

6  John Locke, *Epistola de Tolerantia: A Letter on Toleration*, ed. Raymond Klibansky and J. W. Gough (Oxford: Clarendon Press, 1968), 121–133.
7  Lord Edward Herbert Cherbury, *De Veritate*, trans. and introd. Merich H. Carré (Bristol: Typis Blaeviorum, 1937).
8  Passages quoted and referred to are found in ibid., 85–90, 92–108, 289f., 298–308, 321f.
9  Charles Blount, *The Oracles of Reason* (London: Kessinger Publishing, 1995), 195–209.
10  Matthew Tindal, *Christianity as Old as Creation* (London: Thoemmes Press, 1995 [1730]), 157–208.
11  Ibid., 90–99; Cherbury, *De Veritate*, 289; Blount, *Oracles*, 195.
12  William Warburton, *The Divine Legation of Moses Demonstrated on the Principles of a Religious Deist, from the Omission of the Doctrine of a Future State of Reward and Punishment in the Jewish Dispensation* (London: F. Gyles, 1738); cf. Jan Assmann, *Religio Duplex: Ägyptische Mysterien und europäische Aufklärung* (Berlin: Verlag der Weltreligionen, 2010), 98–114.
13  Warburton, *Divine Legation*, xxi, 20.
14  Ibid., 60, 78f.
15  For the quotations and passages cited, see Warburton, *Divine Legation*, xxi, 20, 24–32, 39f., 50, 56–60, 78f., 108–110; Lord Henry St John Bolingbroke, *Works*, vol. 4 (London: Mallet, 1841), 108ff. In all further notes of this kind below, the order of the page numbers corresponds to the order of the quotations and references in the text.
16  Warburton, *Divine Legation*, 51f., 54, 100–122.
17  Johann Joachim Spalding, *Die Bestimmung des Menschen: Kritische Aufgabe* I/I (Tübingen: Mohr Siebeck, 2006), xxxix, 1, 13, 20–23.
18  Hermann Samuel Reimarus, *Die vornehmsten Wahrheiten der natürlichen Religion in zehn Abhandlungen auf eine begreifliche Art erkläret und gerettet* (Hamburg: Bohn, 1766), foreword, 1–5, 196ff., 450ff., 746ff., 749.
19  Bolingbroke, *Works*, vol. 4, 109.
20  Lord Edward Herbert Cherbury, *De Religione Gentilium* (Amsterdam: no publisher, 1663).
21  Reimarus, *Wahrheiten*, 450–466.
22  David Hume, *The Natural History of Religion*, ed. H. E. Root (Stanford, CA: Stanford University Press, 1957), 21.
23  Ibid., 24, 26f., 40–43.
24  Ibid., 70.
25  Ibid., 42, 49–53, 53f., 63.
26  Jürgen Osterhammel, *Die Entzauberung Asiens. Europa und die asiatischen Reiche im 18. Jahrhundert* (Munich: C. H. Beck, 1998).
27  François Delaporte, *Das zweite Naturreich: Über die Fragen des Vegetabilischen im 18. Jahrhundert* (Frankfurt am Main: Ullstein, 1983), 49–70; cf. Ludwig Wittgenstein, *Philosophische Untersuchungen: Kritisch-genetische Edition* (Frankfurt am Main: Suhrkamp, 2001), 613, 793.
28  Eduard Fueter, *Geschichte der neueren Historiographie* (Munich: Oldenbourg, 1936), 265ff., 349–396; Wolf Lepenies, *Das Ende der Naturgeschichte:*

*Wandel kultureller Selbstverständlichkeiten in den Wissenschaften des 18. und 19. Jahrhunderts* (Frankfurt am Main: Suhrkamp, 1978), 9–77; Adalbert Klempt, *Die Säkularisierung der universalhistorischen Auffassung: Zum Wandel des Geschichtsdenkens im 16. und 17. Jahrhundert* (Göttingen: Musterschmidt, 1960); on Linné and Buffon see also John Hedley Brooke, *Science and Religion: Some Historical Perspectives* (Cambridge: Cambridge University Press, 1991), 226–241.

29  Giambattista Vico, *Die neue Wissenschaft: Über die gemeinschaftliche Natur der Völker; Nach der Ausgabe von 1744*, trans. with introd. Erich Auerbach, 2nd edn (Berlin: De Gruyter, 2000); Voltaire (François-Marie Arouet), *Essai sur les Mœurs et l'Esprit des Nations et sur les Principaux Faits de l'Histoire Depuis Charlemagne Jusqu'à Louis XIII* (Paris: Librairie Hachette et Compagnie, 1866 [1756]).

30  David A. Pailin, *Attitudes to Other Religions: Comparative Religion in Seventeenth- and Eighteenth-Century Britain* (Manchester: Manchester University Press, 1984), 2ff.; Peter Harrison, *'Religion' and the Religions in the English Enlightenment* (Cambridge: Cambridge University Press, 1990), 160ff.; Guy G. Stroumsa, *A New Science: The Discovery of Religion in the Age of Reason* (Cambridge, MA: Harvard University Press, 2010), 33f.; Peter Byrne, *Natural Religion and the Nature of Religion: The Legacy of Deism* (London: Routledge, 1989), 51–110. Ernst Feil, *Religio*, vol. 4, *Die Geschichte eines neuzeitlichen Grundbegriffes im 18. und 19. Jahrhundert* (Göttingen: Vandenhoeck & Ruprecht, 2007) is of no use for our discussion as it lacks an understanding of the problems that are at issue.

31  Joseph-François Lafitau, *Die Sitten der amerikanischen Wilden im Vergleich zu den Sitten der Frühzeit* (Leipzig: Edition Leipzig, 1987); Paola von Wyss-Giacosa, *Religionsbilder der frühen Aufklärung: Bernard Picart's Tafeln für die 'Ceremonies et Coutûmes Religieuses de Tous les Peuples du Monde'* (Wabern/Bern: Benteli, 2006), 17–55, 317; Jacques Revel, 'The Uses of Comparison: Religions in the Early Eighteenth Century', in *Bernard Picart and the First Global Vision of Religion*, ed. Lynn Hunt, Margaret Jacob and Wijnan Mijnhardt (Los Angeles: Getty Publications, 2010), 337–341; Hartmut Zedelmaier, *Der Anfang der Geschichte: Studien zur Ursprungsdebatte im 18. Jahrhundert* (Hamburg: Meiner, 2003), 187–191.

32  Lafitau, *Sitten*, 53–59.
33  Ibid., 195–209.
34  Warburton, *Divine Legation*, vol. 2, 265f., 315, 317–321.
35  Ibid., vol. 2, 322–330, 401ff.
36  Ibid., vol. 2, 403, 265ff.
37  Vico, *Neue Wissenschaft*, 124, 22, 126f., 43; see also Gerhart von Graevenitz, *Mythos: Zur Geschichte einer Denkgewohnheit* (Stuttgart: Metzler, 1987), 72–84.
38  Vico, *Neue Wissenschaft*, 133f., 136, 134, 136, 138f.
39  Ibid., 138.
40  Ibid., 132, 78f., 52f.
41  Ibid., 68, 101.
42  Ibid., 50f., 52f., 131ff.
43  Ibid., 88, 133, 52f.
44  Ibid., 92f., 313–322, 86, 98.
45  Ibid., 86, 400–403.
46  Ibid., 411f., 425f.
47  Ibid., 426, 424, 426.

48  Voltaire, *Essai*, 120, 14f.
49  Ibid., 14–17, 53–58.
50  Ibid., 178, 7.
51  Ibid., 8–13.
52  Ibid., 63–81.
53  Ibid., vol. 1, 19f., 40–45, 162, 165–169; vol. 3, 176–181.
54  Osterhammel, *Entzauberung, passim*; cf. also Jürgen Osterhammel, 'Nation und Zivilisation in der britschen Historiographie von Hume bis Maccaulay', in *Geschichtswissenschaft jenseits des Nationalstaats*, ed. Jürgen Osterhammel (Göttingen: Vandenhoeck & Ruprecht, 2001), 103–150.
55  Jean-Jacques Rousseau, *Sozialphilosophische und politische Schriften* (Zurich: Buchclub Verlag, 1989), 279, 380–384, 388f.
56  Ibid., 384–387.
57  Ibid., 385; Jean-Jacques Rousseau, *Émile oder Von der Erziehung* (Zurich: Buchclub Verlag, 1989), 374f., 348f., 336, 340f., 350f., 378, 390, 375f., 353, 357, 379.
58  Rousseau, *Sozialphilosophische Schriften*, 53, 74, 63.
59  Johann Gottfried Herder, *Ideen zur Philosophie der Geschichte der Menschheit* (Wiesbaden: Fourier, 1985), 279ff.
60  Ibid., 103–106.
61  Ibid., 125f., 128f.
62  Ibid., 129, 263–266, 245f.
63  Ibid., 230–233, 237, 230, 236, 225f., 235f.
64  Ibid., 73–76, 121, 85f., 146f.
65  Ibid., 443–447.
66  Benjamin Constant, *De la Religion: Texte Intégral Présenté par Tzvetan Todorov et Étienne Hoffmann* (Paris: Arles Actes Sud, 1999), 39f.
67  Johann Christoph Adelung, *Versuch einer Geschichte der Cultur des menschlichen Geschlechts* (Leipzig: Christian Gottlieb Hertel, 1782).
68  Ibid., 5f., 6–10, 22–29, 59–85, 87–148, 249–254, 287–292, 318–346, 448ff.
69  Ibid., 451f.
70  Philipp Christian Reinhard, *Abriß einer Geschichte der Entstehung und Ausbildung der religiösen Ideen* (Jena: Akademische Buchhandlung, 1794), 249 and *passim*.
71  Christoph Meiners, *Allgemeine kritische Geschichte der Religionen*, 2 vols (Hanover: Helwing, 1806).
72  Ibid., vol. 1, 1f., 5–8.
73  Ibid., 114ff., 120f., 129ff.
74  Constant, *De la Religion, passim*, especially 563–577.
75  Cf. Charles-Louis de Secondat, Baron de la Brède et de Montesquieu, *Vom Geist der Gesetze* (Stuttgart: Philipp Reclam, 1965), book 4, 356ff.
76  Lucian Hölscher (ed.), *Das Jenseits: Facetten eines religiösen Begriffs in der Neuzeit* (Göttingen: Wallstein, 2007).
77  Karl Aner, *Die Theologie der Lessingzeit* (Hildesheim: G. Olms, 1964 [1929]), 236–246, 158–176; Albrecht Beutel and Volker Leppin (eds), *Religion und Aufklärung: Studien zur neuzeitlichen 'Umformung des Christlichen'* (Leipzig: Evangelische Verlagsanstalt, 2004).
78  Harm Klueting (ed.), *Katholische Aufklärung: Aufklärung im katholischen Deutschland* (Hamburg: Meiner, 1993).
79  Rudolf Schlögl, *Glaube und Religion in der Säkularisierung: Die katholische Stadt – Köln, Aachen, Münster 1700–1840* (Munich: Oldenbourg, 1995), 109–124.

80  Friedrich Wilhelm Graf, '"Einfache Dechristianisierung": Zur Problemgeschichte eines kulturpolitischen Topos', in *Säkularisierung: Der europäische Sonderweg in Sachen Religion*, ed. Hartmut Lehmann (Göttingen: Wallstein Verlag, 2004), 32–66; Rudolf Schlögl, 'Der Glaube Alteuropas und die moderne Welt: Zum Verhältnis von Säkularisation und Säkularisierung', in *Zerfall und Wiederbeginn: Vom Erzbistum zum Bistum Mainz (1792/97–1830). Ein Vergleich*, ed. Walter G. Rödel and Regina E. Schwertfeger (Würzburg: Echter, 2002), 63–82.
81  Charles Robert Gosselin, *L'Antiquité Dévoilée au Moyen de la Genèse* (Paris: A. Égron, 1817).
82  Ibid., 147–159, 199, 130f.
83  George Stanley Faber, *The Origin of Pagan Idolatry Ascertained from Historical Testimony and Circumstantial Evidence* (London: A. J. Valpy, 1816), 31–57, 61–74, 105–110, 54.
84  Aner, *Theologie der Lessingzeit*, 276–282.
85  Feil, *Religio*, vol. 4, 876–879.
86  John Hutchinson, *Moses's Sine Principio*, vol. 3, *Represented by Names, by Words, by Types, by Emblems: With an Introduction Shewing the Nature of Body and Soul …*, 3rd edn (London: no publisher, 1748), v, xcii, xxv, xcii.
87  Assmann, *Religio Duplex*, 72–88, 108–110.
88  Christoph Meiners, 'Über die Mysterien der Alten, besonders über die Eleusinischen Geheimnisse', in Christoph Meiners, *Vermischte philosophische Schriften*, part 3 (Leipzig: Weygandsche Buchhandlung, 1776), 164–342; on this see also Assmann, *Religio Duplex*, 115f.
89  Meiners, 'Mysterien', 171–175, 187ff., 206, 209.
90  Ibid., 200–206, 293; Assmann, *Religio Duplex*, 118.
91  Rudolf Schlögl, 'Alchemie und Avantgarde: Das Utopische bei Rosenkreuzern und Freimaurern', in *Die Politisierung des Utopischen im 18. Jahrhundert*, ed. Monika Neugebauer-Wölk and Richard Saage (Tübingen: Niemeyer, 1996), 117–142.
92  Reinhart Koselleck, *Kritik und Krise: Eine Studie zur Pathogenese der bürgerlichen Welt* (Frankfurt am Main: Suhrkamp, 1976), essentially defines this as a reservation concerning state and politics.
93  Étienne Bonnot de Condillac, *Essai sur l'Origine des Connaissances Humaines* (Paris: Libraires Associés, 1822).
94  Ibid., 192–196.
95  Ibid., 197–208, 311–316; cf. Jan Assmann, 'Hieroglyphen als mnemotechnisches System: William Warburton und die Grammatologie des 18. Jahrhunderts', in *Seelenmaschinen: Gattungstraditionen, Funktion und Leistungsgrenzen der Mnemotechniken vom späten Mittelalter bis zum Beginn der Moderne*, ed. Jörg Jochen Berns and Wolfgang Neuber (Cologne/Vienna: Böhlau, 2000), 711–724.
96  Rousseau, *Sozialphilosophische Schriften*, 75–80.
97  Johann Peter Süßmilch, *Versuch eines Beweises, dass die erste Sprache ihren Ursprung nicht vom Menschen, sondern allein vom Schöpfer erhalten habe, in der Akademischen Versammlung vorgelesen und zum Druck gegeben* (Berlin: no publisher, 1766).
98  Johann Gottfried Herder, *Abhandlung über den Ursprung der Sprache: Texte, Materialien, Kommentar*, ed. Wolfgang Proß (Munich/Vienna: Carl Hanser Verlag, 1978).

99   Cordula Neis, *Anthropologie im Sprachdenken des 18. Jahrhunderts: Die Berliner Preisfrage nach dem Ursprung der Sprache* (Berlin/New York: De Gruyter, 2003), 198–229; Herder, *Abhandlung*, 31, 75, 32–36, 107–109; cf. on Herder, see also Maurice Olender, *Die Sprachen des Paradieses: Religion, Philosophie und Rassentheorie im 19. Jahrhundert* (Frankfurt am Main/New York: Campus-Verlag, 1995), 46–58.
100  Charles de Brosses, *Ueber den Dienst der Fetischgötter oder Vergleichung der alten Religionen Egyptens mit der heutigen Religion Nigritiens: Mit einem Einleitungsversuch über Aberglauben, Zauberei und Abgötterei und anderen Zusätzen*, trans. Chr. B. H. Pistorius (Berlin: Gottlieb August Lange, 1785); cf. Hartmut Böhme, *Fetischismus und Kultur: Eine andere Theorie der Moderne* (Berlin: Rororo, 2006), 199–204; Karl-Heinz Kohl, *Die Macht der Dinge: Geschichte und Theorie sakraler Objekte* (Munich: C. H. Beck, 2003), 71–76.
101  Brosses, *Fetischgötter*, 4f., 47, 17–43, 161–168, 141, 185ff., 144–151.
102  Philip C. Almond, *The British Discovery of Buddhism* (Cambridge: Cambridge University Press, 1988), 31; P. J. Marshall (ed.), *The British Discovery of Hinduism in the Eighteenth Century* (Cambridge: Cambridge University Press, 1970), 1–44; Michael Stausberg, *Faszination Zarathustra: Zoroaster und die europäische Religionsgeschichte der Frühen Neuzeit* (Berlin/New York: De Gruyter, 1998), 790–836 (on Anquetil Duperron); Tomoko Masuzawa, *The Invention of World Religions: Or, How European Universalism was Preserved in the Language of Pluralism* (Chicago, IL: University of Chicago Press, 2005), 107–178.
103  Friedrich Creuzer, *Symbolik und Mythologie der alten Völker, besonders der Griechen* (Leipzig: Leske, 1890).
104  Ibid., 51, 38, 21–27, 150–195, 240ff., 794–798, 70ff., 102ff., 56ff., 64ff.
105  Ibid., 30–35, 42.
106  Immanuel Kant, *Werke*, vol. 11, *Der Streit der Fakultäten* (Frankfurt am Main: Suhrkamp, 1977).
107  Ibid., 288f., 285, 301, 285.
108  Immanuel Kant, *Kritik der reinen Vernunft* (Stuttgart: Philipp Reclam jun., 1966), 23–26.
109  Georg Wilhelm Friedrich Hegel, *Werke in 20 Bänden: Auf der Grundlage der Werke von 1832 bis 1845 neu edierte Ausgabe*, vol. 1, *Frühe Schriften*, ed. Eva Moldenhauer and Karl Markus Michel (Frankfurt am Main: Suhrkamp, 1978), 234–237; on the ascription, see Franz Rosenzweig, *Das älteste Systemprogramm des deutschen Idealismus* (Heidelberg: Carl Winter, 1917).
110  Georg Wilhelm Friedrich Hegel, *Werke in 20 Bänden: Auf der Grundlage der Werke von 1832 bis 1845 neu edierte Ausgabe*, vol. 11, *Vorrede zu Hinrichs Religionsphilosophie*, ed. Eva Moldenhauer and Karl Markus Michel (Frankfurt am Main: Suhrkamp, 1970 [1822]), 53.
111  Ibid., 53f.; Hegel, *Werke*, vol. 1, 234.
112  Hegel, *Werke*, vol. 11, 51; Immanuel Kant, 'Träume eines Geistersehers, erläutert durch Träume in der Metaphysik', in *Kants Werke*, vol. 2, *Vorkritische Schriften II: 1757–1777* (Frankfurt am Main: Suhrkamp, 1977), 984, 946.
113  Kant, *Kritik der reinen Vernunft*, 612–620, 667; Immanuel Kant, *Werke*, vol. 7, *Kritik der praktischen Vernunft* (Frankfurt am Main: Suhrkamp, 1978), 252–264; Immanuel Kant, *Werke*, vol. 10, *Kritik der Urteilskraft* (Frankfurt am Main: Suhrkamp, 1979), 413–433.

114 Immanuel Kant, *Werke*, vol. 8, *Religion innerhalb der Grenzen der bloßen Vernunft: Die Metaphysik der Sitten* (Frankfurt am Main: De Gruyter, 1968).
115 Ibid., 650f.
116 Ibid., 761f., 777f., 788.
117 Georg Wilhelm Friedrich Hegel, *Hauptwerke in sechs Bänden*, vol. 2, *Phänomenologie des Geistes* (Hamburg: Felix Meiner Verlag, 1999); on this and on what follows, see Lawrence Dickey, *Hegel: Religion, Economics and the Politics of Spirit* (Cambridge: Cambridge University Press, 1987), 143–179; Cyril O'Regan, *The Heterodox Hegel* (New York: State University of New York Press, 1994), 63f., 169f.
118 Georg Wilhelm Friedrich Hegel, *Vorlesungen über die Philosophie der Religion*, 3 vols, ed. Walter Jaeschke (Hamburg: Felix Meiner Verlag, 1993).
119 Hegel, *Vorrede*, 45, 49, 56, 59, 60f.
120 Hegel, *Hauptwerke*, vol. 2, 21.
121 Hegel, *Phänomenologie des Geistes*, 20f., 29, 238, 365, 368.
122 Hegel, *Vorlesungen*, vol. 1, 266.
123 Ibid., vol. 1, xxii, 266f., 277f., 280f., 291, 102–108; vol. 3, xff., 99–108, 147ff.
124 Ibid., vol. 1, 107.
125 Friedrich Wilhelm Joseph von Schelling, *Sämtliche Werke*, vol. 2.2, *Philosophie der Mythologie* (Stuttgart/Augsburg: Cotta, 1857); Friedrich Wilhelm Joseph von Schelling, *Philosophie der Offenbarung (1841/42)*, ed. Manfred Frank (Frankfurt am Main: Surhkamp Taschenbuch, 1977 [1841/42]).
126 Schelling, *Offenbarung*, 109, 121ff., 145ff.
127 Schelling, *Mythologie*, 21, 35, 39f., 52, 80ff., 124, 127, 69, 79, 295, 363, 259, 264.
128 Schelling, *Offenbarung*, 259, 264.
129 Ibid., 136f., 161, 145ff.
130 Ibid., 198, 212.
131 Karl Rosenkranz, *Die Naturreligion: Ein philosophisch-historischer Versuch* (Iserlohn: Langewiesche, 1831), xvi f., 19, 28ff.
132 Ludwig Feuerbach, *Werke in sechs Bänden*, vol. 5, *Das Wesen des Christentums* (Frankfurt am Main: Suhrkamp, 1976).
133 Ibid., 10f.
134 Ibid., 9–12.
135 Ibid., 17f.
136 Ibid., 25, 30ff., 39.
137 Ibid., 56–85, 95–98, 103–106, 189–198.
138 Ibid., 220–223, 228, 236, 246–249, 270f.
139 Ibid., 282, 325f.
140 Friedrich Nietzsche, *Nietzsches Werke: Taschen-Ausgabe*, vol. 11, *Ecce Homo* (Leipzig: Alfred Kröner, 1923), 387.
141 Karl Marx, *Marx-Engels-Werke*, vol. 3, *Thesen über Feuerbach* (East Berlin: Dietz Verlag, 1969), 5; Karl Marx and Friedrich Engels, *Marx-Engels-Werke*, vol. 3, *Die deutsche Ideologie: Kritik der neuesten deutschen Philosophien in ihren Repräsentanten Feuerbach, B.Bauer und Stirner und des deutschen Sozialismus in seinen verschiedenen Propheten* (East Berlin: Dietz Verlag, 1969).
142 Dieter Mersch, 'Das Ereignis der Setzung', in *Performativität und Ereignis*, ed. Erika Fischer-Lichte (Tübingen: Franke, 2003), 41–56.
143 Joseph von Görres, *Gesammelte Schriften*, vol. 18, *Athanasius*, ed. Wilhelm Schellenberg and Heribert Raab (Paderborn: Ferdinand Schöningh, 1998); Johann Adam Möhler, *Symbolik oder Darstellung der dogmatischen Grundsätze der*

Katholiken und der Protestanten nach ihren öffentlichen Bekenntnisschriften (Mainz: Florian Kupferberg, 1832).

144 Friedrich Schlegel, *Kritische Friedrich-Schlegel-Ausgabe*, vol. 9, *Philosophie der Geschichte: In 18 Vorlesungen gehalten zu Wien im Jahre 1828* (Munich/Paderborn/Vienna: Ferdinand Schöningh, 1971), *passim*, esp. 416–420, 427; cf. Matthias Klug, *Rückwendung zum Mittelalter? Geschichtsbilder und historische Argumentation im politischen Katholizismus des Vormärz* (Paderborn: Ferdinand Schöningh, 1995); Marcus Sandl, 'Heilige Stagnation: Mediale Konfigurationen des Stillstandes in der Großdeutsch-katholischen Geschichtsschreibung des frühen 19. Jahrhunderts', *Historische Zeitschrift* 285 (2007): 529–563.

145 Bernhard Bolzano, *Lehrbuch der Religionswissenschaft: Ein Abdruck der Vorlesungshefte eines ehemaligen Religionslehrers an einer katholischen Universität*, part 3, vol. 2 (Sulzbach: Seidel, 1834); J. D. Vogelsang, *Lehrbuch der christlichen Sittenlehre* (Bonn: Habicht, 1834), especially 4f.; Emerich Coreth, Walter Martin Neidl and Georg Pfligersdorffer (eds), *Christliche Philosophie im katholischen Denken des 19. und 20. Jahrhunderts*, vol. 1, *Neue Ansätze im 19. Jahrhundert* (Graz: Styria, 1987).

146 Friedrich Schleiermacher, *Der christliche Glaube nach den Grundsätzen der evangelischen Kirche im Zusammenhang dargestellt*, 2 vols (Berlin: Reimer, 1821–22), vol. 1, 210–213.

147 Friedrich Schleiermacher, *Über die Religion: Reden an die Gebildeten unter ihren Verächtern (1799)* (Berlin/New York: De Gruyter, 1999), 70, 76–79.

148 Ibid., 84f., 108, 111–117, 86–89.

149 Ibid., 135, 118, 140, 139.

150 Ibid., 192, 186; Schleiermacher, *Christliche Glaube*, vol. 1, 218ff.

151 Schleiermacher, *Reden*, 116, 112f.

152 Ludwig Noack, *Die speculative Religionswissenschaft im encyklopädischen Organismus ihrer besonderen Disciplinen* (Darmstadt: C. W. Leske, 1847), v.

153 Ibid., 32f., 57.

154 Ibid., 17ff., 27, 30–33, 57.

155 Ibid., 80–83, 89.

156 Ibid., 153, 148, 269, 114, 388ff., 337, 391.

157 Volker Bohn (ed.), *Typologie: Internationale Beiträge zur Poetik* (Frankfurt am Main: Suhrkamp, 1988); Erich Auerbach, 'Figura', in *Gesammelte Aufsätze zur romanischen Philologie* by Erich Auerbach (Bern: Francke, 1967), 55–92.

158 Eduard Zeller, 'Die Annahme einer Perfektibilität des Christentums, Historisch und dogmatisch untersucht', *Theologische Jahrbücher* 1 (1842): 1–50; Eduard Zeller, 'Über das Wesen der Religion', *Theologische Jahrbücher* 4 (1845): 26–74, 393–430.

159 Zeller, 'Wesen', 32–45, 47, 55, 65–67, 393, 407, 410f.

160 Zeller, 'Perfektibilität', 2, 11–15, 26–30, 42f.

161 Ibid., 48–50.

162 Zeller, 'Wesen', 425–429.

# Chapter 5

1 Karl Löwith, *Sämtliche Schriften*, vol. 2, *Weltgeschichte als Heilsgeschehen* (Stuttgart: J. B. Metzlersehe Verlagsbuchhandlung, 1983); Hans Blumenberg, *Säkularisierung und*

      *Selbstbehauptung* (Frankfurt am Main: Suhrkamp, 1974); Peter Blickle and Rudolf Schlögl (eds), *Die Säkularisation im Prozeß der Säkularisierung Europas* (Epfendorf: Bibliotheca academica, 2005).
2  Hartmut Lehmann (ed.), *Säkularisierung, Dechristianisierung, Rechristianisierung im neuzeitlichen Europa: Bilanz und Perspektiven der Forschung* (Göttingen: Vandenhoeck & Ruprecht, 1997).
3  Manuel Borutta, 'Genealogie der Säkularisierungstheorie: Zur Historisierung einer großen Erzählung der Moderne', *Geschichte und Gesellschaft* 36 (2010): 347–376; Manuel Borutta, *Antikatholizismus: Deutschland und Italien im Zeitalter der europäischen Kulturkämpfe* (Göttingen: Vandenhoeck & Ruprecht, 2010); Albrecht Koschorke, '"Säkularisierung" und "Wiederkehr der Religion": zu zwei Narrativen der europäischen Moderne', in *Moderne und Religion: Kontroversen um Modernität und Säkularisierung*, ed. Ulrich Willems, Detlef Pollack, Helene Basu, Thomas Gutmann and Ulrike Spohn (Bielefeld: Transcript-Verlag, 2013), 237–260.
4  Numerous examples are given in Alois Hahn, 'Religiöser Wandel in der deutschen Gegenwartsgesellschaft – Kontroversen um seine religionssoziologische Interpretation', in *Religionskontroversen in Frankreich und in Deutschland*, ed. Matthias König and Jean-Paul William (Hamburg: Hamburger Edition, 2008), 240–250.
5  José Casanova, *Public Religions in the Modern World* (Chicago, IL: University of Chicago Press, 1998), 11–15; José Casanova, *Europas Angst vor der Religion* (Berlin: Berlin University Press, 2009), 8–16; Talal Asad, *Formation of the Secular: Christianity, Islam, Modernity* (Stanford, CA: Stanford University Press, 2003), 181f.
6  Johann Caspar Bluntschli, *Psychologische Studien über Staat und Kirche* (Zurich: Beyel, 1844).
7  Friedrich Wilhelm Graf, '"Einfache Dechristianisierung": Zur Problemgeschichte eines kulturpolitischen Topos', in *Säkularisierung: Der europäische Sonderweg in Sachen Religion*, ed. Hartmut Lehmann (Göttingen: Wallstein Verlag, 2004), 32–66.
8  On the term, see Rudolf Schlögl, 'Hierarchie und Funktion: Zur Transformation der stratifikatorischen Ordnung der Frühen Neuzeit', *Zeitsprünge* 15 (2011): 47–63.
9  Peter van der Veer, 'Spirituality in Modern Society', *Social Research* 76 (2009): 1077–1120.
10  Frank Ruda, *Hegels Pöbel: Eine Untersuchung der 'Grundlinien der Philosophie des Rechts'* (Konstanz: Konstanz University Press, 2011).
11  Gabriel Tarde, *Die Gesetze der Nachahmung* (Frankfurt am Main: Suhrkamp, 2003), 100–112.
12  This is also true of the following statement by Luhmann: 'Religion appears to be present … whenever a person has understood why things are not the way one would like them to be'. Niklas Luhmann, *Religion der Gesellschaft* (Frankfurt am Main: Suhrkamp, 2000), 122. The idea that there are processes in the human psyche that do not reach human consciousness was first formulated in the 1830s (Gustav Carus).
13  See the reconstruction of Luhmann's arguments in Hahn, 'Religiöser Wandel', 266.
14  This constellation is the prerequisite for Latour's suggestion that religious speech produces God: Bruno Latour, *Jubilieren: Über religiöse Rede* (Frankfurt am Main: Suhrkamp, 2011), 198–202. On the significance of the theory of signs for religion in the modern age, which discovers language as agent, see Giorgio Agamben, *Signatura rerum: Zur Methode*, trans. Anton Schütz (Frankfurt am Main: Suhrkamp, 2009), 84–87.
15  Pippa Norris and Ronald Inglehardt, *Sacred and Secular: Religion and Politics Worldwide* (Cambridge: Cambridge University Press, 2004).

# Bibliography

Adelung, Johann Christoph. *Versuch einer Geschichte der Cultur des menschlichen Geschlechts*. Leipzig: Christian Gottlieb Hertel, 1782.
Agamben, Giorgio. *Signatura rerum: Zur Methode*, translated by Anton Schütz. Frankfurt am Main: Suhrkamp, 2009.
Albrecht, Ruth, Annette Bühler-Dietrich and Florentine Strzelczy (eds). *Glaube und Geschlecht: Fromme Frauen, spirituelle Erfahrungen, religiöse Traditionen*. Cologne/Vienna: Böhlau, 2008.
Alff, Wilhelm. *Michelets Ideen*. Geneva: Droz, 1966.
Almond, Philip C. *The British Discovery of Buddhism*. Cambridge: Cambridge University Press, 1988.
Altenbernd, Johannes. 'Bibelanstalt, Bibelbund oder Bibelgesellschaft? Bibelverbreitung und Vereinsgründung in der katholischen Kirche zwischen 1805-1830'. In *Weltmission und religiöse Organisationen: Protestantische Missionsgesellschaften im 19. und 20. Jahrhundert*, edited by Arthur Bogner, Bernd Holtwick and Hartmann Tyrell, 249-284. Würzburg: Egon-Verlag, 2004.
Andermann, Kurt. 'Geistliche Staaten am Ende des Alten Reiches'. *Historische Zeitschrift* 271 (2000): 593-619.
Aner, Karl. *Die Theologie der Lessingzeit*. Hildesheim: G. Olms, 1964 [Halle: Niemeyer, 1929].
Arens, Bernhard, S.J. *Die katholischen Missionsvereine: Darstellung ihres Werdens und Wirkens, ihrer Satzungen und Vorrechte*. Freiburg im Breisgau: Herder, 1922.
Aretin, Karl Otmar von. *Das Alte Reich 1648-1806*. Vol. 3, *Das Reich und der österreichisch-preußische Dualismus 1745-1806*. Stuttgart: Klett-Cotta, 1997.
Armstrong, Anthony. *The Church of England: The Methodists and Society 1700-1850*. London: Rowman and Littlefield, 1973.
Arx, Walter von. 'Liturgische Reflexionen im Klerus anhand des Archivs für die Pastoralkonferenzen in den Landkapiteln des Bistums Konstanz'. In *Liturgiewissenschaft: Studien zur Wissenschaftsgeschichte*, edited by Franz Kohlschein and Peter Wünsche, 143-187. Paderborn: Aschendorff Verlag, 1996.
Asad, Talal. *Formation of the Secular: Christianity, Islam, Modernity*. Stanford, CA: Stanford University Press, 2003.
Aspinall, Arthur. *Politics and the Press, c. 1780 1850*. Brighton: Harvester Press, 1973.
Assmann, Jan. 'Hieroglyphen als mnemotechnisches System: William Warburton und die Grammatologie des 18. Jahrhunderts'. In *Seelenmaschinen: Gattungstraditionen, Funktion und Leistungsgrenzen der Mnemotechniken vom späten Mittelalter bis zum Beginn der Moderne*, edited by Jörg Jochen Berns and Wolfgang Neuber, 711-724. Cologne/Vienna: Böhlau, 2000.
Assmann, Jan. *Die Mosaische Unterscheidung oder der Preis des Monotheismus*. Munich: Carl Hanser Verlag, 2003.
Assmann, Jan. *Religio Duplex: Ägyptische Mysterien und europäische Aufklärung*. Berlin: Verlag der Weltreligionen, 2010.

Aston, Nigel. *Religion and Revolution in France 1780-1804*. Washington, D.C.: Catholic University of America Press, 2000.

Auerbach, Erich. 'Figura'. In *Gesammelte Aufsätze zur romanischen Philologie*, by Erich Auerbach, 365-369. Bern: Francke, 1967.

Auerbach, Nina. *Women and the Demon: The Life of a Victorian Myth*. Cambridge, MA: Harvard University Press, 1982.

Aulard, François-Alphonse. *Le Culte de la Raison et le Culte de l'Être Suprême 1793-1794: Essai Historique*. Boston, MA: Elibron Classics, 2003 [Paris: Felix Alcan Éditeur, 1892].

Baader, Franz von. *Gesellschaftslehre*, edited by Hans Grassl. Munich: Kösel Verlag, 1957.

Bade, Klaus Jürgen. *Europa in Bewegung: Migration vom späten 18. Jahrhundert bis zur Gegenwart*. Munich: C. H. Beck, 2002.

Baecker, Dirk. *Studien zur nächsten Gesellschaft*. Frankfurt am Main: Suhrkamp, 1997.

Bahlcke, Joachim. *Ungarischer Episkopat und österreichische Monarchie: Von einer Partnerschaft zur Konfrontation 1686-1790*. Stuttgart: Franz Steiner Verlag, 2005.

Bakker, Willem F., O. J. de Jong, W. Van't Spijker and L. J. Wolthuis. *De Afscheiding van 1834 en Haar Geschiedenis*. Kampen: VBK Media, 1984.

Barclay, David E. 'Ritual, Ceremonial and the "Invention" of a Monarchical Tradition in Nineteenth-Century Prussia'. In *European Monarchy: Its Evolution and Practice from Roman Antiquity to Modern Times*, edited by Heinz Duchhardt, Richard A. Jackson and David Sturdy, 207-220. Stuttgart: Franz Steiner Verlag, 1992.

Barclay, David E. *Anarchie und guter Wille: Friedrich Wilhelm IV und die preußische Monarchie*, translated by Marion Müller. Berlin: Siedler Verlag, 1995.

Barrie, Vivianne. 'Die Anglikanische Kirche'. In *Die Geschichte des Christentums*. Vol. 10, *Aufklärung, Revolution, Restauration (1750-1830)*, edited by Bernard Plongeron, 44-54. Freiburg im Breisgau: Herder, 2000.

Barth, Boris, and Jürgen Osterhammel (eds). *Zivilisierungsmissionen: Imperiale Weltverbesserung seit dem 18. Jahrhundert*. Konstanz: UVK, 2005.

Basdevant-Gaudemet, Brigitte, and Germain Sicard. *Les Communes Françaises: l'Enseignement et les Cultes de la Fin de l'Ancien Régime à nos Jours*. Paris: Honoré Champion Éditeur, 2005.

Bayly, C. A. *The Birth of the Modern World 1780-1914: Global Connections and Comparisons*. London: Wiley-Blackwell, 2004.

Beck, Rainer. 'Der Pfarrer und das Dorf'. In *Armut, Liebe, Ehre*, edited by Richard von Dülmen, 107-143. Frankfurt am Main: Fischer, 1988.

Bedford, R. D. *The Defence of Truth: Herbert of Cherbury and the Seventeenth Century*. Manchester: Manchester University Press, 1979.

Beetham, Margaret. *A Magazine of Her Own? Domesticity and Desire in the Women's Magazine 1800-1914*. London: Routledge, 1996.

Beinert, Wolfgang, and Heinrich Petri (eds). *Handbuch der Marienkunde*. Regensburg: Pustet, 1984.

Ben-Amos, Avner. *Funerals, Politics and Memory in Modern France, 1789-1996*. Oxford: Oxford University Press, 2000.

Bentley, James. *Ritualism and Politics in Victorian Britain: The Attempt to Legislate for Belief*. Oxford: Oxford University Press, 1978.

Berenson, Edward. *Populist Religion and Left-Wing Politics in France 1830-1852*. Princeton, NJ: Princeton Legacy Library, 1984.

Berghoff, Peter. *Der Tod des politischen Kollektivs: Politische Religion und das Sterben und Töten für Volk, Nation und Rasse*. Berlin: De Gruyter, 1997.

Best, Geoffrey F. *Temporal Pillars: Queen Anne's Bounty, the Ecclesiastical Commissioners, and the Church of England*. Cambridge: Cambridge University Press, 1964.
Beutel, Albrecht, and Volker Leppin (eds). *Religion und Aufklärung: Studien zur neuzeitlichen 'Umformung des Christlichen'*. Leipzig: Evangelische Verlagsanstalt, 2004.
Beyer, Peter. *Religion in Globalized Society*. Arlington: Routledge, 2006.
Birtsch, Günther. 'Religions- und Gewissensfreiheit in Preußen von 1780 bis 1817'. *Zeitschrift für historische Forschung* 11 (1984): 177–204.
Blackbourn, David. *Marpingen: Apparitions of the Virgin Mary in Nineteenth-Century Germany*. New York: Knopf, 1994.
Blaschke, Olaf. 'Abschied von der Säkularisierungslegende'. *Zeitenblicke* 5 (2006). Available online: www.zeitenblicke.de/2006/1/blaschke/index_htm (accessed 2 June 2006).
Blessing, Werner K. *Staat und Kirche in der Gesellschaft: Institutionelle Autorität und mentaler Wandel in Bayern während des 19. Jahrhunderts*. Göttingen: Vandenhoeck & Ruprecht, 1982.
Blet, Pierre. *Le Clergé de France et la Monarchie: Études sur les Assemblées Génerales du Clergé de 1615 à 1666*. 2 vols. Rome: Gregorian University Press, 1959.
Blickle, Peter, and Rudolf Schlögl (eds). *Die Säkularisation im Prozeß der Säkularisierung Europas*. Epfendorf: Bibliotheca academica, 2005.
Blitz, Hans M. *Aus Liebe zum Vaterland: Die deutsche Nation im 18. Jahrhundert*. Hamburg: Hamburger Edition, 2000.
Blount, Charles. *The Oracles of Reason*. London: Kessinger Publishing, 1995.
Blumenberg, Hans. *Säkularisierung und Selbstbehauptung*. Frankfurt am Main: Suhrkamp, 1974.
Bluntschli, Johann Caspar. *Psychologische Studien über Staat und Kirche*. Zurich: Beyel, 1844.
Böhme, Hartmut. *Fetischismus und Kultur: Eine andere Theorie der Moderne*. Berlin: Rororo, 2006.
Bohn, Volker (ed.). *Typologie: Internationale Beiträge zur Poetik*. Frankfurt am Main: Suhrkamp, 1988.
Bolingbroke, Henry St John, Lord. *Works*. Vol. 4. London: Mallet, 1841.
Boll, Franz Christian. *Von dem Verfalle und der Wiederherstellung der Religiosität mit besonderer Hinsicht auf das protestantische Deutschland*. 2 pts. Neustrelitz: Ferdinand Albanus, 1809.
Bolton, Charles A. *Church Reform in 18th Century Italy: The Synod of Pistoia 1786*. Den Haag: Springer, 1969.
Bolzano, Bernhard. *Lehrbuch der Religionswissenschaft: Ein Abdruck der Vorlesungshefte eines ehemaligen Religionslehrers an einer katholischen Universität*. Part 3, vol. 2. Sulzbach: Seidel, 1834.
Bonald, Louis de. *Législation Primitive Consideré par la Raison*. Paris: Librairie d'Adrien le Clere, 1847.
Borutta, Manuel. *Antikatholizismus: Deutschland und Italien im Zeitalter der europäischen Kulturkämpfe*. Göttingen: Vandenhoeck & Ruprecht, 2010.
Borutta, Manuel. 'Genealogie der Säkularisierungstheorie: Zur Historisierung einer großen Erzählung der Moderne'. *Geschichte und Gesellschaft* 36 (2010): 347–376.
Bouvier, J.-B. *Dissertatio in sexo decalogi praeceptum et supplementum ad tractatum de Matrimonio*. 9th edn. Paris: Mequignon Juniorem, 1839.
Bowman, Frank P. *French Romanticism: Intertextual and Interdisciplinary Readings*. Baltimore, MD: Johns Hopkins University Press, 1990.

Brandmüller, Walter. *Handbuch der bayerischen Kirchengeschichte*. Vol. 2, *Von der Glaubensspaltung bis zur Säkularisierung*. St Ottilien: EOS Verlag, 1993.
Braun, Albert. *Der Klerus des Bistums Konstanz im Ausgang des Mittelalters*. Münster: De Gruyter, 1938.
Braun, Bettina (ed.). *Geistliche Fürsten und geistliche Staaten in der Spätphase des Alten Reiches*. Epfendorf: Bibliotheca academica, 2008.
Brecht, Martin, Klaus Deppermann, Ulrich Gäbler, and Hartmut Lehmann (eds). *Geschichte des Pietismus*. Vol. 1 and vol. 2 of 4. Göttingen: Vandenhoeck & Ruprecht, 1993–95.
Brentano, Clemens. *Werke*. Vol. 1, edited by Wolfgang Frühwald, Bernhard Gajek and Friedhelm Kemp. Darmstadt: Carl Hanser, 1968.
Brentano, Clemens. *Sämtliche Werke und Briefe*. Vol. 26, *Religiöse Werke (Part V): 1. Das bittere Leiden unseres Herrn Jesu Christ*, edited by Jürgen Behrens and Anne Bohnenkamp-Renke. Stuttgart: Kohlhammer, 1980.
Brettschneider, Karl Gottlieb. *Clementine oder die Frommen und Altgläubigen unserer Tage*. Halle: Schwetschke, 1841.
Brinkmann, Tobias, 'Zivilgesellschaft transnational: Jüdische Hilfsorganisationen und jüdische Massenmigration aus Osteuropa in Deutschland, 1868–1914'. In *Religion und Philanthropie in den europäischen Zivilgesellschaften: Entwicklungen im 19. und 20. Jahrhundert*, edited by Liedtke Rainer and Klaus Weber, 138–157. Munich: Ferdinand Schöningh, 2009.
Brockmeyer, Bettina. *Selbstverständnisse: Dialoge über Körper und Gemüt im frühen 19. Jahrhundert*. Göttingen: Ferdinand Schöningh, 2009.
Brooke, John Hedley. *Science and Religion: Some Historical Perspectives*. Cambridge: Cambridge University Press, 1991.
Brosses, Charles de. *Ueber den Dienst der Fetischgötter oder Vergleichung der alten Religionen Egyptens mit der heutigen Religion Nigritiens: Mit einem Einleitungsversuch über Aberglauben, Zauberei und Abgötterei und anderen Zusätzen*, translated by Chr. B. H. Pistorius. Berlin: Gottlieb August Lange, 1785.
Brown, Callum G. *The Death of Christian Britain: Understanding Secularisation 1800–2000*. 2nd edn. London: Routledge, 2008.
Brown, Stewart J. *The National Churches of England, Ireland and Scotland 1801–1846*. Oxford: Oxford University Press, 2001.
Brückner, Wolfgang. *Die Verehrung des Heiligen Blutes in Walldürn: Volkskundliche und soziologische Untersuchungen zum Strukturwandel barocken Wallfahrens*. Aschaffenburg: Geschichts- und Kunstverein Aschaffenburg, 1958.
Buchheim, Karl. *Ultramontanismus und Demokratie: Der Weg der deutschen Katholiken im 19. Jahrhundert*. Munich: Kösel, 1963.
Budischin, Hans-Jörg. *Der gelehrte Zivilprozeß in der Praxis geistlicher Gerichte des 13. und 14. Jahrhunderts im deutschen Raum*. Bonn: L. Röhrscheid, 1974.
Buisson, Ludwig. *Potestas und Caritas: Die päpstliche Gewalt im Spätmittelalter*. Cologne/Vienna: Böhlau, 1958.
Burke, Edmund. *Betrachtungen über die Französische Revolution*. Zurich: Manesse Verlag, 1986.
Burkhard, Dominik. *Staatskirche, Papstkirche, Bischofskirche: Die 'Frankfurter Konferenzen' und die Neuordnung der Kirche in Deutschland nach der Säkularisation*. Rome/Freiburg im Breisgau: Herder, 2000.
Busch, Norbert. 'Die Feminisierung der ultramontanen Frömmigkeit'. In *Wunderbare Erscheinungen: Frauen und katholische Frömmigkeit im 19. und 20. Jahrhundert*, edited by Irmtraud Götz von Olenhusen, 203–219. Paderborn: Ferdinand Schöningh, 1995.

Büschel, Hubertus. 'Vor dem Altar des Vaterlandes – Verfahren ritueller Sakralisierung von Monarch und Staat zu Beginn des 19. Jahrhunderts'. In *Kultur, ein Netz von Bedeutungen: Analysen zur symbolischen Kulturanthropologie*, edited by Florian Steger, 161–183. Würzburg: Königshausen & Neumann, 2002.

Büschel, Hubertus. *Untertanenliebe: Der Kult um deutsche Monarchen 1770–1830*. Göttingen: Vandenhoeck & Ruprecht, 2006.

Byrne, Peter. *Natural Religion and the Nature of Religion: The Legacy of Deism*. London: Routledge, 1989.

Cabanis, José. *Le Sacre de Napoleon: 2 Décembre 1804*. Paris: Éditions Gallimard, 1970.

Cabanis, José. *Charles X: Roi Ultra*. Paris: Éditions Gallimard, 1972.

Callahan, William. 'The Spanish Church'. In *Church and Society in Catholic Europe of the Eighteenth Century*, edited by William Callahan and David Higgs, 34–50. Cambridge: Cambridge University Press, 1979.

Callahan, William. *Church, Politics, and Society in Spain 1750–1874*. Cambridge, MA: Harvard University Press, 1984.

Cameron, Evan. *Enchanted Europe: Superstition, Reason, and Religion, 1250–1750*. Oxford: Oxford University Press, 2011.

Capitani, François de. 'Schweizerische Stadtfeste als bürgerliche Selbstdarstellung'. In *Stadt und Repräsentation*, edited by Bernhard Kirchgässner and Hans-Peter Becht, 115–126. Sigmaringen: Thorbecke, 1995.

Casanova, José. *Public Religions in the Modern World*. Chicago, IL: University of Chicago Press, 1998.

Casanova, José. *Europas Angst vor der Religion*. Berlin: Berlin University Press, 2009.

*Catéchisme à l'Usage de Toutes les Églises de l'Empire Français*. Paris: Nyon & Nicolle, 1806.

Chadwick, Owen. *The Victorian Church*. Vol. 1, *1829–1859*. London: Hymns Ancient & Modern Ltd, 1970.

Chateaubriand, François-René de. *Essais sur les Révolutions: Génie du Christianisme*. Paris: Arvensa Editions, 1978.

Châtellier, Louis. *L'Europe des Dévots*. Paris: Flammarion, 1987.

Cherbury, Edward Herbert, Lord. *De Religione Gentilium*. Amsterdam: no publisher, 1663.

Cherbury, Edward Herbert, Lord. *De Veritate*, translated with an introduction by Merich H. Carré. Bristol: Typis Blaeviorum, 1937.

Chevallier, Pierre. *Loménie de Brienne et l'Ordre Monastique 1760–1789*. Paris: Librairie Philosophique Vrin, 1959.

Christian, William A., Jr. *Person and God in a Spanish Valley*. Princeton, NJ: Princeton University Press, 1989.

Clark, Jonathan C. D. *English Society, 1660–1832: Religion, Ideology and Politics During the Ancien Regime*. Cambridge: Cambridge University Press, 2000.

Clavadetscher, Otto P. *Die geistlichen Richter des Bistums Chur*. Basel: Helbing & Lichtenhahn, 1964.

Coing, Helmut (ed.). *Handbuch der Quellen und Literatur der neueren europäischen Privatrechtsgeschichte*. Vol. 1. Munich: C. H. Beck, 1973.

Coleridge, Samuel T. *The Collected Works of Samuel Taylor Coleridge*. Vol. 10, *On the Constitution of the Church and State*, edited by John Colmer. London: Princeton University Press, 1976.

Colley, Linda. 'The Apotheosis of George III: Loyalty, Royalty and the British Nation 1760–1820'. *Past and Present* 102 (1984): 94–129.

Colley, Linda. *Britons: Forging the Nation 1707–1837*. New Haven, CT: Yale University Press, 1992.

Collingham, Hugh A., and Robert S. Alexander. *The July Monarchy: A Political History of France 1830–1844*. London: Addison-Wesley, 1988.

Collins, Irene. *The Government and the Newspaper in France 1814–1881*. Oxford: Oxford University Press, 1959.

Condillac, Étienne Bonnot de. *Essai sur l'Origin des Connaissances Humaines*. Paris: Libraires Associés, 1822.

Constant, Benjamin. *Werke in vier Bänden*. Vol. 4, *Politische Schriften*. Berlin: Propyläen, 1972.

Constant, Benjamin. *De la Religion: Texte Intégral Présenté par Tzvetan Todorov et Étienne Hoffmann*. Paris: Arles Actes Sud, 1999.

Cooper, Kate (ed.). *Elite and Popular Religion*. Woodbridge, NY: Ecclesiastical History Society, 2006.

Coreth, Emerich, Walter Martin Neidl and Georg Pfligersdorffer (eds). *Christliche Philosophie im katholischen Denken des 19. und 20. Jahrhunderts*. Vol. 1, *Neue Ansätze im 19. Jahrhundert*. Graz: Styria, 1987.

Cornwall, Robert D., and James E. Bradley (eds). *Religion, Politics and Dissent, 1660–1832: Essays in Honour of James E. Bradley*. Farnham: Routledge, 2010.

Cortés, Juan D. *Der Staat Gottes: Eine katholische Geschichtsphilosophie*, edited by Ludwig Fischer. Darmstadt: Wissenschaftliche Buchgesellschaft, 1966.

Creuzer, Friedrich. *Symbolik und Mythologie der alten Völker, besonders der Griechen*. Leipzig: Leske, 1890.

Croce, Walter. 'Die niederen Weihen und ihre hierarchische Wertung: Eine geschichtliche Studie'. *Zeitschrift für katholische Theologie* 70 (1948): 257–314.

Crowe, Ian. *Patriotism and Public Spirit: Edmund Burke and the Role of the Critic in Mid-Eighteenth-Century Britain*. Stanford, CA: Stanford University Press, 2012.

Curtis, Sarah A. *Educating the Faithful: Religion, Schooling and Society in 19th Century France*. De Kalb, IL: Northern Illinois University Press, 2000.

Danzelot, Jacques. *Die Ordnung der Familie*. Frankfurt am Main: Suhrkamp, 1980.

Darnton, Robert. *Der Mesmerismus und das Ende der Aufklärung in Frankreich*. Frankfurt am Main: Carl Hanser, 1968.

Davis, Horton. *Worship and Theology in England: From Watts and Wesley to Maurice, 1690–1850*. Princeton, NJ: Eerdmans, 1961.

Debreyne, Pierre. *Essai sur la Théologie Morale Considerée dans ses Rapports avec la Physiologie et la Médicine*. Paris: Poussielgue-Rusand, 1844.

Delaporte, François. *Das zweite Naturreich: Über die Fragen des Vegetabilischen im 18. Jahrhundert*. Frankfurt am Main: Ullstein, 1983.

Delius, Walter. *Geschichte der Marienverehrung*. Munich: Ernst Reinhardt, 1963.

Delumeau, Jean. *La Première Communion*. Paris: Desclée de Brouwer, 1987.

Deniel, Raymond. *Une Image de la Famille et de la Société sous la Restauration (1815–1830): Études de la Presse Catholique*. Paris: Éditions ouvrieres, 1965.

Derrida, Jacques. 'Glaube und Wissen: Die beiden Quellen der "Religion" an den Grenzen der bloßen Vernunft'. In *Die Religion*, edited by Jacques Derrida and Gianni Vattimo, 9–106. Frankfurt am Main: Suhrkamp, 2001.

Devlin, Judith. *The Superstitious Mind: French Peasants and the Supernatural in the Nineteenth Century*. New Haven, CT: Yale University Press, 1987.

Dibelius, Otto. 'Friedrich Wilhelms IV und die Idee des christlichen Staates'. *Die Furche* 22 (1936): 40–48.

Dickey, Laurence. *Hegel: Religion, Economics and the Politics of Spirit*. Cambridge: Cambridge University Press, 1987.

*Die Lauheit des Zeitalters gegen Religion und Schrift*.... Leipzig: Bruder und Hofmann, 1806.
Dieringer, Franz. 'Die katholische Journalistik in Deutschland und ihre Aufgabe'. *Der Katholik* 23 (1843): 1–17.
Dinzelbacher, Peter (ed.). *Handbuch der Religionsgeschichte im deutschsprachigen Raum.* Vol. 5, *1750–1900*. Paderborn: Ferdinand Schöningh, 2007.
Ditchfield, Grayson M. *George III: An Essay in Monarchy*. Basingstoke: Palgrave, 2002.
Dory, Daniel, and Raymond Verdier. *La Construction Religieuse du Territoire*. Paris: Éditions L'Harmattan, 1995.
Düding, Dieter. 'Das deutsche Nationalfest von 1814: Matrix der deutschen Nationalfeste im 19. Jahrhundert'. In *Öffentliche Festkultur: Politische Feste in Deutschland von der Aufklärung bis zum Ersten Weltkrieg*, edited by Dieter Düding, Peter Friedemann and Paul Münch, 67–88. Reinbek: Rowohlt Taschenbuchverlag, 1988.
Dülmen, Richard van. 'Antijesuitismus und katholische Aufklärung in Deutschland'. *Historisches Jahrbuch der Görres-Gesellschaft* 89 (1969): 52–80.
Dunn, John. *Locke: A Very Short Introduction*. Oxford: Oxford University Press, 1984.
Durkheim, Émile. *Die elementaren Formen des religiösen Lebens*. Frankfurt am Main: Suhrkamp, 1981.
Ebertz, Michael N. 'Die Bürokratisierung der katholischen "Priesterkirche"'. In *Priesterkirche*, edited by Paul Hoffmann, 132–163. Düsseldorf: Patmos, 1987.
Echterkamp, Jörg. '"Religiöses Nationalgefühl" oder "Frömmelei der Deutschtümler"? Religion, Nation und Politik im Frühnationalismus'. In *Nation und Religion in der deutschen Geschichte*, edited by Heinz-Gerhard Haupt and Dieter Langewiesche, 142–169. Frankfurt am Main: Campus Verlag, 2001.
Edelmann, Nicole. *Voyantes, Guérisseuses et Visionaires en France 1784–1914*. Paris: Albin Michel, 1995.
Ego, Anneliese. *Animalischer Magnetismus oder Aufklärung: Eine mentalitätsgeschichtliche Studie zum Konflikt um ein Heilsprinzip in Frankreich*. Würzburg: Königshausen & Neumann, 1991.
Elster, John. *Alexis de Tocqueville: The First Social Scientist*. Cambridge: Cambridge University Press, 2009.
Engels, Jens Ivo, and Hillard von Thiessen. 'Glauben: Begriffliche Annäherungen anhand von Beispielen aus der Frühen Neuzeit'. *Zeitschrift für historische Forschung* 28 (2001): 333–357.
Erbe, Michael. *Vom Konsulat zum Empire Libéral: Ausgewählte Texte zur französischen Verfassungsgeschichte 1799–1870*. Darmstadt: Wissenschaftliche Buchgesellschaft, 1985.
Erler, Adalbert, and Ekkehard Kaufmann (eds). *Handwörterbuch der Rechtsgeschichte*. Vol. 2. Berlin: Erich Schmidt Verlag, 1978.
Ernst, Robert. *Maria redet mit uns: Marienerscheinungen seit 1830*. Walhorn: Pfarramt Walhorn, 1983.
Escudero, José A. *Perfiles Juridicos de la Inquisicion Espanola*. Madrid: Universidad Complutense, 1992.
Faber, George Stanley. *The Origin of Pagan Idolatry Ascertained from Historical Testimony and Circumstantial Evidence*. London: A. J. Valpy, 1816.
Feil, Ernst. *Religio*. Vol. 4, *Die Geschichte eines neuzeitlichen Grundbegriffes im 18. und 19. Jahrhundert*. Göttingen: Vandenhoeck & Ruprecht, 2007.
Feine, Hans E. *Kirchliche Rechtsgeschichte*. Vol. 1, *Die katholische Kirche*. 2nd edn. Cologne/Vienna: Böhlau, 1972.

Feuerbach, Ludwig. *Werke in sechs Bänden*. Vol. 5, *Das Wesen des Christentums*. Frankfurt am Main: Suhrkamp, 1976.
Fichte, Johann Gottfried. *Reden an die deutsche Nation*, edited by Reinhard Lanth. Hamburg: Meiner, 1978.
Fife, Graeme. *The Terror: The Shadow of the Guillotine; France 1792-1794*. New York: St Martin's Press, 2006.
Figl, Johann (ed.). *Handbuch der Religionswissenschaft: Religionen und ihre zentralen Themen*. Innsbruck: Tyrolia, 2003.
Finkenstaedt, Thomas, and Helene Finkenstaedt. *Die Wieswallfahrt: Ursprung und Ausstrahlung der Wallfahrt zum Gegeißelten Heiland*. Regensburg: Pustet, 1981.
Flade, Paul. *Das römische Inquisitionsverfahren in Deutschland bis zu den Hexenprozessen*. Aalen: Scientia Verlag, 1972.
Foerster, Erich. *Die Entstehung der Preußischen Landeskirche unter der Regierung König Friedrich Wilhelms III: Ein Beitrag zur Geschichte der Kirchenbildung im deutschen Protestantismus*. 2 vols. Tübingen: J. C. B. Mohr (Paul Siebeck), 1905-07.
Forrestal, Alison (ed.). *Politics and Religion in Early Bourbon France*. Basingstoke: Palgrave Macmillan, 2009.
Förster, Cornelia. 'Das Hambacher Fest 1832: Volksfest und Nationalfest einer oppositionellen Massenbewegung'. In *Öffentliche Festkultur. Politische Feste in Deutschland von der Aufklärung bis zum Ersten Weltkrieg*, edited by Dieter Düding, Peter Friedemann and Paul Münch, 113-131. Reinbek: Rowohlt Taschenbuchverlag, 1988.
Foucault, Michel. *Archäologie des Wissens*. Frankfurt am Main: Suhrkamp, 1981.
François, Étienne. *Die unsichtbare Grenze. Protestanten und Katholiken in Augsburg 1648-1806*, translated by Angelika Steiner-Wendt. Sigmaringen: Wißner-Verlag, 1991.
Fransen, Gérard. 'Les Décrétales et les Collections de Décrétales'. In *Typologie des Sources du Moyen Âge Occidental*, vol. 2, edited by Léopold Genicot. Turnhout: Brepols, 1972.
Frederking, Bettina. 'Auf der Suche nach dem "wahren" Frankreich: Das Attentat auf den Duc de Berry am 13. Februar 1820'. In *Konstrukte nationaler Identität: Deutschland, Frankreich und Großbritannien (19. und 20. Jahrhundert)*, edited by Joseph Jurt, Daniel Mollenhauer, Michael Einfalt and Erich Pelzer, 35-57. Würzburg: Ergon Verlag, 2002.
Freitag, Werner. *Pfarrer, Kirche und ländliche Gemeinschaft: Das Dechanat Vechta 1400-1803*. Bielefeld: Verlag für Regionalgeschichte, 1998.
Frevert, Ute. *Die kasernierte Nation: Militärdienst und Zivilgesellschaft*. Munich: C. H. Beck, 2001.
Freytag, Nils. *Aberglauben im 19. Jahrhundert: Preußen und seine Rheinprovinz zwischen Tradition und Moderne (1815-1918)*. Berlin: Duncker & Humblot, 2003.
Fritsch, Matthias J. *Religiöse Toleranz im Zeitalter der Aufklärung: Naturrechtliche Begründung – konfessionelle Differenzen*. Hamburg: Felix Meiner Verlag, 2004.
Fuchs, Peter. *Der Sinn der Beobachtung: Begriffliche Untersuchungen*. Göttingen: Velbrück, 2004.
Fueter, Eduard. *Geschichte der neueren Historiographie*. Munich: Oldenbourg, 1936.
Füßl, Wilhelm. *Professor in der Politik: Friedrich Julius Stahl (1802-1861); Das Monarchische Prinzip und seine Umsetzung in die parlamentarische Praxis*. Göttingen: Vandenhoeck & Ruprecht, 1988.
Gabriels, Jos. 'Patrizier und Regenten: Städtische Eliten in den nördlichen Niederlanden'. In *Bürgerliche Eliten in den Niederlanden und in Nordwestdeutschland*, edited by Heinz Schilling and Herman Diederiks, 37-64. Cologne/Vienna: Böhlau, 1985.

Gadbois, Geneviève. "'Vous êtes Presque la Seule Consolation de L'Eglise": Le Foi de Femmes Face à la Déchristianisation de 1789-1890'. In *La Religion de ma Mère: Le Rôle des Femmes dans la Transmission de la Foi*, edited by Jean Delumeau, 301–325. Paris: Le Cerf, 1992.

Gadille, Jacques, and Jean-Marie Mayeur (eds). *Liberalismus, Industrialisierung, Expansion Europas (1830-1914): Geschichte des Christentums; Religion, Politik, Kultur*. Vol. 11. Freiburg im Breisgau: Herder, 1997.

Gagnol, Paul. *La Dîme Ecclésiastique en France au XVIIIe Siècle*. Geneva: Slatkine, 1974.

Gaume, J. *Handbuch für Beichtväter*. 2nd edn. Aachen: Cremersche Buchhandlung, 1843.

Gause, Ute. *Kirchengeschichte und Genderforschung: Eine Einführung in protestantische Perspektive*. Tübingen: UTB, 2006.

Gebhard, Horst. *Liberté, Egalité, Brutalité: Gewaltgeschichte der Französischen Revolution*. Augsburg: Sankt Ulrich Verlag, 2011.

Geheimes Staatsarchiv Preußischer Kulturbesitz, Berlin X Rep. 40–1497 und Evangelisches Zentralarchiv Berlin 7/2555.

Geishüttner, Joseph. *Versuch einer wissenschaftlichen und populären Dogmatik*. Vienna: Doll, 1818.

Gentz, Friedrich von. *Briefe und vertraute Blätter*. Vol. 3, edited by Gustav Schlesier. Mannheim: Heinrich Hoff, 1838.

Gerbert, Olympe Philipe. *Considération sur le Dogme Générateur de la Piété Catholique*. Paris: Bureau du Mémorial catholique, 1829.

Gerlach, Ernst Ludwig von. 'Friedrich Wilhelm IV: Zwei Aufsätze'. In *Ernst Ludwig v. Gerlach: Aufzeichnungen aus seinem Leben und Wirken*. Vol. 2, *1848-1877*, edited by Jakob von Gerlach, 445–510. Schwerin: Fr. Bahn Verlag, 1903.

Gerlach, Jakob von. (ed.). *Ernst Ludwig v. Gerlach: Aufzeichnungen aus seinem Leben und Wirken*. Vol. 1, *1795-1848*. Schwerin: Fr. Bahn Verlag, 1903.

Gibson, Ralph. *A Social History of French Catholicism 1789-1914*. London: Routledge, 1989.

Gibson, William. *Church, State, and Society 1760-1850*. Basingstoke: Macmillan, 1994.

Gil, Sean. *Women in the Church of England: From the 18th Century to the Present*. London: SPCK, 1994.

Gilbert, Alan D. *Religion and Society in Industrial England: Church, Chapel and Social Change 1740-1914*. London: Longman, 1976.

Gilley, Sheridan, and Brian Stanley (eds). *The Cambridge History of Christianity*. Vol. 8, *World Christianities, ca. 1815-1914*. Cambridge: Cambridge University Press, 2006.

Gißibl, Bernhard. *Frömmigkeit, Hysterie und Schwärmerei: Wunderbare Erscheinungen im bayerischen Vormärz*. Frankfurt am Main: Peter Lang, 2004.

Gladigow, Burkhard. *Religionswissenschaft als Kulturwissenschaft*. Stuttgart: Kohlhammer, 2005.

Gladstone, William R. *The State in Its Relations with the Church*. Vol. 1. London: Gregg International Publishers, 1969.

Goertz, Hans-Jürgen. *Die Täufer: Geschichte und Deutung*. Munich: C. H. Beck, 1980.

Goeters, Johann F., and Joachim Rogge (eds). *Die Geschichte der Evangelischen Kirche der Union*. Vol. 1, *Die Anfänge der Union unter landesherrlichem Kirchenregiment 1817–1850*. Leipzig: Evangelische Verlagsanstalt, 1992.

Gollwitzer, Heinz. *Ludwig I: Königtum im Vormärz; Eine politische Biographie*. Munich: Süddeutscher Verlag, 1986.

Görres, Joseph von. *Die christliche Mystik*. 5 vols, edited by Uta Ranke-Heinemann. Frankfurt am Main: Vito von Eichborn Verlag, 1989.

Görres, Joseph von. *Gesammelte Schriften*. Vol. 18, *Athanasius*, edited by Wilhelm Schellenberg and Heribert Raab. Paderborn: Ferdinand Schöningh, 1998.
Gosselin, Charles Robert. *L'Antiquité Dévoilée au Moyen de la Genèse*. Paris: A. Égron, 1817.
Götz von Olenhusen, Irmtraud. *Klerus und abweichendes Verhalten: Zur Sozialgeschichte katholischer Priester im 19. Jahrhundert. Die Erzdiözese Freiburg*. Göttingen: Vandenhoeck & Ruprecht, 1994.
Goubert, Pierre, and Daniel Roche. *Les Français et l'Ancien Régime*. Vol. 2. Paris: Armand Colin, 1984.
Goy, Jean. *À Reims, Le Sacre des Rois de France*. Reims: Jean Goy, 1980.
Grab, Walter (ed.). *Die Französische Revolution. Eine Dokumentation*. Munich: Nymphenburger, 1973.
Graevenitz, Gerhart von. *Mythos: Zur Geschichte einer Denkgewohnheit*. Stuttgart: Metzler, 1987.
Graf, Friedrich Wilhelm. *Die Politisierung des religiösen Bewusstseins: Die bürgerlichen Religionsparteien im deutschen Vormärz. Das Beispiel des Deutschkatholizismus*. Stuttgart: Frommann-Holzboog, 1978.
Graf, Friedrich Wilhelm. '"Einfache Dechristianisierung": Zur Problemgeschichte eines kulturpolitischen Topos'. In *Säkularisierung: Der europäische Sonderweg in Sachen Religion*, edited by Hartmut Lehmann, 32–66. Göttingen: Wallstein Verlag, 2004.
Graf, Gerhard. *Gottesbild und Politik: Eine Studie zur Frömmigkeit in Preußen während der Befreiungskriege 1813–1815*. Göttingen: Vandenhoeck & Ruprecht, 1993.
Groupe de la Boussièr. *Pratique de la Confession. Des Pères du Désert à Vatican II; Quinze Études d'Histoire*. Paris: Cerf, 1983.
Gruber, Bettina. *Die Seherin von Prevorst: Romantischer Okkultismus als Religion, Wissenschaft und Literatur*. Paderborn: Ferdinand Schöningh, 2000.
Gründer, Horst. *Welteroberung und Christentum: Ein Handbuch zur Geschichte der Neuzeit*. Gütersloh: Gütersloher Verlagshaus, 1992.
Grzywacz, Malgorzata. *Familia Dei: Studien zum Erscheinungsbild der deutschen evangelischen Geistlichkeit in ihren Selbstzeugnissen und der Literatur von der Reformation bis zur Gegenwart*. Poznan: Naukowe UAM, 2002.
Gugerli, David. *Zwischen Pfrund und Predigt: Die protestantische Pfarrfamilie auf der Zürcher Landschaft im ausgehenden 18. Jahrhundert*. Zurich: Chronos, 1988.
Gundert, Wilhelm. *Geschichte der deutschen Bibelgesellschaften im 19. Jahrhundert*. Bielefeld: Chronos, 1987.
Habermas, Rebekka. *Frauen und Männer des Bürgertums*. Göttingen: Vandenhoeck & Ruprecht, 2000.
Hacker, Josef. *Die Messe in den deutschen Diözesan-Gesang- und Gebetbüchern von der Aufklärungszeit bis zur Gegenwart: Mit einem Überblick über die Geschichte dieser Bücher*. Munich: Karl Zink Verlag, 1950.
Hagemann, Karin. '*Männlicher Muth und Teutsche Ehre': Nation, Militär und Geschlecht zur Zeit der antinapoleonischen Kriege Preußens*. Paderborn: Ferdinand Schöningh, 2002.
Hahn, Alois. 'Religiöser Wandel in der deutschen Gegenwartsgesellschaft – Kontroversen um seine religionssoziologische Interpretation'. In *Religionskontroversen in Frankreich und in Deutschland*, edited by Matthias König and Jean-Paul William, 239–271. Hamburg: Hamburger Edition, 2008.
Haller, Carl L. von. *Restauration der Staatswissenschaft: oder Theorie des natürlich-gesellgen Zustandes, der Chimäre des künstlich-bürgerlichen entgegengesetzt*. 6 vols. Aalen: Scientia-Verlag, 1964 [Winterthur: In der Steinerischen Buchhandlung, 1820–34].

Hampton, David, and Myrtle Hill. *Evangelical Protestantism in Ulster Society 1740–1890*. London: Routledge, 1992.
Händler, Gerd (ed.). *Kirchengeschichte in Einzeldarstellungen*. Vols 3–4. Berlin: Berliner Wissenschaftsverlag, 1990–2003.
Harrison, John F. C. *The Second Coming: Popular Millenarianism 1780–1850*. London: Routledge, 1979.
Harrison, Peter. *'Religion' and the Religions in the English Enlightenment*. Cambridge: Cambridge University Press, 1990.
Hartinger, Walter. *Religion und Brauch*. Darmstadt: Wissenschaftliche Buchgesellschaft, 1992.
Hasler, August B. *Pius IX (1846–1878): Päpstliche Unfehlbarkeit und 1. Vatikanisches Konzil; Dogmatisierung und Durchsetzung einer Ideologie*. 2 vols. Stuttgart: Hiersemann Verlag, 1977.
Hasselhorn, Martin. *Der altwürttembergische Pfarrstand im 18. Jahrhundert*. Stuttgart: Kohlhammer Verlag, 1958.
Hauck, Albert. *Kirchengeschichte Deutschlands*. Vol. 5.1. Leipzig: J. C. Hinrichs'sche Buchhandlung, 1911.
Haupt, Heinz Gerhard (ed.). *Das Ende der Zünfte: Ein europäischer Vergleich*. Göttingen: Vandenhoeck & Ruprecht, 2002.
Hausberger, Karl. *Reichskirche, Staatskirche, 'Papstkirche': Der Weg der deutschen Kirche im 19. Jahrhundert*. Regensburg: Pustet, 2008.
Hausen, Karin. 'Die Polarisierung der "Geschlechtscharaktere" – Eine Spiegelung der Dissoziation von Erwerbs- und Familienleben'. In *Sozialgeschichte der Familie in der Neuzeit Europas*, edited by Werner Conze, 363–393. Stuttgart: Klett, 1976.
Hazareesingh, Sudir. *The Saint Napoleon: Celebrations of Sovereignty in Nineteenth-Century France*. Cambridge, MA: Harvard University Press, 2004.
Hebekus, Uwe, Ethel Matala de Mazza and Albrecht Koschorke (eds). *Das Politische: Figurenlehre des sozialen Körpers nach der Romantik*. Munich: Fink, 2003.
Hegel, Georg Wilhelm Friedrich. *Werke in 20 Bänden: Auf der Grundlage der Werke von 1832 bis 1845 neu edierte Ausgabe*. Vol. 1, *Frühe Schriften*, edited by Eva Moldenhauer and Karl Markus Michel. Frankfurt am Main: Suhrkamp, 1978.
Hegel, Georg Wilhelm Friedrich. *Werke in 20 Bänden: Auf der Grundlage der Werke von 1832 bis 1845 neu edierte Ausgabe*. Vol. 11, *Vorrede zu Hinrichs Religionsphilosophie*, ed. Eva Moldenhauer and Karl Markus Michel. Frankfurt am Main: Suhrkamp, 1970 [1822].
Hegel, Georg Wilhelm Friedrich. *Vorlesungen über die Philosophie der Religion*. 3 vols, edited by Walter Jaeschke. Hamburg: Felix Meiner Verlag, 1993.
Hegel, Georg Wilhelm Friedrich. *Hauptwerke in sechs Bänden*. Vol. 2, *Phänomenologie des Geistes*. Hamburg: Felix Meiner Verlag, 1999.
Hegel, Georg Wilhelm Friedrich. *Hauptwerke in sechs Bänden*. Vol. 3, *Wissenschaft der Logik*. Hamburg: Felix Meiner Verlag, 1999.
Hegel, Georg Wilhelm Friedrich. *Hauptwerke in sechs Bänden*. Vol. 5, *Grundlinien der Philosophie des Rechts*. Hamburg: Felix Meiner Verlag, 1999.
*Heiliger Rock Album: Eine Zusammenstellung der wichtigsten Aktenstücke, Briefe, Adressen, Berichte und Zeitungsartikel über die Ausstellung des Heiligen Rockes in Trier*. Leipzig: Mayer und Wigand, 1844.
Heimann, Mary. *Catholic Devotion in Victorian England*. Oxford: Oxford University Press, 1995.

Hendrickson, Kenneth E., III. *Making Saints: Religion and the Public Image of the British Army, 1809-1855*. Cranbury, NJ: Fairleigh Dickinson University Press, 1998.
Heppe, Heinrich. *Geschichte der quietistischen Mystik in der katholischen Kirche*. Berlin: Hertz, 1875.
Herder, Johann Gottfried. *Abhandlung über den Ursprung der Sprache: Texte, Materialien, Kommentar*, edited by Wolfgang Proß. Munich/Vienna: Carl Hanser Verlag, 1978.
Herder, Johann Gottfried. *Ideen zur Philosophie der Geschichte der Menschheit*. Wiesbaden: Fourier, 1985.
Hersche, Peter. *Der Spätjansenismus in Österreich*. Vienna: Verlag der österreichischen Akademie der Wissenschaften, 1977.
Hersche, Peter. *Die Deutschen Domkapitel im 17. und 18. Jahrhundert*. Vol. 2, *Vergleichende sozialgeschichtliche Untersuchungen*. Bern: Peter Hersche, 1984.
Hersche, Peter. '"Chiesa Ricettizia": Ein Modell kommunaler Organisation von Kirche in Unteritalien'. In *Gemeinde, Reformation und Widerstand*, edited by Heinrich R. Schmidt, André Holenstein and Andreas Würgler, 293-308. Tübingen: Bibliotheca academica, 1998.
Hersche, Peter. *Italien im Barockzeitalter 1600-1750: Eine Sozial- und Kulturgeschichte*. Cologne/Vienna: Böhlau, 1999.
Hinchliff, Peter. 'Voluntary Absolutism: British Missionary Societies in the 19th Century'. In *Voluntary Religion*, edited by William J. Sheils and Diana Wood, 363-379. London: Blackwell, 1986.
Hinschius, Paul. *System des katholischen Kirchenrechts mit besonderer Rücksicht auf Deutschland*. Berlin: I. Guttentag, 1869.
Hintze, Otto. 'Epochen des evangelischen Kirchenregiments in Preußen'. In *Gesammelte Abhandlungen*. Vol. 3, *Regierung und Verwaltung: Gesammelte Aufsätze zur Staats- Rechts- und Sozialgeschichte Preußens*, edited by Gerhard Oestreich, 57-96. 2nd edn. Göttingen: Vandenhoeck & Ruprecht, 1967.
His, Eduard. *Geschichte des neueren schweizerischen Staatsrechts*. Vol. 2, *Die Zeit der Restauration und der Regeneration 1814 bis 1848*. Basel: Helbing & Lichtenhahn, 1929.
Hoffmann, C.D.W. *Ein Wort über die herrschenden Irreligiosität und einen zweckmäßigen Religionsunterricht als das wirksamste Mittel dagegen....* Berlin: Frölich, 1804.
Hoffmann, Joachim. *Berlin-Friedrichsfelde: Ein deutscher Nationalfriedhof*. Berlin: Das Neue Berlin, 2001.
Hoffmann, Robert. 'Die katholische Missionsbewegung in Deutschland vom Anfang des 19. Jahrhunderts bis zum Ende der Kolonialgeschichte'. In *Imperialismus und Kolonialismus: Kaiserliches Deutschland und koloniales Imperium*, edited by Klaus Jürgen Baden, 29-50. Wiesbaden: Steiner, 1982.
Hoffmann, Stefan. *Geschichte des Medienbegriffs*. Hamburg: Felix Meiner Verlag, 2002.
Hoffmann-Curtius, Kathrin. 'Altäre des Vaterlandes: Kultstätten nationaler Gemeinschaft in Deutschland seit der Französischen Revolution'. In *Anzeiger des Germanischen Nationalmuseums und Berichte aus dem Forschungsinstitut für Realienkunde*, 283-307. Nürnberg: Das Nazionalmuseum, 1989.
Hole, Robert. *Pulpits, Politics and Public Order in England 1760-1832*. Cambridge: Cambridge University Press, 1989.
Holmes, J. Derek. *The Triumph of the Holy See: A Short History of the Papacy in the Nineteenth Century*. London: Patmos Press, 1978.
Hölscher, Lucian. 'Die Religion des Bürgers: Bürgerliche Frömmigkeit und protestantische Kirche im 19. Jahrhundert'. *Historische Zeitschrift* 250 (1990): 595-630.

Hölscher, Lucian. *Geschichte der protestantischen Frömmigkeit in Deutschland*. Munich: C. H. Beck, 2005.
Hölscher, Lucian (ed.). *Das Jenseits: Facetten eines religiösen Begriffs in der Neuzeit*. Göttingen: Wallstein, 2007.
Holtwick, Bernd. 'Licht und Schatten. Begründungen und Zielsetzungen des protestantischen missionarischen Aufbruchs im frühen 19. Jahrhundert'. In *Weltmission und religiöse Organisationen: Protestantische Missionsgesellschaften im 19. und 20. Jahrhundert*, edited by Arthur Bogner, Bernd Holtwick and Hartmann Tyrell, 225–246. Würzburg: Ergon Verlag, 2004.
Holzem, Andreas. *Konfession und Sektenbildung: Deutschkatholiken, Reformkatholiken und Ultramontane am Oberrhein 1844–1866*. Paderborn: Ferdinand Schöningh, 1994.
Holzem, Andreas. *Religion und Lebensformen: Katholische Konfessionalisierung im Sendgericht des Fürstbistums Münster 1570–1800*. Paderborn: Ferdinand Schöningh, 2000.
Holzem, Andreas. 'Säkularisation in Oberschwaben: Ein problemgeschichtlicher Aufriss'. In *Die Säkularisation im Prozeß der Säkularisierung Europas*, edited by Peter Blickle and Rudolf Schlögl, 261–299. Epfendorf: Bibliotheca academica, 2005.
Hommer, Joseph von. *1760–1836: Meditationes in vitam meam peractam. Eine Selbstbiographie*, edited and translated by Alois Thomas. Mainz: Selbstverlag der Gesellschaft für mittelrheinische Kirchengeschichte, 1976.
Honegger, Claudia. *Die Ordnung der Geschlechter: Die Wissenschaft vom Menschen und das Weib 1750–1850*. Frankfurt am Main: Suhrkamp, 1991.
Hörisch, Jochen. *Der Sinn und die Sinne: Eine Geschichte der Medien*. Frankfurt am Main: Eichborn, 2001.
Horst, Conrad. *Mysteriosophie oder über die Veredelung des protestantischen Gottesdienstes...*. Frankfurt: Varentrapp, 1817.
Hsia, Ronnie Po-chia. *Gegenreformation: Die Welt der katholischen Erneuerung, 1540–1770*. Frankfurt am Main: Fischer Taschenbuch Verlag, 1998.
Huber, Ernst R. (ed.). *Deutsche Verfassungsgeschichte seit 1789*. Vol. 1, *Reform und Restauration 1789 bis 1830*. Stuttgart: W. Kohlhammer Verlag, 1957.
Huber, Ernst R., and Wolfgang Huber (eds). *Staat und Kirche im 19. und 20. Jahrhundert*. Vol. 1, *Staat und Kirche vom Ausgang des alten Reichs bis zum Vorabend der bürgerlichen Revolution*. Berlin: Wissenschaftliche Buchgesellschaft, 1973.
Hudson, Wayne. *The English Deists: Studies in Early Enlightenment*. London: Pickering and Chatto, 2009.
Hume, David. *The Natural History of Religion*, edited by H. E. Root. Stanford, CA: Stanford University Press, 1957.
Hunter, Jan. *The Secularisation of the Confessional State: The Political Thought of Christian Thomasius*. Cambridge: Cambridge University Press, 2007.
Hutchinson, John. *Moses's Sine Principio*. Vol. 3, *Represented by Names, by Words, by Types, by Emblems: With an Introduction Shewing the Nature of Body and Soul...*. 3rd edn. London: no publisher, 1748.
Ideler, Wilhelm. *Der religiöse Wahnsinn, erläutert durch Krankengeschichten: Ein Beitrag zur Geschichte der religiösen Wirren der Gegenwar*. 2 pts. Halle: Schwetschke, 1847.
Imbert-Goubeyre, Antoine. *Les Stigmatisées*. Part 2. Paris: Victor Palmé, 1873.
Imbert-Gourbeyre, Antoine. *La Stigmatisation*. Paris: Bouflet, 1984.
Israel, J. I. *Radical Enlightenment: Philosophy and the Making of Modernity 1650–1750*. Oxford: Oxford University Press, 2001.

Janz, Oliver. *Bürger besonderer Art: Evangelische Pfarrer in Preußen 1850-1915*. Berlin/New York: De Gruyter, 1994.
Jedin, Hubert (ed.). *Handbuch der Kirchengeschichte*, 6 vols. Freiburg im Breisgau: Herder, 1962-79.
Jemolo, Arturo C. *Chiesa e Stato in Italia dalla Unificazione a Giovanni XXIII*. Turin: Einaudi, 1965.
Jones, Raymond. *France and the Cult of the Sacred Heart: An Epic Tale of Modern Times*. Berkeley, CA: University of California Press, 2000.
Jong, Otto Jan de. *Nederlandse Kerkgeschiedenis*. Nijkerk: Callenbach, 1972.
Julia, Dominique. 'Le Clergé Paroissial dans les Diocèse de Reims à la Fin du XVIIIe Siècle'. *Revue d' Histoire Moderne et Contemporaire* 13 (1966): 195-216.
Jung, Franz Wilhelm. *Beitrag zu Ideen über Kirche und Kirchengebäude*. Mainz: no publisher, 1814.
Kant, Immanuel. *Kritik der reinen Vernunft*. Stuttgart: Philipp Reclam jun., 1966.
Kant, Immanuel. *Werke*. Vol. 7, *Kritik der praktischen Vernunft*. Frankfurt am Main: Suhrkamp, 1978.
Kant, Immanuel. *Werke*. Vol. 8, *Religion innerhalb der Grenzen der bloßen Vernunft: Die Metaphysik der Sitten*. Frankfurt am Main: De Gruyter, 1968.
Kant, Immanuel. *Werke*. Vol. 10, *Kritik der Urteilskraft*. Frankfurt am Main: Suhrkamp, 1979.
Kant, Immanuel. *Werke*. Vol. 11, *Der Streit der Fakultäten*. Frankfurt am Main: Suhrkamp, 1977.
Kant, Immanuel. 'Träume eines Geistersehers, erläutert durch Träume in der Metaphysik'. In *Kants Werke*. Vol. 2, *Vorkritische Schriften II: 1757-1777*. Frankfurt am Main: Suhrkamp, 1977.
Kapfinger, Hans. *Der Eoskreis 1828 bis 1832: Ein Beitrag zur Vorgeschichte des politischen Katholizismus in Deutschland*. Munich: Pfeiffer, 1928.
Keller, Adolf. *Church and State on the European Continent: The Social Service Lecture 1936*. London: Epworth Press, 1936.
Kerner, Hanns. *Die Reform des Gottesdienstes: Von der Neubildung der Gottesdienstordnung und der Agende in der evangelisch-lutherischen Kirche in Bayern im 19. Jahrhundert bis zur erneuerten Agende*. Stuttgart: Calwer, 1994.
Kirsch, Martin. *Monarch und Parlament im 19. Jahrhundert: Der monarchische Konstitutionalismus als europäischer Verfassungstyp. Frankreich im Vergleich*. Göttingen: Vandenhoeck & Ruprecht, 1999.
Kirsch, Thomas G. 'Restaging the Will to Believe: Religion, Pluralism, Anti-Syncretism and the Problem of Belief', *American Anthropologist* 106 (2004): 699-709.
Kisky, Wilhelm. *Die Domkapitel der geistlichen Kurfürsten in ihrer persönlichen Zusammensetzung im 14. und 15. Jahrhundert*. Cologne/Vienna: Böhlau, 1906.
Kißener, Michael. *Ständemacht und Kirchenreform: Bischöfliche Wahlkapitulation im Nordwesten des Alten Reiches 1265-1803*. Munich: Ferdinand Schöningh, 1993.
Kittsteiner, Heinz-Dieter. 'Die Abschaffung des Teufels im 18. Jahrhundert: Ein kulturhistorisches Ereignis und seine Folgen'. In *Die andere Kraft: Zur Renaissance des Bösen*, edited by Alexander Schuller and Wolfert von Rahden, 55-92. Berlin: De Gruyter Akademie Forschung, 1993.
Klempt, Adalbert. *Die Säkularisierung der universalhistorischen Auffassung: Zum Wandel des Geschichtsdenkens im 16. und 17. Jahrhundert*. Göttingen: Musterschmidt, 1960.
Kley, Dale van. *The Jansenists and the Expulsion of the Jesuits from France 1757-1765*. New Haven, CT: Yale University Press, 1975.

Kley, Dale van. 'The Church, State, and the Ideological Origins of the French Revolution: The Debate over the General Assembly of the Gallican Clergy in 1765'. *Journal of Modern History* 51 (1979): 629–666.
Klueting, Harm (ed.). *Katholische Aufklärung: Aufklärung im katholischen Deutschland*. Hamburg: Meiner, 1993.
Klueting, Harm (ed.). *Der Josephinismus: Ausgewählte Quellen zur Geschichte der theresianisch-josephinischen Reformen*. Darmstadt: Wissenschaftliche Buchgesellschaft, 1995.
Klug, Matthias. *Rückwendung zum Mittelalter? Geschichtsbilder und historische Argumentation im politischen Katholizismus des Vormärz*. Paderborn: Ferdinand Schöningh, 1995.
Kocka, Jürgen. *Arbeitsverhältnisse und Arbeiterexistenzen: Grundlagen der Klassenbildung im 19. Jahrhundert*. Berlin: Dietz, 1990.
Kohl, Karl-Heinz. *Die Macht der Dinge: Geschichte und Theorie sakraler Objekte*. Munich: C. H. Beck, 2003.
Kondylis, Panajotis. *Konservativismus: Geschichtlicher Gehalt und Untergang*. Stuttgart: Klett-Cotta, 1986.
Konersmann, Frank. *Kirchenregiment und Kirchenzucht im frühneuzeitlichen Kleinstaat: Studien zu den herrschaftlichen und gesellschaftlichen Grundlagen des Kirchenregiments der Herzöge von Pfalz-Zweibrücken 1410–1793*. Speyer: Mohr Siebeck, 1996.
Kopp, Georg L. C. *Die katholische Kirche im 19. Jahrhundert und die zeitgemäße Umgestaltung ihrer Verfassung mit besonderer Rücksicht auf die im ehemaligen Mainzer, später Regensburger Erzstifte hierzu getroffenen Anstalten und Anordnungen*. Mainz: Kupferberg, 1830.
Koschorke, Albrecht. *Körperströme und Schriftverkehr: Mediologie des 18. Jahrhunderts*. Munich: Fink, 1999.
Koschorke, Albrecht. *Die Heilige Familie und ihre Folgen: Ein Versuch*. Frankfurt am Main: Fischer-Taschenbuch-Verlag, 2000.
Koschorke, Albrecht. '"Säkularisierung" und "Wiederkehr der Religion": zu zwei Narrativen der europäischen Moderne'. In *Moderne und Religion: Kontroversen um Modernität und Säkularisierung*, edited by Ulrich Willems, Detlef Pollack, Helene Basu, Thomas Gutmann and Ulrike Spohn, 237–260. Bielefeld: Transcript-Verlag, 2013.
Koschorke, Albrecht, Thomas Frank, Ethel Matala de Mazza and Susanne Lüdemann. *Der fiktive Staat: Konstruktionen des politischen Körpers in der Geschichte Europas*. Frankfurt am Main: Fischer-Taschenbuch-Verlag, 2007.
Koselleck, Reinhart. 'Einleitung'. In *Geschichtliche Grundbegriffe. Historisches Lexikon zur politisch-sozialen Sprache in Deutschland*. Vol. 1, edited by Otto Brunner, Werner Conze and Reinhart Koselleck, xiii–xvii. Stuttgart: Klett-Cotta, 1972.
Koselleck, Reinhart. *Preußen zwischen Reform und Revolution. Allgemeines Landrecht, Verwaltung und soziale Bewegung von 1791 bis 1848*. 2nd edn. Stuttgart: Deutscher Taschenbuchverlag, 1975.
Koselleck, Reinhart. *Kritik und Krise: Eine Studie zur Pathogenese der bürgerlichen Welt*. Frankfurt am Main: Suhrkamp, 1976.
Koselleck, Reinhart. *Zeitschichten: Studien zur Historik*. Frankfurt am Main: Suhrkamp, 2000.
Koselleck, Reinhart. *Begriffsgeschichte: Studien zur Semantik und Pragmatik der politischen und sozialen Sprache*. Frankfurt am Main: Suhrkamp, 2006.
Koselleck, Reinhart, Fritz Gschnitzer, Karl Ferdinand Werner and Bernd Schönemann. 'Volk, Nation, Nationalismus, Masse'. In *Geschichtliche Grundbegriffe: Historisches*

*Lexikon zur politisch-sozialen Sprache in Deutschland.* Vol. 7, edited by Reinhart Koselleck, Werner Conze and Otto Brunner, 141-431. Stuttgart: Klett-Cotta, 1992.

Köser, Silke. *'Denn eine Diakonisse darf kein Alltagsmensch sein': Kollektive Identitäten kaiserswerther Diakonissen 1836–1914.* Leipzig: Evangelische Verlagsanstalt, 2006.

Kovács, Elisabeth. 'Kirchliches Zeremoniell am Wiener Hof des 18. Jahrhunderts im Wandel von Mentalität und Gesellschaft'. *Mitteilungen des Österreichischen Staatsarchivs* 32 (1979): 109–142.

Kremer, Stephan. *Herkunft und Werdegang geistlicher Führungsschichten in den Reichsbistümern zwischen Westfälischem Frieden und Säkularisation: Fürstbischöfe, Weihbischöfe, Generalvikare.* Freiburg im Breisgau: Herder, 1992.

Kriele, Eduard. *Geschichte der Rheinischen Mission.* Vol. 1, *Die Rheinische Mission in ihrer Heimat.* Barmen: Missionshaus, 1928.

Kroen, Sheryl. *Politics and Theatre: The Crises of Legitimacy in Restoration France, 1815–1830.* Berkeley, CA: University of California Press, 2000.

Kroll, Frank-Lothar. *Friedrich Wilhelm IV und das Staatsdenken der deutschen Romantik.* Berlin: Colloquium, 1990.

Krug, Wilhelm Traugott. *Die Kirchenverbesserung und die Gefahren des Protestantismus....* Leipzig: Baumgärtner, 1826.

Kselman, Thomas A. *Miracles and Prophecies in Nineteenth-Century France.* New Brunswick, NJ: Rutgers University Press, 1983.

Kselman, Thomas A. *Death and Afterlife in Modern France.* Princeton, NJ: Princeton University Press, 1993.

Kuhlemann, Frank Michael. *Bürgerlichkeit und Religion: Zur Sozial- und Mentalitätsgeschichte der evangelischen Pfarrer in Baden 1860–1914.* Göttingen: Vandenhoeck & Ruprecht, 2002.

Kupisch, Karl. *Die deutschen Landeskirchen im 19. und 20. Jahrhundert: Die Kirche in ihrer Geschichte: Ein Handbuch.* Vol. 4. 2nd edn. Göttingen: Vandenhoeck & Ruprecht, 1975.

Lafitau, Joseph-François. *Die Sitten der amerikanischen Wilden im Vergleich zu den Sitten der Frühzeit.* Leipzig: Edition Leipzig, 1987.

Lagrée, Michel. *L'Histoire des Curés.* Paris: Fayard, 2005.

Lalor, Stephen. *Matthew Tindal, Freethinker: An Eighteenth-Century Assault on Religion.* London: A&C Black, 2006.

Lampert, Ulrich. *Kirche und Staat in der Schweiz.* Vol. 2. Basel: Rütschi und Egloff Verlag, 1938.

Landes, David S. *The Unbound Prometheus: Technological Change in Industrial Development in Western Europe from 1750 to the Present.* Cambridge: Cambridge University Press, 1969.

Landwehr, Achim. *Geschichte des Sagbaren: Einführung in die Historische Diskusanalyse.* 2nd edn. Tübingen: Campus Verlag, 2004.

Langenwiesche, Dieter. 'Nation und Religion'. In *Europäische Religionsgeschichte: Ein mehrfacher Pluralismus.* Vol. 2, edited by Hans G. Kippenberg, Jörg Rüpke and Kocku Stuckrad, 525–533. Göttingen: Vandenhoeck & Ruprecht, 2009.

Langlois, Claude. *Le Catholicisme au Féminin: Les Congrégations Françaises à Supérieure Génerale au XIXe Siècle.* Paris: Cerf-Histoire, 1984.

Latour, Bruno. 'Gebt mir ein Laboratorium und ich werde die Welt aus den Angeln heben'. In *ANThology: Ein einführendes Handbuch zur Akteur-Netzwerk-Theorie*, edited by Andréa Belliger and David J. Krieger, 103–134. Bielefeld: Transcript-Verlag, 2006.

Latour, Bruno. *Jubilieren: Über religiöse Rede.* Frankfurt am Main: Suhrkamp, 2011.

Latreille, André. *L'Eglise Catholique et la Révolution Française*. 2 vols. Paris: Hachette, 1946–50.
Laufkötter, Franz. 'Weib'. In *Kirchen-Lexikon oder die Enzyklopädie der katholischen Theologie und ihrer Hilfswissenschaften*. Vol. 11, edited by Heinrich J. Wetzer and Benedikt Welte, 820–821. Freiburg im Breisgau: Herder, 1852.
Le Bras, Gabriel. *Institutions Ecclésiastiques de la Chrétienté Médiévale*. Paris: Bloud et Gay, 1964.
Lefort, Claude. *Fortdauer des Theologisch-Politischen*. Vienna: Passagen Verlag, 1999.
Lefton, Jean. *La Crise Révolutionnaire 1789–1856*. Paris: Bloud et Gay, 1949.
Lehmann, Hartmut (ed.). *Säkularisierung, Dechristianisierung, Rechristianisierung im neuzeitlichen Europa: Bilanz und Perspektiven der Forschung*. Göttingen: Vandenhoeck & Ruprecht, 1997.
Lehmann, Maren. *Inklusion: Beobachtungen einer sozialen Form am Beispiel von Religion und Kirche*. Berlin: Humanities Online, 2002.
Lemaire, Suzanne. *La Comission des Réguliers*. Paris: Tenin, 1926.
Leonhard, Jörn. *Liberalismus: Zur historischen Semantik eines europäischen Deutungsmusters*. Munich: Oldenbourg, 2001.
Lepenies, Wolf. *Das Ende der Naturgeschichte: Wandel kultureller Selbstverständlichkeiten in den Wissenschaften des 18. und 19. Jahrhunderts*. Frankfurt am Main: Suhrkamp, 1978.
Lepointe, Gabriel. *L'Organisation et la Politique Financières du Clergé de France sous le Règne de Louis XV*. Paris: Librairie de la Société du Recueil Sirey, 1923.
Lévêque, Laure. *Penser la Nation: Mémoire et Imaginaire en Révolutions*. Paris: Éditions L'Harmattan, 2011.
Lieberknecht, Paul Ernst. *Geschichte des Deutschkatholizismus in Kurhessen*. Marburg: N. G. Elwert, 1915.
Liermann, Christiane. *Rosminis politische Philosophie der zivilen Gesellschaft*. Paderborn: Ferdinand Schöningh, 2004.
Lill, Rudolf. *Die Beilegung der Kölner Wirren 1840–1842: Vorwiegend nach Akten des Vatikanischen Geheimarchivs*. Düsseldorf: L. Schwann, 1962.
Linse, Ulrich. *Geisterseher und Wunderwirker: Heilssuche im Industriezeitalter*. Frankfurt am Main: Fischer Taschenbuch Verlag, 1996.
Locke, John. *Epistola de Tolerantia: A Letter on Toleration*, edited by Raymond Klibansky and J. W. Gough. Oxford: Clarendon Press, 1968.
Löffler, Josias Friedrich Christian. *Über den Wert und die Erhaltung des christlichen Gottesdienstes*. Jena: no publisher, 1811.
Lönne, Karl Egon. *Politischer Katholizismus im 19. und 20. Jahrhundert*. Frankfurt am Main: Suhrkamp, 1986.
Lottes, Günther. 'Die Geistlichen Staaten und die Herrschaftskonkurrenz im Reich'. In *Individualisierung, Rationalisierung, Säkularisierung: Neue Wege der Religionsgeschichte*, edited by Michael Weinzierl, 96–111. Vienna: Oldenbourg Wissenschaftsverlag, 1997.
Löwith, Karl. *Sämtliche Schriften*. Vol. 2, *Weltgeschichte als Heilsgeschehen*. Stuttgart: J. B. Metzlersche Verlagsbuchhandlung, 1983.
Luhmann, Niklas. *Funktionen und Folgen formaler Organisation*. 3rd edn. Berlin: Duncker & Humblot, 1976.
Luhmann, Niklas. *Funktion der Religion*. Frankfurt am Main: Suhrkamp, 1977.
Luhmann, Niklas. *Gesellschaftsstruktur und Semantik: Studien zur Wissenssoziologie der modernen Gesellschaft*. Vol. 1. Frankfurt am Main: Suhrkamp, 1980.

Luhmann, Niklas. *Soziale Systeme: Grundriss einer allgemeinen Theorie*. Frankfurt am Main: Suhrkamp, 1984.
Luhmann, Niklas. *Protest: Systemtheorie und soziale Bewegungen*. Frankfurt am Main: Suhrkamp, 1996.
Luhmann, Niklas. *Die Gesellschaft der Gesellschaft*. 2 vols. Frankfurt am Main: Suhrkamp, 1998.
Luhmann, Niklas. *Die Politik der Gesellschaft*. Frankfurt am Main: Suhrkamp, 2000.
Luhmann, Niklas. *Organisation und Entscheidung*. Opladen: Westdeutscher Verlag, 2000.
Luhmann, Niklas. *Religion der Gesellschaft*. Frankfurt am Main: Suhrkamp, 2000.
Luhmann, Niklas. *Einführung in die Systemtheorie*. Heidelberg: Carl-Auer-Systeme-Verlag, 2002.
Luhmann, Niklas. *Ideenevolution: Beiträge zur Wissenssoziologie*. Frankfurt am Main: Suhrkamp, 2008.
Lyons, Martyn. 'Fires of Expiation: Book-Burnings and Catholic Mission in Restoration France'. *French History* 10 (1996): 240–264.
Mager, Wolfgang. *Frankreich vom Ancien Régime zur Moderne. Wirtschafts-, Gesellschafts- und politische Institutionengeschichte 1630–1830*. Stuttgart: Kohlhammer, 1980.
Maier, Hans. 'Über revolutionäre Feste und Zeitrechnungen'. In *Wie eine Revolution entsteht: Die Französische Revolution als Kommunikationsereignis*, edited by Hans Maier and Eberhard Schmidt, 99–117. Paderborn/Munich/Vienna/Zurich: Schöningh, 1988.
Maistre, Joseph de. *Considérations sur la France; Suivie de: Essai sur le Principe Générateur des Constitutions Politiques et des Autres Institutions Humaines*. Paris: La Société typographique, 1814.
Maistre, Joseph de. *Du Pape*, edited by Jacques Lovie and Joannès Chetail. Geneva: Librairie Droz, 1966.
Manios, Hubert de (ed.). *Maria: Études sur la Sainte Vierge*. 7 vols. Paris: Beauchesne, 1949.
Mannheim, Ernst. *Aufklärung und öffentliche Meinung: Studien zur Soziologie der Öffentlichkeit im 18. Jahrhundert*. Stuttgart: Frommann-Holzboog, 1979.
Mannheim, Karl. *Ideologie und Utopie*. 3rd edn. Frankfurt am Main: Schulte-Bulmke, 1952.
Marin, Juan Sàez. *Datos Sobre la Iglesia Espanola Contemporànea 1768–1868*. Madrid: Editora Nacional, 1975.
Marrus, Michael R. 'Pilger auf dem Weg: Wallfahrten im Frankreich des 19. Jahrhunderts'. *Geschichte und Gesellschaft* 3 (1977): 330–351.
Marshall, P. J. (ed.). *The British Discovery of Hinduism in the Eighteenth Century*. Cambridge: Cambridge University Press, 1970.
Marx, Karl. *Marx-Engels-Werke*. Vol. 3, *Thesen über Feuerbach*. East Berlin: Dietz Verlag, 1969.
Marx, Karl, and Friedrich Engels. *Marx-Engels-Werke*. Vol. 3, *Die deutsche Ideologie: Kritik der neuesten deutschen Philosophien in ihren Repräsentanten Feuerbach, B.Bauer und Stirner und des deutschen Sozialismus in seinen verschiedenen Propheten*. East Berlin: Dietz Verlag, 1969.
Masuzawa, Tomoko. *The Invention of World Religions: Or, How European Universalism Was Preserved in the Language of Pluralism*. Chicago, IL: University of Chicago Press, 2005.
Mathiez, Albert. *Les Origines des Cultes Révolutionaires 1789–1792*. Paris: Société nouvelle de librairie et d'édition, 1904.

Mayeur, Jean-Marie, Luce Pietri, Charles Pietri, André Vauchez and Marc Venard (eds). *Die Geschichte des Christentums: Religion, Politik, Kultur*. Freiburg im Breisgau: Herder, 1991.
Mayntz, Renate. *Soziologie der Organisation*. Hamburg: Rowohlt Taschenbuch Verlag, 1967.
Mazza, Ethel Matala de. *Der verfasste Körper: Zum Projekt einer organischen Gemeinschaft in der politischen Romantik*. Freiburg im Breisgau: Rombach Verlag, 1999.
McAdam, Doug, John D. McCarthy and Mayer N. Zald (eds). *Comparative Perspectives on Social Movements: Political Opportunities, Mobilizing Structures and Cultural Framings*. Cambridge: Cambridge University Press, 1996.
McLeod, Hugh. 'Weibliche Frömmigkeit – männlicher Unglaube? Religion und Kirchen im bürgerlichen 19. Jahrhundert'. In *Bürgerinnen und bürgerliche Geschlechterverhältnisse im 19. Jahrhundert*, edited by Ute Frevert, 134–156. Göttingen: Wallstein, 1988.
McLeod, Hugh. *Secularisation in Western Europe 1848–1914*. New York: St Martin's, 2000.
McManners, John. *French Ecclesiastical Society under the Ancien Régime: A Study of Angers in the Eighteenth Century*. Manchester: Manchester University Press, 1960.
McManners, John. *Church and Society in Eighteenth Century France*. Vol. 1, *The Clerical Establishment and Its Social Ramifications*. Oxford: Oxford University Press, 1998.
Meding, Wichmann von. 'Das Wartburgfest im Rahmen des Reformationsjubiläums 1817'. *Zeitschrift für Kirchengeschichte* 97 (1987): 205–235.
Mehlhausen, Joachim. 'Friedrich Wilhelm IV: Ein Laientheologe auf dem preußischen Königsthron'. In *Vom Amt des Laien in Kirche und Theologie: Festschrift für Gerhard Krause zum 70. Geburtstag*, edited by Henning Schroer and Gerhard Müller, 185–213. Berlin: De Gruyter, 1983.
Mehnert, Gottfried. *Programme evangelischer Kirchenzeitungen im 19. Jahrhundert*. Witten: Luther-Verlag, 1972.
Meiners, Christoph. 'Über die Mysterien der Alten, besonders über die Eleusinischen Geheimnisse'. In *Vermischte philosophische Schriften*. Part 3, 164–342. Leipzig: Weygandsche Buchhandlung, 1776.
Meiners, Christoph. *Allgemeine kritische Geschichte der Religionen*. 2 vols. Hanover: Helwing, 1806.
Meinzer, Michael. *Der französische Revolutionskalender 1792–1805: Planung, Durchführung und Scheitern einer politischen Zeitrechnung*. Munich: Oldenbourg, 1992.
Meiwes, Reilinde. *'Arbeiterinnen des Herrn': Katholische Frauenkongregationen im 19. Jahrhundert*. Frankfurt am Main: Campus, 2000.
Menzel, Wolfgang. *Christliche Symbolik*. 2 pts. Regensburg: G. Joseph Manz, 1854.
Merrick, Jeffrey W. *The Desacralisation of the French Monarchy in the Eighteenth Century*. Baton Rouge, LA: Louisiana State University Press, 1990.
Mersch, Dieter. 'Das Ereignis der Setzung'. In *Performativität und Ereignis*, edited by Erika Fischer-Lichte, 41–56. Tübingen: Francke, 2003.
Michelet, Jules. *Le Prêtre, la Femme et la Famille*, 7th edn. Paris: Chamerot Libraire Éditeur, 1861.
Michelet, Jules. *Geschichte der Französischen Revolution*. Vol. 2. Frankfurt am Main: Eichborn, 1988.
Mieck, Ilja. *Die Entstehung des modernen Frankreich 1450–1610: Strukturen, Institutionen, Entwicklungen*. Stuttgart/Berlin/Cologne/Mainz: Kohlhammer, 1982.
Mitterwieser, Alois. *Geschichte der Fronleichnamsprozession in Bayern*, revised by Torsten Gebhard. Munich: Weinmayer, 1949.

Möhler, Johann Adam. *Symbolik oder Darstellung der dogmatischen Grundsätze der Katholiken und der Protestanten nach ihren öffentlichen Bekenntnisschriften.* Mainz: Florian Kupferberg, 1832.
Molnár, Attila K. 'The Construction of the Notion of Religion in Early Modern Europe'. *Method and Theory in the Study of Religion* 14 (2000): 47–60.
Montalembert, Charles F., Comte de. *De Devoirs des Catholiques dans la Question de la Liberté d'Enseignement.* Paris: L'Univers, 1843.
Montesquieu, Charles-Louis de Secondat, Baron de la Brède et de. *Vom Geist der Gesetze.* Stuttgart: Philipp Reclam, 1965.
Mooser, Josef. 'Konventikel, Unterschichten und Pastoren: Entstehung, Träger und Leistungen der Erweckungsbewegung in Minden-Ravensberg ca. 1820–1850'. In *Frommes Volk und Patrioten: Erweckungsbewegung und soziale Frage im östlichen Westfalen 1800–1858,* edited by Josef Mooser, 16–52. Bielefeld: Verlag für Regionalgeschichte, 1999.
Morgan, Sue. *A Passion for Purity: Alice Hopkins and the Politics of Gender in the Late Victorian Church.* Bristol: University of Bristol, 1999.
Morrien, Rita. *Sinn und Sinnlichkeit: Der weibliche Körper in der deutschen Literatur der Bürgerzeit.* Cologne/Vienna: Böhlau, 2001.
Mosse, George C. *Die Nationalisierung der Massen: Von den Befreiungskriegen bis zum Dritten Reich.* Frankfurt am Main: Ullstein, 1976.
Mostert, Walter. 'Glaube – der christliche Begriff für Religion'. *Zeitschrift für Theologie und Kirche* 95 (1998): 217–231.
Muhs, Rudolf. 'Die Stigmata der Karoline Beller: Ein katholisches Frauenschicksal des Vormärz im Spannungsfeld von Volksreligiosität, Kirche, Staat und Medizin'. In *Wunderbare Erscheinungen: Frauen und katholische Frömmigkeit im 19. und 20. Jahrhundert,* edited by Irmtraud Götz von Olenhusen, 83–130. Paderborn: Ferdinand Schöningh, 1995.
Müller, Adam. *Elemente der Staatskunst.* Berlin: Haug- und Spenersche Verlagsbuchhandlung, 1948.
Müller, Hans. *Säkularisation und Öffentlichkeit am Beispiel Westfalen.* Münster: Mehren und Hobbeling, 1971.
Müller, Joseph. *Die bischöflichen Diözesanbehörden.* Stuttgart: Ferdinand Enke, 1905.
Müller, Max. *Chips from a German Workshop.* Vol. 1, *Essays on the Science of Religion (1867).* New York: Charles Scribner, 1872.
Mulsow, Martin, and Andreas Mahler (eds). *Die Cambridge School der politischen Ideengeschichte.* Berlin: Suhrkamp, 2010.
Mundt, Theodor. *Madonna: Unterhaltungen mit einer Heiligen.* Frankfurt am Main: Athenäum, 1973 [1835].
Muratori, Ludwig A. *Über die Einbildungskraft des Menschen: Mit vielen Zusätzen,* edited by Georg Herman Richartz, 2 pts. Leipzig: Weygand, 1785.
Neill, Stephen. *Geschichte der christlichen Missionen.* 2nd edn. Erlangen: Verlag der Evangelischen Lutherischen Mission, 1990.
Neis, Cordula. *Anthropologie im Sprachdenken des 18. Jahrhunderts: Die Berliner Preisfrage nach dem Ursprung der Sprache.* Berlin/New York: De Gruyter, 2003.
Neugebauer-Wölk, Monika. 'Esoterik in der Frühen Neuzeit: Zum Paradigma der Religionsgeschichte zwischen Mittelalter und Moderne'. *Zeitschrift für historische Forschung* 27 (2000): 321–364.
Nietzsche, Friedrich. *Nietzsches Werke: Taschen-Ausgabe.* Vol. 11, *Ecce Homo.* Leipzig: Alfred Kröner, 1923.

Nipperdey, Thomas. *Deutsche Geschichte 1815–1866*. Munich: C. H. Beck, 1983.
Noack, Ludwig. *Die spekulative Religionswissenschaft im enzyklopädischen Organismus ihrer besonderen Disziplinen*. Darmstadt: C. W. Leske, 1847.
Nockles, P. B. *The Oxford Movement in Context: Anglican High Churchmanship 1760–1857*. Cambridge: Cambridge University Press, 1985.
Norris, Pippa, and Ronald Inglehardt. *Sacred and Secular: Religion and Politics Worldwide*. Cambridge: Cambridge University Press, 2004.
Novalis (Friedrich von Hardenberg). 'Die Christenheit oder Europa'. In *Das philosophisch-theoretische Werk*, edited by Hans J. Mähl, 732–750. Vol. 2 of *Novalis: Werke, Tagebücher und Briefe Friedrich von Hardenbergs*, edited by Hans J. Mähl, Richard Samuel and Hans Jürgen Balmes. Munich: Hanser, 1978.
Nowak, Kurt. *Geschichte des Christentums in Deutschland: Religion, Politik und Gesellschaft vom Ende der Aufklärung bis zur Mitte des 20. Jahrhunderts*. Munich: C. H. Beck, 1995.
Ó Suilleabhain, Séan. *Irish Wake Amusements*. Dublin: Mercier Press, 1967.
Obelkevich, James. *Religion and Rural Society in South Lindsay 1825–1875*. Oxford: Clarendon Press, 1976.
Olender, Maurice. *Die Sprachen des Paradieses: Religion, Philosophie und Rassentheorie im 19. Jahrhundert*. Frankfurt am Main/New York: Campus-Verlag, 1995.
O'Regan, Cyril. *The Heterodox Hegel*. New York: State University of New York Press, 1994.
Orr, Clarissa Campell. 'The Hanoverian Court and the Christian Enlightenment'. In *Monarchy and Religion: The Transformation of Royal Culture in Eighteenth-Century Europe*, edited by Michael Schaich, 317–342. Oxford: Oxford University Press, 2007.
Osterhammel, Jürgen. *Die Entzauberung Asiens: Europa und die asiatischen Reiche im 18. Jahrhundert*. Munich: C. H. Beck, 1998.
Osterhammel, Jürgen. 'Nation und Zivilisation in der britischen Historiographie von Hume bis Maccaulay'. In *Geschichtswissenschaft jenseits des Nationalstaats*, edited by Jürgen Osterhammel, 103–150. Göttingen: Vandenhoeck & Ruprecht, 2001.
Osterhammel, Jürgen. *Die Verwandlung der Welt: Eine Geschichte des 19. Jahrhunderts*. Munich: C. H. Beck, 2009.
Osterhammel, Jürgen. *Sklaverei und die Zivilisation des Westens*. 2nd revised edn. Munich: Carl-Friedrich-von-Siemens-Stiftung, 2009 [2000].
Overton, John H., and Frederic Relton. *The English Church from the Accession of George I to the End of the Eighteenth Century 1714–1800*. New York: AMS Press, 1968 [London: Macmillan, 1906].
Ozouf, Mona. *La Fête Révolutionnaire 1789–1799*. Paris: Éditions Gallimard, 1976.
Pahut, René. 'Religionsfreiheit'. *Theologische Realenzyklopädie* 28 (1967): 565–574.
Pailin, David A. *Attitudes to Other Religions: Comparative Religion in Seventeenth- and Eighteenth-Century Britain*. Manchester: Manchester University Press, 1984.
Paletschek, Sylvia. *Frauen und Dissens: Frauen im Deutschkatholizismus und in den freien Gemeinden 1841–1852*. Göttingen: Vandenhoeck & Ruprecht, 1990.
Pammer, Michael. *Glaubensabfall und wahre Andacht: Barockreligiosität, Reformkatholizismus und Laizismus in Oberösterreich 1700–1820*. Vienna: Verlag für Geschichte und Politik, 1994.
Panzer, Georg W. Friedrich. *Gesammelte Schriften einige Verbesserungen in der römisch-katholischen Kirche betreffend*. Frankfurt: Raspe, 1782.
Papenheim, Martin. *Erinnerung und Unsterblichkeit: Semantische Studien zum Totenkult in Frankreich 1715–1794*. Stuttgart: Klett-Cotta, 1992.

Perronnet, Michel C. *Les Evêques de l'Ancienne France*. 2 vols. Lille: Éditions Garnier Fréres, 1977.
Pfanner, David, 'Charles Blount'. In *The Oxford Dictionary of National Biography*, vol. 6, edited by Matthew Harrison and Brian Harrison. Oxford: Oxford University Press, 2004.
Pfister, Rudolf. *Kirchengeschichte der Schweiz*. Vols 2 and 3. Zurich: Zwingli-Verlag, 1974 and 1985.
Phayer, Michael. 'Politics and Popular Religion: The Cult of the Cross in France 1815–1840'. *Journal of Social History* 11 (1978): 346–365.
Placanica, Augusto. *Cassa Sacra e Beni della Chiesa Nella Calabria del Settecento*. Naples: Giuffré, 1970.
Plongeron, Bernard. *La Vie Quotidienne du Clergé Français au XVIIIe Siècle*. Paris: Hachette, 1974.
Plongeron, Bernard (ed.). *La Religion Populaire dans l'Occident Chrétien: Approches Historiques*. Paris: Edité par Paris, Beauchesne, 1976.
Pohlmeyer, Herrmann Joseph. *Unfehlbarkeit und Souveränität: Die päpstliche Unfehlbarkeit im System der ultramontanen Ekklesiologie des 19. Jahrhunderts*. Mainz: Grünwald, 1975.
Pollack, Detlef. 'Was ist Religion? Probleme der Definition'. *Zeitschrift für Religionswissenschaft* 3 (1995): 163–190.
Priesching, Nicole. *Maria von Mörl (1812–1868): Leben und Bedeutung einer 'Stigmatisierten Jungfrau' aus Tirol im Kontext ultramontaner Frömmigkeit*. Brixen: Verlag A. Weger, 2004.
Prochaska, Frank K. *Women and Philanthropy in 19th Century England*. Oxford: Oxford University Press, 1990.
Raab, Heinrich L. 'Wiederaufbau und Verfassung der Reichskirche'. In *Handbuch der Kirchengeschichte*. Vol. 5, *Die Kirche im Zeitalter des Absolutismus und der Aufklärung*, edited by Hubert Jedin, 152–180. Freiburg im Breisgau: Herder, 1970.
Raab, Heribert. 'Der Untergang der Reichskirche in der großen Säkularisation'. In *Handbuch der Kirchengeschichte*. Vol. 5, *Die Kirche im Zeitalter des Absolutismus und der Aufklärung*, edited by Hubert Jedin, 533–554. Freiburg im Breisgau: Herder, 1970.
Radowitz, Joseph von. *Ausgewählte politische Schriften*. Vol. 1, edited by Wilhelm Corvinus. Regensburg: Habbel, no date.
Rahner, Hugo. *Kirche und Staat im frühen Christentum*. Munich: Kösel, 1961.
Raphael, Lutz, and Heinz Elmar Tenorth (eds). *Ideen als gesellschaftliche Gestaltungskraft im Europa der Neuzeit*. Munich: Oldenbourg, 2006.
Raschke, Joachim. *Soziale Bewegungen: Ein historisch-systematischer Grundriß*. Frankfurt am Main: Campus-Verlag, 1995.
Ravitch, Norman. *Sword and Mitre: Government and Episcopate in France and England in the Age of Aristocracy*. Den Haag: Mouton & Co., 1966.
Rébillon, Armand. 'La Situation Économique du Clergé à la Veille de la Révolution dans les Districts de Rennes, de Fougères et de Vitré'. In *La Révolution Française*, edited by Georges Lefebvre, 328–330. Paris: Alcan, 1930.
Reckwitz, Andreas. *Die Transformation der Kulturtheorien: Zur Entwicklung eines Theorieprogramms*. Weilerswist: Velbrück Wissenschaft, 2000.
Reichardt, Rolf. Das *Blut der Freiheit: Französische Revolution und demokratische Kultur*. Frankfurt am Main: Fischer Taschenbuch-Verlag, 1998.
Reimarus, Hermann Samuel. *Die vornehmsten Wahrheiten der natürlichen Religion in zehn Abhandlungen auf eine begreifliche Art erkläret und gerettet*. Hamburg: Bohn, 1766.

Reinhard, Philipp Christian. *Abriß einer Geschichte der Entstehung und Ausbildung der religiösen Ideen*. Jena: Akademische Buchhandlung, 1794.
Reinhard, Rudolf. 'Die hochadeligen Dynastien in der Reichskirche'. *Römische Quartalsschrift* 83 (1988): 213–235.
Reinhard, Wolfgang. 'Die Verwaltung der Kirche'. In *Deutsche Verwaltungsgeschichte*. Vol. 1, *Vom Spätmittelalter bis zum Ende des Reiches*, edited by Kurt Jeserich, Han Pohl and Georg-Christoph von Unruh, 143–176. 2nd edn. Stuttgart: Deutsche Verlags-Anstalt, 1983.
Reinhard, Wolfgang. 'Die Kirche als Mobilitätskanal der frühneuzeitlichen Gesellschaft'. In *Ständische Gesellschaft und soziale Mobilität*, edited by Winfried Schulze, 333–351. Munich: Oldenbourg, 1988.
Reinhard, Wolfgang. 'Die lateinische Variante von Religion und ihre Bedeutung für die politische Kultur Europas: Ein Versuch in historischer Anthropologie'. *Saeculum* 43 (1992): 231–255.
Reinhard, Wolfgang. *Geschichte der Staatsgewalt: Eine vergleichende Verfassungsgeschichte Europas von den Anfängen bis zur Gegenwart*. 2nd revised edn. Munich: C. H. Beck, 2000.
Reinhold, Franz Hermann von. *System der Christliche Gewissheit*. 2nd completely revised edn. Erlangen: A. Deichert, 1884 [1870–73].
Reinhold, Friedrich Ludwig. *Ideen über das Äußere der evangelischen Gottesverehrung*. Neustrelitz: Ferdinand Albanus, 1805.
Rémond, René. *Religion und Gesellschaft in Europa: Von 1789 bis zur Gegenwart*. Munich: C. H. Beck, 2000.
Reuß, Georg Jakob Ludwig. *Neue evangelische Kirchenagende: Oder was zur gründlichen Untersuchung des protestantischen Cultus in der Kirche und für die Kirche billig zu dieser Zeit geschehen sollte*. Gotha: Beckersche Buchhandlung, 1821.
Revel, Jacques. 'The Uses of Comparison: Religions in the Early Eighteenth Century'. In *Bernard Picart and the First Global Vision of Religion*, edited by Lynn Hunt, Margaret Jacob and Wijnan Mijnhardt, 331–347. Los Angeles: Getty Publications, 2010.
Ribbeck, C. R. *Ueber den Werth des öffentlichen Gottesdienstes und die demselben gebührende Achtung*. Magdeburg: Keil, 1800.
Richter, Ludwig Ämilius. *Geschichte der evangelischen Kirchenverfassung in Deutschland*. Amsterdam: Rodopi, 1970 [Leipzig: Bernh. Tauchnitz, 1851].
Ris, Georg. *Der 'kirchliche Konstitutionalismus': Hauptlinien der Verfassungsbildung in der evangelisch-lutherischen Kirche Deutschlands im 19. Jahrhundert*. Tübingen: Mohr, 1988.
Rosa, Mario. 'The Italian Churches'. In *Church and Society in Catholic Europe of the Eighteenth Century*, edited by William J. Callahan and David Higgs, 66–76. Cambridge: Cambridge University Press, 1979.
Rosenkranz, Gerhard. *Die christliche Mission: Geschichte und Theologie*. Munich: Kaiser, 1977.
Rosenkranz, Karl. *Die Naturreligion: Ein philosophisch-historischer Versuch*. Iserlohn: Langewiesche, 1831.
Rosenzweig, Franz. *Das älteste Systemprogramm des deutschen Idealismus*. Heidelberg: Carl Winter, 1917.
Rousseau, Jean-Jacques. 'Briefe vom Berge'. In *Jean-Jacques Rousseau: Schriften in drei Bänden*. Vol. 2, edited by Henning Ritter, 7–253. Munich/Vienna: Hanser, 1978.
Rousseau, Jean-Jacques. *Gesellschaftsvertrag oder Grundsätze des Staatsrechts*, edited by Hans Brockard. Stuttgart: Reclam, 1979.

Rousseau, Jean-Jacques. *Émile oder Von die Erziehung*. Zurich: Buchclub Verlag, 1989.
Rousseau, Jean-Jacques. *Sozialphilosophische und politische Schriften*. Zurich: Buchclub Verlag, 1989.
Roxborough, John. *Thomas Chalmers: Enthusiast for Mission. The Christian Good of Scotland and the Rise of the Missionary Movement*. Edinburgh: Authentic Media, 1999.
Ruda, Frank. *Hegels Pöbel: Eine Untersuchung der 'Grundlinien der Philosophie des Rechts'*. Konstanz: Konstanz University Press, 2011.
Rule, John. 'Methodism, Popular Beliefs and Village Culture'. In *Popular Culture and Custom in Nineteenth Century England*, edited by Robert D. Storch, 48–70. London: Croom Helm, 1982.
Rupp, Gordon. *Religion in England, 1688–1791*. Oxford: Oxford University Press, 1986.
Rupp, Horst F. '"Jeder Lehrer – ein Religionslehrer": Über den Zusammenhang von Religion und Schule in Deutschland'. In *Beruf und Religion im 19. und 20. Jahrhundert*, edited by Frank-Michael Kuhlemann and Hans-Walter Schmuhl, 86–96. Stuttgart: Kohlhammer, 2003.
Rutz, Andreas. *Bildung, Konfession, Geschlecht: Religiöse Frauengemeinschaften und katholische Mädchenbildung im Rheinland (16.–18. Jahrhundert)*. Mainz: Von Zabern, 2006.
Saint-Simon, Claude-Henri de. *Œvres Completes*. Vol. 23, *Nouveau Christianism: Dialogues entre un Conservateur et un Novateur*. Paris: Anthropos, 1966 [1825].
Sakrausky, Oskar. 'Historische Beschreibung was sich anlässlich des Toleranzpatents in Arriach zugetragen hat'. *Jahrbuch für die Geschichte des Protestantismus in Österreich* 102, no. 3 (1986–87): 3–91.
Sandl, Marcus. 'Heilige Stagnation: Mediale Konfigurationen des Stillstandes in der Großdeutsch-katholischen Geschichtsschreibung des frühen 19. Jahrhunderts'. *Historische Zeitschrift* 285 (2007): 529–563.
Sartori, Joseph von. *Statistische Abhandlung über die Mängel in der Regierungsverfassung der geistlichen Wahlstaaten und von den Mitteln solchen abzuhelfen*. Augsburg: Doll, 1787.
Sassen, Saskia. *Territory, Authority, Rights: From Medieval to Global Assemblages*. Princeton, NJ: Princeton University Press, 2006.
Saurer, Edith. 'Frauen und Priester: Beichtgespräche im frühen 19. Jahrhundert'. In *Arbeit, Frömmigkeit und Eigensinn: Studien zur historischen Kulturforschung*, edited by Richard von Dülmen, 141–170. Frankfurt am Main: Fischer Taschenbuch-Verlag, 1990.
Saurer, Edith. 'Religiöse Praxis und Sinnesverwirrung: Kommentare zur religiösen Melancholiediskussion'. In *Dynamik der Tradition: Studien zur historischen Kulturforschung*, edited by Richard von Dülmen, 213–239, 301–305. Frankfurt am Main: Fischer Taschenbuch-Verlag, 1992.
Savart, Claude. *Les Catholiques en France au XIXe Siècle: Le Témoignage du Livre Religieux*. Paris: Beauchesne, 1985.
Sawicki, Diethart. *Leben mit den Toten, Geisterglauben und die Entstehung des Spiritismus in Deutschland, 1770–1900*. Paderborn/Munich/Vienna/Zurich: Ferdinand Schöningh, 2002.
Schaich, Michael. 'The Funerals of the British Monarchy'. In *Monarchy and Religion*, edited by Michael Schaich, 421–450. Oxford: Oxford University Press, 2007.
Scharfe, Martin. *Evangelische Andachtsbilder: Studien zur Intention und Funktion des Bildes in der Frömmigkeitsgeschichte vornehmlich des schwäbischen Raumes*. Stuttgart: Müller & Gräff, 1968.

Schelling, Friedrich Wilhelm Joseph von. *Sämtliche Werke*. Vol. 2.2, *Philosophie der Mythologie*. Stuttgart/Augsburg: Cotta, 1857.

Schelling, Friedrich Wilhelm Joseph von. *Philosophie der Offenbarung (1841/42)*, edited by Manfred Frank. Frankfurt am Main: Suhrkamp Taschenbuch, 1977.

Schenda, Rudolf. *Volk ohne Buch: Studien zur Sozialgeschichte der populären Lesestoffe 1770-1910*. 3rd edn. Frankfurt am Main: Vittorio Klostermann, 1988 [Munich: Deutscher Taschenbuch Verlag, 1977].

Schieder, Wolfgang. 'Kirche und Revolution: Sozialgeschichtliche Aspekte der Trierer Wallfahrt von 1844'. *Archiv für Sozialgeschichte* 14 (1974): 419-454.

Schilling, Heinz. 'Religion und Gesellschaft in der calvinistischen Republik der Vereinigten Niederlande – "Öffentlichkeitskirche" und Säkularisation. Ehe und Hebammenwesen. Presbyterien und politische Partizipation'. In *Kirche und gesellschaftlicher Wandel in deutschen und niederländischen Städten der werdenden Neuzeit*, edited by Franz Petri, 195-250. Cologne/Vienna: Böhlau, 1980.

Schilling, Heinz. 'Das Calvinistische Presbyterium in der Stadt Gronigen während der Frühen Neuzeit und im ersten Viertel des 19. Jahrhunderts: Verfassung und Sozialprofil'. In *Bürgerliche Eliten in den Niederlanden und in Nordwestdeutschland. Studien zur Sozialgeschichte des europäischen Bürgertums im Mittelalter und in der Neuzeit*, edited by Heinz Schilling and Herman Diedericks, 195-273. Cologne/Vienna: Böhlau, 1985.

Schlaich, Klaus. *Kollegialtheorie: Kirche, Recht und Staat in der Aufklärung*. Munich: Claudius, 1969.

Schlatter, Wilhelm. *Geschichte der Basler Mission 1815-1915*. Vol. 1. Basel: Verlag der Basler Missionsbuchhandlung, 1910.

Schlegel, Friedrich. *Kritische Friedrich-Schlegel-Ausgabe*. Vol. 9, *Philosophie der Geschichte: In 18 Vorlesungen gehalten zu Wien im Jahre 1828*. Munich/Paderborn/Vienna: Ferdinand Schöningh, 1971.

Schleiermacher, Friedrich. *Der christliche Glaube nach den Grundsätzen der evangelischen Kirche im Zusammenhang dargestellt*. 2 vols. Berlin: Reimer, 1821-22.

Schleiermacher, Friedrich. *Über die Religion: Reden an die Gebildeten unter ihren Verächtern (1799)*. Berlin/New York: De Gruyter, 1999.

Schlögl, Rudolf. *Glaube und Religion in der Säkularisierung: Die katholische Stadt – Köln, Aachen, Münster 1700-1840*. Munich: Oldenbourg, 1995.

Schlögl, Rudolf. 'Sünderin, Heilige oder Hausfrau? Katholische Kirche und weibliche Frömmigkeit um 1800'. In *Wunderbare Erscheinungen: Frauen und katholische Frömmigkeit im 19. und 20. Jahrhundert*, edited by Irmtraud Götz von Olenhusen, 13-50. Paderborn: Ferdinand Schöningh, 1995.

Schlögl, Rudolf. 'Alchemie und Avantgarde: Das Utopische bei Rosenkreuzern und Freimaurern'. In *Die Politisierung des Utopischen im 18. Jahrhundert*, edited by Monika Neugebauer Wölk and Richard Saage, 117-142. Tübingen: Niemeyer, 1996.

Schlögl, Rudolf. 'Öffentliche Gottesverehrung und privater Glaube in der Frühen Neuzeit. Beobachtungen zur Bedeutung von Kirchenzucht und Frömmigkeit für die Abgrenzung privater Sozialräume'. In *Das Öffentliche und Private in der Vormoderne*, edited by Gerd Melville and Peter von Moos, 165-209. Cologne/Vienna: Böhlau, 1998.

Schlögl, Rudolf. 'Von der Weisheit zur Esoterik: Themen und Paradoxien im frühen Rosenkreuzerdiskurs'. In *Aufklärung und Esoterik*, edited by Monika Neugebauer-Wölk, 53-86. Hamburg: Meiner, 1999.

Schlögl, Rudolf. 'Der Glaube Alteuropas und die moderne Welt: Zum Verhältnis von Säkularisation und Säkularisierung'. In *Zerfall und Wiederbeginn: Vom Erzbistum zum*

*Bistum Mainz (1792/97–1830). Ein Vergleich*, edited by Walter G. Rödel and Regina E. Schwertfeger, 63–82. Würzburg: Echter, 2002.

Schlögl, Rudolf. 'Rationalisierung als Entsinnlichung religiöser Praxis. Zur sozialen und medialen Form von Religion in der Neuzeit'. In *Die Säkularisation im Prozess der Säkularisierung Europas*, edited by Peter Blickle and Rudolf Schlögl, 37–64. Epfendorf: Bibliotheca-Academia-Verlag, 2005.

Schlögl, Rudolf. 'Kommunikation und Vergesellschaftung unter Anwesenden: Formen des Sozialen und ihre Transformation in der Frühen Neuzeit'. *Geschichte und Gesellschaft* 34 (2008): 155–224.

Schlögl, Rudolf. 'Hierarchie und Funktion: Zur Transformation der stratifikatorischen Ordnung der Frühen Neuzeit'. *Zeitsprünge* 15 (2011): 47–63.

Schlögl, Rudolf. 'Körper, Seele und Verstand: Medien der Subjektivierung in der Frühen Neuzeit'. In *Der Mensch in Gesellschaft: Zur Vorgeschichte des modernen Subjekts in der Frühen Neuzeit*, edited by Michael Hohlstein, Rudolf Schlögl and Isabelle Schürch, 137–177. Paderborn: Ferdinand Schöningh, 2019.

Schmale, Wolfgang, and Nan L. Dodde (eds). *Revolution des Wissens? Europa und seine Schulen im Zeitalter der Aufklärung 1750–1825: Ein Handbuch zur europäischen Schulgeschichte*. Bochum: Winkler, 1991.

Schmidt, Arno. *Fouqué und einige seiner Zeitgenossen*. Zurich: Haffmans, 1987.

Schmidt, Heinrich Richard. '"Verfall der Religion": Epochenwende um 1700'. In *Die Säkularisation im Prozess der Säkularisierung Europas*, edited by Peter Blickle and Rudolf Schlögl, 245–258. Epfendorf: Bibliotheca-Academia-Verlag, 2005.

Schmidt, Kurt Dietrich. *Die katholische Reform und die Gegenreformation*. Göttingen: Vandenhoeck & Ruprecht, 1975.

Schmidt, Kurt Dietrich, and Ernst Wolf (eds). *Die Kirche in ihrer Geschichte: Ein Handbuch*. Göttingen: Vandenhoeck & Ruprecht, 1961–2019.

Schmidt, Peer. *Die Privatisierung des Besitzes der toten Hand in Spanien: Die Säkularisation unter König Karl IV in Andalusien 1798–1808*. Stuttgart: Steiner, 1990.

Schmidt, Peter. *Das Collegium Germanicum in Rom und die Germaniker: Zur Funktion eines römischen Ausländerseminars 1552–1914*. Tübingen: Niemeyer, 1984.

Schmidt-Biggemann, Wilhelm. *Philosphia perennis: Historische Umrisse abendländischer Spiritualität in Antike, Mittelalter und Früher Neuzeit*. Frankfurt am Main: Suhrkamp, 1998.

Schmid-Tschirren, Christina M. *Von der Säkularisation zur Separation: Der Umgang des Staates mit den Kirchengütern in den evangelisch-reformierten und paritätischen Kantonen der Schweiz im 19. Jahrhundert*. Zurich/Basel/Geneva: Schulthess, 2011.

Schmiedl, Joachim. *Mariannische Religiosität in Aachen: Frömmigkeitsformen einer katholischen Industriestadt des 19. Jahrhunderts*. Altenberg: Oros-Verlag, 1994.

Schmitt, Carl. *Römischer Katholizismus und politische Form*. Stuttgart: Klett-Cotta, 1984.

Schnabel, Franz. *Deutsche Geschichte im 19. Jahrhundert*. Vol. 4, *Die religiösen Kräfte*. Freiburg: Herder, 1937.

Schneider, Bernhard. 'Entwicklungstendenzen rheinischer Frömmigkeits- und Kirchengeschichte in der ersten Hälfte des 19. Jahrhunderts: Tradition und Modernisierung'. *Archiv für rheinische Kirchengeschichte* 48 (1996): 57–195.

Schneider, Bernhard. *Katholiken auf die Barrikaden: Europäische Revolutionen und deutsche katholische Presse 1815–1848*. Paderborn/Munich/Vienna/Zurich: Ferdinand Schöningh, 1998.

Scholz, Natalie. *Die imaginierte Restauration: Repräsentationen der Monarchie im Frankreich Ludwigs XVIII*. Darmstadt: Wissenschaftliche Buchgesellschaft, 2006.
Scholz, Natalie, and Christina Schröer (eds). *Représentation et Pouvoir: La Politique Symbolique en France 1789–1830*. Rennes: Presses universitaires de Rennes, 2007.
Schorn-Schütte, Luise. *Evangelische Geistlichkeit in der Frühenneuzeit: Deren Anteil an der Entfaltung frühmoderner Staatlichkeit und Gesellschaft. Dargestellt am Beispiel des Fürstentums Braunschweig-Wolfenbüttel, der Landgrafschaft Hessen-Kassel und der Stadt Braunschweig*. Gütersloh: Gütersloher Verlags-Haus, 1996.
Schorn-Schütte, Luise. 'Zwischen Amt und Beruf: Der Prediger als Wächter, "Seelenhirt" oder Volkslehrer. Evangelische Geistlichkeit im Alten Reich und in der Eidgenossenschaft im 18. Jahrhundert'. In *Evangelische Pfarrer: Zur sozialen und politischen Rolle einer bürgerlichen Gruppe in der deutschen Gesellschaft des 18. bis 20. Jahrhunderts*, edited by Luise Schorn-Schütte and Robert von Friedeburg, 1–35. Stuttgart: Kohlhammer, 1997.
Schrörs, Heinrich. *Die Kölner Wirren 1837: Studien zu ihrer Geschichte*. Berlin: Dümmler, 1927.
Schult, Richard. '"… das Schiff der Revolution in den von ihm bestimmten Hafen zu bringen": Jacques-Louis David und die Krönung Napoleons'. *Geschichte in Wissenschaft und Unterricht* 12 (1992): 728–742.
Schulte, Aloys. *Der Adel und die deutsche Kirche im Mittelalter: Studien zur Sozial-, Rechts- und Kirchengeschichte*. 3rd edn. Darmstadt: Wissenschaftliche Buchgesellschaft, 1958 [Stuttgart: F. Enke, 1910].
Schulte-Umberg, Thomas. *Profession und Charisma: Herkunft und Ausbildung des Klerus im Bistum Münster 1776–1940*. Paderborn/Munich/Vienna/Zurich: Ferdinand Schöningh, 1999.
Schulte-Umberg, Thomas. 'Professionalisierung des katholischen Klerus: Forschungsstrategien und Perspektiven am Beispiel des Bistums Münster'. In *Beruf und Religion im 19. und 20. Jahrhundert*, edited by Frank Michael Kuhlemann and Hans-Walter Schmuhl, 28–50. Stuttgart: Kohlhammer, 2003.
Schwegler, Urban. 'Von Priestermission und Laienmitarbeit: Organisation und Bau katholischer Missionsgesellschaften auf dem Hintergrund der katholischen Weltmission. Am Beispiel der Missionsgesellschaft Bethlehem, Immensee (SMB)'. In *Weltmission und religiöse Organisationen: Protestantische Missionsgesellschaften im 19. und 20. Jahrhundert*, edited by Arthur Bogner, Bernd Holtwick and Hartmann Tyrell, 397–423. Würzburg: Ergon Verlag, 2004.
Schwengelbeck, Matthias. 'Monarchische Herrschaftsrepräsentationen zwischen Konsens und Konflikt: Zum Wandel des Huldigungs- und Inthronisationszeremoniells im 19. Jahrhundert'. In *Die Sinnlichkeit der Macht. Herrschaft und Repräsentation seit der Frühen Neuzeit*, edited by Jan Andres, Alexa Geisthövel and Matthias Schwengelbeck, 123–162. Frankfurt am Main: Campus-Verlag, 2005.
Scoppola, Pietro. *Chiesa e Stato Nella Storia d'Italia: Storia Documentaria dall'Unità alla Republica*. Bari: Laterza, 1967.
Sevrin, Ernest. *Les Missions Religieuses en France sous la Restauration 1815–1830*. Vol. 1. Paris: Procure des Prêtres de la Miséricorde, 1948.
Sharpe, Eric J. *Comparative Religion: A History*. 2nd edn. Eastbourne: Open Court, 1986.
Sicard, Augustin. *L'Ancien Clergé de France: Les Evêques avant la Révolution*. 5th edn. Paris: Gabalda, 1912 [Partis: V. Lecoffre, *c*. 1893].
Simon, Alois. *Le Cardinal Sterckx et son Temps 1792–1867*. 2 vols. Wetteren: Éditions Scaldis, 1950.

Skinner, S. A. *Tractarians and the 'Condition of England': The Social and Political Thought of the Oxford Movement*. Oxford: Clarendon Press, 2004.

Skuy, David. *Assassination, Politics and Miracles: France and the Royalist Reaction of 1820*. London: McGill-Queen's University Press, 2003.

Sösemann, Bernd. 'Preußische Königsjubiläen als Ritual der Kommunikation: Dignitätspolitik in höfischer und öffentlicher Inszenierung von 1701 bis 1901'. In *Preußische Stile. Ein Staat als Kunststück*, edited by Patrick Bahners and Gerd Roellecke, 114–124. Stuttgart: Klett-Cotta, 2001.

Spalding, Johann Joachim. *Die Bestimmung des Menschen: Kritische Ausgabe I/I*. Tübingen: Mohr Siebeck, 2006.

Spamer, Adolf. *Das kleine Andachtsbild vom XVI bis zum XX Jahrhundert*. Munich: Bruckmann, 1930.

St Claire, William. *The Reading Nation in the Romantic Period*. Cambridge: Cambridge University Press, 2004.

Stahl, Friedrich J. *Das monarchisches Prinzip: Eine staatsrechtlich-politische Abhandlung*. Heidelberg: Mohr, 1845.

Stahl, Friedrich J. *Der Protestantismus als politisches Prinzip*. Berlin: no publisher, 1853.

Stahl, Friedrich J. *Der christliche Staat und sein Verhältnis zu Deismus und Judentum: Eine durch die Verhandlungen des Vereinigten Landtags hervorgerufene Abhandlung*. Berlin: Oehmigke, 1858.

Stambolis, Barbara. *Religiöse Festkultur: Tradition und Neuformierung katholischer Frömmigkeit im 19. und 20. Jahrhundert*. Paderborn/Munich/Vienna/Zurich: Ferdinand Schöningh, 2000.

Stamm-Kuhlmann, Thomas. *König in Preußens großer Zeit: Friedrich Wilhelm III: der Melancholiker auf dem Thron*. Berlin: Siedler, 1992.

Stanley, Brian. *The History of Baptist Missionary Societies 1792–1992*. Edinburgh: T&T Clark, 1992.

Stanley, Brian. 'Christian Missions, Antislavery and the Claims of Humanity 1813–1873'. In *The Cambridge History of Christianity*. Vol. 8, edited by Sheridan Gilley and Brian Stanley, 443–458. Cambridge: Cambridge University Press, 2006.

Stausberg, Michael. *Faszination Zarathustra: Zoroaster und die europäische Religionsgeschichte der Frühen Neuzeit*. Berlin/New York: De Gruyter, 1998.

Steins, Achim. 'Der ordentliche Zivilprozeß vor dem bischöflichen Offizial: Ein Beitrag zur Geschichte des gelehrten Prozesses in Deutschland im Spätmittelalter'. *Zeitschrift für Rechtsgeschichte* 59 (1973): 191–262.

Stollenwerk, Alexander. *Der Deutschkatholizismus in den Preußischen Rheinlanden*. Mainz: Gesellschaft für Mittelrheinische Kirchengeschichte, 1971.

Stolz, Fritz. *Grundzüge der Religionswissenschaft*. Göttingen: Vandenhoeck & Ruprecht, 1985.

Stroumsa, Guy G. *A New Science: The Discovery of Religion in the Age of Reason*. Cambridge, MA: Harvard University Press, 2010.

Süßmilch, Johann Peter. *Versuch eines Beweises, dass die erste Sprache ihren Ursprung nicht vom Menschen, sondern allein vom Schöpfer erhalten habe, in der Akademischen Versammlung vorgelesen und zum Druck gegeben*. Berlin: no publisher, 1766.

Sykes, Norman. *Church and State in England in the XVIIIth Century*. Hamden, CT: Archon Books, 1962.

Tackett, Timothy. *Priest and Parish in Eighteenth-Century France: A Social and Political Study of the Curés in a Diocese of Dauphiné 1750–1791*. Princeton, NJ: Princeton University Press, 1977.

Tackett, Timothy. *Religion, Revolution, and Regional Culture in Eighteenth-Century France: The Ecclesiastical Oath of 1791*. Princeton, NJ: Princeton University Press, 1986.
Tarde, Gabriel. *Die Gesetze der Nachahmung*. Frankfurt am Main: Suhrkamp, 2003.
Targoff, Ramie. *Common Prayer: The Language of Public Devotion in Early Modern England*. Chicago, IL: University of Chicago Press, 2001.
Tholuck, August. *Die Lehre von der Sünde und vom Versöhner oder die wahre Weihe des Zweiflers*. Hamburg: Friedrich Perthes, 1823.
Thomasius, Friedrich Christian. *Ueber Veredelung des christlichen Kultus durch Hilfe der Aesthetik: Mit Hinsicht auf die kirchliche Verfassung auf die preußischen Provinzen in Franken*. Nürnberg: no publisher, 1803.
Tindal, Matthew. *Christianity as Old as Creation*. London: Thoemmes Press, 1995 [London: Thomas Astley, 1730].
Tocqueville, Alexis de. *L'Ancien Régime et la Révolution*. Revised and corrected edn. Paris: Éditions Gallimard, 1967.
Tocqueville, Alexis de. *Der alte Staat und die Revolution (1856)*. Munich: Deutscher Taschenbuch-Verlag, 1978.
Toscani, Xenio. *Il Clero Lombardo dall'Ancien Regime alla Restaurazione*. Bologna: Il Mulino, 1979.
Tylor, Edward Burnett. *Primitive Culture*. Vol. 2, *Religion in Primitive Culture*. New York: Harper & Row, 1958 [London: John Murray, 1871].
Tyrell, Hartmann. 'Weltgesellschaft, Weltmission und religiöse Organisation – Einleitung'. In *Weltmission und religiöse Organisationen. Protestantische Missionsgesellschaften im 19. und 20. Jahrhundert*, edited by Arthur Bogner, Bernd Holtwick and Hartmann Tyrell, 13–134. Würzburg: Ergon Verlag, 2004.
Valjavec, Fritz. 'Das Woellnersche Religionsedikt und seine geschichtliche Bedeutung'. In *Fritz Valjavec: Ausgewählte Aufsätze*, edited by Karl A. Fischer and Mathias Bernath, 294–306. Munich: Oldenbourg, 1963.
Veer, Peter van der. 'Spirituality in Modern Society'. *Social Research* 76 (2009): 1077–1120.
Veit, Ludwig Andreas, and Ludwig Lenhart. *Kirche und Volksfrömmigkeit im Zeitalter des Barock*. Freiburg: Herder, 1956.
Venard, Marc. *Das Zeitalter der Vernunft*. Freiburg im Breisgau: Herder, 1998.
Vico, Giambattista. *Die neue Wissenschaft: Über die gemeinschaftliche Natur der Völker; Nach der Ausgabe von 1744*, translated with introduction by Erich Auerbach. 2nd edn. Berlin: De Gruyter, 2000.
Virgin, Peter. *The Church in an Age of Negligence: Ecclesiastical Structure and Problems of Church Reform 1700–1840*. Cambridge: Clarke, 1989.
Vogelsang, J. D. *Lehrbuch der christlichen Sittenlehre*. Bonn: Habicht, 1834.
Voltaire (François-Marie Arouet). *Essai sur les Mœurs et l'Esprit des Nations et sur les Principaux Faits de l'Histoire Depuis Charlemagne Jusqu'à Louis XIII*. Paris: Librairie Hachette et Compagnie, 1866.
Vovelle, Michel. *Religion et Révolution: La Déchristianisation de l'An II*. Paris: Hachette, 1976.
Vovelle, Michel. 'Die andere Entchristianisierung'. In *Sozialgeschichte der Aufklärung in Frankreich*. Part 2, edited by Hans Ulrich Gumbrecht, Rolf Reichardt and Thomas Schleich, 201–228. Munich: Oldenbourg, 1981.
Walder, Ernst. *Staat und Kirche in Frankreich*. Vol. 2, *Vom Kultus der Vernunft zur napoleonischen Staatskirche*. Bern: Lang, 1953.
Wandruszka, Adam. *Leopold II: Erzherzog von Österreich, Großherzog von Toskana, König von Ungarn und Böhmen, Römischer Kaiser*. 2 vols. Munich: Herold, 1965.

Waquet, Françoise. *Les Fêtes Royals sous la Restauration ou l'Ancien Régime Retrouvé*. Geneva: Edité par Arts et Métiers Graphiques, 1981.
Warburton, William. *The Divine Legation of Moses Demonstrated on the Principles of a Religious Deist, from the Omission of the Doctrine of a Future State of Reward and Punishment in the Jewish Dispensation*. London: Printed for F. Gyles, 1738.
Ward, Reginald. 'John Wesley'. *Theologische Realenzyklopädie* 35 (2003): 657–666.
Ward, William R. 'The Tithe Question in England in the Early Nineteenth Century'. *Journal of Ecclesiastical History* 16 (1965): 67–81.
Ward, William. *Religion and Society in England 1790–1850*. London: Batsford, 1972.
Wayne, Hanley. *The Genesis of the Napoleonic Propaganda 1796–1799*. New York: Columbia University Press, 2005.
Weber, Christoph. *Aufklärung und Orthodoxie am Mittelrhein 1820–1850*. Munich/Paderborn/Vienna: Ferdinand Schöningh, 1973.
Weber, Christoph. *Familienkanonikate und Patronatsbistümer: Ein Beitrag zur Geschichte von Adel und Klerus im neuzeitlichen Italien*. Berlin: Duncker & Humblot, 1988.
Weedon, Alexis. *Victorian Publishing: The Economics of Book Production for a Mass Market 1836–1916*. Aldershot: Routledge, 2003.
Wehler, Hans-Ulrich. *Deutsche Gesellschaftsgeschichte*. Vol. 1, *Vom Feudalismus des Alten Reiches bis zur defensiven Modernisierung der Reformära 1700–1815*. Munich: Beck, 1987.
Wehler, Hans-Ulrich. *Deutsche Gesellschaftsgeschichte*. Vol. 2, *Von der Reformation bis zur industriellen und politischen 'Deutschen Doppelrevolution' 1815–1845/49*. 2nd edn. Munich: Beck, 1989.
Weiss, Otto. *Die Redemptoristen in Bayern (1790–1909): Ein Beitrag zur Geschichte des Ultramontanismus*. Vol. 2. Munich: EOS, 1977.
Weiss, Otto. 'Der Ultramontanismus: Grundlagen – Vorgeschichte – Struktur'. *Zeitschrift für bayerische Landesgeschichte* 41 (1978): 821–877.
Weißenbach, Josef Anton. *Von dem Mißbrauch beim Mariendienst und was da abzuschaffen, einzuschränken, beyzubehalten sey: Ein Hausbuch wider die Glaubensfeger*. No place, 1786.
Weltecke, Dorothea. *'Der Narr spricht: Es ist kein Gott': Atheismus, Unglauben und Glaubenszweifel vom 12. Jahrhundert bis zur Neuzeit*. Frankfurt am Main: Campus-Verlag, 2010.
Werminghoff, Albert. *Verfassungsgeschichte der deutschen Kirche im Mittelalter*, 2nd edn. Leipzig: Teubner, 1913.
Wernle, Paul. *Der schweizerische Protestantismus im XVIII. Jahrhundert*. 2 vols. Tübingen: Mohr, 1923.
Wessenberg, Ignaz Heinrich von. *Ueber Schwärmerei: Historisch-philosophische Betrachtungen mit Rücksicht auf die jetzige Zeit*. Heilbronn: Landherr, 1835.
Wiebel-Fanderl, Olivia. *Die Wallfahrt Altötting: Kultformen und Wallfahrtsleben im 19. Jahrhundert*. Passau: Verein für Ostbairische Heimatforschung, 1982.
Wienfort, Monika. *Monarchie in der bürgerlichen Gesellschaft. Deutschland und England von 1640 bis 1848*. Göttingen: Vandenhoeck & Ruprecht, 1993.
Wigelsworth, Jeffrey. *Deism in Enlightenment England: Theology, Politics and Newtonian Public Science*. Manchester: Manchester University Press, 2009.
Willms, Johannes. *Napoleon: Eine Biographie*. Munich: Beck, 2005.
Windischmann, Carl Joseph Hieronimus. *Ueber Etwas, das der Heilkunst notthut: Ein Versuch der Vereinigung dieser Philosophie mit der christlichen Philosophie*. Leipzig: Cnobloch, 1824.

Winkel, Heidemarie. 'Christliche Religion und ihre Sinnformen der Selbstbeschreibung: Mission und Ökumene als Grundpfeiler des Wandels religiöser Wissensformen'. *Geschichte und Gesellschaft* 36, no. 2 (2010): 285–316.
Wirth, Jean. 'La Naissance du Concept de Croyance (XIIe–XVIIIe Siècle)'. *Bibliothèque d'Humanisme et Renaissance* 44 (1983): 7–58.
Wirth, Johann G. *Das Nationalfest der Deutschen zu Hambach, unter Mitwirkung eines Redaktionsausschusses beschrieben*. 2 vols. Neustadt: Christmann, 1832.
Wittgenstein, Ludwig. *Philosophische Untersuchungen: Kritisch-genetische Edition*. Frankfurt am Main: Suhrkamp, 2001.
Wolf, Hubert. *Index: Der Vatikan und die verbotenen Bücher*. Munich: Beck, 2006.
Wolffe, John. *Great Deaths: Grieving, Religion and Nationhood in Victorian and Edwardian Britain*. Oxford/New York: Oxford University Press, 2000.
Wülfing, Wulf. 'Die heilige Luise von Preußen: Zur Mythisierung einer Figur der Geschichte in der deutschen Literatur des 19. Jahrhunderts'. In *Bewegung und Stillstand in Metaphern und Mythen: Fallstudien zum Verhältnis von elementarem Wissen und Literatur im 19. Jahrhundert*, edited by Jürgen Link and Wulf Wülfing, 233–258. Stuttgart: Klett-Cotta, 1984.
Wyss-Giacosa, Paola von. *Religionsbilder der frühen Aufklärung: Bernard Picart's Tafeln für die 'Ceremonies et Coutûmes Religieuses de Tous les Peuples du Monde'*. Wabern/Bern: Benteli, 2006.
Yorke, Henri Redhead. *Paris et la France sous le Consulat: Les Homes, les Institutions, les Mœurs*, translated by Guillaume Lerolle. Paris: Librairie académique Perrin & Co., 1921.
Zander, Helmut. 'Höhere Erkenntnis: Die Erfindung des Fernrohrs und die Konstruktion der erweiterten Wahrnehmungsfähigkeit zwischen dem 17. und dem 20. Jahrhundert'. In *Trancemedien und Neue Medien um 1900: Ein anderer Blick auf die Moderne*, edited by Markus Hahn and Erhard Schüttpelz, 17–56. Bielefeld: Transcript-Verlag, 2009.
Zedelmaier, Helmut. *Der Anfang der Geschichte: Studien zur Ursprungsdebatte im 18. Jahrhundert*. Hamburg: Meiner, 2003.
Zeller, Eduard. 'Die Annahme einer Perfektibilität des Christentums, Historisch und dogmatisch untersucht'. *Theologische Jahrbücher* 1 (1842): 1–50.
Zeller, Eduard. 'Über das Wesen der Religion'. *Theologische Jahrbücher* 4 (1845): 393–430.
Ziehmann, Benjamin. 'Säkularisierung, Konfessionalisierung, Organisationsbildung: Dimensionen der Sozialgeschichte der Religion im langen 19. Jahrhundert'. *Archiv für Sozialgeschichte* 47 (2007): 485–508.

# Index

Aachen 157, 164
Abel, Karl von 82
abstract concept of religion 208–23
Act of Union (1801) 79
Adelung, Johann Christoph 219
*Agende* 83
agrarian economy 38, 72, 74
*Allgemeines Landrecht für die Preußischen Staaten* 29, 76, 82–3
altar 84, 116, 117, 207
*Altbayern* 39
Amort, Eusebius 189
Anabaptists 18, 28, 177
angels 186
Anglican Church *see* Church of England
animal magnetism 189, 257
anthropology 92, 168, 222
anti-clericalism 38
Apostolic church 100
Aquinas, Thomas 197
archdeacons 14, 134
aristocracy 12–13
　high clergy 15, 22, 23–4, 32–3, 34, 35–6, 71, 134
　Reformed Church and 29, 30
armies 126
Arndt, Ernst Moritz 123
Arndt, Johannes 143
Arnim, Achim von 111
Asad, Talal 250
atheism 66, 199
atomization 89–91
Auerbach, Erich 242
*Aufheben* 196
Augustinian theology 47, 251
Aulard, Alphonse 57
autonomy 138–42
Awakened Christians 149, 172

Baader, Franz von 87, 96, 152
Bacon, Francis 208
baptism 160, 161

Baptist Missionary Society 149
Baptists 144
Barat, Sophie 185
Baroque piety 52, 168
Basel Evangelical Missionary Society 149
Batavian Revolution 29
Bauer, Friedrich Christian 241–2
Bavaria 19, 39, 53–4, 71, 82, 103, 108, 118–19, 168
Bayle, Pierre 199
Beck, Louise 173
Becker, Karoline 174
Belgium 49, 134
Benedict XIV (Pope) 189
benedictions 107
benefices 14, 16, 32, 43, 44, 72, 73, 74
Berlin Missionary Association 150
Berry, Charles Ferdinand, Duc de 106, 113, 114, 164
Bible societies 150
bishops 14, 17, 134
　episcopal independence 132
　Gallican Church 35, 37
　prince-bishops 71
　Reformed churches 29, 31
Blarer, Melchior 52
Blount, Charles 196, 198, 200
Blumenberg, Hans 249
Bluntschli, Johann Caspar 251, 256
body politic 40
Bolingbroke, Henry St John, 1st Viscount 200, 201
Bonaparte, Joseph 70
Bonaparte, Napoleon 56, 67–8, 69, 77, 229
　coronation 106, 125
　monarchical legacy 103, 105–6, 108–9, 118, 120, 121–2
Book of Common Prayer 170–1
Borutta, Manuel 249
Bossuet, Jacques-Bénigne Lignel 22, 171, 205
Brennwald, Leonhard 40

Brentano, Clemens 111, 152, 165, 183
Brienne, Loménie de (Bishop) 58
British and Foreign Bible Society 150
British national identity 120–1
Brunner, Otto 174
Buffon, Georges-Louis Leclerc, Comte de 205, 224
bulls of circumscription 82
*Bundesakte* 81, 84
bureaucratization 131
Burke, Edmund 55, 75, 87, 89, 90
*Burschenschaften* 118

calendar 65, 105, 113, 118
Calvinism 18, 19
    Netherlands 27–8, 29
camarilla 182
canon law 13, 15
canonizations 132, 189
canons 14, 20, 24
Capellari, Mauro 133
Cardano, Girolamo 199
Carlsbad Decrees (1817) 102, 136
Casanova, José 250
Catherine the Great 49
Catholic Church *see* Gallican Church; Roman Catholic church
Catholic Emancipation 112, 255
celibacy 37, 44, 177, 188, 191
censorship 102
central Europe 252
charisma 80, 89, 98, 108, 144, 145, 146, 148, 152, 164, 165, 171–2
charity 176, 185
Charles X of France 109, 111, 118, 122
Charlotte Augusta, Princess of Wales 113–14
Chastenet, Antoine-Hyacinthe, comte de 172
chastity 188
Chateaubriand, René de 78, 85, 87, 88, 92, 106, 110, 114
Cherbury, Edward Herbert, 1st Baron 196, 197–8, 200, 201, 206
Chevaliers du Foi 109–10, 152
*chiesa ricettizia* 43
chivalric novels 163
Christian Mission Society 149
Christian Socialism 87, 97

Christian symbolism 105, 106, 108, 169, 170
Church Act (1836) 74
church maintenance funds 27
church membership 140
Church of England 18
    Book of Common Prayer 170–1
    church and state 137, 141
    civil society and 94, 111–12
    clerical training and duties 138
    decline in the influence of the institutional church 155, 156, 157, 160, 161
    elementary school system 142
    liturgy and ritual 169, 170
    mixed marriages 141
    Oxford Movement 139, 152, 158
    parish clergy 43
    plurality and 79–81
    property 20, 55
        hierarchy and 26–7
    secularization and 72–5
    social and organizational structure 26, 27
    Tractarians 170
Church of Scotland 137–8
church organization 17–19
    autonomy and membership 138–42
    hierarchy and elites 32–7
    hierarchy and property 19–27
    institution of grace 131–5, 151
    institutionalization 31
    Methodism 145–6
    nationalization 30
    parish churches 17, 18, 19, 27–31
    parish clergy 37–8
        income and background 39–43, 73
        patronage 43–5
        spiritual callings 42, 45
    Protestant state churches 135–8
    reforms 45–6, 68, 69
        France 46–8
        Habsburg empire 49–54
        Jesuits 46, 48–9
church property 13–14, 32
    pre-Revolutionary Europe 13–14, 16, 19–27
    secularization and 68
        England 72–5

Imperial Church 71–2
Italy and Spain 69–70
church services 167–9
rites of passage 159–161, 256
Cicero 213
citizen kings 253
civil marriages 83, 84, 140
civil society 85–6 (*see also* pluralism; secularization)
atomization 89–91
church as political form 97–101
concept of the nation 104, 116–24
constitutions 103, 107
de-Christianization during the French Revolution 61–3
family 88–9
monarchy and 96, 98–100, 101, 103–4, 105–16, 124
morality 86–8
natural religion and 196, 197–200, 201, 202
political religion 91–7
political space of participation 101–5
religion and politics 124–7
tradition 90–1
civil wars 75, 197
clairvoyance 172–3
Clapham Sect 152
Clausewitz, Carl von 11
Clement XIII (Pope) 33
Clement XIV (Pope) 49
clergy (*see also* bishops; parish clergy)
aristocratic high clergy 15, 22, 23–4, 134
French Revolution and 61–2, 63–4
pre-Revolutionary Europe 14–15
training 135, 138
clientilism 44
Codex Juris Canonici 13, 15
Coke, Thomas 156, 157
Coleridge, Samuel Taylor 89, 94, 100
collegialism 31
Collegium Germanicum 34
Cologne Troubles 83, 162
colonialism 195
commonwealth 89
communication structures 193, 194, 195, 226–8

Communion 11, 52, 80, 84, 106, 118, 140, 155–7, 160, 168, 169, 171
comparative phenomenology of religion 214, 242
Condillac, Étienne Bonnot de 226, 227
confession/confessors 187, 190–1
confessionalization 18, 19, 127, 130
plurality 77–85
Congress of Vienna 69, 98, 131
consciousness 253–5, 237, 242
conservatism
England 89, 100
Prussia 98–9, 111
Roman Catholic church 87, 93, 98
consistories 11
Lutheran church 29, 30
Constant, Benjamin 219, 221
*constitution civile* 58–61
*Constitution Civile du Clergé* 60
constitutions 103, 107
Contract of Poissy (1561) 22
convents 14
conversion experiences 130, 196
coronation ceremonies 11, 12, 105–6, 107, 119, 125
Corporation Act (1661) 26, 79
Cortés, Juan Donoso 87, 88, 89–90, 98
Council of Trent 14, 46, 119, 131, 134
Creuzer, Georg Friedrich 229–30, 241
Cudworth, Ralph 207
Cult of Reason 66, 67, 252
Cult of the Supreme Being 58, 66–7, 252
culture *see* religion as culture

David, Jacques-Louis 66, 67, 120, 125
de Bonald, Louis 87, 88, 90, 92, 133, 185
de Brosses, Charles 228
de-Christianization 61–3, 157, 249
de Maistre, Joseph 87, 88, 90, 97–8, 106, 133
deaconesses 177
deacons 28, 36
deaneries 134
Debreyne, Pierre 190
*Declaration of the Rights of Man and of the Citizen* 55, 56, 104
deism 196–200, 246
religion as culture 202–4
theodicy 200–2

Deutscher Bund 82
devil 172
Diderot, Denis 12
Dissenters 26, 72, 73, 74, 80, 81, 112, 129, 130, 143, 144,149,156, 158
　elementary school system and 141–2
　mixed marriages 141
division of labour 56
divorce 185
dynasties 112–13

ecclesiastical and secular rule 12–17
ecclesiastical courts 15–16, 17
ecclesiastical electoral states 20
ecclesiastical property 13–14, 32
ecclesiology 132, 133 (*see also* church organization)
economy of salvation 50, 167, 177
Edict of Nantes 19
Egyptian culture 207, 208, 225, 229
Eichhorn, Johann Albrecht Friedrich 111
*Eigenkirchen* 32
elders 28
elementary school system 130, 141–2, 177–8, 185
elites 32–7 (*see also* aristocracy)
Emmerich (Emerick), Anna Katharina 165, 183
emotion 170, 171, 174
Engels, Friedrich 238
England (*see also* Church of England; United Kingdom)
　conservatism 89, 100
　Dissent *see* Dissenters
　feminine ideals 187–8
　general male suffrage 102
　women's societies and associations 180–1
Enlightenment 11, 22, 46, 52, 63, 65, 167, 177
　Catholicism and 223
　relativism 76
　secret societies 226
　social theory 64
enthusiasm 170
episcopal independence 132
episcopal sees 20 (*see also* bishops)
episcopalism 31
*Erblande* 51

eroticism 189, 191
eschatology 200
European identity 205
Evangelicals 185, 186, 188, 191
exorcisms 172, 189
Eylert, Rulemann Friedrich 110

Faber, F. W. 170
Faber, George Stanley 224
*fabrica ecclesiae* 27
Fall 198
family relationships 88–9
　piety and 159–61, 256
fanaticism 213
Fawcett, Millicent 181
Febronian reforms 21, 46, 54
*Feldprobst* 30
feminization of religion 175, 177, 178, 180, 181, 183, 256
Ferdinand VII of Spain 70
fervent/inspired networks 152–3
festivals 109, 118
　calendar 65, 105, 113, 118
Feuerbach, Ludwig 236–9, 242, 243, 244, 258
Fichte, Johann Gottlieb 95, 111
Filmer, John 184
flagellation 190
Formula of Concord (1577) 44
Fouché, Joseph 62, 65
Fouqué, Friedrich de la Motte 111
Fourier, Charles 175
France (*see also* Gallican Church; French Revolution)
　Bourbon monarchy 109, 114
　decline in the influence of the institutional church 160–1
　Dôme des Invalides 120
　Panthéon 64, 119–20
　re-Christianizing 122–3, 185
　religious publishing houses 163
　Restoration 57, 109, 121–3, 185
　state formation and monarchy 21
　women's congregations 178–80
Francis I of France 21
Francke, August Hermann 30
Frank, H. R. von 171
Frankfurt Parliament 84
Frederick, Duke of York 121

Frederick I of Prussia 30
Frederick II of Prussia 11, 30, 49, 117, 123
Frederick William I of Prussia 107
Frederick William II of Prussia 108, 119
Frederick William III of Prussia 83, 84, 103, 110, 115, 123, 136
Frederick William IV of Prussia 84, 87, 98, 99–100, 107–8, 110–11, 119, 137, 139, 152, 184, 254
freedom of conscience 75, 82, 85
Freemasons 67, 226
Freethinkers 160
French Revolution
    Burke's critique of 55, 89, 90
    concept of the nation 116–17, 119–20
    Convention 62, 63, 65–6
    cult of the dead 119–20
    effect on church and religion 55, 56, 96
    legacy 252
    National Assembly 55, 59, 60, 61, 62, 63, 64, 68
    religion during the Revolution 57–8
    *constitution civile* 58–61
    de-Christianization 61–3
    revolutionary cult 58, 63–7
    revolutionary calendar 65
Friends of the Light 147, 148, 162, 182
fundamentalism 250, 255
funerals 160, 161
Fürstenbund 71

Gallican Articles 22
Gallican Church 11
    bishops 35, 37
    clergy 23–4, 39, 41, 42
    French Revolution and 58
    hierarchy and elites 34–6, 56
    Napoleon and 105–6
    reforms 46–8
    relationship with Rome 21–2, 134
    Restoration 109–10, 121–3
    state influence 18
    taxation 22–4
    wealth and property 19, 20
Ganzes Haus 174
Gassner, Johann Joseph 172, 189
*Gemeine Herrschaft* 76
Gentz, Friedrich 87, 91

George III of England 103, 108, 111–12, 113, 120, 121
Gerbert, Olympe Philipe 170, 171
Gerlach, Ernst Ludwig von 87, 111, 124, 152
Gerlach, Ludwig Friedrich Leopold von 111, 152
German Catholics 147–8, 162, 182
German Confederation 136
German idealism 231–2
Germany (*see also* Bavaria; Prussia)
    brotherhoods 170
    church and state 134, 137
    concept of the nation 117–18
    decline in the influence of the institutional church 155, 157, 160
    Federal Act (1815) 81, 84
    *Landeskirchen* 18, 157, 160, 162, 168, 181
    Lutheran state churches 100
    newspapers and journals 161–2, 164
    Pietism *see* Pietism
    religious book production 163
    women's congregations 180–1
ghosts 171–2
Gladstone, William 87, 88, 93, 94, 169
Gnosticism 172
Goethe, Johann Wolfgang von 85
Goeze, Johann Melchior 200
Golden Bull (1356) 20
Görres, Joseph von 78, 87, 93, 152, 157, 162, 165, 191, 236, 239, 241, 242
Gosselin, Charles Robert 223–4
Greek mythology 212, 220, 221, 224, 227, 229
Gregory VII (Pope) 16
Gregory XV (Pope) 132
Gregory XVI (Pope) 69, 79
Groningen 28, 29, 36

Habsburg Empire 11, 33, 49–54, 76
Hahnemann, Samuel 192
Halle Pietism 30 (*see also* Pietism)
Haller, Albrecht von 184, 185
Haller, Karl Ludwig von 87, 88, 89–90, 92, 93, 98
Hardenberg, Friedrich von (Novalis) 85, 87, 90, 91, 96, 101, 103, 115

Hegel, Georg Wilhelm Friedrich 95, 175, 195, 196, 231, 232, 233–5, 236, 237, 238, 241, 242, 243, 246, 247, 256, 257
Hengstenberg, Ernst Ludwig 139, 162
Hengstenberg, Wilhelm 111
Henry VIII of England 26
Herberstein, Karl Graf von 52
Herder, Johann Gottfried 217–18, 227–8, 230, 246
heresy 143
Hermes, Georg 133
'hidden churches' 28
historicization of religion 245–6
 abstract notion of religion 208–23
 deism 201–2, 204–5
 early phase 205–8
 placeless Christianity 223–4
 Schleiermacher 241
 Zeller 243, 244
Hobbes, Thomas 87, 215
*Hochstifte* 71
Holbach, Paul Henri Thiri, Baron d'Holbach 216
Holy Roman Empire 16, 18, 20, 46, 56
 pastoral clergy 39, 42
Holy See 132 (*see also* Papacy)
Homer 210
Hommer, Josef von 168
Hontheim, Nikolaus von 54
Hugo, Victor 107
Huguenots 19, 28, 206
humanism 18
Hume, David 202–4, 246, 257
Hutchinson, John 225, 226
hypnosis 173, 183, 189

Ideler, Wilhelm 189
Ideologies 193
Illuminati 226
immanence 194–5, 259
immortal soul 200, 201
Imperial Church 21, 32, 34, 56
 secularization 71–2
incense 168
inclusion 254–6
Indian reductions 48
individualization 89, 130, 154, 160, 161, 258

indulgences 151
industrialization 72, 87, 158, 174, 176, 256
Ingolstadt Mass Association 151
Innocent XI (Pope) 22
Inquisition 70
inspired networks 152–3
institution of grace 131–5, 151
institutional transformation 193
introspection 202
Investiture Controversy 16–17
Ireland 79–80
Isabella II of Spain 70
Islam 213–14
Italian church 25
Italy 20
 aristocracy 34
 secularization 69

Jahn, Friedrich Ludwig 123
Jansenists 47, 52, 54, 188
Jaricot, Pauline Mari 151
Jesuits 46, 48–9, 70, 132, 177–8
Jews 23, 50, 61
Joseph II, Emperor of Austria 12, 33, 46, 49, 50–2
journals 102, 161–2
Judaism 208, 210, 218
July Monarchy 78
July Revolution 79, 120
Jung-Stilling, Heinrich 172
*Junker* 30
*jus circa sacra* 31
*jus in sacra* 29

Kant, Immanuel 172, 192, 231, 232–3, 236, 247, 257
*Katholische Kirchenzeitung* 161
Kieser, Dietrich Georg 172
*Kirchenmeister* 27
Kleist, Heinrich von 111, 115, 192
Knights of Malta 71
Kölner Wirren (Cologne Troubles) 83, 162
Körner, Theodor 115
Koschorke, Albrecht 250
Koselleck, Reinhart 196
Krug, Wilhelm Traugott 192
Kügelgen, Wilhelm von 187
Kulturkampf 84

La Rochefoucauld, François de 110
Lactantius 206
Lafayette, Gilbert du Motier, Marquis de 116–17
Lafitau, Joseph-François 206–7, 208, 214
laity
    missionary associations and Bible societies 151
    pre-Revolutionary Europe 14–15
Lamennais, Hugues Félicité Robert de 87
*Landeskirchen* 18, 157, 160, 162, 168, 181
*Landgemeinden* 78
landgraviate 40
language 226–8
Lateran Council II 13
Latin Christianity 13 *see also* Roman Catholic church
Lavater, Johann Caspar 172
Lepelletier de Saint-Fargeau, Michel 120
legitimacy, monarchy and 98, 99, 103, 105
Leo XII (Pope) 69, 132
Leopold, Grand Duke of Tuscany 46, 53
liberalism 86, 134
liberty 199
liturgy 168, 169
Locke, John 184, 196, 226
London City Mission 181
London Missionary Society 149
Louis XIV of France 22, 35
Louis XV of France 12, 48
Louis XVI of France 11, 12, 122
Louis XVIII of France 103, 106–7, 109, 118, 119, 120, 122
Louis Philippe, King of France 120
Louise, Queen of Prussia 115–16, 117
Löwith, Karl 249
Luhmann, Niklas 194, 251
Luther, Martin 143, 174, 251
Lutheran Church 28, 30
    church services 168
    Old Lutherans 84
    state churches 79, 100
Lutheran theology 18, 76, 200–1

*Mainzer Katholik* 161
Mainzer Kreis 162
Malthus, Robert 73
Mandeville, Bernard 199, 201, 247, 258
Mannheim, Karl 194

Marat, Jean-Paul 120
Maria Theresa, Habsburg Empress 11, 33, 46, 49
Marian piety 132, 164, 165, 179, 182, 183, 188–9, 192
Marie Antoinette 122
marriage 22, 160, 161
    civil marriages 83, 84, 140
    mixed marriages 83, 130, 140–1
mass media 161–5, 176, 256
Marx, Karl 238, 257
masturbation 190
Mathiez, Albert 57
meaning 193, 194, 256–8
media events 125, 130
Meiners, Christoph 220–1, 225–6
Melbourne, William Lamb, Lord Melbourne 74
Mennonites 28
mesmerism 172, 173, 174, 182, 189, 239
Methodism 45, 73, 79, 80, 81, 129, 144–7, 156, 158, 166, 170
    elementary school system 142
    John Wesley 144–6, 149, 151, 182
    printed texts 162, 164
    role of women 181, 182, 191–2
Methodist Society for the Establishment of Missions amongt the Heathen 149
Michelet, Jules 57, 186, 190–1, 256
Migazzi, Cardinal Christoph Anton 52
military values 123, 126
millenarians 171, 182
Millman, Henry H 121
Mirabeau, Honoré Gabriel Riqueti, Comte de 64, 119
missionary societies 122–3, 132, 149–51
    women and 177, 181, 185
mixed marriages 83, 130, 140–1
modernity 249, 250
Möhler, Johann Adam 239
Mohr, Heinrich 164
monarchy 11–12, 21–2, 34, 36
    citizen kings 253
    civil society and 96, 98–100, 101, 103–4, 105–16, 124
    coronation ceremonies 11, 12, 105–6, 107, 119, 125
    dynasties 112–13

legitimacy 98, 99, 103, 105
  Prussia 98–100, 107–8, 110–11, 115–16, 119
  resacralization 106–16
  Restoration 78, 85, 86, 109
monasteries 14, 46–7, 51, 57, 69, 70
monotheism 203, 206, 213, 214, 219, 220, 222, 228
Montalembert, Charles Forbes René de 124
Montmorency, Mathieu de 110
morality 86–8, 199
Moravians 144, 147
More, Hannah 181
Mörl, Maria von 165, 174
Müller, Adam 88, 90, 95, 111
Muratori, Ludovico Antonio 53, 191
mysticism 28, 165, 168, 171, 173, 182, 237, 238
myths 210, 229–30
  Greek mythology 212, 220, 221, 224, 227, 229

Nadere Reformatie 28
Napoleon III 78
nation, concept of 104, 116–24
National School Society 142
natural law 11, 209
natural religion 196, 198, 201, 202 (*see also* deism)
Neale, John Masen 158–9
Nelson, Horatio, Lord Nelson 121
neo-Platonism 172, 207, 225
Netherlands 21, 27–9, 78–9, 141
Nettelbladt, Daniel 31
New Toleration Act (1813) 80, 147
Newman, John Henry 170
newspapers 102, 161–2, 164, 256
Nietzsche, Friedrich 238
Noack, Ludwig 241–2
nobility *see* aristocracy
Novalis (Friedrich von Hardenberg) 85, 87, 90, 91, 96, 101, 103, 115
novels 163, 187

*Oberkirchenrat* 98
O'Connell, Daniel 80
Oeuvre de la Propagation du Foi 150, 151
Old Lutherans 84
Organic Articles 77

organizational forms *see* church organization
organizations vs social movements 142–3, 196
original sin 5, 105, 189, 192, 258
orthodoxy 76, 98, 110, 112, 162, 220, 240
Oxford Movement 139, 152, 158

Paley, William 184
pantheism 237
Papacy
  Holy See 132
  infallibility 98, 133
  spiritual and secular power 14, 17
papal encyclicals 132, 134
Papal States 25, 68, 131
parish churches 17, 18, 19, 27–31
  sociation beyond the local level 129
parish clergy 37–8
  income and background 39–43, 73
  patronage 43–5
  spiritual callings 42, 45
Parti Prêtre 109
participatory political order 101–5
pastoral care 14, 15, 23, 38, 41, 42, 45, 46, 47, 51, 52, 68, 69, 73, 74, 123, 134, 135, 138
patronage 17, 43–5
pauperism 87
Peace of Augsburg 71, 75
Peace of Westphalia 20, 71, 82
perennialism 18, 207, 210, 222
perfectibility 243
personal conversion 130
Perthes, Friedrich 123
Pfaff, Christoph Matthäus 31
Pfeilschifter, Johann Baptiste von 161
Pfuel, Ludwig von 44
phenomenology of religion 214, 242
philanthropy 176, 177
philosophy of religion 230–1
  absolutely free being 231–3
  *potentia existendi* 235–6
  re-instating religion's foundations 239–45
  self-relationships 236–9
  spirit that observes itself 233–5
Picart, Bernard 206
Pietism 28, 30, 143, 147, 148, 174, 177
piety 130, 142, 144, 147, 153–4, 168

decline in the influence of the institutional church 155–9
family context 159–61, 256
media and 161–5
perceiving the next world 171–4
prayer books 166–7, 171
    Book of Common Prayer 170–1
religious enthusiasm and excitement 170, 171
transcendence 153, 165–71, 182, 257
pilgrimages 11, 50, 52, 157, 164, 168, 255
Pitt, William, 1st Earl of Chatham 121, 152
Pius VI (Pope) 51, 62, 68
Pius VII (Pope) 69, 8, 132
Pius VIII (Pope) 132
Plato 212
pluralism 77–85, 245
political religions 91–7
political space 101–5
politics, religion and 124–7
Polybius 211
polycentricity 259
polytheism 203, 206, 219, 220, 221, 223, 225, 226
Popes
    Benedict XIV 189
    Clement XIII 33
    Clement XIV 49
    Gregory VII 16
    Gregory XV 132
    Gregory XVI 69, 79, 132
    Innocent XI 22
    Leo XII 69, 132
    Pius VI 51, 62, 68
    Pius VII 69, 80, 132
    Pius VIII 132
popular beliefs 171–2
popular piety *see* piety
popular sovereignty 56, 77, 85, 87
*potentia existendi* 235–6
power structures: Roman church 13–17
prayer books 166–7, 171
    Book of Common Prayer 170–1
    for women 188, 189, 191
preachers 28, 29
    John Wesley 144–5, 147
predestination 28, 200, 258
prince-bishops 71
print media 161–5

processions 169
professionalization 135, 138
proprietary churches 43
prostitutes 188
Protestantism
    as a political principle 95–6, 99
    church organization 27–31, 36–7
        autonomy and membership 139
        parish clergy 40–1, 43
        sociation beyond the local level 130
        state churches 135–8
    church services 167
    decline in the influence of the institutional church 158, 160
    French Revolution and 61, 62
    national identity and 123
    newsletters and pious texts 162, 164
    pluralism and 77, 78
    reason and 201
    religious publishing 163
    role of women 180, 181, 182, 187, 191–2
    toleration and 76
    universal priesthood 28, 99
Prussia 29–30, 40, 82–4, 102
    church and state 136–7
    concept of the nation 117, 123–4
    monarchy and civil society 96, 98–100, 107–8, 110–11, 115–16, 119
    religiosity 123–4
Prussian Main Bible Society 150
psychograph 173
public order 76
*publieke kerk* 27
Pufendorf, Samuel 31
Puritans 144, 170
Puységur, Amand-Marie-Jacques de Chastenet, Marquis de 172

Quakers 112, 144, 149, 182
Quietism 171

Radowitz, Karl Maria von 87, 90
Rauhes Haus 162
Rautenstrauch, Stefan Franz 51
Rauch, Christian Daniel 115
reason 197, 201, 202, 203, 212, 213
Redemptorists 173
reflexivity 229–30

Reformation 17, 18, 91
    church membership and 140
    necessity of 239
    perfectibility and 243
    political impact 99
Reformed church 27–31, 36–7
Reichsdeputationshauptschluss 71
Reichskirche 21
Reichsschluss 71
Reichstag 20
Reimarus, Samuel 201, 202
Reims/Rheims 11, 12, 107
Reinhard, Philipp Christian 219–20
relativism 76
religion
    history of *see* historicization of religion
    phenomenology 214
    philosophy of *see* philosophy of religion
religion as culture 202–4, 224–5
    communication: God and language 226–8
    deism 202–4
    reflexivity: symbols and myths 229–30
    self-revelation 225–6
religious communication 193, 194, 195, 226–8
    creation of meaning 193, 194, 256–8
religious education 141
religious festivals 109, 118
    calendar 65, 105, 113, 118
religious mania 189
religious orders 47–8, 70, 132, 177–8
religious studies 239, 242
religious tolerance 26–7, 50, 56, 75–7, 196, 255
religious violence 76, 196–7, 210–11, 213
Remonstrants 28
revelation 237, 239, 243
Rheims/Reims 11, 12, 107
Ricci, Scipione de 53
Richartz, Georg Hermann 191
rites of passage 159–61, 256
ritual 169, 170
Robespierre, Maximilien 66, 67
Roman Catholic church
    brotherhoods 170

Catholic Emancipation 112, 255
conservatism 87, 93, 98
constructions of gender and sinfulness 188
Council of Trent 14, 46, 119, 131, 134
decline in the influence of the institutional church 155, 158
ecclesiology 132, 133
Enlightenment and 223
French Revolution and 56, 60–3
Habsburg empire 50
Imperial Church 21, 32, 34, 56
    secularization 71–2
indulgences 151
institution of grace 131–5, 151
Ireland 80–1
liturgy 168
missionary associations 150, 151
Napoleon and 105–6
Netherlands 27
newspapers and journals 161–2, 164
organizational structures 131–5
pluralism and 77, 78, 79
post-Reformation 18
post-Tridentine 45, 143
power structures 13–17
processions 169
secularization and 70, 71–2
seminaries 135
toleration and 76
Ultramontanism 61, 83, 93, 96, 98, 133, 134, 135, 139, 152, 161
veneration of Virgin Mary 132, 164, 165, 179, 183, 188–9, 192
Romantic movement 56, 87, 100, 115, 127, 183, 184, 185, 231
Romme, Guilbert 65
Ronge, Johannes 148, 182
Rosenkranz, Karl 236
Rosicrucians 226
Rosmini, Antonio 92
Rousseau, Jean-Jacques 64, 66, 76, 90, 101, 104, 120, 215–17, 227, 228, 246
rural deans 134

sacraments 170
Sacred Heart, devotion to 164, 165, 170, 182, 183, 185
Saint-Simon, Henri de 57, 87, 97, 101
saints 203
salvation economy 50, 167, 177
Santa Clara, Abraham a 166
Sartori, Joseph Edler von 32
Savigny, Karl Friedrich von 111
Schadow, Johann Gottfried 117
Schelling, Friedrich Wilhelm Joseph von 195, 235–6, 242, 244
Schlegel, Friedrich 87, 236, 239, 242
Schleiermacher, Friedrich 85, 101, 126, 136, 157, 170, 219, 232, 240–1, 242, 243, 247, 251, 257, 258
Schmitt, Carl 98
school system 130, 135, 141–2, 177–8, 185
science 97, 101, 102, 165, 170, 171, 172, 173, 189, 190, 230, 231, 232, 240, 245, 250, 251
Scotland 137–8
Scottish Society for the Propagation of Christian Knowledge 149
scriptural authority 198
secret societies 109, 111, 118, 152, 226
sects 142, 152
secular rule 16
and ecclesiastical rule during the *ancien régime* 12–17
French Revolution 56–7
Reformation and 18
secularization 67–9, 130, 156, 167
communication and the creation of meaning 256–8
differentiation and 252–4
England 72–5
Imperial Church and 71–2
inclusion and 254–6
Italy and Spain 69–70
process of 249–52, 258–9
self-consciousness 233–5, 237, 242
self-descriptions 194, 195, 196
self-interest 199
self-relationships 236–9
self-revelation 225–6
semantics 194
seminaries 135, 138
sensory experience 168, 169

*sentiment religieux* 219, 221
separation of powers 56
sexuality
female 190, 192
order of the sexes 175–6
religious construction of gender, social order and sinfulness 183–92
slavery, abolition of 149, 152
Smith, Adam 56, 199, 247, 251, 257, 258
social contract/*contrat social* 104
social inclusion 254–6
social mobility 15
social movements 142–3, 196
social order 193, 195
social systems 194, 195
socialism 87, 96–7
sociation 125, 129
bureaucratization 131
religion as a social movement 142–4
fervent and inspired networks 152–3
German Catholics 147–8, 162
Methodists 144–7
missionary associations and Bible societies 148–51, 176–81
piety *see* piety
Société des Missions 150
Society for Christianity 149
Society for the Abolition of Slavery 149
Society for the Propagation of Christian Knowledge 141
Society for the Propagation of the Gospel in the Foreign Parts of the World 149
sociology of knowledge 194
somnambulism 173, 177, 183, 189
Sonderbund War 251
sovereignty of the people 56, 77, 85, 87
Spain 19
Bourbon kings 24–5
secularization 69–70
Spalding, Johann Joachim 200, 201
Spaur, Joseph Philip Graf 52
Spener, Jakob 143
spirit realm 171–4, 177, 182, 183
spiritual callings 42, 45
Stahl, Friedrich Julius 87, 95–6, 98, 99, 152
state churches 79, 100, 135–8
state funerals 119–21

state power 12, 57
Sterne, Lawrence 73
stigmata 165, 174, 177, 183
Strict Observance 226
structural transformation 193
sublation 196
*summus episcopus* 29, 31
superstition 171–2, 199
Supreme Being 58, 66–7, 206
Süßmilch, Johann Peter 44, 227, 228
Swedenborg, Emanuel 172
Switzerland 19, 21, 27, 28, 39, 41, 76, 78, 158, 251
symbols 229–30
    Christian symbolism 105, 106, 108, 169, 170
Synod of Dort 28, 29
systems 194, 195

Talleyrand, Charles-Maurice, Duke of Périgord and Bishop of Autun 59, 116
Tamburini, Pietro 53
taxation 16, 17
    Church of England 26
    Gallican Church 19
    pre-Revolutionary France 22–4
Temples of Reason 63
Terme, Johann Baptist de 52
Test Act (1673) 28, 79, 80, 112
theism 203
theodicy 166, 200–2
theological training 135, 138
theology 239–40 (*see also* philosophy of religion)
Thornton, Henry 152
Tindal, Matthew 196, 198
tithes 16, 38, 72, 74
Toland, John 196
tolerance 26–7, 50, 56, 75–7, 196, 255
Toleration Act (1689) 26, 80
Tocqueville, Alexis de 57
Tories 87 (*see also* conservatism)
tract societies 163
Tractarians 169, 170
tradition 90–1
transcendence
    conflict and 197
    historical origins of religion 210, 218, 222

immanence and 194–5, 259
introspection and 202
Latin Christianity 13
philosophy of religion 239, 258
piety and 153, 165–71, 257
*potentia existendi* 235
reason and 201
women and 182
treasury of grace 47
treasury of salvation 50
Treaty of Hubertusburg (1763) 50
Trier 20, 148, 152, 157, 164, 168
Trinity 224, 237
truth 197
Tübinger Stift 43

Ultramontanism 61, 83, 93, 96, 98, 133, 134, 135, 139, 152, 161
Union of Free Religious Communities 148
Unitarians 80
United Kingdom (*see also* England; Scotland)
    army 126
    Catholic Emancipation 112, 255
    natural religion 196, 198, 202 (*see also* deism)
    religious book production 163
    state events 125
general male suffrage 102
universal priesthood 28, 99
urbanization 158, 176, 256
Urlsperger, Johannes 149
utopian socialism 96–7

van Eß, Leander 150
veneration of Virgin Mary 132, 164, 165, 179, 183, 188–9, 192
Venn, Henry 184
*Vergemeinschaftung* 64
vicars-general 35
Vico, Giambattista 205, 208–11, 212, 214, 246, 258
Victoria, Queen of England 121
Virginian Declaration of Rights 56
virginity 180
Vischering, Droste 83
visions 165, 173, 174, 177, 182, 183
Voltaire (François-Marie Arouet) 64, 119, 205, 211–14, 228

Wake, William (Archbishop of Canterbury) 184
Warburton, William 197–8, 199–200, 208
Wartburg Festival 118
Watson, Richard 112
Weber, Max 108, 250
Wecker, Karl Theodor 175
Wellington, Arthur Wellesley, 1st Duke 121, 126
Welte, Benedikt 176
Werner, Zacharias 115
Wesley, John 144–6, 149, 151, 182
Wessenberg, Ignaz Heinrich von 183, 187, 256
Westphalian church order (1815) 136, 137
Wetzer, Heinrich J. 176
Wichern, Ernst 162
Wieland, Christoph Martin 174
Wilberforce, John 152
Wilberforce, William 185
William I, King of the Netherlands 79
William IV, King of England 121
witches 171, 172, 182
Wittola, Max Anton 52

Woellner, Johann Christoph 75, 110, 156
women
    changing roles 174
    charity, philanthropy and missionary work 176–81, 185
    congregations 178–80
    education 178
    female sexuality 190, 192
    feminization of religion 175, 177, 178, 180, 181, 183, 256
    mystical experiences 165
    order of the sexes 175–6
    religious construction of gender, social order and sinfulness 183–92
    resistance to de-Christianization 63
    visionaries 173, 174, 177, 183
    working careers 179, 180–1
Württemberg 31, 40, 43, 82, 103, 117, 138

Zeller, Eduard 243–5, 254
Zinzendorf, Nicolaus 144
Zoe, Marie 191
Zurich 40, 43

www.ingramcontent.com/pod-product-compliance
Lightning Source LLC
Chambersburg PA
CBHW070011010526
44117CB00011B/1506